R. Gupta's®

POPULAR MASTER GUIDE

DSSSB–TEACHERS

PGT

ENGLISH

Recruitment Exam

by

RPH Editorial Board

2026
EDITION

RAMESH PUBLISHING HOUSE, NEW DELHI

Published by
O.P. Gupta *for* Ramesh Publishing House
Admin. Office
12-H, New Daryaganj Road, Opp. Officers' Mess,
New Delhi-110002 ✆ 23275224, 23245124

E-mail: info@rameshpublishinghouse.com
For Online Shopping: www.rameshpublishinghouse.com

Showroom
• Balaji Market, Nai Sarak, Delhi-110006 ✆ 23282525 📱 9354373464
• 4457, Nai Sarak, Delhi-110006

Book Code: R-1305

ISBN: 978-93-5012-004-0

Price: ₹ 445

Printed at: Deepak Offset, Delhi

CONTENTS

ENGLISH LANGUAGE

ENGLISH LITERATURE

Scheme of Examination

DSSSB will conduct **One Tier Exam** for PGT posts having two section:

Section-I

S.No.	Subject	Questions	Marks
1.	Mental Ability and Reasoning Ability	20	20
2.	General Awareness	20	20
3.	English Language & Comprehension	20	20
4.	Hindi Language & Comprehension	20	20
5.	Numerical Aptitude & Data Interpretation	20	20
	Total	**100**	**100**

Section-II

S.No.	Subject	Questions	Marks
1.	MCQs pertaining to Post-Graduation qualification and teaching methodology required for the post.	**200**	**200**

Previous Years' Paper

Delhi Subordinate Services Selection Board (DSSSB)

PGT (English) Recruitment Exam, 2025

(Exam held on 11-07-2025)

Subject Knowledge – English & Teaching Methodology

1. Which of the following is a key characteristic of 'Third Wave Feminism'?

1. The rejection of digital activism and popular culture in feminist discourse
2. An emphasis on individual identity, intersectionality, and the diversity of women's experiences
3. A focus on universal female identity and their shared experiences
4. A primary focus on securing women's right to vote and basic legal equality

2. In corpus-based analysis, which of the following is primarily used to identify the frequency and distribution of words or phrases across large collections of texts?

1. Pragmatic markers
2. Thematic analysis
3. Collocation analysis
4. Concordance lines

3. According to Wordsworth, the poet's language should be free from:

1. artificial expressions
2. any connection to neoclassicism
3. emotional depth and intensity
4. metaphor and symbolism

4. How does the play 'A Dance of the Forests' begin?

1. The Dead Man and Dead Woman coming up out of the soil
2. Obaneji appearing in human form
3. Demoke pushing his apprentice out of the tree
4. Aroni casting a spell

5. What literary technique does Miller most prominently use to blur the lines between past and present in 'Death of a Salesman'?

1. Stream of consciousness
2. Allegory
3. Foreshadowing
4. Flashback

6. Which of the following works is a complex and scathing commentary on the white liberals?

1. July's People
2. My Son's Story
3. Burger's Daughter
4. The House Gun

7. Which of the following sentences demonstrates correct hierarchical sentence structure?

1. Running late, the meeting was already in progress when she arrived.
2. Although the book was interesting, the ending disappointed many readers.
3. The student who studies hard pass the exam easily.
4. Him and me went to the library to study for the exam.

8. How would you describe Gemmy's character in 'Remembering Babylon'?
1. Confident and assertive, with strong leadership qualities
2. Fearful of others and completely withdrawn
3. Lost and disoriented, struggling to find his identity
4. Strong and independent, with no dependence on others

9. Which modernist theme is featured in these lines about the character of Peter?
"For Peter, the city was a vast, impersonal machine, a place where people were reduced to mere cogs and wheels."
1. Mortality
2. Madness
3. Alienation
4. Inner life and emotions

10. In 'Adventures of Huckleberry Finn', which river do Huck and Jim travel on during their journey to freedom?
1. The Colorado River
2. The Ohio River
3. The Mississippi River
4. The Missouri River

11. How does Look Back in Anger critique the Welfare State?
1. By advocating for government control over the economy
2. By presenting it as the only solution to class tensions
3. By questioning its failure to create real social equality
4. By supporting conservative policies over social reforms

12. Who among the following introduced the concept of implicature?
1. HP Grice
2. JL Austin
3. Penelope Brown
4. Stephen Levinson

13. Why is the postcolonial legacy ambiguous according to postcolonial theorists?
1. Because the age of Enlightenment was also an age of empire, and the connection between those two historical epochs is more than incidental.
2. Because the age of restoration was also an age of monks, and the connection between those two historical epochs is more than inspirational.
3. Because the era of amusement was also an era of epoch, and the connection between those two romantic movements is more than accidental.
4. As the concept of postcolonialism was the idea of distant feelings of king and queens, and the competition between those ideas and epochs is more than transcendental.

14. For Marx, what distinguishes one type of society from another type?
1. The nature of its technology and divisions of labour
2. The mode of its treatment with the society
3. Its mode of distribution
4. The nature of its consumption and segments of earnings

15. In Marxist literary criticism, the relationship between base and superstructure suggests that:
1. the superstructure is completely independent of the economic base
2. literature exists outside the influence of economic and material conditions
3. the economic base shapes the superstructure, but the superstructure can also influence the base
4. the superstructure determines the base, making economic conditions secondary to cultural factors

16. What is the significance of Abel's return to the reservation in 'House Made of Dawn'?

1. It symbolises his complete assimilation into the dominant culture.
2. It represents his attempt to find peace and healing after his traumatic experiences.
3. It signals his desire to leave the past behind and start over.
4. It marks his rejection of both his Native American identity and modern society.

17. What is Milton's first dramatic representation of the contention between good and evil, a theme recurring in his later literary masterpieces?

1. Paradise Regained
2. Paradise Lost
3. Comus
4. On His Blindness

18. Yeats's 'Sailing to Byzantium' sings of the rich art and culture of Byzantium. Which of the following is the current location of Byzantium?

1. Egypt 2. Spain
3. Turkey 4. Italy

19. In 'A Passage to India', when Aziz and Fielding are united two years after the trial, they had to go on separate paths due to an outcrop of rocks as they rode through the jungles. What does this symbolise?

1. They were morally on different planes.
2. Both Aziz and Fielding are lost in their own way, and neither knows the right path.
3. Sociological hierarchy places an Indian behind an Englishman, for they shouldn't travel together despite their friendship.
4. The racial politics caused a breach in their friendship.

20. How did 'Orientalism' emerge in terms of postcolonialism?

1. The ideas got popularity in the west as a thought-provoking movement that most of the critics in the western world found to be new and alluring in the early 18th till the late 19th centuries.
2. It emerged as a field of study and a set of ideas in the context of European colonialism and imperialism in the 18th and 19th centuries.
3. It emerged as a set of courses and fundamental ideas woven with the context of eastern colonialism and imperialism in the late 18th and early 19th centuries.
4. Most of the critics of the postcolonial era supported these ideas because they provided them with a new vision to write against the western world during the 18th and 19th centuries.

21. Which of the following challenges the assumption of fixed meanings in a text by exposing contradictions, ambiguities and the instability of language?

1. Structuralism 2. Hermeneutics
3. Deconstruction 4. Phenomenology

22. The letters in 'The Color Purple' are written in the first person. How does this narrative technique affect the portrayal of the theme of oppression?

1. It provides a distant and objective view of the events.
2. It reduces the emotional impact of Celie's experiences by focusing on third-party perspectives.
3. It makes the novel feel more like a history lesson than a personal story.
4. It makes the theme of oppression feel more personal and immediate, as the reader experiences Celie's suffering directly.

23. Which of the following phonological processes involves the replacement of one sound with another due to influence from a nearby sound?

1. Assimilation 2. Epenthesis
3. Elision 4. Metathesis

24. Which literary figure critiqued Wordsworth's views on poetic diction?

1. Lord Byron 2. PB Shelley
3. ST Coleridge 4. John Keats

25. How does the structure of 'Remembering Babylon' contribute to its themes?

1. By following a linear timeline
2. By adhering to a strict chronological order
3. Through fragmented and non-linear narration
4. By using a single narrative perspective

26. Which of the following best describes a dialect?

1. A fixed and unchanging form of a language with slight regional differences
2. A non-standard way of speaking that is considered incorrect or ungrammatical
3. A separate language with some relation to the standard language but no mutual intelligibility
4. A regional or social variety of a language characterised by distinct vocabulary, grammar and pronunciation

27. 'A structure is an operational group with an indefinite meaning, bringing together any number of elements with an unspecified content, and a finite number of relationships of an unspecified nature but whose function and certain results concerning the elements are defined'.

Whose statement is this about structuralism?

1. Michael Moore 2. Edward Creep
3. Benzamin Ray 4. Martial Gueroult

28. What does Shaw's Pygmalion suggest about wealth and morality?

1. That wealth automatically leads to greater wisdom and kindness
2. That economic prosperity should define a person's moral worth
3. That financial success does not equate to ethical superiority
4. That money is the only factor that determines one's character

29. What is the term for a language variety used by a particular social group?

1. Lingua franca 2. Morphology
3. Orthography 4. Dialect

30. Which riots broke out in India after Prime Minister Indira Gandhi was assassinated, inspiring The Shadow Lines?

1. The 1984 Anti-communal riots
2. The 1980 Anti-Sikh riots
3. The 1984 Anti-Sikh riots
4. The 1980 Anti-communal riots

31. Which of the following is NOT a theme of Yeats's *Sailing to Byzantium*?

1. Old age and mortality
2. Artistic significance
3. Unrequited love and regret
4. Spiritual transcendence

32. In 'Pride and Prejudice', why did Charlotte marry Mr. Collins?

1. It was because she had always been jealous of Elizabeth and she thought it was a victory over her that she married and improved her station in life while Elizabeth couldn't.
2. Mr. Collins was the heir to Charlotte's family estate as she was an only child and the only way she could save her family home and estate was by marrying him.
3. The pressure for marriage was acute for women like Charlotte who were plain faced with no independence and without parity in property, rights and economic opportunities. Thus, Mr. Collins' proposal would have been her first and last option to gain autonomy and economic prospects.
4. Mr. Collins was distraught after Elizabeth rejected his marriage proposal and Charlotte married him out of the kindness of her heart.

33. 'The Shadow Lines' won Sahitya Akademi award in the year:

1. 1989 2. 1988
3. 1987 4. 1985

34. How did Orientalist scholarship and representations help justify and legitimise colonial domination?

1. By presenting the east as forward, rational and in need of eastern civilisation
2. By portraying the Orient as backward, irrational and in need of Western civilisation
3. Through portraying the Orient as outstanding, rational and in need of contemporary social reforms
4. By commanding their literary works through new ideas which were taken as backward, outdated and in need of modern civilisation

35. Which of the following statements is INCORRECT?

A. Childe Roland is a recurring character from ballads that has been mentioned in European literature as a symbol of the lost one.

B. The title of Browning's poem has been taken from 'King Lear'.

C. Browning in his poem 'Childe Roland to the Dark Tower Came' has used Roland as a symbol of being in the wrong profession as he contemplates on his current situation as a middle-aged Victorian poet who is not yet successful and famous.

D. Roland is a cripple in Browning's poem.

1. B 2. D
3. A 4. C

36. In Poetics, Aristotle differentiates between history and poetry, asserting that poetry is superior because:

1. it deals with what could happen rather than what has happened
2. it is written in verse and history could only be relayed through prose
3. it focusses on particular events rather than universal truths
4. it presents events in a cause-and-effect manner to reveal universal principles

37. Select the most appropriate option to complete the statement regarding postcolonial theory.

The 'Ethnic Studies' concerns itself generally with art and literature produced by _____.

1. excluded ethnic groups which come from a remote place and show a greater concern for the supremacy of the ethnic class
2. contemporary ethnic groups which dominate in the cultural race of the society through a dominating position and greater number of members in the ethnic society
3. identifiable ethnic groups either marginalised or in a subordinate position to a dominant culture
4. specific ethnic groups either in a dominating or in a seductive position to a passive cultural movement

38. What does the tree represent in *Waiting for Godot*?

1. Only stability and life
2. Only stability
3. Stability, life and hope
4. Only life and hope

39. Which literary device is most frequently employed by Whitman in 'Leaves of Grass' to convey a sense of unity and inclusiveness?

1. Anaphora 2. Allegory
3. Hyperbole 4. Irony

40. What does the 'American Dream' primarily signify in Death of a Salesman?

1. Material wealth and success
2. Personal freedom and self-expression
3. Family unity and love
4. Intellectual and artistic achievement

41. Select the correct option to complete the sentence.

In 'House Made of Dawn', the character of Francisco plays a crucial role in _____.

1. representing the younger generation's break from tradition
2. encouraging Abel to leave the reservation and seek a new life
3. passing on Native American traditions and teachings to Abel
4. advocating for the assimilation of Native Americans into mainstream society

42. In 'Half of a Yellow Sun', which Nigerian ethnic group is primarily associated with the Republic of Biafra?

1. Igbo
2. Fulani
3. Hausa
4. Yoruba

43. Complete the sentence given below.

In his poems, Les Murray often uses language to _____.

1. celebrate the simplicity, hardships and beauty of rural life
2. reject traditional poetic forms in favour of experimental styles
3. glorify urban environments and technology
4. focus on international issues rather than local concerns

44. Identify the lines that are written about a ghost in 'Wuthering Heights'.

1. "I'm afraid of him, Miss," Nelly said, her voice trembling. "He's not like other folks. He's got a wicked heart, and he'll do us harm if we don't watch out."
2. "He's more myself than I am. Whatever our souls are made of, his and mine are the same."
3. "I began to feel a strange, creeping sensation in my fingers, and a cold, clammy feeling in my heart. I looked up, and saw Catherine's face, pale and wan, with her eyes fixed on me."
4. "I've had the most terrible dreams, Nelly," Catherine said, her voice trembling. "I've seen Heathcliff's face, and it's haunted me."

45. Which of the following is a fundamental principle of structuralist analysis in literature?

1. The emphasis on the historical context of a text
2. The exploration of deep structures underlying cultural phenomena
3. The focus on the author's intentions
4. The interpretation of texts based on reader response

46. Which of the following concepts did Louis Althusser introduce to explain how ideology functions in society?

1. Ideological State Apparatuses
2. Ideological Superstructures
3. Dialectical Materialism
4. Cultural Hegemony

47. What does Lena Grove symbolise in 'Light in August'?

1. Destruction and chaos
2. Wealth and power
3. Innocence and renewal
4. Fear and paranoia

48. Which city serves as the primary setting for the events of the novel Ice-Candy-Man?

1. Karachi
2. Lahore
3. Amritsar
4. Hyderabad

49. Why is Nick Carraway considered a somewhat unreliable narrator in 'The Great Gatsby'?

1. He tends to glorify Gatsby while being critical of other characters.
2. He openly admits to lying throughout the novel.
3. He is emotionally detached from the characters and events.
4. He often withholds information from the reader.

50. Match the following characters with the correct novels, written by Mulk Raj Anand.

List A	List B
1. The Road	(*a*) Lalu Singh
2. Coolie	(*b*) Ananta
3. The Big Heart	(*c*) Bhikhu
4. The Sword and the Sickle	(*d*) Munoo

1. 1-(*a*), 2-(*b*), 3-(*c*), 4-(*d*)
2. 1-(*c*), 2-(*a*), 3-(*b*), 4-(*d*)
3. 1-(*d*), 2-(*a*), 3-(*b*), 4-(*c*)
4. 1-(*c*), 2-(*d*), 3-(*b*), 4-(*a*)

51. In 'An Astrologer's Day', how does the astrologer recognise the man who threatens him?

1. By his voice
2. By his unique clothing
3. By the scar on his forehead
4. By his questions

52. What Renaissance ideal does Faustus represent in Marlowe's Doctor Faustus?

1. The complete submission to divine authority
2. The thirst for knowledge and limitless power
3. The idea that monarchy is the true source of power
4. The rejection of art and literature as distractions

53. Which of the following symbolises the deterioration of the Usher family in 'The Fall of the House of Usher'?

1. The shattered vase in the drawing-room
2. The crumbling mansion
3. The dead tree in the garden
4. The broken mirror in Roderick's room

54. According to Aristotle, what is considered the highest form of art?

1. Lyric Poetry 2. Comedy
3. Epic Poetry 4. Tragedy

55. What was the impact of the dislocation of the characters in A House for Mr. Biswas, descendants of Indian labourers brought to Trinidad from India?

1. A sense of belongingness and contentment
2. A sense of happiness
3. A sense of rootlessness and alienation
4. A sense of anger

56. In 'Sister Carrie', which theme is reflected through Carrie's rise in social status and her pursuit of wealth?

1. Feminism and gender equality
2. The tension between individual desires and societal expectations
3. The corruption of innocence
4. The search for true love

57. In 'Sister Carrie', which of the following characters represents the theme of materialism?

1. Drouet 2. Ames
3. Hurstwood 4. Carrie

58. The character Saleem Sinai has a unique ability that represents magic realism in 'Midnight's Children'. What is this ability?

1. The ability to manipulate reality through storytelling
2. The power to become invisible at will
3. The power to travel through time and witness historical events
4. Telepathy that connects him to all the other children born at the moment of India's independence

59. Select the option that is correct regarding the following two statements labelled Assertion (A) and Reason (R).

Assertion (A): In *The Bluest Eye, Pecola Breedlove* believes that having blue eyes will make her life better and earn her love and acceptance.

Reason (R): Blue eyes are portrayed as the societal standard of beauty and success imposed by a racist culture.

1. Both (A) and (R) are true, but (R) is not the correct explanation of (A).
2. (A) is false, but (R) is true.
3. (A) is true, but (R) is false.
4. Both (A) and (R) are true, and (R) is the correct explanation of (A).

60. Identify the thematic setting of Spenser's 'Sonnet 67'.

1. In this poem, the poet tries to connect physical beauty with spiritual virtue in a way that the erotic is linked with the spiritual and the sacred.
2. In this poem, the poet is feeling lost in a sea of trouble, without the guidance or solace of his beloved, because he has lost access to her but he hopes that when the storm has passed, she will shine again as his guiding star.
3. In this poem, the hunter and the prey are engaged in their typical routine of trying to escape and trying to capture; however, the poem ends with a new mutuality and reciprocity resulting in willful surrender that thematically alludes to the willing surrender to love.
4. The poet complains in this poem that his beloved is tyrannical in her stance, and his love for her is the object of her oppression.

61. Which of the following statements regarding Fra Lippo Lippi's character is INCORRECT?

A. Fra Lippo Lippi is an astute and knowledgeable character who presents a treatise of realism through his monologue.
B. Psychologically, he is in a state of tug of war between pursuing the spiritual life into which he was forced as an orphan to sustain himself and the sensual life of freedom and liberty that sustains all art.
C. He argues whether an artist should immortalise human beings through an idealist perception of their souls or an artist should portray life and human beings honestly in their flesh and blood and as close to reality as possible so as to keep the art closer to its subject.
D. He is apprehended by two watchmen/policemen for dressing obscenely in a red light area when we are introduced to him.

1. B
2. C
3. D
4. A

62. Whom does General R and Lt. Koina believe to have betrayed Kihika?

1. Karanja
2. Mumbi
3. Gikonyo
4. Mugo

63. Walcott uses images of genetic hybridity and cultural diversity to express the extremity of his identity crisis in which of the following poems?

1. The Sea is History
2. The Schooner Flight
3. Another Life
4. A Far Cry from Africa

64. What does nature symbolise in Whitman's Leaves of Grass?

1. A place of punishment
2. The interconnectedness of life
3. A chaotic and uncontrollable force
4. A trivial background

65. What is the most powerful theme of 'Postcolonial' writings?

1. The celebration of metropolitan modernity
2. The erasure of native traditions in favor of progress
3. The glorification of colonial achievements
4. Loss and recovery of cultural identity

66. How does Miller address the theme of personal freedom in 'Black Spring'?

1. By emphasising the importance of conforming to societal rules
2. By presenting characters who reject societal expectations and embrace individualism
3. By showing how personal freedom leads to self-destruction and failure
4. By illustrating the peace found in living a traditional, structured life

67. Select the correct option to complete the sentence.

The novel's title, 'House Made of Dawn', most likely refers to _____.

1. the spiritual and cultural connection of the protagonist to his ancestral lands
2. the dawn of a new era for Native American people
3. the bright future that Abel envisions after his struggles
4. a literal house that Abel builds at the end of the novel

68. What is the primary characteristic of a regional dialect?

1. It is specific to a particular geographic area.
2. It is spoken by the elite class.
3. It is influenced by the speaker's profession.
4. It is the same across different social classes.

69. Which of the following best illustrates the practical use of pragmatics in communication?

1. Understanding the literal meaning of a sentence without considering context
2. Analysing the phonetic structure of spoken language
3. Identifying and correcting grammatical errors in a sentence
4. Interpreting an indirect request based on social and situational context

70. What does 'Postcolonial Criticism' investigate?

1. The bonding between critics and the works of the colonisation period
2. The relationships between writers and colonised readers the period post-colonisation
3. The relationships between colonisers and colonised in the period post-colonisation
4. The antithesis based on the expectations of the colonised writers and their criticism

71. Which of the following options is correct about the given statements?

A. Thematically, the line 'You know that the soot cannot spoil your white hair' shows the development from innocence to maturity.

B. The above lines ironically suggest that now the beautiful white hair won't be tainted by the dark soot; however, the incident of shaving the head will forever be impressed upon the innocent mind of the child as a reminder of the dark realities of the world. The child who consoles his friend with the above lines is still viewing the world in an optimistic light despite the circumstances but the child who has been tonsured can't share this optimism.

1. Both (A) and (B) are correct, but (B) does not support the claim made by (A).
2. (A) is false, but (B) is true.
3. (A) is true, but (B) is false.
4. Both (A) and (B) are true, and (B) supports the claim that (A) makes.

72. In the South African context presented in July's People, what social structure coincides with and goes hand in hand with apartheid?

1. Matriarchy
2. Egalitarianism
3. Patriarchy
4. Colonialism

73. What is ironic about the motif of prayer in Tughlaq?

1. Prayer is the time for murdering the people.
2. Through prayer all the evil doers as well as good-intentioned people get strength.
3. By prayer, the Sultan earned the goodwill of even his enemies and the revolters.
4. Prayer brought both the Hindus and the Muslims together to support the Sultan's ideal plans.

74. How does Mahesh Dattani's play 'Tara' address the issue of gender discrimination?

1. By depicting a family where the male child is given preferential treatment over the female child due to societal norms
2. By illustrating a community where women have more opportunities and are celebrated more than men
3. By focusing on the positive impact of gender equality on the family's dynamics and future
4. By showing that gender roles and stereotypes are equally distributed between men and women in the society portrayed

75. In 'Death of a Salesman', which of the following symbolises Willy Loman's unattainable aspirations and the illusion of success?

1. The car
2. The refrigerator
3. The garden
4. The stockings

76. Literary criticism suggests that women in literature:

1. have been historically presented as objects seen from a male's perspective
2. have been majorly presented as objects seen from a female's perspective
3. have been ironically presented as subjects seen from an essayist's perspective
4. have been formally presented as objects seen from a publisher's perspective

77. How is Miss Minnie Cooper characterised in the novel 'Light in August'?

1. As an innocent and compassionate woman
2. As a nurturing mother figure to the town
3. As a strong and independent female character
4. As a woman who embodies both racial prejudice and personal shame

78. What is Uhuru?

1. Unity of Tribes
2. A tribal festival
3. Independence from Britain
4. The beginning of colonialism

79. What does the title of the novel Samskara: A Rite for a Dead Man signify?

1. The importance of rites and rituals during death
2. The spiritual connotations of rituals conducted during death anniversaries
3. The society's responsibility of burying the dead irrespective caste and creed
4. The socio-religious purification ritual associated with the death of a Brahmin

80. In 'The Catcher in the Rye', why does Holden Caulfield admire his younger sister Phoebe?

1. She is intelligent, kind and represents the innocence he longs to protect.
2. She reminds him of his favorite childhood teacher.
3. She encourages him to leave New York and start a new life.
4. She shares his cynical view of the world.

81. Which aspect of *Waiting for Godot* best reflects the philosophy of Absurdism?

1. A meaningless repetition of actions and dialogue
2. Heroic actions of the main characters
3. A clear moral lesson given at the end
4. A well-organised plot structure

82. How does Nathaniel Hawthorne explore the theme of individual versus society in the Scarlet Letter?

1. By showing the Puritan community's acceptance of Hester
2. By highlighting the importance of conformity
3. By focusing on the political conflicts of the time
4. By depicting Hester's isolation and ostracism

83. Which of the following terms refers to a variant pronunciation of a phoneme that does NOT change word meaning?

1. Morpheme 2. Syllable
3. Phoneme 4. Allophone

84. Who is the narrator of 'Kanthapura'?

1. Rangamma 2. Moorthy
3. Achakka 4. Bhatta

85. In 'Midnight's Children', the line between history and fiction is often blurred. What literary device does Rushdie use to achieve this effect?

1. Paradox 2. Hyperbole
3. Irony 4. Intertextuality

86. Many 19th-century Australian poets wrote about the lives of bushrangers. What does this reflect about Australian identity during that period?

1. Fascination with rebellion and independence
2. A disdain for rural life
3. A focus on urbanisation and modernisation
4. A desire to imitate European aristocracy

87. Which of the following is NOT a function of intonation?

1. Conveying the speaker's attitude or emotion
2. Highlighting focus or emphasis in a sentence
3. Signaling sentence type
4. Indicating vowel length

88. In 'The Last of the Mohicans', the story is mostly told from whose perspective?

1. Uncas
2. Hawkeye (Natty Bumppo)
3. Cora Munro
4. Magua

89. Which of the following images has been used by Pope in 'An Epistle to Dr. Arbuthnot' to describe 'scribblers who write hastily'?

1. Spiders 2. Grub
3. Butterfly 4. Mosquito

90. Which of the following reasons does NOT justify the title of Joseph Conrad's *Heart of Darkness* in the context of the novel?

1. It refers to the entire process of colonisation that dehumanises the natives.
2. It also refers to the inherented evil and wickedness in human beings.
3. It refers to the forests of Africa that were unexplored then.
4. It alludes to the kindness in the hearts of native Africans.

91. The given lines from Spenser's Sonnet 77 describe which of the following parts of his beloved?

Exceeding sweet, yet voyd of sinfull vice;
That many sought, yet none could ever taste;
Sweet fruit of pleasure, brought from Paradice
By Love himselfe, and in his garden plaste.

1. Breasts 2. Lips
3. Eyes 4. Heart

92. In 'Remembering Babylon', how is Gemmy Fairley best described?

1. A heroic and noble figure
2. A wealthy landowner in colonial Australia
3. A runaway convict seeking refuge in the wilderness
4. A European who has lived among Indigenous Australians

93. Which of the following factors primarily determines the choice of register in communication?

1. The speaker's native dialect and accent
2. The grammatical complexity of the language being spoken
3. The historical evolution of the language
4. The social context, audience and purpose of the interaction

94. How does Emerson view nature's role in human life?

1. It has no spiritual significance.
2. It is a teacher and a source of inspiration.
3. It is purely recreational.
4. It distracts from intellectual pursuits.

95. "Mrs. Dalloway is a novel that explores the complexities of colonialism and imperialism... Woolf's use of multiple narrative voices creates a sense of multiplicity and diversity... It is a novel that challenges dominant discourses and power structures."
Which of the following critics have remarked the above about Mrs. Dalloway?

1. Sandra Gilbert
2. Jacques Derrida
3. Toril Moi
4. Gayatri Chakravorty Spivak

96. Which of the following is NOT a theme of 'A triumph of life'?

1. The corruptibility of life and the inevitability of life's ultimate destination
2. The quest for knowledge and deeper meanings
3. The illusiveness of power and glory
4. Surrender to God and faith in his compassion

97. In 'An Epistle to Dr. Arbuthnot', Pope has used the poetic technique of satire. Which of the following characters is a satirical representation of Charles Montagu, Earl of Halifax?

1. Bubo
2. Sporus
3. Atticus
4. Bufo

98. In 'The Fall of the House of Usher', what is the main reason for Roderick Usher's increasing madness?

1. The influence of his wife
2. The illness of his brother
3. His obsession with supernatural occurrences
4. His isolation from society

99. What is the term for a single vowel that changes its quality noticeably during its pronunciation?

1. Monophthong
2. Open vowel
3. Diphthong
4. Cardinal vowel

100. "Mrs. Dalloway is a novel that explores the complexities of language and meaning... Woolf's use of modernist techniques creates a sense of instability and undecidability... It is a novel that challenges traditional notions of truth and reality."
Which of the following critics has remarked the above about 'Mrs. Dalloway'?

1. Jacques Derrida
2. James Wood
3. Hermione Lee
4. Gayatri Chakravorty Spivak

101. In Raja Rao's Kanthapura, how does the concept of Satyagraha (the force of truth) play a role in shaping the villagers' struggle against the British?

1. The villagers are indifferent to the concept of Satyagraha and rely only on passive resistance.
2. The villagers use violent methods to resist British rule.
3. The villagers focus solely on economic boycotts, ignoring the political struggle.
4. The villagers emphasise the moral power of truth to resist colonial authority without resorting to violence.

102. In 'I'm Nobody! Who are you?', Dickinson critiques which societal concept?

1. Pursuit of success
2. Social isolation
3. Passage of time
4. Fame and public recognition

103. What does 'False consciousness' refer to in terms of Marxist view of literature?

1. The set of beliefs and convictions that prevent an individual from perceiving the truth about social economic and realities.
2. The model of texts and convictions that hinders an individual from searching the hidden about social and political realities.
3. The set of tasks and responsibilities that allures any individual from making the rules about studies and economic realities.
4. The set of ideas and projections that motivate an individual from perceiving the fact about social and economic realities.

104. Which of the following historical crises forms a theme of Adiche's 'Half of a Yellow Sun'?

1. Starvation and economic prosperity
2. Classism and speciesism
3. The savagery of war on women
4. The psychological impact of Western imperialism

105. 'The God of Small Things' confounding of fantasy and reality connects the novel with which of the following styles?

1. Surrealism 2. Minimalism
3. Existentialism 4. Hysterical realism

106. Select the most appropriate option to fill in the blank.

In Book VI of 'The Paradise Lost', Milton describes the battle between the good and evil angels; the defeat of the latter results in their _____.

1. expulsion from heaven
2. entry to the heaven
3. rivalry for the throne
4. expulsion from hell

107. What does Karnad mean by the statement "What struck me absolutely about Tughlaq's history was that it was contemporary."?

1. There was parallelism between the realities of the 14th century India, ruled by a Sultan and the 20th century democratic country governed by a Prime Minister and his colleagues in the Cabinet.
2. The dramatist lived during Sultan Tughlaq's reign and so he experienced the realities of life.
3. There were many countries showing a strong influence of Sultan Tughlaq's vision and mission in their administration.
4. Sultan Tughlaq's modus operandi in administration was followed by all the administrators of the world.

108. Who among the following directed the play 'Tara' and is also said to have first spotted and encouraged Mahesh Dattani's talent and given him the confidence to venture into a career in theatre?

1. Alyque Padamsee
2. Habib Tanvir
3. Girish Karnad
4. Vijay Tendulkar

109. In The Scarlet Letter, what is the significance of the meteor that appears in the sky the night Hester, Pearl and Dimmesdale meet on the scaffold?

1. It is interpreted as a sign of hope for Hester.
2. It is seen as a sign of Dimmesdale's guilt.
3. It symbolises Chillingworth's vengeance.
4. It marks the beginning of a new season.

110. How does 'The Floating Opera' reflect Post-war concerns?

1. Absurdity, uncertainty
2. Heroic protagonist
3. Traditional values
4. Patriotism

111. In 'Night of the Scorpion', what is the scorpion a symbol of?

1. Peace and calm
2. Good fortune
3. Fear and suffering
4. Wealth and prosperity

112. How does psychological criticism deal with a work of literature?

1. Primarily as an expression, in an indirect and fictional form, of the state of mind
2. Primarily as an identification, in a direct and rhetoric form, of the state of human behaviour
3. It presents life with a distant perception in a direct and romantic form
4. Basically in a manner where the human feelings and their interpretations are kept away with the real work of art

113. How does Faulkner's portrayal of the character of Homer Barron contribute to the Southern Gothic atmosphere of the story 'A Rose for Emily'?

1. By embodying the grotesque and unsettling aspects of Southern life
2. By emphasising his role as a strict authority figure who enforces social norms
3. By representing a figure of social progress and modernity
4. By presenting him as a traditional Southern gentleman who upholds community values

114. What emotions coloured Hagar Shipley's relationships with others in Margaret Laurence's 'The Stone Angel'?

1. Fear and suspicion of the world
2. Joy and acceptance of the world
3. Love and compassion of the world
4. Trust and confidence of the world

115. 'The Shadow Lines' is set against the backdrop of which of the following historical events?

1. Swadeshi movement
2. Partition of India
3. Communal riots of 1963-64 in Dhaka and Calcutta
4. Second World War

1. Only 1 and 2
2. 1, 2, 3 and 4
3. Only 1, 3 and 4
4. Only 1, 2 and 3

116. What is/are the major poetic technique(s) engaged by Walcott in his poems?

1. His use of vivid imagery
2. Complex metaphors
3. A blend of European literary traditions with Caribbean oral storytelling
4. Rhythm and musicality in his verse

1. Only 2
2. 1, 2, 3 and 4
3. Only 1, 2 and 3
4. Only 1

117. Select the correct option to complete the sentence.

The theme of spirituality in 'The Color Purple' is closely tied to _____.

1. the way Celie gradually builds a personal relationship with God that empowers her
2. the strict, authoritarian figures in Celie's life who dictate her faith
3. Celie's formal religious education at church
4. the rejection of all forms of religion throughout the novel

118. How does 'House Made of Dawn' explore the theme of alienation?

1. Abel's alienation is primarily caused by his rejection of modernity
2. Abel integrates successfully into white American society
3. Abel finds solace in city life after leaving the reservation
4. Abel feels disconnected from both his Native American roots and the dominant culture

119. Which type of evidence do Wimsatt and Beardsley argue should be used in literary criticism?

1. External evidence from the author's life
2. Psychological evidence about the reader's response
3. Internal evidence from the text itself
4. Biographical evidence about the author

120. The Partition of India serves as a backdrop in 'Clear Light of Day'. Which character is most directly affected by the communal tensions during this period?

1. Bim 2. Tara
3. Baba 4. Raja

121. Which century of slavery was depicted in the novel Beloved by Toni Morrison?

1. 20th century
2. 18th century
3. 17th century
4. 19th century

122. In Bapsi Sidhwa's 'Ice-Candy-Man', how is disability represented in the context of the partition of India, and what does this representation reveal about societal attitudes towards disability?

1. The portrayal of disability in the novel focusses on medical and rehabilitative solutions highlighting progressive attitudes towards disability and an emphasis on medical intervention.
2. The novel represents disability as a source of shame and marginalisation, revealing how individuals with disabilities are often excluded from the socio-political discourse and deemed as burdens during times of crisis.
3. Disability is portrayed as a minor issue that is easily resolved within the broader narrative of the partition, reflecting a lack of significant societal impact.
4. Disability is depicted as a symbol of strength and resilience, demonstrating that societal attitudes towards disability are predominantly positive and supportive.

123. In 'Voss', what is the purpose of Johann Ulrich Voss's expedition?

1. Establish trade routes with indigenous communities
2. Map uncharted territories in the Australian outback
3. Escape his troubled past in Germany
4. Discover a lost city in the Australian desert

124. In Wole Soyinka's 'A Dance of the Forests', how does the portrayal of Yoruba culture contribute to the play's exploration of traditional values and societal critiques?

1. It emphasises Yoruba culture's focus on individual achievements and personal success rather than communal values and responsibilities.
2. It showcases the Yoruba cultural rituals and beliefs as means to reflect upon the importance of adhering to traditional values and customs in resolving societal problems, as well as, engaging with traditions in a way that is dynamic and relevant to the present.
3. It highlights the Yoruba culture's emphasis on modernity and the rejection of traditional practices in favour of Western values.
4. It presents Yoruba culture as irrelevant to the play's themes, focussing instead on universal themes that transcend cultural specifics.

125. Based on the following Statement and Assertion, select the most appropriate option.

Statement (S): Wuthering Heights is a masterful blend of the Gothic and the Romantic.

Assertion (A): Emily Bronte's use of the Gothic mode allows her to explore the darker aspects of human nature, while her Romantic sensibility enables her to create a sense of transcendence and timelessness.

1. (S) is true, but (A) is false.
2. Both (S) and (A) are true and (A) justifies (S).
3. Both (S) and (A) are true, but (A) cannot justify (S).
4. (S) is false, but (A) is true.

126. Identify those lines from 'Mrs. Dalloway' that do not represent a modernist theme.

1. "Regent's Park was a haven of tranquility, a green oasis in the midst of the bustling city. The flowers bloomed, the birds sang, and the sun shone down, casting a warm, golden light over the scene."
2. "The war had changed everything. The old certainties were gone, and in their place was a sense of uncertainty, of flux."
3. "For reality was not a fixed, unchanging thing, but a fluid, ever-shifting illusion that refused to be pinned down."
4. "For human beings, experience was a fragmented, disjointed thing, full of gaps and fissures that refused to cohere into a meaningful whole."

127. In Ethnographic Discourse Analysis, which approach is most crucial for capturing the dynamic relationship between language and social practices within a specific community?

1. Using experimental methods to test language comprehension in controlled settings
2. Engaging in prolonged participant observation and contextualised discourse transcription.
3. Conducting large-scale corpus analysis to identify linguistic trends
4. Relying solely on surveys and interviews to gather self-reported language use

128. Which of the following are the major problems dealt in the novel Tamas by Sahni?

1. Immigrant experience and sense of belonging
2. Party politics and religious fanaticism
3. Natural disaster and struggle for life
4. Racial and gender discrimination

129. Select the most appropriate option to fill in the blank.

The last two poems of John Milton's _____, a brief epic in four books, and a dramatic poem 'Samson Agonistes' were published in one volume in the year 1671.

1. Penseroso
2. Paradise Lost
3. Paradise Regained
4. L'Allegro

130. What is the theme of Becket's final sermon in Murder in the Cathedral?

1. Power is greater than faith
2. Suffering is meaningless
3. Martyrdom should be selfless
4. Politics must rule religion

131. How does the motif of seeing and being seen shape the racial and social dynamics of the novel in Morrison's The Bluest Eye?

1. Through Pecola's obsession with mirrors
2. Through the portrayal of white media
3. Through the community's surveillance and judgment
4. Through the Breedlove family's social interactions

132. Identify the poetic technique being used in the given lines.

If they be two, they are two so
As stiff twin compasses are two;
Thy soul, the fixed foot, makes no show
To move, but doth, if the other do.

1. Alliteration 2. Metaphor
3. Assonance 4. Conceit

133. What is the central existential theme in 'Floating Opera'?

1. The quest for power
2. The absurdity of life
3. The search for utopia
4. The celebration of tradition

134. In Freudian theory, which term describes the psychological mechanism by which unacceptable thoughts are pushed into the unconscious?

1. Projection 2. Repression
3. Displacement 4. Sublimation

135. Which of the following characters in Coolie symbolises the exploitation of child labour in colonial India?

1. Ganpat 2. Mr. England
3. Munoo 4. Babu Nathoo Ram

136. Moorthy, the protagonist of 'Kanthapura', is primarily influenced by which historical figure?

1. Subhas Chandra Bose
2. B.R. Ambedkar
3. Jawaharlal Nehru
4. Mahatma Gandhi

137. Match the two columns given below based on the characters from the novel 'Great Expectations' and their dominant traits.

(Characters)	(Their Dominant Traits)
1. Wemmick	(*a*) Bitterness
2. Jaggers	(*b*) Kindness
3. Ms. Havisham	(*c*) Loyalty
4. Joe	(*d*) Moral Ambiguity

1. 1-(*c*), 2-(*a*), 3-(*d*), 4-(*b*)
2. 1-(*d*), 2-(*c*), 3-(*b*), 4-(*a*)
3. 1-(*c*), 2-(*d*), 3-(*a*), 4-(*b*)
4. 1-(*b*), 2-(*a*), 3-(*d*), 4-(*c*)

138. Select the correct option to complete the sentence.

The setting of 'House Made of Dawn' is significant because it highlights ____.

1. the urbanisation of Native American life
2. the isolation of Native Americans in a distant land
3. the peaceful coexistence of Native American and European cultures
4. the clash between Native American traditions and modern American society

139. How does the theme of female empowerment manifest through the character of Celie in 'The Color Purple'?

1. She learns to assert her voice and embrace her independence.
2. She relies on her relationship with men for validation and strength.
3. She becomes more submissive to men over time.
4. She remains isolated and does not change throughout the novel.

140. In 'Voss' by Patrick White, where do we find the theme of death and redemption most evident?

1. The collapse of Voss's leadership under extreme desert conditions
2. The internal conflicts among the expedition members during their journey
3. The death of key expedition members early in the journey
4. The symbolic impact of Voss's death on Laura's understanding of herself

141. Select the correct future tense form of the verb in brackets to fill in the blank.

By next summer, Linda ____ (bartend) for a year.

1. will bartend
2. will have been bartending
3. will bartending
4. will be bartending

142. How does the use of ethos in persuasive writing contribute to the effectiveness of the argument?

1. By creating vivid imagery
2. By providing logical reasoning and evidence
3. By appealing to the reader's emotions
4. By establishing the writer's credibility and ethical stance

143. Which of the following sentences best exemplifies the use of personification in descriptive writing?

1. The mountain stood tall against the sky.
2. The clouds floated by lazily.
3. The flowers bloomed in the garden.
4. The river murmured softly as it wound through the valley.

144. Identify the structure of the following passage.

The invention of Braille was a major turning point in the history of disability. The writing system of raised dots used by visually impaired people was developed by Louis Braille in nineteenth-century France. In a society that did not value disabled people in general, blindness was particularly stigmatised, and lack of access to reading and writing was a significant barrier to social participation. The idea of tactile reading was not entirely new, but existing methods based on sighted systems were difficult to learn and use. As the first writing system designed for blind people's needs, Braille was a groundbreaking new accessibility tool. It not only provided practical benefits but also helped change the cultural status of blindness.

1. Topic sentence, description, explanation, persuasion
2. Explanation, description, persuasion, topic sentence
3. Significance, description, topic sentence, explanation
4. Topic sentence, description, significance, explanation

145. In 'Adventures of Huckleberry Finn', which character serves as a moral compass for Huck, despite being a slave?

1. Jim
2. Pap Finn
3. Tom Sawyer
4. The Duke

146. Which of the following techniques used by Lawrence in 'Sons and Lovers' helped him achieve a high degree of psychological realism?

1. Dialogues
2. Third person narrator's foreshadowing
3. Stream of consciousness
4. Contrasting parallels

147. Which of the following best describes the impact of a well-structured argument on the coherence of an essay?

1. It enhances the overall coherence by ensuring each part of the argument logically follows from the previous one.
2. It provides a detailed and thorough explanation, allowing the reader to grasp the full scope of the argument.
3. It allows for flexibility in idea development, ensuring a smooth transition between diverse points of view.
4. It simplifies complex ideas, making the argument more accessible without losing its depth.

148. Even though *Middlemarch* is known for its realistic representation of the then society, which of the following social classes is missing from the novel?

1. Aristocracy
2. Clergymen
3. Landed gentry
4. Labourers

149. Which of the following is true of the snowflake method for outlining a plot of the story?

1. Writing character summary is the beginning of the snowflake method of outlining the plot of a narrative.
2. It is important to begin the story with a crucial event in the snowflake method of outlining a plot.
3. The snowflake method of designing the plot outline begins with an introduction of a character with the name.
4. In the snowflake method of plot outlining, one-sentence summary is written first and then it is expanded into a long story.

150. Which revision strategy is the most effective for improving the overall clarity of a text?

1. Removing redundancies and unnecessary details
2. Changing the font size
3. Adding more adjectives and adverbs
4. Rewriting the text in a different language

151. Which of following options is correct about the given statements?

A. Sylvia Plath's 'Daddy' is a confessional piece of poetry with several autobiographical elements.

B. However, the description of a fascist and Nazi father, the "daddy" in the poem becomes a symbol for patriarchy as a whole who subjugates women with 'the boot in the face' and has to be killed multiple times so that a woman could survive.

1. A is false, but B is true.
2. A is true, but B is false.
3. Both A and B are true, but B is arguable.
4. Both A and B are true, and B is justified.

152. In an argumentative essay, why is it important to address counterarguments?

1. To lengthen the essay
2. To seem scholarly and well-read
3. To weaken the opposing side's arguments
4. To show a balanced understanding of the issue and strengthen the original argument

153. In narrative writing, what role does a subplot typically play in relation to the main plot?

1. It distracts the reader from the main events.
2. It complements and enhances the main plot by introducing additional conflicts or themes.
3. It serves as an irrelevant side story.
4. It only serves to increase the length of the narrative.

154. Select the sentence that is NOT in the future tense.

1. They had already finished their work before we arrived.
2. I will visit my grandparents next summer.
3. She is going to bake a cake for the party.
4. He shall complete his assignment by tomorrow.

155. Select the correct present perfect continuous tense form of the underlined verb in the given sentence.

My aunt <u>live</u> in Korea for five years.

1. has lived 2. has been living
3. is living 4. lives

156. Which of the following is a common pitfall that can obscure the purpose of expository writing?

1. Diverging into personal opinions and irrelevant topics
2. Providing ample supporting details
3. Maintaining an objective tone
4. Staying focussed on the central idea

157. In structuralism, the concept of 'binary oppositions' refers to ______.

1. the dual narrative perspectives in a novel
2. the contrast between the protagonist and antagonist in a story
3. the comparison of two different literary genres
4. the underlying oppositional relationships that structure meaning in language and texts

158. Many poems from the 'Songs of Innocence and Experience' represent parallel situations representing the states before and after exposure to the cruelties and realities of adult world. Identify the pair that does NOT fall in this category.

1. The Blossom and The Sick Rose
2. The Divine Image and The Human Abstract
3. The Shepherd and London
4. The Lamb and The Tyger

159. The opening lines of 'Tom Jones', 'An author ought to consider himself, not as a gentleman who gives a private or eleemosynary treat, but rather as one who keeps a public ordinary, at which all persons are welcome for their money', introduce a recurring motif in the novel. Identify that motif.

1. Food 2. Lust
3. Deceit 4. Failure

160. Which organisational strategy is most effective when writing a comparative essay?
1. Circular argumentation
2. Chronological order
3. Narrative structure
4. Block method and point-by-point method

161. Select the correct present continuous tense form of the underlined verb in the given sentence.

I meet the girls at seven.

1. met
2. meets
3. has met
4. am meeting

162. Whose gossip and judgement emphasises themes of conformity and societal pressures in Patrick White's, The Solid Mandala'?
1. The neighbours
2. The relatives
3. The twins
4. The friends

163. Select the correct future tense form of the verb in brackets to fill in the blank.

This time tomorrow, I _____ (perform) on the big stage.

1. will be performing
2. am performing
3. will have been performing
4. will perform

164. Four sentences related to a topic are given below in jumbled order. Three of them can form a meaningful paragraph. Select the ODD sentence.

A. If we want to prevent the concentration of all wealth and power in the hands of a small elite, the key is to regulate the ownership of data.

B. In the 21st century, however, data will eclipse both land and machinery as the most important asset, and politics will be a struggle to control the flow of data.

C. Facebook's crucial test will come when an engineer invents a new tool that causes people to spend less time buying stuff online and more time in meaningful offline activities with friends.

D. The race to obtain the data is already on, headed by data giants such as Google, Facebook, Baidu and Tencent.

1. D
2. B
3. A
4. C

165. Select the correct present perfect tense form of the underlined verb in the given sentence.

My aunt work at the factory for seven years.

1. is working
2. has been working
3. has worked
4. worked

Direction (Qs. No. 166 to 170): *Read the given passage and answer the questions that follow.*

In the modern world, progress is often synonymous with improvement. However, as we race towards technological advancements and societal changes, we sometimes fail to recognise the paradoxical nature of progress. While we have developed unprecedented conveniences, from smartphones to artificial intelligence, we have also encountered unforeseen consequences. The more we advance, the more we seem to distance ourselves from nature and the essence of human interaction. Environmental degradation, social isolation and the erosion of traditional values are the darker side effects of our relentless pursuit of progress.

Progress, in its pursuit of efficiency and speed, has inadvertently created a world where people are increasingly disconnected from one another. The rise of social media, while allowing for instant communication, has made personal interactions more superficial. The promise of technological advancement has failed to deliver the profound sense of fulfillment that many expected. While the conveniences of modern life are undeniable, they come at the cost of our emotional and environmental well-being. We may have solved many practical problems, but at the expense of losing touch with the deeper human connections that once defined our societies. In our relentless race forward, we have ignored the profound need for balance between advancement and maintaining the values that make life meaningful. As we continue on this path, it is essential to pause and reflect on whether the price we are paying for progress is truly worth it. Can we achieve a balance between technological development and maintaining a connection to our roots? Can we truly progress without losing the human aspects that make life meaningful?

166. Select the most appropriate ANTONYM of the word 'isolation' as used in the passage.

1. Separation 2. Connection
3. Distinction 4. Seclusion

167. How does the theme of the passage relate to real-life situations?

1. The passage encourages abandoning technology to return to a simpler, traditional lifestyle.
2. It highlights the growing concern over how environmental issues are linked to industrial progress.
3. The passage reflects how our daily use of smartphones has improved communication.
4. It shows that technological advancements have no impact on human interactions.

168. Identify the central theme of the passage.

1. Traditional values are outdated and irrelevant.
2. Progress only harms the environment.
3. Technological advancements are always beneficial.
4. Progress brings both benefits and unintended consequences.

169. Select the summary that best captures the essence of the given passage.

1. Although progress has brought technological improvements it also comes with side effects like social isolation and environmental harm.
2. Progress is all about the conveniences and technologies we use every day.
3. The future holds limitless potential for progress, with no drawbacks.
4. The passage highlights how technology and nature can coexist perfectly.

170. Identify the most suitable title for the passage.

1. The Effect of Advancement
2. The Age of Innovation
3. The Cost of Convenience
4. The Paradox of Progress

Direction (Qs. No. 171 to 175): *Read the given passage and answer the questions that follow.*

The 21st century has witnessed an unprecedented evolution in artificial intelligence (AI), reshaping the way humans interact with technology. With the advent of neural networks, machine learning and deep learning, AI has infiltrated nearly every sector, from healthcare to finance and from entertainment to governance. While some celebrate AI as the dawn of a new intellectual revolution, others express deep concerns about its ethical implications. The ability of AI to process vast amounts of data within milliseconds presents both an opportunity and a threat—enabling innovations while simultaneously raising issues regarding surveillance, privacy and job displacement.

Historical parallels exist; the Industrial Revolution, for example, mechanised production but also displaced workers, leading to socio-economic shifts. Today, AI is at a similar crossroads, and the world must carefully navigate the balance between innovation and ethical responsibility. Policymakers, technologists and ethicists must engage in continuous dialogue to ensure that AI serves humanity rather than undermining it. The core question remains: Will AI empower society, or will it exacerbate inequalities? The answer depends on how humans choose to wield this transformative power.

Beyond economic and ethical concerns, AI also raises philosophical questions about human identity and creativity. As AI-generated content becomes more sophisticated, distinguishing between human and machine-made works is increasingly challenging. The implications for authorship, intellectual property and artistic expression are profound. If AI can compose music, write literature and generate paintings, what does it mean to be truly creative? These concerns further highlight the necessity of ethical oversight and regulation. While AI has the potential to revolutionise industries and elevate human capabilities, unchecked advancements may lead to unforeseen consequences that reshape the very fabric of society. Thus, a balance between technological progress and ethical vigilance is essential for a sustainable future.

171. What is the central theme of the passage?

1. Comparison between AI and the Industrial Revolution
2. The ethical and societal implications of AI
3. The role of policymakers in regulating AI
4. The economic consequences of AI implementation

172. How is the passage structured?

1. A chronological history of AI development
2. A balanced discussion weighing the pros and cons of AI
3. A cause-and-effect analysis of AI's influence
4. A personal opinion on the impact of AI

173. Select the summary that best captures the essence of the given passage.

1. AI will inevitably lead to global job loss and economic collapse.
2. AI is a technological advancement that benefits all sectors without any disadvantages.
3. AI is a powerful tool with both benefits and risks, requiring careful ethical consideration.
4. The Industrial Revolution and AI are identical in their impact on society.

174. How does the passage connect to real-world issues?

1. It discusses how AI is irrelevant to modern-day society.
2. It focuses solely on the futuristic possibilities of AI.
3. It relates the rise of AI to previous technological revolutions and ethical concerns.
4. It ignores any real-world connection and remains theoretical.

175. How is the tone of the passage?

1. Alarmist and pessimistic
2. Satirical and dismissive
3. Enthusiastic and overly optimistic
4. Neutral and analytical

Direction (Qs. No. 176 to 180): *Read the given passage and answer the questions that follow.*

Speculative fiction has given way to pressin realism in the conversation about artificia intelligence (AI) in recent years. As AI is use more and more in fields like healthcare, educatior finance and national security, stakeholders ar facing previously unheard-of ethical, societal an legal ramifications. Although AI systems have th potential to boost productivity and creativity, the also bring up difficult issues with accountability transparency and prejudice. Algorithmic bia in which AI systems mirror or even magnif preexisting societal disparities is one particular controversial topic. Facial recognition softwa frequently misidentifies members of minori groups more frequently than others, according studies. Similar to this, even if gender or rac is not specifically included in the algorithm, A driven hiring tools may prejudice applicants bas on these factors. These results highlight the ne for inclusive data sets and stricter managemer

Furthermore, a major problem with ma AI models, especially those based on de learning, is their opacity. Known as 'bla box' systems, these models are capable producing incredibly precise forecasts withc offering clear explanations. This inability to be interpreted damages public confidence and makes regulatory actions more difficult. The challenge of how to strike a balance between innovation and accountability still stands as governments and institutions start to design frameworks for AI governance. It is not just ideal, but crucial to use a multidisciplinary strategy that includes ethicists, technologists, legal experts and impacted populations. AI's transformational potential can only be realised for equitable advancement through proactive regulation and inclusive discourse.

176. What conclusions concerning public confidence in AI systems can be drawn from the passage?

1. Efficiency is causing it to develop gradually.
2. It has little influence over policy decisions.
3. Media coverage is a major factor.
4. Lack of transparency undermines it.

177. What does the passage's use of the word 'opacity' most closely mean?

1. No clarity
2. Absence of visibility
3. Rejection to regulation
4. Effectiveness

178. Which of the following is deemed necessary for the development of AI in a responsible manner?

1. Leadership in the private sector
2. Regulatory avoidance
3. A multidisciplinary strategy
4. Greater automation

179. What is meant by 'algorithmic bias'?

1. Mathematical computation errors
2. AI's incapacity to handle massive data sets
3. AI systems figuring out how to fix social problems
4. AI systems that replicate or exacerbate preexisting social injustices

180. What is the passage about?

1. The economic advantages of AI
2. The evolution of AI
3. The difficulties and consequences of using AI
4. Deep learning's technical components

181. Which philosophy underpins Assessment for Learning (AfL)?

1. Behaviourism
2. Positivism
3. Constructivism
4. Essentialism

182. What does 'language across the curriculum' primarily emphasise?

1. Using language in all subject areas
2. Teaching only through the mother tongue
3. Learning grammar rules in isolation
4. Using language only in language classes

183. What does the term gender bias refer to?

1. Neutral attitude towards gender
2. A preference for science subjects
3. Unequal treatment based on gender
4. Biological difference between sexes

184. In the context of lesson planning, what does the term 'differentiation' refer to?

1. Implementing technology in the classroom
2. Teaching different subjects each day
3. Using various assessment methods
4. Tailoring instruction to meet individual student needs

185. According to Taba (1962), which principle ensures logical progression and increasing complexity in curriculum content?

1. Moral education
2. Cultural assimilation
3. Vertical articulation
4. Horizontal integration

186. Which of the following is a formative assessment practice?

1. National standardised test
2. Final term examination
3. Weekly quiz with feedback
4. Annual performance report

187. What is the term for a child's ability to control impulses and delayed gratification?

1. Metacognition 2. Concrete thinking
3. Self-regulation 4. Perseverance

188. Which of the following best describes a student who prefers experiential learning?

1. Memorizes facts without understanding
2. Learns only through lectures
3. Learns through abstract symbols
4. Learns by doing and hands-on activities

189. What does cross-curricular planning in subject pedagogy enhance?

1. Subject rigidity
2. Interdisciplinary understanding
3. Siloed knowledge
4. Examination burden

190. What is the role of the teacher in constructivist learning best described as?

1. Disciplinarian
2. Passive evaluator
3. Facilitator of learning
4. Source of knowledge

191. With which approach is inquiry-based learning strategy best aligned?

1. Classical conditioning
2. Humanist
3. Behaviourist
4. Constructivist

192. Which principle is violated if curriculum content is culturally biased or ignores minority perspectives?

1. Scope 2. Appropriateness
3. Inclusiveness 4. Comprehensiveness

193. What is the process of transforming disciplinary knowledge into teachable content called?

1. Curriculum reduction
2. Instructional automation
3. Content elimination
4. Pedagogical transformation

194. Which perspective views learning as a response to external stimuli?

1. Behaviourist 2. Humanist
3. Constructivist 4. Cognitive

195. According to the Index for Inclusion, which of the following is one key dimension of inclusive practice?

1. Building community
2. Reducing flexibility
3. Ranking students
4. Focusing on exams

196. Which classroom strategy is best for encouraging aesthetic learning?

1. Dramatisation
2. Silent reading tests
3. Repetition drills
4. Closed-ended worksheets

197. What does 'hidden curriculum' in schools refer to?

1. Gender-neutral teaching practices
2. Specialised training material
3. The official syllabus taught in class
4. Unstated norms and values implicitly taught

198. What does the principle of Zero Rejection Policy under inclusive education ensure?

1. No child is denied admission based on disability
2. Neurotypical students are admitted on priority
3. Gifted children are separated from slow Learners
4. All students pass an entrance test

199. Which of the following should planning for subject pedagogy take into account?

1. Single teaching method
2. Uniform content delivery
3. Learner diversity
4. Only textbook exercises

200. The integration of environmental science with geography and biology is an example of:

1. narrow subject teaching
2. disciplinary breakdown
3. interdisciplinary learning
4. unstructured learning

ANSWERS

1	**2**	**3**	**4**	**5**	**6**	**7**	**8**	**9**	**10**
2	4	1	1	4	1	2	3	3	3
11	**12**	**13**	**14**	**15**	**16**	**17**	**18**	**19**	**20**
3	1	1	3	3	2	3	3	4	2
21	**22**	**23**	**24**	**25**	**26**	**27**	**28**	**29**	**30**
3	4	1	3	3	4	4	3	4	3
31	**32**	**33**	**34**	**35**	**36**	**37**	**38**	**39**	**40**
3	3	1	2	2	4	3	4	1	1
41	**42**	**43**	**44**	**45**	**46**	**47**	**48**	**49**	**50**
3	1	1	3	2	1	3	2	1	4
51	**52**	**53**	**54**	**55**	**56**	**57**	**58**	**59**	**60**
3	2	2	4	3	2	4	4	4	3
61	**62**	**63**	**64**	**65**	**66**	**67**	**68**	**69**	**70**
3	1	4	2	4	2	1	1	4	3
71	**72**	**73**	**74**	**75**	**76**	**77**	**78**	**79**	**80**
4	3	1	1	3	1	4	3	4	1
81	**82**	**83**	**84**	**85**	**86**	**87**	**88**	**89**	**90**
1	4	4	3	2	1	4	2	1	4
91	**92**	**93**	**94**	**95**	**96**	**97**	**98**	**99**	**100**
1	4	4	2	4	4	4	4	3	1
101	**102**	**103**	**104**	**105**	**106**	**107**	**108**	**109**	**110**
4	4	1	3	1	1	1	1	2	1
111	**112**	**113**	**114**	**115**	**116**	**117**	**118**	**119**	**120**
3	1	1	1	2	2	1	4	3	4
121	**122**	**123**	**124**	**125**	**126**	**127**	**128**	**129**	**130**
4	2	2	2	2	1	2	2	3	3
131	**132**	**133**	**134**	**135**	**136**	**137**	**138**	**139**	**140**
3	4	2	2	3	4	3	4	1	4
141	**142**	**143**	**144**	**145**	**146**	**147**	**148**	**149**	**150**
2	4	4	4	1	3	1	1	4	1
151	**152**	**153**	**154**	**155**	**156**	**157**	**158**	**159**	**160**
3	4	2	1	2	1	4	3	1	4
161	**162**	**163**	**164**	**165**	**166**	**167**	**168**	**169**	**170**
4	1	1	4	3	2	2	4	1	4

171	172	173	174	175	176	177	178	179	180
2	2	3	3	4	4	1	3	4	3
181	**182**	**183**	**184**	**185**	**186**	**187**	**188**	**189**	**190**
3	1	3	4	3	3	3	4	2	3
191	**192**	**193**	**194**	**195**	**196**	**197**	**198**	**199**	**200**
4	3	4	1	1	1	4	1	3	3

EXPLANATORY ANSWERS

1. Third Wave Feminism emerged in the 1990s as a response to the perceived limitations of the second wave. It emphasized individual identity, intersectionality, and the diversity of women's experiences. Unlike earlier waves that often focused on a universal female identity, the third wave recognized how race, class, sexuality, and culture intersect to shape different forms of womanhood. It also embraced popular culture and digital activism as legitimate spaces for feminist expression.

2. In corpus-based analysis, researchers examine large collections of texts (corpora) to identify patterns in language use. The tool primarily used to explore the frequency and distribution of words or phrases is the concordance line, which displays instances of a word in context, allowing analysts to see how it's used across texts. While collocation analysis shows word associations, concordance lines directly reveal frequency and context.

3. According to William Wordsworth, in his Preface to Lyrical Ballads, a poet's language should be that of ordinary men—natural, spontaneous, and free from artificial expressions. He rejected the overly ornate and stylized diction of neoclassical poetry, favoring simplicity and emotional authenticity to express genuine human feelings.

4. Wole Soyinka's play A Dance of the Forests opens with The Dead Man and Dead Woman coming up out of the soil. This scene symbolizes the resurfacing of the past to confront the living, setting the stage for the play's exploration of Nigeria's historical and moral complexities.

5. In Arthur Miller's Death of a Salesman, the playwright blurs the boundaries between past and present primarily through the use of flashbacks. Willy Loman's mind slips between memories and reality, allowing the audience to experience his psychological collapse and the weight of unfulfilled dreams. This narrative technique deepens the tragedy by intertwining illusion with reality.

6. Nadine Gordimer's July's People is a scathing critique of white liberalism in apartheid South Africa. The novel follows the Smales family, liberal whites forced to rely on their Black servant July during a civil war. This role reversal exposes the fragility of their liberal ideals, their dependence on privilege, and the failure of true communication between races. The Smales' attachment to possessions further highlights the superficiality of their beliefs.

7. A hierarchical sentence structure organizes ideas with main and subordinate clauses properly connected. The sentence "Although the book was interesting, the ending disappointed many readers", correctly uses a subordinating conjunction ("although") to form a dependent clause linked to an independent clause. The other options contain grammatical or structural errors.

8. In David Malouf's Remembering Babylon, Gemmy is portrayed as lost and disoriented, struggling to find his identity. Having lived between the white settlers and the Aboriginal people, he embodies the theme of alienation and cultural in-betweenness. His fragmented sense of belonging highlights the tensions of colonial identity and displacement.

9. The description of Peter's perception of the city as "a vast, impersonal machine" reflects the modernist theme of alienation. Modernist literature often depicts individuals feeling isolated, dehumanized, and disconnected within the mechanized and impersonal modern world. The imagery of "cogs and wheels" symbolizes loss of individuality in urban life.

10. In Mark Twain's Adventures of Huckleberry Finn, Huck and Jim travel on the Mississippi River, which serves as both a literal and symbolic route to freedom. The river represents escape from societal constraints and moral hypocrisy, allowing the characters to explore themes of friendship, race, and freedom.

11. Look Back in Anger critiques the Welfare State by exposing its failure to create true social equality. Jimmy Porter's anger reflects disillusionment with post-war Britain, where promised equality remains unfulfilled despite economic reforms.

12. H. P. Grice introduced the concept of implicature, explaining how speakers convey meanings indirectly through conversational context and implied understanding.

13. The postcolonial legacy is ambiguous because the age of Enlightenment was also an age of empire, linking ideals of freedom with colonial domination.

14. For Marx, societies differ based on their technology and division of labour, which determine class relations and production systems.

15. In Marxist criticism, the economic base shapes the superstructure (culture and ideology), though the superstructure can also influence the base.

16. In N. Scott Momaday's House Made of Dawn, Abel's return to the reservation symbolizes his search for peace and healing after his trauma and alienation in the modern world. It marks a spiritual reconnection with his Native roots and traditions.

17. John Milton's first dramatic representation of the struggle between good and evil appears in Comus, a masque blending poetry and moral allegory, foreshadowing themes developed later in Paradise Lost.

18. In W.B. Yeats's Sailing to Byzantium, Byzantium represents an ideal world of art, spirituality, and eternal beauty, standing apart from the decay of mortal life. Historically, Byzantium refers to the ancient city that became Constantinople, and today it is Istanbul in modern-day Turkey. Yeats uses it as a symbol of transcendence through artistic and spiritual perfection.

19. In E.M. Forster's A Passage to India, when Aziz and Fielding âre separated by rocks during their final ride, it symbolises the inevitable divide created by racial politics. Despite their genuine friendship, the colonial realities of British rule make true equality impossible. The physical separation mirrors the social and cultural distance that the political climate enforces between them.

20. Orientalism emerged as a field of study and set of ideas in the context of European colonialism and imperialism during the 18th and 19th centuries, shaping how the West represented and dominated the East.

21. The theory that challenges fixed meanings in texts by revealing contradictions, ambiguities, and linguistic instability is Deconstruction. Developed by Jacques Derrida, it argues that meaning is never stable or absolute but constantly shifting through language and interpretation.

22. In Alice Walker's The Color Purple, the first-person epistolary narrative makes the theme of oppression deeply personal and immediate. Celie's letters allow readers to experience her pain, growth, and empowerment directly through her voice, creating intimacy and emotional authenticity.

23. Assimilation is a phonological process where one sound changes to become more like a neighboring sound. For example, in "input" pronounced as "imput", the /n/ changes to /m/ under the influence of the following /p/.

24. S.T. Coleridge critiqued Wordsworth's views on poetic diction, arguing in his Biographia Literaria that Wordsworth's claim to use the "language of common men" was inconsistent and that poetic language should still elevate expression while remaining natural.

25. In David Malouf's Remembering Babylon, the fragmented and non-linear structure mirrors the themes of displacement, identity, and cultural fragmentation. This narrative style reflects the characters' psychological and cultural confusion, blurring boundaries between past and present, civilization and wilderness.

26. A dialect is a regional or social variety of a language distinguished by its own vocabulary, grammar, and pronunciation. Dialects reflect local identity and culture but remain mutually intelligible with the standard language.

27. The statement defining a structure as an operational group with indefinite meaning and finite relationships was made by Martial Gueroult, a structuralist philosopher who emphasized relationships over fixed elements in meaning-making.

28. In George Bernard Shaw's Pygmalion, the play suggests that financial success does not equate to moral superiority. Through characters like Henry Higgins and Eliza Doolittle, Shaw shows that wealth and class do not inherently grant virtue, empathy, or refinement.

29. A dialect is a language variety used by a particular social or regional group, marked by unique vocabulary, pronunciation, and grammar. It reflects the identity, culture, and social background of its speakers. For example, British and American English are dialects of the same language. Dialects show how language varies across communities while remaining largely intelligible.

30. The 1984 Anti-Sikh riots in India, following Prime Minister Indira Gandhi's assassination, inspired Amitav Ghosh's The Shadow Lines. The novel examines memory, violence, and the blurred boundaries of identity and nationhood.

31. In W.B. Yeats's Sailing to Byzantium, the key themes include old age, mortality, artistic immortality, and spiritual transcendence. The poem does not focus on unrequited love and regret—that theme appears in some of Yeats's other works, not this one.

32. In Pride and Prejudice, Charlotte Lucas marries Mr. Collins because of economic and social necessity. As a plain, unmarried woman with limited prospects, she saw his proposal as her only chance at security and independence within a restrictive society that offered few options to women.

33. Amitav Ghosh's The Shadow Lines won the Sahitya Akademi Award in 1989. The novel explores themes of memory, identity, and the blurred boundaries between nations and personal histories.

34. Orientalist scholarship justified colonial domination by portraying the Orient as backward, irrational, and in need of Western civilisation. This created a false binary where the West was seen as progressive and rational, legitimizing imperial control as a "civilizing mission".

35. In Browning's Childe Roland to the Dark Tower Came, Roland is not depicted as a cripple; he is a weary but determined knight seeking purpose and redemption. The title indeed comes from King Lear, and Roland symbolizes perseverance amid despair.

36. In Poetics, Aristotle says poetry is "more philosophical" than history because it treats the universal—what could or is likely to happen—whereas history records the particular—what actually has happened. Hence, poetry's superiority lies in its engagement with possibilities and general truths, not mere facts.

37. In postcolonial theory, Ethnic Studies focuses on art and literature produced by identifiable ethnic groups that are marginalized or subordinate to dominant cultures. It seeks to highlight their voices, histories, and cultural identities often suppressed by mainstream narratives.

38. In Samuel Beckett's Waiting for Godot, the tree symbolizes life, hope, and stability, yet it also becomes a source of uncertainty and existential doubt. Its sudden appearance of leaves between the acts suggests a fragile sign of renewal, but its barrenness and ambiguity reflect the characters' confusion about meaning and purpose in a bleak, absurd world. Thus, it embodies both hope and existential crisis.

39. Walt Whitman frequently uses anaphora—the repetition of words or phrases at the beginning of lines—in Leaves of Grass to create rhythm, unity, and inclusiveness, reflecting the democratic and collective spirit of his poetry.

40. In Arthur Miller's Death of a Salesman, the American Dream represents the pursuit of material wealth and success as the measure of a man's worth. Willy Loman's tragedy stems from his blind belief that financial success defines happiness and personal value.

41. In N. Scott Momaday's House Made of Dawn, Francisco plays a crucial role in passing on Native American traditions and teachings to Abel. Through stories, rituals, and memories, he connects Abel to his cultural roots, guiding him toward spiritual healing and identity.

42. In Chimamanda Ngozi Adichie's Half of a Yellow Sun, the Igbo ethnic group is primarily associated with the Republic of Biafra, which declared independence during the Nigerian Civil War (1967–1970).

43. In his poetry, Les Murray uses language to celebrate the simplicity, hardships, and beauty of rural life in Australia. His work often reflects empathy for rural people, their struggles, and their connection to nature and landscape.

44. The line that refers to a ghostly encounter in Wuthering Heights is:

"I began to feel a strange, creeping sensation in my fingers, and a cold, clammy feeling in my heart. I looked up, and saw Catherine's face, pale and wan, with her eyes fixed on me."

This depicts Catherine's ghost appearing to Lockwood, creating one of the novel's most haunting scenes.

45. A fundamental principle of structuralist analysis in literature is the exploration of deep structures underlying cultural phenomena. Structuralists study patterns, systems, and relationships in texts rather than focusing on authors or historical context.

46. Louis Althusser introduced the concept of Ideological State Apparatuses (ISAs) to explain how ideology functions in society. These include institutions like schools, churches, and the media that shape individuals' beliefs to maintain the dominance of the ruling class.

47. In William Faulkner's Light in August, Lena Grove symbolizes innocence and renewal. Her calm perseverance and maternal purity contrast with the novel's darker themes, representing hope, continuity, and the enduring human spirit amid chaos.

48. The primary setting of Bapsi Sidhwa's Ice-Candy-Man is Lahore, during the time of India's Partition in 1947. The city's transformation mirrors the communal tensions and human suffering of that period.

49. In The Great Gatsby, Nick Carraway is considered a somewhat unreliable narrator because he glorifies Gatsby while being critical of others, revealing bias and selective sympathy. His partiality clouds the objectivity of his narration.

50. In Mulk Raj Anand's novels, each protagonist reflects the struggles of the Indian working class and oppressed groups:

- In The Road, Bhikhu represents the outcast who fights for dignity and social inclusion.
- In Coolie, Munoo is a poor orphan whose tragic life exposes the exploitation of child labor and colonial injustice.
- In The Big Heart, Ananta, a coppersmith, symbolizes the conflict between tradition and industrial change.
- In The Sword and the Sickle, Lalu Singh embodies the awakening of the peasantry and the rise of socialist ideals.

51. In R.K. Narayan's An Astrologer's Day, the astrologer recognises the man who threatens him by the scar on his forehead. The scar reveals that the man is Guru Nayak, whom the astrologer once attacked and left for dead years earlier.

52. In Christopher Marlowe's Doctor Faustus, Faustus embodies the Renaissance ideal of the thirst for knowledge and limitless power. His desire to go beyond human limitations and master all fields of learning reflects the spirit of intellectual ambition that characterized the Renaissance.

53. In Edgar Allan Poe's The Fall of the House of Usher, the crumbling mansion symbolizes the decay and deterioration of the Usher family. Its physical collapse at the end mirrors the psychological and moral disintegration of its last surviving members.

54. According to Aristotle, tragedy is the highest form of art, as it evokes pity and fear, leading to catharsis—the emotional purification of the audience. Tragedy deals with noble characters and universal human truths, making it superior to other forms.

55. In V.S. Naipaul's A House for Mr. Biswas, the descendants of Indian labourers in Trinidad experience a profound sense of rootlessness and alienation. Cut off from their ancestral homeland and struggling to find identity and stability, their displacement defines the novel's central theme.

56. In Theodore Dreiser's Sister Carrie, Carrie's rise in social status and pursuit of wealth reflect the theme of the tension between individual desires and societal expectations. Her ambition for success and comfort clashes with moral conventions, exposing the materialistic values of modern urban life.

57. In Theodore Dreiser's Sister Carrie, the character who most centrally represents the theme of materialism is Carrie herself. Her journey from a poor country girl to a successful actress illustrates her belief that happiness and fulfillment come through wealth, comfort, and social status. However, despite achieving material success, she remains emotionally unfulfilled, revealing the emptiness of such pursuits.

58. In Salman Rushdie's Midnight's Children, Saleem Sinai has telepathic powers that connect him with all the other children born at the exact moment of India's independence. This ability symbolizes the nation's diversity and shared destiny, embodying magic realism.

59. In Toni Morrison's The Bluest Eye, Pecola Breedlove believes blue eyes will bring her love and acceptance because society idealizes white beauty standards. Thus, both the assertion and the reason are true, and the reason correctly explains the assertion.

60. In Edmund Spenser's Sonnet 67, the poet presents a hunter-prey allegory that ends with mutual surrender, symbolizing love's willing submission. The beloved, once elusive, now yields freely, suggesting harmony through genuine affection.

61. In Robert Browning's Fra Lippo Lippi, the monk-painter is a realist who struggles between spiritual restraint and sensual freedom, arguing that art should portray life truthfully. However, the incorrect statement is D, since he is not apprehended for dressing obscenely but for wandering the streets at night, which arouses suspicion.

62. In Ngugi wa Thiong'o's A Grain of Wheat, General R and Lieutenant Koina initially believe that Karanja is the one who betrayed Kihika to the colonial authorities. However, it is later revealed that Mugo was the true betrayer. This mistaken belief adds to the novel's tension and themes of guilt, sacrifice, and moral ambiguity.

63. Derek Walcott's poem "A Far Cry from Africa" explores genetic hybridity and cultural diversity to express the poet's identity crisis between his African ancestry and British colonial heritage. The poem reflects deep inner conflict about belonging and divided loyalty.

64. In Walt Whitman's Leaves of Grass, nature symbolizes the interconnectedness of all life. It embodies unity, equality, and the divine presence in every living being, reinforcing Whitman's democratic and transcendental vision.

65. The most powerful theme of postcolonial writings is the loss and recovery of cultural identity. Such literature addresses the struggles of formerly colonized peoples to reclaim their heritage, language, and selfhood after the disruptions of imperial rule.

66. In Henry Miller's Black Spring, the theme of personal freedom is explored through characters who reject societal expectations and embrace individualism. Miller celebrates artistic and sexual liberation, challenging conventional morality and affirming self-expression as a path to authenticity.

67. The title House Made of Dawn symbolizes the spiritual and cultural connection of the protagonist, Abel, to his ancestral lands. It alludes to a Navajo prayer, representing healing, harmony, and the cyclical renewal of life central to Native American spirituality.

68. A regional dialect is specific to a particular geographic area, reflecting distinct pronunciation, vocabulary, and grammar that mark speakers from that region.

69. Pragmatics deals with how meaning is shaped by context. Its practical use is interpreting an indirect request based on social and situational context, such as understanding that "Can you pass the salt?" is a polite request, not a question about ability.

70. Postcolonial Criticism investigates the relationships between colonisers and the colonised in the period post-colonisation, examining power, identity, representation, and the lingering effects of empire on culture and literature.

71. Thematically, the line "You know that the soot cannot spoil your white hair" reflects the loss of innocence and movement toward maturity. It contrasts childlike optimism with the harsh reality of suffering. Both statements (A) and (B) are correct, and (B) supports (A) by explaining how the experience transforms the child's understanding of the world.

72. In July's People, the social structure that coincides with apartheid is patriarchy. Both systems reinforce domination and control—apartheid through race, patriarchy through gender—reflecting power hierarchies deeply rooted in society.

73. In Girish Karnad's Tughlaq, the irony of the motif of prayer lies in the fact that prayer becomes a time for murder. The Sultan's religious devotion is corrupted by political violence, exposing the hypocrisy and moral decay of his rule.

74. In Mahesh Dattani's Tara, gender discrimination is addressed by depicting a family where the male child is given preference over the female child. The play exposes societal norms that value sons more, showing how Tara's life is limited by her gender despite equal potential.

75. In Death of a Salesman, the garden symbolizes Willy Loman's unattainable dreams and illusion of success. His attempt to plant seeds reflects his desire to leave a legacy, yet the lack of sunlight shows the futility of his efforts—nothing can grow, just as his ambitions cannot flourish.

76. Literary criticism, especially feminist criticism, observes that women in literature have historically been presented as objects seen from a male perspective. This idea aligns with the concept of the "male gaze", where female characters are depicted through patriarchal ideals rather than as independent subjects.

77. In William Faulkner's Light in August, Miss Minnie Cooper is portrayed as a woman embodying both racial prejudice and personal shame. Her false accusation against a Black man reflects her internal frustration and the deep-seated racism of her society.

78. In the context of Ngugi wa Thiong'o's A Grain of Wheat, Uhuru means independence from Britain. It marks Kenya's liberation from colonial rule and symbolizes the struggle, hope, and contradictions surrounding freedom.

79. The title Samskara: A Rite for a Dead Man signifies the socio-religious purification ritual associated with the death of a Brahmin. It reflects both the literal funeral rite and the metaphorical spiritual cleansing of the community confronting moral decay.

80. In J.D. Salinger's The Catcher in the Rye, Holden Caulfield admires his sister Phoebe because she is intelligent, kind, and represents the innocence he longs to protect. She embodies the purity and honesty missing in the adult world he despises.

81. In Samuel Beckett's Waiting for Godot, the meaningless repetition of actions and dialogue best reflects the philosophy of Absurdism. The play illustrates the futility of human existence and the search for meaning in an indifferent universe.

82. In Nathaniel Hawthorne's The Scarlet Letter, the theme of individual versus society is explored through Hester Prynne's isolation and ostracism. Her punishment by the Puritan community exposes the tension between personal freedom, moral strength, and rigid social norms.

83. An allophone is a variant pronunciation of a phoneme that does not change word meaning. For example, the /p/ sounds in pin and spin are different allophones of the same phoneme /p/.

84. In Raja Rao's Kanthapura, the story is narrated by Achakka, an old village woman. Her oral storytelling style gives the novel an authentic, traditional Indian voice and frames historical events through a communal perspective.

85. In Salman Rushdie's Midnight's Children, the blurring of history and fiction is achieved through intertextuality, blending real historical events with imaginative storytelling to question the nature of truth and narrative.

86. The 19th-century Australian poets' fascination with bushrangers—outlaws who defied authority—reflects the nation's spirit of rebellion and independence. These figures became symbols of resistance, freedom, and the rugged individualism central to Australian identity.

87. Intonation helps convey emotion, emphasis, and sentence type, but it does not indicate vowel length, which is a phonetic rather than prosodic feature.

88. In James Fenimore Cooper's The Last of the Mohicans, the story is mainly told from the perspective of Hawkeye (Natty Bumppo), the frontiersman who bridges Native American and European cultures.

89. In Alexander Pope's An Epistle to Dr. Arbuthnot, the image of spiders is used to describe scribblers who write hastily. Pope compares such writers to spiders who spin webs out of themselves — producing intricate but ultimately worthless creations. This metaphor criticizes self-absorbed authors who generate verbose works without real substance or inspiration.

90. The title Heart of Darkness does not refer to the kindness in the hearts of native Africans. Instead, it symbolizes the moral corruption of imperialism, the darkness of human nature, and the literal darkness of the African continent as perceived by Europeans.

91. In Edmund Spenser's Sonnet 77, the lines — "Exceeding sweet, yet void of sinful vice;/ That many sought, yet none could ever taste;/ Sweet fruit of pleasure, brought from Paradice/ By Love himselfe, and in his garden plaste" — allegorically describe the beloved's breasts. The imagery of "sweet fruit of pleasure" and "brought from Paradise" symbolizes purity, chastity, and divine beauty—desirable yet untouched. This reflects Spenser's theme of virtuous love within sacred union.

92. In David Malouf's Remembering Babylon, Gemmy Fairley is best described as a European who has lived among Indigenous Australians. His identity between two cultures embodies the themes of alienation, belonging, and the clash of civilizations.

93. The choice of register in communication primarily depends on the social context, audience, and purpose. Speakers adjust their language formality and tone to suit different situations, such as casual talk versus formal speech.

94. Ralph Waldo Emerson views nature as a teacher and a source of inspiration. In his essay Nature, he presents it as a divine reflection that nurtures the human spirit and connects people with the transcendental truth of the universe.

95. The statement about Mrs. Dalloway—emphasizing colonialism, multiple voices, and power structures—aligns with the postcolonial perspective of Gayatri Chakravorty Spivak, who critiques imperial and patriarchal dominance in literature.

96. In Shelley's A Triumph of Life, themes include the corruptibility of life, the quest for meaning, and the illusion of power and glory. However, surrender to God and faith in His compassion is not a theme, as the poem questions divine order rather than affirms it.

97. In Alexander Pope's An Epistle to Dr. Arbuthnot, Bufo is a satirical representation of Charles Montagu, Earl of Halifax. Pope mocks him as a shallow patron of letters—ostentatious in generosity but insincere and driven by vanity.

98. In Edgar Allan Poe's The Fall of the House of Usher, Roderick Usher's increasing madness results mainly from his isolation from society, which heightens his fears and obsessions, blurring the boundary between reality and imagination.

99. A diphthong is a single vowel sound that changes its quality noticeably during pronunciation, as in the words coin or loud.

100. The statement about Mrs. Dalloway—emphasizing instability of meaning, undecidability, and challenges to truth—reflects the deconstructionist approach of Jacques Derrida, known for analyzing the fluidity of language and meaning.

101. In Raja Rao's Kanthapura, the concept of Satyagraha (the force of truth) shapes the villagers' anti-colonial struggle by emphasizing moral power and non-violence. Inspired by Gandhian ideals, they resist British authority through truth, faith, and passive endurance rather than aggression.

102. In Emily Dickinson's "I'm Nobody! Who are you?", she critiques fame and public recognition, valuing anonymity and authenticity over the superficiality of social attention and popularity.

103. In Marxist theory, false consciousness refers to the set of beliefs and convictions that prevent individuals from perceiving the truth about social and economic realities, keeping them unaware of class exploitation and inequality.

104. In Chimamanda Ngozi Adichie's Half of a Yellow Sun, one key theme is the savagery of war on women, portraying the trauma, loss, and resilience of female characters amid the Biafran War.

105. Arundhati Roy's The God of Small Things blends fantasy and reality through vivid, symbolic, and nonlinear storytelling—characteristic of surrealism, where dreamlike imagery reflects emotional truth and memory.

106. In Book VI of Paradise Lost, Milton depicts the battle between the good and evil angels, where the rebellious angels led by Satan are expelled from Heaven after their defeat. This expulsion marks the fall of Lucifer and his followers.

107. When Girish Karnad said "What struck me absolutely about Tughlaq's history was that it was contemporary", he meant that the political and social realities of 14th-century India under Sultan Tughlaq paralleled those of 20th-century democratic India, showing corruption, idealism, and disillusionment in leadership.

108. The play Tara was directed by Alyque Padamsee, who also discovered and encouraged Mahesh Dattani's talent, giving him the confidence to pursue a career in theatre.

109. In Nathaniel Hawthorne's The Scarlet Letter, the meteor that appears when Hester, Pearl, and Dimmesdale stand on the scaffold is interpreted as a sign of Dimmesdale's guilt, forming an "A" in the sky—a celestial reflection of his hidden sin.

110. John Barth's The Floating Opera reflects post-war concerns of absurdity and uncertainty. The novel questions meaning, morality, and existence in a chaotic world, aligning with postmodern and existentialist thought.

111. In Nissim Ezekiel's "Night of the Scorpion", the scorpion symbolizes fear and suffering. Its sting causes physical pain to the poet's mother and emotional turmoil to the villagers, reflecting human helplessness and superstition.

112. Psychological criticism interprets a literary work as an expression, in an indirect and fictional form, of the author's or characters' state of mind. It explores motives, desires, and subconscious elements influencing behavior and creation.

113. In William Faulkner's "A Rose for Emily", Homer Barron contributes to the Southern Gothic atmosphere by embodying the grotesque and unsettling aspects of Southern life. His mysterious relationship with Emily and his corpse's later discovery heighten the story's eerie tone.

114. In Margaret Laurence's The Stone Angel, Hagar Shipley's relationships are coloured by fear and suspicion of the world. Her pride, emotional repression, and inability to express love isolate her from those closest to her.

115. Amitav Ghosh's The Shadow Lines is set against the backdrop of multiple major historical events — the Swadeshi movement, the Partition of India (1947), the communal riots of 1963–64 in Dhaka and Calcutta, and references to the Second World War. Each of these events deepens the novel's exploration of memory, identity, and the blurred boundaries between nations and people.

116. Derek Walcott's poetry is renowned for its vivid imagery, complex metaphors, and a blend of European literary traditions with Caribbean oral storytelling, all infused with rhythm and musicality. Together, these techniques shape his rich, hybrid poetic voice.

117. In Alice Walker's The Color Purple, the theme of spirituality is tied to Celie's gradual, personal relationship with God, which evolves from passive faith to an empowering inner spirituality that helps her find strength and self-worth.

118. In N. Scott Momaday's House Made of Dawn, the theme of alienation is portrayed through Abel's disconnection from both his Native American roots and the dominant white culture, reflecting his struggle to find identity and belonging.

119. Wimsatt and Beardsley, in their theory of the "Intentional Fallacy", argue that literary criticism should rely on internal evidence from the text itself, rather than the author's intention or biography.

120. In Anita Desai's Clear Light of Day, the Partition of India most directly affects Raja, whose admiration for Muslim culture and closeness to the Hyder Alis lead to tension and separation within his Hindu family during the communal unrest.

121. Toni Morrison's Beloved is set in the aftermath of American slavery during the 19th century, exploring the psychological scars and intergenerational trauma of formerly enslaved people after the Civil War.

122. In Bapsi Sidhwa's Ice-Candy-Man, disability is portrayed as a source of shame and marginalisation, reflecting how disabled individuals are excluded and devalued during the Partition crisis. This depiction exposes society's prejudiced and dismissive attitudes toward disability in times of chaos.

123. In Patrick White's Voss, Johann Ulrich Voss's expedition aims to map uncharted territories in the Australian outback, symbolising not only exploration but also spiritual and existential questing.

124. In Wole Soyinka's A Dance of the Forests, the portrayal of Yoruba culture—through rituals, myths, and ancestral spirits—serves to reflect the need to engage with traditional values dynamically and meaningfully to confront modern societal problems.

125. Wuthering Heights indeed blends Gothic and Romantic elements. The Gothic mode exposes passion, vengeance, and the darkness of human nature, while Romantic sensibility brings transcendence and emotional depth. Thus, both [illegible] true and (A) justifies (S).

126. The lines from Mrs. Dalloway that do not represent a modernist theme are the ones describing an idealised, static scene — "Regent's Park was a haven of tranquility..." — as this reflects traditional, descriptive realism rather than modernist fragmentation or psychological depth.

127. In Ethnographic Discourse Analysis, the most crucial method is prolonged participant observation and contextualised discourse transcription, which allows the researcher to capture how language functions within real social interactions and cultural contexts.

128. Bhisham Sahni's Tamas primarily deals with party politics and religious fanaticism, portraying the chaos, manipulation, and communal hatred surrounding the Partition of India.

129. The last two poems of John Milton's Paradise Regained, along with the dramatic poem Samson Agonistes, were published together in 1671.

130. In T. S. Eliot's Murder in the Cathedral, Becket's final sermon emphasizes that martyrdom should be selfless—a submission to divine will, not a pursuit of personal glory or pride.

131. In Toni Morrison's The Bluest Eye, the motif of seeing and being seen shapes racial and social dynamics through the community's surveillance and judgment. The constant gaze—both white and Black—defines beauty and worth, reinforcing racial hierarchies and Pecola's tragic internalization of inferiority.

132. In John Donne's A Valediction: Forbidding Mourning, the comparison of lovers' souls to the "stiff twin compasses" is an example of a conceit—an extended, intricate metaphor linking two seemingly unrelated things to express spiritual and emotional unity.

133. The central existential theme in John Barth's The Floating Opera is the absurdity of life. The novel reflects post-war disillusionment, questioning the purpose of existence and rejecting absolute mora[l] or philosophical meaning.

134. In Freudian theory, repression is the mechanism by which unacceptable or distressing thought[s] are pushed into the unconscious, preventing the[m] from reaching conscious awareness.

135. In Mulk Raj Anand's Coolie, Munoo symbolises the exploitation of child labour in colonial India. His tragic life journey—from servant to factory worker—exposes systemic oppression and the dehumanizing effects of poverty under colonial rule.

136. In Raja Rao's Kanthapura, Moorthy is primarily influenced by Mahatma Gandhi. He adopts Gandhian ideals of non-violence, truth (Satyagraha), and spiritual resistance, leading his village in the freedom struggle.

137. (*c*) **Wemmick** - Loyalty (especially to Pip and his father, the Aged Parent)

(*d*) **Jaggers** - Moral Ambiguity (a lawyer who is both just and corrupt)

(*a*) **Ms. Havisham** - Bitterness (after being jilted, she lives in resentment)

(*b*) **Joe** - Kindness (gentle, compassionate, and forgiving)

138. The setting of House Made of Dawn is significant because it highlights the clash between Native American traditions and modern American society, reflecting Abel's alienation and struggle for identity between two conflicting worlds.

139. In Alice Walker's The Color Purple, Celie's journey toward female empowerment manifests as she learns to assert her voice, achieve self-worth, and embrace independence through sisterhood and personal growth.

140. In Patrick White's Voss, the theme of death and redemption is most evident in the symbolic impact of Voss's death on Laura's understanding of herself, where his spiritual connection and death bring transcendence and self-realisation to Laura

141. This sentence — "By next summer, Linda _____ (bartend) for a year." — requires the future perfect continuous tense, which expresses an action that will have been ongoing for a certain period up to a point in the future. It shows duration and continuity of an activity that will still be in progress by that time.

142. The use of ethos in persuasive writing appeals to the reader's sense of trust and morality. It helps establish the writer's credibility, reliability, and ethical stance, making the argument more convincing and authoritative.

143. The sentence — "The river murmured softly as it wound through the valley". — uses personification, a poetic device that attributes human qualities to non-human entities. The river is described as "murmuring", which evokes a calm, human-like sound and creates vivid imagery.

144. The passage about Braille begins with a topic sentence introducing its importance, followed by a description of its origin and purpose. It then highlights its significance as a groundbreaking accessibility tool and ends with an explanation of its broader cultural and social impact.

145. In Adventures of Huckleberry Finn, Jim acts as Huck's moral compass. Despite being enslaved, Jim embodies compassion, honesty, and wisdom. His moral strength helps Huck develop empathy and question the corrupt values of his society, leading to Huck's ethical growth.

146. D.H. Lawrence achieved a remarkable level of psychological realism in Sons and Lovers through the use of the stream of consciousness technique. This narrative method allows readers to access the characters' inner thoughts, emotions, and conflicts directly, capturing the complexity of human psychology and emotional depth.

147. A well-structured argument enhances the coherence of an essay by ensuring that each part logically connects to the previous one. This logical flow helps readers follow the progression of ideas smoothly, making the essay persuasive and unified in thought and structure.

148. While Middlemarch offers a comprehensive and realistic portrayal of provincial English society—depicting the clergy, professionals, and middle classes—the aristocracy is notably absent. George Eliot focuses on the moral and intellectual struggles of the middle class rather than the elite, reflecting her interest in ordinary human experiences rather than the privileges of the upper ranks.

149. The snowflake method of outlining a story begins with a one-sentence summary that captures the essence of the plot. This sentence is then gradually expanded into a paragraph, a page, and eventually a full narrative, allowing the story to develop organically while maintaining structural integrity.

150. The most effective revision strategy for improving clarity in writing is removing redundancies and unnecessary details. This helps make the text concise, focused, and easy to understand, allowing the main ideas to stand out without distraction.

151. Sylvia Plath's "Daddy" is a confessional poem deeply rooted in her personal trauma and psychological struggles, drawing from autobiographical elements such as her relationship with her father. The depiction of the Nazi father figure symbolically represents patriarchy and the oppressive systems that subjugate women. The poem's violent imagery and defiance highlight the need for metaphorical destruction of male dominance for female survival.

152. Addressing counterarguments in an argumentative essay is crucial because it demonstrates an understanding of multiple perspectives. This approach not only shows fairness and intellectual honesty but also strengthens the original argument by refuting opposing views with logic and evidence.

153. In narrative writing, a subplot serves to complement and enhance the main plot. It introduces secondary conflicts or themes that mirror or contrast with the central storyline, thereby enriching character development and deepening the overall narrative complexity.

154. The sentence "They had already finished their work before we arrived." is in the past perfect tense, not the future tense. It describes an action completed before another past event. The other options use future constructions.

155. The correct present perfect continuous tense form of the verb "live" in the sentence "My aunt live in Korea for five years." is "has been living." This tense indicates an action that began in the past and continues up to the present.

156. A common pitfall in expository writing is diverging into personal opinions and irrelevant topics, which undermines the objectivity and clarity essential to this form. Expository writing's main purpose is to explain or inform, and introducing subjective viewpoints can obscure the focus and confuse readers.

157. In structuralism, the concept of binary oppositions refers to the underlying oppositional relationships (such as life/death, good/evil, nature/culture) that structure meaning in language and literature. Meaning is generated not through isolated concepts but through their contrast with opposing terms.

158. In Blake's Songs of Innocence and Experience, most poem pairs contrast innocence with experience. However, "The Shepherd" and "London" do not form such a direct parallel — the former portrays pastoral peace and purity, while the latter explores oppression and corruption, with no direct pairing between the two collections.

159. The opening lines of Tom Jones establish food as a recurring motif symbolising human appetite, indulgence, and moral consumption. Fielding uses feasting imagery to mirror society's excesses, connecting physical nourishment with moral and social behavior throughout the novel.

160. In a comparative essay, the most effective organisational strategies are the block method (discussing each subject separately) and the point-by-point method (alternating between subjects for each key aspect). Both structures ensure logical coherence and clear comparison.

161. The correct present continuous tense form of the verb "meet" in the sentence "I meet the girls at seven" is "am meeting". This tense indicates an action that is planned or happening around the present moment.

162. In Patrick White's The Solid Mandala, the gossip and judgment of the neighbours highlight the themes of conformity and societal pressure. Their observations emphasize how society imposes norms and expectations on individuals who are different, particularly the twin brothers.

163. The correct future continuous tense form of the verb "perform" in the sentence "This time tomorrow, I ____ on the big stage" is "will be performing." It expresses an action that will be in progress at a specific time in the future.

164. Sentence C ("Facebook's crucial test will come when an engineer invents a new tool...") is the odd one out because it shifts focus to Facebook's business model rather than the broader theme of data ownership and political control discussed in the other sentences.

165. The correct present perfect tense form of the verb "work" in the sentence "My aunt work at the factory for seven years" is "has worked". This tense indicates an action that began in the past and continues up to the present.

166. The word "isolation" in the passage refers to the state of being separated or disconnected from others. Its most appropriate antonym is "connection", which signifies togetherness and social interaction—the very quality the passage laments losing in modern life.

167. The passage's theme connects to real life by highlighting the growing concern over how environmental issues are linked to industrial progress. It shows that while technology and industry bring comfort, they also cause environmental harm and emotional detachment.

168. The central theme of the passage is that progress brings both benefits and unintended consequences. While technological and social advancements have made life more convenient, they have also led to isolation, environmental degradation, and the loss of meaningful human connections.

169. The summary that best captures the essence of the passage is: Although progress has brought technological improvements, it also comes with side effects like social isolation and environmental harm. This statement balances both the positive and negative aspects of progress discussed in the passage.

170. The most suitable title for the passage is "The Paradox of Progress". This title aptly reflects the central idea that progress, while beneficial, also produces negative consequences, creating a paradox between advancement and loss.

171. The central theme of the passage is the ethical and societal implications of AI. It explores how artificial intelligence offers immense potential for progress while simultaneously posing risks related to privacy, job loss, and the definition of human creativity.

172. The passage is structured as a balanced discussion weighing the pros and cons of AI. It presents both the advantages of AI in innovation and the associated ethical, philosophical, and societal challenges, maintaining an objective analytical tone.

173. The summary that best captures the essence of the passage is: AI is a powerful tool with both benefits and risks, requiring careful ethical consideration. This reflects the author's central argument about balancing technological progress with moral responsibility.

174. The passage connects to real-world issues by relating the rise of AI to previous technological revolutions and ethical concerns. It draws a parallel between the Industrial Revolution and modern AI developments, showing how innovation can create both progress and disruption.

175. The tone of the passage is neutral and analytical. The author neither glorifies nor condemns AI but critically examines its implications, calling for balance between innovation and ethics.

176. The passage suggests that lack of transparency undermines public confidence in AI systems. When algorithms operate as "black boxes" without offering explanations for their decisions, it damages trust and makes it harder for people to rely on or regulate these technologies.

177. The word 'opacity' in the passage most closely means "no clarity". It refers to the fact that deep learning systems often work in ways that are not easily understood or explained, creating confusion about how they reach conclusions.

178. The passage clearly states that a multidisciplinary strategy—involving ethicists, technologists, legal experts, and affected populations—is essential for the responsible development of AI. This ensures fairness, accountability, and inclusivity.

179. The term 'algorithmic bias' refers to AI systems that replicate or exacerbate preexisting social injustices. This happens when biased data or flawed models lead to unfair outcomes, such as misidentification or discrimination in hiring or policing.

180. The passage primarily discusses the difficulties and consequences of using AI—including bias, lack of transparency, and the need for regulation and ethical oversight. It stresses the importance of balancing innovation with accountability.

181. The philosophy that underpins Assessment for Learning (AfL) is Constructivism. This approach emphasises that learners actively construct their own understanding through feedback, reflection, and continuous assessment rather than rote memorisation or external rewards.

182. The concept of 'language across the curriculum' primarily emphasises using language in all subject areas. It recognises that language is central to learning and should be integrated across disciplines to enhance comprehension and expression, not confined to language classes alone.

183. The term 'gender bias' refers to unequal treatment based on gender. It involves favouring one gender over another in opportunities, expectations, or representation, leading to discrimination and perpetuating stereotypes.

184. In lesson planning, 'differentiation' means tailoring instruction to meet individual student needs. Teachers modify content, process, or learning outcomes based on learners' abilities, interests, and learning styles to ensure inclusivity and effectiveness.

185. According to Hilda Taba (1962), the principle that ensures logical progression and increasing complexity in curriculum content is Vertical articulation. It refers to the sequential arrangement of learning experiences that build upon prior knowledge and skills.

186. A formative assessment practice is one that provides ongoing feedback to help students improve during the learning process rather than merely evaluating them at the end. A weekly quiz with feedback fits this definition as it allows for reflection and adjustment in learning.

187. The ability of a child to control impulses and delay gratification is known as self-regulation. It involves managing emotions, behaviour, and attention to achieve long-term goals — an essential aspect of emotional intelligence and learning readiness.

188. A student who prefers experiential learning learns best by doing and through hands-on activities. This approach connects theory with practice, encouraging deeper understanding through experience rather than passive observation or memorisation.

189. Cross-curricular planning enhances interdisciplinary understanding by linking concepts and skills across different subjects. It encourages students to see connections between areas of knowledge, promoting critical thinking and holistic learning.

190. In constructivist learning, the teacher's role is best described as a facilitator of learning. Instead of merely transmitting knowledge, the teacher guides, supports, and encourages learners to construct their own understanding through exploration and inquiry.

191. The inquiry-based learning strategy is best aligned with the Constructivist approach. This method encourages students to ask questions, explore, and discover knowledge through active engagement, thereby constructing their own understanding rather than passively receiving information.

192. When curriculum content is culturally biased or ignores minority perspectives, it violates the principle of Inclusiveness. This principle ensures that all cultural, linguistic, and social groups are represented and respected in educational materials and pedagogy.

193. The process of transforming disciplinary knowledge into teachable content is called Pedagogical transformation. It involves adapting complex academic knowledge into simplified, learner-friendly material suitable for classroom instruction.

194. The Behaviourist perspective views learning as a response to external stimuli. According to behaviourism, behaviour is shaped and reinforced through conditioning—either classical or operant—rather than internal thought processes.

195. According to the Index for Inclusion, one key dimension of inclusive practice is building community. It emphasises creating a welcoming, collaborative environment where diversity is valued and every learner feels a sense of belonging.

196. The classroom strategy best for encouraging aesthetic learning is dramatization. This approach engages imagination, creativity, and emotional expression, helping students appreciate beauty, art, and human experience through performance and interpretation.

197. The term 'hidden curriculum' refers to the unstated norms, values, and beliefs that are implicitly taught in schools through daily interactions, routines, and institutional culture—beyond the formal syllabus. These lessons often shape students' social attitudes and behaviour.

198. The Zero Rejection Policy under inclusive education ensures that no child is denied admission based on disability. It upholds every child's right to education, promoting equal opportunities and inclusive participation for all learners regardless of their abilities.

199. Planning for subject pedagogy must take into account learner diversity. Effective teaching requires adapting methods, materials, and assessments to accommodate students' varying needs, interests, learning styles, and abilities.

200. The integration of environmental science with geography and biology exemplifies interdisciplinary learning, where knowledge from multiple subjects is combined to provide a more holistic understanding of concepts and their real-world applications.

YOUR SPACE

Previous Paper (Solved)

Delhi Subordinate Services Selection Board

DSSSB–PGT (English) Recruitment Exam, 2023*

Subject Knowledge – English & Teaching Methodology

1. Thomas Heywood's *An Apology for Actors* appears in three brief treatises. Which of the following is NOT a part of the mentioned work?
   A. The true use of their quality
   B. Their ancient dignity
   C. Their antiquity
   D. Their apology

2. Who is considered as the prime mover of the Modernist movement in English literature?
   A. TS Eliot B. WH Auden
   C. GB Shaw D. Walt Whitman

3. Which novel by Leo Tolstoy has Napoleon's invasion of Russia in 1812 as its theme?
   A. War and Peace
   B. The Prisoner of Caucasus
   C. Resurrection
   D. Anna Karenina

4. Select the option that expresses the given sentence in passive voice.

   I have often told you to switch off the lights.
   A. Often, I have told you to switch off the lights.
   B. To switch off the lights have been often told to you by me.
   C. You were being often told to switch off the lights.
   D. You have often been told to switch off the lights by me.

5. In which of the following books by JM Coetzee do we come across the character of a hallucinating Magda?
   A. Dusk Lands
   B. In the Heart of the Country
   C. Waiting for the Barbarian
   D. Disgrace

6. What is William Wordsworth's opinion about poetic diction?
   A. "...there is an essential difference between the language of prose and metrical composition."
   B. "A language near to the language of men."
   C. "The richest treasure that our wit affords."
   D. "An operative language for poetry."

7. To whom does Michael Henchard, a character in Thomas Hardy's *The Mayr of Caster-bridge* sell his wife and daughter?
   A. To a passing sailor
   B. To a landlord of the town
   C. To the furmity seller
   D. To the mayor of the town

8. Which of the following poems is an elegy on Abraham Lincoln?
   A. Walt Whitman's *O Caption, My Caption!*
   B. Robert Frost's *Mending Wall*
   C. Emily Dickenson's *Success is Counted*
   D. Langston Hugh's *I, Too*

9. What is the study of the pronunciation of a particular language, within a specific language tradition called?
   A. Orthoepy
   B. Phonetics
   C. Accent
   D. Phonology

* Exam held on 21/06/2023.

10. Select the ***most appropriate*** verb form to fill in the blank.

He used to visit the library every week, but he ______ now.

A. has rarely come B. comes
C. is rarely coming D. rarely comes

11. Which of the following is NOT an example of a dystopian novel?

A. *The Handmaid's Tale* (1985) by Margaret Atwood
B. *Brave New World* (1932) by Aldous Huxley
C. *Men Like Gods* (1923) by HG Wells
D. *Atlas Shrugged* (1957) by Ayn Rand

12. Who among the following wrote two sonnets and sent them to his mother as a New Year's gift from Cambridge?

A. George Herbert B. Andrew Marvell
C. Samuel Johnson D. Herbert Grierson

13. Who among the following writers wrote during the Augustan age?

A. Oliver Goldsmith B. Alexander Pope
C. John Milton D. John Dryden

14. *The Story of Cain and Abel* is an example of a ______.

A. pagan play B. mystery play
C. miracle play D. religious play

15. In which famous poem do the given lines appear?

"I saw a Rose-Bud open this morn;
I'll swear The blushing Morning open'd not more fair."

A. Samuel Johnson's *The Vanity of Human Wishes*
B. Andrew Marvell's *To His Coy Mistress*
C. Abraham Cowley's *The Spring*
D. John Donne's *The Good Morrow*

16. Who among the following critics advocates a close textual and verbal analysis of poetry?

A. Ronald Barthes
B. TS Eliot
C. George Saintsbury
D. IA Richards

17. Who among the following is NOT a Latin American story writer?

A. Gabriel Garcia Marquez
B. Tony Morrison
C. Judith Ortiz Cofer
D. Rosario Ferre

18. What gives a word its principle meaning?

A. A base or root of the morphemes
B. A language units consisting of one word or several words
C. The representative words of phonographic words
D. The graphic representation of words

19. Which of the following works of Virgil does Edmund Spenser emulate in his poetic work *The Shepheard's Calendar?*

A. Eclogues B. Ciris
C. Georgics D. Aeneid

20. What brings the differences between academic or business writing, or regional uses of English?

A. Style of language
B. Rules of language
C. Objectivity in the use of language
D. Flexibility in the use of language

21. Whom does Dryden condemn in his true-blue satirical work *Mac Flecknoe*?

A. Thomas Heywood
B. Thomas Shadwell
C. Oliver Goldsmith
D. James Shirley

22. In which of the following poems by John Donne do these lines, "For God's sake hold your tongue, and let me love" appear?

A. The Good Morrow
B. The Canonization
C. The Sun Rising
D. A Valediction: Forbidding Morning

23. When a group of students brainstorm, write down ideas, develop an outline and draft a good write-up, what does this exercise denote?

A. Exercise of discursive writing
B. Writing narratives
C. Exercise on descriptive writing
D. Personal writing practice

24. Which of the following is NOT a salient feature of Neoclassical poems?
A. Intense use of imagination
B. Grand and expressive style
C. Use of sublime
D. Scholarly allusions

25. Who among the following Shakespearean tragic heroes was bestowed with the 'Thane of Cawdor' title?
A. Bassanio B. Othello
C. Macbeth D. Hamlet

26. Which of the following tales from *The Canterbury Tales* has a long prologue with a condemnation of celibacy?
A. The Knight's tale
B. The Cook's tale
C. The Wife of Bath's tale
D. The Frier's tale

27. "He holds him with his skinny hand,
There was a ship, 'quoth he.
Hold off! unhand me, grey-beard loon!'
Eftsoons his hand dropt he."

Who is the 'grey-beard loon' in the above lines?
A. Don Juan
B. Marino Faliero
C. The Ancient Mariner
D. Kubla Khan

28. What is the 'Freewriting exercise' popularised by Peter Elbow in 1973 also termed as?
A. Automatic writing
B. Invented writing
C. Essay writing
D. Scribbling

29. Which epic imagery is used while referring to Belinda's petticoat as a 'sev'nfoldfence' guarding her, below the waist, from potential violators?
A. Achille's heels
B. Aeneas's quest to the underworld of Hades
C. Shield of Ajax
D. Ixion, an ancient Greek king

30. Who among the following Elizabethan poets wrote *Musophilus: Containing a General Defense* of *Learning*, a long poem having a dialogue between a courtier and a man of letters?
A. Thomas Campion
B. Ben Johnson
C. Christopher Marlow
D. Samuel Daniel

31. "The winged seeds, where they lie cold and low,
Each like a corpse within its grave, until
Thine azure sister of the Spring shall blow"
What does the phrase "Thine azure sister of the Spring" imply?
A. The poet uses the phrase to suggest the cyclic nature of the seasons.
B. The poet here emphasises on the creative and generative force of nature.
C. The poet refers to the spring wind and implies that the two winds are sisters since they work together in bringing about change.
D. The poet refers to the West Wind as the creator and destroyer.

32. In which of the following novels of DH Lawrence do we come across the protagonist, Connie Reid?
A. Lady Chatterley's Lover
B. Sons and Lovers
C. Woman in Love
D. The Rainbow

33. Which of the following was Aravind Adiga's debut novel?
A. Last Man in Tower
B. Amnesty
C. The White Tiger
D. Between the Assassinations

34. The three R's of stylistic analysis stipulate that stylistic analysis should be all of the following EXCEPT:
A. replicable B. retrievable
C. responsive D. rigorous

35. Which of the following can be considered as an INCORRECT style option while writing formally?
A. Use of complicated language to provide simple instructions
B. Use of quotation marks to denote speech
C. Use of a clear and accurate style
D. Consistency

36. Who among the following supported the idea of the author's psychic life finding unconscious revelation in his work?
A. Ellen Willis B. Karl Jung
C. Sigmond Freud D. Ronald Barthes

37. Who wrote the essay, 'The Metaphysical Poets'?
A. TS Eliot B. Herbert Grierson
C. Samuel Johnson D. Andrew Marvell

38. What are lexemes?
A. Words with similar meaning
B. A language unit consisting of one word or several words
C. Words having similar sounds
D. Words having similar phonetic script

39. What does Philip Sidney intend in his work, *The Defence of Poesy*, 1595 with his argumentative manoeuvre, "the poet, he nothing affirms, and therefore never lieth"?
A. To affirm Renaissance as a period of revival
B. To defend Aristotle against Plato's attack in Republic
C. To advocate the classical arts of ancient Rome and Greece
D. To appreciate the spirit of adventure in Elizabethan Era

40. "There shall be
In that rich earth a richer dust concealed;
A dust whom England bore, shaped, made aware,
Gave, once, her flowers to love, her ways to roam;
A body of England's, breathing English air,
Washed by the rivers, blest by suns of home."

In which of the following poems do the above lines appear?
A. Wilfred Owen's *Anthem for Doomed Youth*
B. WH Auden's *The Unknown Citizen*
C. WB Yeats' *An Irish Airman Foresees His Death*
D. Rupert Brooke's *The Soldier*

41. Which of the following works deals with the harshness of the Great Depression and arouses sympathy for the struggles of migrant farmworkers?
A. Sinclair Lewi's *Arrowsmith*
B. Earnest Hemmingway's *To Have and Have Not*
C. Toni Morrison's *Sula*
D. John Steinbeck's *The Grapes of Wrath*

42. Which of the following plays exposes the vanities and vices of mankind and most notably greed-induced credulity?
A. Ben Johnson's *Alchemist*
B. John Webster's *The White Devil*
C. Thomas Kyd's *The Spanish Tragedy*
D. John Fletcher's *The Tamer Tamed*

43. Who among the following literary figures from America is NOT a Nobel Laureate?
A. Ernest Hemingway
B. Isabel Allende
C. TS Eliot
D. Pearl C Buck

44. Which medieval epic has Inferno, Purgatorio and Paradiso as its integral parts?
A. Cursor Mundi
B. Troilus and Criseyde
C. The Divine Comedy
D. Siege of Jerusalem

45. *My Story* is an autobiographical work of which famous Indian female writer?

A. Toru Datta
B. Kamala Markandaya
C. Kamala Das
D. Nayantara Sahgal

46. Identify the kind of determiner of the underlined word in the given sentence.

He has rather a pleasant personality.

A. Numeral B. Qualifier
C. Ordinal D. Pre-determiner

47. Which rhyming scheme was used in *Troilus and Criseyde*, an epic poem written by Geoffrey Chaucer?

A. Spenserian Stanza B. Alliteration
C. Rime Royale D. Ottava Rima

48. Which of the following works by Khushwant Singh harps on the issue of partition and its resultant trauma?

A. Delhi: A Novel
B. The Sikhs
C. Train to Pakistan
D. The End of India

49. In which of the following poems do the given lines appear?

"My vegetable Love should grow
Vaster than Empires, and more slow.
A hundred years should go to praise
Thine Eyes, and on thy Forehead Gaze."

A. Andrew Marvell's *To His Coy Mistress*
B. Samuel Johnson's *The Vanity of Human Wishes*
C. John Donne's *The Good Morrow*
D. George Herbert's *The Altar*

50. What is 'The Lord Chamberlain's Men'?

A. The lead actors in Shakespearean dramas
B. The professional company running famous Elizabethan theatre
C. The performance hall of Oxford and Cambridge University
D. Elizabethan theatre

51. Which of the following is an example of a Stream-of-Consciousness novel?

A. DH Lawrence's *The Rainbow*
B. VS Naipaul's *The Mystic Masseur*
C. Joseph Conrad's *Heart of Darkness*
D. James Joyce's *Ulysses*

52. Who is considered as the first author in the symbolist tradition?

A. Charles Baudelaire
B. Arthur Rimbaud
C. Ezra Pound
D. William Butler Yeats

53. Which novel by Charles Dickens is set in London and Paris during the French Revolution?

A. The Tale of Two Cities
B. David Copperfield
C. Oliver Twist
D. The Great Expectation

54. Which of the following theories by Coleridge harps on "the avoidance of critical thinking or logic in examining something unreal or impossible in reality"?

A. Tradition and Individual talent
B. Theory of 'sublime'
C. Objective co-relative
D. Willing suspension of disbelief

55. What do the critics call Elizabeth Bishop's poems for their detached, descriptive, deliberate and unmoved qualities?

A. Epigrammatical B. Close to painting
C. Abstract D. Free verse

56. In which of Achebe's novels do we come across the following quote?

"Procrastination is a lazy man's apology."

A. Anthills of Savannah
B. Arrow of God
C. A Man of the People
D. Things Fall Apart

57. What are orthographic words?

A. The phonic representation of words
B. The graphic representation of words
C. The pictorial representation of words
D. The representative words of phonographic words

58. Identify the type of clause in the given sentence.

We sow so that we may reap.

A. Adverb clause of result/consequence
B. Adverb clause of manner
C. Adverb clause of comparison
D. Adverb clause of concession

59. Which literary genre does Eliot employ to elucidate the feelings of isolation and inadequacy in *The Love Song of J Alfred Prufrock*?

A. Dramatic monologue
B. Lyric
C. Epic
D. Ballad

60. Which of the following inferior poets does Alexander Pope NOT mention in his satirical work, *An Epistle to Dr. Arbuthnot*?

A. Harvey B. Bishop Philips
C. Jonathan Swift D. Colley

61. Select the ***most appropriate*** modal auxiliary to fill in the blank.

A bridge was built so that the dangerous ferry ________ be avoided.

A. Has to B. would
C. may D. Need to

62. Which of the following poems of William Wordsworth does NOT fall under the category of the Lucy poems?

A. A Slumber Did My Spirit Seal
B. She dwelt among the untrodden ways
C. Strange Fits of Passion Have I Known
D. She Was a Phantom of Delight

63. Which of the following works was edited by the Scottish literary scholar and editor, Sir Herbert Grierson?

A. The Metaphysical Lyrics and the Poems of the Seventeenth Century
B. The Metaphysical Club: A Story of Ideas in America
C. The Complete Metaphysical Poems
D. The Metaphysical Poets

64. In which of the following novels do we find colonialism and racism as the prime subject?

A. Joseph Conrad's *Heart of Darkness*
B. DH Lawrence's *Sons and Lovers*
C. VS Naipaul's *Mr. Stone and the Knight's Companion*
D. James Joyce's *Ulysses*

65. Which of the following poems by WB Yeats describes the metaphorical journey of a man pursuing his own vision of eternal life?

A. The Second Coming
B. The Tower
C. Easter, 1916
D. Sailing to Byzantium

66. Which of the following novels is a prequel of Charlotte Bronte's *Jane Eyre*?

A. Return of the Native
B. Sula
C. Brave New World
D. Wide Sargasso Sea

67. Where are the thirty pilgrims in Chaucer's *The Canterbury Tales* going?

A. The shrine of Thomas Becket
B. Santiago de Compostela
C. Temple Mount
D. Church of the Holy Sepulchre

68. What is a careful word by word and line by line review of a written draft called?

A. Drafting B. Proof-reading
C. Revising D. Outlining

69. Who among the following writers is famous as a children's author?

A. Sarojini Naidu B. RK Lakshman
C. Ruskin Bond D. Khushwant Singh

70. Identify the type of clause in the given sentence.

All that glitters is not gold.

A. Adverb clause of concession
B. Adverb clause of condition
C. Adjective clause
D. Noun clause

71. Which of the following is a story version of Arthurian Romance?
A. The Wedding of Sir Gawain and Dame Rangel
B. The Book of Duchess
C. Roman de la Rose
D. Troilus and Criseyde

72. What is the process that encouraged a freeing of the mind from rational and utilitarian values and constraints as well as moral and aesthetic judgement?
A. Absolutism
B. Psychic automatism
C. Imaginative idealism
D. Gothic realism

73. Who defines Romanticism as liberalism in literature?
A. Victor Hugo B. Dr. Johnson
C. James Thomson D. Sir Philip Sidney

74. Who among the following feminist thinkers does NOT fall under the category of radical feminist thinker?
A. Shulamith Firestone
B. Julie Bindel
C. Elaine Showalter
D. Ellen Willis

75. What do we call the verse form that consists of eight iambic pentameter lines, followed by a ninth line of six iambic feet (an alexandrine)? The rhyme scheme is *ababbcbcc*.
A. Free Verse B. Rime Royale
C. Ottava Rima D. Spenserian Stanza

76. In which phase of writing does the writer imitate the given texts?
A. Advanced writing B. Free writing
C. Guided writing D. Controlled writing

77. What is a historical account, or a biography, written from personal knowledge called?
A. Memoir
B. Personal development
C. First person narrative
D. Personal narrative

78. Of [Jane] Austen he said he "couldn't possibly share her sentimental ambitions, her sentimental sense of the world". Who made this controversial statement about Jane Austen?
A. VS Naipaul
B. TS Eliot
C. George Bernard Shaw
D. Joseph Conrad

79. What do we call writing that is expressive and original?
A. Prose writing
B. Generative writing
C. Creative writing
D. Fiction writing

80. Which genre conveys information grounded in real life or facts?
A. Prose B. Fiction
C. Non-fiction D. Autobiography

81. Think'st thou that I, who saw the face of God
And tasted the eternal joys of heaven.
Am not tormented with ten thousand hells
In being deprived of everlasting bliss?

In which of the following works do we come across the above mentioned lines?
A. Christopher Marlowe's *Dr. Faustus*
B. Thomas Kyd's *The Spanish Tragedy*
C. John Webster's *The White Devil*
D. Ben Johnson's *Alchemist*

82. For which literary work did Sir VS Naipaul receive the Booker Prize in 1971?
A. Half a Life
B. In a Free State
C. A House for Mr. Biswas
D. An Area of Darkness

83. Which of the following CANNOT be considered as an aspect of Romantic Revival?
A. An exuberant intellectual curiosity
B. Insistence upon bringing reform through didacticism
C. Sense of mystery
D. An instinct for the elemental simplicities of life

84. What do we call any written account of a series of related events and experiences?
A. Narrative B. Fiction
C. Prose D. Non-fiction

85. "So long as men can breathe or eyes can see,
So long lives this, and this gives life to thee."

What do these two lines from the ending couplets of William Shakespeare's sonnet boast of?
A. The reign of Queen Elizabeth
B. The British Empire in the Elizabethan period
C. The post-Renaissance cultural revival
D. The poetry during English Renaissance

86. Who among the following critics propounded the theory of the anxiety of influence?
A. Ronald Barthes B. Harold Bloom
C. IA Richards D. George Saintsbury

87. 'Good fences make good neighbours.'
In which of the following poems by Robert Frost do we come across the above mentioned lines?
A. The Road Not Taken
B. Stopping by a Wood on a Snowy Evening
C. Mending Wall
D. Birches

88. Which of the following can help in understanding the meaning of literature?
A. Morphology B. Graphology
C. Stylistics D. Phonetics

89. Select the ***most appropriate*** verb form to fill in the blank.

By 2040, artificial intelligence ______ many of the jobs that people do now.
A. have been taking over
B. will be taking over
C. will have taken over
D. shall be taking over

90. What, according to AC Bradley, is responsible for setting in motion a certain chain of actions leading to the demise of the tragic characters with reference to Shakespearean Tragedies?
A. Mimesis
B. Fatal flaw
C. Balance of the universe
D. Catharsis

91. Which famous writer authored the book titled *Pride, Prejudice, and Punditry*?
A. Shashi Tharoor B. Vikram Seth
C. Shashi Deshpande D. Amitav Ghosh

92. In which of the following poems do the given lines appear?

"Can that for true love pass
When a fair woman courts her glass?
Something unlike must in love's likeness be:
His wonder is one and variety.
For he whose soul nought but a soul can move
Does a new Narcissus prove
And his own image love."

A. Abraham Cowley's *Platonic Love*
B. Andrew Marvell's *To His Coy Mistress*
C. Samuel Johnson's *The Vanity of Human Wishes*
D. John Donne's *The Good Morrow*

93. To which iconic Nobel Prize winning writer is Rabindranath Tagore compared pertaining to the theme of post-colonial translation?
A. Earnest Hemmingway
B. WB Yeats
C. TS Eliot
D. GB Shaw

94. In which of the following Caribbean islands was Hemmingway's *The Old Man and the Sea* set?
A. Jamaica B. Trinidad
C. Cuba D. Tobago

95. ______ deals with the words in a language.
A. Phonetics B. Linguistics
C. Phonology D. Morphology

96. "... Than Oars divide the Ocean,
Too silver for a seam,
Or Butterflies, off Banks of Noon,
Leap, plashless as they swim."

Where do we find the above mentioned beautiful lines?

A. Emily Dickinson's *A Bird Came down the Walk*
B. Langston Hugh's *I, Too*
C. Robert Frost's *Mending Wall*
D. Sylvia Plath's *Tulip*

97. Who among the following Romantic poets does NOT fall under the category of the Lake poets?

A. William Wordsworth
B. Robert Southey
C. Thomas Gray
D. ST Coleridge

98. Where is the name 'the Augustan age' derived from?

A. The poem titled *Augustus*
B. The book written by the name of *Augustus*
C. The movement held in the empire of *Augustus*
D. The Roman emperor, *Augustus*

99. In which novel does RK Narayan use mythological reference and juxtaposes them with the facets of modern life?

A. Waiting for the Mahatma
B. The Guide
C. The Man-Eater of Malgudi
D. The English Teacher

100. Who wrote the late 14th century poem, *Confessioamantis*?

A. John Gower
B. Giovanni Boccaccio
C. Dante Alighieri
D. Geoffrey Chaucer

101. Which of the following novels of Mulk Raj Anand deals with the wretched plight of workers on the tea – plantations?

A. Untouchable
B. Two Leaves and a Bud
C. Across the Black Water
D. The Sword and the Sickle

102. Who wrote *Hullaballooin Guava Orchard*?

A. Kiran Nagarkar B. Kiran Desai
C. Aravind Adiga D. Shashi Tharoor

103. Which of the following modern plays deals with the theme of an intellectual yet disaffected and disillusioned young man?

A. Samuel Beckett's *Waiting for the Godott*
B. George Osborne's *Look Back in Anger*
C. Galsworthy's *Skin Game*
D. TS Eliot's *The Family Reunion*

104. Who among the following contemporaries of Petrarch wrote *The Decameron*?

A. Giovanni Boccaccio
B. Dante Alighieri
C. Pietro Bembo
D. Geoffrey Chaucer

105. Which of the following theories stresses on the poet's role as "...not to express personal emotion but rather to serve as a medium for the collective emotions of the mind of Europe"?

A. Tradition and individual talent
B. Dissociation of sensibility
C. Anxiety of authorship
D. Objective co-relative

106. Which of the following poets does NOT fall under the category of the precursors of the Romantic Revival in English literature?

A. William Collins
B. William Wordsworth
C. William Blake
D. William Cowper

107. Which of the following poems uses the conceit of God as a landlord and humanity as a tenant farmer seeking a "new [...] lease"?

A. John Milton's *The Paradise Lost*
B. Abraham Cowley's *The Spring*
C. John Donne's *The Valedictory Forbidding Morning*
D. George Herbert's *Redemption*

108. In which of Amitav Ghosh's novels do we come across the character Tha'mma?

A. Flood of Fire
B. The Shadow Lines
C. River of Smoke
D. The Hungry Tides

109. Which unfinished satirical work by Lord Byron furnishes a witty and satirical commentary on the hypocrisy of various social and sexual conventions?
A. The Vision of Judgement
B. The Prophesy of Dante
C. Marino Faliero
D. Don Juan

110. Which of the following plays by George Bernard Shaw is a human comedy about the English class system?
A. Pygmalion
B. Oliver Twist
C. The Arms and the Man
D. The Doctor's Dilemma

111. In layman's terminology, POA, in phonology, is ______ the consonant is produced.
A. where B. how
C. here D. when

112. Who among the following considers Shakespeare's works as 'Just representation of general nature'?
A. Dr. Johnson B. ST Coleridge
C. IA Richard D. TS Eliot

113. In which of the following novels does Kamala Markandaya explore the tension between the East and the West - between superstition and science, faith and reason?
A. A Handful of Rice
B. Possession
C. Nectar in a Sieve
D. A Silence of Desire

114. Which of the following is the title of Meena Alexander's memoir?
A. Shadow Lines
B. Fault Lines
C. My Story
D. Prison and Chocolate Cake

115. Which book by Khalid Husseini deals with Afghan American identity, a generation of people who fled the Soviet Invasion of Afghanistan to the US?
A. A Thousand Splendid Suns
B. The Kite Runner
C. And the Mountain Echoed
D. Sea Prayer

116. Which of Atwood's novels presents a funny, engaging account of emotional cannibalism between a couple?
A. Surfacing B. The Edible Woman
C. Oryx and Crake D. Cat's Eye

117. Who among the following is the exponent of confessional poetry in American literature?
A. Anne Sexton B. Phillis Wheatley
C. Sylvia Plath D. Emily Dickinson

118. When a writer, through his writing, tries to convince his readers and persuade them with logic and moral appeal, what is such writing termed as?
A. Exercise of discursive writing
B. Exercise on descriptive
C. Exercise on persuasive writing
D. Personal writing practice

119. Which poetic form is used by John Keats in his *La Belle Dame sans Merci*?
A. Ballad B. Pastoral elegy
C. Ode D. Lyric

120. Sandra Gilbert and Susan Guber's *The Mad Woman in the Attic* deals with ______.
A. the place of women in American literary tradition
B. women writers and the 19th century literary imagination
C. the issue related to franchise
D. the anxiety of female authorship

121. Who among the following emphasises on the universality and essentiality of tradition?
A. Dr. Johnson B. IA Richard
C. ST Coleridge D. TS Eliot

122. Which of the following poems by Edgar Allen Poe does NOT fall under the category of dark poem?

A. To Helen B. The Raven
C. A Valentine D. Annabel Lee

123. Select the ***most appropriate*** modal auxiliary to fill in the blank.

He was so tired that he ______ scarcely stand.

A. can B. may
C. could D. should

124. Which traditional form of poetry did Alexander Pope use for his poem?

A. Rime Royale B. Heroic Couplets
C. Split Couplets D. Spenserian Stanza

125. What was Renaissance poetry based on?

A. The political tension in British Empire
B. The spirit of adventure
C. Tradition and culture of Medieval England
D. The classical arts of ancient Rome and Greece

126. Which of the following is the title of the preface of *The Medall* (1682) by John Dryden?

A. An Epistle to Dr. Arbuthnot
B. A Modcst Proposal
C. Apology of an Idler
D. Epistle to the Whigs

127. Which of the following poems of John Milton deals with Christ's Incarnation and his overthrow of earthly and Pagan powers?

A. Paradise Lost
B. On the Morning of Christ's Nativity
C. Lycidas
D. II Penseroso

128. Why is Andrew Marvell's poem *To His Coy Mistress* called a 'carpe diem' poem?

A. It offers moral instructions.
B. It encourages the reader to transcend the mundane and recognise the power of each moment.
C. It focusses on the pleasure that life offers.
D. It combines two heterogenous ideas.

129. "Her mother shed a tear or two but wasn't really crying. It was the thing to do, so she did it enjoying every moment."

In which of Nissim Ezekiel's poems do the above mentioned lines appear?

A. The Hill
B. Philosophy
C. Jewish Wedding in Bombay
D. Night of the Scorpion

130. Which book by VS Naipaul conveys the sense of disillusionment which the author experiences on his first visit to India?

A. India: A Wounded Civilization Now
B. The Loss of El Dorado
C. Flag on the Island
D. Area of Darkness

131. Which of the following novels by Amitav Ghosh is NOT a part of his Ibis trilogy?

A. Sea of Poppies B. River of Smoke
C. Flood of Fire D. The Hungry Tides

132. In which of Goldsmith's poems do we come across these beautiful lines?

"The naked negro, panting at the line,
Boasts of his golden sands and palmy wine,
Basks in the glare, or stems the tepid wave,
And thanks his gods for all the good they gave."

A. Retaliation: A Poem
B. The Deserted Village
C. The Traveller
D. Memory

133. Who is credited with the rediscovery of Cicero's letter and founding the Renaissance humanism?

A. Petrarch
B. Geoffrey Chaucer
C. Giovanni Boccaccio
D. Dante Alighieri

134. Which of the following Shakespeare's plays deals with the story of blossoming love, secret marriage and eventual deaths of two teenagers from feuding families?

A. Antonio and Cleopatra
B. Romeo and Juliet
C. All's Well That Ends Well
D. The Merchant of Venice

135. "No mockeries now for them; no prayers nor bells;
Nor any voice of mourning save the choirs,—
The shrill, demented choirs of wailing shells;
And bugles calling for them from sad shires."

In which of the following poems do the above lines appear?
A. WH Auden's *The Unknown Citizen*
B. WB Yeat's *An Irish Airman Foresees His Death*
C. Rupert Brooke's *The Soldier*
D. Wilfred Owen's *Anthem for Doomed Youth*

136. What does the comprehensibility skill for writing include?
A. Effectively communicating messages and information
B. Testing writing skills
C. Testing vocabulary
D. Building relationship between ideas and expressions

137. Who among the following literary figures received the Nobel Prize for "Lifting the Memory of Slavery into the Realm of Myth"?
A. Isabel Allende
B. Pearl C Buck
C. Sinclair Lewis
D. Toni Morrison

138. Identify the kind of determiner of the underlined word in the given sentence.

There were <u>many</u> people at the station.
A. Ordinal
B. Quantifier
C. Numeral
D. Possessive determiner

139. Which of the following poem was written by Ben Johnson in response to bad reviews received by his plays?
A. Beginning Another
B. An Ode to Himself
C. A Fit of Rhyme against Rhyme
D. To Celia

140. Who named Edmund Spenser as a 'poet's poet'?
A. Charles Lamb
B. Christopher Marlow
C. Ben Johnson
D. AC Bradley

141. Which section from TS Eliot's *The Waste Land* encourages the individual to liberate himself (or herself) from suffering through detachment?
A. The Burial of the Dead
B. A Game of Chess
C. Death by Water
D. The Fire Sermon

142. "Though an excellent actor, he prefers force to fraud, and in his world, there is no general illusion as to his true nature. Again, to compare Iago with the Satan of *Paradise Lost* seems almost absurd, so immensely does Shakespeare's man exceed Milton's Fiend in evil."

In which of the following critical works do we come across the above lines?
A. TS Eliot's *Shakespeare Criticism, Discovery, and Advance*
B. *Shakespearean Tragedy* by AC Bradley
C. Coleridge's *Essays and Lectures on Shakespeare*
D. Dr. Johnson's *Preface to Shakespeare*

143. Identify the type of clause in the given sentence.

Stand still if you value your life.
A. Adverb clause of concession
B. Adverb clause of condition
C. Adverb clause of comparison
D. Adverb clause of manner

144. Which of the following elegies bemoans the death of ordinary and common men?

A. When Lilacs Last in the Dooryard Bloom'd
B. In Memoriam
C. Lycidas
D. Elegy Written in a Country Churchyard

145. In which literary genre does Shri Aurobindo's poem *The Golden Light* fall?
A. Ballad B. Lyric
C. Sonnet D. Ode

146. Which of the following Romantic poets is also known for writing historical novels?
A. Robert Southey B. Robert Burns
C. Sir Walter Scott D. Thomas Gray

147. "...any text is not a discrete whole but contains several irreconcilable and contradictory meanings"

Which literary theory supports the above statement?
A. Structuralism
B. Reader Response Theory
C. Deconstruction
D. The Theory of Impersonal

148. Which of the following tells us about how a sentence is worded and structured?
A. Syntax B. Morphemes
C. Lexemes D. Phonics

149. Virginia Woolf's novel, *A Room of One's Own* is an extension of her own essay. What was the topic of that essay which she later extended into a novel?
A. Literature and history are a male construct
B. Education and women
C. Women and economy
D. Literature and women

150. What is an iambic verse consisting of stanzas of three lines called?
A. Terza Rima B. Blank verse
C. Ottava Rima D. Rhyme royale

151. Who among the following poets was the poet laureate from 1813 till his death?
A. ST Coleridge B. Lord Byron
C. Robert Southey D. PB Shelly

152. Which of the following works of TS Eliot deals with the theme of man's relationship with time, the universe and the divine?
A. The Waste Land
B. Four Quartets
C. The Cocktail Party
D. The Hollow Men

153. Who is considered as a founder of the Imagist movement in English literature?
A. Ezra Pound B. TS Eliot
C. Walt Whitman D. WH Auden

154. "In the village churchyard there grows an old yew,
Every spring it blossoms anew:
Old passports can't do that, my dear, old passports can't do that."

In which famous modern poem do we come across the above lines?
A. TS Eliot's *The Hollow Men*
B. Ezra Pound, *In a Station of the Metro*
C. WH Auden, *The Refugee Blues*
D. WB Yeats' *The Tower*

155. What was Thomas Campion known for?
A. Lyrics B. Epics
C. Masquerades D. Sonnets

Directions (Qs. No. 156-160): *Read the given passage and answer the questions that follow.*

Idleness so called, which does not consist in doing nothing, but in doing a great deal not recognised in the dogmatic formularies of the ruling class, has as good a right to state its position as industry itself. It is admitted that the presence of people who refuse to enter in the great handicap race for sixpenny pieces is at once an insult and a disenchantment for those who do. A fine fellow (as we see so many) takes his determination, votes for the sixpences, and in the 42 emphatic Americanism, 'goes for' them. And while such an one is ploughing distressfully up the road, it is not hard to understand his resentment, when he perceives cool persons in the meadows by the wayside, lying with a handkerchief over their ears and a glass at their elbow.

Alexander is touched in a very delicate place by the disregard of Diogenes. Where was the glory of having taken Rome for these tumultuous barbarians, who poured into the Senate house, and found the Fathers sitting silent and unmoved by their success? It is a sore thing to have laboured along and scaled the arduous hilltops, and when all is done, find humanity indifferent to your achievement. Hence physicists condemn the unphysical; financiers have only a superficial toleration for those who know little of stocks; literary persons despise the unlettered; and people of all pursuits combine to disparage those who have none.

156. Who is referred to as 'the tumultuous barbarian'?
A. The man relaxing in the wayside meadow
B. The physicist
C. Alexander and his soldiers
D. Diogenes and the other senate members

157. Why was Alexander, the Great touched after taking Rome?
A. He learnt that his people knew very little about the importance of working hard.
B. He discovered that Diogenes and the other senate members were indifferent to his achievement.
C. He found that his soldiers wish to relax in the wayside meadows.
D. He found that his subjects are barbarians.

158. Who/What, according to the writer, has a right to state its position?
A. Disenchanted B. Idleness
C. Industry D. Hardship

159. What, according to the writer, made the hard-working man ploughing up the road feel distressful?
A. Finding that others are scaling the hilltops
B. Learning that his fellowmen knew very little about the stocks
C. Finding that humanity is indifferent to his achievement
D. Seeing the idler lying coolly by the wayside

160. Who are referred to as being part of "the great handicap race"?
A. The idlers
B. Industrious person
C. The tumultuous barbarians
D. Diogenes and his senators

Directions (Qs. No. 161-165): *Read the given passage and answer the questions that follow.*

Although religion does not inhibit the acquisition of wealth, although it does not hold up large fortunes as evil, the tenor of its teaching, by and large, is to induce an attitude of indifference to worldly things, things which gratify one's lower self and keep one engrossed in money-making. The student should be made to realise that the real goods of life are spiritual, love of things of the spirit and service of one's fellowmen, joy of an ordered disciplined life. These are blessings money cannot buy. What is wealth before such things of the spirit? Of all religious teachers, Jesus Christ has dealt more comprehensively than any other with the problem of wealth in all its aspects. He may be called the greatest exponent of the science of wealth. With only four words "Blessed are ye poor!" he changed altogether the values which man attached to human existence and human happiness and acquisition and possession of wealth. Real bliss consisted, he taught, not in riches nor in anything else which the world regarded as prosperity or felicity, but in the joy and happiness derived from being at peace with one's fellowmen through perfect love and fellowship and selfless service and sacrifice.

The word "poor" on the lips of the Master had a spiritual significance–the poor so far as they were poor in spirit, humble before God, simple, God-fearing, teachable, faithful, it could surely not have been his intention to hold up destitution and privation as a blessing in itself, that would have turned life into a terrible ordeal and it would have been heartless to exhort the poor to believe that money was not necessary for one's sustenance or the joys and blessings of life. Even things of the spirit cannot be had without money. Extreme poverty

179. Where do we find the origin of Renaissance madrigal?
A. Italy B. Minnesota
C. France D. England

180. What distinguished Madrigal from the earlier forms of vocal music?
A. They were religious.
B. They were always secular.
C. The style was traditional.
D. The verses were written in English language.

181. Inclusive teaching refers to inclusion in the classroom of:
A. special children
B. different classes of normal children
C. normal and handicapped children
D. physically and mentally handicapped children

182. How many parts of Dhrupad singing styles are there?
A. One B. Six
C. Five D. Three

183. Who said the following?
"It (Curriculum) is a tool in the hands of the artist (teacher) to mould his material (pupil) according to his ideal (objective) in his studio (school)."
A. Alexander Cunningham
B. CV Good
C. RK Mukherjee
D. Gordon Willard Allport

184. In which year was the POCSO Act' introduced?
A. 2010 B. 2012
C. 2013 D. 2011

185. The five-step method in teaching is associated with ______.
A. Brandon Glover
B. FP Graves
C. Johann Heinrich Pestalozzi
D. Herbert Spencer

186. Teaching is a/an ______.
A. basic art B. performing art
C. art and science D. fashion

187. According to Cole and Bruce, "______ is a unique stage of emotional development".
A. Adult stage B. Childhood stage
C. Infant stage D. Adolescent stage

188. What is the meaning of 'culture'?
A. Social group
B. The achievement of objectives of society
C. Social awareness
D. Way of living

189. In which year was the Rehabilitation Council of India Act passed?
A. 1991 B. 1997
C. 1995 D. 1992

190. Curriculum is ______.
A. a part of thinking
B. a complete set of organised experiences in the school
C. general education
D. a body of knowledge

191. Who is considered as the 'Father of Kindergarten'?
A. Aristotle
B. William Heard Kilpatrick
C. Friedrich Wilhelm August Froebel
D. Maria Montessori

192. Teaching is NOT a variable of ______.
A. Syllabus B. Teacher
C. Student D. Society

193. Khayal is a singing style. From which language did the word 'khayal' come from?
A. Sanskrit B. Urdu
C. Arabic D. Hindi

194. Democratic education system does NOT include:
A. providing equal opportunities
B. universal education
C. paid education
D. child-centred education

195. What is the full form of LAC?
A. Learning across the classroom
B. Language across the classroom
C. Language across the curriculum
D. Learning across the curriculum

172. Who, according to the narrator, had an invincible distaste for anything to do with pens and paper?
A. The governor of Samoa
B. Natives
C. Walker
D Mackintosh

173. "What the hell do I care about grammar?" What prompts Walker to utter the above line?
A. He did not understand the intelligible phrases.
B. The expressions used in the report were childish.
C. The report is delayed due to Mackintosh's dilatoriness.
D. He had an invincible distaste for neatness.

174. Which expression in the passage describes the report initially prepared for the governor?
A. Concise and neatly official
B. Neglected to prepare
C. Pencilled in some insertion
D. Childish in expression and faulty in language

175. Identify the word in the passage which means 'tending or intended to cause delay'.
A. Sneering B. Remonstrated
C. Dilatoriness D. Vindictively

Directions (Qs. No. 176-180): *Read the given passage and answer the questions that follow.*

The definition of a madrigal is a song for several voices that is a setting of a poem. Popular from about 1520 to 1650, performers mostly sang madrigals acapella, meaning without instrumental accompaniment. The style originated in Italy but flourished in many other European countries. What is the Renaissance madrigal? It developed from a form of secular vocal music and verse in the 14th century, but singers transformed it in the 16th century. The Renaissance madrigal used richer poetry and developed much more complex music. From its origins in Italy, the madrigal flourished in many other European countries in the 16th and 17th centuries. In England, the form was immensely popular in Elizabethan times. The English madrigal was the only version that differed substantially from its Italian counterpart. In about the 1520s in Italy, peopie began to write manuscripts of madrigals. These musical pieces were quite different from their 14th century counterparts. The older versions were for two, or rarely three, voices, with much ornamentation. Their verse was mostly pastoral, consisting of two or three stanzas of three lines each, plus a final couplet. At this point, the music was composed for performance by skilled amateur singers.

What distinguished madrigals from earlier forms of vocal music was that they were always secular. Previously, most music had been religious, and madrigals were among the first styles to depart from that tradition. Their themes were social, and composers wrote the verses they used in the vernacular rather than the Latin of sacred music. Where sacred music had been smooth and predictable, madrigals might include dissonance and sudden shifts of melody or rhythm. Renaissance madrigals were also through-composed, meaning that each line of verse had its own music with no internal repetition as there had been in earlier years. Even if lines of verse were repeated, music rarely was.

176. What does the word 'a capella' signify?
A. A song for several voices
B. Secular vocal music
C. Without instrumental accompaniment
D. Verse in the 14th century

177. When did Madrigal become immensely popular?
A. In Elizabethan times
B. During Italian Renaissance
C. During French Revolution
D. In the medieval period

178. What was the theme of Madrigals?
A. Amateur B. Social
C. Sacred D. Traditional

196. Which of the following is NOT an assessment tool?
A. Seminar
B. Test
C. Interview
D. Observation

197. Grading of learning outcomes is known as:
A. diagnosis assessment
B. summative assessment
C. formative assessment
D. continuous assessment

198. Curriculum is considered ______.
A. to be organised by scholar
B. to be organised by parents
C. to be organised by the students
D. the heart of any learning institution

199. Discipline is not a ______.
A. behaviour that needs to be maintained in the school
B. punishment
C. substantial body of knowledge, based upon which research is conducted
D. mode of life in accordance with certain rules and regulation

200. Who gave the theory of moral development?
A. Stanley Hall
B. Jean Jacques Rousseau
C. Lawrence Kohlberg
D. John Dewey

ANSWERS

1. (D)	2. (D)	3. (A)	58. (A)	59. (A)	60. (C)
4. (D)	5. (B)	6. (B)	61. (C)	62. (D)	63. (A)
7. (A)	8. (A)	9. (D)	64. (A)	65. (D)	66. (D)
10. (D)	11. (C)	12. (A)	67. (A)	68. (B)	69. (C)
13. (B)	14. (B)	15. (C)	70. (C)	71. (A)	72. (B)
16. (D)	17. (B)	18. (A)	73. (A)	74. (C)	75. (D)
19. (A)	20. (A)	21. (B)	76. (C)	77. (A)	78. (A)
22. (B)	23. (A)	24. (A)	79. (C)	80. (C)	81. (A)
25. (C)	26. (C)	27. (C)	82. (B)	83. (B)	84. (A)
28. (A)	29. (C)	30. (D)	85. (D)	86. (B)	87. (C)
31. (C)	32. (A)	33. (C)	88. (C)	89. (C)	90. (B)
34. (C)	35. (A)	36. (C)	91. (A)	92. (A)	93. (B)
37. (A)	38. (B)	39. (B)	94. (C)	95. (D)	96. (A)
40. (D)	41. (D)	42. (A)	97. (C)	98. (D)	99. (C)
43. (B)	44. (C)	45. (C)	100. (A)	101. (B)	102. (B)
46. (D)	47. (C)	48. (C)	103. (B)	104. (A)	105. (A)
49. (A)	50. (B)	51. (D)	106. (B)	107. (D)	108. (B)
52. (A)	53. (A)	54. (D)	109. (D)	110. (A)	111. (A)
55. (B)	56. (A)	57. (D)	112. (A)	113. (D)	114. (B)

115. (B)	**116. (B)**	**117. (C)**	**160. (A)**	**161. (A)**	**162. (D)**
118. (C)	**119. (A)**	**120. (B)**	**163. (D)**	**164. (C)**	**165. (B)**
121. (D)	**122. (C)**	**123. (C)**	**166. (B)**	**167. (D)**	**168. (D)**
124. (B)	**125. (D)**	**126. (D)**	**169. (C)**	**170. (C)**	**171. (C)**
127. (B)	**128. (B)**	**129. (C)**	**172. (C)**	**173. (A)**	**174. (A)**
130. (D)	**131. (D)**	**132. (C)**	**175. (C)**	**176. (C)**	**177. (A)**
133. (A)	**134. (B)**	**135. (D)**	**178. (B)**	**179. (A)**	**180. (B)**
136. (A)	**137. (D)**	**138. (B)**	**181. (C)**	**182. (D)**	**183. (A)**
139. (B)	**140. (A)**	**141. (D)**	**184. (B)**	**185. (D)**	**186. (C)**
142. (B)	**143. (B)**	**144. (D)**	**187. (B)**	**188. (D)**	**189. (D)**
145. (C)	**146. (C)**	**147. (C)**	**190. (C)**	**191. (C)**	**192. (D)**
148. (A)	**149. (A)**	**150. (A)**	**193. (C)**	**194. (C)**	**195. (C)**
151. (C)	**152. (B)**	**153. (A)**	**196. (A)**	**197. (B)**	**198. (D)**
154. (C)	**155. (C)**	**156. (C)**	**199. (B)**	**200. (C)**	
157. (B)	**158. (B)**	**159. (D)**			

Previous Paper (Solved)

Delhi Subordinate Services Selection Board

DSSSB–PGT (English) Recruitment Exam, 2021*

Subject Knowledge – English & Teaching Methodology

1. Select the quantifier determiner in the given sentence.
I have some money in my purse.
A. purse B. have
C. money D. some

2. Fill in the blank with the correct form of the verb.
The sun .... in the west direction. (set)
A. settled B. set
C. setted D. sets

3. Select the most appropriate option.
.... indicates an action that hasn't happened yet and will happen.
A. Present Continuous
B. Past Tense
C. Present Tense
D. Future Tense

4. I did play basketball is an example of .... tense.
A. Future Tense
B. Simple Past Tensc
C. Past Perfect Tense
D. Past Continuous Tense

5. I expect that I shall get a prize. Which clause is there in this sentence?
A. Coordinate Clause B. Adverbial Clause
C. Noun Clause D. Relative Clause

6. Determiners are the words that are known to modify the ....
A. Nouns B. Adjectives
C. Verbs D. Adverbs

7. Present Progressive Tense is also called ....
A. Present Indefinite
B. Present Perfect
C. Present Continuous
D. Past Perfect

8. Which of the following is an example of Quantitative Determiner?
A. Some B. An
C. Those D. This

9. Fill in the blank.
I have read .... Bible many times.
A. The B. An
C. A D. Those

10. Which one of the following options falls under the category of the definite article?
A. Some B. An
C. The D. A

11. Whatever we study increases our knowledge. Identify the type of clause.
A. Noun Clause
B. Coordinate Clause
C. Adverb Clause
D. Adjective Clause

12. Which clause is there in the sentence:
'To err is human, to forgive divine.'
A. Noun Clause
B. Adverbial Clause
C. Coordinate Clause
D. Relative Clause

13. They serve God well who serve His children. Identify the type of clause.

* Online exam held on 30/06/2021.

A. Adverb Clause
B. Coordinate Clause
C. Noun Clause
D. Adjective Clause

14. Fill in the blank with appropriate option.

I .... (buy) a car last month.

A. bought B. buying
C. have bought D. will buy

15. Which tense is used to describe the Universal Truth or Habitual Action?

A. Present Perfect
B. Present Perfect Continuous
C. Present Indefinite
D. Present Continuous

16. How many types of clauses are there?

A. 6 B. 8
C. 2 D. 5

17. Fill in the blank with the appropriate option.

.... Himalayas are prone to the landslides.

A. The B. An
C. This D. A

18. Pick up the possessive determiner from the given list.

A. their B. this
C. An D. that

19. The dog followed the boy wherever he went. Identify the type of clause.

A. Adjective Clause
B. Coordinate Clause
C. Noun Clause
D. Adverb Clause

20. Select the most appropriate option.

'I do' is an example of .... tense.

A. Past Perfect
B. Present Indefinite
C. Present Continuous
D. Present Perfect

21. Fill in the blanks.

A clause is a group of words having a .... and .... of its own, but it forms part of a sentence.

A. verb ; adjective
B. subject ; verb
C. adjective ; verb
D. verb ; adverb

22. Chaucer was the first to use Ottava Rima in English. What is the rhyme scheme of Ottava Rima?

A. ABBAABBA B. AABBAABB
C. ABABABCC D. ABABBCBC

23. You .... fall ill if you eat all of that.

A. but B. should
C. would D. will

24. In which month did Chaucer and his pilgrims go to Canterbury?

A. May B. March
C. January D. April

25. The modal '............' expresses the ability to do something.

A. Can B. Have to
C. Need not D. Must

26. What will be the passive form of 'I write a book?'

A. A book is written by me.
B. I wrote a book.
C. A book was written by me.
D. A book will be written by me.

27. .... is used to express less possibility of anything.

A. Shall B. Will
C. Might D. Must Not

28. "My leg aches" is an example of ....

A. Active Voice B. Passive Voice
C. Future Tense D. Past Tense

29. How many types of voices are there in English?

A. 5 B. 3
C. 2 D. 4

30. Select the most appropriate option.

.... expresses pure future.

A. Could B. Must
C. Can D. Will

31. '............' is the past tense of will.
A. Must B. Would
C. Should D. Could

32. What would be the passive form of 'Shut the Window?'
A. Window was shut.
B. Shut the window.
C. Let the window be shut.
D. I will shut the window.

33. Which modal from the following is used for seeking permission?
A. Can B. Should
C. Will D. Must

34. Change the following into passive voice. Somebody has eaten the last piece of cake.
A. The last piece of cake had been eaten.
B. The last piece of cake will be eaten.
C. The last piece of cake was eaten.
D. The last piece of cake has been eaten.

35. What is the name of the host and owner of Tabard Inn?
A. Alison Bailey B. Harry Bailey
C. John Bailey D. Hurbert Bailey

36. Fill in the blank with appropriate modal. He .... come today. (possibility)
A. but B. as
C. because D. may

37. What would be the active form of 'The bicycle was ridden by the kids.'
A. The kids rode the bicycle.
B. The kids would ride the bicycle.
C. The kids have ridden the bicycle.
D. The kids will ride the bicycle.

38. Which form of verb is used in changing active voice to passive voice?
A. 4th Form B. 3rd Form
C. 1st Form D. 2nd Form

39. In which poem did Chaucer use the heroic couplet for the first time?
A. Troilus and Criseyde
B. The Legend of Good Women
C. The Book of the Duchess
D. The House of Fame

40. The modal .... expresses an invitation or request.
A. because B. must
C. but D. will

41. Amoretti is an Italian word which means ....
A. Little love secrets
B. Sonnets from Italy
C. Colin Clout Come Home Again
D. Little love poems

42. Who is the author of the lines, 'I find no peace and all my war is done; I fear and hope, I burn and freeze like ice'?
A. Sir Thomas Wyatt
B. Edmund Spenser
C. Sir Philip Sidney
D. Earl of Surrey

43. How many eclogues are there in Shepheardes Calendar?
A. 11 B. 10
C. 6 D. 12

44. 'Ad Fontes' was the rallying cry during the Renaissance. What does this phrase mean?
A. Back to foundation
B. To the origin
C. Back to the sources
D. Back to fundamentals

45. Who regarded Edmund Spenser as 'Poet's Poet'?
A. William Langland
B. Charles Lamb
C. William Shakespeare
D. Geoffrey Chaucer

46. What is the name of the most leading figure of Christian Humanism in Europe?
A. John Wycliffe B. John Lydgate
C. Thomas More D. Erasmus

47. Which royal dynasty has been celebrated in Spenser's Fairie Queene?
A. Plantagenet B. Tudor
C. Stuart D. Anjou

48. Renaissance is a .... word which means ....

A. Spanish, reduce
B. Dutch, recuperate
C. German, rejuvenate
D. French, rebirth

49. The Peasant's Revolt also called Wat Tyler's Rebellion started in the year ....
A. 1381 B. 1383
C. 1382 D. 1380

50. Who had quoted about Chaucer's characters "Here is god's plenty"?
A. Samuel Johnson
B. Alexander Pope
C. John Dryden
D. William Langland

51. What is the rhyme scheme of Spenserian Stanza?
A. ABCABCDCD B. ABDABCDAB
C. ABABBCBCC D. ABBAABBCD

52. The Miller's Tale is about a carpenter. What is the name of the carpenter?
A. Roger B. John
C. Robin D. Alison

53. Which of the following poets is not associated with Metaphysical poetry?
A. Andrew Marvell B. George Herbert
C. Henry Vaughan D. Philip Sidney

54. Whose court does the Wife of Bath talk about in her tale?
A. King David B. King Charles
C. King Arthur D. King Solomon

55. It is widely known that Spenser's Fairie Queene was addressed to Queen Elizabeth. What is her name in the text?
A. Eliza B. Britomart
C. Gloriana D. Una

56. Which of the following works is not written by Spenser?
A. The Lady of May
B. The Tears of the Muses
C. Astrophel
D. Prothalamion

57. Name the poetic device used in the given line from Chaucer's Prologue to the Canterbury Tales "Nor that a monk, when he is cloisterless, is like unto a fish that's waterless."
A. Personification B. Metaphor
C. Simile D. Litotes

58. Chaucer's life can be categorized into three periods. Which one does he not belong to?
A. Spanish B. Italian
C. French D. English

59. How many legends are there in Chaucer's The Legend of Good Women?
A. 11 B. 8
C. 10 D. 9

60. The Progress of the Soul is authored by ....
A. John Bunyan B. John Donne
C. John Lyly D. John Milton

61. Samuel Butler's famous satire is known as ....
A. MacFlecknoe
B. Hudibras
C. The Dunciad
D. Absalom and Achitophel

62. In Absalom and Achitophel, King Charles II is allegorical representation of ....
A. King Solomon B. King Amon
C. King Josiah D. King David

63. In the Essay of Dramatick Poesie, Dryden is represented by Neander. What does Neander mean?
A. New man B. New logic
C. New hope D. New ideas

64. What is the name of Belinda's maid in the mock-epic 'The Rape of the Lock'?
A. Dennis B. Arabella
C. Betty D. Bush

65. What is the name of John Milton's heavenly muse?
A. Urania B. Umbriel
C. Raphael D. Gloriana

66. Which game does Belinda play in the, 'Hampton Court'?
A. Ombre B. Chess
C. Golf D. Carrom

67. Who quotes the following: The mind is its own place, and in itself can make heaven of hell, a hell of heaven?
A. Moloch B. Adam
C. God D. Satan

68. What is the name of the pastoral elegy written by John Milton on the death of Edward King?
A. Lycidas
B. The Pilgrim's Progress
C. Paradise Regained
D. Samson Agonistes

69. Who authored, 'The Essay on Man: Epistle I'?
A. Alexander Pope B. Ben Jonson
C. John Dryden D. John Milton

70. Complete the line taken from T.S. Eliot's poem 'The Love Song of J. Alfred Prufrock'. I have measured my life out with ....
A. Scale B. Mornings
C. Coffee Spoons D. Evenings

71. Which poem was written by Dryden on the restoration of King Charles II?
A. The Hind and the Panther
B. Astraea Redux
C. Religio Laici
D. Absalom and Achitophel

72. What form is Milton's epic poem Paradise Lost written in?
A. Rhyme Royal B. Blank Verse
C. Ottava Rima D. Heroic Couplets

73. The Great Fire of London broke out in the year ....
A. 1662 B. 1665
C. 1666 D. 1660

74. Name the poetic device used in the given line from Andrew Marvell's, poem, 'To His Coy Mistress': "And you should, if you please, refuse."
A. Assonance B. Metaphor
C. Repetition D. Simile

75. What is the full title of Milton's masque Comus written in 1634?
A. The Masque of Blackness
B. Lovers Made Men
C. A Masque Presented at Ludlow Castle
D. The Masque of Beauty

76. Who quoted about John Milton "Milton was on the devil's party without knowing it."
A. William Blake
B. John Dryden
C. Alexander Pope
D. William Wordsworth

77. What is the subtitle of 'Alexander's Feast' by John Dryden?
A. The Power of Music
B. The Power of Song
C. The Power of the Soul
D. The Power of Food

78. Who quoted the following statement? "We hate poetry that has a palpable design upon us."
A. William Wordsworth
B. John Keats
C. P.B. Shelley
D. Lord Byron

79. Who guards the gates of Eden in Milton's Paradise lost?
A. Ariel B. Raphael
C. Gabriel D. Uriel

80. Which meter does the blank verse use?
A. Dactyllic Hexameter
B. Iambic Pentameter
C. Trochaic Tetrameter
D. Iambic Hexameter

81. Which of the following novels is not authored by R.K. Narayan?
A. The Guide
B. Malgudi Days
C. The God of Small Things
D. My Days

82. Doctor Faustus was a well-known .. scholar.
A. German B. French
C. English D. Spanish

83. Peter Philip Carey is a/n .... novelist.
A. Indian B. American
C. French D. Australian

84. What is the name of Hester Prynne's husband in The Scarlet Letter?
A. Mister Hibbins
B. Roger Chillingworth
C. Arthur Dimmsdale
D. Governor Bellingham

85. Who amongst the following is not a Bennet sister?
A. Jane B. Mary
C. Sophie D. Elizabeth

86. "Our sweetest songs are those that tell of saddest thought" is a famous line from ....
A. Wordsworth's 'The Solitary Reaper'
B. Keats' 'Ode to a Nightingale'
C. Shelley's 'To a Skylark'
D. Coleridge's 'Christabel'

87. What do you mean by phonology?
A. A branch of linguistics that deals with the system of sounds.
B. A branch of linguistics that deals with sentence structure.
C. A branch of linguistics that deals with words and their origin.
D. A branch of linguistics that deals with language.

88. Why was Shelley expelled from the Oxford University?
A. He refused to deny authorship of a pamphlet called The Necessity of Atheism.
B. He openly rebelled against the University Chancellor's decision to segregate classes based on race.
C. He married Mary Wollstonecraft.
D. He indulged in the same sex relationship.

89. Who is associated with the Imagist Poetry from the following poets?
A. Robert Browning
B. Alfred Lord Tennyson
C. Ezra Pound
D. Elizabeth Barret Browning

90. An Imaginary Life tells the story of Roman poet ....
A. Horace B. Socrates
C. Aristotle D. Ovid

91. The phrase 'Ut Pictura Poesis' appears in .... .
A. The Republic B. Ars Poetica
C. Arcadia D. Defence of Poetry

92. .... is Mohun Biswas's wife in A House for Mr Biswas.
A. Tara B. Shama
C. Tulsi D. Padma

93. Shelley's 'Ode to the West Wind' was published in the collection of poems, named ....
A. Poetry and Prose
B. Poetical Works
C. Prometheus Unbound
D. The Romantic Poets

94. What is the name of Okonkwo's son in Things Fall Apart?
A. Unoka B. Ezeudu
C. Nwoye D. Mr. Brown

95. Who is the narrator of the novel Moby Dick?
A. Starbuck B. Captain Boomer
C. Ishmael D. Captain Ahab

96. Keats' 'Hyperion' is ....
A. Haiku B. Free Verse
C. Sonnet D. Blank Verse

97. The setting of Keats' 'Eve of St. Agnes' is ....
A. Modern B. Elizabethan
C. Victorian D. Medieval

98. Tridib is a protagonist in Amitav Ghosh's ....
A. Sea Poppies
B. Gun Island
C. The Shadow Lines
D. The Hungry Tide

99. Who tells Hamlet about his father's demise?
A. His Lover B. His Mother
C. His Uncle D. The Ghost

100. What is the study of meaning, reference, and truth called?
A. Lexicon B. Vocabulary
C. Syntax D. Semantics

101. Which of the following is not a poetry collection by Thomas Hardy?
A. Poems of the Past and Present
B. The Hollow Men
C. Moments of Vision
D. Wessex Poems

102. Which of the following are the founders of Imagism, an early Modernist school of poetry?
A. T.S. Eliot & W.B. Yeats
B. Ezra Pound, Hilda Dolittle & Richard Arlington
C. Wallace Stevens & Ezra Pound
D. Philip Larkin, Seamus Heaney and W.B. Yeats

103. Who symbolises 'pride' and 'prejudice' in Jane Austen's novel 'Pride and Prejudice'?
A. Lydia Bennet & Charles Bingley
B. Jane Bennet & George Wickham
C. Mrs. Bennet & Mr. Bennet
D. Darcy & Elizabeth Bennet

104. Which of the following Jane Austen's novels has a character named Wickham?
A. Persuasion
B. Mansfield Park
C. Pride and Prejudice
D. Emma

105. In G.B. Shaw's 'Pygmalion', Colonel Pickering returned to London, after travelling to a foreign country, to meet Professor Higgins. Which foreign country was that?
A. Italy B. France
C. India D. Ireland

106. Which poem by Keats deals with the enigma of 'truth' and 'beauty'?
A. Ode on a Grecian Urn
B. To a Nightingale
C. Fall of Hyperion
D. Eve of St. Agnes

107. What happens to Faustus at the end of the play, Dr. Faustus?
A. He returned to study theology and medicine.
B. He was carried off to Hell.
C. A serpent bit him.
D. He killed himself.

108. Which of the following is not one of the parts of 'The Waste Land'?
A. The Holy Grail
B. The Fire Sermon
C. The Burial of the Dead
D. A Game of Chess

109. "Frailty, thy name is woman! / A little month, or ere those shoes were old / With which she follow'd my poor father's body." These lines appear in Shakespear's 'Hamlet' ....
A. Act 2, Scene I B. Act 2, Scene II
C. Act 1, Scene I D. Act I, Scene II

110. Who amongst the following was not a 'trench poet'?
A. Seigfried Sassoon
B. Wilfred Owen
C. Ezra Pound
D. Isaac Rosenberg

111. Which socio-political event is referred to in Eliot's play, 'Murder in the Cathedral'?
A. Assassination of Charles II of Spain
B. Assassination of Archbishop, Thomas Becket
C. Assassination of Henry VIII
D. Murder of Queen Mary

112. Who is the speaker in the following lines? : "I want to be a lady in a flower shop stead of selling at the corner of Tottenham Court Road. But they won't take me unless I can talk more genteel. He said he could teach me."
A. Raina from 'Arms and the Man'
B. Ann Whitefield from 'Man and Superman'
C. Eliza in 'Pygmalion'
D. Miss Proserpine Garnett from 'Candida'

113. Which of the following is not true of 'Hamlet's' "Grave digging" scene?
A. It foreshadows the final tragedy.
B. It provides criticism of the organized religion.
C. It serves as comic relief.
D. There were three grave diggers in the scene.

114. Which of the following is not a character in Shakespeare's 'Hamlet'?
A. Orlando B. Horatio
C. Polonius D. Ghost

115. In his 'Prayer for My Daughter' Yeats does not want his daughter to be like one particular person. Who is that person?
A. Florence Farr
B. Lady Gregory
C. Olivia Shakespeare
D. Maud Gonne

116. Which city does Faustus visit extensively in Scene 7 of Christopher Marlowe's 'Dr. Faustus'?
A. London B. Rome
C. Jerusalem D. Paris

117. Which rhyme scheme did Shelley use in his famous ode 'Ode to the West Wind'?
A. Rhyme Royal B. Ottava Rima
C. Terza Rima D. Enclosed Rhyme

118. Which romantic poet has the following epitaph inscribed on his tombstone, "Here lies one whose name was writ in water"?
A. P.B. Shelley
B. ST. Coleridge
C. John Keats
D. William Wordsworth

119. "When the evening is spread out against the sky Like a patient etherized upon a table". These lines are taken from ....
A. Seamus Heaney's Digging
B. Philip Larkin's Whitsun Weddings
C. W.B. Yeats's 'Byzantium'
D. T.S. Eliot's 'Love Song of J. Alfred Prufrock'

120. What was the profession of Philip Larkin before he became a full time writer?
A. Librarian B. Stage actor
C. Doctor D. School teacher

121. From which language does the word 'Linguistics' derive its meaning from?
A. Latin B. French
C. Sanskrit D. Greek

122. "I am an American linguist, philosopher, cognitive scientist, studied at the University of Pennsylvania, and writer of an anti-war essay "The Responsibility of Intellectuals"." Who am I?
A. Edward Sapir
B. Ferdinand de Saussure
C. Roman Jakobson
D. Avram Noam Chomsky

123. Which literary theory/age are we referring to if we talk about the art movements like Cubism, Dadaism, Surrealism, and Futurism?
A. Post-Structuralism
B. Post-Modernism
C. Structuralism
D. Modernism

124. .... is the study of word derivation and word inflection in terms of constituent morphemes.
A. Phonology B. Lexicology
C. Semantics D. Morphology

125. Read both the sentences carefully and choose the current option.
(*a*) Structuralism derives ultimately from linguistics.
(*b*) Post-Structuralism derives ultimately from philosophy.
A. Both (*a*) & (*b*) are false.
B. Both (*a*) & (*b*) are true.
C. (*a*) is false & (*b*) is true.
D. (*a*) is true & (*b*) is false.

126. "It was the best of times, it was the worst of times, it was the age of wisdom, it was the age of foolishness...". Which novel begins with these lines?
A. The Heart of the Matter.
B. Hard Times
C. A Passage to India
D. A Tale of Two Cities

127. Which of the following is not one of the themes of, 'A Passage to India'?

A. Safe travel to India
B. Colonialism & Imperialism
C. Race & Culture
D. Religious Unity

128. Which of the following pair is not correctly matched?

A. Great Expectations : Miss Havisham
B. Hard Times : Stephen Blackpool
C. David Copperfield : Thomas Grandgrind
D. Oliver Twis't : Artful Dodger

129. Stanley Fish's in his book, 'Is There a Text in this Class? The Authority of Interpretive Communities' writes that ....

A. all interpretations are myth.
B. it is interpretive communities, rather than either the text or reader, that produce meanings.
C. an author plays very important role in the interpretation of the text.
D. the text has a fixed meaning.

130. In 'Heart of Darkness', when Marlow said that Kurtz "had kicked himself loose of the earth", what does he imply there?

A. That Kurtz is free from all the restraints of the basic morality of what is wrong and right.
B. That Kurtz is nothing more than dirt.
C. That now Kurtz has no human passion left for anyone.
D. That Kurtz has dug the earth by kicking with his legs.

131. Who among the following linguists introduced 'phonology', 'morphology, and 'syntax' as three levels of Linguistics?

A. Robert A. Hall B. Victor Yngve
C. R.H. Robins D. Panini

132. Which of the following novels by Charles Dickens was first published in an episodic form?

A. Hard Times
B. David Copperfield
C. Great Expectations
D. The Pickwick Papers

133. The special features which affect speech sounds such as pitch, intonation, stress and junction are called ....

A. Prosody B. Phonology
C. Ellipsis D. Suprasegmental

134. Which of the following is not a correct match?

A. T.S. Eliot : 'Tradition and the Individual Talent'
B. Mathew Arnold : 'The Study of Poetry'
C. William Wordsworth : 'An Essay on Man'
D. S.T. Coleridge : 'Biographia Literaria'

135. Shantih shantih shantih is the last line of T.S. Eliot's ....

A. The Hollow Men
B. Four Quartets
C. The Waste Land
D. Ash Wednesday

136. What are the three sections which the novel, 'The Passage to India' is divided into?

A. 'Mosque', 'Cave', and 'Church'
B. 'Mosque', 'Church', and 'Temple'
C. 'Mosque', 'Club', and 'Temple'
D. Mosque', 'Cave', and 'Temple'

137. .... is the author of the book 'S/Z,' which attempts a structural analysis of Balzac's thirty-page story 'Sarrasine'?

A. Jonathan Culler B. Roland Barthes
C. Frank Kermode D. Terence Hawkes

138. Which of the following finds out how a certain set of people use a language at a given time?

A. Synchronic Linguistics
B. Cultural Linguistics
C. Sociological Linguistics
D. Diachronic Linguistics

139. Which two cities are mentioned in Charles Dickens's 'A Tale of Two Cities'?

A. Paris & New York
B. London & New York
C. London & Paris
D. Paris & Rome

140. Ethnolinguistics is the study of language relating to ....

A. topographical factors
B. historical factors
C. geographical factors
D. ethnic types and behaviour

141. Which of the following thinkers introduced the 'Theory of Mimesis'?

A. Plato B. Aristotle
C. Dante D. Sophocles

142. Which work of R.K. Narayan has received Sahitya Academy Award for Literature?

A. Bachelor of Arts
B. The Guide
C. Malgudi Days
D. Vendor of Sweets

143. Who is the author of the famous existentialist play, 'The Hairy Ape'?

A. Arthur Miller
B. Eugene O'Neill
C. Tennessee Williams
D. William Faulkner

144. Who drafted the document, "The Declaration Of Independence"?

A. Abraham Lincoln
B. John Adams
C. H.D. Thoreau
D. Thomas Jefferson

145. 'Evolution', a powerful poem by a Native American poet, Sherman Alexie illustrates ....

A. the systematic degradation of the Native American people and their culture
B. how American writers have evolved the technique of writing poetry
C. the theory of evolution of the human race
D. the sci-fi narration of evolution of another new world

146. Most of Jhumpa Lahiri's fiction deals with the theme of ....

A. Marriage and its failure most Indian household displays
B. Indian politics
C. Diasporic Indians' dilemma and search for rootedness.
D. Poverty and squalor of Indian cities

147. Nissim Ezekiel's 'Goodbye Party for Miss Pushpa T.S.' satirizes ....

A. the way Indians use the English Language
B. the humour of a woman named Pushpa T.S.
C. the way Indians are fond of partying
D. the school politics involved in farewell parties

148. In the years from 1958 to 1966, Chinua Achebe published four novels in which he traced the history of Nigeria from pre-colonial to post-colonial times. These novels are 'Things Fall Apart', 'No Longer at Ease', 'Arrow of God' and ....

A. Beware, Soul-Brother
B. Morning Yet on Creation Day
C. A Man of the People
D. Nervous Conditions

149. Which famous novel of Toni Morrison begins with the following line: "124 is spiteful"?

A. Sula B. The Bluest Eyes
C. Beloved D. Tar Baby

150. "Comedy aims at representing men as worse, Tragedy as better than in actual life," are the words of ....

A. Aristotle B. Sophocles
C. Dante D. Plato

151. The play 'Tughlaq' is an allegory on ....

A. the role of an Emperor in governing the state
B. the Mughal dynasty
C. the Nehruvian era
D. the Hindu – Muslim relationship

152. My Story is an autobiographical work of ......

A. Kamala Markandya
B. Shobha De
C. Anita Desai
D. Kamala Das

153. V.S. Naipaul's Indian Travel Trilogy consists of 'An Area of Darkness', 'India: A Wounded Civilization' and ....

A. The Enigma of Arrival
B. India: A Million Mutinies Now
C. A Bend in the River
D. A House of Mr. Biswas

154. "I am obnoxious to each carping tongue/ That says my hand a needle better fits.". These are the words of the first published American woman poet. Who is she?
A. Mary Hutchinson
B. Emily Dickinson
C. Mary Wollstonecraft
D. Anne Bradstreet

155. Who among the following has not won a Noble Prize in Literature?
A. William Faulkner
B. Walt Whitman
C. Toni Morrison
D. Sinclair Lewis

156. Which of the following is not a part of New Literatures in English?
A. British English Literature
B. Commonwealth Literature
C. Post-Colonial Literature
D. Third World Literature

157. Which of the given options is not correct of Tennessee Williams' plays?
A. The Glass Menagerie: Amanda Wingfield
B. Cat on the Hot Tin Roof: Big Daddy
C. The Street Car Named Desire: Blanche DuBois
D. The Night of the Iguana: Jim O'Connor

158. Which of the following sequences is correct about Anita Desai's novels, arranged according to the year they were published?
A. 'Fire on the Mountain', 'Journey to Ithaca', 'Clear Light of Day', 'In Custody'
B. 'Fire on the Mountain', 'Clear Light of Day', 'In Custody', 'Journey to Ithaca'.
C. 'Clear Light of Day', 'Fire on the Mountain', 'In Custody', 'Journey to Ithaca'
D. 'Fire on the Mountain', 'In Custody', 'Clear Light of Day', 'Journey to Ithaca'.

159. 'The Purloined Letter' is a ....
A. detective short story by Edgar Allan Poe
B. famous novel by Henry Melville
C. narrative poem by Walt Whitman
D. prose piece of Ralph Waldo Emerson

160. Which of the following poems by Robert Frost, became an inspirational poem for former Indian Prime Minister, Pandit Jawaharlal Nehru?
A. After Apple Picking
B. Stopping By Woods on a Snowy Evening
C. Mending Wall
D. The Road Not Taken

161. Who among the following is regarded as the first Aboriginal writer in Australian Literature?
A. Marcia Langton B. David Unaipon
C. Sally Morgan D. Noel Pearson

162. What is the nationality of the author of the famous Booker Prize winner novel, the 'Life of Pi'?
A. Canadian B. Australian
C. Indian D. British

163. Which of the following is not true of Margaret Atwood's 'The Handmaid's Tale'?
A. It is an utopian novel.
B. The Testament is its sequel novel.
C. It is set in an imaginary state known as Gilead.
D. It is a dystopian novel.

164. At Shagger's Funeral is a poem by ....
A. Chris Wallace B. Gwen Harwood
C. Les Murray D. Bruce Dawe

165. In which genre of literature does 'The Getting of Wisdom' by Henry Handel Richardson fall?
A. Children's Literature
B. Autobiography
C. Detective Fiction
D. Gothic Fiction

166. Which of the following real life persons influenced the character of Johann Ulrich Voss, in Patrick White's novel 'Voss'?

A. Ludwig Leichhardt
B. Christopher Columbus
C. Marco Polo
D. Ferdinand Magellan

167. Name a South African Nobel Laureate whose most of the works document South African apartheid.
A. Dorris Lessing
B. Nadine Gordimer
C. Bessie Head
D. Pauline Smith

168. Who is the protagonist of Michael Ondantjee's 'English Patient'?
A. Kip B. Hana
C. Almásy D. Katharine Clifton

169. "The creature or spirit in him had spoken up, having all along had the words in there that would betray him and which, when they came hooting out of his mouth, so astonished him: Do not shoot. I am a B-b-British object." are famous lines from ....
A. 'True History of the Kelly Gang' by Peter Carey
B. Voss' by Patrick White
C. 'Remembering Babylon' by David Malouf
D. 'The Removalists' by David Williamson

170. Which novel by Sidhwa served as the basis for Deepa Mehta's movie, 'Earth'?
A. Ice Candy Man
B. Water: A Novel
C. City of Sin and Splendour: Writings on Lahore
D. The Bride

Directions (Qs. 171-175): *Read the passage carefully and choose the best answer to each question out of the four alternatives.*

There is consistent, strong evidence to prove that the SARS-CoV-2 virus, behind the COVID-19 pandemic, is predominantly transmitted through the air, according to a new assessment published on Friday in The Lancet journal. The analysis by six experts from the UK, the US and Canada says public health measures fail to treat the virus as predominantly the airborne route leave people unprotected and allow the virus to spread. Although some studies in the past have suggested that COVID-19 may spread through air, overall scientific literature on the subject has been inconclusive. In July last year, over 200 scientists from 32 nations wrote to the WHO, saying there is evidence that the coronavirus is airborne, and even smaller particles can infect people. "The evidence supporting airborne transmission is overwhelming, and evidence supporting large droplet transmission is almost non-existent," said Jose-Luis Jimenez, from the University of Colorado Boulder in the US. "It is urgent that the World Health Organization and other public health agencies adapt their description of transmission to the scientific evidence so that the focus of mitigation is put on reducing airborne transmission," Jimenez said. Studies have confirmed these events cannot be adequately explained by close contact or touching shared surfaces or objects, the researchers said in their assessment.

They noted that transmission rates of SARS-CoV-2 are much higher indoors than outdoors, and transmission is greatly reduced by indoor ventilation. The team cited previous studies estimating that silent—asymptomatic or presymptomatic — transmission of SARS-CoV-2 from people who are not coughing or sneezing accounts for at least 40 per cent of all transmission.

171. What, according to Jimenez, is expected from WHO and other public health organisations?
A. To find scientific ways to reduce the airborne transmission
B. To guide people to wear masks.
C. To find a scientific cure for permanent extinction of the virus.
D. To find the scientific evidence of their description of transmission of SARS-CoV-2 to reduce its transmission.

172. Find a word from the passage which is the antonym of 'disproof'.
A. Evidence B. Predominance
C. Assessment D. Focus

173. Which of the following statements is not true about the transmission of SARS-CoV-2?

A. It is transmitted through air.
B. It is transmitted via close contact or touching shared surfaces or objects.
C. It could be transmitted through Asymptomatic patients to a healthy person.
D. It is transmitted much higher outdoors than indoors.

174. Find a word from the passage which means same as 'alleviation'.
A. description
B. Mitigation
C. transmission
D. predominance

175. What did six experts from the UK, the US and Canada analyse about SARS-CoV-2 virus?
A. The public health measures fail to treat the virus as people do not use protection.
B. The virus cannot be transmitted through air.
C. The virus spread is uncontrollable and cannot be treated now.
D. The virus spreads fast as it is airborne.

Directions (Qs. 176-180): *Read the poem carefully and choose the best answer to each question out of the four alternatives.*

One day I wrote her name upon the strand,
But came the waves and washed it away:
Again I wrote it with a second hand,
But came the tide, and made my pains his prey.
"Vain man," said she, "that dost in vain assay,
A mortal thing so to immortalize;
For I myself shall like to this decay,
And eke my name be wiped out likewise."
"Not so," (quod I) "let baser things devise
To die in dust, but you shall live by fame:
My verse your virtues rare shall eternize,
And in the heavens write your glorious name:
Where when as death shall all the world subdue,
Our love shall live, and later life renew."

176. What is the rhyme scheme of the above poem?
A. ABAB BCBC CDCD EF
B. AABB AABB AABB CC
C. ABBA ABBA CDDC EE
D. ABAB BCBC CDCD EE

177. What message is conveyed in the final couplet?
A. Everyone must die one day.
B. There is life after death.
C. Love is immortal.
D. Life after death promises fulfillment of love.

178. "Again I wrote it with a second hand, But came the tide, and made my pains his prey". What do these lines symbolise?
A. That the lover is tired of writing his beloved's name on the shore.
B. That the tide takes pleasure in erasing the name.
C. That time will destroy all man-made things.
D. That the poet wrote the name of his beloved with his left hand.

179. How will the beloved be immortalised?
A. By her name written on the shore.
B. By the verse of the poet lover.
C. By dying as an old woman.
D. By praying to God.

180. Find a word from the passage which is the opposite of 'successful'.
A. Eternize
B. Vain
C. Subdue
D. Devise

181. Which type of learning is concerned with perception of things to be learned by primary sensory organs?
A. Verbal
B. Cognition
C. Discrimination
D. Sensory

182. What involves two cell divisions during which the chromosome number is halved?
A. Genes
B. Heterozygous
C. Meiosis
D. Homozygous

183. Which assessments are in-process evaluations of student learning that are typically administered multiple times during a unit, course, or academic program?

A. Pre-assessments
B. Summative assessments
C. Formative Assessments
D. High stake assessments

184. Which type of attention makes an individual exercise his will power in a single act to assign a work?
A. Implicit
B. Involuntary
C. Explicit
D. Non-formal education

185. Phonetics is classified into three types according to the production, perception and ....
A. dialect B. articulatory
C. auditive D. transmission

186. Which type of hearing loss is the result of damage to the delicate sensory hair cells of the inner ear?
A. Sensorineural hearing loss
B. Mixed hearing loss
C. Conductive hearing loss
D. Central hearing loss

187. Which type of text is associative with the purpose of communicating ideas and information between individuals?
A. Narrative B. Transactional
C. Reflective D. Expository

188. Name the set of three hierarchical models that is used to classify educational learning objectives in cognitive, affective and sensory domains.
A. Bloom's Taxonomy
B. Multilingualism
C. Schema
D. Dialect

189. .... is the way in which men and women are treated or behave differently in society, either with their own gender or with each other.
A. Gender mainstreaming
B. Gender analysis
C. Gender parity
D. Gender Dynamics

190. In which custom did wives immolated themselves while their husbands went to perform Saka?
A. Jauhar B. Devadasi
C. Sati D. Child Marriage

191. In which stage of cognitive development by Jean Piaget do the children begin to think logically about concrete events?
A. Formal Operational Stage
B. Pre-operational Stage
C. Concrete Operational Stage
D. Sensory Motor Stage

192. Name the statement that was released in 1994 (UNESCO) which led to a large number of developing countries reformulate their policies to promote the inclusion of students with disabilities into mainstream schools.
A. Statement on Race
B. Peace Statement
C. Statement on Racial Prejudice
D. Salamanca Statement

193. Which educational method includes many different kinds of learners in the same classroom, instead of separating students according to their learning abilities?
A. Parity B. Inclusive
C. Equity D. Mainstreaming

194. In which stage of Erik Erikson's theory of Psycho-social Development is the period of Initiative versus Guilt?
A. Stage III B. Stage I
C. Stage IV D. Stage II

195. A .... is a multi-purpose scoring guide for assessing student products and performances.
A. Grade card B. Rubric
C. Report card D. Analysis

196. Which form of art helps develop kinesthetic skills in the students and provides a medium to experience life in a different form?
A. Visual and media
B. Dance
C. Music
D. Creative writing

197. Which approach to assessment is formative rather than summative?
A. Assessment as learning
B. Constructivist
C. Assessment of learning
D. Assessment for learning

198. Which law of the Gestalt principle of perceptual organisation states that if enough shape is indicated, people perceive the whole by filling in the missing information?
A. Law of Similarity
B. Law of Proximity
C. Law of Closure
D. Law of Common Fate

199. Which approach sought to challenge root causes of gender inequality and increase women's access to resources and decision-making?
A. Gender in Developmental Approach
B. Post Structuralism Theory
C. Human Rights based Approach
D. Women in Developmental Approach

200. Forum Theatre is coordinated by an 'anchor' who is called a ....
A. Joker
B. Host
C. Protagonist
D. Oppressor

ANSWERS

1	2	3	4	5	6	7	8	9	10
D	D	D	B	C	A	C	A	A	C
11	**12**	**13**	**14**	**15**	**16**	**17**	**18**	**19**	**20**
A	C	D	A	C	C	A	A	D	B
21	**22**	**23**	**24**	**25**	**26**	**27**	**28**	**29**	**30**
B	C	D	D	A	A	C	A	C	D
31	**32**	**33**	**34**	**35**	**36**	**37**	**38**	**39**	**40**
B	C	A	D	B	D	A	B	B	D
41	**42**	**43**	**44**	**45**	**46**	**47**	**48**	**49**	**50**
D	A	D	C	B	D	B	D	A	C
51	**52**	**53**	**54**	**55**	**56**	**57**	**58**	**59**	**60**
C	B	D	C	C	A	C	A	D	B
61	**62**	**63**	**64**	**65**	**66**	**67**	**68**	**69**	**70**
B	D	A	C	A	A	D	A	A	C
71	**72**	**73**	**74**	**75**	**76**	**77**	**78**	**79**	**80**
B	B	C	A	C	A	A	B	C	B
81	**82**	**83**	**84**	**85**	**86**	**87**	**88**	**89**	**90**
C	A	D	B	C	C	A	A	C	D
91	**92**	**93**	**94**	**95**	**96**	**97**	**98**	**99**	**100**
B	B	C	C	C	D	D	C	D	D
101	**102**	**103**	**104**	**105**	**106**	**107**	**108**	**109**	**110**
B	B	D	C	C	A	B	A	D	C

111	112	113	114	115	116	117	118	119	120
B	C	D	A	D	B	C	C	D	A
121	**122**	**123**	**124**	**125**	**126**	**127**	**128**	**129**	**130**
A	D	D	D	B	D	A	C	B	A
131	**132**	**133**	**134**	**135**	**136**	**137**	**138**	**139**	**140**
A	D	D	C	C	D	B	A	C	D
141	**142**	**143**	**144**	**145**	**146**	**147**	**148**	**149**	**150**
A	B	B	D	A	C	A	C	C	A
151	**152**	**153**	**154**	**155**	**156**	**157**	**158**	**159**	**160**
C	D	B	D	B	A	D	B	A	B
161	**162**	**163**	**164**	**165**	**166**	**167**	**168**	**169**	**170**
B	A	A	D	A	A	B	C	C	A
171	**172**	**173**	**174**	**175**	**176**	**177**	**178**	**179**	**180**
D	A	D	B	D	D	C	C	B	B
181	**182**	**183**	**184**	**185**	**186**	**187**	**188**	**189**	**190**
D	C	C	A	D	A	B	A	D	A
191	**192**	**193**	**194**	**195**	**196**	**197**	**198**	**199**	**200**
C	D	D	A	B	B	B	C	A	A

Previous Paper (Solved)

Delhi Subordinate Services Selection Board

DSSSB–PGT (English) Recruitment Exam, 2018*

Subject Knowledge – English & Teaching Methodology

Directions (Qs. No. 1-10): *Read the following passage and answer questions.*

Near the end of the 19th century, economist Thorstein Veblen came up with the idea of conspicuous consumption. Coincidentally (or maybe not), around this time French perfumers mastered the art of selling an inexpensively-produced product as a symbol of decadent luxury. In fact, historian Eugénie Briot points out that the marketing of scents through clever branding, rather than real differences in what's being sold, originated in 19th-century France.

Industrialisation transformed the perfume business in the 19th century. Steam engines allowed for mass production on a radically new scale. Between 1880 and 1905, one factory went from a 6-horsepower machine to a 500-horsepower alternative. Machines ground iris root and extracted and infused scents. Factories could now dry perfumed soaps in less than a tenth of the time it had previously taken.

In the 1870s, French perfumers also quietly began swapping flowers and other organic materials out for artificial compounds. Scents created with piperonal, a synthetic chemical that happened to smell like the heliotrope flower, quickly became popular with the upper classes. But, as the cost of producing the chemical fell, "heliotrope" perfumes descended the class ladder. By the late 1890s, it was associated with disreputable members of the lower class. The price of other scent compounds, including vanillin and artificial musk, also dropped precipitously in these years.

Some perfumers celebrated the newly widespread availability of perfumes. "One of the outstanding features of the social history of our time is the ascent of the humble classes toward well-being, a luxury, as we could say, until then reserved only to the privileged," one wrote. "Today, the humblest craftsman uses perfumed soap, which he or she can obtain at infinitesimal prices."

While some perfume-makers gravitated toward a high-volume, low-price business, others developed ways to keep selling at high prices. The different perfumes were "easily interchangeable," Briot writes, so manufacturers found new ways to sell them.

It helped that in the second half of the century, perfumers also achieved a new social status. Some were knighted, and others were elected to public office. This fame allowed some of them to transform their names into brands. As competition heated up, Briot writes, "Capitalising on their names was among the first, and best, ways to achieve dominance."

Other tactics for selling expensive perfumes to wealthy buyers included displaying them in fancy boutiques and using elaborate packaging. And in a move echoed today in "sponsored content" stories on news sites, high-end perfumers also placed ads disguised as society gossip columns in which high-society ladies praised their products. As Briot puts it, perfumers differentiated "their products by conferring a highly symbolic value on them".

1. Which one of the following statements is FALSE?

* Online exam held on 02/07/2018.

A. Labourers like bathing with perfumed soaps because they can afford them.
B. Upmarket boutiques, more fantastic bottles and the swankiest packaging presented ordinary perfumes as exotic products.
C. Extracting and infusing scents into soaps remained harder and expensive unlike drying soaps, due to industrialisation.
D. Perfumes were considered a decadent luxury in France.

2. The sixth paragraph shows how:
A. perfumers rose in society and used their names as brands to make their perfumes famous
B. brands moved upwards on the social-ladder when the manufacturers became celebrities
C. as brands became more famous and expensive, perfumers gained greater social status
D. branding in the market place is a consequence of labelling of people in the wider society

3. Which one of the following statements is true?
A. Swapping flowers and other organic materials out for artificial compounds led to better smelling perfumes.
B. Society gossip columns employing high-society ladies to praise perfumes made the poor spurn them.
C. The shift of the humble classes toward well-being made luxury items affordable to them.
D. Branding and name and fame are discrete phenomena, as has been shown by the perfume industry.

4. Identify the most appropriate meaning of the highlighted word in the sentence below, according to the context in which it is used in the passage:

... economist Thorstein Veblen came up with the idea of **conspicuous** consumption.
A. attention-grabbing B. understandable
C. elegant D. arrogant

5. Identify the correct synonym of the highlighted word in the sentence given below, according to the context in which it is used in the passage:

Today, the humblest craftsman uses perfumed soap, which he or she can obtain at **infinitesimal** prices.
A. unimportant B. limitless
C. countless D. negligible

6. What main idea/topic is developed in the third paragraph?
A. How perfumes came to be associated with the 'vermin' of society
B. How perfumes became cheaper in all senses of the word
C. The discovery, production and popularisation of synthetic perfumes and their consequences
D. How piperonal replaced heliotrope flowers in perfumes

7. When the writer observes, 'The different perfumes were easily interchangeable,' he implies that:
A. there were no cost differences between the higher-end and the popular perfumes
B. there were no social differences between the higher-end and the popular perfumes
C. there were no substantial differences between the higher-end and the popular perfumes
D. there were no price differences between the higher-end and the popular perfumes

8. What is this passage about?
A. The origins of the French perfume industry
B. The branding and marketing of French perfumes
C. How French perfumes became popular and came to be used by all classes of people
D. Changes in the branding, marketing and consumption of French perfumes

9. The manufacturing process of the French perfume industry and business underwent fundamental changes:
A. when perfumers became celebrities

B. when the labouring-class started using perfumes
C. when chemicals replaced flowers
D. when the industrial revolution happened

10. Which one of the following options provides an accurate interpretation of the following statement?

... as the cost of producing the chemical fell, ''heliotrope" perfumes descended the class ladder.

A. ... as the cost of producing "heliotrope" perfumes fell, it was considered a popular perfume.
B. ... as the cost of producing the chemical fell, "heliotrope" perfumes naturally went downhill.
C. ... as the cost of producing the chemical fell, "heliotrope" perfumes were used by labourers and working-class people.
D. ... when the base chemical became cheaper, "heliotrope" perfumes became cheaper, came to be used by ordinary folk and lost its 'rich' tag.

Directions (Qs. No. 11-20): *Read the following passage and answer questions.*

In the early- to mid-19th century, Americans heard or ignored 'sounds' depending on their ideological predispositions, and perhaps to some extent we still do. After all, this summer many of us will head out for a week of camping in the woods or hiding out in a beachside cabin, eager for the peace and quiet of nature. But why do we think of nature as quiet, when there are squawking birds, crashing waves, and maybe a raucous thunderstorm rolling in? Environmental historian Peter A. Coates points out that what we think of as noise is as much a matter of ideology as decibels.

Coates writes that city dwellers have always complained about noise, starting long before industrialisation. "Possessing the power to drive genteel folks to distraction were hammering tinsmiths, carpet-beating maids, whip-cracking, foul-mouthed animal drovers, and, not least, the purveyors of so-called 'rough music,'" he writes. Horse-drawn carriages made such a racket on city cobblestones that people in the 1890s actually looked forward to the horseless electric carriage as a quieter alternative.

But in some times and places, it was nature that was understood as noisy while the sounds of civilised society were considered a gentle comfort. Quoting historian Mark Smith, Coates notes that European settlers in America found the noise of an axe striking a tree an "aural victory over howling wilderness"— "howling" evoking Old Testament language suggesting both wild beasts and "equally blood-thirsty and ignoble human savages whose keynote sound was a blood-curdling war whoop".

To 19th-century modernists, Coates writes, "mechanical sounds and the noisy bustle of commerce bespoke prosperity" while quiet "was synonymous with indolence, backwardness, and stagnation". But romantics like Nathaniel Hawthorne heard the "long shriek" of a distant train whistle as an affront to both the natural sounds of birds and leaves and the preindustrial human sounds of the village clock or the cowbell. "It tells a story of busy men, citizens, from the hot streets," Hawthorne wrote. "It brings the noisy world into the midst of our slumberous peace."

In the 20th century, natural quiet—or, rather, the absence of radios and car horns and the presence of honking geese and howling wolves—became central to the conservation movement and the creation of natural parks. One founder of the Wilderness Society suggested in 1932 that designated wild areas would "interest the folks in the inexpensive joys of nature in lieu of the jarring jams of jazz".

In contrast, "wise use" advocates of the late 20th century hoped human sounds could coexist harmoniously with nature. In 1990, future Interior Secretary Gale Norton argued for the "right to make noise"— for example by enjoying the natural world from the seat of a snowmobile.

When city-dwellers head out into nature this summer, they might just find that the quiet they seek is not external after all.

11. Which one of the following statements is true?

A. Noise is not defined or seen in terms of decibels as the term is restricted to scientific use.

B. Modernists are right in arguing that development is heard in industrial sounds.

C. Ideology influences noise-perception more significantly as civilisation advances.

D. The preindustrial human sounds of the village clock or the cowbell can be irritating to the ear of a rustic dweller.

12. Identify the correct synonym of the highlighted word in the sentence given below, according to the context in which it is used in the passage:

Coates notes that European settlers in America found the noise of an axe striking a tree an "aural victory over **howling** wilderness".

A. honking B. spiteful

C. wailing D. brash

13. Identify the most appropriate meaning of the highlighted word in the sentence below, according to the context in which it is used in the passage:

Hawthorne wrote, "It brings the noisy world into the midst of our **slumberous** peace."

A. Quiet B. Nocturnal

C. Lethargic D. Refreshing

14. The fifth paragraph develops which of the following ideas?

A. Natural quiet became important to conservation movements which came into being in the 20th century.

B. Sounds of animals in nature are unobtrusive, unlike those of the cities.

C. Designated wild areas and nature parks would provide the inexpensive joy of 'natural quiet'.

D. Natural parks provided people sick of the 'sounds of life' the opportunity to hear and enjoy the 'sounds' of animals.

15. What did the "wise use" advocates of the late 20th century hope for?

A. That both human sounds and sounds of nature could exist as a synced stereo.

B. That human noise would upset the ecology of nature's quietude.

C. The coterminous existence of industrial and natural sounds.

D. That both human sounds and the quietude of nature could coalesce.

16. Which one of the following statements is FALSE?

A. Definitions of noise and quietude differ both, according to perception and predisposition.

B. The noise of wild nature being civilised is more welcome to everybody than the dangerous quiet of wild animals.

C. That European settlers in America found the noise of an axe striking a tree sweet proves attitudes to noise are a matter of ideology too.

D. The sounds of civilised society can be more comforting than the sounds of nature.

17. Which one of the following options provides an accurate interpretation of the following statement?

In 1990, future Interior Secretary Gale Norton argued for the "right to make noise''—for example by enjoying the natural world from the seat of a snowmobile.

A. This statement adds a new feature to the hope that it is possible for human sounds to coexist with nature's sounds.

B. This statement exemplifies the hope that it is possible for human sounds to coexist with nature's sounds.

C. This statement takes the attention away from the hope that it is possible for human sounds to coexist with nature's sounds.

D. This statement negates the hope that it is possible for human sounds to coexist with nature's sounds.

18. What can be concluded from the following sentence?

When city-dwellers head out into nature this summer, they might just find that the quiet they seek is not external after all.

A. People go seeking for peace and quiet, lacking it in their minds and hearts.
B. Quietude and disquietude are conditions related to one's state of mind, feelings and thoughts.
C. Only city-dwellers would head out to nature as they are the ones who would aspire for and seek 'quietude'.
D. Nature might help people discover the fact that quietude is in them and not outside, just as an ideology is.

19. According to the passage, 'noise is as much a matter of ideology as decibels'. Extending this, which one of the following options will encompass both and disturb us as noise.

A. A couple quarreling in the market
B. A bomb detonated in a quarry
C. A child crying in a public place
D. A jet flying overhead

20. Identify the option that finds and states the main idea that is developed in the passage:

A. Modernists considered quiet to be a sound of laziness, while Romantics found the buzz of industries a violator of natural sounds.
B. The difference between quiet and 'noise' is a matter of likes and dislikes and the perception of it has varied across centuries, people and habitats.
C. The quiet that man seeks is in him and not in the external world — that definitions of noise and its origin vary shows people have not realised it.
D. City dwellers have always been against noise, especially the industry-produced one; the rural residents of villages may consider the sounds of animals and birds 'noise' or unwanted sound.

Directions (Qs. No. 21-30): *Read the following passage and answer questions.*

On the popular Twitter hashtag #notalion, medieval historians and aficionados share the most un-leonine lions from the Middle Ages. One on the edge of an illuminated manuscript smiles gently, its flat face almost human; another from the 11th century seems to smirk with pride at the glory of his mane that radiates like the sun.

Why do these lions look, well, not like lions? In early Christian and Romanesque sculpture, "the physiognomy of the lion gradually loses more and more of its animal aspect, and tends, though quaintly, to the human". The obvious explanation is that there weren't that many lions in medieval Europe to model for artists, and the accessible representations for copying had the same lack of realism.

However, an art historian points out, there actually were a number of lions on the continent, imported from Africa and Asia: There are many accounts of their presence and even their breeding, first at various courts and then in the cities; they were kept in Rome by the popes as early as 1100. The city of Florence had lions in the 13th century; lions were at Ghent's court in the 15th century. So, it's not impossible that first-hand accounts of lions were available to artists – an artist made a drawing of a lion 'al vif' ['from life'] in the 13th century – though where he saw the animal is unknown.

The inaccuracy of medieval lions may have been a stylistic preference, particularly in a bestiary, or compendium of beasts. Because the artists chose to illustrate the animals rather than their accompanying moralisations, they had more freedom of choice in their imagery. For example, the picture in the 12th or 13th century Ashmole Bestiary, in which a big lion is depicted as cowering in terror at a rooster, relates this supposed cowardly attribute of the lion!

Lions were also prevalent on medieval door knockers, where they were represented as stern guardians. They regularly appeared on the heraldry of European royalty, their predatory poses symbolising authority and a noble independence. There was likely some hearsay involved in the imperfect medieval lions, yet the artists were often breaking with nature to express an idea. Rather than mistakes, these #notalion specimens can be viewed as artistic decisions, albeit ones which appear delightfully strange to our modern eyes.

21. Identify the most appropriate meaning of the highlighted word in the sentence below, according to the context in which it is used in the passage:

Because the artists chose to illustrate the animals rather than their accompanying **moralisations,** they had more freedom of choice in their imagery.

A. Ethics B. Reformations

C. Explanations D. Sermons

22. Which of the following inferences may be made from this sentence in the passage?

"They regularly appeared on the heraldry of European royalty, their predatory poses symbolising authority and a noble independence ..."

A. Only predators could have authority and nobility.

B. Authority and nobility were associated with a predatory nature.

C. Authority, nobility and a soft nature go hand in hand.

D. Only a stern and strong person can exude authority and nobility.

23. When a big lion is depicted as cowering in terror at a rooster, it is done so because:

A. the artists are not required to offer any explanations

B. the artists are not concerned with verisimilitude

C. the artists want to show the lion as a cowardly animal

D. the artist is merely illustrating a quality of a creature for a compendium

24. What is the first paragraph about?

A. It debates the qualities of medieval lions as represented in illustrations.

B. It discusses why medieval lions are so un-leonine in their representative illustrations.

C. It defines medieval lions, where they are seen as illustrations and what is strange about them.

D. It describes a phenomenon which is problematised in the paragraph that follows.

25. Which of the following options provides an accurate paraphrase of the following statement?

It's not impossible that first-hand accounts of lions were available to artists.

A. First-hand accounts of lions may not have been available to artists

B. First-hand accounts of lions could have been available to artists

C. First-hand accounts of lions would have been available to artists

D. First-hand accounts of lions should have been available to artists

26. What does the author imply by the following sentence from the passage?

In early Christian and Romanesque sculpture, "the physiognomy of the lion gradually loses more and more of its animal aspect, and tends, though quaintly, to the human".

A. While the evidence is empirical, the reasons for such representations require conjectures and rationalisations.

B. Romanesque sculpture was highly imaginative and had 'Man as the measure of all'.

C. Early Christians humanised animals to nullify any remnant of pagan influences.

D. There need not be or cannot be any logical explanation for the stated fact.

27. Which one of the following statements is true?

A. Medieval representations of creatures lacked realism as symbolism was considered more important then.

B. To give lions human emotions and expressions was normal in medieval representations.

C. That there is an illustration of a lion 'from life' in the middle ages makes it necessary to consider an explanation from the artist's point of view to explain humanoid lions.

D. Both, Twitter #tags and strange and funny artistic decisions are subject to scrutiny for approval.

28. What is the passage about?

A. While illustrations of medieval lions are strange, their oddity being not traceable to the absence of lions, and are ineffable as other representations have normal expressions, they could be expressions of artists' values.

B. The popular Twitter hashtag #notalion and its sharing of medieval lions, which are abnormal, anthropoid and are strange not only to the modern eye but to the artists of that time too.

C. Europe had real lions during the middle ages as models for their drawings, yet artists' medieval lions are not leonine enough, but this could not be an expression of values associated with them by artists.

D. The portrayal of lions in medieval Europe in unreal terms is to be seen as a stylistic preference and an expression of artistic freedom, and to be traced to the absence of lions then.

29. Identify the correct synonym of the highlighted word in the sentence given below, according to the context in which it is used in the passage:

Lions were also prevalent on medieval door knockers, where they were **represented** as stern guardians.

A. Replaced B. Selected
C. Meant D. Portrayed

30. Which one of the following statements is FALSE?

A. The physiognomy of the lion shares many features with the physiognomy of humans.

B. Lions were bred and kept in medieval rich houses, perhaps as pet animals.

C. The use of lions in heraldry and knockers reveal the love of lions in medieval ages.

D. Stylistic preferences of artists cannot be discounted when examining medieval lions' strange expressions.

Directions (Qs. No. 31-40): *Read the following passage and answer questions.*

Readers of adventure stories such 'Treasure Island' or 'Sherlock Holmes' might remember how the seemingly harmless "black spot," a mere scrap of paper, or an envelope of just five orange pips, were a palpable source of fear for those who knew the code of the secret society who used them. Being singled out, or "marked for death" in this way, rather than an obscure joke, was nothing less than a threat for those who understood the symbol. Language can encode many more nuances than just literal meanings or grammatical functions, even when it comes to humble punctuation, secret languages or the register of a particular subculture.

Interestingly, even in ordinary, everyday language use, the very words and expressions we use are already marked for our cultural and social biases, so much so that we're often not even aware of it. It reveals our underlying assumptions about what we may consider normal, default, regular—even positive or desirable in certain contexts. This has an impact on how we view their opposites—the abnormal, unusual, irregular, negative, undesirable. Take a pair of simple antonyms, such as happy/unhappy. The word "happy" is considered more of a default, normal, perhaps more desirable state in English, while "unhappy" is considered more "marked," and we know this because it's actively morphologically marked with a prefix – un.

This idea, known as markedness, is a concept that is applied from linguistics to psychology, cognitive science and sociology; the concept is particularly useful for describing certain contrasts and constructs. To put it very simply, the insight into markedness is this: in a contrasting pair, you might expect an equal binary relationship, but you'll often find that the relationship is not equal, it's asymmetric. One is usually considered generic (the unmarked) and in many cases, is a default state favoured above the other (the marked).

Unmarked words in English are often favoured as more positive, such as in happy/sad, friendly/unfriendly, clean/unclean or duty, even when there may be no overt morphological marking.

Researchers have noted how pairs like man/woman, while considered politically or socially equal, linguistically are unequal, not just because "woman" is marked, but because "man" can still be understood as a generic for the human race while "woman" is never used in that way.

It's revealing how we mark these words in common expressions that are not even politically charged at all, like "she's four feet tall"!

31. Identify the option that completes the statement INAPTLY/ UNACCEPTABLY:

When we linguistically mark something ________

A. we are trying to establish the norm and the atypical

B. we have assumptions about 'default' and 'exception'

C. we are essentially qualifying it as a "specialised" form

D. we are not sure of the "generic" form

32. Identify the correct synonym of the highlighted word in the sentence given below, according to the context in which it is used in the passage:

Language can encode many more **nuances** than just literal meanings.

A. Shades B. Traces
C. Points D. Qualities

33. Identify the most appropriate meaning of the highlighted word in the sentence below, according to the context in which it is used in the passage:

It's **revealing** how we mark these words in common expressions that are not even politically charged at all, like "she's four feet tall"!

A. Exposing B. Divulging
C. Uncovering D. Telling

34. The third paragraph ________.

A. argues that binaries, contrasting pairs, and default values characterise markedness as a concept and construct.

B. compares and contrasts default and marked values and the lack of symmetry that underlies markedness.

C. shows how binaries, contrasting pairs and default values characterise markedness as a concept and construct.

D. exemplifies how markedness is used to distinguish between default assumptions and loaded meanings.

35. Identify the option that is FALSE and makes a wrong claim.

Familiarity with markedness helps us understand ________

A. the default values that words carry

B. the binaries that operate in languages

C. the codification of language-systems

D. how to load special meaning on words

36. Which one of the following statements is FALSE?

A. Cognitive Psychology does not recognise markedness.

B. 'She is four feet short' is an ambiguous statement.

C. Markedness refers to how we process the differences inherent in a word in our mind

D. 'Sheep' and 'Goats, are a marked pair in what they connote.

37. The concept/construct of markedness is used in psychology, cognitive science and sociology. Study the examples below and identify the option in which markedness cannot be perceived:

A. Brunch sounds officious; lunch, expansive

B. Lady indicates respect; girl, affection; woman could be pejorative

C. Tests indicate teachers and schools; examinations, public agencies

D. Bedouin is respectable; nomad is neutral; gypsy is pejorative

38. What is this passage about?

A. It describes how the use of codes creates markedness and defines and exemplifies it and explains how it is a linguistic phenomenon

B. It shows how language is full of default assumptions and is used to indicate status and establish power equations, markedness being one such thing

C. It introduces and explains markedness with examples, and explains how using binary codes brings it to play across social domains

D. It introduces and defines the concept of markedness, explains its forms, functions and semantic potential in common usage, with the help of examples

39. Which one of the following statements is FALSE?

A. Codes have to be symbolic in nature if they have to communicate information.

B. Markedness questions the very existence of antonyms in a language.

C. The pair 'witch/wizard' reveals social and cultural bias – pejorative versus admiration.

D. Defining and non-defining relative clauses, superficially distinguished through the presence or absence of commas, are an example of markedness in grammar.

40. Which one of the following options provides an accurate interpretation of the following statement?

Readers of adventure stories such 'Treasure Island' or 'Sherlock Holmes' might remember how the seemingly harmless "black spot," a mere scrap of paper, or an envelope of just five orange pips, were a palpable source of fear for those who knew the code of the secret society who used them.

A. The use of codes and secret signals were restricted to secret societies in novels

B. Language is a code; codes are reduced languages, initially described in popular fiction

C. Secret societies in fiction used to convey threats in a code, shared among the members of the society only

D. Secret societies, such as the mafia, convey threats only in an unfamiliar code, shared among the members of the society only

Directions (Qs. No. 41-50): *Read the following passage and answer questions.*

Nationalism and national identity are not just ideological constructs. Rather, they are created and enforced through a bureaucracy that produces censuses, surveys and identity documents. This bureaucracy and its technologies of surveillance (photography, fingerprinting, statistics) are very recent, but they have become an indelible part of our lives. Holding a passport is a sign of citizenship or legal residency recognised by any other sovereign state in the world.

But even before modern states could attempt to control the movement of their populations, people weren't free to move around as they pleased. For most of history, large segments of the population, including serfs, slaves, and indentured servants, required privately created passes or papers to legitimate their movement. But as the global economy expanded, and New World frontiers and early industrial factories developed an insatiable demand for labour, these private controls fell away. The European empires of the late 19th century imposed new rights, responsibilities, and identities on their citizens through education, conscription, and taxation. The prevailing liberalism, the vagueness of nationality in an imperial context, and the limits of surveillance meant millions upon millions were able to move to settler colonies in the Americas, South Africa and Oceania—with often the notable exclusion of Asians.

This diplomatic-surveillance regime changed after WWI. Nation-states claiming to represent exclusive nationalities replaced empires. The rise of communist parties in Russia and elsewhere in Europe gave rise to suspicion of foreign agents. Moreover, the demand for labour was easing. National working classes constituted political interest groups that protested the labour competition of new immigrant classes.

With the hardening of border security and immigration quotas between these new nation states, and the spread of cheap photography, passports became both standardised, mandatory travel documents and ritual tools reinforcing national identity. Indeed, holders of passports from more powerful nations enjoy privileges abroad that others do not. Meanwhile, many of the fragments of empires that failed to form nation states, or unwanted minority groups, have at times been made "stateless" populations. These groups have ranged from Russian expatriates after the Bolshevik Revolution, to European Jews during the Holocaust and Palestinian refugees after the creation of Israel. Lacking a passport in a worldwide system of nation states is the ultimate negation of agency.

But national identity doesn't even mean all that it used to. Much of the new nationalism expressed as xenophobia and racism is rooted in nostalgia, accurate or not, for a time when national membership meant certain shared experiences and rights bridging social classes. The march of de-industrialisation, the decline of welfare services and the widening of income inequality mean that the global elite are everywhere carving out private zones of privilege guarded by fences and private security. The value of a passport as diplomatic currency is losing ground to another currency— the almighty dollar.

41. The vagueness of nationality in an imperial context ________.

A. did not affect the people of Asia
B. was caused by the absence of passports
C. resulted in the collapse of empires
D. enabled migration and the advent of new colonies

42. Identify the most appropriate meaning of the highlighted word in the sentence below, according to the context in which it is used in the passage:

Much of the new nationalism expressed as xenophobia and racism is **rooted** in nostalgia.

A. Based on B. Embedded in
C. Surrounded D. Set in

43. What happens when the country of your origin ceases to exist as an independent nation, according to the passage?

A. You have no identity and you are not free to move; you stagnate and become powerless to act
B. You become part of a fringe group, are tagged 'stateless' or 'non-state' and suffer reduced status as a citizen of the world.
C. You become a citizen of another country after immigration; you are now seen as a refugee and a stateless being.
D. Your country cannot issue passports which other nations will recognise and thus deprive you of the free will to act, compelling you to become a refugee or a dependent.

44. Nationalism and national identity are not just ideological constructs but ______ .

A. are a way of conducting everyday life in the modern world by contemporary man
B. are manifested practically as documents developed by bureaucrats to create and maintain national identities
C. are problematic conceptions as they engender racism and xenophobia
D. have become practical issues/ considerations in the world of passports

45. Which of the following statements is FALSE according to the passage?

A. Settler colonies in the Americas, South Africa and Oceania were created by nation-states before passports became a norm.
B. Political parties which depended on labour unions protested the labour competition of new immigrant classes.
C. The spread of cheap photography helped standardisation of passports.
D. Education, conscription and taxation were methods used by sovereign nations to enforce citizens' identity.

46. Identify the main idea discussed in the fourth paragraph.

A. Passports opens many a door and provides many an opportunity; lack of a passport closes all such doors and deny one all opportunities.
B. Passports and national identities are intertwined, so the absence of one will mean the absence of the other.

C. There is a class division in passports themselves – a Bangladeshi passport and a Swedish one are not 'equal' in their diplomatic reach and influence.

D. In the present world, passports are mandatory, and they help establish national identity; 'stateless' and 'powerless' human beings can be empowered with a passport.

47. Which one of the following options provides an accurate interpretation of the statement given below?

The value of a passport as diplomatic currency is losing ground to another currency—the almighty dollar.

A. Where a passport opened the doors of alien nations due to diplomatic exigencies, there the all-powerful dollar now opens such doors for the privileged.

B. A passport is becoming cheaper even while the dollar is gaining more power and influence.

C. As money is becoming an object of worship, relationships between nations are souring and have become insignificant.

D. Today dollars are all powerful and influential; once upon a time, passports used to be so.

48. Which of the following statements is true according to the passage?

A. Dollars cannot replace passports even though they have greater purchasing power.

B. Immigration quotas in the USA at present are a by-product of the enhanced status of American passports.

C. Privileges and rights are conferred by nations only to passport holders.

D. Photography, fingerprinting and statistics were brought into passports by bureaucrats.

49. Identify the option that sums up the ideas and views expressed in the passage correctly and fully:

A. Empires and nations of the world have always kept an eye on the movements of their people – the Indian toll-gates prove that. A passport helps them do this systematically.

B. Passports reify national identities; they helped surveil people and their movements but now control their migration and travel; they can be used to offer or deny exclusive privileges of citizenships which themselves can now be bought.

C. Tracing the origins of passports and understanding the changes geopolitics experienced would show that passports offer privileges which become noticeable only when one is denied a passport.

D. A passport means you are the citizen of a world; like passes and permits, it enables the state to check and monitor your movement. Passports have become common and are obligatory tokens of identity.

50. Identify the correct synonym of the highlighted word in the sentence given below, according to the context in which it is used in the passage:

Nation-states claiming to represent **exclusive** nationalities replaced empires.

A. Specific B. Special

C. Controlled D. Chosen

Directions (Qs. No. 51-60): *Read the following passage and answer questions.*

Children's books may not form part of the recruitment process for most businesses, but for shoe repair and key-cutting business Timpson, the key to its hiring process is whether the prospective candidate resembles say, Mr Happy or Miss Quick, characters in children's books. "Other than specialist roles in finance or IT, we really don't bother about CVs or qualifications and we certainly don't take much notice of the words written on an application form," Timpson says. "The only thing that matters is personality."

As well as more unorthodox methods, firms are turning to AI and other forms of tech to recruit. L'Oreal has introduced virtual reality to its approach, whereby graduates don a headset, take a virtual tour of the French beauty giant's offices, and experience a virtual meeting while having their personality and judgement assessed. Byte London, a marketing technology agency, recently introduced a chatbot (a computer programme that conducts a conversation) to help find employees. Replacing the initial application process, the Facebook Messenger chatbot, named Space Gentleman, asks applicants a series of 10 questions such as: "Do you have the right to work in the UK?", "We wanted to reduce the cost of hiring candidates, improve the quality of candidates applying to Byte and make the application more enjoyable." He adds: "We're also using it as a soft sell for the agency's personality, helping people work out if they'd be a good fit."

Last year, the mini bakery store chain Bagelman ditched the CV as part of the recruitment process, instead encouraging prospective staff to attend a recruitment workshop, where the company could identify people who matched the job. "We were hiring individuals who looked great on paper with impressive qualifications, but it soon became apparent they didn't share our values. We realised that no matter the qualifications on the CV, it was the person in front of us that mattered." Now Bagelman runs workshops where candidates have to participate in various set tasks. "Candidates who stand out for us will show great customer service, the ability to think on their feet and retain information. A CV can't show us any of that and is open to interpretation."

Chris Rowley, a professor at Cass Business School, says companies should be more creative with recruiting but warns that while some methods can reduce the problems with CVs and applications forms, which he says have "poor reliability as predictors of job performance", you need to be able to justify that decisions are not based on characteristics such as gender, ethnicity or age, but on the job criteria. He advises companies use a mix of CVs, application forms, and semi-structured interviews and tests.

51. CVs and application forms ________.
- A. are ignored by modern business networks as they are ancient methods of recruiting
- B. are not capable of defining personality which is crucial in the job market
- C. are poor reflectors of future ability and have to be replaced partially or wholly with other recruitment methods
- D. are no longer credible or indicative of skills possessed

52. What is the main idea that the passage develops?
- A. Personality and on-the-job-performance are more important than academic qualifications and so smart business networks use smart techniques and modern methods to recruit.
- B. Companies are doing everything to recruit a good employee, using children's literature, virtual reality, chatbots and even workshops. CVs and letters of application are not to be trusted.
- C. Small business networks have intelligently started adopting advances in technology to recruit people; admittedly, CVs and applications have poor reliability, but they need not be done away with.
- D. As times are changing, and as CVs and applications do not give a clue to the actual skills of applicants, modern business firms are successfully using novel recruiting methods.

53. Which of the statements below is true in light of your understanding of the passage?
- A. Chatbots can work like initial questionnaires and help filter out completely unfit applicants.
- B. Resemblance to children's favourite character is a good predictor of future performance in all jobs.
- C. Reactions while being taken on a virtual tour will always reveal aspects of one's personality and attitude which are crucial on-the-job requirements.

D. CVs and application forms have become useless and obsolete in the world of computers, AI and virtual reality.

54. A marketing technology agency recently introduced a chatbot (a computer programme that conducts a conversation) to help find employees. What will chatbots be able to reveal? What can't it access and show?

A. A computer programme that conducts a conversation cannot be very different from Napoleon's recruiting methods for soldiers; it lacks flexibility.

B. A chatbot can sell the company's soft skills and help in the initial selection of candidates; but it cannot reveal their skills or help final selection.

C. A chatbot will be economical and a time- and cost-saving technique; but computers cannot say whether candidates are prevaricating or not.

D. Use of a chatbot will reveal the attitude of candidates to computers; but it will not help reveal their attitude in the real world.

55. Identify the meaning that is closest to the highlighted word in the sentence below, according to the context in which it is used in the passage:

As well as more **unorthodox** methods, firms are turning to AI and other forms of tech to recruit.

A. Innovative B. Rebellious

C. Blasphemous D. Heretical

56. Identify the correct synonym of the highlighted word in the sentence given below, according to the context in which it is used in the passage:

L'Oreal has introduced **virtual** reality to its approach, whereby graduates don a headset.

A. Holy B. Fake

C. Righteous D. Simulated

57. Which of the following inferences may be drawn from the following statement?

Chris Rowley ______ warns that ______ you need to be able to justify that decisions are not based on characteristics such as gender, ethnicity or age, but on the job criteria.

A. Gender; ethnicity and age are not as reliable as the CV for recruitment.

B. Gender; ethnicity and age are reliable criteria for recruitment.

C. Gender; ethnicity and age are just as reliable as job criteria for recruitment.

D. Gender; ethnicity and age are not acceptable criteria for recruitment.

58. Which of the following options provides an accurate interpretation of the following statement?

CVs and applications forms _______ have "poor reliability as predictors of job performance".

A. CVs and applications forms are tokens of loyalty but are poor clairvoyants of future performance

B. CVs and applications forms are constant and so they cannot be analysed to recruit people

C. CVs and application forms are not un-dependable per se but they cannot tell beforehand how someone will perform later

D. CVs and applications forms are trustworthy and are highly prophetic in their indications

59. Which of the following options is UNACCEPTABLE and FALSE and will NOT complete the statement correctly?

Recruitment workshops ________

A. cast a better net than chatbots, virtual tours or 'resemblance familiar characters' when it comes to recruiting chefs, but may not be enough to recruit other professionals.

B. and appointing apprentices serve similar purposes – fitting man for machine.

C. are like 'demonstration lessons' used to hire teachers, however what is demonstrated may not indicate what will be needed on the job.

D. are a novel and non-traditional method of selecting the right people in terms of the jobs they will perform.

60. Why are new methods of hiring cost-efficient?

A. There are no tests or face-to-face interviews requiring travel for all, thus saving a lot of money.

B. They don't depend on CVs and application forms alone, but employ interviews and tests.

C. The cost of initial filtering is negligible and the process itself is fast, making the new methods cheaper and faster.

D. They adopt selection methods that are tailored for their needs, with an awareness of the required profile of future employees.

61. Fill in the blanks to make the following sentence complete, correct and meaningful:

The corporates ____ that only consolidation _______ the development of better seed varieties and the innovations needed to avert global hunger and malnutrition, as the world population ______ to around 10 billion people in a few decades time.

A. argue; brings; climbs
B. argue; can bring; climbed
C. argue; can bring; climbs
D. argued; could bring; climbs

62. Parts of a sentence (or two) are given as options and they are jumbled up. One of the options contains an error that renders the unjumbled sentence wrong and ungrammatical. Identify the part/option which contains the error:

A. their affinities for such laws, to hold very broadly
B. of universally applicable laws but humans
C. unlike atoms, are not consistent enough in
D. the dictates of logic requires the existence

63. In the sentence given below a phrase clause is missing, indicated through a blank. Identify the option that can fill in the blank and complete the sentence correctly and meaningfully:

To point the finger at farming as the cause of environmental degradation through intensification makes no sense, _____ in that time – increased house building, more roads, and more cars on those roads – and the impact they have had on the country's landscape.

A. especially when you would have considered other changes that have taken place
B. though when you consider the other changes that have taken place
C. particularly when you considered the other changes that have taken place
D. especially when you consider the other changes that have taken place

64. In the sentence given below a phrase/clause is missing, indicated through a blank. Identify the option that can fill in the blank and complete the sentence correctly and meaningfully:

Instead of working in a well-funded research institute, _____ Deb is now part of the worldwide farmers' movement to limit corporate control and to redefine what knowledge is, and who owns it.

A. as might be expected in a Fulbright biotech scholar,
B. as might be expected of Fulbright biotech scholar,
C. as might be expecting of a Fulbright biotech scholar,
D. as might be expected of a Fulbright biotech scholar,

65. Fill in the blanks to make the following sentence complete, correct and meaningful:

Backed ______ governments and enabled _____ world trade rules and intellectual property laws, Bayer-Monsanto has been allowed to control much _______ the world's supply ______ seeds.

A. by; by; at; at
B. by; by; of; of
C. at; by; of; of
D. by; at; of; at

66. Parts of a sentence (or two) are given as options and they are jumbled up. One of the options contains an error that renders the unjumbled sentence wrong and ungrammatical. Identify the part/option which contains the error:

A. Bayer and Monsanto whom concentrate on
B. grows forgotten crops and is the antithesis of
C. developing a small number of blockbuster staple crops
D. an Indian plant researcher Debal Deb

67. Fill in the blanks to make the following sentence complete, correct and meaningful:

______ there is a major hiccup in the next few days, an incredibly powerful company will shortly be given a license to dominate world farming.

A. As if
B. Although
C. Unless
D. Until

68. Parts of a sentence (or two) are given as options and they are jumbled up. One of the options contains an error that renders the unjumbled sentence wrong and ungrammatical. Identify the part/option which contains the error:

A. is not philanthropy and the extension of an age-old
B. system of mutualised farming that has provided
C. social stability and dietary diversity for many
D. the seed-sharing of "landraces", or local varieties

69. Parts of a sentence (or two) are given as options and they are jumbled up. One of the options contains an error that renders the unjumbled sentence wrong and ungrammatical. Identify the part/option which contains the error:

A. richer than non-democracies,
B. are less likelier to go to war
C. and have a better record of fighting corruption
D. democracies are on average

70. Parts of a sentence (or two) are given as options and they are jumbled up. One of the options contains an error that renders the unjumbled sentence wrong and ungrammatical. Identify the part/option which contains the error:

A. they are logical, ignoring human beings' whims and greed
B. logical grand plans for the betterment of mankind
C. but much ideas almost always fail precisely because
D. history records many well-conceived and apparent

71. Parts of a sentence (or two) are given as options and they are jumbled up. One of the options contains an error that renders the unjumbled sentence wrong and ungrammatical. Identify the part/option which contains the error:

A. the legal and biological grip of seed corporates
B. on global farming will tighten, threatening
C. environmentalists in developing countries say
D. farther the small farmer who used to feed the world

72. Fill in the blanks to make the following sentence complete, correct and meaningful:

Bayer-Monsanto will have an indirect impact ____ every consumer and a direct one _____ most farmers _____ Britain, the EU and the US. It will effectively control most _____ the world's GM crop genetic traits, as well as much of the data _____ what farmers grow where, and the yields they get.

A. on; in; in; of; about
B. in; on; on; of; about
C. on; on; in; of; about
D. in; on; on; by; about

73. In the sentence given below a phrase/clause is missing, indicated through a blank. Identify the option that can fill in the blank and complete the sentence correctly and meaningfully:

I was shocked to find a six-year-old girl who did not know what a potato was. She agreed that she liked eating chips and crisps, but was very skeptical that ______ .

A. this dirty, hard, brown thing have anything to do with them
B. this hard, dirty brown thing had anything to do with them
C. the brown, hard, dirty thing had everything to do in them
D. this hard, dirty brown thing have anything to do with them

74. Parts of a sentence (or two) are given as options and they are jumbled up. One of the options contains an error that renders the unjumbled sentence wrong and ungrammatical. Identify the part/option which contains the error:

A. governments and research organisations are blinded by the prospect of
B. new technologies and have paid a little attention to farmers traditional knowledge,
C. a veritable storehouse of wisdom, which is essential
D. if the world is to adapt to climate change and population growth.

75. In the sentence given below a phrase/clause is missing, indicated through a blank. Identify the option that can fill in the blank and complete the sentence correctly and meaningfully:

Improving the way we farm in harmony with wildlife, while not decreasing food production, _____ that focuses purely on agriculture.

A. must not be achieved through any sort of knee-jerk blame game
B. will not be achieved on some sort of knee-jerk blame game
C. should be achieved through some sort of knee-jerk blame game
D. will not be achieved through some sort of knee-jerk blame game

76. Parts of a sentence (or two) are given as options and they are jumbled up. One of the options contains an error that renders the unjumbled sentence wrong and ungrammatical. Identify the part/option which contains the error:

A. besides many varieties that can grow in brackish water
B. 4 to 5 ft of water, and dozens that are drought-tolerant,
C. growing in 12ft of water, some that can grow in
D. Deb has discovered rice varieties that are capable of

77. Parts of a sentence (or two) are given as options and they are jumbled up. One of the options contains an error that renders the unjumbled sentence wrong and ungrammatical. Identify the part/option which contains the error:

A. and only gives his seeds to people he trusts
B. Deb kept the exact location of his farm secret
C. claiming that spies have been sent to steal his seeds
D. and that companies want to claim them as their own

78. Parts of a sentence (or two) are given as options and they are jumbled up. One of the options contains an error that renders the unjumbled sentence wrong and ungrammatical. Identify the part/option which contains the error:

A. of hundreds of Indian rice varieties and also an act
B. the immense reach of the likes of Monsanto and Bayer
C. the community seed bank is a living repository
D. of effective ecological and political defiance upon

79. In the sentence given below a phrase/clause is missing, indicated through a blank. Identify the option that can fill in the blank and complete the sentence correctly and meaningfully:

There is actually quite a broad consensus on many of the most fundamental questions of public life: _______ and in politics there is a similarly support for representative democracy and governments that place a high value on fairness and diversity.

A. in economics there is a wide support for a regulating market economy flanked by a big state
B. in economics there is wide supported for a regulated market economy flanked by a big state
C. in economics there is wide support for a regulated market economy flanked by a big state
D. in economics their is wide support for a regulated market economy flanking by a big state

80. Fill in the blanks to make the following sentence complete, correct and meaningful:

_______ powerful lobbying in Europe and _______ political arm-twisting on several continents, the path has been cleared for Monsanto, the world's ______ seed company, to be taken over by Bayer.

A. Subsequent; a lot of; largest
B. Subsequent to; lots of; largest
C. Subsequent to; lot of; larger
D. Subsequent to; a lot of; largest

81. The parts of a sentence given below, when rearranged, form a grammatical sentence. Identify the option that presents the correct order:

1. the name 'applied science' could be given, but
2. there exists no category of science to which
3. we have science and the applications of science
4. which are united as the fruit is to the tree

A. 3, 2, 4, 1 B. 4, 1, 2, 3
C. 2, 3, 4, 1 D. 2, 1, 3, 4

82. Identify the option that converts the statement below into a question, without any distortion:

We describe the variety of ecological and evolutionary consequences that may result from humans encountering wildlife.

A. Shall we describe the variety of ecological and evolutionary consequences that may result from humans encountering wildlife?
B. May we describe the variety of ecological and evolutionary consequences that may result from humans encountering wildlife?
C. Can evolutionary consequences result from humans encountering wildlife and do we describe the variety of ecological and evolutionary consequences?
D. Do we describe the variety of ecological and evolutionary consequences that may result from humans encountering wildlife?

83. Rewrite the statement below into a question, so as to derive the highlighted part as the answer:

The expression 'food desert' calls to mind desolate places, not **places with enormous potential**.

A. When the expression 'food desert' calls to mind desolate places, what does the expression fail?
B. When the expression 'food desert' calls to mind desolate places, what does the expression fail to evoke?
C. When the expression 'food desert' calls to mind desolate places, what it does fail to evoke?
D. When the expression 'food desert' calls to mind desolate places, why does the expression fail to evoke places with enormous potential?

84. Identify the option that restates the given statement using a positive adjective, without any change of meaning:

Wireless is the most preferred mode of operation today.

A. A mode of operation much preferred today is wireless.
B. Other modes of operation, unlike wireless, are not preferred today.

C. Wireless is preferred than many other modes of operation today.

D. No other mode of operation today is as much preferred as wireless.

85. Identify the option that converts the statement below into a question, without any distortion:

America's sustainable food movement has been steadily growing yet the movement is predominantly white.

A. Unless America's sustainable food movement has been steadily growing, isn't the movement predominantly white?

B. Lest America's sustainable food movement has been steadily growing, won't the movement predominantly white?

C. Though America's sustainable food movement has been steadily growing, is the movement predominantly white?

D. Though America's sustainable food movement has been steadily growing, isn't the movement predominantly white?

86. Identify the option that restates the comparison using a positive adjective, without any change of meaning:

We use the computers in our pockets, known as 'phones', more than those on our desks or laps.

A. The computers on our desks and laps are less used by us than those, known as 'phones', in our pockets.

B. The computers on our desks and laps are not used by us as much as those, known as 'phones', in our pockets.

C. The computers in our pockets, known as 'phones', are used as much as the computers on our desks or laps.

D. We use the computers on our desks and laps as much as those, known as 'phones', in our pockets.

87. The parts of a sentence given below, when rearranged, form a grammatical sentence. Identify the option that presents the correct order:

1. and far from being relaxing, having nothing to do, to get through
2. so many so-called "empty workers" find it really tough as
3. the day, they had to work on a novel, played video games or just slept
4. their workloads take up less than half the time spent at work

A. 3, 2, 4, 1 B. 2, 1, 4, 3
C. 2, 4, 1, 3 D. 2, 1, 3, 4

88. Identify the option that restates the comparison using a positive adjective, without any change of meaning:

Nature-based tourism is huge as more people visit natural areas than there are people on Earth!

A. Nature-based tourism is huge as there are not as many people on Earth as those who visit natural areas!

B. Nature-based tourism is huge as there are as many people on Earth as those who visit natural areas!

C. Nature-based tourism is huge as many people on Earth visit natural areas!

D. Nature-based tourism is huge as those who visit natural areas are not as many as there are on Earth!

89. Fill in the blanks with the appropriate modal verbs:

The Judge pointed out to the plaintiff-wife, "The contract says '_____ to give alimony' – there is no obligation or compulsion. Notwithstanding this, we _____ admit what the contract says earlier, '_____ a stipend for her lifetime' which makes payments to you compulsory and obligatory."

A. shall decide; shall; can be given

B. may decide; shall; shall be given

C. may decide; have to; shall be given

D. must decide; will; may be given

90. Identify the option that will fill in the blanks with appropriate modal verbs:

It is raining heavily. You _____ go to school today.

A. not have to B. don't have to
C. must not D. haven't have to

91. Identify the option that restates the given statement using the comparative adjective, without any change of meaning:

The belief that everyone coding would solve anyone's problems has been shown up as the most ludicrous one.

A. The belief that everyone coding would solve anyone's problems has been shown up as more ludicrous than any other belief.
B. The belief that everyone coding would solve anyone's problems has been shown up as much ludicrous as any other belief.
C. The belief that everyone coding would solve anyone's problems has been shown up as very ludicrous than any other belief.
D. he belief that everyone coding would solve anyone's problems has been shown up as much ludicrous than any other belief.

92. The parts of a sentence given below, when rearranged, form a grammatical sentence. Identify the option that presents the correct order:

1. and, tragically, never seen from the other half of the Earth
2. forever but at some point in the far future reach a stable
3. John's hypothesis is that the moon will not retreat from Earth
4. distance when it will be visible only from one half of Earth

A. 3, 2, 4, 1 B. 2, 3, 4, 1
C. 1, 3, 4, 2 D. 4, 3, 2, 1

93. Identify the option that converts the statement below into a question, without any distortion:

If all school children were given free, healthy breakfasts and lunches they would have less room in their stomachs for junk.

A. If all school children were given free, healthy breakfasts and lunches, could they have some room in their stomachs for junk?
B. If all school children were given free, healthy breakfasts and lunches, would they have much room in their stomachs for junk?
C. If all school children were given free, healthy breakfasts and lunches, should there be any room in their stomachs for junk?
D. If all school children were given free, healthy breakfasts and lunches, would they have any room in their stomachs for junk?

94. Rewrite the given sentence, using modal verbs, without any change of meaning or distortion:

The weather bureau announced the likelihood of the deep depression becoming stronger and the possibility of it turning into a cyclone.

A. The weather bureau announced the deep depression shall become stronger and must turn into a cyclone.
B. The weather bureau announced the deep depression shall become stronger and would turn into a cyclone.
C. The weather bureau announced the deep depression could become stronger and might turn into a cyclone.
D. The weather bureau announced the deep depression might become stronger and could turn into a cyclone.

95. Rewrite the statement below into a question, so as to derive the highlighted part as the answer:

The idea that giving people the ability to grow their own food and giving up soda for water would make people's conditions better is ridiculously naive.

A. How is the idea to make people's conditions better ridiculously naive?
B. Which idea to make people's conditions better is ridiculously naive?
C. What is the idea to make people's conditions better ridiculously naive?
D. Why is the idea to make people's conditions better ridiculously naive?

96. Fill in the blanks with the appropriate modal verbs:

I _____ wear the regimental sash to attend the funeral parade of my former Commander. So, I _____ instruct my orderly to keep it ready.

A. may; must B. have to; may
C. have to; must D. must; have to

97. The parts of a sentence given below, when rearranged, form a grammatical sentence. Identify the option that presents the correct order:

1. given that obesity is more prevalent among
2. in health inequality between the rich and the poor
3. lower socioeconomic classes, interventions
4. such as the Daily Mile could help to close the gap

A. 1, 3, 4, 2
B. 3, 2, 4, 1
C. 4, 3, 1, 2
D. 1, 2, 3, 4

98. The parts of a sentence given below, when rearranged, form a grammatical sentence. Identify the option that presents the correct order:

1. "digital nutrition", likens media diets to
2. what's on our plates; rather than counting calories
3. or screen time, think about what you're eating
4. a psychologist who specializes in the concept of

A. 4, 3, 1, 2
B. 2, 3, 4, 1
C. 3, 2, 4, 1
D. 4, 1, 2, 3

99. Identify the option that restates the given statement using the comparative adjective, without any change of meaning:

Simple nature-based tourism is supposed to be not as good as ecotourism, natural-area tourism driven by concern for environmental conservation, social welfare, and local economic development.

A. Ecotourism, natural-area tourism driven by concern for environmental conservation, social welfare, and local economic development, is better than simple nature-based tourism.
B. Ecotourism, natural-area tourism driven by concern for environmental conservation, social welfare, and local economic development, is supposed to be better than simple nature-based tourism.
C. Simple nature-based tourism is supposed to be as good as ecotourism, natural-area tourism driven by concern for environmental conservation, social welfare, and local economic development.
D. Ecotourism, natural-area tourism driven by concern for environmental conservation, social welfare, and local economic development, is the best tourism.

100. Fill in the blanks with the appropriate modal verbs, making sure the sentences are grammatical:

The indifferent chocolate industry, if it wants, _____ to prevent the spread of health myths associated with chocolate. Chocolate is a treat you, as a rule, _____ enjoy occasionally and in small portions, not a health food.

A. could do more; should
B. will do more; would
C. must do more; can
D. should do more; should

101. Convert the following sentence into a compound sentence:

Without a bus service, a village dies. Some people can't even stay in their own homes. They must go into care homes.

A. Not even being able to stay in their own homes and having to go into care homes, some people in a village, without a bus service, dies.
B. Some people not even being able to stay in their own homes and have to go into care homes, a village, without a bus service, dies.

C. Some people are not able to stay in their own homes and having to go into care homes, a village, without a bus service, dies.

D. Some people not even being able to stay in their own homes and having to go into care homes, a village, without a bus service, dies.

102. Read the sentence below, which states an open condition. Identify the option that converts it correctly into a sentence that states an unreal and imaginary condition:

If we want to close the boardroom gender gap, we need to stop helping women and start fixing workplaces.

A. If the boardroom gender gap is to be closed, we would need to stop helping women and start fixing workplaces.

B. If we were to close the boardroom gender gap, we will need to stop helping women and start fixing workplaces.

C. If the boardroom gender gap were to close, we would need to stop helping women and start fixing workplaces.

D. If we were to close the boardroom gender gap, we would need to stop helping women and start fixing workplaces.

103. Convert and rewrite the sentence below into a sentence with just one independent clause:

Some scholars are keen to believe that genuine traditions lie beneath the superficial literary encrustation, while others are inclined to minimise these elements.

A. Other scholars being inclined to minimise these elements, some are keen to believe that genuine traditions lie beneath the superficial literary encrustation.

B. Some scholars being keen to believe that genuine traditions lie beneath the superficial literary encrustation, others are inclined to minimise these elements.

C. Some scholars are keen to believe that genuine traditions lie beneath the superficial literary encrustation, and others being inclined to minimise these elements.

D. Other scholars are inclined to minimise these elements and some are keen to believe that genuine traditions lie beneath the superficial literary encrustation.

104. Rewrite the sentence in direct speech into its corresponding reported speech:

"It has taken us all by surprise. Customers are saying can you do more," he said. "I think the vegan and flexitarian market is the first major food trend that has come out of social media."

A. He said that it had taken them all by surprise. He added that customers were asking whether they can do more. He concluded that he thinks the vegan and flexitarian market was the first major food trend that had come out of social media.

B. He said that it has taken them all by surprise. He added that customers are asking whether they can do more. He concluded that he thought the vegan and flexitarian market was the first major food trend that had come out of social media.

C. He said that it had taken them all by surprise. He added that customers were asking whether they can do more. He concluded that he thought the vegan and flexitarian market is the first major food trend that has come out of social media.

D. He said that it had taken them all by surprise. He added that customers were asking whether they can do more. He concluded that he thought the vegan and flexitarian market was the first major food trend that had come out of social media.

105. Convert the following sentence into a compound sentence:

Most council leaders, who decide how to spend the transport budget, are men.

A. Most council leaders are men and they decide how to spend the transport budget.

B. Most council leaders, being men, decide how to spend the transport budget.

C. Most council leaders are men because they decide how to spend the transport budget.

D. Most council leaders are men but they decide how to spend the transport budget.

106. Read the sentence below, which states an open condition. Identify the option that converts it correctly into a sentence that states an unreal and rejected condition:

If more studies show how antibiotics interfere with immunotherapy, it may be possible to show how intestinal flora can help new cancer treatments.

A. Had more studies shown how antibiotics interfere with immunotherapy, it would have been possible to show how intestinal flora could have helped new cancer treatments.

B. Had more studies not shown how antibiotics do not interfere with immunotherapy, it would have been possible to show how intestinal flora could have helped new cancer treatments.

C. Had more studies shown bow antibiotics interfere with immunotherapy, it would have been possible to show how intestinal flora can help new cancer treatments.

D. Had more studies shown how antibiotics interfere with immunotherapy, it may be possible to show how intestinal flora could have helped new cancer treatments.

107. Change the voice of the following sentence without changing its meaning.

Archaeologists unearthed the figurine in 2017 during excavations at a site called 'Abel Beth Maacah'.

A. The figurine will be unearthed by archaeologists in 2017 during excavations at a site called 'Abel Beth Maacah".

B. The figutrine is unearthed by archaeologists in 2017 during excavations at a site called 'Abel Beth Maacah".

C. The figurine was unearthed **by** archaeologists in 2017 during excavations at a site called 'Abel Beth Maacah".

D. The figurine had been unearthed by archaeologists in 2017 during excavations at a site called 'Abel Beth Maacah'.

108. Convert the following sentence into a simple sentence:

Expensive train commutes are for the all important middle class, while buses ferry about the poor.

A. Buses ferry about the poor, expensive train commutes is for the all-important middle class.

B. Even as buses ferrying about the poor, expensive train commutes are for the all-important middle class.

C. Buses ferrying about the poor, expensive train commutes are for the all-important middle class.

D. Buses ferry about the poor, expensive train commutes are for the all-important middle class.

109. Rewrite the sentence into the other voice, without changing its meaning.

Antarctic ice cores provide a history of the atmosphere for thousands of years and make known carbon dioxide levels reached a distinct minimum around 1610.

A. A history of the atmosphere for thousands of years will be provided and that carbon dioxide levels reached a distinct minimum around 1610 would have been made known by Antarctic ice cores.

B. A history of the atmosphere for thousands of years was provided and that carbon dioxide levels reached a distinct minimum around 1610 is made known by Antarctic ice cores.

C. A history of the atmosphere for thousands of years is provided and that carbon dioxide levels reached a distinct minimum around 1610 has been made known by Antarctic ice cores.

D. A history of the atmosphere for thousands of years is provided and that carbon dioxide levels reached a distinct minimum around 1610 is made known by Antarctic ice cores.

110. Rewrite the sentence in direct speech into its corresponding reported speech:

He told the reporter. "When someone is murdered it is clear: the courts must prosecute the criminal. Yet when we talk about genocide, or crimes against humanity, people start looking for arguments."

A. He said that when someone is murdered it is always clear that the courts must prosecute the criminal. However, when we talk about genocide, or crimes against humanity, people start looking for arguments.
B. He told the reporter that when someone is murdered it is clear that the courts has to prosecute the criminal. He added that, however, when we talk about genocide, or crimes against humanity, people will start looking for arguments.
C. He told the reporter that when someone is murdered it is clear that the courts must prosecute the criminal. He added that, however, when we talk about genocide, or crimes against humanity, people start looking for arguments.
D. He told the reporter that when someone was murdered it is clear that the courts must prosecute the criminal. He added that, however, when we talked about genocide, or crimes against humanity, people would start looking for arguments.

111. Rewrite the sentence into the other voice without changing its meaning.

Exciting young people about STEM and its endless possibilities will set them on an exciting path and could lead to a fulfilling and rewarding career in engineering and technology.

A. When young people are excited about STEM and its endless possibilities, they will be set on an exciting path and led to a fulfilling and rewarding career in engineering and technology.
B. When young people excited about STEM and its endless possibilities, will be set on an exciting path and could be led to a fulfilling and rewarding career in engineering and technology.
C. When young people are excited about STEM and its endless possibilities, they will be set on an exciting path and could be led to a fulfilling and rewarding career in engineering and technology.
D. When young people will be excited about STEM and its endless possibilities, they are set on an exciting path and could lead to a fulfilling and rewarding career in engineering and technology.

112. Identify the option that converts and restates the following sentence using a rejected, impossible condition:

If they fail, the future of food will go into the hands of three giant companies that are wedded to genetic modification.

A. They fail and the future of food will go into the hands of three giant companies that are wedded to genetic modification.
B. Were they to fail, the future of food would go into the hands of three giant companies that are wedded to genetic modification.
C. Had they failed, the future of food would have gone into the hands of three giant companies that are wedded to genetic modification.
D. As they fail, the future of food will go into the hands of three giant companies that are wedded to genetic modification.

113. Convert the following sentence into a compound sentence:

A majority strongly self-identifies as English. The only subset exceptions, though they are important ones, are black and minority-ethnic adults.

A. A majority strongly self-identifies as English, even as the only subset exceptions, though they are important ones, are black and minority-ethnic adults.
B. A majority strongly self-identifies as English and the only subset exceptions, though they are important ones, are black and minority-ethnic adults.

C. A majority strongly self-identifies as English but the only subset exceptions, though they are important ones, are black and minority-ethnic adults.

D. A majority strongly self-identifies as English yet the only subset exceptions, though they are important ones, are black and minority-ethnic adults.

114. Rewrite the sentence into the other voice, without changing its meaning.

Researchers suggest effects of the colonial era can be detected in rocks or even air.

A. That one can detect effects of the colonial era in rocks and even air is suggested by researchers.

B. That one could have detected effects of the colonial era in rocks and even air was suggested by researchers.

C. One can detect effects of the colonial era in rocks and even air is suggested by researchers.

D. That one can detect effects of the colonial era in rocks and even air was suggested by researchers.

115. Identify the option that converts the sentence fully and correctly into a sentence that states a real and open condition:

Many of the poorest farmers use the system of rice intensification (SRI), which dramatically increases yields of rice, wheat, and potato.

A. Had the yields of rice, wheat, and potato not increased dramatically, many of the poorest farmers would not have used the system of rice intensification (SRI).

B. If rice, wheat and potato yields were to increase dramatically, many of the poorest farmers would use the system of rice intensification (SRI).

C. If yields of rice, wheat, and potato will increase dramatically, many of the poorest farmers will opt to use the system of rice intensification (SRI).

D. If many of the poorest farmers will not use the system of rice intensification (SRI), yields of rice, wheat, and potato will not increase dramatically.

116. Rewrite the sentence in direct speech into its corresponding reported speech:

She said, "Younger people are talking about veganism on social media and old shoppers are keen to buy into the idea of being 'flexitarian'."

A. She remarked that younger people are talking about veganism on social media and that old shoppers are keen to buy into the idea of being 'flexitarian'.

B. She remarked that younger people will be talking about veganism on social media and that old shoppers be keen to buy into the idea of being 'flexitarian'.

C. She remarked that younger people talked about veganism on social media and old shoppers were keen to buy into the idea of being 'flexitarian'.

D. She remarked that younger people were talking about veganism on social media and that old shoppers were keen to buy into the idea of being 'flexitarian'.

117. Rewrite the sentence into the other voice, without change of meaning.

Waitrose this week launched dedicated vegan sections in more than 130 stores.

A. Dedicated vegan sections in more than 130 stores launched by Waitrose.

B. Dedicated vegan sections in more than 130 stores are being launched by Waitrose.

C. Dedicated vegan sections in more than 130 stores were launched by Waitrose.

D. Dedicated vegan sections in more than 130 stores are launched by Waitrose.

118. Convert the following sentence into a compound sentence:

The Children's Commissioner has warned that social media firms must switch off addictive technology.

A. The Children's Commissioner has warned that social media firms must switch off addictive technology and that it deliberately keeps children hooked online.

B. Warning that social media firms must switch off addictive technology, the Children's Commissioner said that it deliberately keeps children hooked online.

C. The Children's Commissioner has warned that social media firms must switch off addictive technology but that it deliberately keeps children hooked online.

D. The Children's Commissioner has warned that social media firms must switch off addictive technology and yet that it deliberately keeps children hooked online.

119. Convert and rewrite the sentence below into a compound one, with two independent clauses:

Slowly slices of Britain's hidden history are being revealed as the public learn more and more about the activities of undercover police officers.

A. Slowly slices of Britain's hidden history are being revealed and the public are learning more and more about the activities of undercover police officers.

B. Slowly slices of Britain's hidden history has been revealed and the public have learnt more and more about the activities of undercover police officers.

C. Slowly slices of Britain's hidden history are being revealed as the public are learning more and more about the activities of undercover police officers.

D. Slowly slices of Britain's hidden history are revealed but the public learn more and more about the activities of undercover police officers.

120. Rewrite the sentence into the other voice without changing its meaning.

The weight of evidence indicates that humans are not unique in possessing the neurological substrates that generate consciousness.

A. That humans are not unique in possessing the neurological substrates that generate consciousness has been indicated by the weight of evidence.

B. That humans are not unique in possessing the neurological substrates that generate consciousness is indicated by the weight of evidence.

C. That humans are not unique in possessing the neurological substrates that generate consciousness is being indicated by the weight of evidence.

D. That humans are not unique in possessing the neurological substrates that generate consciousness will be indicated by the weight of evidence.

121. Study the formal letter given below:

Abracada Industries Dt 10 Jan 2020
SEZ, Feral Land

To

Manacles Pvt. Ltd
SEZ, Ash Land

Dear John,

Remember the conversation we had about your last consignment? You seem more concerned about settlement from our end than looking into our complaints! You kept talking about dues and turned a deaf ear to out complaints.

This cannot go on

Call me and confirm action at your end regarding replacing defective items and then we will start thinking about paying you.

Hope you understand things better now.

Yours sincerely,
Henry

The letter violates all that we associate with a formal letter.

Identify the superficial features of this letter, unacceptable as they are, which you will IMMEDIATELY change, before you go on to revise the letter and make its language, tone and style formal.

A. Change alignment and use of different fonts

B. Replace the idiom used

C. Remove the underlining in the body

D. Change salutation and use of first names

122. Which ONE of the following options is a proper thesis-statement, fit to be developed into an argumentative essay?

A. 'The Great Gatsby' is a great novel.

B. The Great Gatsby', though it conveys the message that the notion of the American dream is illusory, does not argue that Americans must stop dreaming.

C. Though critics point out that Scott Fitzgerald's 'The Great Gatsby' is about how the notion of the American dream is illusory, or how it portrays the loss of innocence, or portrays the Jazz Age, its true fame lies in capturing the shadows of evil yet to come.

D. 'The Great Gatsby', of course, conveys the message that the notion of the American dream is illusory, but more importantly it ushers American fiction into a new narrative world, as evident in T.S. Eliot's observation: 'the first step that American fiction has taken since Henry James'.

123. You are required to make an official announcement at your workplace, which will not be private or individual to individual. For the message to have the utmost impact on the audience, you will get it printed and distributed later. Which one of the following given options would you employ?

A. A signed letter

B. An e-mail

C. A business memo

D. A notice on the notice-board

124. Identify the correct sequence of ideas and the letter of the sentence that disrupts the unity of the paragraph.

The organic movement was founded on the pioneering work of Sir Alfred Howard.

1. There are other agricultural models, such as biodynamic farming and permaculture.
2. Organic and biodynamic meats have labels, regenerative farming, as yet, does not – so you need to investigate your farmer yourself.
3. More recently some innovators have been fusing technology with environmental principles
4. It is still relatively small – in Europe 5.7% of agricultural land is under this movement - but influential.
5. Agroforestry, silvopasture, or regenerative agriculture create farming methods which all encompass carbon sequestration, high biodiversity and good animal welfare.

A. 3, 4, 5, 1 – omit 2

B. 2, 1, 3, 5 – omit 4

C. 2, 5, 3, 4 – omit 1

D. 4, 1, 3, 5 – omit 2

125. The sentences of a paragraph are given in a jumbled order and labelled 1, 2, 3, 4 and 5 below. One of the sentences offers a digression. Identify the digressing sentence:

1. Indian Buddhist analysis of the mind spans a period of some 15 centuries, from the earliest discourses of the Buddha to the systematic developments of late Mahayana Buddhism.
2. Perhaps no other classical philosophical tradition, East or West, offers a more complex and counter-intuitive account of mind and mental phenomena than Buddhism.
3. Philosophical accounts of mind emerge within scholastic traditions but tracing their roots necessarily uniquely to Buddha's teachings of the not-self doctrine is fanciful.
4. Rather, Buddhist theories of mind center on the doctrine of not-self, which postulates that human beings are reducible to the physical and psychological constituents and processes which comprise them.
5. While Buddhists share with other Indian philosophers the view that the domain of the mental encompasses a set of interrelated faculties and processes, they do not associate mental phenomena with the activity of a substantial, independent, and enduring self or agent.

A. 3 B. 5
C. 1 D. 4

126. Once you employ a chart in your report/essay, what should you NOT attempt in explaining it and developing your ideas in the body?

A. Use clear language and avoid acronyms.
B. Make sure apples and oranges are not compared and that correlation is not taken as causation.
C. Ensure through queries or a summary that the readers have perceived and understood the essential trends or movements.
D. Use direct labeling wherever possible, avoiding indirect look-up.

127. Identify the option that provides the missing phrases in the paragraphs given below:

The argument and thought-experiment now generally known as the 'Chinese Room Argument' was first published in a paper in 1980 by American philosopher John Searle. It has become one of the best-known arguments in recent philosophy.

(*a*) _________ following a computer program for responding to Chinese characters slipped under the door, Searle understands nothing of Chinese, and yet, by following the program for manipulating symbols and numerals just as a computer does, he produces appropriate strings of Chinese characters.

(*b*) _______ the narrow conclusion of the argument is that programming a digital computer may make it appear to understand language but does not produce real understanding. Hence the "Turing Test" is inadequate. Searle argues that the thought experiment underscores the fact that computers merely use syntactic rules to manipulate symbol strings, but have no understanding of meaning or semantics.

(*c*) _______ that the theory that human minds are computer-like computational or information processing systems is refuted. Instead minds must result from biological processes; computers can at best simulate these biological processes. Thus the argument has large implications for semantics, philosophy of language and mind, theories of consciousness, computer science and cognitive science generally.

(*d*) _________ there have been many critical replies to the argument.

A. (*a*) As a result
(*b*) Searle imagines himself alone in a room
(*c*) that fool those outside into thinking there is a Chinese speaker in the room
(*d*) The broader conclusion of the argument is

B. (*a*) Searle imagines himself alone in a room
(*b*) that fool those outside into thinking there is a Chinese speaker in the room
(*c*) The broader conclusion of the argument is
(*d*) As a result

C. (*a*) As a result
(*b*) The broader conclusion of the argument is
(*c*) Searle imagines himself alone in a room
(*d*) that fool those outside into thinking there is a Chinese speaker in the room

D. (*a*) The broader conclusion of the argument is
(*b*) that fool those outside into thinking there is a Chinese speaker in the room
(*c*) Searle imagines himself alone in a room
(*d*) As a result

128. Identify the option that does not deal with this specific issue:

How does a writer communicate better with his audience? It could be a letter to the editor, an essay, a report or any such piece of continuous writing {composition}?

A. Employ sentences that are not too long or dense; be economical with words; define jargon only where needed – defining a term which your audience is familiar with is either insulting to them or challenging to them.

B. Introduce not only the essay but also each paragraph in a multi-paragraph essay, but make sure the introductions act as advance organisers.
C. Make sure your adjectives and determiners are specific to the idea; make doubly sure the adjectives are derived ones and attributive in nature; condense sentences with many 'technical adjectives'.
D. Exemplify, even in a text that deals with a technical issue, ideas; the examples should match schemata that audience have interest in and easily relate to the discussed idea.

129. Which one of the following options is a proper thesis-statement, fit to be developed into an argumentative essay?
A. Government educational institutions will become better once they imitate 'corporate' colleges and schools and their pedagogic processes.
B. Government educational institutions will become better once the controversy surrounding commercialisation of education dies down and people understand more money means more knowledge and skills via education.
C. As the history of nationalisation of banks shows, just as private banking did not disappear or become less influential or popular, or just as the working style of the public banks did not become customer-friendly, the writer argues that closing 'corporate' colleges and schools will not necessarily make government, public educational institutions 'better'.
D. Government educational institutions will become better once 'corporate' colleges and schools are closed.

130. This is a condensed version of a business report; it includes a conclusion and (a set of) recommendations. It does NOT indicate the writer's orientation, agenda or significance-understanding. What is it called?
A. Summary
B. Executive summary
C. Cover letter
D. Business memo

131. When you send an e-mail in your official capacity as the CEO of an organisation to the CEO of another one, who happens to be a vendor, whose absence will sever the supply chain' escalating an old complaint, what will be your initial and last sentences in the body, after your greeting and before your signing off?
A. This is with reference to the complaints from our production team about the last two batches of xxxxxx, which have come to my attention... Hoping for a final solution from you.
B. I am afraid you are taking advantage of the fact that without your products our factory will close down... Help us avoid further delays and losses.
C. We are recording our complaint ... Take immediate action if you don't want us to terminate your contract.
D. It was nice meeting you in the club and getting to know your views on the last budget... Please do what you can at your end.

132. Read the two sentences given below:
- Films will continue to entice insecure teenagers who have been hypnotised by the glamour and the glamourous lifestyle of those associated with it and who dream of the money they would earn and adult-addicts for their love of the medium.
- Films will continue to entice adult-addicts for their love of the medium and insecure teenagers who have been hypnotised by the glamour, who dream of the money they would earn and the glamorous lifestyle of those associated with it.

Teachers of 'Writing' would advise you to use the second sentence (or similar structures). Identify the option that properly explains the reasons for such a preference:

A. Mercenary instincts alone cannot be the reason, and since personalised satisfaction is more important, the second sentence has the better sequence.
B. The second sentence moves down from 'adults' to 'teenagers', it follows the right hierarchical order and reflects reality better.
C. Since the coordinated parts move from the shorter to the longer in the second sentence, a rhythmically more attractive line is created in the second sentence.
D. Love for medium is more important than glamour. The second sentence gets the order right.

133. Identify the option that continues the following discussion appropriately:

- The melting of Antarctica is accelerating at an alarming rate.
- An international team of ice experts said in a new study that about 3 trillion tons of ice have disappeared since 1992.
- From 1992 to 2011, Antarctica lost nearly 84 billion tons of ice a year (76 billion metric tons).
- ______________
- ______________
- All that water made global oceans rise about three-tenths of an inch (7.6 millimeters).

A. • From 2012 to 2017, the melt rate decreased to more than 241 billion tons a year (219 billion metric tons).
 • In the last quarter century, the southernmost continent's ice sheet – a key indicator of climate change- melted into enough water to cover Texas to a depth of nearly 13 feet (4 meters).

B. • From 2012 to 2017, the melt rate increased to more than 241 billion tons a year (219 billion metric tons)
 • In the last quarter century, the southernmost continent's waters – a key indicator of climate change - solidified into enough ice to cover Texas to a depth of nearly 13 feet (4 meters).

C. • From 2012 to 2017, the melt rate increased to more than 241 billion tons a year (219 billion metric tons)
 • In the last quarter century, the southernmost continent's ice sheet – a key indicator of climate change- melted into enough water to cover Texas to a depth of nearly 13 feet (4 meters).

D. • In the last quarter century, the southernmost continent's ice sheet – a key indicator of climate change – melted into enough water to cover Texas to a depth of nearly 13 feet (4 meters).
 • From 2012 to 2017, the melt rate increased to more than 241 billion tons a year (219 billion metric tons).

134. Identify the option that suggests a **better sequencing of Ideas** expressed in the bulleted list, keeping in mind the proposition developed in the sentence itself:

Throughout human history the hunting and farming of meat has been part of our stories and mythologies and some of our legal and religious systems:

1. even the roasted wild boars consumed at the end of every adventure by Asterix and Obelix.
2. the sacrificial sheep to mark the beginning of Eid Al-Adha
3. the medieval forest laws that created areas where no one but English royalty could hunt
4. the fatted calf for the prodigal son

A. Only the statement about 'the sacrificial sheep' needs to be moved up as it is sacred
B. The royal practice and laws are factual and must be stated first
C. The given sequence is acceptable as it moves from comics to serious stories
D. Reflecting the order stated, the fatted calf should be the first one, followed by the royal laws and the sacrificial sheep; Asterix and Obelix should be the last one.

135. The first five sentences of the paragraph given below are in a jumbled order. Identify the option that gives their correct order:

1. Of the total vehicular pollution, 40% to 45% comes from two-wheelers and another 30% to 35% from four wheelers.
2. The movement away from kerosene, coal and wood fires for cooking will have a big impact on domestic activity.
3. The other area that is already critical and will keep getting worse, unless checked, is vehicular emission.
4. We need to speed up the journey towards LPG and solar-powered stoves.
5. Just vehicular pollution contributes around 35% of the total PM 2.5 emissions today.

In a future with internal combustion engines (ICE) vehicles, urban pollution will continue to remain 25% to 30% above safe global standards because of the growth in automobiles. This is where our focus needs to be.

A. 5, 4, 3, 2, 1
B. 1, 2, 3, 4, 5
C. 3, 5, 1, 2, 4
D. 2, 4, 3, 5, 1

136. Which option provides the two missing sentences, *a* and *b* in the paragraph given below?

On 7 March 2014 at 16:42, flight MH370 departed from KL bound for Beijing. Initially, everything about the flight proceeded as normal. The Mode S transponder system on board the aircraft was responding as expected to interrogation from the ATC Secondary Surveillance Radar up to the time when it was lost on the ATC radar screen at 17:21:13.

(*a*) __________

(*b*) __________

This message conutained a collation of six reports generated ar five-minute intervals by the system from 16:41:43 until 17:06:43. These reports contained information about the aircraft position and motion such as latitude, longitude, altitude, air temperature, air speed, wind direction, wind speed, and true heading.

A. (*a*) The last recorded radio transmission with the crew of MH370 occurred at 17:19:30 as the aircraft was instructed to contact Vietnamese ATC on leaving the Malaysian Flight Information Region.
(*b*) The ACARS position reports are scheduled to be transmitted at thirty-minute intervals during cruise.

B. (*a*) No message was received from the aircraft to report a system failure.
(*b*) Similarly, the on-board Aircraft Communications Addressing and Reporting System (ACARS) reported as expected at 17:07:29.

C. (*a*) The ACARS position reports are scheduled to be transmitted at thirty-minute intervals during cruise.
(*b*) The next scheduled report at 17:37 was not received.

D. (*a*) The last recorded radio transmission with the crew of MH370 occurred at 17:19:30 as the aircraft was instructed to contact Vietnamese ATC on leaving the Malaysian Flight Information Region.
(*b*) No message was received from the aircraft to report a system failure.

137. Study the paragraph given below:

Two sentences, other than the first one, state the same idea. It is enough if one of them is retained and the other can be dropped. Identify the pair – keep it in mind that either of them could be deleted.

1. What is the carbon bubble and what will happen if it bursts?
2. This carbon bubble has been estimated at between \$1 trillion and \$4 trillion (£3 trillion), a large chunk of the global economy's balance sheet.
3. Investments amounting to trillions of dollars in fossil fuels – coal mines, oil wells, power stations, conventional vehicles – will lose their value when the world moves decisively to a low-carbon economy.

4. Fossil fuel reserves and production facilities will become stranded assets, having absorbed capital but unable to be used to make a profit.
5. Currently, fossil fuel prices do not reflect the environmental damage the fuels do, in climate change and air and water pollution.
6. As the world moves towards a low-carbon economy, fossil fuel investments worth trillions of dollars, from oil wells to cars, will lose their value.

A. 3 or 2　　B. 6 or 5
C. 3 or 6　　D. 5 or 4

138. Identify the option that gives the correct order of the sentences below, and helps it become a paragraph:

1. There is an early need to standardise charging infrastructure equipment to ensure interoperability and make it widespread.
2. The country aims to set up more than 4.8 million charging points at an investment of almost $20 billion by 2020.
3. Similarly, China has standardised charging infrastructure to ensure increased usage and set up 16,000 charging points across the country.
4. For the alternative mobility technologies to settle, an enabling infrastructure is required.
5. European OEMs have formed a consortium, 'Ionity', to provide interoperable charging points across the continent.
6. China has regulations to include charging infrastructure in all residential buildings. India needs to start learning from global examples to push enabling infrastructure.

A. 1, 4, 3, 5, 6, 2
B. 1, 5, 4, 3, 2, 6
C. 4, 1, 5, 3, 2, 6
D. 4, 1, 3, 5, 2, 6

139. Which one of the following is NOT an effective feature of an e-cover letter?

A. Reiterating and keeping the channel open in the conclusion
B. Attaching the cover letter to the main e-mail
C. Pinpointing challenges you would like to face and advertising your skills
D. Attempting a greater specification in the subject line

140. Which one of the following should a letter of complaint AVOID and NOT include?

A. Threats of future legal action
B. Suggestions about how the complaint could be redressed
C. Details that would help the recipient to act
D. Specific details of the complaint

141. Identify the correct option.

Which one of the following plays by Shakespeare makes use of a framing structure called Induction?

A. Much Ado About Nothing
B. The Twelfth Night
C. The Taming of the Shrew
D. Merry Wives of Windsor

142. Identify the option that names the poet and the poem from which these lines are taken.

We decay
Like corpses in a charnel.
the creative spirit of Adonais,
like a star,
Beacons from the abode where the Eternal are.

A. Milton, 'Lycidas'
B. Tennyson, 'In Memorium'
C. Shelley, 'Adonais'
D. Arnold, 'Thyrsis'

143. Identify the play/correct option:

Dr. Johnson made this observation about a play by Shakespeare: *to waste criticism upon unresisting imbecility; upon faults too evident for detection, and too gross for aggravation.*

A. Macbeth
B. The Twelfth Night
C. Hamlet
D. Cymbeline

144. The Shakespearean sonnet consisted of:

A. three quatrains and a couplet

B. seven couplets
C. an octave and a sestet
D. au indivisible 14-line unit

145. Read the letter below.

Identify the option that specifies the defect in this letter:

It is not surprising to see the continued hounding of author Perumal Murugan for exercising his fundamental right to freedom of speech and expression ('Murugan, wife apply for transfer from college to avoid book row', IE, February 4). The Indian constitution safeguards freedom of speech. So do many nations. I remember discussing this issue with a few Americans in Washington. Washington is such an impressive city, full of administrators? That is why Amartya Sen immortalised the idea of "the argumentative Indian". I am with you, Mr. Murugan, and with many others like you.
- nd
XXX

A. Lack of references
B. Lack of ideas
C. Lack of examples
D. Lack of unity

146. Which one of the following plays by Shakespeare does NOT employ a chorus or a character playing a role similar to that of a chorus?

A. Pericles
B. Macbeth
C. Henry V
D. The Winter's Tale

147. Read the 'letter to the editor' given below:

Identify the option that describes the relationship between the second and the third sentences:

This refers to 'Sanitation and state capacity' by xxxx (Xx October 14). I couldn't agree more with the writer on why "Swachh Bharat must go beyond building physical infrastructure". Cooperation across departments as well as roping in civic bodies and, most importantly, citizens remain the most critical bottlenecks for many of the government's *abhiyans*. Waste management must be addressed as a priority. Issues like recycling and processing domestic and commercial electronic waste, which is growing exponentially, require a more sophisticated approach than landfill dumping.
IS
Yyy

A. Addition
B. Specification
C. Exemplification
D. Generalisation

148. • 'Thyrsis', [a monody] is an elegiac poem by Matthew Arnold. It is considered one of Arnold's finest poems.
• 'Thyrsis' is a traditional Greek name for a shepherd-poet.

A. Arthur Hugh Clough
B. Alfred Tennyson
C. William Wordsworth
D. Percy Bysshe Shelley

149. Identify what Sidney **DID NOT** say about or on history.

A. Poetry can reward virtue and punish vice/ evil; History reflects life 'where sinners can prosper'
B. Poetry liberates itself through reality; History is constrained by reality.
C. Poetry uses examples [like historians] and precepts [as philosophers do]
D. Poetry can portray the ideal; History cannot, as it is bound by truth/reality

150. • This famous novel by Sir Walter Scott has Elizabeth I as a character.
• It is centered around the life and death of the Countess of Leicester and the ambition of her husband – sharing the crown of his sovereign. Elizabeth I

Identify the novel.

A. Ivanhoe
B. Rob Roy
C. Kenilworth
D. Waverley

151. Read the 'letter to the editor' given below:

Identify the option that describes the relationship between the second and the third sentences:

The recent hype created by the media over the mauling of a visitor by a white tiger at the Delhi Zoo portrays the animal as a bloodthirsty monster ('A zoo tragedy', xx, September 24). While it is sad that a young life was lost due to the negligence of the zoo authorities, it is certainly wrong to paint an animal born and raised in captivity as an evil brute. Given the shouting and the stones being pelted on the tiger, even the calmest animal could be provoked into turning aggressive. There should be greater focus on instilling discipline among people who visit the zoo.

- BS

zzz

A. Giving a reason
B. Substantiating a stance announced
C. Adding details to what has been stated
D. Exemplifying a statement

152. Comedy of humours use the Medieval and Renaissance medical theory that the human body held a balance of four liquids. When properly balanced, these humours were thought to give the individual a healthy mind in a healthy body. The options below lists the four humours, bur one of them is INCORRECT.

Identify the INCORRECT option:

A. sanguine B. choler
C. blood D. phlegm

153. Gothic novels are tales of mystery and horror. They rely heavily on ____ .

Identify the wrongly attributed feature.

A. an innocent young heroine, normally a governess
B. a supernatural, exotic environment
C. a nonlinear plot narrated through letters
D. the presence of the devil and/or ghosts

154. The Romantic period, which ran between the publication of 'Lyrical Ballads' and the passing of 'Reform bills', emphasised the following mentioned in the options. One of the options is not related to the ideals of the Romantic period. Identify it:

A. Comprehensive and inclusive rationalisation
B. An exaltation of Nature, seen symbolically
C. Intense focus on human subjectivity
D. Focus on childhood and spontaneity

155. Which of the options does NOT describe an essential feature of a 'blank verse'?

A. A blank verse does not suit the 'high seriousness' of epics such as 'Paradise Lost'
B. A blank verse uses unrhymed five-stress lines, *i.e.*, iambic pentameters.
C. A blank verse is closest to the rhythms of normal, everyday English speech.
D. The blank verse did not disappear and could be found in later schools of poetry, including T. S. Eliot's.

156. In which of the following poems did Milton invoke the goddesses of Mirth and Melancholy?

A. 'On having attained the age of three and twenty' and 'On his blindness'
B. 'Comus' and 'Lycidas'
C. 'L'Allegro and 'Il Penseroso'
D. 'Paradise Lost' and 'Paradise Regained'

157. Which of the, tragic heroes of Shakespeare exemplify the Aeschylean notion of "knowledge through suffering" (redemption)?

A. Macbeth in 'Macbeth'
B. Antony in 'Antony and Cleopatra '
C. Hamlet in 'Hamlet'
D. Lear in 'King Lear'

158. These lines are from Herbert's 'Redemption'. The poem uses an extended metaphor and is allegorical in nature. It is also a parable – a parable of tenants.

At length I heard a ragged noise and mirth
Of theeves and murderers; there I him espied.
Who straight, Your suit is granted, said, & died.

Identify the best possible inference and generalisation of the poem:

A. A request that he pays less rent for the land he has taken from the landlord.

B. A prayer that he be allowed to change the rental terms in a new contract.

C. An appeal that he be allowed to punish his body less for the purification of his soul.

D. A plea that he allowed to make fewer sacrifices to be 'redeemed' – that his soul be saved.

159. Identify the option that specifies the defect in the following letter:

I DO not agree with the editorial, 'Take Rajasthan's cue' (Xx, September 24). Toilets and playgrounds are integral to any learning environment. It should also periodically review the pedagogy. A lower emphasis on toilets is also likely to have a negative impact on girls' education, since the lack of toilets in schools is a major reason for them dropping out. The government should address the issue of learning outcomes through a multi-pronged approach. It should raise the standard for teacher selection. The suggestion of overlooking the teacher-student ratio criteria is ironic, since that is also bound to affect learning outcomes.

-AS

XXx

A. Lack of unity

B. Lack of coherence

C. Lack of development

D. Lack of reference

160. 'The practice of recording conversations and sayings of the famous became especially popular in the 17th century. This material is especially useful for biographers and can be a form of literary biography in itself· One of the best-known examples of this is:

A. Lytton Strachey's 'Eminent Victorians'

B. Jerome K. Jerome's 'My Life, and Times'

C. James Boswell's biography of Samuel Johnson

D. William Hazlitt's Table-Talk, a collection of essays

161. What is the name of the old man in London who teaches young homeless boys how to be pickpockets and then fences their stolen goods and is executed for complicity in a murder in Dickens's 'Oliver Twist'?

A. Mr. Bumble

B. The Artful Dodger

C. Fagin

D. Bill Sikes

162. Identify the correct option.

Mulk Raj Anand's Munoo in 'The Coolie' is essentially and ultimately a victim of different oppression in society compared to that which Bakha in 'The Untouchables' goes through in a day. What is *the other crucial difference between the two characters,* when all that is stated and on the surface is understood, that could be inferred?

A. Bakha suffers untouchability, Munoo is a victim of exploitation

B. Bakha can be redeemed by a leader, Munoo's redemption is death

C. Bakha is a boy throughout the novel, Munoo grows into a man

D. Bakha can dream, Munoo has to exist

163. Miller wrote in 1949. "The quality in such plays [i.e., tragedies] that does shake us ... derives from the underlying fear of being displaced, the disaster inherent in being torn away from our chosen image of what and who we are in this world. Among us today this fear is as strong, and perhaps stronger, than it ever was. **In fact, It is the common man who knows this fear best."**

Which play of his illustrates the highlighted clause?

A. The Last Yankee

B. All My Sons

C. Death of a Salesman

D. The Crucible

164. What makes women writers in Indian Writing in English stand out?

A. Women writers continue to define the borders of the community, class, and race.
B. Women writers are more concerned with exploitation in the name of patriarchy and write from the victims' point of view.
C. Women writers are barely directly affected by colonial oppression and colonialism
D. Women writers are sensitive to what Indian women have suffered under 'double colonisation' – patriarchal and colonial yokes simultaneously

165. Fill in the blank by choosing the correct option:

Hemingway employs _______ to narrate the tale of 'The Old Man and the Sea'.
A. a multivocal narrative
B. a fly-on-wall technique
C. first-person narration
D. a third person omniscient narrator

166. What is the fly in Emily Dickinson's poem 'I heard a fly buzz- when I died'?
A. A metaphor for her soul leaving her body – an aural image of death; fly here connotes death
B. A housefly, the symbol of a carrier of infection and death, telling her in her ear that her death is imminent
C. An imaginary fly accompanying her in her death; she could hear it in her dying moments in her mind
D. A butterfly, that buzzed to remind her of the mystery and miracle of the world and life at the moment of her death

167. Identify the correct option.
Which of the following authors below CANNOT be classified under 'Caribbean Literature'?
A. Derek Walcott B. Nadine Gordimer
C. VS Naipaul D. CLR James

168. The tortuous initiation into modern life, mimicked *sans* philosophical over, or undertones, in an imaginary land, the part-feudal, part-modern setting of inchoate longing and vague dissatisfactions and intellectual impotence of the marginalised upper caste protagonists, and the confused inner life of a fragmented makeshift pre-colonial society that has yet to figure out its past or future are ***the concerns of this novelist,*** according to a critic.

Identify the novelist.
A. Raja Rao
B. Rabindranath Tagore
C. Mulk Raj Anand
D. RK Narayan

169. Identify the correct option.

'The Road' by Soyinka depicts the Nigerian experiences during the middle of the twentieth century, and it reflects the roles played by drugs, criminals, corrupt policemen, and unscrupulous politicians. This line is from 'The Road' of Wole Soyinka: "May we never walk when the road waits, famished." Explain the significance of this line.
A. It is a prayer to Ogun, the god of the road (in Yoruba cosmology), and not simply the road itself, that waits, hungry.
B. The Professor's occupation promotes a personal quest for the meaning of death, which encounters him at the end of 'The Road'.
C. It is an adage that cautions against driving on the road and advocates walking on it, instead.
D. Soyinka's fascination with the predatory quality of the road. This beast of prey which lies in wait is "a monstrous man-eater; an inescapable doom."

170. This dramatist was the first to use characters pared down to basic existential elements and as symbols to reiterate his Stygian[= unpleasantly dark] view of the human condition; he is also known as the one who initiated the Theatre of the Absurd.

Identify the dramatist from the options given.
A. Harold Pinter B. Bertolt Brecht
C. Joe Orton D. Samuel Beckett

171. Yeats laments in Easter 1916, *"All changed, changed utterly:/A terrible beauty is born."* Explain the nature of the change and the terrible beauty referred to here.

A. The Irish rising and the English reaction
B. Maud Gonne's change of mind and heart
C. The dawn and influence of modernism
D. A growing indifference to nature after WWI

172. In the following lines, what is it that Nissim Ezekiel is referring to?

There is a place to which I often go,
Not by planning to, but by a flow
Away from all existence, to a cold
Lucidity, whose will is uncontrolled.
Here, the mills of God are never slow.

A. Warmth of homeland
B. Inevitability of death
C. Finiteness of graveyard
D. Understanding life in death

173. Identify the correct option and complete the observation:

In the novels seeking the most objective narrative method of all, the device of the storyteller who does not understand the story he is telling, the technique of the "unreliable observer" was used by James Joyce and other writers. The reader, understanding better than the narrator, has the illusion of receiving the story directly. The device that Joyce employs towards achieving this is known ________.

A. echoes of famous lines and allusions
B. stream of consciousness [interior monologue]
C. fantastic incidents and shadowy characters
D. parody of other narrative styles

174. Name the play by George Bernard Shaw which is about war between the gender, shows woman as conqueror and posits that in the battle between instinct and intelligence, instinct always wins. This play has Don Juan as a Shavian hero in England at the turn of the century.

A. Man and Superman
B. Candida
C. Mrs. Warren's Profession
D. The Devil's Disciple

175. In this poem, TS Eliot reflects upon language, time, and history. The poem itself could be read as a clear meditation on time. Identify the poem.

A. Ash Wednesday
B. The Waste Land
C. Four Quartets
D. The Love Song of J. Alfred Prufrock

176. What does the scarlet letter stand for in 'The Scarlet Letter'? Why is the colour scarlet used here?

A. The scarlet letter was a letter the narrator discovers: he is forced to chase the mystery- scarlet signifies danger
B. The scarlet letter is a mystery and the theme of the novel; scarlet indicates danger
C. It is the letter A of the alphabet; the colour scarlet was the colour of Christ's blood and indicates 'a martyr'- punished for no sin of his or her
D. It is the letter A of the alphabet; its colour is a Biblical reference to the Whore of Babylon who was dressed in purple and scarlet

177. Mahbub Ali in Kipling's 'Kim' tells Kim. 'Here begins the great game.' Identify the option that offers the most relevant and clear interpretation of the statement.

A. It refers to the battle for supremacy in Asia between Britain and Russia in the 19th century
B. It seeds the spy stories of le Carre around Kim [Philby] where espionage was a (deadly) game
C. It hints at the battle between the races, in which Kim would ultimately become a 'chela'
D. It predicts the cold war between the West and Russia in the 20th century

178. Who said this?

Magic realism, at least as practiced by Marquez, is a development out of Surrealism that expresses a genuinely "Third World" consciousness......... He is not writing about Middle-earth, but about the one we all inhabit. Macondo exists. That is its magic.

A. Homi Bhabha B. Salman Rushdie
C. Vikram Seth D. Edward Said

179. Hopkins's 'Pied Beauty' is a unique example of a curtal sonnet. Explain the significance of these lines and the ***echo of an image*** by another poet.

All things counter, original, spare, strange;
Whatever is fickle, freckled (who knows how?)
With swift, slow; sweet, sour; adazzle, dim;
He fathers-forth whose beauty is past change:

A. Hopkins, in this hymn, a paean, reinforces this notion of a changeless God divinely creating dappledness, complexity, variety and flux, similar to a kind God creating the Lamb and a punitive one, the Tyger in Blake
B. Hopkins observes here that the whole spectrum of nature in all its beauty is mysteriously germinated by Him, who is worthy of praise and tries to imitate the tone and affect of the psalms.
C. Hopkins in these lines employs a telling alliterative rhythm – the sounds are similar, but signify contrary and different values, as early English poets used to
D. Hopkins is exploring his relationship with God through experimental stress patterns, syntax and language, which is similar to Eliot's in 'The Waste Land'

180. The Oxford Dictionary defines **drama** as 'a play for theatre, radio, or **television**, as a genre or style of literature and as the activity of acting'. What is the impact of television on the literariness of English drama? In which aspect of drama as theatre is the influence most palpable'?

A. Dialogue delivery and authentic language
B. Costumes and presentation
C. Awareness of the images constructed for viewers
D. The emergence of 'closet dramas'

181. Which of these is NOT an assessment method?

A. Simulations
B. Discussion board threads
C. Posters
D. Students watching a cartoon audiovisual

182. Which of these is NOT a level of cognitive domain?

A. Synthesis B. Articulates
C. Application D. Evaluation

183. Which of these is NOT an advantage while using the teaching-derived materials for teaching?

A. Institutionally prepared materials may enhance the reputation of the institution by demonstrating its commitment to providing materials specifically for its students.
B. Quality materials take time to produce and adequate staff time as well as resources need to be allocated.
C. Materials can be produced that are directly relevant to students' and institutional needs and that reflect local content, issues, and concerns.
D. Materials produced within the institution can be revised or adapted as needed, giving them greater flexibility.

184. Which of these statements on audiovisuals (AV) is NOT correct?

A. AV helps in developing perception
B. AV helps in transfer of training
C. AV helps in gaining attention of distracted students
D. AV helps in assimilation of knowledge

185. Which of these sentences is NOT true about the factors that affect inclusive education?

A. Expenses are a constraint to meet up to the needs of all the children
B. Differently-abled students can never be made a part of normal students in any given classroom
C. Societies negative attitudes towards children of different abilities
D. Accessibility to the students to reach the classroom

186. A teacher wants to develop the gross motor skills of the students. Which one of these activities would NOT be appropriate for developing gross motor skills?

A. Ball throwing
B. Stretching
C. Climbing
D. Newspaper scrunch

187. Which of these is NOT a blog tool?

A. Blogger B. Permalink
C. Edublog D. WordPress

188. When the test measures what it claims to measure along with what is worth measuring, then the test is said to be:

A. reliable B. valid
C. authentic D. fair

189. Which of these examples need NOT necessarily reflect teacher evaluation?

A. Meghana scored 90% in mathematics in the board exams
B. The average marks of the class were 62.8%
C. Students complain that they must wait long for their homework books to be returned
D. The students feel very happy to attend Mr John's class as he involves them in lot of curricular activities

190. Identify the attitude to be developed in a student through teaching social sciences from the given options.

A. Respect and appreciation for accomplishments of man throughout history in solving problems
B. Ability to use simple tools like maps, graphs, etc.
C. Ability to participate constructively as a member or leader in group discussions
D. Knowledge to find the sources of given information

191. The aim of which scheme launched in 2001 is to provide useful and relevant elementary education for all children in the age group of 6-14 years?

A. Jan Shikshan Sansthans
B. Rashtriya Madhyamik Shiksha Abhiyan
C. The State, Resource Centre(s)
D. Sarva Shiksha Abhiyan

192. In a particular mathematics class, a student suggests alternative methods to a problem. Which stage of cognitive domain is the student exhibiting?

A. Application B. Knowledge
C. Skill D. Understanding

193. Which of these examples does NOT integrate art, dance, music, craft with other subjects?

A. Students explore Indian mythology using puppets in social science class.
B. Tamil students learn the difference between translating and interpreting the language using music and the literary works of RD Burman
C. History students watch a movie on Akbar in an open-air auditorium to know the good works of the emperor.
D. Mathematics students manipulate flower garlands to understand the patterns.

194. The skills of speaking and writing are called ______ skills.

A. active B. arbitrator
C. programmed D. passive

195. Which of these is NOT necessarily a method of motivation to promote self-learning in students?

A. Success and failure techniques
B. Reward techniques
C. Never blame techniques
D. Knowledge of result

196. Which of these is NOT a major aspect in playwriting?

A. Plot B. Genre
C. Dialogue D. Cliche

197. Which of these options is a barrier in inclusive education?

A. Constructing a curriculum that meets to the needs of all the children.
B. Friendship and social skills develop.
C. Children develop a positive understanding of themselves and their society.

D. Parents' vision of giving their differently-abled a child a normal life can be made true.

198. Identify the learning style from the given description:

Rita is given a project on saving environment. She prefers using charts, diagrams, visual aids over the written words. What kind of learning preference does Rita exhibit?

A. Visual / Non-verbal Learning style
B. Tactile Learning style
C. Visual / Verbal Learning style
D. Auditory Learning style

199. Which of these is NOT a part of social science?

A. Anthropology
B. Law
C. Biology
D. Statistics

200. Understanding that there are socially determined difference between men and women, and that these influence access to and control of resources is known as:

A. gender parity
B. gender awareness
C. gender equality
D. gender equity

ANSWERS

1	**2**	**3**	**4**	**5**	**6**	**7**	**8**	**9**	**10**
C	B	C	A	D	C	C	D	D	D
11	**12**	**13**	**14**	**15**	**16**	**17**	**18**	**19**	**20**
B	C	C	C	A	B	B	D	B	B
21	**22**	**23**	**24**	**25**	**26**	**27**	**28**	**29**	**30**
C	B	A	D	B	A	C	A	D	A
31	**32**	**33**	**34**	**35**	**36**	**37**	**38**	**39**	**40**
D	A	B	C	C	A	A	D	B	C
41	**42**	**43**	**44**	**45**	**46**	**47**	**48**	**49**	**50**
D	A	D	D	A	D	A	A	B	A
51	**52**	**53**	**54**	**55**	**56**	**57**	**58**	**59**	**60**
B	C	A	B	A	D	A	C	C	D
61	**62**	**63**	**64**	**65**	**66**	**67**	**68**	**69**	**70**
C	D	D	D	B	A	C	A	B	C
71	**72**	**73**	**74**	**75**	**76**	**77**	**78**	**79**	**80**
D	C	B	B	D	A	B	D	C	D
81	**82**	**83**	**84**	**85**	**86**	**87**	**88**	**89**	**90**
D	D	B	D	D	B	C	A	C	B
91	**92**	**93**	**94**	**95**	**96**	**97**	**98**	**99**	**100**
A	A	D	D	B	C	A	D	B	A
101	**102**	**103**	**104**	**105**	**106**	**107**	**108**	**109**	**110**
D	D	A	D	A	A	C	C	D	C
111	**112**	**113**	**114**	**115**	**116**	**117**	**118**	**119**	**120**
C	C	B	A	D	D	C	A	A	B

121	122	123	124	125	126	127	128	129	130
A	D	C	D	A	C	B	C	C	B
131	**132**	**133**	**134**	**135**	**136**	**137**	**138**	**139**	**140**
C	C	C	D	D	B	C	C	B	A
141	**142**	**143**	**144**	**145**	**146**	**147**	**148**	**149**	**150**
C	C	D	A	D	B	B	A	B	C
151	**152**	**153**	**154**	**155**	**156**	**157**	**158**	**159**	**160**
B	A	C	A	A	C	D	D	B	C
161	**162**	**163**	**164**	**165**	**166**	**167**	**168**	**169**	**170**
C	B	C	D	D	A	B	D	A	D
171	**172**	**173**	**174**	**175**	**176**	**177**	**178**	**179**	**180**
A	D	B	A	C	D	A	B	A	C
181	**182**	**183**	**184**	**185**	**186**	**187**	**188**	**189**	**190**
D	B	B	C	B	D	B	B	A	A
191	**192**	**193**	**194**	**195**	**196**	**197**	**198**	**199**	**200**
D	A	C	A	C	D	A	A	C	B

Previous Paper (Solved)

DSSSB—PGT (ENGLISH) Exam-2015

SECTION-B

POST SPECIFIC SUBJECT-RELATED QUESTIONS

1. The last book of Gulliver's travels is:
A. Voyage to Lilliput
B. Voyage to Brobdingnag
C. Voyage to Houyhnhnms
D. Voyage to Laputa

2. Venus and Adonis is a long narrative poem by:
A. Edmund Spenser B. Sydney
C. Dryden D. Shakespeare

3. In Charlotte Bronte's Jane Eyre, the mad woman in the attic is:
A. Blanche Ingram B. Celine Varens
C. Bertha Mason D. Grace Poole

4. The author of Leviathan is:
A. Thomas Hobbes
B. Jonathan Swift
C. John Lyly
D. Francis Bacon

5. To which kind of poetry does 'The Canterbury Tales' belong?
A. Epic B. Dramatic
C. Lyrical D. Narrative

6. Dr. Johnson's 'The Lives of the Poets' is an example of:
A. Psychoanalytical criticism
B. Biographical criticism
C. Historical criticism
D. Archetypal criticism

7. A metre in which an unaccented syllable precedes the accented is called:
A. Dactylic B. Iambic
C. Catalectic D. Anapaestic

8. Who of the following did the critic Hugh Walker Call "The Prince among English Essayists"?
A. Francis Bacon B. Joseph Addison
C. Charles Lamb D. Oliver Goldsmith

9. The author of the short story "The Owl who was God" is:
A. George Orwell
B. James Thurber
C. Ernest Hemingway
D. Oscar Wilde

10. "Saki" is the pen name of:
A. Somerset Maugham
B. K.A. Abbas
C. Wilkie Collins
D. Hector Hugh Munro

11. .... is known as the father of detective stories.
A. Edgar Allen Poe
B. Anton Chekov
C. Arthur Conan Doyle
D. Judith Wright

12. The author of "Beowulf" is:
A. Caedmon B. Cynewulf
C. John Gower D. None of these

13. The pilgrims in the "Canterbury Tales" were going to:
A. Shrine of St. Agnes at Canterbury
B. Shrine of St. Lucas of Jerusalem
C. Shrine of St. Thomas at Canterbury
D. Shrine of St. Mark in Southwark

*Tier-I Exam

14. In Langland's Piers the Plowman, Piers finally appears as:
- A. King
- B. The Holy Trinity
- C. Jesus
- D. The Good Samaritan

15. The first tragedy written in English is:
- A. Edward II
- B. Doctor Faustus
- C. The Jew of Malta
- D. Gorboduc

16. Reflection on the French Revolution is a work by:
- A. Mathew Arnold
- B. Edmund Burke
- C. Wordsworth
- D. Edward King

17. .... is a morality play revived in the modern age.
- A. Everyman
- B. A Parting
- C. Abraham and Isaac
- D. Shepherd's Garland

18. Thomas Kyd was the founder of:
- A. Romantic tragedy
- B. Romantic comedy
- C. Historic tragedy
- D. Restoration comedy

19. The lines "The luantic, the lover and the poet./Are of imagination all compact" are spoken by:
- A. Theseus B. Bottom
- C. Pyramus D. Thisbey

20. Falstaff is a character in Shakespeare's :
- A. Henry I
- B. Measure for Measure
- C. Henry VIII
- D. Henry IV

21. The Fox is the sub-title of:
- A. The Alchemist
- B. Volpone
- C. Everyman in His Humour
- D. None of these

22. The Jungle Book is a collection of .... stories for children.
- A. Ghost stories B. Animal stories
- C. Horror stories D. Detective

23. The only novel written by Rudyard Kipling is:
- A. Lord Jim
- B. The Jungle Book
- C. The Secret Agent
- D. Kim

24. The expression "Ancestral Voices Prophesying War" occurs in:
- A. Christabel
- B. Rime of the Ancient Mariner
- C. Kubla Khan
- D. Frost at Midnight

25. The soul of tragedy, according to Aristotle is:
- A. Character B. Plot
- C. Diction D. Spectacle

26. The correct chronological sequence of the following books is:
- A. The Medal; Astrea Redux; Annus Mirabilis; Absalom and Achitophel
- B. Astrea Redux; Annus Mirabilis; Absalom and Achitophel; The Medal
- C. Annus Mirabilis; Absalom and Achitophel; The Medal; Astrea Redux
- D. Astrea Redux; Annus Mirabilis; The Medal; Absalom and Achitophel

27. 'Diction' means:
- A. Severity of prose
- B. Devices of metre and rhyme
- C. Syntax and word order
- D. Poetic device

28. Arthur Miller's "The Death of a Salesman" is chiefly about:
- A. American dream
- B. American imperialism

C. American pragmaticism
D. American transcendentalism

29. The figure of speech used in the expression "Murderous innocence of the sea" is:
A. Onomatopoeia B. Personification
C. Oxymoron D. Simile

30. Mrs. Malaprop is a character in:
A. The Dolls House
B. Pygmalion
C. The Maid's Tragedy
D. The Rivals

31. Samuel Butler's Hudibras is modelled upon:
A. Astrophel and Stella
B. Don Quixote
C. Pilgrims Progress
D. Volpone

32. "Essays of Elia" is:
A. Political ideology
B. Social Criticism
C. Personal impressions
D. Literary criticism

33. 'Dream Play' is a famous work of:
A. Strindberg B. Zota
C. A.C. Swinburne D. Amy Lowell

34. Who is ***not*** a member of the Bloomsbury Group?
A. E.M. Forster B. Leonard Woolf
C. Lytton Strachey D. G.B. Shaw

35. Who is the Pioneer of the Aesthetic Movement?
A. Walter Pater
B. John Henry Newman
C. Stevenson
D. Oscar Wilde

36. The Oxford Movement was fundamentally a movement for:
A. Social reform
B. Religious reform
C. Political reform
D. Economic reform

37. The author of "Les Fleurs du mal" is:
A. Flaubert B. Mallarme
C. Baudelaire D. Gautier

38. Which novel of Hardy portrays a girl 'Simple, Sensuous and Passionate' who never comes to terms with the world?
A. The Return of the Native
B. Tess of the D'Urbervilles
C. The Mayor of Casterbridge
D. The Woodlanders

39. Which of the following works by Stevenson illustrates the doubleness of man's nature?
A. Treasure Island
B. Kidnapped
C. Weir of Hermiston
D. Dr. Jekyll and Mr. Hyde

40. The novel 'The Man who was Thursday' was written by:
A. Joseph Conrad B. G.K. Chesterton
C. Rudyard Kipling D. H.G. Wells

41. In his novels, H.G. Wells portrays the character of :
A. Lower middle class
B. The Aristocratic class
C. Lower class
D. The Capitalists

42. 'Weena' is a character in H.G. Wells' novel:
A. The Invisible Man
B. The Wheels of Chance
C. Kipps
D. The Time Machine

43. Joseph Conrad's novels deal with the adventure and romance of:
A. Mountain life B. Sea life
C. City life D. Social life

44. Walter de la Mare is a poet of:
A. the Georgian period
B. the Romantic period
C. the Victorian period
D. the Edwardian period

45. In Shaw's play, ... a professor changes the life of a flower girl.
A. Candida
B. Widower's House
C. The Apple Cart
D. Pygmation

46. Conrad's novel, ... is set in Tsarist Russia.
A. Under Western Eyes
B. Nostromo
C. Almayer's Folly
D. The Nigger of the Narcissus

47. In Shaw's St. Joan, Joan tries to free .... from the English armies:
A. Italy B. Austria
C. France D. Germany

48. "Relations" is a poem by:
A. A.K. Ramanujan B. Sarojini Naidu
C. Toru Dutt D. Nissim Ezeklel

49. The story in which Kamala Das refer to a Lesbian relationship is:
A. Iqbal
B. The Guest
C. The Doll for the child prostitute
D. In love

50. The author of 'The Home and The World' is:
A. Manmohan Ghose
B. Sri Aurobindo
C. Rabindranath Tagore
D. Mulk Raj Anand

51. In which of the following novels, the incidents relating to the declaration of emergency in India figure?
A. Bombay Duck
B. A Suitable Boy
C. Such a long Journey
D. English, August : An Indian story

52. "She is inspired but diabolically inspired". Who does this line refer to:
A. Candida
B. Saint Joan
C. Major Barbara
D. Ann White Field

53. "American Dream" is the name of character in Edward Albee's:
A. American Dream
B. A Zoo Story
C. The Death of Bessie Smith
D. Who's Afraid of Virginia Woolf

54. "Anagnorisis" is a term used by Aristotle for describing:
A. the moment of discovery by the protagonist
B. the reversal of fortune for the protagonist
C. the crisis reaching its height
D. the character giving vent to his emotions

55. Walt Whitman's "O Captain, My Captain" is an elegy on:
A. John F. Kennedy
B. Abraham Lincoln
C. Boswell
D. His father

56. Who of the following is known for aphoristic prose style?
A. William Hazlitt B. Charles Lamb
C. G.K. Chesterton D. Francis Bacon

57. "Imagism" is associated with:
A. D.H. Lawrence
B. Benedetto Croce
C. T.S. Eliot
D. T.E. Hulme

58. "Beyond Interpretation" is a famous essay by:
A. Jonathan Culler
B. Walter Benjamin
C. Terry Eagleton
D. Barthes

59. An "Idyll" is usually a poem about a:
A. Picturesque city life
B. Panoramic view of nature
C. Picture of industrial society
D. Picturesque country life

60. The term "stream of consciousness" is derived from the writing of:
A. Virginia Woolf B. Wiliam James
C. Gertrude Stein D. D.H. Lawrence

61. The lines "Not that he wished is greatness to create for politicians neither love nor hate" occur in:
A. Mac Flecknoe
B. The Rape of the Lock

C. Absalom and Achitophel
D. Essay on Man

62. "Our birth is but a sleep and a forgetting" is a line from:
A. Preludes
B. Dejection : An Ode
C. Immortality Ode
D. Tintern Abbey

63. U.R. Ananthamurthy's novel Samskara was translated from Kannada into English by:
A. H.S. Shivaprakash
B. A.K. Ramanujan
C. G. Parthasarathi
D. Shiv K. Kumar

64. "Understanding Poetry" by Brooks and Warren encapsulates the principles of:
A. New criticism
B. New historicism
C. Reader-response theory
D. Marxist criticism

65. "Imagined Communities" is a concept propounded by:
A. Gayathri Spivak
B. Ashish Nandy
C. Benedict Anderson
D. Walter Benjamin

66. Which of the following novels has the theme of freedom of Muslim Women?
A. Sunlight on a Broken Column
B. In Custody
C. Dark Holds No Terror
D. The Shadow Lines

67. The phrase, "Monuments of unageing intellect" occurs in Yeats':
A. Byzantium
B. Among School Children
C. Adam's Curse
D. Sailing to Byzantium

68. Who among the following is a Canadian critic?
A. Terry Eagleton B. F.R. Levis
C. Northrop Frye D. Cleanth Brooks

69. "Ripeness is all" is a line from:
A. Macbeth B. Julius Ceasar
C. Hamlet D. King Lear

70. The technique used in the line, "Something there is, that doesn't love a wall" is:
A. An epithet B. Inversion
C. Litotes D. Neologism

71. "There is nothing outside the text" is an important aspect of:
A. Reader-response theory
B. New criticism
C. Deconstruction
D. Structuralism

72. The letter 'A' at different points in "The Scarlet Letter" stands for the following ideas except:
A. Adultery B. Able
C. Angel D. Appetite

73. John Crowe Ransom's "God without Thunder : An Unorthodox Defence of Orthodoxy" is an attack on:
A. Politicalization of life
B. Moral disintegration
C. Science for destroying the mystery of God
D. Science for not bringing man the promised happiness

74. "Poetry sheds no tears 'such as Angels weep', but natural and human tears;" are lines by:
A. Wordsworth B. Shelley
C. Coleridge D. Keats

75. Arnold was the first English critic to stress upon the necessity of:
A. Dialectical criticism
B. Comparative criticism
C. Functional criticism
D. Classical criticism

76. In his major criticism D.H. Lawrence makes a distinction between:
A. Knowledge and power
B. Sensitive mind and intellectual awareness
C. Education and ignorance
D. Intuition and the mind, instinct of the body and intellect of the mind

77. The phrase "dissociation of sensibility" was first used by Eliot in his:
A. Frontiers of criticism
B. Tradition and individual talent
C. Metaphysicai poets
D. Essay on Hamlet

78. "The Principles of Literary Criticism" is a famous work of:
A. I.A. Richards
B. Cleanth Brooks
C. William Empson
D. John Crowe Ransom

79. The pen-name 'Alpha of the Plough' refers to the essayist:
A. W.M. Thackerey B. A.G. Gardiner
C. E.V. Lucas D. Oliver Goldsmith

80. 'The Negro Artist and the Racial Mountain : The Manifesto of the Harlem Renaissance' is a short essay by:
A. Larry Neal B. James Baldwin
C. Alaine Locke D. Langston Hughes

81. Who of the following wrote "Eros and Civilization"?
A. Jacquer Lacan B. Sigmund Freud
C. Karl Jung D. Herbert Marcuse

82. What is the common factor in literature written by Commonwealth writers?
A. Colonial experience and English Language
B. Christianity
C. British Influence on Governance
D. Superiority of English Language

83. "Marg" a reputed Indian journal of arts was edited by:
A. Raja Rao
B. Mulk Raj Anand
C. Bhabani Bhattacharya
D. G. Parthasarathi

84. Which of the following novels by R.K. Narayan has a character, called Susila?
A. Mr. Sampath
B. The Dark Room
C. The English Teacher
D. Grand Mother's Tale

85. Which novel of Kamala Markandaya explores the evil and ugly nature of racial prejudice?
A. Nectar in a sieve
B. Possession
C. Some inner fury
D. The Nowhere Man

86. .... is an untouchable in "The God of Small Things."
A. Father Mulligan B. Velutha
C. Esthappen D. Pappachi

87. "Lajja" is a well known work of:
A. Manju Kapur
B. Kamala Das
C. Taslima Nasreen
D. Shashi Deshpande

88. Salman Rushdie's first novel is:
A. Shame
B. Midnights Children
C. Grimus
D. The Satanic Versus

89. Ratan Rathor is a character in Arun Joshi's novel:
A. The Strange Case of Billy Biswas
B. The Apprentice
C. The Last Labyrinth
D. The City and the River

90. The author of "The Great Indian Novel" is:
A. Amitav Gosh
B. Humayun Kabir
C. Upamanyu Chatterjee
D. Shashi Tharoor

91. Ngugi in "Weep Not, Child" calls the Kenyan youth to:
A. Rebel
B. Protest
C. Build the nation
D. Identify and understand the features of their heritage

92. The author of the paradoxical phrase— "To gain his freedom, the author must give up his freedom"
A. Wole Soyinka B. Ngugi
C. Chinua Achebe D. Nadine Gordimer

93. "Diaspora" means:
A. Exile
B. Movement
C. Going away from home
D. The movement of people to a country away from their own

94. What is the chronological sequence of Chinua Achebe's African Triology?
A. Things Fall Apart – No Longer at Ease – Arrow of God
B. No Longer at Ease – Things Fall Apart – Arrow of God
C. Arrow of God – Things Fall Apart – No Longer at Ease
D. Things Fall Apart – Arrow of God – No Longer at Ease

95. "I am the enemy you killed, my friend/I knew you in this dark" are the lines from:
A. The Soldier
B. Strange Meeting
C. Ulysses
D. To his dead body

96. Periphrasis, which is a round about way of speech or writing is also known as:
A. Allusion B. Synecdoche
C. Litotes D. Circumlocution

97. Who among the following writers belonged to the American Beat Movement?
A. Charles Beard B. Isaac McCaslin
C. Allen Ginsberg D. Thomas Paine

98. Which of the following is a Parody of Gothic novels?
A. Frankenstein B. Northanger Abbey
C. Mysteries of Udolfo D. Jane Eyre

99. Verse that has no set theme, no regular metre, rhyme or stanzaic pattern is called:
A. Blank verse B. Flexible Verse
C. Heroic Verse D. Free Verse

100. The terms "resonance" and "wonder" are associated with:
A. Willium Empson
B. Terence Hawkes
C. Roland Barthes
D. Stephen Greenbiatt

ANSWERS

1	2	3	4	5	6	7	8	9	10
C	D	C	A	D	B	B	C	B	D
11	**12**	**13**	**14**	**15**	**16**	**17**	**18**	**19**	**20**
A	D	A	C	D	B	A	B	A	D
21	**22**	**23**	**24**	**25**	**26**	**27**	**28**	**29**	**30**
B	B	D	C	B	B	C	A	C	D
31	**32**	**33**	**34**	**35**	**36**	**37**	**38**	**39**	**40**
B	C	A	D	A	B	C	B	D	B
41	**42**	**43**	**44**	**45**	**46**	**47**	**48**	**49**	**50**
A	D	B	A	D	A	C	A	A	C
51	**52**	**53**	**54**	**55**	**56**	**57**	**58**	**59**	**60**
C	B	A	A	B	D	D	A	D	B
61	**62**	**63**	**64**	**65**	**66**	**67**	**68**	**69**	**70**
C	C	B	A	C	A	D	C	D	B
71	**72**	**73**	**74**	**75**	**76**	**77**	**78**	**79**	**80**
C	D	C	A	B	D	C	A	B	D
81	**82**	**83**	**84**	**85**	**86**	**87**	**88**	**89**	**90**
D	A	B	C	D	B	C	A	B	D
91	**92**	**93**	**94**	**95**	**96**	**97**	**98**	**99**	**100**
C	D	D	A	B	D	C	B	D	D

English Language

1 Comprehension Passages

Directions: *Read the following passages and answer the questions given below each.*

PASSAGE-1

In the Roman times, defected enemies were generally put to death as criminals for having offended the emperor of Rome. In the middle ages, however, the practice of ransoming of returning prisoners in exchange for money became common. Though some saw this custom as a step towards a most humane society, the primary reasons behind it were economic rather than humanitarian.

In those times, rulers had only a limited ability to raise taxes. They could neither force their subject to fight nor pay them to do so. The promise of material compensation in the form of goods and ransom was therefore the only way of inducing combatants to participate in a war. In the middle ages, the predominant incentive for the individual soldiers was the expectation of spoils. Although collecting ransom clearly brought financial gain, keeping a prisoner and arranging for his exchange had its cost. Consequently, procedures were devised to reduce transaction costs.

One such device was a rule asserting that the prisoner had to assess his own value. This compelled the prisoner to establish a value *without too much distortion;* indicating too low a value would increase, the captive's chances of being killed, while indicating too high a value would either ruin him financially or create a prohibitively expensive ransom that would also result in death.

1. It can be inferred from the passage that a medieval soldier

A. was less likely to kill captured members of opposing armies than was a soldier of the Roman Empire

B. was similar to a 20th century terrorist in that he operated on a basically independent level and was motivated solely by economic incentives

C. had few economic options and chose to fight because it was the only way to earn an adequate living

D. was motivated to spare prisoners' lives by humanitarian rather than economic ideals

2. Which of the following best describes the change in policy from executing prisoners in Roman times to ransoming prisoners in the middle ages?

A. The emperors of Rome demanded more respect than did medieval rulers and thus Roman subjects went to greater lengths to defend their nation

B. It was a reflection of the lesser degree of direct control medieval ruler had over subjects

C. It became a show of strength and honour warrior of the middles ages to be able to capture and return their enemies

D. Medieval soldiers were not as humanitarian as their ransoming practices might have indicated

3. The primary purpose of the passage is to
   A. discuss the economic basis of the medieval practice of exchanging prisoners for ransom
   B. examine the history of the treatment of prisoner of war
   C. emphasize the importance of a warrior's code of honour during the middle ages
   D. explore a way of reducing the cost of ransom
4. The author uses the phrase *"without too much distortion"* in order to
   A. indicate that prisoners would fairly assess their worth
   B. emphasize the important role medieval prisoners played in determining whether they should be ransomed
   C. explain how prisoners often paid more than an appropriate ransom in order to increase their chances for survival
   D. suggest that captors and captives often had understanding relationships

PASSAGE-2

The factor of geographical distribution is equally, possibly even more, significant that English is spoken as first or native language in at least four continents of the world, Russian in two, Chinese and the Indian languages in one. English is without question the closest approach to a world language today. It goes without saying that no two persons ever have an identical command of their common language. Certainly, they have not precisely the same vocabulary. There are at least minor differences in pronunciation, indeed the same individual will not pronounce his vowels and consonants in absolutely identical fashion everytime he utters them. Everyone possesses, in addition, certain individual traits of grammatical form and syntactical order, constituting that peculiar and personal quality of language which we term as style. All of this is implicit in the well-known phrase, 'Style is the man.' No men are identical, no two styles are the same. If this be true of but two persons, the potential of differences resident in a language spoken by more than 200 million truly staggers imagination.

1. The author argues that English is the closest approach to a world language because
   A. there are more native speakers of English than of any other language
   B. English has less number of mutually unintelligible dialects
   C. the geographical distribution of English covers a much greater area
   D. other languages are much too complex to be world languages
2. The fact that the same individual will not pronounce his vowels and consonants identically everytime shows that
   A. literary style varies from person to person
   B. mutual intelligibility is a myth
   C. vocabulary varies from individual to individual
   D. no two persons speak the same language exactly the same way
3. It is evident from the passage that style is
   A. a strange type of language
   B. a language where one does not have to be particular about correctness and grammar
   C. language used in a particular way by an individual
   D. a question of grammatical and syntactic correctness
4. According to some authorities
   A. more people speak Chinese dialect than English
   B. more people speak English as an auxiliary language than as a first language
   C. more people speak English in the UK than in England
   D. about one-fourth of the world's population speaks English
5. The overall implication of the passage is that
   A. to suppose that 230 million people speak English as a native language would certainly be an underestimate
   B. the 55 million inhabitants of the British Isles speak like the 30 million inhabitants of the dominions and colonies
   C. a little less than half the native English speakers in the world live in the US

D. about one-tenth of the total English-speaking world population lives in British dominions and colonies

PASSAGE-3

What is the future which awaits our children? The underlying assumption of the question, that Indian children have a common future, is itself dubious. It can legitimately be asked whether a student who is well-fed, attending a boarding school in the salubrious climate of the hills and learning to use computers has any future in common with a malnourished child who goes to a school with no blackboards, if indeed he does go to school. The latter may have no worthwhile future at all. And it might be worthwhile to analyse the significance of this marginalisation of more than 75 per cent of the children of this country.

The failure to provide an infrastructure for primary education in the villages of India more than 40 years after independence is in sharp contrast with the sophisticated institutions, for technical institutes of higher education are funded by the government, which essentially means that the money to support them comes from taxes. And, since indirect taxation forms a substantial part of the taxes collected by the government, the financial burden is borne by all the people. L.K. Jha put it graphically when he observed that 25 paise of every rupee spent on educating an IIT student comes from the pockets of men and women whose children may never enter a proper classroom.

1. The author is trying to highlight which of the following?
   A. Faulty system of direct taxes
   B. The greatness of L.K. Jha
   C. Need of sophisticated education for rural poor
   D. Need to have common future for Indian children

2. Which of the following pairs have been termed as 'sharp contrast' by the author?
   (*i*) Infrastructure for technical education
   (*ii*) Lack of infrastructure for rural primary schools
   (*iii*) 25 paise of every rupee earned by Government is spent on education
   (*iv*) The financial burden of higher technical education is borne by all people
   (*v*) 75% of children have limited opportunities
   A. (*ii*) and (*iv*) B. (*ii*) and (*iii*)
   C. (*iii*) and (*iv*) D. (*i*) and (*ii*)

3. Which of the following statements is not true?
   (*i*) The author welcomes Govt.'s initiative on primary education
   (*ii*) 75% of the children have a bright future
   (*iii*) 25% cost of educating a technocrat comes from poor people
   A. Only (*i*) B. Only (*ii*)
   C. Only (*iii*) D. Only (*i*) and (*ii*)

4. According to the author, who among the following does not have a hopeful and prosperous future?
   (*i*) All students from technical institutes
   (*ii*) All students financially supported by the Government
   A. Only (*i*) B. Only (*ii*)
   C. Both (*i*) and (*ii*) D. Neither (*i*) nor (*ii*)

5. What seems to be the likely answer of the author to the question posed by him in the first sentence of the passage?
   (*i*) There is no common future for the Indian children
   (*ii*) The future is worthwhile for majority of Indian children
   (*iii*) The majority may never enter a proper classroom
   A. Only (*i*) B. Only (*ii*)
   C. Only (*iii*) D. Both (*i*) and (*ii*)

6. What seems to be the purpose of the author in writing this passage?
   A. Setting goals for children of upper middle class
   B. Questioning the legitimacy of public schools
   C. Highlighting lack of infrastructural facilities for primary education
   D. Focusing on inequality in educational opportunities.

PASSAGE-4

It all started twenty-five years ago. I was teaching Economics at a university in Bangladesh. The country was in the middle of a famine. I felt terrible. Here I was, teaching the **elegant** theories of Economics in the classroom with all the **enthusiasm** of a brand-new Ph.D. from the United States. But I would walk out of the classroom and see skeletons all around me, people waiting to die.

I felt that whatever I had learned, whatever I was teaching, was all make-believe stories, with no meaning for people's lives. So I started trying to find out how people lived in the village next door to the university campus. I wanted to find out whether there was anything I could do as a human being to delay or stop the death, even for one single person. I **abandoned** the bird's-eye view that lets you see everything from above, from the sky. I assumed a worm's-eye view, trying to find whatever comes right in front of you—smell it, touch it, see if you can do something about it.

One particular incident took me in a new direction. I met a woman who was making bamboo stools. After a long discussion, I found out that she made only two U.S. pennies each day. I couldn't believe anybody could work so hard and make such beautiful bamboo stools yet make such a tiny amount of profit. She explained to me that because she didn't have the money to buy the bamboo to make the stools, she had to borrow from the trader- and the trader imposed the condition that she had to sell the product to him alone, at a price that he decided.

And that explains the two pennies—she was virtually in bonded labour to this person. And how much did the bamboo cost? She said, "Oh, about twenty cents. For a very good one twenty-five cents." I thought, "People suffer for twenty cents and there is nothing anyone can do about it?" I debated whether I should give her twenty cents, but then I came up with another idea—let me make a list of people who needed that kind of money. I took a student of mine and we went around the village for several days and came up with a list of forty-two such people. When I added up the total amount they needed, I got the biggest shock of my life : It added up to twenty-seven dollars! I felt ashamed of myself for being part of a society which could not provide even twenty-seven dollars to forty-two hard-working, skilled human beings.

To escape that shame, I took the money out of my pocket and gave it to my student. I said, "You take this money and give it to those forty-two people that we met and tell them this is a loan, but they can pay me back whenever they are able to. In the meantime, they can get a good price. After receiving the money, they were very excited.

1. Which of the following can be inferred about the author?

A. He studied in Bangladesh
B. He also belonged to a poor family
C. His Ph.D. was on poverty in Bangladesh
D. His Ph.D. was in Economics

2. The author of the passage seems to have–

A. inspired several people through his lecture to make a living
B. transformed himself into an action-oriented person to eradicate poverty
C. continued his teachings excellently and with a lot of enthusiasm
D. helped his students in their endeavour to eradicate poverty

3. Which of the following is ***MOST OPPOSITE*** of the word **'Elegant'** as used in the passage?

A. Irrelevant B. Diluted
C. Crude D. Ignoble

4. The contents of the passage prove that poverty can be alleviated if ....

(*i*) there is a strong will to do so.
(*ii*) some funds and/or other resources are available.
(*iii*) there is a vision to identify and remedy the problems

A. Only (*i*) and (*ii*) B. Only (*ii*) and (*iii*)
C. Only (*i*) and (*iii*) D. All the three

5. The woman described in the passage could not earn reasonably good money because ....

A. the quality of the goods she made was short of excellence

B. the sale of her products was very scanty
C. the raw material required to make finished products was in short supply
D. None of these

6. The trader's act to compel the woman to sell the stools only to him can be termed as..........
A. an act of kindness towards the needy woman
B. an ethical business strategy to maximize profit
C. sheer exploitation of the hopeless and needy people
D. contributing some help to the famine-stricken victims

7. What made the author feel ashamed of himself?
A. He lacked in thorough knowledge of Economics and therefore wanted to study more
B. He was ignorant of the fact that even a small help was also going to be significant
C. He was a party to the exploitation of the poor by the trader
D. He was not in a position to take the culprit trader to task

8. The survey conducted by the author revealed that............
A. the amount needed to help the village poor to make a living was not very big'
B. it was an unmanageable task for the author to help the needy people of the village
C. there were forty-two traders who were engaged in the act of exploitation of the poor
D. the number of the needy people in the village was very large

Directions (9-10) : *Choose the word/group of words which is most nearly the* ***SAME*** *in meaning as the word given in bold as given in passage.*

9. ABANDONED

A. Gave up B. Escaped from
C. Accepted D. Took away

10. ENTHUSIASM

A. Excellence B. Happiness
C. Force D. Zeal

PASSAGE-5

Cyber crime is the branded stigma defacing the culture and magnanimity of computer technology. It is upkeeping the flag with indomitable triumph against developing computer technology worldwide.

Modern age is striding with marching steps of technology revolution beating the past decade of ancestral belief with ultimate care. Computer invention has unfolded the mystery of quick access with the objective of minimum manpower and cutting the time consumption parameters.

As each coin has dual face of its portrait, likewise computer technology is sick of creeping virus. Synthetic manmade dilemma of site hackers activation is causing setback to the expanding anchor of revolutionary device with great loss of time, economy and data profile as suffered by consumers. A recent report from Internet security firm Websense estimates that 85.6 per cent of all the unwanted e-mails contained links to spam sites. The company's data suggests that the number of malicious sites grew 233 per cent in the last six months and saw 671 per cent growth in the number of malicious sites during the last year. In June alone, the total number of e-mails detected as containing viruses increased by 600 per cent compared to May.

Chat rooms, blogs and message-boards where the users post comments have been identified as the top targets of hackers and spammers due to the high traffic these attract. According to Websense, 95 per cent of user-generated comments to blogs, chat rooms and message-boards during the first half of 2009 were malicious.

It is advisable not to click on spurious links and stay away from keying in passwords at unknown sites as they are most likely to be spammed. Hackers can steal your passwords and log in to your account and access critical information like account numbers and contact details among other things.

1. The above passage is:
A. an advisory for the computer users.
B. an advisory for the Internet users.

C. a warning against possible threat to the Internet users.
D. related to chat rooms, blogs and message boards.

2. People who use chat rooms and blogs,
A. are safe and have no threats from spam.
B. are more prone to malicious e-mails.
C. create virus and hack the accounts of others.
D. are unsafe.

3. According to the writer, it is not safe to:
A. log on to spurious links.
B. access one's own account frequently.
C. have essential information stored in a computer.
D. include data-stealing code.

4. Hackers and spammers, according to the writer, are:
A. a new threat to the Internet users and the economy.
B. only pranksters and not serious threat to the system.
C. trained, professional technocrats who are an asset.
D. not expert professionals.

5. Which word in the passage is synonym of *weblog*?
A. blog B. password
C. site D. e-mail

6. Which agency has assessed the data record with spam sites?
A. Microsoft
B. Internet security from Google
C. Websense
D. Spammers

7. Which month dominates the e-mails detection data record?
A. May B. June
C. Last six months D. Last year

PASSAGE-6

All cultures, even the simplest, seem to be in a continuous state of change. The earlier anthropologists, as opposed to the moderns, assumed that cultures with relatively simple technology and political structure represented only slightly modified survivors of the ancient conditions of our own ancestors and for that reason dubbed them primitive. Also, largely as a device for simplifying their own theoretical studies, they assumed that such cultures were static or nearly so, persisting unchanged over long time periods. Actually, we have plenty of evidence that this is not the case. Not only do all archaeological records, fragmentary as they are, show change through time, but wherever explorers have visited a primitive tribe at intervals of a generation or more, their reports show that changes have taken place. Since there is always the possibility that these changes have been set in motion by the first explorer's visit or by contacts with other Europeans during the intervals, the archaeological evidence is more reliable. From this it appears that changes in technology are the only part of culture on which it provides conclusive evidence, were exceedingly slow during the first nine-tenths of human existence. Thousands of years have gone without the introduction of any new tool or appliance. However, during the last twenty-five or thirty thousand years, there has been a progressive speeding up of cultural change. In their operation, the process of cultural change falls into a definite sequence. The first step is the presentation to the society of a potential addition to its culture. This is followed by the new elements' acceptance or rejection. If accepted there are further processes of modification and integration by which the new elements and the pre-existing culture are brought into adjustment. Lastly, there is usually, but not always, the elimination of an older culture element, or elements where functions have been taken over by the new elements.

A potential element of culture may be invented or borrowed. In either case, the new idea or appliance originates with some individual or at work with a small series of individuals who have either pooled their ingenuity to solve a problem or contributed to improving details during the developments of the invention. There can be no invention or cultural change without an inventor. The main difference between invention and borrowing is that if the new thing originates within the setting provided by the society and its culture, we refer to it as culture borrowing, The processes of acceptance or rejection or integration will be the same, although the attitude of the receiving society towards the one in which the potential element originated may influence acceptance.

1. According to the passage,
   A. modern anthropologists are more systematic and accurate than earlier ones
   B. a relatively simple society will see progress as spasmodic, resulting from the borrowing of cultural elements
   C. the last twenty years have seen societies rapidly becoming cultured
   D. cultural interaction is necessary for the cultural progress of primitive societies
2. According to the passage,
   A. foreign cultural elements are never assimilated in their original form
   B. assimilation of a cultural element is partly dependent on the attitude of the borrower society to the source society
   C. the process of cultural change is usually random
   D. self-sufficient societies rely on inventions rather than cultural borrowings
3. According to the author, earlier anthropologists assumed some cultures to be static because
   A. of insufficient interaction with them
   B. of poor or unreliable analysis
   C. it made their task of studying these cultures more simple
   D. of fragmentary archaeological evidence
4. According to the passage,
   A. a culture with simple technologies and political structure is likely to be static
   B. explorers seem to have begun a process of change in many societies
   C. much of the culture seen today is the result of changes in the recent past
   D. all cultures seem to have continuous rates of change
5. All the following are essential to the process of borrowing cultural elements, except
   A. the projection of a particular cultural element as attractive to and suitable for the recipient society
   B. the displacement of the cultural element performing the same task in the recipient society
   C. the modification of cultural elements to suit the recipient society
   D. the widespread acceptance of the new element within the recipient society
6. According to the passage,
   A. "cultural borrowing" is primarily dependent on the relationship between the donor and recipient societies
   B. the process of assimilation of a new element, whether borrowed or indigenous, will be the same once the society becomes receptive to it.
   C. borrowing a new element carries the risk of conflict between the new element and the original element that performed the same task
   D. a technologically more complex society will always be a donor to a technologically simpler society
7. No cultural change is really possible without
   A. a willingness to learn and imbibe from alien cultures
   B. a process of integration, which brings the culture and the innovation into a state of adjustment
   C. the human element which acts as a source of all innovation
   D. a society's receptivity to change
8. From the passage, we can infer that
   A. a society takes much longer to integrate a "culture borrowing" than an "invention"
   B. altering the sequence of cultural assimilation will result in unintegrated cultural elements in a society

C. a society with a simpler political and technological structure is more likely to be receptive to new cultural elements

D. as the political and technological structure of a society becomes complex, cultural change becomes faster

PASSAGE-7

The Indian economy rests on agricultural base and for decades and generations the picture that India presented to the world was one of famine and of an unchanging peasantry reluctant to depart from the cultural practices handed down to them by their forefathers. Indian agriculture, it was said, was a gamble on the rains. Some visionaries and civil servants had sought to change all this. Their experiments at rural transformation were watched with amused interest and if their efforts did not meet with more than temporary and isolated success, it was because they were operating individuals and in very limited areas within what was basically an inhospitable and unresponsive administrative environment. The scale of effort was enlarged during the Second World War with the launching of the "grow more food campaign." But, the administrative structure remained largely unaltered.

It was to change all this, that the Community Development Programme was introduced. There were three problems that had to be tackled. First, if the farmer was to change methods, he had to be educated to see the possibility to change through actual demonstration in his field at no cost to himself. If the farmer tilled the land in the same manner as his father before him, it was because tradition had no optimised risks and the farmer had no margin on the basis of which to gamble on strange new practices and risk not merely a financial loss but his very survival. Second, there was no one agency to whom the farmer could turn for assistance or advice. If he wanted better seeds, he had to go to the Agriculture Department. For irrigation he had to knock at the doors of the Irrigation Department. Roads were the responsibility of the Public Works Department. Land problems had to be taken up with the revenue authorities and so on. In short, the administration was totally fragmented at the point which touched the life of the farmer. Coordination was difficult and the totality of the farmer's problem could never be adequately comprehended, let alone ameliorated, by the administration. Third, even if the administration sought to promote rural transformation and the farmers were willing, how was the new knowledge to be transmitted not merely to every village but to each cultivator?

The Community Development Programme sought to provide answers to these three problems. Something in the nature of the single-line administration was established under a chain of command running through the District Development Officer and Block Development Officer to the multipurpose village-level worker. Instead of having to go to several departments to get anything done, the farmer could now deal with a single community development authority with which all the executive agencies involved in rural development were associated. The many thousands of field demonstrations laid out under the Community Development Programme demonstrated the possibility of change in a manner that carried conviction and at no risk to the peasant. Once the farmer was persuaded, his alleged age-old conservatism vanished and the next problem was to satisfy his evergrowing demands. Meanwhile, the establishment of a National Extension Service first time created a permanent transmission system for the propagation and demonstration of new ideas and methods, not just in isolated pockets, but over very wide areas.

1. The success of the efforts put in for rural transformation was limited because

A. of their limited field of operation in an advanced environment

B. their experiments were watched with amusement

C. their focus was on temporary achievements

D. None of these

2. Which of the following was the objective of launching Community Development Programme?

A. To eradicate illiteracy of the rural folk

B. To switch over to mechanisation in agro-sector
C. To solve the diverse problems of farmers on a single platform
D. To minimise farmer's financial losses and risks

3. For the people in the world, the image of Indian village is that of
A. an opponent of traditionalism and conservatism
B. a rule-bound, conservative and culture-groomed person
C. a visionary and a perfect gambler
D. an inhospitable and unresponsive person

4. The experiments undertaken by some visionaries were aimed at
A. changes in administrative environment
B. temporary and isolated success
C. evolution of new operational strategies
D. upliftment of peasants and rural development

5. What was the probable disadvantage of the fragmented administration to the farmers?
A. Loss of time, money and energy
B. Exposure to novel techniques and strategies
C. Availability of manures, fertilisers and seeds
D. Uncertainty of rains during the crop season

6. If the administration and also the farmers were willing to promote rural transformation, which was the main hindering factor in their way?
A. Comprehension of the farmers' problems
B. Lack of coordination among different agencies
C. Lack of availability of facilities for cultivation
D. None of these

7. What was the impact of these demonstrations on the farmers?
A. Their unreasonable demands increased disproportionately
B. Their tendency to cling to past traditions vanished
C. National Extension Service was established by them
D. Their standard of living remained unaltered

8. The apparent plus-point of the Community Development Programme demonstrations was that
A. they were free from any cost or risk to the farmers
B. they were not against the farmers' traditional practices
C. they were conducted by multipurpose workers
D. the changes as demonstrated were all familiar to the farmers

PASSAGE-8

The University Grants Commission's directive requiring college and university lecturers to spend a minimum of 22 hours a week in direct teaching is the product of budgetary cutbacks rather than pedagogic wisdom. It may seem odd, at first blush, that teachers should protest about teaching a mere 22 hours. However, if one considers the amount of time academics require to prepare lectures of good quality as well as the time they need to spend doing research — it is clear that most conscientious teachers work more than 40 hours a week. In university systems around the world, lecturers rarely spend more than 12 to 15 hours in direct teaching activities a week. The average college lecturer in India does not have any office space. If computers are available, Internet connectively is unlikely. Libraries are poorly stocked. Now the UGC says universities must implement a complete **freeze** on all permanent recruitment, abolish all posts which have been vacant for more than a year, and cut staff strength by 10 percent. And it is in order to ensure that these cutbacks do not affect the quantum of teaching that existing lecturers are being asked to work longer. Obviously, the quality of teaching — and academic work in general — will decline. While it is true that some college teachers do not take their classes regularly, the UGC and the institutions concerned must find a proper way to hold them accountable. An absentee teacher will continue to play truant even if the number of hours he is required to teach goes up.

All of us are well aware of the unsound state that the Indian higher education system is in today. Thanks to years of **sustained** financial neglect, most Indian universities and colleges do no research worth the name. Even as the number of students entering colleges has increased dramatically, public investment in higher education has actually declined in relative terms. Between 1995 and 2007, when public expenditure on higher education as a percentage of outlays on all levels of education grew by more than 60 per cent in Malaysia and 20 per cent in Thailand, India showed a decline of more than 10 per cent. Throughout the world, the number of teachers in higher education per million population grew by more than 10 per cent in the same period; in India, it fell by one per cent. Instead of transferring the burden of government apathy on to the backs of the teachers, the UGC should insist that the needs of the country's university system are adequately catered for.

1. Why does the UGC want to increase the direct teaching hours of university teachers?
A. UGC feels that the duration of contact between teacher and the taught should be more
B. UGC wants teachers to spend more time in their departments
C. UGC wants teachers to devote some time to improve university administration
D. UGC does not have money to appoint additional teachers

2. Which of the following is the reason for the sorry state of affairs of the Indian Universities as mentioned in the passage?
A. The poor quality of teachers
B. Involvement of teachers in extracurricular activities
C. Politics within and outside the departments
D. Not getting enough financial assistance

3. Which of the following statement(s) is/are ***TRUE*** in the context of the passage?
(*i*) Most colleges do not carry out research worth the name.
(*ii*) UGC wants lecturers to spend minimum 22 hours a week in direct teaching.
(*iii*) Indian higher education system is in unsound state.
A. Only (*i*) and (*iii*)
B. All (*i*), (*ii*) and (*iii*)
C. Only (*iii*)
D. Only (*ii*)

4. Besides direct teaching, University teachers spend considerable time in/on.....
A. administrative activities such as admissions
B. supervising examinations and correction of answer papers
C. carrying out research in the area of their interest
D. maintaining research equipment and libraries

5. Which of the following statements is ***NOT TRUE*** in the context of the passage?
A. UGC wants teachers to spend minimum 40 hours in a week in teaching
B. Some college teachers do not engage their classes regularly
C. The average collect teacher in India does not have any office space
D. UGC wants universities to abolish all posts which have been vacant for more than a year

6. Between 1995 and 2007, the number of teachers in higher education per million population, in India........
A. increased by 60%
B. increased by 20%
C. decreased by 22%
D. decreased by 1%

7. Which of the following statements is ***NOT TRUE*** in the context of the passage?
A. Indian universities are financially neglected.
B. All over the world, the university lecturers hardly spend more than 12 to 15 hours a week in direct teaching
C. Indian universities are asked to reduce staff strength by 10%
D. Public investment in higher education has increased in India

8. Choose the world which is ***SIMILAR*** in meaning as the word **'freeze'** as used in the passage.
   A. Cold B. Halt
   C. Decay D. Control
9. What is the UGC directive to the universities?
   A. Improve the quality of teaching
   B. Spend time on research activities
   C. Do not appoint any permanent teacher
   D. Provide computer and internet facilities
10. Choose the world which is ***SIMILAR*** in meaning as the word **'sustained'** as used in the passage.
   A. Continuous B. Frequent
   C. Careless D. Deliberate

PASSAGE-9

Progress in life depends a good deal on crossing one threshold after another. Some time ago, a man watched his little nephew try to write his name. It was hardwork, very hardwork. The little boy had arrived at an effort threshold. Today he writes his name with comparative ease. No new threshold confronts him. This is the way with all of us. As soon as we cross one threshold, as soon as we conquer one difficulty, a new difficulty appears, or should appear. Some people make the mistake of steering clear of thresholds. Anything that requires genuine thinking and use of energy they avoid. They prefer to stay in a rut where thresholds are not met. Probably, they have been at their job a number of years. Things are easy for them. They make no effort to seek out new obstacles to overcome. Real progress stops under such circumstances.

Some middle-aged and elderly people greatly enrich their lives by continuing to cross thresholds. One man went into an entirely new business when he was past middle life and made success of it, De Morgan didn't start to write novels until he was past sixty. Psychologists have discovered that man can continue to learn throughout his life. And it is undoubtedly better to try and fail than not to try at all. There one can be placed in the category of the Swiss mountaineer of whom it was said, *"He died climbing"*. When a new difficulty arises to obstruct your path, do not complain. Accept the challenge. Determine to cross this threshold as you have crossed numerous other thresholds in your past. In the words of a poet, do not rest but strive *to pass from dream to grander dream.*

1. What obstructs real progress in life?
   A. Remaining at one and the same post
   B. Avoiding the thinking and energy
   C. Shunning every work
   D. Stopping education
2. What does progress in life depend upon?
   A. Good habits
   B. Hardwork
   C. Overcoming one difficulty after another
   D. Spirit of service and cooperation
3. What does *'He died climbing'* signify?
   A. He died when he was climbing the hill
   B. He died before getting at the top
   C. He strove hard till the last moment of life
   D. He climbed the hill and then died
4. What does *'to pass from dream to grander dream'* mean?
   A. Always having greater and greater aspiration in life
   B. Seeing one good dream and then greater aspiration in life
   C. Making plan after plan
   D. Seeing one dream after the other
5. What did the man entering a new business past middle life do of his business?
   A. He miserably failed in it
   B. He achieved partial success
   C. He dropped the business after sometime
   D. He achieved good success in it
6. How can you accomplish the most difficult tasks?
   A. By mobilizing all possible resources
   B. By avoiding all obstacles
   C. By sticking to hardwork
   D. By doing it bit by bit and persisting in the effort
7. What does De Morgan's life teach?
   A. That it is futile to learn many things
   B. That one is never old in case he has vigour
   C. That it is never too late to learn
   D. That creative writing can be made even late in life

8. How do middle-aged and elderly people add brilliance to their lives?
   A. By overcoming difficulty one after another
   B. By getting sycophants to surround them
   C. By making fine speeches
   D. By acquiring resourcefulness
9. What should we do when a new difficulty obstructs our path?
   A. Run away from it
   B. Be bold and face it
   C. Manoeuvre to get it removed
   D. Enlist other people's help to get it over
10. When did De Morgan start to write novels?
   A. When he was sixty years old
   B. When he was below sixty
   C. When he studied psychology
   D. None of these

PASSAGE-10

Peace and order are necessary, not just in our own country but also at the international level, if we are to secure national progress and development. The different countries in the world are coming closer today due to faster means of transport and communication. Economically, they are becoming increasingly interdependent. If peace is disturbed in one part of the world, it has adverse effects in other parts of the world as well. Nuclear weapons have already threatened the world with nuclear war. If the conflicts between different nations are not settled in time, they might *culminate* in a nuclear war destroying the whole world. It is therefore, in our own interest that the world is free of conflicts. If at all there are any, they must be settled promptly and peace should be restored. That is why we have declared the establishment of international peace and understanding as an objective of our foreign policy.

We need the help and cooperation of other countries for our scientific, industrial and economic development, especially in those fields where we have yet to achieve self-sufficiency. We obtain the latest machinery, technology and financial aid from the developed countries. On our part we, too, offer help to the under-developed countries. We are keen on maintaining friendly relations with other countries. Such friendly relations *foster* international understanding.

We have always exerted ourselves to see that the disputes arising between the different nations are settled through peaceful negotiations. We play an active role in the United Nations, the South Asian Association for Regional Cooperation, the Commonwealth of Nations and other such international organisations. We make it a point to participate in the international conferences on issues like energy crisis, environmental imbalance, nuclear arms race etc. We always offer a helping hand to other nations affected by natural calamities such as famines, earthquakes, floods and so on. We strive to maintain peaceful and friendly relations with our neighbouring countries. *Why do we do all this!* We sincerely believe that conflicts in today's world should be minimised, making way for better cooperation among the nations. If this is achieved, human resources will no longer be wasted in things like war or aggression. There will be no destruction of wealth. We believe that, in a peaceful world, there will be greater scope for the economic and cultural development of countries.

1. According to the passage, maintaining friendly relations with other countries facilitate
   A. developing international understanding
   B. exchange of scientists and technologists
   C. strategic planning in defence matters
   D. import and export of several vital commodities
2. If conflicts between nations do not cease
   A. international bodies will have to take up these issues
   B. international understanding will not be fostered
   C. nuclear war will destroy the whole world
   D. the means of transport and communication will be disrupted
3. Which of the following is obtained by us from the developed countries, according to the passage?
   A. Fertilisers B. Foodgrains
   C. Leather Products D. Technology

4. Which of the following according to the passage, is facilitating the process of different countries coming together?
A. Emerging world order
B. Asian Association for Regional Cooperation
C. Our participation in international conferences
D. Faster means of transport and communication

5. Minimising the conflicts and making way for better cooperation among the nations will result in
A. useful and purposive utilisation of human resources
B. better utilisation of means of transport and communication
C. culmination of nuclear war destroying the world
D. keenness on maintaining friendly relations with other countries

6. Which of the following statements is not true in the context of the passage?
A. International conflicts must be settled promptly
B. We try to maintain friendly relations with our neighbours
C. We participate in many international conferences
D. Each country can be considered isolated and insulated from the effects of other countries

7. Which of the following words is largely ***SIMILAR*** in meaning of the word **'culminate'** as used in the passage?
A. Reach the highest point
B. Stretch to the maximum
C. Absolute standards
D. Total destruction

8. Which of the following words is most ***OPPOSITE*** in meaning of the word **'foster'** as used in the passage?
A. Advocate B. Hinder
C. Obviate D. Facilitate

9. The question *"Why do we do all this!"* is asked in the passage in which of the following contexts?
A. We always offer a helping hand to other nations in improving their technology
B. We endeavour to maintain peaceful and friendly relations with our neighbours
C. We obtain the latest machinery, technology and financial aid from the developed countries
D. We have shaped our foreign policy in a balanced and purposeful manner

10. Does any of the following sentences contain any idea expressed in the passage?
A. We have to make conscious efforts to preserve our national unity
B. Our country is huge in size and population where many languages are spoken
C. We have adopted the objective of democracy in the interest of overall development of our country
D. None of these statements contain any idea expressed in the passage

PASSAGE-11

There is a fairly universal sentiment that the use of nuclear weapon is clearly contrary to morality and that its production does not go far enough. These activities are not only opposed to morality but also to law and if the legal objection can be added to the moral, the argument against the use and the manufacture of these weapons will considerably be reinforced. Now the time is ripe to evaluate the responsibility of scientists who knowingly use their expertise for the construction of such weapons which has *deleterious* effect on mankind.

To this must be added the fact that more than 50 per cent of the skilled scientific manpower in the world is now engaged in the armaments industry. How appropriate it is that all this valuable skill should be *devoted* to the manufacture of weapons of death in a world of poverty is a question that must touch the scientific conscience.

A meeting of biologists on the Long-Term Worldwide Biological Consequences of Nuclear War added frightening dimensions to those forecasts. Its report suggested that the long biological effects resulting from climatic changes may at least be as serious as the immediate ones.

Sub-freezing temperatures, low light levels and high dose of ionizing and ultraviolet radiation extending for many months, after a large-scale nuclear war, could destroy the biological support systems of civilization, at least in the Northern Hemisphere. Productivity in natural and agricultural ecosystems could be severely restricted for a year or more. Post-war survivors would face starvation as well as freezing conditions in the dark and be exposed to near-lethal dose of radiation. If, as now seems possible, the Southern Hemisphere were affected also, global disruption of the biosphere could ensue. In any event, there would be severe consequences, even in the areas not affected directly, because of the interdependence of the world economy. In either case the extinction of a large fraction of the earth's animals, plants, and microorganisms seems possible. The population size of Homo sapiens conceivably could be reduced to pre-historic levels or below and extinction of the human species itself cannot be excluded.

1. The author's most important objective of writing the above passage seems to
A. highlight the use of nuclear weapons as an effective population control measure
B. illustrate the devastating effects of use of nuclear weapons on mankind
C. duly highlight the supremacy of the nations which possess nuclear weapons
D. summarise the long biological effects of use of nuclear weapons

2. The scientists possessing expertise in manufacturing destructive weapons are
A. very few in number
B. irresponsible and incompetent
C. more than half of the total number
D. engaged in the armaments industry against their desire

3. According to the passage, the argument against the use and manufacture of nuclear weapons
A. does not stand the test of legality
B. possess legal strength although it does not have moral standing
C. is acceptable only on moral grounds
D. becomes stronger if legal and moral considerations are combined

4. Which of the following is one of the consequences of Nuclear War?
A. Fertility of land will last only for a year or so
B. Post-war survivors being very few will have abundant food
C. Lights would be cooler and more comfortable
D. Southern hemisphere would remain quite safe in the post-war period

5. Choose the word which is most ***OPPOSITE*** in meaning of the word **'deleterious'** as used in the passage.
A. Beneficial B. Harmful
C. Irreparable D. Non-cognizable

6. The author of the passage seems to be of the view that
A. utilization of scientific skills in manufacture of weapons is appropriate
B. the evaluation of the scientists' expertise show their incompetence
C. manufacture of weapons of death would help eradication of poverty
D. utilization of valuable knowledge for manufacture of lethal weapons is inhuman

7. Which of the following best explains the word **'devoted'** as used in the passage?
A. dedicated for a good cause
B. utilized for betterment
C. abused for destruction
D. underutilized

8. It appears from the passage that the use of nuclear weapons is considered against morality by
A. only such of those nations who cannot afford to manufacture weapons

B. almost all the nations of the world
C. only the superpowers who can afford to manufacture and sell weapons
D. a minority group of scientists who have the necessary skill and competence

9. Which of the following statement(s) (*i*), (*ii*) and/ or (*iii*) is/are definitely true in the context of the passage?
(*i*) Living organisms in the areas which are not directly affected by the consequences of nuclear war would also suffer
(*ii*) There is a likelihood of extinction of the human species as a consequence of nuclear war
(*iii*) The post-war survivors would be exposed to the risk of near-lethal radiation
A. Only (*i*) B. Only (*ii*)
C. Only (*iii*) D. All the three

10. The biological consequences of nuclear war as given in the passage include all the following except
A. fall in temperature below zero degree celsius
B. ultraviolet radiation
C. high dose of ionizing
D. None of these

PASSAGE-12

During the first year that Mr Wordsworth and I were neighbours, our conversation turned frequently on the two *cardinal* points of poetry, the power of exciting the sympathy of the reader by a faithful *adherence* to the truth of nature and the power of giving the interest of novelty by the modifying colours of imagination. The sudden charm, which *accidents* of light and shade, which moonlight or sunset diffused, over a known and familiar landscape, appeared to represent the practicability of combining both. These are the poetry of nature. The thought suggested itself that a series of poems might be composed of two sorts. In the one, the incidents agents were to be, in part at least, supernatural; and the excellence aimed at was to consist in the interesting of the affections by the dramatic truth of such emotions, as would naturally accompany such situations, supposing them real. And real in the sense they have been to every human being who, from whatever source of delusion, has at any time believed himself under supernatural agency. For the second class, subjects were to be chosen from ordinary life; the characters and incidents were to be such as will be found in every village and its vicinity, where there is a *meditative* and feeling mind to seek after them or to notice them, when they present themselves.

In this idea originated the plan of "Lyrical Ballads" in which it was agreed, that my endeavours should be directed to persons and characters supernatural, or at least romantic; yet so as to transfer from our inward nature a human interest and a semblance of truth sufficient to procure for these shadows of imagination that willing suspension of disbelief for the moment, which constitutes poetic faith. Mr Wordsworth, on the other hand, was to propose to himself as his object, to give the charm of novelty to things of everyday and to excite a feeling analogous to the supernatural, by awakening the mind's attention to the *lethargy* of custom and directing it to the loveliness and the wonders of the world before us; and inexhaustible treasure, but for which, in consequence of the *film* of familiarity and selfish *solicitude,* we have eyes, yet see not, ears that hear not, and hearts that neither feel nor understand.

1. The dialogue between the author and Mr Wordsworth usually centred around
A. the sympathy which the reader feels for the poet
B. importance of adhering to the truth of nature
C. contribution of imagination to poetic creation
D. the most prominent characteristic of poetry

2. Which of the following can be inferred from the statement "And real.... supernatural agency"?
A. The author believes that the supernatural is real
B. He does not believe in the existence of the supernatural agencies
C. He thinks supernatural events have no place in poetry
D. None of these

3. According to the author, despite having senses people fail to enjoy beauty because of the fact that
A. beauty is in the eyes of the viewer
B. they spend most of their time alone
C. only a poetic mind can appreciate it
D. the things which are out of sight are often out of mind

4. What sort of objects/phenomena was most likely to blend the two cardinal points of poetry?
A. Natural phenomena coupled with familiar objects
B. Diffused moonlight or sunset
C. The charm in thunder and lightning
D. Modifying colours of imagination

5. Which of the following is referred to as unending wealth?
A. Loveliness and wonders of the world
B. Familiarity with nature's objects
C. Selfless inner vision
D. Control over senses

6. According to the passage, the author and Mr Wordsworth differed in their
A. ideas of the two cardinal points of poetry
B. perceptions of the supernatural objects
C. choice of subject matter
D. plans for the organisation of "Lyrical Ballads"

7. Which of the following statements (*i*), (*ii*) and (*iii*) is/are *definitely true* in the context of the passage?
(*i*) The two subjects of poems as discussed in the passage are supernatural and those rrom ordinary life
(*ii*) "Lyrical Ballads" are poems based on delusion and are far from reality
(*iii*) The author of the passage was a contemporary of Mr Wordsworth
A. Only (*i*) is true B. Only (*ii*) is true
C. Only (*iii*) is true D. (*i*) and (*ii*) are true

Directions (Qs. 8 to 11): *Choose the word or group of words which is most nearly the SAME in meaning as the word given in bold capitals as used in the passage.*

8. **FILM**
A. covering B. photograph
C. movie D. surface

9. **SEMBLANCE**
A. perversion B. coating
C. likeness D. distortion

10. **CARDINAL**
A. ordinary B. exceptional
C. chief D. terminal

11. **ACCIDENTS**
A. tragic incidents
B. natural phenomena
C. man-made things
D. unromantic happenings

Directions (Qs.12 to 15): *Which of the following is most **OPPOSITE** in meaning of the word printed in bold capitals as used in the passage.*

12. **ADHERENCE**
A. clinging B. abandoning
C. cohesion D. forsaken

13. **MEDITATIVE**
A. immediate B. divergent
C. unconscious D. contemplating

14. **LETHARGY**
A. sluggishness B. awakening
C. mobility D. action

15. **SOLICITUDE**
A. motive B. nature
C. disrespect D. negligence

PASSAGE-13

There was an old weaver in a village, who had been praying to Lord Shiva for the last twenty-five years to give them enough money to live in comfort. Each morning and evening, he would walk round the Shiva temple one hundred and one times, prostrate himself before the image and then come back home. In spite of having prayed for such a long period, there was no sign of wealth coming to him. He, however, never lost faith in God and waited for the time to come.

As time passed, the poor weaver grew old. It was difficult for him to go round and round the temple and he was to help himself through a stick to walk. Lord Shiva did hear the weaver's prayer but did nothing to help him. However, Parvati, Shiva's wife, felt sorry at this and spoke to her husband. "Why are you so hard on that old weaver who has been worshipping you for such a long time? He is grown so old now that he cannot even walk properly. Why don't you make life easier for him?" Shiva smiled and replied to Parvati, "Do you think I would have refused to give him wealth if he could make use of it? What can I do for someone who is not destined to be rich?" Parvati, however, was not convinced with the view that a man cannot make use of wealth if it is given to him.

One day both Shiva and Parvati came down to earth and went to that temple. Shiva put a pot of gold on the way of the weaver when he was taking a round of the temple so that he can pick it up. The weaver walked on. "Oh, my Lord", he prayed, "How long have I to continue this *wretched* life? You have not been kind enough to me. But I can still play my trade. My eyes are still good. How fortunate I am that even in my old age I can still weave well." Then a terrible thought struck the weaver. "Suppose I were to lose my eyesight. But still I would be able to walk round the temple. Let me try. I could walk like this." He *firmly* closed his eyes and walked on. He passed by the pot of gold with his eyes closed. He smiled when he opened his eyes. "Yes," he said, "I need not worry. Even if I become blind, I can still walk round the temple." The weaver then went home. Shiva looked at Parvati and said, "But there is something I can do for him. He will not lose all interest in wealth. He will be very happy."

1. According to this passage, what made Parvati feel sorry?
   A. The old age of the weaver
   B. The attitude of the weaver
   C. Shiva not helping the weaver
   D. Shiva not listening to her appeal
2. Why did the weaver think himself fortunate?
   A. That he could carry out his profession in old age
   B. That he could walk around the temple even without eyesight
   C. That Parvati was kind enough to convince Shiva for him
   D. Not given in the passage
3. When the weaver opened his eyes
   A. he found the pot of gold
   B. he was cheerful
   C. he was worried
   D. he saw Shiva and Parvati
4. The weaver took how many rounds of the temple everyday?
   A. 101 B. 102
   C. 111 D. 202
5. Which of the following statements is not true regarding the weaver?
   A. He lost faith in God
   B. He worshipped for more than 25 years
   C. He continued taking rounds of temple even in old age
   D. He spent a miserable life
6. On which of the following views did Shiva and Parvati have differences of opinion?
   A. Every devotee can be blessed with the fulfilment of his wish
   B. Without eyesight one can locate the pot of gold
   C. Taking a positive attitude towards the weaver
   D. One cannot make use of the wealth if it is given to him
7. Had the weaver got enough money from the God, he would
   A. have a peaceful life
   B. have an easy life with no financial constraints
   C. not have further prayed to the God
   D. not have to stick to the weaver's job any more
8. After keeping the pot of gold on the passage around the temple, Shiva and Parvati
   A. returned to heaven
   B. hid themselves near the temple
   C. closely watched the weaver as invisible entities
   D. Not given in the passage

9. How did Shiva favour the old weaver?
   A. By availing him the pot of gold
   B. By giving him strength to work
   C. By asking Parvati to help him
   D. Not given in the passage

Directions (Qs. 10 to 12): *Choose the word which is most nearly **SAME** in meaning as the word printed in bold capitals as used in the passage.*

10. FELT
A. realised B. thought
C. expressed D. told

11. WRETCHED
A. unsatisfactory B. dirty
C. poor D. difficult

12. HARD
A. rigorous B. cruel
C. indifferent D. strict

Directions (Qs. 13 to 15): *Choose the word which is most **OPPOSITE** in meaning of the word printed in bold as used in the passage.*

13. STRUCK
A. prevented B. occurred
C. avoided D. slipped

14. FIRMLY
A. liberally B. openly
C. lightly D. closely

15. LOSE
A. collect B. gain
C. obtain D. restore

PASSAGE-14

It is *heartening* to know that if one had not had any heart attack earlier and he stops smoking, his chances of having a heart attack *drop* to that of a non-smoker in about six months' time. Stopping of smoking is also the single most effective means of secondary prevention (recurrence of a heart attack) in heart patients.

Smoking leads to pain and stiffness in the legs while walking. No amount of drugs can help. The only remedy is to give up smoking. If women smoke during pregnancy, there is an increased risk of death of the baby in the womb or soon after birth. Even where the baby survives, there is likelihood of delayed physical and intellectual development of the baby till it reaches 11 years of age.

Still worse the fact about smoking is that passive smoking is equally dangerous. Passive smokers are those who do not smoke but being in the company of smokers have to inhale smoke exhaled by the smokers They are equally prone to heart diseases, lung cancer and bronchitis, for no fault of theirs. It is seen that the incidence of these diseases is greater among women whose husbands are *heavy* smokers As such, every non-smoker has a fundamental right to safeguard himself against the danger of passive smoking. "Your smoking is injurious to my health and I have a right to stop you from smoking" could be the slogan against passive smoking. It is a great threat to the health of the individual, the family and the society. In fact one has to choose between health and smoking including passive smoking. *One cannot have both.*

Another matter of *grave concern* about smoking is the long time interval between the start of smoking habit and the manifestation of deadly diseases like cancer, chronic bronchitis and heart attack. People are generally not aware of the link between smoking and the misery they have to undergo years later and younger people often fall victim to this menacing habit under the wrong impression that they are *immune* to its disastrous effects, not realising that they are *heading* towards catastrophe. The prolonged incubation period of many tobacco-related diseases has prevented recognition of the size of the threat and the *grim* picture of chronic and life-threatening diseases.

1. What is "passive smoking"?
   A. Giving up the habit of smoking abruptly
   B. Exhaling smoke by a non-smoker
   C. Unintended intake of smoke exhaled by smokers
   D. Smoking cigarettes which are harmless in nature

2. The effects of passive smoking are more and more prominently observed among
   A. the children
   B. the smokers

C. the wives of smokers
D. the non-smokers

3. Which of the following is a heartening thing, according to the author?
A. People who have had a heart attack stop smoking
B. It takes only six months for any person to quit smoking
C. The smoker carries the risk of heart attack for six months
D. None of these

4. Which of the following statements is/are false in the context of the passage?
(*i*) Passive smokers are not free from risk of heart diseases
(*ii*) Intake of certain medicines helps recover pain and stiffness in legs caused by smoking
(*iii*) Younger people are immune to the disastrous effects if their regular smoking is under control
A. (*i*) and (*ii*) only B. (*ii*) and (*iii*) only
C. (*ii*) only D. (*iii*) only

5. Which of the following is not mentioned in the passage as a likely result of smoking by women during pregnancy?
A. Death of baby before birth
B. Death of baby after birth
C. Survival of baby with some abnormality
D. Abnormal delay in the childbirth

6. Which of the following is considered by the author as a matter of "grave concern"?
A. Inordinate delay in appearance of symptoms of hazards of smoking
B. Long time required for giving up the habit of smoking
C. Manifestation of deadly diseases like cancer, bronchitis, etc.
D. Lack of awareness of people regarding the hazards of smoking

7. The youth feel that they are immune to the hazardous effects of smoking because
A. these effects of smoking are not visible within a short time span
B. they do not realise that they are heading towards disaster
C. they feel a great thrill in acquiring the habit of smoking
D. the link between smoking and its disastrous effects cannot be established

8. Which factor prevents people from realising the extent of threat of smoking hazards?
A. Their lack of awareness of civic responsibilities
B. Their firm belief that they are not immune to these hazards
C. The less disastrous effects of tobacco-related diseases
D. None of these

9. The last sentence of the third para *"One cannot have both"* means
A. active smoking and passive smoking
B. smoking and risk of heart diseases
C. threat to the individual and also to the family
D. None of these

Directions (Qs. 10 to 12): *Choose the word which is most nearly the **SAME** in meaning as the word given in bold capitals as used in the passage.*

10. **HEADING**
A. crowning B. marching
C. adorning D. title

11. **HEAVY**
A. excessive B. bulky
C. large D. thick

12. **DROP**
A. roll B. escape
C. remove D. reduce

Directions (Qs. 13 to 15): *Choose the word which is most nearly the **OPPOSITE** in meaning of the word given in bold capitals as used in the passage.*

13. **GRIM**
A. dim B. dark
C. presentable D. pleasant

14. **IMMUNE**
A. free B. vulnerable
C. powerful D. weak

15. HEARTENING

A. cheerful　　B. miserable
C. frightening　　D. dangerous

PASSAGE-15

The happy man is the man who lives objectively, who has free affections and wide interests, who secures his happiness through these interests and affections and through the fact that they, in turn, make him an object of interest and affection to many others. To be the recipient of affection is a potent cause of happiness, but the man who demands affection is not the man upon whom it is *bestowed.* The man who receives affection is, speaking broadly, the man who gives it. But it is useless to attempt to give it as a calculation, in the way in which one might lend money at interest, for a calculated affection is not genuine and is not felt to be so by the recipient.

What then can a man do who is unhappy because he is encased in self? So long as he continues to think about the causes of his unhappiness, he continues to be self-centred and therefore does not get outside the vicious circle, if he is to get outside it, it must be genuine interests, not by simulated interests adopted merely as a medicine. Although this difficulty is real, there is nevertheless much that he can do if he has rightly diagnosed his trouble. If, for example, his trouble is due to a sense of sin, conscious or unconscious, he can first persuade his conscious mind that he has no reason to feel sinful and then proceed, to plant his rational conviction in his unconscious mind, concerning himself meanwhile with some more or less neutral activity. If he succeeds in *dispelling* the sense of sin, it is possible that genuine objective interests will arise spontaneously. If his trouble is self-pity, he can deal with it in the same manner after first persuading himself that there is nothing extraordinarily unfortunate in his circumstances.

If fear is his trouble, let him practise exercises designed to give courage. Courage has been recognised from time immemorial as an important virtue, and a great part of training of boys and young men has been devoted to producing a type of character capable of fearlessness in battle. But moral courage and intellectual courage have been much less studied, they also, however, have their technique. Admit to yourself everyday atleast one painful truth, you will find this quite useful. Teach yourself to feel that life still be worth living even if you were not, as of course you are, immeasurably superior to all your friends in virtue and in intelligence. Exercises of this sort prolonged through several years will at last enable you to admit facts *without flinching* and will, in so doing, free you from the empire of fear over a very large field.

1. Who according to the passage is the happy man?
A. who is encased in self
B. who has free affection and wide interests
C. who is free from worldly passions
D. who has externally centre passions

2. According to the passage, calculated affection
A. appears to be false and fabricated
B. makes other pen-on to love you
C. turns into permanent affection over a period of time
D. leads to self-pity

3. Which of the following virtues, according to the passage, has been recognised for long as an important virtue?
A. Patriotism　　B. Sacrifice
C. Courage　　D. Self-consciousness

4. Which of the following, according to the passage, has not been studied much?
A. Feeling of guilt and self-pity
B. The state of mind of an unhappy man
C. How to get absorbed in other interests
D. Moral and intellectual courage

5. If a man is suffering from a sense of sin
A. he should invite opinion of others
B. he should admit his sin at once
C. he should consciously realize that he has no reason to feel sinful
D. he should develop a fearless character

6. What happens to a man who demands affection?
A. His feelings are reciprocated by others
B. He tends to take a calculated risk
C. He becomes a victim of a viscious circle
D. None of these

7. What should a man do who is suffering from the feeling of self-pity?
A. He should control his passions and emotions
B. He should persuade himself that everything is alright in his circumstances
C. He should seek affection from others
D. He should develop a feeling of fearlessness

8. How to get out of the viscious circle mentioned in the passage?
A. By practicing skills of concentration
B. By inculcating the habits of self-absorption
C. Being true to others and one's internal circumstances
D. None of these

9. Which of the following statements is not *true* in the context of the passage?
A. Happy man has wide interests
B. Courage has been recognized as an important virtue
C. Unhappy man is encased in self
D. Issue of intellectual courage has been extensively studied

10. Which of the following words is ***SIMILAR*** in meaning of the word **'bestowed'** as used in the passage?
A. Conferred B. Accommodated
C. Trusted D. Withdrawn

11. Which of the following statements is *true* in the context of the passage?
A. All passions stem from unhappiness
B. The happy man lives in subjectively
C. Any virtue has a dark side also
D. One feels happy if one receives affection

12. Which of the following words is ***SIMILAR*** in meaning to the word **'flinching'** as used in the passage?
A. Wincing B. Convincing
C. Explaining D. Debating

13. What happens when you think about cause of your unhappiness?
A. You try to introspect and look critically at yourself
B. You realize that the life can be lived in different ways
C. You try to practice exercise designed to give courage
D. You remain a self-centred person

14. What according to the passage is the real cause of happiness?
A. Material rewards and incentives received
B. Critical analysis of the happy state of mind
C. Affection received from others
D. Calculated risks taken

15. Which of the following words is ***OPPOSITE*** in meaning of the word **'dispelling'** as used in the passage?
A. Giving B. Accumulating
C. Projecting D. Scattering

PASSAGE-16

Education, particularly higher education is the obvious but crucially important instrument for nation building. As Confucious has said:

"If you are thinking of one year, plant rice. If you are thinking of a decade, plant trees. If you are thinking of a century, educate the people."

When we set about the task of higher education, we should be absolutely clear in our perception of the goals of education in the specific context of our nation's development. No *doubt*, one of the important aims of education would be to create the required range and nature of trained manpower assessed to be needed by different sectors of national growth. The entire educational apparatus must be geared progressively to fulfill the requirements of different phases of our growth in every sector—primary, secondary and *tertiary.* The aim must be to ensure that our country does not experience either *paucity,* or a *surfeit* of trained manpower in any specific segment of our economy. The requirements of our country, as a free, democratic, secular, socialist, nation, *aspiring* for rapid development, *entail* a specific recipe for our educational institutions.

Today's educational institutions must therefore be developed accordingly and must regulate themselves to give the country the precise nature and quantum of trained manpower as projected by the requirements of our planned economy.

1. The author has quoted thoughts of Confucious to stress
A. importance of planting trees for human beings
B. the worthless efforts in planting rice
C. the benefits of investing in education
D. the need for assessing manpower requirement

2. Which statement cannot be made on the basis of the passage?
A. Higher education should keep in view the requirements of national economy
B. Higher education has not been employed for nation building
C. All levels of education have a role to play in nation's growth
D. In our country we need to have a specially planned educational system

3. The writer believes that
A. there are no problems related to higher education
B. investment in education is of long-range
C. higher education should be used to assess manpower needs
D. aims of higher education in India are absolutely clear

4. The author's expectations from higher education, are essentially
A. unrealistic B. confusing
C. critical D. vague

5. The writer indicates that
A. higher education did not play any role in national growth
B. primary education did not play any role in national growth
C. our nation experiences paucity of trained manpower in many sectors
D. today's higher education has no precise goals to achieve

6. Author has used the word 'apparatus' to indicate the
A. scientific nature of education
B. complicated organization demanded by education
C. readily visible benefits of education
D. entire equipment of education to perform particular function

7. Which of the following has not been conveyed by the passage?
A. Education at any level can contribute in nation building
B. Manpower needs in many areas can be fulfilled through higher education
C. Rapid development of our nation is possible through higher education
D. Present higher education does not ensure surfeit of trained manpower

8. This passage is likely to be addressed to
A. politicians only
B. scientists only
C. students only
D. cannot be said

9. Choose a suitable title to the passage:
A. Manpower Planning in India
B. Importance of Higher Education
C. Demands of Higher Education
D. Role of Higher Education in India

Directions (Qs.10 to 12): *Choose the word which is most nearly the **SAME** in meaning as the word given in bold capitals as used in the passage.*

10. DOUBT
A. suspicion B. certain
C. definite D. sure

11. TERTIARY
A. last B. important
C. third D. terminal

12. ASPIRING
A. inquiring B. awaiting
C. involving D. striving

Directions (Qs.13 to 15): *Choose the word which is most **OPPOSITE** in meaning as the word given in bold capitals as used in the passage.*

13. PAUCITY
A. moderate
B. enormity
C. mediocrity
D. littleness

14. SURFEIT
A. abundance
B. redundancy
C. repletion
D. lack

15. ENTAIL
A. entitled
B. ensure
C. dismiss
D. retain

PASSAGE-17

Globalisation, liberalisation and free-market are some of the most significant modern trends in economy. Most economists in our country seem *captivated* by the spell of the free-market. Consequently, nothing seems good or normal that does not accord with the requirements of the free market. A price that is determined by the seller or, for that matter, established by anyone other than the aggregate of consumers seems *pernicious.* Accordingly, it requires a major act of will to think of price-fixing as both normal in all industrialised societies because the industrial system itself provides, as an effortless consequence of its own development, the price-fixing that it requires. Modern industrial planning requires and rewards great size. Hence, a comparatively small number of large firms will be competing for the same group of consumers. That each large firm will act with consideration of its own needs and thus avoid selling its products for more than its competitors charge is commonly recognised by *advocates* of free-market economic theories. But each large firm will also act with full consideration of the needs that it has in common with the other large firms competing for the same customers. Each large firm will thus avoid significant price-cutting, because price-cutting will be prejudicial to the common interest in a *stable* demand for products. Most economists do not see price-fixing when it occurs because they expect it to be brought about by a number of *explicit* agreements among large firms; it is not.

Moreover, those economists who argue that allowing the free-market to operate without interference is the most efficient method of establishing, prices have not considered the economics of non-socialist countries. Most of these economics employ intentional price-fixing by cartel and informal price-fixing by agreements covering the members of an industry are common place. Were there something peculiarly efficient about the free-market and inefficient about price-fixing, the countries that have avoided the first and used the second would have suffered drastically in their economic development. There is no indication that they have.

Socialist industry also works within a framework of controlled prices. In the early 1970's the Soviet Union began to give firms and industries some flexibility in adjusting prices that a more informal evolution has accorded the capitalist system. Economists in the USA have hailed the change as a return to the free-market. But the then Soviet firms were not in favour of the prices established by a free-market over which they exercised little influence; rather, Soviet firms acquired some power to fix prices.

1. Considering the literal meaning and connotations of the words used in the passage, the author's attitude towards "most economists" can best be described as
A. derogatory and antagonistic
B. impartial and unbiased
C. spiteful and envious
D. critical and condescending

2. The author's primary objective of writing the passage seems to
A. belie the popular belief that the free-market helps enhance development of industrial societies
B. advocate that price-fixing is unavoidable and it is beneficial to the economy of any industrialised society
C. explain the methodology of fixing price to stabilise free-market
D. prove that price-fixing and free-market are compatible and mutually beneficial to industrialised societies

3. Which of the following statements (*i*), (*ii*) and/ or (*iii*) is/are *true* in the context of the information given in the passage? The information in the passage is helpful to
(*i*) know some of the ways in which prices can be fixed
(*ii*) identify the products for which price-fixing can be more beneficial
(*iii*) differentiate between the economics; of various countries
A. Only (*i*)
B. Only (*ii*)
C. Only (*iii*)
D. Only (*i*) and (*ii*)

4. The author feels that price fixed by seller seems pernicious because
A. people don't have faith in large firms
B. people don't want the Government to fix prices
C. most economists believe that consumers should determine prices
D. most economists believe that no one group should determine prices

5. What was the result of the then Soviet Union's change in economic policy in the 1970's?
A. They showed greater profits
B. They had less control over the free-market
C. They were able to adjust to techno-advancement
D. They became more responsive to free-market

6. According to the passage, price-fixing in non-socialistic countries is generally
A. intentional and widespread
B. illegitimate but beneficial
C. conservative and inflexible
D. legitimate and innovative

7. Which of the following statements about the socialist industry is/are false?
(*i*) It works under certain price restrictions
(*ii*) it has no authority to determine prices
(*iii*) It hails the strategy of price-fixing, as a major deviation
A. Only (*i*) is false
B. Only (*ii*) is false
C. Only (*iii*) is false
D. (*i*) and (*ii*) are false

8. The author's primary concern seems to
A. summarise conflicting viewpoints
B. make people aware of recent discoveries
C. criticise a point of view
D. predict the probable results of a practice

9. Which of the following statements is definitely *true* in the context of the passage? Price-fixing is
A. a profitable result of economic development
B. an inevitable result of the industrial system
C. the joint result of a number of carefully organised decisions
D. a phenomenon uncommon to industrialised societies

Directions (Qs. 10 to 12): *Choose the word which is most* ***OPPOSITE*** *in meaning of the word given in bold capitals as used in the passage.*

10. **OVERT**
A. unambiguous B. concealed
C. manifest D. inexplicable

11. **PERNICIOUS**
A. harmful B. deadly
C. promotive D. extravagant

12. **CAPTIVATED**
A. repelled B. seized
C. tamed D. enchanted

Directions (Qs. 13 to 15): *Choose the word which is most nearly the* ***SAME*** *in meaning as the word or group of words given in bold capitals as used in the passage.*

13. **EXPLICIT**
A. clean B. implied
C. obvious D. specifically

14. **ADVOCATES**
A. lawyers B. experts
C. recommends D. supporters

15. **STABLE**
A. uniform B. fluctuating
C. permanent D. restored

PASSAGE-18

Books are a great treasurehouse of knowledge. They are the living examples of man's *march* on the path to higher and higher civilisation. The great men who died long ago, live in their books. We feel their very personality and existence when we read their books. We feel as if they were conversing with us.

Books not only store civilization but also carry it forward. All coming generations get the light of knowledge from the books written by their ancestors and try to improve upon that knowledge. Civilization cannot make much *headway* in a country where there are not many *great* books. We get through books the latest knowledge in the fields of arts, science, commerce, etc. This knowledge is helpful to us and *enables* us to achieve success in the field of our choice.

Books are never failing friends. They never *desert* us, not even when all fair-weather friends have deserted us. They dispel the dark clouds of gloom from our minds and increase our happiness if we are already happy. Through the ages, the scriptures and other great books have provided immeasurable *solace* to the wounded and strife-torn humanity.

There may be books prescribed for some course or profession, but then there are books for general study. The books of literature—poetry, drama, novel, short stories, etc., are generally highly thrilling and inspiring if they are written by a good author. There may be tragic, comical or humorous books. The question is that of an individual's choice.

To be a lover of books, though not to be bookworm, is a sign of good luck. A voracious reader gets much *more pleasure* from reading books than a miser gets in hoarding money. The knowledge embedded in books is valueless; so is pleasure obtained from reading them. A good book absorbs the whole spirit of man; the reader's pleasure is indescribable.

1. Which of the following, according to the passage, is not true about books?
A. They are source of inspiration
B. They are source of knowledge
C. They are source of happiness
D. They are means of livelihood

2. How do the books help in progress of civilization?
A. Based on the earlier books new knowledge is obtained
B. The books provide solution to many problems
C. The books inspire the scientists
D. Not mentioned in the passage

3. How do the books make people more happy?
A. They help the reader to overcome the shadows of uncertainty
B. They help bring in joy by amusing the reader through their content
C. They help the reader to understand the darker side of life
D. Not mentioned in the passage

4. Which of the following is the author's view about the knowledge and pleasure derived from books?
(*i*) We get more of knowledge and less of pleasure
(*ii*) We get more of pleasure and less of knowledge
(*iii*) We get knowledge and pleasure in equal measure
A. only (*i*) B. only (*ii*)
C. either (*i*) or (*ii*) D. only (*iii*)

5. The high quality of books produced by a country indicates:
A. it has a high rate of literacy
B. it has a progressive civilization
C. it is not an industrialised nation
D. it has learned ancestors

6. Why are the books, according to the passage, called never-failing friends?
A. Books do not betray individuals
B. Books are inanimate

C. Books always give companionship to the reader
D. Books are available in the market anytime unlike others

7. How do the books help in bringing peace in the minds of people?
A. Books provide information about the past civilization
B. Books help people learn to take correct steps with the help of the recorded information
C. Books act as a window to the minds of the great men
D. Not mentioned in the passage

8. Which of the following has been described as a sign of good luck?
A. Being a miser
B. Having lot of money
C. Advancing the culture
D. A passion for books

Directions (Qs. 9 to 12): *Choose the word which is most nearly the **SAME** in meaning as the word given in bold capitals as used in the passage.*

9. **SOLACE**
A. peace B. tranquillity
C. calmness D. console

10. **ENABLES**
A. helps B. succeeds
C. promotes D. stops

11. **HEADWAY**
A. higher B. forge
C. movement D. improve

12. **MARCH**
A. move B. progress
C. pass D. register

Directions (Qs. 13 to 15): *Choose the word which is most **OPPOSITE** in meaning of the word given in bold capitals as used in the passage.*

13. **GREAT**
A. small B. thin
C. short D. ordinary

14. **PLEASURE**
A. displeasure B. pain
C. happiness D. hardship

15. **DESERT**
A. waterhole B. bitter
C. accompany D. propel

PASSAGE-19

The world dismisses curiosity by calling it idle or mere idle curiosity—even though curious persons are seldom idle. Parents do their best to extinguish curiosity in their children because it makes life difficult to be faced everyday with a string of unanswerable questions about what makes fire hot or why grass grows. Children whose curiosity survives parental discipline are invited to join our university. With the university, they go on asking their questions and trying to find the answers. In the eyes of a scholar, that is what a university is for. Some of the questions which the scholars ask, seem to the world to be scarcely worth asking, let alone answering. They asked questions too minute specialised for you and me to understand without years of explanation. If the world inquires of one of them why he wants to know the answer to a particular question he may say especially if he is a scientist, that the answer will in some obscure way make possible a new machine or weapon or gadget. He talks that way because he knows that the world understands and respects utility.

But to you who are now part of the university, he will say that he wants to know the answer simply because he does not know it, the way the mountain climber wants to climb a mountain, simply because it is there. Similarly a historian asked by an outsider why he studies history may come out with the argument that he has learnt to repeat on such occasions, something about knowledge of the past making it possible to understand the present and mould the future. But if you really want to know why a historian studies the past, the answer is much simpler, something happened and he would like to know what. All this does not mean that the answers which scholars find to their questions have no consequences. They may have enormous consequences but these seldom form the reason for asking the questions or pursuing the answers. It is true that scholars can be put to work answering questions for the sake of the consequences as thousands are working, now, for example, in search of a cure for cancer. But this is not the primary function of the scholars. For the consequences are usually subordinate to the satisfaction of curiosity.

1. According to the passage, the children make life difficult for their parents
   A. by their ceaseless curiosity
   B. by unceasing bombardment of questions
   C. by asking irrelevant questions
   D. by posing profound questions
2. The common people consider some of the questions that the scholars ask unimportant
   A. as they are too lazy and idle
   B. as they are too modest
   C. as it's beyond their comprehension
   D. as it is considered a waste of time
3. A historian really studies the past
   A. to comprehend the present and to reconstruct the future
   B. to explain the present and plan the future
   C. to understand the present and make fortune
   D. to understand the present and mould the future
4. Children whose curiosity survives parental discipline means
   A. children retaining their curiosity in spite of being discouraged by their parents
   B. children pursuing their mental curiosity
   C. children's curiosity subdued due to parents' intervention
   D. children being disciplined by their parents
5. According to the passage, parents do their best to discourage curiosity in their children
   A. because they have no time
   B. because they have no patience to answer them
   C. because they feel that their children ask stupid questions continuously
   D. because they are unable to answer all their questions

PASSAGE-20

I do not suggest that the cultural side of education should be ignored. On the contrary, I think, it is essential to the production of the sort of adult who best fits the modern world. But I think that what is important in cultural education should be conveyed, at any rate in the early stages, by methods far more attractive than those now usual. History and Geography should be taught at first by means of the cinema. When taught this way, they will give pleasure; attention will be spontaneous and therefore the impression will be less temporary. In spite of reforming movements, there is still among educators a feeling that what is enjoyed without effort cannot have much educational value. I would have children made aware of the manners and customs of tribes and nations utterly remote from their own. Education conducted on these lines would do more than many books *to cure provincialism in space and time* and to make children realise that actual human beings with actual feelings can be outwardly very different from the people among whom they live, but inwardly composed of the same human material. A Zulu would not appear strange, remote or savage but one like themselves.

1. The writer criticised traditional educators for not
   A. using cinema as a method of teaching
   B. making learning an enjoyable activity
   C. imparting information about remote tribes
   D. imparting information about various cultures
2. The writer thinks that the cultural side of education is needed to make man
   A. appreciate one's heritage
   B. appreciate other civilisations
   C. suitable for modern civilisation
   D. admire his environment

3. The expression *"to cure provincialism in space and time"* means to get rid of
   A. regional feelings
   B. obscure ideas
   C. narrow views
   D. selfish opinion

4. One of the goals of education should be to make children realise that
   A. human culture is diverse
   B. regional cultures should not be ignored.
   C. they must respect values of alien culture
   D. there is a unified system of human values underneath cultural diversity

5. The response of the learners to teaching through cinema is
   A. absorbing B. long-lasting
   C. enthusiastic D. superficial

ANSWERS

PASSAGE-1

1	2	3	4
A	B	A	A

PASSAGE-2

1	2	3	4	5
A	D	C	D	A

PASSAGE-3

1	2	3	4	5
D	A	D	A	A
6				
D				

PASSAGE-4

1	2	3	4	5
D	B	D	C	D
6	7	8	9	10
C	B	A	A	D

PASSAGE-5

1	2	3	4	5
A	D	A	A	A
6	7			
C	B			

PASSAGE-6

1	2	3	4	5
A	B	C	A	B
6	7	8		
B	B	C		

PASSAGE-7

1	2	3	4	5
D	C	B	C	A
6	7	8		
D	B	A		

PASSAGE-8

1	2	3	4	5
D	D	B	C	A
6	7	8	9	10
D	D	B	C	A

PASSAGE-9

1	2	3	4	5
A	C	C	A	D
6	7	8	9	10
D	B	A	B	D

PASSAGE-10

1	2	3	4	5
A	C	D	D	A
6	7	8	9	10
D	A	B	B	D

PASSAGE-11

1	2	3	4	5
B	C	D	A	A
6	7	8	9	10
D	C	B	D	D

PASSAGE-12

1	2	3	4	5
C	D	D	A	A
6	7	8	9	10
A	C	D	C	C
11	12	13	14	15
B	B	D	C	D

PASSAGE-13

1	2	3	4	5
B	D	A	A	B
6	7	8	9	10
A	A	C	C	A
11	12	13	14	15
B	B	B	B	A

PASSAGE-14

1	2	3	4	5
C	C	D	B	D
6	7	8	9	10
A	A	D	D	B
11	12	13	14	15
A	D	D	B	C

PASSAGE-15

1	2	3	4	5
B	A	C	D	C
6	7	8	9	10
D	B	D	D	A
11	12	13	14	15
D	D	D	C	B

PASSAGE-16

1	2	3	4	5
D	D	C	D	D
6	7	8	9	10
D	A	D	B	A
11	12	13	14	15
C	D	B	D	C

PASSAGE-17

1	2	3	4	5
B	B	A	C	D
6	7	8	9	10
A	C	A	B	B
11	12	13	14	15
C	A	C	D	C

PASSAGE-18

1	2	3	4	5
D	A	D	D	B
6	7	8	9	10
A	D	D	D	A
11	12	13	14	15
D	B	D	B	C

PASSAGE-19

1	2	3	4	5
A	C	D	A	D

PASSAGE-20

1	2	3	4	5
B	A	C	D	B

2 Sentence Correction

The most common errors in English are of spellings, grammar and usage of words. By regular practice, the errors can be easily spotted and minimised.

COMMON ERRORS WITH NOUNS AND NOUN-PHRASES

	Incorrect	Correct
1.	I have bought new *furnitures.*	I have bought new *furniture.*
2.	The wages of sin *are* death.	The wages of sin *is* death.
3.	She told these *news* to her mother.	She told her mother this *news.*
4.	He took *troubles* to do his work.	He took *trouble* (or pains) over his work.
5.	The *cattles* were grazing.	The *cattle* were grazing.
6.	He showered *many abuses* on me.	He showered *much abuse* on me.
7.	I spent the holidays with my *family members.*	I spent the holidays with my *family.*
8.	There is no *place* in this compartment.	There is no *room* in this compartment.
9.	Write this new *poetry* in your *copy.*	Write this new *poem* in your *note-book.*
10.	He took *insult* at this.	He took *offence* at this.
11.	Put your *sign* here.	Put your *signatures* here.
12.	She is my *cousin sister.*	She is my *cousin.*
13.	*Sunil's* my *neighbour's* house was burgled.	*Sunil* my *neighbour's* house was burgled.
14.	I lost a *ten-rupees* note.	I lost *a ten-rupee* note.
15.	Road closed for *repair.*	Road closed for *repairs.*
16.	His house is out of *repairs.*	His house is out of *repair.*
17.	What is the *reason* of an earthquake?	What is the *cause* of an earthquake?
18.	This building is made of *stones.*	This building is made of *stone.*
19.	I disapprove of *these kinds* of games.	I disapprove of *this kind* of games.
20.	Veena's and Sheela's father is ill.	Veena and Sheela's father is ill.
21.	His *son-in-laws* are doctors.	His *sons-in-law* are doctors.
22.	*Alms* is given to the *poor.*	*Alms* are given to the poor.

Incorrect	Correct
23. He always keeps his words.	He always keeps his *word.*
24. I carried the *luggages.*	I carried the *luggage.*
25. *Two-third* of the work is left.	*Two-thirds* of the work is left.

COMMON ERRORS WITH PRONOUNS

Incorrect	Correct
1. Both did not go.	Neither went.
2. We all did not go.	None of us went.
3. Each of these boys play.	Each of these boys plays.
4. Whoever does best he will get a prize.	Whoever does best will get a prize.
5. One should not waste his time.	A man should not waste his time.
6. I and she are sisters.	She and I are sisters.
7. He is wiser than me.	He is wiser than I.
8. Between you and I, Anil is not to be trusted.	Between you and me, Anil is not to be trusted.
9. Nobody was there but I.	Nobody was there but me.
10. Who is there ? It is me.	Who is there ? It is I.
11. Only he and me can use this card.	Only he and I can use this card.
12. Let you and I go now.	Let you and me go now.
13. Everyone got one's pay.	Everyone got his pay.
14. Everyone is frightened when they see a tiger.	Everyone is frightened when he sees a tiger.
15. These two friends are fond of one another.	These two friends are fond of each other.
16. I did not like him coming at that hour.	I did not like his coming at that hour.
17. Who do you think I met?	Whom do you think I met?
18. You should avail this opportunity.	You should avail yourself this opportunity.
19. When you have read these books, please return the same to me.	When you have read the books, please return them to me.
20. They that are humble need fear no fall.	Those that are humble need fear no fall.

COMMON ERRORS WITH ADJECTIVES

Incorrect	Correct
1. These all oranges are good.	All these oranges are good.
2. He held the book in the both hands.	He held the book in both hands.
3. Both men have not come.	Neither man has come.
4. That man should do some or other work.	That man should do some work or other.
5. He is elder than I.	He is older than I.

	Incorrect	Correct
6.	Shakespeare is greater than any other poets.	Shakespeare is greater than any other poet.
7.	He is a coward man.	He is a cowardly man.
8.	Many villagers cannot write his own name.	Many villagers cannot write their own name.
9.	Each of us loves our home.	Each of us loves his home.
10.	Much efforts bring their reward.	Much effort brings its reward.
11.	He found hundred rupees.	He found a hundred rupees.
12.	He had leave of four days.	He had four days leave.
13.	This is a worth seeing sight.	This is a sight worth seeing.
14.	He will spend his future life here.	He will spend the rest of his life here.
15.	There is a best teacher in that class.	There is a very good teacher in that class.
16.	Of the two plans this is the best.	Of the two plans this is the better.
17.	He is becoming strong every day.	He is becoming stronger every day.
18.	He is worst than I.	He is worse than I.
19.	Jaipur is hot than Delhi.	Jaipur is hotter than Delhi.
20.	In our library the number of books is less.	In our library the number of books is small.
21.	From the three he is more clever.	He is the cleverest of the three.
22.	India is the first peace-loving country in the world.	India is the foremost peace-loving country in the world.
23.	Verbal instruction will not do.	Oral instruction will not do.
24.	Her command over French is most excellent.	Her command over French is excellent.
25.	He has not some money with him.	He has not any money with him.
26.	I have visited Bombay many a times.	I have visited Bombay many a time.
27.	Death is more preferable to dishonour.	Death is preferable to dishonour.
28.	I gave him a few books I had.	I gave him the few books I had.
29.	If he wants farther help send him to me.	If he wants further help, send him to me.
30.	She is so cunning as a fox.	She is as cunning as a fox.

COMMON ERRORS WITH VERBS

	Incorrect	Correct
1.	He asked had we taken our luggage.	He asked if we had taken our luggage.
2.	She asked what are you doing.	She asked what we were doing.
3.	Rama asked to Anil why he is angry.	Rama asked Anil why he was angry.
4.	He does not care for his money.	He does not take care of his money.
5.	He does not care for his work.	He takes no care over his work.
6.	No one cared for him after his mother died.	No one took care of him after his mother died.
7.	He got angry before I said a word.	He got angry before I had said a word.

	Incorrect	Correct
8.	I met a man who was my tutor 20 years ago.	I met a man who had been my tutor twenty years ago.
9.	I had been for walking yesterday.	I went for a walk yesterday.
10.	If I shall do this I shall be wrong.	If I do this I shall be wrong.
11.	I have left trekking.	I have given up trekking.
12.	I came to know as to how he did this.	I learnt how he did this.
13.	I came to know why he was sad.	I found out why he was sad.
14.	He knows to swim.	He knows how to swim.
15.	The criminal's head was cut.	The criminal's head was cut off.
16.	I said to him to go.	I told him to go.
17.	I told the teacher to excuse me.	I asked the teacher to excuse me.
18.	He is troubling me.	He is giving me trouble.
19.	I have got a hurt on my leg.	I have hurt my leg.
20.	She gave a speech.	She made a speech.
21.	He has given his examination.	He has sat for his examination.
22.	He took out his shoes.	He took off his shoes.
23.	I have ordered for a new car.	I have ordered a new car.
24.	He would not hear me.	He would not listen to me.
25.	I struck a blow on his face.	I struck him in the face.
26.	He denied to come.	He refused to come.
27.	He lived there for a day.	He stayed there for a day.
28.	The book is not found.	The book is lost.
29.	Shut the light.	Turn off the light.
30.	I must revenge my brother.	I must avenge my brother.

COMMON ERRORS IN SUBJECT-VERB AGREEMENT

	Incorrect	Correct
1.	The owners of this factory *is* very rich.	The owners of this factory *are* very rich.
2.	The pleasures of nature that one can experience at Shimla *is* beyond description.	The pleasures of nature that one can experience at Shimla *are* beyond description.
3.	There *is* no street lights in our colony.	There *are* no street lights in our colony.
4.	He and I *am* entrusted with the job.	He and I *are* entrusted with the job.
5.	Rice and curry *are* his favourite dish.	Rice and curry *is* his favourite dish.
6.	The honour and glory of our country *are* at stake.	The honour and glory of our country *is* at stake.
7.	Time and tide *waits* for none.	Time and tide *wait* for none.
8.	All the passengers with the driver *was* killed.	All the passengers, with the driver, *were* killed.

	Incorrect	Correct
9.	The teacher, with her students, *were* going out.	The teacher, with her students, *was* going out.
10.	I as well as they *am* tired.	I as well as they *are* tired.
11.	Not only the soldiers but their captain also *were* captured.	Not only the soldiers but their captain also *was* captured.
12.	Neither you nor I *were* selected.	Neither you nor I *was* selected.
13.	Either of these two applicants *are* fit for the job but neither want to accept it.	Either of these two applicants *is* fit for the job but neither wants to accept it.
14.	One of these students are sure to stand first.	One of these students *is* sure to stand first.
15.	Everyone of these workers want a raise.	Everyone of these workers wants a raise.
16.	None of these letters has been answered so far.	None of these letters *have* been answered so far.
17.	None of the girls were present at the party.	None of the girls *was* present at the party.
18.	Many a battle were fought on Indian soil.	Many a battle *was* fought on Indian soil.
19.	A lot of work remain to be done.	A lot of work *remains* to be done.
20.	The majority of these girls likes music.	The majority of these girls *like* music.
21.	The number of admissions are encouraging.	The number of admissions *is* encouraging.
22.	A large number of boys was present.	A large number of boys *were* present.
23.	A variety of books was on display.	A variety of books *were* on display.
24.	Variety are the spice of life.	Variety *is* the spice of life.
25.	If my estimates are correct. I will need another hundred rupees.	If my estimate is correct, I will need another hundred rupees.
26.	Mathematics *are* my favourite subject.	Mathematics *is* my favourite subject.
27.	'Gulliver's Travels' *are* written by Swift.	'Gulliver's Travels' *is* written by Swift.
28.	Ten miles *are* a long distance to cover on foot.	Ten miles *is* a long distance to cover on foot.
29.	A new pair of shoes *are* to be purchased.	A new pair of shoes *is* to be purchased.
30.	The Committee *have* issued its report.	The Committee *has* issued its report.
31.	I, who am your friend, *has* always been on your side.	I, who am your friend, *have* always been on your side.
32.	I am the person who *have* always stood by you.	I am the person who *has* always stood by you.
33.	This is one of the best novels that *has* been published this year.	This is one of the best novels that *have* been published this year.
34.	Less than half the amount *have* been wasted.	Less than half the amount *has* been wasted.
35.	A lot of people *has* turned up for the show.	A lot of people *have* turned up for the show.
36.	Much of their honour *are* un-deserved.	Much of their honour *is* un-deserved.
37.	More than a decade *have* passed since this house was built.	More than a decade *has* passed since this house was built.
38.	Either she or he *are* mistaken.	Either she or he *is* mistaken.
39.	Plenty of information *are* available on the subject.	Plenty of information *is* available on the subject.
40.	Plenty of pamphlets *is* available on the subject.	Plenty of pamphlets *are* available on the subject.

COMMON ERRORS IN USE OF WILL, SHALL, WOULD, SHOULD, MAY, MIGHT, MUST

	Incorrect	Correct
1.	When I shall see him I shall tell him this.	When I *see* him, I shall tell him this.
2.	If I should do wrong, he would punish me.	If I *did* wrong, he would punish me.
3.	Until he will have confessed his fault, he will be kept in prison.	Until he *has* confessed his fault, he will be kept in prison.
4.	She will obey me.	She *shall* obey me.
5.	You would work hard.	You *should* work hard.
6.	You shall find him in the garden.	You *will* find him in the garden.
7.	He must have died of exposure, but we cannot be certain.	He *might* have died of exposure, but we cannot be certain.
8.	You might not show disrespect to your elders.	You *must* not show disrespect to your elders.
9.	You may take exercise in order to maintain good health.	You *must* take exercise in order to maintain good health.
10.	He must be a crook for all we know.	He *may* be a crook for all we know.

COMMON ERORRS IN THE USE OF ADVERBS

(Very, Much, Too, Enough, Quite, Hardly, Scarcely, Before, Ago, Since, Yet, Still, etc.)

	Incorrect	Correct
1.	He is very much angry.	He is *very* angry.
2.	She was very good enough to help me.	She was *good enough* to help me.
3.	She runs much fast.	She runs *very* fast.
4.	She runs very faster than Seema.	She runs *much* faster than Seema.
5.	It is bitter cold today.	It is *bitterly* cold today.
6.	He is a much learned man.	He is a very learned man.
7.	She is thinking very hardly.	She is thinking very hard.
8.	To tell in brief the film was boring.	*In short* the film was boring.
9.	He told the story in details.	He told the story *in detail.*
10.	I did it anyhow.	I *managed to do* it somehow.
11.	Aeroplanes reach Europe soon.	Aeroplanes reach Europe quickly.
12.	Before long there were dinosaurs on the earth.	*Long ago,* there were dinosaurs on the earth.
13.	This book is too interesting.	This book is *very* interesting.
14.	He lives miserly.	He lives in *a miserly* way.
15.	Just I had gone when she came.	I had just gone when she came.
16.	He sings good.	He sings *well.*
17.	He sings good than I.	He sings *better* than I.

	Incorrect	Correct
18.	Really speaking it is cold.	*As a matter of fact* it is cold.
19.	He is enough tall to reach the ceiling.	He is *tall enough* to reach the ceiling.
20.	He went directly to his college.	He went *direct* to his college.
21.	He is presently at Delhi	He is at Delhi *at present.*
22.	Last night she returned lately.	Last night she *returned late.*
23.	He was even blamed by his friends.	He was *blamed even* by his friends.
24.	I only employed him for a week.	I employed him for a week only.
25.	I met him four months before.	I met him four *months ago.*
26.	Anil seldom ever goes to school.	Anil *seldom goes* to school.
27.	I will wait here until you do not go.	I will wait here until *you go.*
28.	I never remember having met her before.	I *do not remember* having met her before.
29.	She has not been here too long to have many friends.	She has not *been here long* enough to have many friends.
30.	Hardly I have had any rest since one week.	Hardly have *I had* any rest for a week.
31.	Scarcely the water crossed the danger level, the warning signals were sounded.	Scarcely *had the* water *crossed the* danger level, when the warning signals were sounded.
32.	She is neat but fairly slow.	She is *neat* but rather slow.
33.	It is a rather good film.	It is a *fairly good* film.
34.	We yet have time to catch the bus.	We *still have* time to catch the bus.
35.	She has not still spent all her money.	She has *not yet* spent all her money.

COMMON ERRORS IN THE USE OF CONJUNCTIONS

	Incorrect	Correct
1.	As he is fat so he runs slowly.	As he is fat *he* runs slowly.
2.	If he is fat then he will run slowly.	If he is fat, he will run slowly.
3.	Though he is fat still he runs fast.	Though he is fat, *he runs* fast.
4.	*As* I pulled the trigger at the sametime he shook my arm.	As I pulled the trigger, he shook my arm.
5.	No sooner I had spoken than he left.	No sooner *had* I spoken than he left.
6.	Not only he will go, but also he will stay there.	Not only *will he* go, but he *will also* stay there.
7.	Neither he comes nor he writes.	Neither *does he* come nor *does he* write.
8.	Scarcely he entered the room than the telephone rang.	Scarcely *had* he entered the room *when the* telephone rang.
9.	Hardly she had left the house than it began to rain.	Hardly *had she* left the house *when* it began to rain.
10.	He is the fastest runner and he comes last.	He is the fastest runner *but* he comes last.
11.	She is as innocent as if she looks.	She is as innocent as she looks.

	Incorrect	Correct
12.	Until he does not try he must be punished.	He must be punished unless he tries.
13.	I want to know as to why you are late.	I want to know why you are late.
14.	I am fond of Chinese food as for example sweet and sour prawns.	I am fond of Chinese food, for example, sweet and sour prawns.
15.	He was angry therefore I ran away.	He was angry so I ran away.
16.	I was trying to work, at that time he was disturbing me.	While I was trying to work, he was disturbing me.
17.	Supposing if he is late, what will happen?	Supposing he is late (or if he is late) what will happen?
18.	He asked me that why I was late.	He asked me why I was late.
19.	Let us catch a taxi lest we should not get late.	Let us catch a taxi lest we should get late.
20.	She dresses herself like the teacher does.	She dresses herself as the teacher does.
21.	Wait while I come.	Wait *until* (or *till*) I come.
22.	Until, there is corruption in India, there can be little progress.	*As long* as there is corruption in India there can be little progress.
23.	I have never told a lie nor cheated anybody.	I have never told a lie *nor have I* cheated anybody.
24.	Both Mohan as well as Arun are responsible for this action.	Both Mohan *and* Arun are responsible for this action.
25.	Hindus and Muslims both are to blame for the riots.	*Both Hindus* and Muslims are to blame for the riots.
26.	I have bought paintings, books, records, and etc.	I have bought paintings, books *and records etc.*
27.	He as well as you is a fool.	He as well as you *are* a fool.
28.	He is so poor and he cannot save anything.	He is so *poor that* he cannot save anything.
29.	Such a book that you want is not available.	Such a book *as* you want is not available.
30.	Such was her condition as everyone was moved to pity.	Such was her condition that everyone was moved to pity.

COMMON ERRORS IN THE USE OF PREPOSITIONS

	Incorrect	Correct
1.	I will not listen him.	I will not listen *to* him.
2.	Copy this word by word.	Copy this word *for* word.
3.	He enquired from her where she lived.	He enquired *of* her where she lived.
4.	Sign here with ink.	Sign here *in* ink.
5.	Has she come in train or by foot?	Has she come *by* train or *on* foot?
6.	She said this at his face.	She said this *to* his face.
7.	Open the book on page one.	Open the book *at* page one.

Incorrect	Correct
8. I was invited for lunch.	I was *invited to* lunch.
9. I am ill since three months.	I have been *ill for* three months.
10. This paper is inferior than that.	This paper is inferior *to* that.
11. This resembles to that.	This *resembles* that.
12. My brother is superior than you in strength.	My brother is superior *to* you in strength.
13. He wrote me.	He wrote *to* me.
14. I shall explain them this.	I shall explain this *to* them.
15. Send this letter on my address.	Send this letter *to* my address.
16. He suggested me this.	He suggested this *to* me.
17. He goes *on his* work.	He goes *to his* work.
18. He *reached to* Nagpur.	He *reached* Nagpur.
19. He told *to me* to go.	He told *me* to go.
20. The term begins *from* July 1st.	The term begins *on* July 1st.
21. There are many advantages *from* this.	The advantages *of* this are many.
22. We waste much time *in* trifles.	We waste much time *on* (or *over)* trifles.
23. He sat *on* a tree.	He sat *in* a tree.
24. This is a comfortable house to *live*.	This is a comfortable house to *live in*.
25. This is the road to *go*.	This is the road to *go by*.
26. He married *with* an Indian lady.	He *married an Indian* lady.
27. He accompanied *with* his friend.	He *accompanied his* friend.
28. He went *for doing some* business.	He went away *on* business.
29. He went for *riding*.	He went *for a ride*.
30. I *pitied on* him.	I *pitied* him.
31. When this was searched it was found.	When this was searched *for* it was found.
32. I shall inform them *this*.	I shall inform them *of* this.
33. *Due to illness* I cannot go to school.	*Owing* to illness I cannot go to school.
34. He went *to the back side* of the house.	He went *behind* (or to the back of) the house.
35. I must go; there is no *help*.	I must go; there is no help *for it*.
36. I *met with your* friend there.	I *met your* friend there.
37. The First World War was fought *during* 1914-1918.	The First World War was fought *between* 1914-1918.
38. England grew prosperous *between* Queen Victoria's reign.	England grew prosperous *during* Queen Victoria's reign.
39. He asked a holiday.	He asked *for* a holiday.
40. I am obliged of you for this good turn.	I am obliged *to* you for this good turn.
41. There is no harm to try.	There is no harm *in trying*.

MISCELLANEOUS ERRORS

(Including Ambiguities and Indianisms)

	Incorrect	Correct
1.	Many *homes* are lying vacant.	Many *houses* are lying vacant.
2.	It is cool in the *shadow* of the tree.	It is cool in the *shade* of the tree.
3.	She *keeps* good health.	She *enjoys* good health.
4.	My leg is *paining*.	*I am feeling pain* in my leg.
5.	*See* this word in the dictionary.	*Look up* this word in the dictionary.
6.	The train will arrive *just now.*	The train will arrive *shortly.*
7.	They are *pulling* on well.	They are *getting* on well.
8.	The river has *over flown* its bank.	The river has *over flown* its banks.
9.	He was appointed *on* the post.	He was appointed *to* the post.
10.	Last but not *the least,* we have to discuss the problem of over population.	Last but not *least,* we have to discuss the problem of over population.
11.	*Cities* after *cities* fell.	*City* after *city* fell.
12.	What is the use Munir going there?	What is the use of Munir going there?
13.	He *did many mischief.*	He *made much mischief.*
14.	It is exact five *in* my watch.	It is exact five *by* my watch.
15.	I will dine with them on *next Sunday.*	I will dine with them *Sunday next.*
16.	Misfortunes when faced bravely and *manly* become less troublesome.	Misfortunes when faced bravely and *manfully* become less troublesome.
17.	I am *laid down* with fever.	I am *laid up* with fever.
18.	He is habituated to smoking.	He is *addicted* to smoking.
19.	*According to my opinion* he is right.	*In my opinion* (or according *to me)* he is right.
20.	Could you please *open* this knot?	Could you please *untie* this knot?

MULTIPLE CHOICE QUESTIONS

Directions: *Read each sentence to find out whether there is any grammatical error in it. The error, if any, will be in one part of the sentence marked A, B or C. The letter of that part is the answer. If there is no error, the answer is 'D'. (Ignore the errors of punctuation, if any).*

1. (A) He managed to make sense of the book/ (B) even though it was the first time/(C) he read anything on the subject./(D) No error.

2. (A) A large scale exchange of nuclear weapons/(B) will produce unprecedented amounts of radiation/(C) that can penetrate into the biological tissue./(D) No error.

3. (A) No sooner did I open the door/(B) when the rain, heavy and stormy, rushed in/(C) making us shiver from head to foot./(D) No error.

4. (A) After opening the door/(B) we entered into the room/(C) next to the kitchen/(D) No error.

5. (A) Locke's treatises on government toleration and education/(B) show a mind fully awake in /(C) the possibilities of social reconstruction. /(D) No error.

6. (A) There was very heavy rain last night,/(B) and the rivers have overflown their banks/(C) causing severe hardship to the people living by them./(D) No error.

7. (A) A leading textile manufacturer, one of the fastest growing in the industry,/(B) is looking for a marketing manager/(C) to look up the marketing network of the company./(D) No error.

8. (A) Last month we celebrated/(B) the wedding of our sister for whom/(C) we have been looking for a suitable alliance for three years./ (D) No error.

9. (A) The method suggested in the lecture/(B) enables a student to learn more quickly/(C) and to have remembered for a longer period of time./(D) No error.

10. (A) She is/(B) no longer popular as she has/ (C) a friends./(D) No error.

11. (A) He said that he/(B) will mind if/(C) I refused his offer./(D) No error.

12. (A) He ensured his bank manager/(B) that he would soon/(C) repay the loan./(D) No error.

13. (A) Both of you two/(C) can come with me/ (C) to the play tonight./(D) No error.

14. (A) Mr. Smith was accused for murder/(B) but the court found him not guilty/(C) and acquitted him./(D) No error.

15. (A) If I had known/(B) this yesterday/(C) I will have helped him./(D) No error.

16. (A) Not one of the hundreds/(B) of striking workers/(C) were allowed to go near the factory./(D) No error.

17. (A) The meeting adjourned abruptly/(B) by the Chairman after/(C) about three hours of deliberation./(D) No error.

18. (A) Having read a number of stories/(B) about space travel,/(C) his dream now is about to visit the moon./(D) No error.

19. (A) The news of the disturbance/(B) was broadcasted/(C) the same evening./(D) No error.

20. (A) Everyone visiting the house asked the young girl/(B) how could she kill the wolf/ (C) single handed and without a weapon./(D) No error.

21. (A) While walking slowly in the park/(B) on a quiet summer afternoon/(C) a mad dog suddenly attacked him from behind/(D) No error.

22. (A) Since the attachment of air-conditioned sleeping cars to all important trains,/(B) travelling became very pleasant,/(C) especially during the summer season./(D) No error.

23. (A) It is the newspaper/(B) that exposes us to the widest range/(C) of human experiences and behaviour./(D) No error.

24. (A) When the dentist came in/(B) my tooth was stopped aching/(C) out of fear that I might lose my tooth./(D) No error.

25. (A) Emphasis on equality of life ensures/(B) for the health and happiness/(C) of every individual./(D) No error.

26. (A) The students were/(B) awaiting for/(C) the arrival of the chief guest./(D) No error.

27. (A) You will come/(B) to my party tomorrow,/ (c) isn't it?/(D) No error.

28. (A) All the four sons/(B) of the old man/(C) quarrelled between themselves./(D) No error.

29. (A) I have never seen/(B) so large animal/(C) before./(D) No error.

30. (A) If she will be promoted/(B) she will get/ (C) a higher salary./(D) No error.

31. (A) He accused/(B) one of his friends/(C) of stealing his watch./(D) No error.

32. (A) One of my favourite actor/(B) is acting/ (C) in this play also./(D) No error.

33. (A) I have read/(B) too many books/(C) by R.K. Narayan./(D) No error.

34. (A) He says that/(B) his car does/(C) eight kilometres in a litre/(D) No error.

35. (A) On the busy Ring Road/(B) we witnessed a collusion/(C) between a truck and an auto./ (D) No error.

36. (A) I have/(B) an appointment/(C) on the 9th September on five o'clock/(D) No error.

37. (A) Jayesh is getting/(B) fatter because he/(C) does not take exercise at all/(D) No error.

38. (A) If you listen with/(B) the questions carefully/(C) you will be able to answer them easily/ (D) No error.

39. (A) Had you not/(B) reached in time/(C) he would have lost all our belongings./(D) No error.

40. (A) Neeraj said/(B) that he would rather fail than copying/(C) in the examination/(D) No error.

41. (A) He is generally/(B) more hungry/(C) than she is./(D) No error.

42. (A) She walked in/(B) the room where the murder/(C) had taken place./(D) No error.

43. (A) Do the roses in your garden smell/(B) more sweetly/(C) than those in ours?(D) No error.

44. (A) He told to the story in detail/(B) and the children listened/(C) to it with great interest./ (D) No error.

45. (A) Having received your letter/(B) this morning, we are writing/(C) to thank you for the same./(D) No error.

46. (A) I fail to understand/(B) why he replied in negative/(C) when the proposal was in his favour./(D) No error.

47. (A) Though he stoutly persisted in denying his involvement in the case,/(B) the facts made it very clear/(C) that he had hand in the cruel murder of his wife./(D) No error.

48. (A) Please try to understand/(B) that the dispute on this issue is between my brother and myself,/(C) and concerns nobody else./ (D) No error.

49. (A) Regretfully, profits earned by your company/(B) fell by 20 per cent last year/(C) despite higher sales./(D) No error.

50. (A) In the interim period, various student groups, in small numbers,/(B) met me and informed that the notice for strike/(C) was issued without proper consultation./(D) No error.

51. (A) A team of three Indians, two Canadians and three Japanese/(B) was successful in climbing the highest mountain peak on/(C) its third attempt./(D) No error.

52. (A) He enquired me/(B) why I had not seen him the previous day/(C) as I had promised to do./(D) No error.

53. (A) I am sure that all my monthly expenses/ (B) would exceed the income/(C) If I do not economic/(D) No error.

54. (A) He explained the matter/(B) at great length/(C) but I was not the wiser/(D) No error.

55. (A) Salim and Antony are such good friends/ (B) that one won't go to the pictures/(C) without his coming too./(D) No error.

56. (A) He loved/(B) none but/(C) his neighbour's daughter./(D) No error.

57. (A) It does not matter how you do it;/(B) what I want is that/(C) you should finish the work within a month./(D) No error.

58. (A) Most of the members at the meeting felt/ (B) that the group appointed for investigating the case/(C) were not competent to do the job efficiently./(D) No error.

59. (A) Samir, who is a close friend of mine,/(B) told me that he was smelling/(C) the rice from a distance of fifty yards while coming to my house./(D) No error.

60. (A) She hardly knew how to do that problem,/ (B) and so went to her teacher. and asked her,/ (C) "How this problem is to be solved?"/(D) No error

61. (A) The course provide/(B) not only theoretical inputs/(C) but also practical training/(D) No error.

62. (A) Since we are friends/(B) there should be no secret/(C) between you and I./(D) No error.

63. (A) Shanghai is/(B) bigger than any city/(C) of the world/(D) No error.

64. (A) The person which was/(B) recommended for the position/(C) did not fulfil the prescribed qualifications./(D) No error.

65. (A) It is time/(B) we should accept all our people as equals/(C) and as partners in the task of building a strong and united nation./(D) No error.

66. (A) Every motorist knows,/(B) road signs—whether symbols or colour codes—have an immediacy/(C) that neither the spoken nor the written word can match./(D) No error.

67. (A) I had hoped to have met him yesterday/(B) to discuss the matter with him/(C) but he was not in his house, and so I could not meet him./(D) No error.

68. (A) He speaks/(B) not only Tamil/(C) but Telugu as well./(D) No error.

69. (A) Troy was taken by Greeks;/(B) this formed the basis of a story/(C) which has become famous./(D) No error.

70. (A) Our conception of/(B) what should a science of mental life be/(C) has changed considerably since James' time./(D) No error.

71. (A) In these days of inflation/(B) a ten rupee's note will not buy you/(C) even an ordinary meal./(D) No error.

72. (A) The retiring principal asked his old pupils/(B) to take the interest in the school/(C) after he has retired./(D) No error.

73. (A) It is difficult/(B) for anyone/(C) to past time thus./(D) No error.

74. (A) When I get a cold/(B) it takes me weeks/(C) to shake it off./(D) No error.

75. (A) You must/(B) remember me/(C) to post this letter./(D) No error.

76. (A) I am thinking of/(B) to go to Agra/(C) for my cousin's marriage./(D) No error.

77. (A) Had I/(B) known it earlier/(C) I would contact you./(D) No error.

78. (A) He was sure/(B) that he should/(C) win the Prize./(D) No error.

79. (A) He is wiring/(B) for the/(C) last four hours./(D) No error.

80. (A) He was in such hurry/(B) that he didn't/(C) wait for me./(D) No error.

81. (A) Will you lend me/(B) little money/(C) to tide over this crisis./(D) No error.

82. (A)The President had hardly spoken/(B) a few words/(C) when the microphone stopped functioning./(D) No error.

83. (A) In an English paper/(B) examiners should give as much weightage to language/(C) as they give to contents./(D) No error.

84. (A) My father is going/(B) to the office/(C) five day week./(D) No error.

85. (A) The thief broke in the/(B) house at the/(C) dead of night./(D) No error.

86. (A) The long-awaited moment at last came,/(B) and we set out for the station,/(C) as merry a band of children as I have ever seen before or since./(D) No error.

87. (A) In a report issued by Indian Statistical Institute,/(B) the Iron and Steel Industry is investing more than any other/(C) Indian industry in fighting pollution./(D) No error.

88. (A) Block of Residential flats/(B) are coming up/(C) near our house./(D) No error.

89. (A) The test will not need/(B) more than one and half hour/(C) to finish./(D) No error.

90. (A) Will you be/(B) at Board meeting/(C) on next Wednesday?/(D) No error.

91. (A) If you will work hard,/(B) you will get goods grades/(C) in examinations./(D) No error.

92. (A) Do you know/(B) to play/(C) the guitar?/(D) No error.

93. (A) At the station,/(B) I'll hire a coolie/(C) to carry my baggages/(D) No error.

94. (A) The geography teacher/(B) told the class that/(C) the earth was round./(D) No error.

95. (A) There is still/(B) little tea/(C) left in the cup./(D) No error.

96. (A) He has not been attending/(B) English classes/(C) since one month./(D) No error.

97. (A) He persisted/(B) to do it/(C) in spite of my advice/(D) No error.

98. (A) You can get/(B) all the information that you want/(C) in this book./(D) No error.

99. (A) I am hearing/(B) a lot about/(C) the problem of AIDS these days./(D) No error.

100. (A) It is easy to see that/(B) a lawyer's demeanour in court/(C) may be prejudicial against the interests of his client./(D) No error.

ANSWERS

1	2	3	4	5	6	7	8	9	10
C	C	B	B	B	B	C	C	C	C
11	**12**	**13**	**14**	**15**	**16**	**17**	**18**	**19**	**20**
B	A	A	A	C	C	A	C	B	B
21	**22**	**23**	**24**	**25**	**26**	**27**	**28**	**29**	**30**
A	B	D	B	B	B	C	C	B	A
31	**32**	**33**	**34**	**35**	**36**	**37**	**38**	**39**	**40**
D	A	B	C	B	C	B	A	C	B
41	**42**	**43**	**44**	**45**	**46**	**47**	**48**	**49**	**50**
D	A	B	D	D	A	C	B	A	C
51	**52**	**53**	**54**	**55**	**56**	**57**	**58**	**59**	**60**
D	B	C	B	C	D	B	C	D	A
61	**62**	**63**	**64**	**65**	**66**	**67**	**68**	**69**	**70**
A	C	B	A	B	D	A	C	A	B
71	**72**	**73**	**74**	**75**	**76**	**77**	**78**	**79**	**80**
B	B	C	A	B	B	C	B	A	A
81	**82**	**83**	**84**	**85**	**86**	**87**	**88**	**89**	**90**
B	D	D	C	A	C	C	A	B	C
91	**92**	**93**	**94**	**95**	**96**	**97**	**98**	**99**	**100**
C	B	C	D	B	C	B	B	A	D

3 Sentence Improvement

One may use the same words in many ways but the best way is only one that makes the perfect usage of the words and conveys the proper meaning of the expression. Try it yourself in the following questions.

MULTIPLE CHOICE QUESTIONS

Directions: *In these questions, a part of the sentence is bold. Below are given alternatives to the bold part at A, B and C which may improve the sentence. Choose the correct alternative. In case no improvement is needed, your answer is D.*

1. For most people who exercise **at the** morning, there is no getting around the question: Eat and run? Or run and eat later?
A. in the B. in
C. at the time of D. No Improvement

2. Are ad agencies even attempting to peer into the keyhole of this indulgence sanctum to garner consumer insights **ahead of** the curve?
A. above B. over
C. within D. No Improvement

3. Too many people rush into the world of credit and don't stop to think about how **their actions could affect their** credit score and ability to qualify for credit in the future.
A. their actions may affect their
B. their actions might affect their
C. their actions will affect their
D. No Improvement

4. According to the report, **number of deal with** vaccines were energized by concerns around avian flu, SARS, and biodefense products, while looming patent expirations led to more deals in generics.
A. number of deals in
B. number of deal in
C. number of deals with
D. No Improvement

5. This is how the Bombay High Court responded to the state government's purported **moral stand which** dance bars were causing grave harm to society.
A. moral stand in
B. moral stand at
C. moral stand that
D. No Improvement

6. If you have a high credit limit, use **at least a** third of it.
A. atleast a B. at last a
C. utmost a D. No Improvement

7. Fitness experts will say that **first eating provides** fuel for a proper workout.
A. eating in the beginning provides
B. first eat provides
C. eating first provides
D. No Improvement

8. One study that examined the claim directly in 1995 found that a group of people did **burned**

much calories from fat on days when they exercised on an empty stomach than on days when they had a small breakfast first.

A. burn more calories from fat on days
B. burn more calorie from fat on days
C. burnt more calories from fat on days
D. No Improvement

9. Carefree children spent their afternoons **to run about barefoot**, their clothes dusty, and telltale twigs of the neighbour's mango tree in their hair.

A. running barefoot in the sun
B. run about barefoot in the sun
C. running about barefoot in the sun
D. No Improvement

10. A year ago, a 13-year-old girl attempted suicide because her mother **refuses to pay his** mobile bills.

A. refuses to pay her B. refused to pay her
C. refused to pay his D. No Improvement

11. Discreet salience **is extremely important** to create that 'irresistible-yet-unattainable' image for brands that want to take India seriously

A. was extremely important
B. is mainly important
C. was important extremely
D. No Improvement

12. This, over a designer outfit that he wanted for a friend's party and **that his sensitive** parents refused him.

A. which his sensitive
B. which his insensitive
C. that his insensitive
D. No Improvement

13. Goa was full of non-Goa property hunters **rushing about buying up the place** like tomorrow was an expired lease.

A. rushing in buying up the place
B. rushed about buying up the place
C. rushing about to buy up the place
D. No Improvement

14. Property hunting is a **tired and hungry** making business.

A. is a tiresome and hungry
B. is a tiring and hungry
C. is a tiring and waste
D. No Improvement

15. Cultural differences aside, **till luxury need speaks** in a manner that befits.

A. luxury still needs to speak
B. luxury still need to speak
C. luxury till need to speak
D. No Improvement

16. Indian food—the culinary avatar of the subcontinent's social history presented on a platter—**is without doubt the best food** in the world.

A. is undoubtly the greatest food
B. is without doubt greatest food
C. is best food without doubt
D. No Improvement

17. It must retain the language of poetry. **It needed to create** stories, and not statements.

A. It needed creating B. It needs creating
C. It needs to create D. No Improvement

18. In 2005, Asia-Pacific has become the first region **to reach aggregate profiting** in biotech.

A. to reach aggregated profitability
B. to reach aggregate profitability
C. to reach aggregate of profit
D. No Improvement

19. India is deviating to embrace the West. If Western luxury brands deviate a little, **albeit selectively**, they will find rich Indian arms open far and wide.

A. though selectively
B. however selectively
C. albeit selectedly
D. No Improvement

20. China and India continued to attract attention and deals, motivated by the desire to increase access to these **largest and growing** drug markets and by the need to lower the costs of drug development.

A. larger and growing B. large and growing
C. larger and grown D. No Improvement

21. Luxury brands are **still above of the** clover curve here, with their elite (small) audiences.
A. still ahead of the B. still in the
C. still far of the D. No Improvement

22. Agencies **hence needed to be** sure of returns before investing, say ad men.
A. hence needs to be B. so needs to be
C. hence need to be D. No Improvement

23. India is still a nascent market and that's the spirit everyone's **looking at it**.
A. looking for it B. looking in it
C. looking with it D. No Improvement

24. Questioning the state's move to allow women to serve liquor but not dance in bars **of the ground that** dancing aroused physical lust.
A. on the grounds that
B. of the grounds that
C. over the grounds that
D. No Improvement

25. For England the positives from their crushing series lose come in the shape of James Anderson and Kevin Pietersen, **both of which** have made significant strides up the rankings.
A. both of which B. both of whom
C. both of who D. No Improvement

26. International campaigns can work well for luxury here, **but context cannot be** ignored.
A. so context cannot be
B. but context cannot
C. but context couldn't
D. No Improvement

27. For one, the Indian luxury context, **while evolved rapidly**, still has its own meaning, and its own implications.
A. while evolved rapid
B. which evolving rapidly
C. while evolving rapidly
D. No Improvement

28. But too much of availability can compromise a luxury brand or **made it lose** its lustre.
A. make her lose B. make him lose
C. make it lose D. No Improvement

29. Still, it's under-the-upper **layers themselves who** are aspiring for slivers of luxury.
A. layers themselves which
B. layer itself who
C. layers themself which
D. No Improvement

30. It is like saying Hindi movies, with skimpily dressed dancers, would **effect public** order.
A. effect your B. affect public
C. affected public D. No Improvement

31. The court held that a few women being involved in prostitution was no **justice to deny other** bar girls the right to livelihood.
A. justification to declare other
B. justification to deny other
C. justice to let other
D. No Improvement

32. All-rounder Irfan Pathan has also made some progress **over the** player rankings.
A. above the B. at the
C. up the D. No Improvement

33. Former PM V.P. Singh on Sunday **joined hands** with suspended SP Lok Sabha member Raj Babbar to float a new political outfit.
A. folded hands
B. walked hand in hand
C. shaked hands
D. No Improvement

34. Pakistan's former PMs Benazir Bhutto and Nawaz Sharif will meet in London on Monday **to ask** a strategy to return home from exile.
A. to chalk out B. to negotiate
C. to create D. No Improvement

35. It's a family potboiler, medical thriller and political drama **all in one**–except that it's all too real and all too grim.
A. all 3 in one
B. all coupled into one
C. all rolled into one
D. No Improvement

36. India's efforts to get international support for its civil nuclear energy programme got **a go ahead on** Sunday as Germany indicated it would not come in the way of the India-US nuclear deal.
A. a life in B. a boost on
C. a boost at D. No Improvement

37. Is it time for old bungalows to **bite the dust**?
A. go down B. get down
C. come down D. No Improvement

38. The bungalows was an outward manifestation of a certain **way in life,** and with that era gone.
A. way for life B. way of life
C. way at life D. No Improvement

39. The builder Mittals will reportedly **raise their money**-raking high-rise behind it.
A. highten their money
B. rise their money
C. raise there money
D. No Improvement

40. The impatient present has usually demolished **more of the** past before we wake up to the irretrievable loss.
A. much of B. much of their
C. much of the D. No Improvement

41. Preservation is a romantic notion; demolition **quiet** more practical reasons.
A. has many, B. had many,
C. have many, D. No Improvement

42. You must get back to your **charming self** and impress the audience with your social skills.
A. own self B. main self
C. own uniqueness D. No Improvement

43. Stay focused on your goals and don't **get disturbed by** non-materialistic possessions.
A. get involved by B. get betrayed by
C. get distracted by D. No Improvement

44. You may appear more optimistic than your detractors **may want it to be.**
A. want you to be
B. wish yourself to be
C. seek you be
D. No Improvement

45. There are a number of mineral springs in the Czech territory, which **has been used** for medicinal purposes since the early 15th century.
A. have been used
B. had been used
C. has being used
D. No Improvement

46. The picturesque mountains **offers** excellent bungee jumping spots.
A. shows B. provides
C. offer D. No Improvement

47. Begin your **meal with** traditional faves like potato soup, beef soup with liver dumplings or dill soup made from sour milk.
A. meals with B. meal in
C. meals of D. No Improvement

48. You can also **go to the** National Museum building and the famous Prague State Opera.
A. went to B. visit the
C. saw D. No Improvement

49. If they close the Gulf for a **length of time** to shipping, then certainly we could look at $150, probably higher.
A. larger amount of time
B. larger duration of time
C. larger amount of hours
D. No Improvement

50. **More of them** are owned by the state and even the privately-owned ones are open to the public.
A. Most of which B. Most of them
C. Most of all D. No Improvement

51. Constructed in the ninth century by the Prince Booivoj, the castle has transformed **oneself** from a wooden fortress surrounded by earthen bulwarks to the imposing form it has today.
A. himself B. herself
C. itself D. No Improvement

52. Apart from frequent art exhibitions, **their are also** permanent collections devoted to archaeology, anthropology, mineralogy, natural history and numismatics.
A. there is also B. there are also
C. their are also D. No Improvement

53. You can visit the Czech Museum of Fine Arts, **at a** permanent exhibition on Czech Kubism.
A. with a B. for a
C. in a D. No Improvement

54. Tensions **above** Iran come at a time of strong demand for energy.
A. under B. inside
C. over D. No Improvement

55. Because its shores line the narrow Straits of Hormuz, Iran **could quickly hit** both military and commercial shipping.
A. will quickly hit
B. shall quickly hit
C. will be quick hitting
D. No Improvement

56. US **can launch** strikes at uranium enrichment facilities in Iran.
A. might launch B. could launch
C. might launched D. No Improvement

57. Trust your instincts and **see** all hurdles.
A. get freedom from B. visualize
C. overcome D. No Improvement

58. You may lose the war, but with calm, poise and serenity you will win the big battle **that may be following**.
A. that may follows
B. that may follow
C. that might be following
D. No Improvement

59. **There is times** when your best efforts could prove fruitless because of wrong timing.
A. There are time B. There are times
C. There is time D. No Improvement

60. You'll be a little more romantic and may want to **go away** from the hustle-bustle around you.
A. get away B. have get away
C. got away D. No Improvement

61. All you want are a few more hugs of affection, which will not be too difficult **to come**.
A. to come by B. to came
C. to come in D. No Improvement

62. People **around you** could get too sensitive, but try to respect them for that perhaps it will help you during pay-back time.
A. by you B. about you
C. near you D. No Improvement

63. Success **is a made up of** good fortune and hard work.
A. is B. is a
C. is a blend of D. No Improvement

64. The flower style and placement can completely change **the feel of** a room.
A. the feeling of B. the feeling for
C. an feel of D. No Improvement

65. The material (of artificial flower), style of arrangement and location should **complementing each other.**
A. complement one another
B. complement each other
C. complement other
D. No Improvement

66. Houses with **more of** carvings in their interiors, can go for gerberas.
A. many B. lots of
C. lot of D. No Improvement

67. For an artistic look, have lots of cherry blossoms **put together** in a vase.
A. together B. jumbled together
C. made together D. No Improvement

68. If you **have heavy carving** furniture, go for an arrangement in a container with an antique touch.
A. have heavy carved B. had heavy carved
C. had heavy carving D. No Improvement

69. For a traditional party, such as Diwali or Holi, traditional marigold and jasmine are **a best option**.
A. the better option B. the best option
C. the best options D. No Improvement

70. Don't expose to direct sun or keep them **under fan and near an AC**.
A. under fan or near an AC
B. beside fan or near an AC
C. under fan or under an AC
D. No Improvement

71. Use of disprin and aspirin **help the** buds to bloom faster.
A. helped the B. helps in the
C. helps the D. No Improvement

72. If you prefer the lived-in comfy look, clear glass flower vases **make for** cheerful addition.
A. makes for B. make for a
C. makes for a D. No Improvement

73. Cut the stem of the flower every other day. This helps it to consume water and last for a **longer duration of time.**
A. longer span of time
B. longer period of time
C. larger period of time
D. No Improvement

74. The ability to trust others, and understand the needs of others, is **directly relates** to touching.
A. directly relating B. directly related
C. direct relation D. No Improvement

75. Touch and positive attitudes **has been proven** to go together.
A. have been proven B. have been proved
C. have been prove D. No Improvement

76. New Delhi **was watching the** political thriller unfold in the hilly kingdom with apparent nervousness.
A. was watching the B. is watching the
C. was watching a D. No Improvement

77. Anti-monarch agitators cheer **on top of a** bus in Kathmandu on Tuesday.
A. above a B. at the top of a
C. above the D. No Improvement

78. Indian Railway Catering and Tourism Corporation an autonomous body under the railways ministry, **has drawing up** a plan to open 2000 such stalls which would serve standard food.
A. has drawed up B. have drawn up
C. has drawn up D. No Improvement

79. The stalls are **to come** up at ''A'' and ''B'' grade station.
A. likely to be coming
B. likely to come
C. like to come
D. No Improvement

80. To avoid controversies, IRCTC also **plans to continue** samosa-chai stalls which currently dot stations.
A. plan to continue B. plan's to continue
C. plan to continuing D. No Improvement

81. Airbus has been quietly pitching the standing-room only option to Asian carriers, though **none had agreed** to it yet.
A. none have been agreed
B. none have being agreed
C. none have agreed
D. No Improvement

82. High fuel costs, for example, are **making it difficult for** carriers to turn a profit.
A. making difficult for
B. making difficulty for
C. making it as difficult as
D. No Improvement

83. The new seat technology alone, **when used in** add more places for passengers, can add millions in additional annual revenue.
A. used to B. when used to
C. when using to D. No Improvement

84. While you may never win the lottery, **able to** get cash for paper assets is a sure bet.
A. being able to B. getting able to
C. in being able to D. No Improvement

85. At Chattarpur Enclave, **the first thing** that hits you is a massive under construction illegal building where work has been stopped.
A. a first thing
B. one of the first thing
C. the first best thing
D. No Improvement

86. Multi-storeyed housing units would be constructed through public private partnership **at the land** occupied by slum-dwellers.
A. in the land B. on the land
C. over the land D. No Improvement

87. In view of the **few availability of** land, the ministry has decided to take up rehabilitation work on a self-sustaining basis.
A. little availability of
B. some availability of

C. scarce availability of
D. No Improvement

88. A new notification by the urban development ministry now **makes land available to school** only through auction.
A. makes land available to schools
B. making land available to schools
C. making land available to school
D. No Improvement

89. One of the first **lesson that a** young MNC manager learns is that "God is in the details."
A. lesson which a
B. lessons that a
C. lessons which a
D. No Improvement

90. Likewise, investors are more interested in crunching numbers than **they are for** fielding calls from potential sellers.
A. they are in
B. they are at
C. they are in favour of
D. No Improvement

91. With each passing day your memories **grow deep**, your loving nature will always be cherished.
A. grew deep B. grew deeper
C. grow deeper D. No Improvement

92. It may not beat winning the lottery, **but money** you can take to the bank.
A. but it's money
B. so it's money
C. but it's money that
D. No Improvement

93. Wisdom, Vision, Ideals & Thought **continue to guide** us every moment in our Journey ahead.
A. continue to guiding
B. continuously guide
C. continuing at guiding
D. No Improvement

94. Delhi government **are now blaming** DDA for stalling big infrastructure projects in the Capital.
A. is now putting blaming on
B. is now blaming
C. is now blaming the
D. No Improvement

95. Be happy with the status quo and **preserve it by** conciliating others.
A. preserve that by B. it is preserved
C. preserving it by D. No Improvement

96. Have graceful movements, liquid eyes, and a gliding walk, **although** overweight.
A. though B. even if
C. even D. No Improvement

97. But people resent that most of the poverty funds **are lost for** corruption and administrative expenses.
A. are lost in B. are lost at
C. is lost in D. No Improvement

98. It is **very difficult** to store and save almost everything—money, possessions, energy words food, fat.
A. most difficult
B. very much difficult
C. highly difficult
D. No Improvement

99. Now Pause Live TV & watch **with your convenience** and also Record your favorite TV programme.
A. at your convenient
B. your convenience
C. at your convenience
D. No Improvement

100. To avoid **last hour rushing**, please immediately deposit VAT and file your Monthly and Quarterly DVAT return.
A. last rush
B. last minute rush
C. last minute rushing
D. No Improvement

ANSWERS

1	2	3	4	5	6	7	8	9	10
A	D	C	A	C	D	C	A	C	C
11	**12**	**13**	**14**	**15**	**16**	**17**	**18**	**19**	**20**
D	C	D	B	A	D	C	C	D	B
21	**22**	**23**	**24**	**25**	**26**	**27**	**28**	**29**	**30**
C	C	D	A	C	D	C	C	C	C
31	**32**	**33**	**34**	**35**	**36**	**37**	**38**	**39**	**40**
B	C	C	A	C	B	D	B	D	C
41	**42**	**43**	**44**	**45**	**46**	**47**	**48**	**49**	**50**
A	D	C	A	D	C	A	B	D	B
51	**52**	**53**	**54**	**55**	**56**	**57**	**58**	**59**	**60**
C	B	A	C	D	A	C	B	B	A
61	**62**	**63**	**64**	**65**	**66**	**67**	**68**	**69**	**70**
A	C	C	D	B	B	D	A	B	A
71	**72**	**73**	**74**	**75**	**76**	**77**	**78**	**79**	**80**
C	D	B	B	A	A	D	C	B	C
81	**82**	**83**	**84**	**85**	**86**	**87**	**88**	**89**	**90**
C	D	B	A	D	B	C	A	B	A
91	**92**	**93**	**94**	**95**	**96**	**97**	**98**	**99**	**100**
C	A	A	B	D	B	A	D	C	B

4 Spelling Errors

The most common errors in English are of spellings of words. Even the most learned men are sometimes confused about the correct spellings of some words. One must keep and use a dictionary religiously. Never ignore and let pass a new word casually without checking its spelling and meaning.
A number of questions to test your knowledge of spellings are compiled here. Try to solve as many as you can.

MULTIPLE CHOICE QUESTIONS

Directions: *Find the correctly spelt words.*

1. A. Abandon B. Abanddon C. Abendon D. Abbandon

2. A. Embarassment B. Emberrassement C. Embarrassment D. Embbaresment

3. A. Veneration B. Venration C. Venneration D. Venerration

4. A. Tacciturnity B. Taciturnity C. Taciturrnity D. Tacitturnity

5. A. Despponding B. Despending C. Desponding D. Dessponding

6. A. Bueyant B. Buoyant C. Bueeyant D. Buoyent

7. A. Eccintric B. Eccentrie C. Eccentric D. Eccintrie

8. A. Corrigible B. Corigible C. Corregible D. Corrigiblle

9. A. Amandable B. Amendable C. Amenddable D. Amendablle

10. A. Occasional B. Occassional C. Occesional D. Occessional

11. A. Philanthropist B. Philenthropist C. Phelanthropist D. Philanthropest

12. A. Ephameral B. Ephimeral C. Ephemeral D. Ephemerel

13. A. Fanaticism B. Fenaticism C. Faneticism D. Fanatecism

14. A. Profesional B. Professionel C. Professional D. Profissional

15. A. Ameteur B. Amateur C. Amataur D. Amateor

16. A. Philenderer B. Philandarer C. Philanderer D. Philonderer

17. A. Honorary B. Henorary C. Honerary D. Honorery

18. A. Darmatologist B. Dermatologist C. Dermetologist D. Dermatologest

19. A. Compansation B. Compensetion C. Compensotion D. Compensation

20. A. Quadruplets B. Quedruplets C. Quadroplets D. Quadruplats

21. A. Durment B. Dorment C. Doormant D. Dormant

22. A. Aristocracy B. Arestocracy C. Arestocracy D. Aristocrecy

23. A. Lagislature B. Legislature C. Lageslature D. Legesleture

24. A. Dormetory B. Dormitery C. Dormitory D. Dermitory

25. A. Garulous B. Garrulaus C. Gorrulous D. Garrulous

26. A. Regecide B. Regicide C. Rigecide D. Ragicide

27. A. Epicurean B. Epecurean C. Epicurian D. Epicorean

28. A. Commetti B. Commitee C. Committee D. Comitte

29. A. Inemitable B. Inimitable C. Inimetable D. Inimitabli

30. A. Pletocray B. Plitocracy C. Plotocracy D. Plutocracy

31. A. Discriminate B. Discremineta C. Discremenate D. Discriminat

32. A. Juddicious B. Judiceous C. Judicious D. Judiceus

33. A. Accompalish B. Ackmplesh C. Acomplush D. Accomplish

34. A. Damage B. Dammage C. Damaige D. Dammege

35. A. Lackdaisical B. Lackadaisical C. Lckadaisicle D. Lackadisical

36. A. Efficiant B. Effecient C. Efficient D. Eficient

37. A. Survellance B. Surveilance C. Surveillance D. Survaillance

38. A. Schedule B. Schdule C. Schedale D. Schedeule

39. A. Occurad B. Occurred C. Ocurred D. Occured

40. A. Licentious B. Licontious C. Licenttious D. Licientious

41. A. Ribut B. Rebit C. Rebut D. Rebute

42. A. Sychologist B. Psycologist C. Psychologist D. Psychogist

43. A. Neucteus B. Neucleus C. Nucleus D. Neocleus

44. A. Negotcate B. Negociate C. Negotiate D. Nagotiate

45. A. Skelled B. Skilled C. Skiled D. Skillid

46. A. Logecal B. Logical C. Lagical D. Logicle

47. A. Effecency B. Efficiency C. Eficiency D. Efficency

48. A. Cumpartment B. Compartment C. Compartant D. Comportent

49. A. Continuous B. Cuntinuous C. Continus D. Contineuous

50. A. Valuable B. Valueable C. Valuabel D. Valoble

51. A. Tasiturn B. Taciturn C. Taceturn D. Tacitorn

52. A. Omnevorous B. Omnivorous C. Omniverous D. Omnivarous

53. A. Feud B. Fued C. Fiud D. Feued

54. A. Pselm B. Slam C. Psalm D. Salm

55. A. Haphazard B. Hapahazard C. Haphzard D. Haphazrd

56. A. Peevishness B. Pievishness C. Peivishness D. Peeveshness

57. A. Gelactic B. Galectic C. Galactic D. Galactec

58. A. Imbibision B. Imbision C. Embibition D. Imbibition

59. A. Zoparasite B. Zooparaset C. Zooparasite D. Zoprasite

60. A. Neuralgia B. Nuraliga C. Neurolgia D. Neuraltia

61. A. Adequate B. Edequate
C. Adaquete D. Edaquete

62. A. Exparienced B. Experianced
C. Experienced D. Experrienced

63. A. Flatering B. Fletering
C. Flattering D. Fletaring

64. A. Cuttiveted B. Culltrivated
C. Cultivated D. Caltivated

65. A. Materialistic B. Materielistic
C. Meterialistic D. Matterialistic

66. A. Praiceworthy B. Peiseworthy
C. Praiseworthy D. Praisaworthy

67. A. Tranquil B. Trenquil
C. Tranquel D. Trinquil

68. A. Neggardly B. Nigardly
C. Niggerdly D. Niggardly

69. A. Magnanimity B. Megnanimity
C. Magnenimity D. Magnanimety

70. A. Darogate B. Derogate
C. Derogeta D. Deragate

71. A. Incradulous B. Incredulous
C. Incridulous D. Incredalous

72. A. Uncivilized B. Uncevilized
C. Uncivillized D. Uncevelized

73. A. Osttentatious B. Ostentetious
C. Ostentatious D. Ostenttatious

74. A. Extravagant B. Extreragent
C. Extreregant D. Extravegent

75. A. Missunderstood B. Miesunderstood
C. Misunderstood D. Misunderstod

76. A. Belligerent B. Beligirent
C. Belligarant D. Belligerrent

77. A. Pasiveness B. Passiveness
C. Passeveniss D. Passivines

78. A. Astonished B. Astronished
C. Astoneshed D. Asstonished

79. A. Obnosious B. Obnoxeous
C. Obnoxious D. Obnoseous

80. A. Polyendry B. Poliendry
C. Pollyendry D. Polyandry

81. A. Exeggerate B. Exaggerate
C. Exadgerate D. Exagerate

82. A. Fariegn B. Forein
C. Foriegn D. Foreign

83. A. Rennaissance B. Rennaisance
C. Renaisance D. Renaissance

84. A. Excesive B. Excessive
C. Exccessive D. Exccesive

85. A. Forcaust B. Forcast
C. Forecast D. Forecaste

86. A. Valuptuous B. Volluptous
C. Voluptuous D. Volupttuous

87. A. Entrepraneur B. Entreprenuer
C. Entrapreneur D. Entrepreneur

88. A. Paralleled B. Paralelled
C. Parralleled D. Parallelled

89. A. Ocasion B. Occassion
C. Occasion D. Ocassion

90. A. Boquet B. Bouquet
C. Bouquete D. Bouquette

91. A. Courteous B. Curteous
C. Corteous D. Courtus

92. A. Prophecy B. Phropecy
C. Propecy D. Propheci

93. A. Lonesome B. Lonsome
C. Lonesum D. Lonsum

94. A. Formedable B. Formidable
C. Formidabul D. Formdable

95. A. Inibriated B. Enibrited
C. Inebriated D. Inubrited

96. A. Guellible B. Guiellible
C. Guillibel D. Gullible

97. A. Subsequent B. Subsiquent
C. Subsequint D. Subquent

98. A. Alein B. Alien
C. Abein D. Abien

99. A. Misogynesm B. Mesogynism
C. Misogynism D. Misosogesim

100. A. Sanguini B. Sangune
C. Sangiune D. Sanguine

101. A. Reluctant B. Riluctant C. Reluctent D. Relictunt

102. A. Desparge B. Disparage C. Disperage D. Disparege

103. A. Maegre B. Meager C. Meagre D. Megre

104. A. Accedental B. Aceedent C. Accidantle D. Accidental

105. A. Cheapiness B. Chaepness C. Chepness D. Cheapness

106. A. Febulous B. Fabulus C. Fabulous D. Fibulous

107. A. Colusion B. Collision C. Colision D. Collison

108. A. Eradicated B. Erradicated C. Eradecated D. Eradiceted

109. A. Ageonise B. Agonise C. Agonice D. Agonisee

110. A. Comit B. Commiet C. Commit D. Commite

111. A. Immortal B. Emortal C. Immortel D. Immortol

112. A. Perrhic B. Pyrrhic C. Pyrrhec D. Porrhec

113. A. Chauvinism B. Chouvinism C. Chevinism D. Cauvinism

114. A. Rumenate B. Ruminote C. Rimunote D. Ruminate

115. A. Teciturn B. Tociturn C. Tecitorn D. Taciturn

116. A. Verteran B. Viteran C. Veterain D. Veteran

117. A. Antitode B. Antedote C. Antidote D. Autitote

118. A. Audeble B. Audible C. Audcble D. Audebli

119. A. Bellicose B. Billicose C. Bellecose D. Belicose

120. A. Pilferage B. Peliferage C. Pilfarege D. Poliferage

121. A. Chancelery B. Chancellery C. Chancellary D. Chancelary

122. A. Itenerary B. Itinarery C. Itinarary D. Itinerary

123. A. Grieff B. Grief C. Grieef D. Grrief

124. A. Indipenseble B. Indispansible C. Indispensable D. Indipensable

125. A. Guarantee B. Garuntee C. Guaruntee D. Gaurantee

126. A. Meddicine B. Medicine C. Medicene D. Medicinne

127. A. Benefeted B. Benefitted C. Benifited D. Benefited

128. A. Kleptomonia B. Kleptemonia C. Kleptomania D. Klaptomania

129. A. Sepalchrle B. Sepalchral C. Sepulchrle D. Sepulchral

130. A. Acommodation B. Acomodation C. Accomodation D. Accommodation

131. A. Sincerely B. Sencerely C. Sincerelly D. Sincerrely

132. A. Efflorascence B. Eflorescene C. Effllorescence D. Efflorescence

133. A. Vulnarable B. Valnerable C. Velnerable D. Vulnerable

134. A. Rigourous B. Rigerous C. Rigorous D. Regerous

135. A. Omenous B. Ominous C. Ommineous D. Omineous

136. A. Puerille B. Puerrile C. Puerile D. Purrile

137. A. Satellite B. Sattellite C. Satelite D. Sattelite

138. A. Pesanger B. Passenger C. Pessenger D. Pasanger

139. A. Humurous B. Humorous C. Humoreus D. Humorrous

140. A. Equinimity B. Equanimmity C. Equannimity D. Equanimity

141. A. Exemplary B. Eximplary
C. Exemplari D. Examplary

142. A. Sycophants B. Sicophants
C. Sycopants D. Sycophints

143. A. Petchy B. Patchy
C. Patchi D. Patche

144. A. Impassi B. Impasse
C. Impase D. Inpassi

145. A. Aceelerate B. Accilerate
C. Accelerate D. Accelerati

146. A. Vendictive B. Vindective
C. Vindictive D. Vindictivi

147. A. Prudint B. Prudient
C. Prudente D. Prudent

148. A. Superfluons B. Superfleos
C. Superflous D. Superfluous

149. A. Expidite B. Expedeti
C. Expedite D. Expedit

150. A. Livity B. Levity
C. Levety D. Levite

151. A. Econemist B. Economest
C. Economist D. Econimist

152. A. Catholic B. Cetholic
C. Cathelic D. Cathilic

153. A. Unfevourable B. Unfevaurable
C. Unfavourable D. Unfivourable

154. A. Bombastic B. Bombestic
C. Bombostic D. Bombastie

155. A. Posthumaus B. Posthomous
C. Posthumous D. Pasthumous

156. A. Epitaph B. Epetaph
C. Epiteph D. Epitoph

157. A. Falicitate B. Felicitate
C. Falecitate D. Falecetate

158. A. Schezophrenia B. Schizaphrenia
C. Schizophrenia D. Schizophrania

159. A. Claustrophobia B. Cloustrophobia
C. Claustraphobia D. Claustraphabia

160. A. Connoiseur B. Connaisseur
C. Connaissour D. Connoisseur

161. A. Teracherous B. Treacherous
C. Treacheraus D. Treachereans

162. A. Querrelsome B. Quarrelsame
C. Quarrelsome D. Querralsome

163. A. Farmament B. Farmement
C. Fermament D. Fremament

164. A. Sympathetic B. Smypathetic
C. Sympothetic D. Sympethetic

165. A. Pecification B. Pacification
C. Pecifacation D. Pecefication

166. A. Meritricious B. Merefrecious
C. Meretricious D. Merritricious

167. A. Hypocritical B. Hypocretical
C. Hypocriticel D. Hypocirticel

168. A. Vaingloriaus B. Vainglorious
C. Vainglerious D. Vaingloreus

169. A. Imprecticability B. Impracticebility
C. Impracticibility D. Impracticability

170. A. Prograssive B. Progressive
C. Progresive D. Prograsive

171. A. Loquacieous B. Lequacious
C. Loquacious D. Lequocious

172. A. Cataclysm B. Cataclism
C. Catacilysm D. Cataclesm

173. A. Chettering B. Chaterring
C. Chattering D. Chatering

174. A. Fulfilment B. Fulffilment
C. Fulfilmient D. Fullfilment

175. A. Conjectore B. Conjecture
C. Cenjecture D. Cenjectire

176. A. Endication B. Endicaltion
C. Indication D. Indicetion

177. A. Splendour B. Spllendour
C. Splandour D. Splendeur

178. A. Excllusion B. Exclussion
C. Exclusion D. Exclosion

179. A. Discourage B. Disscourage
C. Discourege D. Discaurage

180. A. Curageous B. Courageous
C. Courrageous D. Couregeous

181. A. Exttirpate B. Extirpete C. Extirpate D. Exterpate

182. A. Vorecious B. Varacious C. Voarcious D. Voracious

183. A. Insolvent B. Insolvant C. Insollvent D. Insolvvent

184. A. Querrel B. Querral C. Quarrel D. Quarel

185. A. Contrebution B. Contribution C. Contributtion D. Conterbution

186. A. Desgrace B. Disgrece C. Disgrice D. Disgrace

187. A. Harassment B. Herassment C. Harasment D. Harassmient

188. A. Tranquilitty B. Tranquility C. Trenquility D. Tranquillity

189. A. Imaginative B. Imeginative C. Imagenative D. Imaginetive

190. A. Suficient B. Suficiant C. Sufficient D. Sufficiant

191. A. Transperency B. Transparency C. Transpirency D. Tranporency

192. A. Superanuation B. Superennuation C. Superannuation D. Superannuetion

193. A. Antiquated B. Antiqueted C. Antequated D. Antiquatted

194. A. Adalescent B. Addescant C. Adolescent D. Adolascent

195. A. Newrologist B. Neurologist C. Neurologest D. Newrologest

196. A. Obstatrician B. Obstitrician C. Obstetrician D. Obstetracian

197. A. Illiterate B. Iliterate C. Illitarate D. Illiterete

198. A. Thioretical B. Theoretical C. Theoratical D. Theoritical

199. A. Mersenary B. Marcenary C. Marcenery D. Mercenary

200. A. Archeic B. Arcaic C. Archeic D. Archaic

ANSWERS

1	2	3	4	5	6	7	8	9	10
A	C	A	B	C	B	C	A	B	A
11	12	13	14	15	16	17	18	19	20
A	C	A	C	B	C	A	B	D	A
21	22	23	24	25	26	27	28	29	30
D	A	B	C	D	B	A	C	B	D
31	32	33	34	35	36	37	38	39	40
A	C	D	A	B	C	C	A	B	A
41	42	43	44	45	46	47	48	49	50
C	C	C	C	B	B	B	B	A	A
51	52	53	54	55	56	57	58	59	60
B	B	A	C	A	A	C	D	C	A
61	62	63	64	65	66	67	68	69	70
A	C	C	C	A	C	A	D	A	B
71	72	73	74	75	76	77	78	79	80
B	A	C	A	C	A	B	A	C	D
81	82	83	84	85	86	87	88	89	90
B	D	D	B	C	C	D	A	C	B

91	92	93	94	95	96	97	98	99	100
A	A	A	B	C	D	A	B	C	D
101	102	103	104	105	106	107	108	109	110
A	B	C	D	D	C	B	A	B	C
111	112	113	114	115	116	117	118	119	120
A	B	A	D	D	D	C	B	A	A
121	122	123	124	125	126	127	128	129	130
C	D	B	C	A	B	B	C	D	D
131	132	133	134	135	136	137	138	139	140
A	D	D	C	B	C	A	B	B	D
141	142	143	144	145	146	147	148	149	150
A	A	B	B	C	C	D	D	C	B
151	152	153	154	155	156	157	158	159	160
C	A	C	A	C	A	B	C	A	D
161	162	163	164	165	166	167	168	169	170
B	C	C	A	B	C	A	B	D	B
171	172	173	174	175	176	177	178	179	180
C	A	C	A	B	C	A	C	A	B
181	182	183	184	185	186	187	188	189	190
C	D	A	C	B	D	A	B	A	C
191	192	193	194	195	196	197	198	199	200
B	C	A	C	B	C	A	B	D	D

5 One Word Substitution

There are many words in English language which can be perfectly used for a number of words. These words help in expressing ideas in a short and correct manner for the right occasion. Such words not only enhance the vocabulary but also enable you to economise in the use of words to a great extent. Here is a categorywise list of many such words.

Pertaining to Sciences and Arts

The study of all heavenly bodies and the earth in relation to them	*astronomy*
The science of land management	*agronomics*
The study of mankind	*anthropology*
The study of physical life or living matter	*biology*
The study of plants	*botany*
The art of beautiful hand-writing	*calligraphy*
The science which deals with the varieties of human race	*ethnology*
The study of the origin and history of words	*etymology*
The study of coins	*numismatics*
The study of human face	*physiognomy*
The art of making fireworks	*pyrotechnics*
The study of birds	*ornithology*
The study of languages	*philology*
At home equally on land or in water	*amphibious*
The inside of a nut	*kernel*
The central or innermost part of fruit	*core*
The animals of a certain region	*fauna*
The plants and vegetation of a certain region	*flora*
Absence of rain for a long time	*drought*
To supply land with water by artificial means	*irrigate*
One who studies plant and animal life	*naturalist*
A cud-chewing animal, *e.g.* the cow	*ruminant*

A gnawing animal, *e.g.* the rat	*rodent*
A four-footed animal	*quadruped*
Animals which carry their young in a pouch, *e.g.* kangaroo	*marsupials*
Soil composed largely of decayed vegetable matter	*humus*
A preparation for killing insects	*insecticide*
A plant or animal growing on another	*parasite*
Living for many years	*perennial*

Pertaining to Professions

One who attends to the diseases of the eye	*oculist*
One who tests eyesight and sells spectacles	*optician*
One who attends to the teeth	*dentist*
One skilled in the care of hands and feet	*chiropodist*
A physician who assists women at child-birth	*obstetrician*
One who drives a motor-car	*chauffeur*
One who makes or sells candles	*chandler*
One who preserves the skins of animals and mounts them so as to resemble the living animals	*taxidermist*
One who compiles a dictionary	*lexicographer*
One who writes books	*author*
One skilled in the treatment of diseases of animals	*veterinarian*
A tradesman who manages funerals	*undertaker*
One who draws up contracts and lends money on interest	*scrivener*
One who lends money and keeps goods as security	*pawnbroker*
A teacher who travels from place to place to give instruction	*peripatetic*
One who travels from place to place selling miscellaneous articles	*hawker, pedlar*
One who collects postage stamps	*philatelist*
One who lends money at exorbitant interest	*usurer*
One who takes care of a building	*janitor*
One who sells sweets and pastries	*confectioner*
One who works in a coal-mine	*collier*
One who flies an aeroplane	*pilot, aviator*
One who studies rocks and soils	*geologist*
One who shoes horses	*farrier*
A professional rider in horses races	*jockey*
One who deals in silks, cotton, woollen, and linen goods	*mercer*
One who deals in wines	*vintner*
One who deals in fish	*fishmonger*
One who deals in iron and hardware	*ironmonger*

One who sells fruits, vegetables, etc. from a barrow	*costermonger*
One who sets type (in a printing office)	*compositor*

Pertaining to Marriage and Children

One who marries a second wife or husband while the legal spouse is alive	*bigamist*
One vowed to a single or unmarried life	*celibate*
One engaged to be married	*fiancé, fiancee*
A child whose parents are dead	*orphan*
A hater of marriage	*misogamist*
One who has more than two wives at a time	*polygamist*

Pertaining to Religion

One who believes that man can have no knowledge of God but only of natural phenomena	*agnostic*
One who renounces his religious vows or forsakes his religious principles	*apostate*
One who does not believe in existence of God	*atheist*
One intolerantly devoted to a particular creed	*bigot*
To utter profane language against God or anything holy	*blaspheme*
A breaker of church images	*iconoclast*
Worship of images or idols	*idiolatory*
One who believes in one God	*monotheist*
One who believes in many Gods	*polytheist*

Pertaining to Government

To give up a throne or other office of dignity	*abdicate*
Absence of government	*anarchy*
Government by Sovereign of uncontrolled authority	*autocracy, despotism*
Government by departments of states	*bureaucracy*
Government of the people, for the people and by the people	*democracy*
Government by the nobility	*aristocracy*
The right of self-government	*autonomy*
Government by a few	*oligarchy*
Government by the wealthy	*plutocracy*
Government by divine guidance	*theocracy*
To decide a political question by the direct vote of the whole electorate	*referendum*
Sweeping governmental change	*revolution*
The science of government	*politics*

Pertaining to the Literary Sphere

A work whose writer is unknown	*anonymous*
A record of one's life written by oneself	*autobiography*
The history of the life of a person	*biography*
The heading or short description of a newspaper article, chapter of a book etc.	*caption*
A humorous play, having a happy ending	*comedy*
A list of books in a library	*catalogue, bibliography*
A book in which the events of each day are recorded	*diary*
A books containing the words of a language with their definitions, in alphabetical order	*dictionary*
A book of names and addresses	*directory*
A short speech by a player at the end of a play	*epilogue*
A brief summary of a book	*epitome*
A book containing information on all branches of knowledge	*encyclopaedia*
To remove the offensive portions of a book	*expurgate*
A speech delivered without earlier preparation	*extempore*
A noisy or vehement speech intended to excite passions	*harangue*
A written account, usually in book form of the interesting and memorable experiences of one's life	*memoirs*
A note to help the memory	*memorandum*
A declaration of plans and promises put forward by a candidate for election, political party or a sovereign	*manifesto*
A short speech by a player at the beginning of a play	*prologue*
Literary theft, or passing off an author's original work as one's own	*plagiarism*
Speaking aloud to oneself	*soliloquy*
A play with a sad or tragic end	*tragedy*

Pertaining to Medicine

A substance which destroys or weakens germs	*antiseptic*
Any medicine which produces insensibility	*anaesthetic*
A medicine to counteract poison	*antidote*
Want or poorness of blood	*anaemia*
A medicine which alleviates pain	*anodyne*
To cut off a person's body a part which is infected	*amputate*
One who is recovering from illness	*convalescent*
To be able to tell the nature of disease by its symptoms	*diagnose*
A disease affecting many persons at the same place and time	*epidemic*
A disease confined to a particular district or place	*endemic*
To disinfect by smoke	*fumigate*
Free or exempt from infection	*immune*
A person who is sick	*invalid*

A cure for all diseases	*panacea*
A disease widely epidemic	*pandemic*
Confinement to one place to avoid spread of infection	*quarantine*

Pertaining to Death

Dead and decaying flesh (esp. of animals)	*carrion*
A monument set up for persons who are buried elsewhere	*cenotaph*
To preserve a dead body from putrefaction	*embalm*
Words inscribed on a tomb	*epitaph*
An examination of dead body	*postmortem, autopsy*
An account in the newspaper of the funeral of one deceased	*obituary*
The property left to someone by a will	*legacy*
Occurring after death	*posthumous*
The act of killing a human being	*homicide*
Murder of a new born child	*infanticide*
Murder of a brother	*fratricide*
Murder of a sister	*sororicide*
Murder of a mother	*matricide*
Murder of a father	*patricide*
Murder of a parent	*parricide*
Murder of a king	*regicide*

Denoting Numbers

A collection of poems	*anthology*
A number of merchant ships protected by warships (in war-time)	*convoy*
A number of stars grouped together	*constellation*
A number of hired applauders, *i.e.* persons paid to clap	*claque*
A number of people at church	*congregation*
A number of people gathered together for some common purpose	*gathering, assembly, society*
A group of people who get together to work for some cause of common interest	*coterie*
A number of workmen, prisoners, thieves	*gang*
A number of sheep	*flock*
A number of geese	*gaggle*
A number of leopards	*leap*
A number of lions, monkeys	*pride, troop*
A number of herrings, mackerel	*shoal*
A number of fish taken in a net	*catch, haul*
A number of whales, porpoises	*school, gam*
A number of oxen or horses (two or more) harnessed together	*team*
A number of ships	*fleet*

Pertaining to War

An unprovoked attack by an enemy	*aggression*
Shells, bombs, military stores	*ammunition*
A place where naval or military weapons are made or stored	*ordnance*
An agreement between belligerents to stop fighting	*armistice*
A general pardon of offenders	*amnesty*
To reduce to nothing	*annihilate*
Nations carrying on warfare	*belligerents*
To surround a place with the intention of capturing	*besiege*
To camp in the open air without tents or covering	*bivouac*
To seize for military use	*commandeer*
A person who is forced by law to become a soldier	*conscript*
An order prohibiting ships to leave the ports	*embargo*
A number of firearms being discharged continuously	*fusillade*
To make an examination or preliminary survey of enemy territory or military objectives	*reconnoitre*

Denoting Places

A place where bees are kept	*apiary*
A place where birds are kept	*aviary*
A place where fishes are kept	*aquarium*
A dwelling-place of an animal underground	*burrow*
A squirrel's home	*drey*
A nest of a bird of prey	*eyrie, aerie*
A place where spirituous liquors are produced	*distillery*
A place where clothes are washed and ironed	*laundry*
A place where Government records are kept	*archives*
A place where treasures of art, curiosities, etc. are preserved or exhibited	*museum*
A place where fruit trees are grown	*orchard*

Pertaining to Characteristics and Actions

One who devotes his life to the welfare and interests of other people	*altruist*
One who can use both hands with equal case	*ambidexterous*
One who fishes with a rod	*angler*
One who kills secretly or by surprise	*assassin*
A person who collects things belonging to ancient times	*antiquary*
One who is always finding faults	*censorious*
One living at the same time as another	*contemporary*

One who sneers at the aims and beliefs of his fellowmen	*cynic*
One who delights in speaking about oneself	*egotist*
One who exalts his own opinion	*egoist*
One who dies for a noble cause	*martyr*
One who retires from society to live a solitary life	*recluse, hermit*
One who maliciously sets fire to buildings	*incendiary*
One who is banished from his home or his country	*exile*
One who takes refuge in a foreign country	*refugee, alien*
One who runs away from justice or the law	*fugitive*
One who walks in his sleep	*somnambulist*
One who looks on the bright side of things	*optimist*
One who looks on the dark side of things	*pessimist*
A hater of mankind	*misanthropist*
One who knows everything	*omniscient*
One who is all powerful	*omnipotent*
One who is present everywhere	*omnipresent*
One who devotes his service or wealth for the love of mankind	*philanthropist*
One new to anything	*novice, tyro, neophyte*
One who engages in any pursuit for the love of it, and not for gain	*amateur*
One who journeys to a holy place	*pilgrim*
A leader of the people who can sway his followers by his oratory	*demagogue*
One who has special skill in judging art, music, tastes, etc.	*connoisseur*
One whose reasoning is clever yet false	*sophist*
One who makes a display of his learning	*pedant*
One who is indifferent to pain or pleasure	*stoic*
One who loves his country and serves it devotedly	*patriot*
One devoted to the pleasures of eating and drinking	*epicure*
One who poses to be what he is not	*hypocrite, impostor*
One who foretells events	*prophet*
One who pretends to know a great deal about everything	*mountebank, charlatan, quack*
One versed in many languages	*linguist*
One who cannot pay one's debts	*insolvent*
One who takes over after another in office or employment	*successor*
One who has been before another in office or employment	*predecessor*
One who is opposed to intellectual progress	*obscurant*
One who abstains from alcoholic drinks	*teetotaller*
One who hides away on a ship to obtain a free passage	*stowaway*
One who spends very little	*miser*
One who spends too much	*spendthrift*

Miscellaneous

Loud enough to be heard	*audible*
Not distinct enough to be heard	*inaudible*
Fit for food	*edible*
Unfit for human consumption	*inedible*
Fit to be chosen or selected	*eligible*
Not having the qualities for being chosen	*ineligible*
(Writing) that is easy to read	*legible*
Writing that is difficult to decipher	*illegible*
Able to read	*literate*
Unable to read	*illiterate*
Born of married parents	*legitimate*
Born of unmarried parents	*illegitimate*
To send back a person to his own country	*repatriate*
To banish from one's country	*expatriate*
To move from one country to another	*migrate*
One who leaves his country to settle in another	*emigrant*
One who comes into a foreign country to settle there	*immigrant*
Incapable of being redeemed from evil, *i.e.* beyond correction	*incorrigible*
That which cannot be rubbed out or blotted out	*ineffaceable, indelible*
That which cannot be conquered	*invincible*
Incapable of making errors	*infallible*
That which cannot be avoided or prevented	*inevitable*
Incapable of being burnt	*incombustible*
That which easily catches fire	*inflammable, flammable*
That which cannot be seen	*invisible*
Living for ever	*immortal*
Increase the gravity of an offence	*aggravate*
Ordinary or commonplace remark	*platitude*
That which cannot be satisfied	*insatiable*
That which cannot be repaired	*irreparable*
That which cannot be imitated	*inimitable*
Persons (or efforts) that cannot be wearied	*indefatigable*
One who eats too much	*glutton*
To destroy completely	*annihilate*
A statement open to more than one interpretation	*ambiguous*
A round about way of speaking	*circumlocution*
Cautious observation of events, etc.	*circumspection*
That which cannot be hurt	*invulnerable*

MULTIPLE CHOICE QUESTIONS

Directions: *Below are given some statements each of which is capable of being expressed by one word only. Each statement is followed by four such words of which only one is correct. Out of the given alternatives A, B, C and D choose the correct word which very closely fits each definition.*

1. One who is indifferent to pains and pleasure of life:
A. stoic B. metaphysical
C. pessimist D. sceptic

2. List of names of persons showing duties to be performed by each in turn:
A. notice B. bulletin
C. roster D. agenda

3. Long angry speech of criticism or accusation:
A. track record B. tirade
C. taut D. outburst

4. One who is in favour of never drinking alcoholic drinks:
A. idealist B. uxorious
C. teetotaller D. unalcoholic

5. Trying to win favour by flattery and charm:
A. smarmy B. shrewish
C. toady D. loquacious

6. A decision on which one cannot go back:
A. incorrigible B. irrevocable
C. rigid D. invulnerable

7. The science that studies the varieties of human race:
A. phrenology B. physiology
C. sociology D. ethnology

8. A person who hates women:
A. philogynist B. philatelist
C. misogamist D. misogynist

9. A group of people in a particular grade in an organisation:
A. colleague B. staff
C. echelon D. commission

10. Honourably discharged from service:
A. emeritus B. latitudinarian
C. infallible D. meritorious

11. Partial or total loss of memory:
A. alexia B. anorexia
C. anexia D. amnesia

12. A word made by rearranging the letters of another word like eat–tea:
A. acronym B. anagram
C. byword D. dossier

13. A mass of snow and ice sliding down from a mountain:
A. avalanche B. glacier
C. icebery D. azure

14. To speak irreverently of God:
A. impious B. irreligious
C. immoral D. blasphemy

15. Sudden increase in business:
A. bonanza B. boom
C. bounce D. booze

16. Object of laughter or ridicule:
A. butt B. but
C. divert D. hurtle

17. A pioneer of a reform movement:
A. sinecure B. sycophant
C. gallant D. apostle

18. Art of handwriting:
A. cartography B. choreography
C. calligraphy D. graph

19. One who takes a low view of human nature:
A. coquette B. cynic
C. crony D. coy

20. Document that is handwritten by the author:
A. autograph B. holograph
C. editorial D. preface

21. Talking to one's own self:
A. pessimism B. introvert
C. soliloquy D. brooding

22. One who pretends to have more knowledge than he really has:
A. hypocrite B. charlaton
C. paragon D. lackadaisical

23. Brief biography of a person:
A. profile B. bibliography
C. synopsis D. resume

24. Very small allowance or wage:
A. lumpsum B. consolidated
C. pittance D. paltry

25. Purely spiritual love:
A. devotion B. platonic
C. passionate D. divine

26. Place where people often meet:
A. common room B. discotheque
C. roster D. rendezvous

27. A completely perfect person:
A. upright B. straightforward
C. paragon D. intellectual

28. Commencement of words with the same alphabet:
A. symmetry B. pun
C. phonetic D. alliteration

29. A person who loves everybody:
A. ascetic B. philander
C. philistine D. cosmopolitan

30. A government where the powers are concentrated in the hands of one person:
A. dictatorship B. autocracy
C. plutocracy D. anarchy

31. One who does not believe in the existence of God:
A. atheist B. altruist
C. agnostic D. flippant

32. The large money paid for an early retirement:
A. gold mine B. golden handshake
C. gratuity D. lion's share

33. A hater of learning and knowledge:
A. misologist B. misogynist
C. philologist D. philanthropist

34. One who lives and acts for the welfare of others:
A. misanthrope B. credulous
C. altruist D. gregarious

35. Mental weariness for want of occupation:
A. desperate B. depression
C. fatigue D. ennui

36. That which makes it difficult to recognise the presence of real of somebody or something:
A. cover B. mask
C. make-up D. camouflage

37. To *bear a hand* in one's new business.
A. partnership B. interfere
C. assist D. join

38. One who renounces the world and practices self- discipline in order to attain salvation:
A. devotee B. ascetic
C. theist D. parsimonious

39. A place where gambling is practiced:
A. hotel B. motel
C. casino D. stadium

40. A sad song is a:
A. dirge B. elegy
C. ditty D. knell

41. Record of events by someone with first hand knowledge:
A. novice B. report
C. memoir D. itinerary

42. A mode of talk familiar to a particular group or profession:
A. jargon B. colloquial
C. slang D. abuses

43. Person who is crazy:
A. lackadaisical B. tarter
C. scrupulous D. loony

44. A person who readily believes others:
A. hasty B. immature
C. credulous D. credible

45. One who eats human flesh:
A. beast B. cannibal
C. maneater D. carnivorous

46. Intentional destruction of racial groups:
A. genocide B. homicide
C. fratricide D. communal riot

47. One with weakness of mind caused by old age:
A. dastard B. dotard
C. fop D. philanderer

48. Study of insects:
A. zoology B. philology
C. entomology D. etymology

49. A critical judge of any art particularly fine arts:
A. connoisseur B. veteran
C. philistine D. dilettante

50. One who introduces items of an entertainment:
A. consort B. compere
C. director D. introducer

51. Incapable of being wounded:
A. inevitable B. invulnerable
C. indomitable D. indefatigable

52. A short description of a picturesque scene or event of rural life:
A. narration B. panorama
C. idyll D. passage

53. The act of violating the sanctity of church:
A. sacrilege B. dissenter
C. immorality D. desecration

54. A dishonest dealing:
A. hanky-panky B. hocus-pocus
C. hoity-toity D. hilly-billy

55. A short and stout person:
A. lilliput B. hussy
C. humpty-dumpty D. paragon

56. Word that reads the same backwards as forwards (like did, dad, noon):
A. paradox B. palindrome
C. kowtow D. ragtag

57. Walking in sleep:
A. delusion B. somniloquism
C. somnabulism D. lethargic

58. Glamour and excitement:
A. razzle-dazzle B. razzmatazz
C. kudos D. winsome

59. Violent and bad tempered woman:
A. virago B. moll
C. concubine D. profane

60. One who pays excessive attention to preserving his health:
A. pagan B. bellicose
C. sycophant D. fop

61. A set of papers giving information about a person or event:
A. editorial B. agenda
C. dossier D. clippings

62. List and explanations of technical, difficult, etc. terms:
A. preface B. glossary
C. bibliography D. appendix

63. One who pays too much care to his clothes and personal appearance:
A. conscious B. dandy
C. cynosure D. leer

64. A child born after death of father:
A. effeminate B. immature
C. fatherless D. posthumous

65. A person who is hard to please:
A. insensible B. hypocrite
C. egoist D. fastidious

66. Complete failure in something attempted:
A. fiasco B. vain
C. falsies D. flop

67. A word which can be interpreted in any way:
A. confusing B. misnomer
C. ambiguous D. precise

68. A group of persons united by common interests:
A. society B. class
C. clique D. coterie

69. A person who is inexperienced and easily deceived:
A. fool B. immature
C. blackhorn D. greenhorn

70. Instruction by question and answer:
A. interrogatory B. catechism
C. bulletin D. alibi

71. A person who forsakes religion:
A. irreligious B. non-religious
C. fatalist D. apostle

72. Speaker or agitator who can stir the emotions of the masses:
A. demagogue B. dexterous
C. diligent D. reformist

73. Uncontrollable craving for alcohol:
A. dyspepsia B. delirium
C. edict D. dipsomania

74. A lady who remains unmarried:
A. concubine B. alien
C. spinster D. damsel

75. State payment to an unemployed person:
A. pension B. dole
C. increment D. grant in aid

76. Person slow at learning:
A. adroit B. dubious
C. dunce D. agile

77. One who has a good taste for food and enjoys it:
A. gourmet B. sensitive
C. deleterious D. debonair

78. One who is fond of gossip:
A. flippant B. flibbertigibbet
C. fuddy-duddy D. gregarious

79. A long, loud and angry speech:
A. incongruous B. hyperbole
C. hullabaloo D. harangue

80. A person chosen by the opposing parties to settle their differences:
A. mediator B. prude
C. paramour D. arbitrator

81. That which is outdated or out of use or fashion:
A. discarded B. obsolete
C. classic D. antic

82. Calendar giving information about sun, moon, stars and sometimes also the future:
A. almanac B. appendix
C. horoscope D. chronology

83. Collection in one volume of works by various authors:
A. panorama B. anthology
C. autobiography D. bibliography

84. One who takes part in a study, game, etc. for the love of it and not for professional gain:
A. apologist B. august
C. amateur D. avant-garde

85. A thing that causes annoyance:
A. bugbear B. arduous
C. anathema D. shrill

86. An allowance for support made to a wife by her husband after their legal separation:
A. alimony B. compensation
C. settlement D. ex-gratia

87. Place for hiding treasure, food, weapons, etc.:
A. store B. cache
C. stock D. armoury

88. A person who is stubborn in resisting change:
A. irresistible B. die-hard
C. dead beat D. terse

89. Able to use the left hand or the right hand equally well:
A. ambidextrous B. epicurean
C. apostle D. arbiter

90. A man who rarely speaks the truth:
A. liar B. unreliable
C. hypocrite D. bellicose

91. A combination of business firms:
A. enterprise B. franchise
C. cartel D. autonomous

92. Freeing of suppressed emotions:
A. catastrophe B. catharsis
C. epilogue D. chagrin

93. One who believes in the power of fate:
A. optimist B. pessimist
C. fearful D. fatalist

94. The murder of brother:
A. genocide B. homicide
C. salvage D. fratricide

95. Additional to proper payment:
A. premium B. overtime
C. ex-gratia D. fringe

96. A person or thing used to tempt somebody into a position of danger:
A. decoy B. provocateur
C. jinx D. scapegoat

97. Custom of having more than one husband at the same time:
A. polygamy B. polyandry
C. bigamy D. sexagenary

98. A person of refined taste in food and drink:
A. emeritus B. epicure
C. glutton D. gourmand

99. A tombstone inscription:
A. epithet B. encomium
C. epistle D. epitaph

100. An office which has no work but high salary:
A. fortuitous B. gratuitous
C. sinecure D. ceremonial

ANSWERS

1	2	3	4	5	6	7	8	9	10
A	C	B	C	A	B	D	D	C	A
11	**12**	**13**	**14**	**15**	**16**	**17**	**18**	**19**	**20**
D	B	A	D	B	A	D	C	B	B
21	**22**	**23**	**24**	**25**	**26**	**27**	**28**	**29**	**30**
C	B	A	C	B	D	C	D	D	B
31	**32**	**33**	**34**	**35**	**36**	**37**	**38**	**39**	**40**
A	B	A	C	D	D	C	B	C	A
41	**42**	**43**	**44**	**45**	**46**	**47**	**48**	**49**	**50**
C	A	D	C	B	A	B	C	A	B
51	**52**	**53**	**54**	**55**	**56**	**57**	**58**	**59**	**60**
B	C	D	A	C	B	C	B	A	A
61	**62**	**63**	**64**	**65**	**66**	**67**	**68**	**69**	**70**
C	B	B	D	D	A	C	C	D	B
71	**72**	**73**	**74**	**75**	**76**	**77**	**78**	**79**	**80**
D	A	D	C	B	C	A	B	D	D
81	**82**	**83**	**84**	**85**	**86**	**87**	**88**	**89**	**90**
B	A	B	C	A	A	B	B	A	C
91	**92**	**93**	**94**	**95**	**96**	**97**	**98**	**99**	**100**
C	B	D	D	D	A	B	B	D	C

6 Synonyms and Antonyms

English is the most popular language of the world. It comprises thousands of words. No one can remember all the words and their meanings but everyone must try to read and learn the maximum number of words and their meanings. Readers must keep and use a dictionary religiously. Several important words are listed below with their synonyms and antonyms. Learn as many as you can.

ABANDON
Syn.: discard, desert, discontinue, renounce, relinquish, abnegate, forsake, surrender, give up, quit.
Ant.: retain, maintain, uphold, stay, remain.

ABATE
Syn.: lessen, decrease, diminish, subside, slacken, subside, allay, reduce, curtail.
Ant.: increase, enlarge, heighten, intensify, raise.

ABBREVIATE
Syn.: shorten, abridge, compress, curtain, condense, contract, prune, truncate, reduce.
Ant.: enlarge, expand, lengthen, extend, elongate, prolong, protract.

ABILITY
Syn.: competence, aptitude, capability, talent, intelligence, cleverness, capacity.
Ant.: inability, incompetence, incapacity, incapability, inaptitude.

ABLE
Syn.: capable, competent, intelligent, talented, efficient, skilful.
Ant.: unable, incapable, inefficient, incompetent.

ABRUPT
Syn.: sudden, curt, steep, hasty, unexpected, disconnected, disjointed, brusque, rough.
Ant.: expected, anticipated, gradual, courteous, smooth.

ABSURD
Syn.: illogical, irrational, inconsistent, silly, inane, unreasonable, funny, ridiculous, laughable, ludicrous, nonsensical, fatuous.
Ant.: logical, reasonable, rational, consistent, sensible, sound, proper, sane.

ACCURATE
Syn.: exact, precise, correct, actual, just, right, correct.
Ant.: incorrect, inexact, improper, fallacious, inaccurate, misleading, erroneous.

ADEQUATE
Syn.: ample, abundant, enough, sufficient, plentiful, copious.
Ant.: inadequate, insufficient, meagre, scant, scantly, skimpy.

AFFABLE
Syn.: urbane, polite, friendly, courteous, amiable, suave, good-tempered.
Ant.: impolite, unfriendly, discourteous, haughty.

AKIN
Syn.: kindred, similar, allied, cognate, alike, related, analogous.
Ant.: dissimilar, unrelated, unallied, unconnected, different, unlike, separate.

ALERT
Syn.: wary, vigilant, watchful, attentive, heedful, cautious, lively, fully awake.
Ant.: unwatchful, sluggish, relaxed, quiet, restful.

ABNORMAL
Syn.: unusual, irregular, anomalous, unnatural, odd, strange, erratic.
Ant.: usual, regular, natural, normal, customary.

ACTIVE
Syn.: brisk, energetic, lively, nimble, agile.
Ant.: inactive, indolent, sluggish, lazy, passive, torpid.

ACTUAL
Syn.: real, genuine, authentic, true, concrete, factual, existing.
Ant.: unreal, implied, assumed, false, imaginary, fictitious.

AMBIGUOUS
Syn.: vague, uncertain, undecided, undefined, obscure, doubtful, indistinct, dubious, perplexing.
Ant.: lucid, plain, clear, obvious, unambiguous, unmistakable, indisputable.

APT
Syn.: appropriate, apposite, suitable, fitting, pertinent, germane, relevant, congruent, harmonious, congruous.
Ant.: inapt, inappropriate, incongruous, improper, unsuitable, inapposite, irrelevant.

ARDENT
Syn.: fervid, fervent, warm, impassioned, plowing, intense, eager, earnest, passionate, hearty, cordial, enthusiastic.
Ant.: cool, indifferent, apathetic, nonchalant, unimpassioned.

ATROCIOUS
Syn.: nefarious, heinous, cruel, outrageous, beastly, horrible, horrendous.
Ant.: noble, humane, honourable, laudable, admirable, moral.

AUDACIOUS
Syn.: bold, daring, fearless, impudent, brash, rash, reckless, impertinent, madcap, insolent, brave, disrespectful, intrepid.
Ant.: cowardly, timid, fearful, meek, humble, afraid, frightened, scared, different, panicky, apprehensive, shy, mousy, timorous, fidgety.

AUTHENTIC
Syn.: genuine, real, trustworthy, true, reliable, accurate, authoritative, sound, tangible, definite, actual, precise, exact, correct, factual, veritable, sterling.
Ant.: apocryphal, unreliable, spurious, false, fictitious, fake, sham, imaginary, counterfeit, baseless, untrue.

BEAUTIFUL
Syn.: catching, prepossessing, fetching, cute, enticing, engaging, attractive, charming, fascinating, captivating, alluring, tempting, lovely, bewitching, reductive, pretty, enchanting, winning, comely.
Ant.: ugly, unattractive, unprepossessing, repulsive, gaunt, haggard, unpleasing, revolting, hideous.

BITTER
Syn.: tart, harsh, pungent, unpalatable, acrid, spiteful, cutting, stinging, sour, unpleasant, sarcastic, resentful, biting, sardonic, caustic, severe, acrimonious, poignant, distasteful.
Ant.: tasty, toothsome, tasteful, palatable, pleasant, delicious, warm.

BRIGHT
Syn.: brilliant, shining, luminous, lustrous, radiant, sparkling, quick-witted, cheerful, clever, resplendent, flashing, lucid, limpid, sagacious, keen, astute, shrewd, brainy, intelligent.
Ant.: dull, ignorant, cheerless, imbecile, murky, dark, gloomy, sullen.

BRIEF
Syn.: compendious, concise, short, terse, laconic, curt, succinct, condensed, compact, pithy.
Ant.: long, lengthy, prolonged, protracted, elongated, lengthened, extended, detailed, prolix, verbose, wordy.

BRUTAL
Syn.: atrocious, savage, beastly, brutish, fiendish, devilish, barbarous, cruel, ruthless, merciless, crude, ferocious, bestial, heinous.
Ant.: humane, gentle, civilised, merciful, polished, sympathetic, tender, liberal, considerate, good-natured.

CANDID

Syn.: frank, outspoken, sincere, impartial, honest, artless, ingenuous, straightforward.

Ant.: sly, wily, insincere, reserved, unfair, evasive.

CAPRICIOUS

Syn.: unpredictable, impulsive, fickle, changeable, inconstant, whimsical.

Ant.: constant, firm, steadfast, unswerving.

CARELESS

Syn.: heedless, inattentive, indifferent, negligent, remiss, lax, unmindful.

Ant.: cautious, vigilant, careful, mindful, attentive.

CERTAIN

Syn.: indisputable, reliable, sure, definite, undisputed, unmistakable, positive, absolute.

Ant.: uncertain, disputable, doubtful, indefinite, ambiguous, dubious, questionable.

CHEEK

Syn.: impudence, impertinence, effrontery, gall, temerity, audacity, insolence, sauce, sass.

Ant.: politeness, courtesy, humility, gentleness, respect.

☛ *Cheek* also means either side of the face below the eye.

Examples: She has healthy rosy *cheeks*.
They are dancing *cheek* to *cheek*.

CHEERFUL

Syn.: genial, happy, jolly, merry, jovial, pleasant, lively, cheery, sunny, jocund, gay.

Ant.: cheerless, joyless, dejected, unhappy, doleful, sorrowful, mournful, glum, dreary, dismal.

CHARM (Verb)

Syn.: fascinate, attract, please, delight, influence, entice, enchant, entrance, enrapture, allure, captivate, bewitch, ravish, tempt, lure, seduce, beguile, enthral, thrill.

Ant.: repel, repulse, rebuff, snub, disgust, deter, disturb, irritate, annoy, alarm, frighten, terrify.

COMFORTABLE

Syn.: cosy, snug, pleasant, pleasing, pleasurable, satisfied.

Ant.: uncomfortable, disagreeable, dissatisfied, disturbed, displeasing, irritating, miserable, wretched, troubled, cheerless.

COMPLETE (Adj)

Syn.: whole, thorough, total, entire, full, perfect, exhaustive, consummate.

Ant.: incomplete, imperfect, partial, unfinished, uncompleted, unaccomplished, deficient, skimpy, sketchy.

CORDIAL

Syn.: sincere, friendly, earnest, warm, hearty, ardent, heartfelt, amiable, affable.

Ant.: unfriendly, insincere, cold, distant, formal, reserved.

COURAGE

Syn.: bravery, boldness, valour, heroism, fearlessness, intrepidity, nerve, gallantry, pluck, fortitude, daring.

Ant.: cowardice, timidity, pusillanimity, fear, funk.

CURIOUS

Syn.: inquisitive, inquiring, prying, strange, unusual, nosey, meddlesome.

Ant.: incurious, uninquiring, uninquisitive, uninterested, unconcerned, indifferent, common, usual.

CORRECT (Adj)

Syn.: accurate, proper, exact, precise, right, true, regular, perfect.

Ant.: incorrect, improper, inexact, wrong, untrue, irregular, imperfect.

DAFT

Syn.: silly, crazy, irrational, foolish, unreasonable, reckless, insane, imbecile, lumpish.

Ant.: sane, sound, sensible, deft, rational, reasonable.

DAINTY

Syn.: pretty, neat, delicate, refined, tasty, delicious, fastidious, elegant, toothsome, exquisite, cute, tasteful, palatable.

Ant.: inelegant, coarse, vulgar, rough, crude, rude, nasty, dirty.

DEEP

Syn.: abstruse, profound, intense, learned, sagacious, extreme, devious, vivid, submerged,

bottomless, unfathomable, abysmal, mysterious, knotty, astute, recondite, intricate.
Ant.: shallow, apparent, familiar, artless, commonplace, ordinary, trite, naive, superficial, cursory, simple, banal.

DELIGHT
Syn.: joy, pleasure, rapture, ecstasy, enjoyment, bliss, gratification, gusto, comfort.
Ant.: displeasure, discomfort, sorrow, distress, misery, anguish, suffering, agony, woe, despair, depression.

DETRIMENTAL
Syn.: harmful, injurious, hurtful, pernicious, damaging, noxious.
Ant.: good, beneficial, valuable, useful, profitable, harmless, inoffensive, unobnoxious.

DIFFICULT
Syn.: hard, troublesome, perplexing, tough, laborious, irksome, toilsome, arduous, knotty, burdensome, uphill, herculean, enigmatic.
Ant.: easy, uncomplicated, intelligible, lucid, plain, simple, facile, manageable, tractable, elementary, rudimentary.

DILIGENT
Syn.: industrious, laborious, hard-working, attentive, assiduous, observant, mindful, vigilant, watchful, wakeful, careful.
Ant.: careless, heedless, inattentive, indifferent, unobservant, unmindful.

DISHONEST
Syn.: untrustworthy, false, fraudulent, deceitful, crooked, tricky, deceptive, treacherous, unjust, unfair, unreliable.
Ant.: trustworthy, reliable, fair, just, candid, frank, sincere, upright, truthful, veracious, honest.

DOCILE
Syn.: pliant, tractable, amenable, teachable, yielding, compliant, tame, submissive, gentle, unresisting, dutiful, passive, acquiescent, unassertive, manageable, governable, obsequious.
Ant.: obstinate, stubborn, intractable, self-willed, dogged, defiant, insolent, resistant, resisting, obdurate, disobedient, wilful, uncompromising, unyielding, refractory, recalcitrant.

DOUBTFUL
Syn.: questionable, uncertain, unsure, unlikely, improbable, disputable, debatable, dubious, controversial, fishy, moot, ambiguous.
Ant.: certain, sure, probable, indisputable, unquestionable, positive, absolute, definite, clear, unmistakable, reliable, trustworthy, undoubted, undeniable, indubitable.

DROLL
Syn.: amusing, laughable, funny, comic, sarcastic, whimsical, comical, odd, queer, farcical, ludicrous, ridiculous, absurd, diverting, rompish.
Ant.: sad, lamentable, lugubrious, tragic, painful, dolorous, hurtful, distressing, grievous, woeful, rueful, mournful, deplorable, touching.

DULL
Syn.: stupid, boring, monotonous, foolish, unintelligent, cheerless, gloomy, uninteresting, spiritless, blunt, doltish, sad, stolid, dismal, dowdy, drab, unfashionable, insensible.
Ant.: sensible, cheerful, bright, intelligent, clever, lively, animated, brilliant, sharp, talented, jolly, merry, joyful, gay, jocund, energetic, keen, active, intense, brisk, lively, trenchant, rousing.

EAGER
Syn.: ardent, earnest, zealous, keen, fervent, fervid, vehement, intent, agog, avid, excited, impatient, curious, anxious, enthusiastic, wistful, hearty, cordial, desirous.
Ant.: indifferent, disinterested, cool, loath, unconcerned, apathetic, reluctant, unwilling, disinclined.

EFFICIENT
Syn.: capable, able, competent, gifted, effective, effectual, efficacious, skilful, proficient, talented, intelligent, adept.
Ant.: inefficient, incompetent, ineffectual, unskilled, inexpert.

ELIGIBLE
Syn.: fit, suitable, desirable, worthy, qualified, acceptable, right.
Ant.: unfit, unsuitable, unworthy, unacceptable, undesirable, unqualified.

EMPHEMERAL

Syn.: short-lived, transitory, transient, fleeting, momentary, fugitive, evanescent, fugacious, temporary.

Ant.: eternal, perpetual, perennial, permanent, intransient, lifelong, everlasting, long-lived, prolonged, protracted.

ENORMOUS

Syn.: immense, gigantic, colossal, huge, vast, gargantuan, monstrous, prodigious, stupendous, plentiful, plenteous, copious.

Ant.: trivial, insignificant, ordinary, average, small, little, tiny, diminutive.

ENOUGH

Syn.: plenty, ample, sufficient, abundant, adequate.

Ant.: insufficient, inadequate, meagre, scanty, deficient, scant, jejune, skimpy.

ENTHUSIASM

Syn.: verve, ardour, zeal, fervour, fanaticism.

Ant.: apathy, indifference, detachment, ennui, unconcern, lethargy, weariness, exhaustion, lassitude, languor.

EXPERT (Adj)

Syn.: adept, skilled, adroit, proficient, skilful, deft, dexterous, versed, accomplished.

Ant.: inexpert, unskilful, unskilled, maladroit, clumsy, lungling, unqualified, raw, inexperienced, green, incompetent.

FACE (V)

Syn.: confront, oppose, defy, meet, encounter, resist.

Ant.: avoid, shun, elude, avert, eschew.

FAITHFUL

Syn.: loyal, trustworthy, conscientious, true, accurate, devoted, exact, reliable, staunch, steadfast, constant, dependable, compliant.

Ant.: disloyal, untrustworthy, inaccurate, inexact, unreliable, unfaithful, treacherous, undependable, untrue, fickle.

FICKLE

Syn.: inconstant, disloyal, unfaithful, capricious, impulsive, unpredictable, changeable, unstable, variable, vacillating, wavering, fanciful, whimsical, mutable, irresolute, erratic, unreliable, fitful.

Ant.: steady, steadfast, unchangeable, unwavering, constant, loyal, faithful, reliable, dependable, stable, immutable, invariable.

FIT (Adj)

Ant.: suitable, appropriate, proper, advantageous, sound, well, meet, becoming, fitting, qualified, apt, apposite, decent, decorous, congruent, congruous, concordant, harmonious, eligible.

Ant.: unfit, unsuitable, unbecoming, disadvantageous, unwell, indecent, indecorous, improper, inappropriate, inapt, incongruent, ineligible.

FOOLISH

Syn.: silly, stupid, unwise, ridiculous, absurd, asinine, imbecile, indiscreet, irrational, idiotic, brainless, senseless, nonsensical, witless, preposterous, inane, fatuous, imprudent, inconsistent, illogical, laughable, paradoxical, dotty.

Ant.: wise, sane, prudent, discreet, sound, sensible, rational, sagacious, judicious, sage.

FRIENDLY

Syn.: kindly, pleasantly, amicable, cordial, hearty, warm-hearted, affable, genial, well-inclined, good-tempered, amiable, favourable, pleasing, sociable, companionable, nice, neighbourly, benevolent, well-disposed.

Ant.: hostile, unsociable, unfavourable, unfriendly, adverse, inimical, antagonistic, distant, reserved, cool, ill-inclined, ill-disposed, resistant, opposed.

FUNDAMENTAL

Syn.: basic, primary, essential, cardinal, indispensable, original, rudimentary, elementary, radical, most important, prime, chief.

Ant.: secondary, subordinate, minor, inferior, resultant, second-rate, subsidiary.

FUNNY

Syn.: amusing, jocular, jocose, laughable, eccentric, absurd, droll, comical, comic, playful, ludicrous, farcical, humorous, ridiculous, odd, queer, diverting, strange.

Ant.: sad, serious, solemn, sober, sedate, staid, grave, sorrowful, mournful.

GARRULOUS

Syn.: talkative, chatty, verbose, loquacious, communicative, glib, voluble, prolix, wordy, long-winded, diffuse, profuse, discussive, rambling, circumlocutory, maundering, periphrastic.

Ant.: laconic, reticent, silent, taciturn, uncommunicative, terse, reserved, short-spoken.

GENUINE

Syn.: authentic, sound, true, real, pure, veritable, unadulterated, unalloyed, unaffected, natural, factual, actual, legitimate, undistorted, tangible, valid, sterling.

Ant.: sham, spurious, fictitious, artificial, adulterated, alloyed, impure, apocryphal, untrue, fallacious, unsound, invalid.

GIFTED

Syn.: talented, intelligent, sagacious, competent, wise, able, proficient, efficient, capable, shrewd, inventive, skilful, ingenious, experienced.

Ant.: foolish, doltish, silly, stupid, idiotic.

GLORIOUS

Syn.: famous, beautiful, splendid, magnificent, enjoyable, pleasant, grand, exalted, lofty, majestic, sublime, noble, bright, radiant, renowned.

Ant.: base, ignoble, low, ordinary, ridiculous.

GOOD (N)

Syn.: benefit, profit, advantage, virtue, boon, weal, prosperity, blessing, gain, welfare, righteousness, merit.

Ant.: harm, injury, corruption, wickedness, depravity, detriment, disadvantage, ill, calamity, loss, evil, curse.

GRACEFUL

Syn.: elegant, pleasing in style and attitude, polite, considerate, comely, beautiful, attractive, lithe, lissom, svelte, sylphlike, willowy.

Ant.: ungainly, awkward, lumbering, uncouth, ill mannered, not refined.

GRAND

Syn.: august, exalted, stately, splendid, majestic, lofty, superb, imposing, dignified, noble, princely, magnificent, big, pompous, gorgeous, sublime, impressive.

Ant.: mean, common, insignificant, secondary, inferior, unimportant, little, undignified, unimposing, petty, paltry, beggarly, lowly.

GRIM

Syn.: fearful, stern, fierce, ruthless, horrible, determined, strong-willed, horrid, repellent, frightful, ghastly, gristly, gloomy, severe, unrelenting, unpleasant, depressing, determined, repulsive, dingy, drab, savage, appalling, ferocious, ugly, sullen, hideous.

Ant.: handsome, pretty, graceful, elegant, gentle, gracious, friendly, humane, benign, mild, docile, attractive.

GRUFF

Syn.: rough, surly, blunt, harsh, rude.

Ant.: affable, courteous, mild, smooth.

HARMFUL

Syn.: detrimental, pernicious, prejudicial, deleterious, injurious, noxious, hurtful, mischievous, obnoxious, inauspicious, oppressive, baneful, baleful, menacing, malignant, unhealthful, vitiated, damaging.

Ant.: helpful, profitable, beneficial, advantageous, harmless, useful, favourable, good, salutary, healthful, inoffensive, unobnoxious.

HARMONIOUS

Syn.: congruous, concordant, uniform, proportioned, consistent, tuneful, melodious, sweet-sounding, agreeable, friendly, amicable, cordial.

Ant.: unfriendly, hostile, unfavourable, adverse, opposing, opposed, antagonistic, contrary, discordant, conflicting, inconsistent.

HARSH

Syn.: rough, stern, cruel, severe, blunt, coarse, gruff, discordant, raucous, hoarse, rugged, severe, shrill, strident, austere, acrimonious, ungenial, sharp, sour, ungracious, brutal, heartless.

Ant.: gentle, mild, smooth, soft, melodious.

HEALTHY

Syn.: robust, strong, vigorous, lusty, hearty, sound, well, hygienic, salubrious, wholesome, salutary, bracing, invigorating, harmless, healthful, hale and hearty, inoffensive, laudable, moral.

Ant.: diseased, delicate, infirm, injurious, frail, noxious, sick, ailing, ill, sick.

HEARTY

Syn.: warm, earnest, sincere, heartfelt, cordial, sound, ardent, friendly, enthusiastic, cheerful, healthy, fervent, fervid.

Ant.: cool, reserved, taciturn, insincere.

HONEST

Syn.: frank, sincere, direct, fairly earned, truthful, upright, virtuous, right, sincere, genuine, trustworthy.

Ant.: dishonest, untrustworthy, tricky, deceitful, fraudulent, insincere.

HONOUR (N)

Syn.: privilege, probity, integrity, glory, distinction, great respect, glory, dignity, reverence, grandeur, high-mindedness, eminence, renown, fame.

Ant.: dishonour, disrespect, contempt, irreverence, disgrace, degradation, slight, infamy, perfidy, treachery, improbity, scorn, disdain.

HUMOROUS

Syn.: droll, amusing, ludicrous, funny, jocular, merry, comic, jocose, waggish, farcical.

Ant.: solemn, serious, sober, grave, composed, sedate, dignified.

IDLE

Syn.: indolent, lazy, inactive, unemployed, useless, unoccupied, slothful, futile.

Ant.: active, busy, occupied, working, industrious, employed.

INDUSTRIOUS

Syn.: diligent, hard-working, laborious, assiduous, sedulous.

Ant.: lethargic, inactive, apathetic, lazy, idle, indolent, slothful, torpid, sluggish, shiftless, slack, lax, supine.

IMPORTANT

Syn.: significant, valuable, weighty, influential, momentous, prominent, material, essential, remarkable, eventful.

Ant.: insignificant, unimportant, petty, trivial, mean, secondary, minor, uninfluential, worthless, valueless, immaterial, inferior.

INGENIOUS

Syn.: adroit, clever, dexterous, quick-witted, skilful, talented, smart, bright, sharp, adept, original, inventive, expert, intelligent.

Ant.: unskilled, dull, foolish, clumsy, awkward, stupid, unskilful, inexpert, maladroit, incompetent, inexperienced, unconversant, ungainly.

INGENUOUS

Syn.: innocent, open, candid, frank, sincere, straightforward, truthful, artless, honest, naive, simple, trusting, unaffected, outspoken.

Ant.: insincere, reserved, sly, wily, contrived, disingenuous, mean, pretentious, sham, affected, priggish.

INFINITE

Syn.: boundless, endless, unlimited, unbounded, limitless, immeasurable, interminable, stupendous, eternal, immense, vast, incalculable, numberless, countless, bottomless, unfathomable, inexhaustible, indefinite, perpetual.

Ant.: finite, limited, restricted, bounded, conditioned, confined, definite, determinate, circumscribed.

INTELLIGENT

Syn.: brainy, clever, bright, brilliant, keen, sagacious, quick-witted, discerning, sharp, shrewd, astute, canny, perspicacious, perceptive, nimble, well-informed, enlightened.

Ant.: foolish, doltish, dull, stupid, unintelligent, stolid, obtuse, silly, inane.

INTEGRITY

Syn.: honesty, probity, uprightness, rectitude, truthfulness, sincerity, trustworthiness, fairness, wholeness, completeness, oneness, totality, entirety, indivisibility.

Ant.: dishonesty, duplicity, unfairness, deceit, fraud, improbity.

IRRITABLE

Syn.: peevish, touchy, irascible, testy, short-tempered, fretful, splenetic, petulant, grumpy, pettish, snappish, choleric, peppery, churlish, cantankerous, fractious, crabbed.

Ant.: calm, composed, agreeable, gracious, cheerful, genial, good-natured, blithe, jaunty, buoyant, lively, animated.

JEALOUS

Syn.: envious, invidious, suspicious, resentful, covetous, jaundiced, distrustful, apprehensive, intolerant.

Ant.: unenvious, unjealous, tolerant, liberal, genial, indifferent, unsuspecting.

JOLLY

Syn.: genial, jovial, jubilant, lively, gay, joyful, merry, mirthful, cheerful, light-hearted, jocular, jocund, blithe.

Ant.: cheerless, joyless, sad, mournful, gloomy, morose, sullen, lugubrious, sorrowful, melancholy, dismal, unhappy.

JUST

Syn.: fair, honest, proper, right, reasonable, well-founded, deserved, impartial, true, upright, exact, precise, proportioned, normal.

Ant.: unfair, unjust, improper, unreasonable, partial, untrue, inexact, abnormal, ill-proportioned, prejudiced, biased.

KEEN

Syn.: acute, sharp, penetrating, astute, clever, cunning, quick, shrewd, wily, eager, enthusiastic, intense, deep, strong, cutting, ardent, nippy, avid, fervent.

Ant.: indifferent, blunt, dull, languid, indifferent, cool, careless, half-hearted, unconcerned, lukewarm, impervious, insouciant.

KIND (Adj)

Syn.: friendly, gentle, mild, obliging, benign, lenient, helpful, sympathetic, favourable, benevolent, amiable, good-natured, cordial, courteous, gracious, warm-hearted, humane, compassionate, generous, philanthropic.

Ant.: unfriendly, unfavourable, discourteous, unkind, harsh, severe, hard, callous, cruel, inhumane.

KNOWLEDGE

Syn.: understanding, learning, information, instruction, acquaintance, cognition, cognizance, awareness, comprehension, apprehension, consciousness, familiarity, ken, enlightenment, experience, attainments, scholarship, education.

Ant.: ignorance, nescience, illiteracy, incomprehension, inexperience, unawareness.

LABORIOUS

Syn.: diligent, hard-working, industrious, toilsome, tedious, tiresome, irksome, arduous, assiduous, wearisome, strenuous, painstaking, uphill.

Ant.: easy, light, feasible, indiligent, lazy, indolent, simple, idle.

LACONIC

Syn.: curt, terse, concise, pithy, short, brief, succinct, crisp, compendious, compact.

Ant.: lengthy, prolix, wordy, circumlocutory, verbose, discursive, long-winded, rambling, roundabout, copious, diffuse.

LAX

Syn.: negligent, careless, remiss, sluggish, inattentive, neglectful, heedless, vague, desultory, unmethodical, loose, slack, relaxed.

Ant.: careful, meticulous, attentive, methodical, severe, strict, heedful, regardful, cautious, prudent, discreet.

LESSEN

Syn.: shorten, abate, curtail, decrease, reduce, diminish, abridge, mitigate, contract, deduct, subtract, shrink, allenuate.

Ant.: increase, enlarge, augment, extend, expand, grow, amplify, enhance, magnify.

LIVELY

Syn.: high-spirited, vigorous, energetic, active, animated, brisk, bright, blithe, frolicsome, merry, playful, spirited, forceful, sprightly, vivacious, joyous, joyful, gay.

Ant.: dull, listless, insipid, vapid, inactive, uninteresting, depressed, languid, torpid, apathetic, indifferent, sluggish, dejected, joyless, cheerless, unlively, spiritless.

LOGICAL

Syn.: cogent, convincing, sound, valid, effective, reasonable, natural, rational, sane, relevant.

Ant.: illogical, invalid, ineffective, unreasonable, unnatural, irrational, insane, irrelevant, fallacious.

MADDEN

Syn.: infuriate, enrage, incense, derange, craze, anger, offend, displease, embitter, exasperate, rankle, affront, irritate, provoke, nettle, inflame, annoy.

Ant.: placate, pacify, soothe, calm, assuage, appease, mollify.

MALICIOUS

Syn.: spiteful, malignant, malevolent, evil-minded, hostile, rancorous, virulent, wicked, malign,

pernicious, vicious, harmful, maleficent, ill-disposed, ill-intentioned.
Ant.: benign, kind, good-natured, benevolent, cordial, unselfish, sympathetic, gracious, well-intentioned, humane, warm-hearted, affectionate.

MASTERLY
Syn.: skilful, adept, deft, dexterous, expert, skilled, consummate, perfect, masterful, dominating.
Ant.: unskilled, maladroit, clumsy, inexpert.

METHODICAL
Syn.: orderly, logical, systematic, regular, procedural, planned, arranged, tidy.
Ant.: disorderly, illogical, irregular, unsystematic, unmethodical, untidy, desultory, unarranged, disarranged, sloppy, chaotic, anarchical.

MODEST
Syn.: moderate, inexpensive, not showy or splendid in appearance, not vain or boastful, shy, bashful, humble, meek, reserved, unassuming, unpretentious, diffident, unobtrusive, coy.
Ant.: immodest, showy or splendid in appearance, vain, boastful, ostentatious, pretentious, proud, arrogant, bold, conceited, haughty, disdainful, pert, imperious, domineering, priggish, smug, self-satisfied, egotistic, self-important.

MOMENTOUS
Syn.: important, prominent, significant, weighty, material, pressing, influential, grave, consequential, serious, notable, solemn, memorable, remarkable.
Ant.: unimportant, immaterial, inconsequential, insignificant, mean, petty, trivial, slight, niggling, trifling.

NATURAL
Syn.: innate, inherent, original, normal, spontaneous, unaffected, characteristic, typical, native, unstudied, inborn, naive, ingenuous, inbred, ingrained, usual, intrinsic.
Ant.: unnatural, abnormal, artificial, affected, forced, irregular, unusual, inconsistent, fictitious.

NECESSARY
Syn.: requisite, needful, essential, inevitable, unavoidable, indispensable.
Ant.: unnecessary, optional, unessential, dispensable, voluntary, discretional, casual.

NICE
Syn.: pleasant, agreeable, friendly, kind, fine, subtle, respectable, scrupulous, dainty, attractive, fastidious, tasteful, delicate, choosy, refined, palatable, delectable, pleasing, pleasurable.
Ant.: disagreeable, coarse, unscrupulous, rough, nasty, rueful, mournful, woeful, deplorable, distressing.

NIMBLE
Syn.: agile, sharp, active, brisk, lively, spry, quick.
Ant.: slow, sluggish, clumsy, inert, lazy, indolent, awkward, slothful.

NOVICE
Syn.: beginner, tyro, neophyte, apprentice, greenhorn, learner, acolyte, rookie.
Ant.: expert, adept, master, teacher, trainer, instructor.

OBEDIENT
Syn.: observant, dutiful, complying, compliant, loyal, faithful, devoted, fractable, docile, submissive, pliable, pliant, yielding.
Ant.: disloyal, unfaithful, intractable, uncomplying, uncompliant, unruly, unsubmissive, refractory, resisting, contumacious, recalcitrant.

OBSTINATE
Syn.: stubborn, obdurate, dogged, tenacious, persistent, insistent, headstrong, pertinacious, unyielding, determined, self-willed, wilful, resolute.
Ant.: irresolute, subservient, yielding, submissive, amenable, wavering.

OFFENSIVE (Adj)
Syn.: insulting, annoying, disgusting, repulsive, aggressive, distasteful, foul, aggressive, obnoxious, nasty.
Ant.: pleasant, defensive, inoffensive, harmless, blameless, unaggressive, innocuous.

OWN (V)
Syn.: possess, confess, admit, avow, acknowledge, have, hold, concede.
Ant.: deny, disclaim, disavow, renounce, disown, abjure, abandon.

PEEVISH
Syn.: irritable, touchy, testy, tetchy, irascible, fretful, bad-tempered, crabbed, pettish, petulant,

snappish, waspish, fractious, hot-headed, crabby, churlish.

Ant.: affable, genial, good-natured, good-tempered, pleasant, cordial, hearty, jolly, soft-spoken, polite, urbane.

PERFECT (Adj)

Syn.: complete, excellent, ideal, exact, precise, total, absolute, thorough, faultless, indefective, indeficient, immaculate, impeccable, sound, spotless, entire, utter, consummate.

Ant.: imperfect, incomplete, inexact, deficient, faulty, unsound, deformed, impaired, blemished, crude.

PLEASANT

Syn.: enjoyable, polite and friendly, pleasurable, agreeable, pleasing, delectable, palatable, delightful, cheerful, delicious, jocular, merry.

Ant.: unpleasant, disagreeable, unlively, lugubrious, dismal, sad, mournful, offensive, unpleasing, disgusting, obnoxious, nasty.

PLENTIFUL

Syn.: ample, abundant, copious, profuse, plenteous, prolific, bounteous, bountiful, lavish.

Ant.: scanty, meagre, limited, skimpy, insufficient, sparing, scarce, deficient, rare.

POMPOUS

Syn.: self-important, ostentatious, high-flown, bombastic, grandiose, arrogant, haughty, grand, imposing, lofty, magnificent, majestic, statcly, sublime, dignified, showy, pretentious, assuming, turgid, magniloquent.

Ant.: unassuming, plain-mannered, unpretending, modest, unobtrusive, humble-minded, unpretentious, bashful, coy.

PRECISE

Syn.: exact, accurate, definite, correct, punctilious, fastidious, particular, proper.

Ant.: inexact, inaccurate, indefinite, incorrect, improper, vague, ambiguous, rough, circumlocutory.

PREPOSSESSING

Syn.: attractive, charming, taking, alluring, engaging, winning, appealing, winsome.

Ant.: unattractive, repulsive, ugly, unprepossessing, ill-looking.

PREPOSTEROUS

Syn.: outrageous, absurd, unreasonable, ridiculous, foolish, silly, stupid, inconsistent, irrational, nonsensical, laughable, idiotic, illogical, ludicrous.

Ant.: consistent, reasonable, rational, logical, sensible, sound, just, fair, right, moderate.

PRINCIPAL (Adj)

Syn.: chief, main, foremost, prime, leading, most important, pre-eminent, outstanding, excellent, conspicuous, highest, first-rate, cardinal, fundamental, primary, paramount, supreme, predominant.

Ant.: minor, inferior, subordinate, secondary, auxiliary, subsidiary.

PUSHY

Syn.: aggressive, offensive, forceful, belligerent, bold, impudent, rude, disrespectful, insolent, self-assertive.

Ant.: cowardly, timid, defensive.

QUESTIONABLE

Syn.: doubtful, uncertain, suspicious, dubious, disputable, debatable, arguable, fishy, controversial.

Ant.: certain, indisputable, obvious, evident, unquestionable, sure.

QUICKEN

Syn.: hasten, hurry, speed, accelerate, refresh, animate, rush, expedite.

Ant.: retard, slacken, moderate, curb, shorten, slow, relax, delay, impede, hinder, obstruct.

QUIET (Adj)

Syn.: calm, peaceful, serene, hushed, silent, modest, restrained, subdued, gentle, unostentatious, restful, relaxed, leisurely, unhurried, reposeful, tranquil, quiescent, unobtrusive, passive, undisturbed, motionless, still, mild, modest.

Ant.: loud, agitated, disturbed, perturbed, noisy.

QUIET (N)

Syn.: calm, calmness, hush, peace, repose, rest, silence, stillness, tranquility, serenity, quiescence, quietude.

Ant.: agitation, disturbance, uproar, noise, din, noisiness, loudness, tumult, excitement, turmoil, commotion, unrest.

RAPID

Syn.: speedy, quick, swift, fast, prompt, expeditious, hasty, hurried.

Ant.: slow, sluggish, slack, tardy, leisurely, gradual, languid.

REASONABLE

Syn.: sensible, logical, moderate, tolerable, acceptable, average, sound, fair, rational, inexpensive, sober, temperate.

Ant.: unreasonable, absurd, unfair, illogical, irrational, intolerable, immoderate, expensive, senseless, preposterous, ridiculous, silly, excessive, obstinate.

REGULAR

Syn.: proper, systematic, symmetrical, normal, usual, habitual, constant, orderly, steady, methodical, consistent.

Ant.: irregular, improper, abnormal, unusual, disorderly, inconstant, desultory, unmethodical, changeable, erratic, sporadic.

REMARKABLE

Syn.: unusual, exceptional, august, impressive, extra-ordinary, uncommon, splendid, singular, notable, noteworthy, striking, distinguished, wonderful, famous, prominent, conspicuous, imposing.

Ant.: ordinary, average, inconspicuous, normal, usual, common, customary, undistinguished.

RESPONSIBLE

Syn.: answerable, trustworthy, dependable, accountable, liable, chargeable, reliable.

Ant.: irresponsible, untrustworthy, undependable, unreliable, unaccountable, unanswerable.

RICH

Syn.: wealthy, affluent, prosperous, opulent, nourishing, abundant, ample, fruitful, fertile, luxuriant, vivid, bountiful, sumptuous, gorgeous, sonorous, weil-to-do, plentiful, fecund, well-heeled, productive, wholesome, nutritious.

Ant.: poor, needy, penniless, beggarly, indigent, destitute, barren, sterile, unfruitful, unproductive, impecunious, hard up, necessitous.

SCHOOL (V)

Syn.: train, teach, direct, lead, guide, educate, instruct, control, discipline, inform, enlighten, tutor.

Ant.: misdirect, mislead, misguide, deceive, delude.

SCRUPULOUS

Syn.: absolutely honest, extremely careful and thorough, paying great attention to details, exact, meti-culous, punctilious, upright, moral, conscientious, veracious, truthful, right-minded, high-principled.

Ant.: dishonest, deceitful, tricky, fraudulent, unscrupulous, careless, unprincipled, conscienceless, knavish.

SILLY

Syn.: foolish, doltish, indiscreet, stupid, unwise, childish, inane, fatuous, senseless, absurd, ridiculous, idiotic, nonsensical, irrational, preposterous, outrageous, imprudent.

Ant.: wise, prudent, rational, sane, discreet, sound, intelligent, sensible, sapient, sagacious, discerning, perspicacious, brainy, brilliant, well-advised, judicious, astute, shrewd.

SLY

Syn.: foxy, wily, crafty, cunning, deceitful, secretive, furtive, roguish, mischievous, stealthy, underhand, surreptitious.

Ant.: open, frank, candid, ingenuous, sincere, artless.

SOFTEN

Syn.: mollify, soothe, ease, calm, comfort, quiet, temper, moderate, mitigate, abate, allay, alleviate, assuage, diminish, lessen, extenuate, relieve.

Ant.: harden, stiffen, augment, irritate, increase, aggravate, worsen, enhance, heighten, intensify, infuriate, indurate.

SUITABLE

Syn.: appropriate, proper, fitting, right, becoming, apposite, eligible, seemly, apt, meet, decorous, seasonable.

Ant.: unsuitable, improper, unbecoming, inapt, indecorous, unseemly, ineligible, inappropriate, inapposite.

TEDIOUS

Syn.: boring, tiresome, wearisome, irksome, monotonous, dreary, uninteresting, dull, humdrum, drab.

Ant.: interesting, amusing, entertaining, exciting, delightful, brisk.

TERRIBLE

Syn.: horrible, alarming, fearful, shocking, frightful, awesome, appalling, dreadful, terrifying, frightening, formidable, terrific, horrid, terrible, fearsome.

Ant.: pleasing, encouraging, safe, secure, joyous, informidable, unastounding.

TOLERABLE

Syn.: endurable, bearable, passable, sufferable, acceptable.

Ant.: intolerable, unbearable, unacceptable, unendurable.

TOTALLY

Syn.: fully, wholly, completely, entirely, absolutely, thoroughly, perfectly, utterly.

Ant.: partially, partly, incompletely, somewhat.

TRUE

Syn.: accurate, actual, unerring, correct, authentic, exact, real, veracious, constant, faithful, loyal, genuine, precise, veritable, reliable, rightful, sincere, factual, legitimate.

Ant.: untrue, inaccurate, incorrect, inexact, unreal, unfaithful, disloyal, unreliable, insincere, false, spurious, fictitious, erroneous, inconstant, fickle, fallacious, apocryphal.

UNASSUMING

Syn.: modest, reserved, retiring, humble, diffident, bashful, shy, coy, unpretentious, unostentatious.

Ant.: arrogant, boastful, haughty, proud, vain, immodest, pretentious, ostentatious, pert, vainglorious, imperious, smug, priggish, domineering.

URBANE

Syn.: suave, affable, polite, civil, courteous, refined, well-bred, well-mannered, accomplished, sophisticated, courtly, amiable.

Ant.: uncivil, uncouth, rude, ill-mannered, discourteous, impolite, boorish, impertinent.

UTTER (Adj)

Syn.: complete, entire, thorough, full, whole, perfect, absolute, sheer, total, downwright, consummate, arrant.

Ant.: incomplete, imperfect, partial, meagre, lacking, wanting, deficient, sketchy, skimpy.

VALID

Syn.: binding, sound, legal, logical, effective, cogent, operative, weighty, well-grounded, just.

Ant.: invalid, illegal, illogical, unjust, unsound, ineffective, null and void, inoperative.

VANITY

Syn.: pride, egotism, arrogance, conceit, immodesty, self-esteem, smugness, priggishness, vainglory, boasting, boast, bombast, bluster, brag, rodomontade.

Ant.: modesty, humility, meekness, simplicity, unostentatiousness.

VIGOROUS

Syn.: energetic, active, strong, potent, powerful, mighty, forceful, animated, lively, spirited, sprightly, brisk, vivacious, intense.

Ant.: powerless, ineffective, ineffectual, dull, feeble, unsound, impotent, flabby.

VITAL

Syn.: essential, indispensable, necessary, basic, cardinal, paramount, energetic, lively, dynamic.

Ant.: unessential, unimportant, dispensable, immaterial, insignificant.

WELCOME (Adj)

Syn.: pleasing, agreeable, acceptable, gratifying, pleasant, pleasurable.

Ant.: unwelcome, unacceptable, disagreeable, distasteful, unpleasant, offensive, repugnant, repulsive, unpalatable.

WISE

Syn.: prudent, sagacious, sage, learned, profound, well-advised, judicious, scholarly, well-informed, well-read, shrewd.

Ant.: unwise, foolish, shallow, silly, stupid, inane, fatuous, injudicious, imprudent, ill-advised, doltish, uneducated, unschooled.

WRONG (Adj)

Syn.: erroneous, incorrect, unjust, inaccurate, mistaken, faulty, untrue, unprecise, improper, bad, amiss, inappropriate, unsuitable, false, unfair, unfit.

Ant.: right, correct, true, proper, suitable, exact, just, precise, fair, accurate.

YEARLING

Syn.: youngling, colt, filly, cub, whelp, puppy.

Ant.: elder, doyen, old-timer, veteran.

YEARN
Syn.: desire, strongly, pine, long, hanker, grieve, mourn.
Ant.: hate, detest, despise, loathe, dislike, abominate.

YIELDING
Syn.: pliant, tractable, docile, submissive, compliant, flexible, soft, manageable.
Ant.: intractable, unmanageable, awkward, stubborn, obstinate, obdurate, unyielding, inflexible, hard, unruly, recalcitrant.

YOUNG
Syn.: youthful, new, fresh, inexperienced, immature, youngish, teen-age, juvenile, adolescent, green, puerile.
Ant.: old, elderly, experienced, aged, senior, mature, full-grown.

ZANY (Adj)
Syn.: ridiculous, eccentric, amusing, ludicrous, foolish, doltish, silly, inane, fatuous, stupid, droll, funny, whimsical, dull, drab.
Ant.: wise, intelligent, accomplished, well-informed, shrewd, brisk, active.

ZANY (N)
Syn.: merry-andrew, buffoon, clown, madcap, fool, comedian, jester, nitwit, dunce, dolt, nincompoop, ninny, simpleton, numbskull, oaf, loon, dullard, dunderhead, blockhead, goof, idiot, booby, bonehead, dunce, imbecile.
Ant.: sage, scholar, genius, wise person, intelligent person.

ZEAL
Syn.: enthusiasm, energy, verve, keenness, vim, vigour, heartiness, earnestness, spirit, eagerness, warmth, ardour, fervour, devotion, dash, briskness, alacrity, intensity, vehemence.
Ant.: apathy, indifference, unconcern, ennui, detachment, coldness, torpor, torpidity.

ZEALOUS
Syn.: eager, keen, enthusiastic, deep, strong, intense, earnest, passionate, spirited, ardent, warm, energetic, fervent, fervid, impassioned, vehement.
Ant.: cold, apathetic, indifferent, nonchalant, calm and casual, cool.

ZENITH
Syn.: acme, top, summit, apex, climax, vertex, culmination, peak, prime, highest point.
Ant.: nadir, lowest point or part, base, bottom, foot.

ZEST
Syn.: gusto, relish, enthusiasm, exhilaration, thrill, great enjoyment or excitement.
Ant.: distaste, disrelish, dislike, insipidity.

MULTIPLE CHOICE QUESTIONS

Directions (Qs.1 to 50): *In the following questions choose the word which best expresses the meaning of the given word.*

1. INDICT
   A. Condemn B. Reprimand
   C. Accuse D. Allege
2. SCINTILLATING
   A. Smouldering B. Gilittering
   C. Touching D. Warming
3. REFECTORY
   A. Restaurant B. Parlour
   C. Living Room D. Dining Room
4. DISTINCTION
   A. Diffusion B. Disagreement
   C. Different D. Degree
5. IMPROVEMENT
   A. Advancement B. Betterment
   C. Promotion D. Preference
6. ADVERSITY
   A. Failure B. Helplessness
   C. Misfortune D. Crisis
7. TURN UP
   A. Land up B. Show up
   C. Crop up D. Come up

8. DEIFY
A. Flatter B. Challenge
C. Worship D. Face

9. ERROR
A. Misadventure B. Misgiving
C. Ambiguity D. Blunder

10. SHALLOW
A. Artificial B. Superficial
C. Foolish D. Worthless

11. MASSACRE
A. Murder B. Stab
C. Assissinate D. Slaughter

12. COMBAT
A. Conflict B. Quarrel
C. Feud D. Fight

13. VORACIOUS
A. Wild B. Hungry
C. Angry D. Quick

14. IMPROMPTU
A. Offhand B. Unimportant
C. Unreal D. Effective

15. RABBLE
A. Mob B. Noise
C. Roar D. Rubbish

16. TEPID
A. Hot B. Warm
C. Cold D. Boiling

17. MAYHEM
A. Jubilation B. Havoc
C. Excitement D. Defeat

18. TIMID
A. Fast B. Slow
C. Medium D. Shy

19. CANTANKEROUS
A. Quarrelsome B. Rash
C. Disrespectful D. Noisy

20. PRECARIOUS
A. Cautious B. Critical
C. Perilous D. Brittle

21. TACITURNITY
A. Dumbness B. Changeableness
C. Hesitation D. Reserve

22. INEBRIATE
A. Dreamy B. Stupefied
C. Unsteady D. Drunken

23. HARBINGER
A. Massenger B. Steward
C. Forerunner D. Pilot

24. INTIMIDATE
A. To hint B. Frighten
C. Bluff D. Harass

25. IRONIC
A. Inflexible
B. Bitter
C. Good-natured
D. Disguisedly sarcastic

26. STRINGENT
A. Tense
B. Stringy
C. Strict
D. Causing to shrink

27. ECSTATIC
A. Animated B. Bewildered
C. Enraptured D. Illful

28. COMMENSURATE
A. Measurable B. Proportionate
C. Beginning D. Appropriate

29. DESTITUTION
A. Humility B. Moderation
C. Poverty D. Beggary

30. ASCEND
A. Leap B. Grow
C. Deviate D. Mount

31. UNCOUTH
A. Ungraceful B. Rough
C. Slovenly D. Dirty

32. LYNCH
A. Hang B. Madden
C. Killed D. Shoot

33. LAUD
A. Lord B. Eulogy
C. Praise D. Extolled

34. CORRESPONDENCE
A. Agreements B. Contracts
C. Documents D. Letters

35. VENUE
A. Place B. Agenda
C. Time D. Duration

36. STERILE
A. Barren B. Arid
C. Childless D. Dry

37. SYNOPSIS
A. Index B. Mixture
C. Summary D. Puzzle

38. GERMANE
A. Responsible B. Logical
C. Possible D. Relevant

39. PONDER
A. Think B. Evaluate
C. Anticipate D. Increase

40. CANNY
A. Obstinate B. Handsome
C. Clever D. Stout

41. ABUNDANT
A. Ripe B. Cheap
C. Plenty D. Absent

42. CONSEQUENCES
A. Results B. Conclusions
C. Difficulties D. Applications

43. SHIVER
A. Shake B. Rock
C. Tremble D. Move

44. DILIGENT
A. Progressive B. Brilliant
C. Inventive D. Hard-working

45. DISTANT
A. Far B. Removed
C. Reserved D. Separate

46. FORAY
A. Excursion B. Contest
C. Ranger D. Intuition

47. FRUGALITY
A. Foolishness B. Extremity
C. Enthusiasm D. Economy

48. GARNISH
A. Paint B. Garner
C. Adorn D. Abuse

49. VIGOUR
A. Strength B. Boldness
C. Warmth D. Enthusiasm

50. CANDID
A. Apparent B. Explicit
C. Frank D. Bright

Directions Directions (Qs. 51 to 100): *In the following questions choose the word which is the exact opposite of the given words.*

51. DEAR
A. Priceless B. Free
C. Worthless D. Cheap

52. FLAGITIOUS
A. Innocent B. Vapid
C. Ignorant D. Frivolous

53. LIABILITY
A. Property B. Assets
C. Debt D. Teasure

54. VIRTUOUS
A. Wicked B. Corrupt
C. Vicious D. Scandalous

55. ENCOURAGE
A. Dampen B. Disapprove
C. Discourage D. Warn

56. MORTAL
A. Divine B. Immortal
C. Spiritual D. Eternal

57. LEND
A. Borrow B. Cheat
C. Pawn D. Hire

58. COMIC
A. Emotional B. Tragic
C. Fearful D. Painful

59. ADDITION
A. Division B. Enumeration
C. Subtraction D. Multiplication

60. MINOR
A. Big B. Major
C. Tall D. Heavy

61. REPEL
A. Attend B. Concentrate
C. Continue D. Attract

62. ARTIFICIAL
A. Red B. Natural
C. Truthful D. Solid

63. CAPACIOUS
A. Limited B. Caring
C. Foolish D. Changeable

64. PROVOCATION
A. Vocation B. Pacification
C. Peace D. Destruction

65. METICULOUS
A. Mutual B. Shaggy
C. Meretricious D. Slovenly

66. ABLE
A. Disable B. Inable
C. Unable D. Misable

67. COMFORT
A. Uncomfort B. Miscomfort
C. Discomfort D. None of these

68. GAIN
A. Loose B. Fall
C. Lost D. Lose

69. SYNTHETIC
A. Affable B. Natural
C. Plastic D. Cosmetic

70. ACQUITTED
A. Freed B. Burdened
C. Convicted D. Entrusted

71. STRINGENT
A. General B. Vehement
C. Lenient D. Magnanimous

72. FLIMSY
A. Frail B. Filthy
C. Firm D. Flippant

73. BUSY
A. Occupied B. Engrossed
C. Relaxed D. Engaged

74. ADAPTABLE
A. Adoptable B. Flexible
C. Yielding D. Rigid

75. LOVE
A. Villainy B. Hatred
C. Compulsion D. Force

76. BALANCE
A. Disbalance B. Misbalance
C. Debalance D. Imbalance

77. RELINQUISH
A. Abdicate B. Renounce
C. Possess D. Deny

78. MOUNTAIN
A. Plain B. Plateau
C. Precipice D. Valley

79. FICKLE
A. Courageous B. Sincere
C. Steadfast D. Humble

80. PERENNIAL
A. Frequent B. Regular
C. Lasting D. Rare

81. RARELY
A. Hardly B. Definitely
C. Frequently D. Periodically

82. STARTLED
A. Amused B. Relaxed
C. Endless D. Astonished

83. ADHERENT
A. Detractor B. Enemy
C. Alien D. Rival

84. QUIESCENT
A. Indifferent B. Troublesome
C. Weak D. Unconcerned

85. CONDENSE
A. Expand B. Distribute
C. Interpret D. Lengthen

86. BENIGN
A. Malevolent B. Soft
C. Friendly D. Unwise

87. OBSCURE
A. Implicit B. Obnoxious
C. Explicit D. Pedantic

88. HYPOCRITICAL
A. Gentle B. Sincere
C. Amiable D. Dependable

89. EVASIVE
A. Free B. Honest
C. Liberal D. Frank

90. INDUSTRIOUS
A. Indifferent B. Indolent
C. Casual D. Passive

91. EXTRICATE
A. Manifest B. Palpable
C. Release D. Entangle

92. LUCID
A. Glory B. Noisy
C. Obscure D. Distinct

93. INSIPID
A. Tasty B. Stupid
C. Discreet D. Feast

94. OBEYING
A. Ordering
B. Following
C. Refusing
D. Contradicting

95. VICTORIOUS
A. Defeated B. Annexed
C. Destroyed D. Vanquished

96. COMMISSIONED
A. Started B. Closed
C. Finished D. Terminated

97. VANITY
A. Pride B. Humility
C. Conceit D. Ostentious

98. ZENITH
A. Acme B. Top
C. Nadir D. Pinnacle

99. TANGIBLE
A. Ethereal B. Concrete
C. Actual D. Solid

100. REPRESS
A. Inhibit B. Liberate
C. Curb D. Quell

ANSWERS

1	**2**	**3**	**4**	**5**	**6**	**7**	**8**	**9**	**10**
C	B	D	C	B	C	B	C	D	B
11	**12**	**13**	**14**	**15**	**16**	**17**	**18**	**19**	**20**
D	D	B	A	A	B	B	D	A	B
21	**22**	**23**	**24**	**25**	**26**	**27**	**28**	**29**	**30**
D	D	C	B	D	C	C	B	C	D
31	**32**	**33**	**34**	**35**	**36**	**37**	**38**	**39**	**40**
A	C	C	D	A	A	C	D	A	C
41	**42**	**43**	**44**	**45**	**46**	**47**	**48**	**49**	**50**
C	A	C	D	A	A	D	C	A	C
51	**52**	**53**	**54**	**55**	**56**	**57**	**58**	**59**	**60**
D	A	B	C	C	B	A	B	C	B
61	**62**	**63**	**64**	**65**	**66**	**67**	**68**	**69**	**70**
D	B	A	B	D	C	C	D	B	C
71	**72**	**73**	**74**	**75**	**76**	**77**	**78**	**79**	**80**
C	C	C	D	B	D	C	D	C	D
81	**82**	**83**	**84**	**85**	**86**	**87**	**88**	**89**	**90**
D	B	B	A	C	A	C	B	B	B
91	**92**	**93**	**94**	**95**	**96**	**97**	**98**	**99**	**100**
D	C	A	A	A	D	B	C	A	B

7 Pair of Words

There are many words in English which seem or sound similar and cause confusion and errors in their usage. Go through some such words and their usage here and answer the questions thereafter.

1. **Abject** (*miserable; degraded*) : Many of our labourers live in a state of abject poverty.

   Object (*aim; purpose*) : His only object in life is to make money.

2. **Abstain** (*keep oneself from a thing*) : The doctor advised Arun to abstain from alcoholic drinks if he wanted to keep fit.

   Refrain (*keep oneself from an act or from doing something*) : Asha would be popular if only she refrained from grumbling at everything.

3. **Accede** (*to agree*) : The teacher acceded to the student's request.

   Exceed (*to go beyond*) : He has to borrow money by the end of the month as his expenditure always exceeds his income.

4. **Accept** (*consent to receive; answer affirmatively*) : He readily accepted the offer of a job.

   Except (*leaving out*) : All except Sunil came to the party.

5. **Access** (*approach*) : A popular leader is generally easy of access.

   Excess (*more than necessary*) : He has ruined his health because he eats and drinks in excess.

6. **Accident** (*an unexpected or chance happening*) : (i) She died in an accident. (ii) My getting a prize was a pure accident.

   Incident (*event*) : The explorer related to us some of the interesting incidents of his life.

7. **Adapt** (*to fit or adjust*) : We must adapt ourselves to our surroundings if we want to lead a contented life.

   Adept (*skilled*) : He is adept in the art of flattery.

   Adopt (*1. to take up*) : Students these days adopt unfair means to get through examinations. (*2.* take a person into a relationship he did not previously *occupy*) Having no child of their own, Mr. and Mrs. Sharma have decided to adopt one.

8. **Affect** (*1. to produce material effect*) : The drought has adversely affected agriculture production. (*2. to pretend*) He affected ignorance of the situation in order to escape the police inquiry.

   Effect (noun *result*) : The drought has had little effect on agricultural production this year. (*verb to bring about*): The necessary changes have been effected in the time-table.

9. **Allude** (*to make an indirect reference*) : The speaker alluded more than once to the moral degeneration of today's youth.

   Elude (*to escape; evade*) : The criminal eluded the police for a long time.

10. **Allusion** (*indirect reference*) : This essay is full of historical allusions.

    Illusion (*a deception; false notion*) : She is suffering from the illusion that she is the most intelligent girl in the class.

11. **Altar** (*place of worship*) : He lit a lamp at the altar before kneeling down to pray.

Alter (*to change*) : I had to alter my plans because of the sudden airlines strike.

12. **Alternate** (*coming by turns*) : Every alternate Saturday we have a regional film on the television

Alternative (*a choice between two things*) : Having missed the last bus he had no alternative but to walk home.

13. **Alteration** (*change*) : Some alterations in the programme had to be made to accommodate the new item.

Altercation (*quarrel*) : There was a minor altercation between the two friends over a torn book

14. **Apathy** (*indifference; want of feeling*) : The apathy of the general public towards accident victims is shocking.

Antipathy (*dislike; hostility*) : I like coffee but I have an antipathy for tea. Arun's antipathy towards Sunil is affecting their business partnership.

15. **Apposite** (*suitable*) : He made the apposite congratulatory remarks while giving out the prizes.

Opposite (*1. facing in front of*) : He stood opposite me. (2. *contrary*) His opinion on the matter is opposite to me.

16. **Appreciable** (*capable of being estimated*) : No appreciable progress has been made in the negotiations.

Appreciative (*full of appreciation or high esteem*) : Her graceful dancing deserved the appreciative comments of the critics.

17. **Apprehensive** (*1. having a feeling of fear*) She was apprehensive that her unexpected arrival might cause inconvenience to her hosts. (2. *perceptive*) : He was fully apprehensive of the beauty of the painting.

Comprehensive (*1. including much*) : He wrote a comprehensive letter to explain all aspects of the situation. (2. *of understanding*) : He has a remarkable comprehensive faculty; he can master those topics in a day's time.

18. **Ardent** (*enthusiastic, eager*) : He is an ardent admirer of Western music and never misses a concert in town

Arduous (*hard to achieve; strenuous*) : It is only after arduous practice that he has become a great musician.

19. **Artistic** (*concerned with art*) : Her artistic taste is reflected in the things she buys.

Artful (*skilful, cunning*) : His artful schemes did not succeed; they were seen through.

Artificial (*not natural*) : If we could invent artificial rain our agricultural production need not be affected by drought.

20. **Ascent** (*climbing up*) : The ascent to the top of the mountain tired the boys.

Assent (*consent*) : Without the Principal's assent the children could not leave the school.

21. **Aspire** (*to desire eagerly*) : He has always aspired to fame as an explorer.

Expire (*to come to an end*) : As his contract with the firm has expired, he is on the look out for some other job.

22. **Avocation** (*minor occupation*) : Music is an avocation with many a scientist.

Vocation (*profession; employment*) : He wanted to take up medicine as his vocation but circumstances forced him to become a teacher.

Vacation (*holiday of a fixed period from work*) : During the summer vacation many students go in for activities like trekking.

23. **Award** (*what is conferred; adjustment*) : Satyajit Ray has won many awards for his directorial skill.

Reward (*what is given in return for something done or received*) : The salesman got a reward for his honest action of returning the bag of money left by a customer.

24. **Bail** (*release on security given for appearance*) : As the man had been accused of murdering, the magistrate refused him bail.

Bale (*package; bundle*) : Many bales of cotton were destroyed in the recent fire in the godown.

25. **Bare** (*uncovered; unclothed; undisguised*) : The bare truth of the matter is that there is a lack of political will to improve the conditions of the poor.

Bear (*1. carry*) : He had to bear the heavy box all the way from the station. (*2. endure*) : Delhi's summers are too hot to bear with all these power cuts.

26. **Beneficial** (*advantageous*) : The extra classes will be beneficial for the weak students.

Beneficent (*showing active kindness*) : His beneficent nature was well in evidence during the recent floods when he distributed free blankets and food to the victims.

27. **Berth** (*sleeping place; proper place for anything*) : As I am undertaking a long journey by train I would like to reserve a berth for me.

Birth (*bring forth offspring; origin*) : The birth of a child is generally an occasion of joy.

28. **Beside** (*by the side of*) : We decided to have our lunch beside the lake.

Besides (*in addition to*) : Besides Arun, there were eleven people at the meeting.

29. **Born** (*come into the world by birth*) : He was born at midnight on November *30, 2012*.

Borne (*past participle of bear*) : He has borne his responsibilities with cheerful efficiency.

30. **Bridal** (*relating to bride or wedding*) : It is a custom to distribute the bridal cake among the guests.

Bridle (*head-gear of a horse by which it is controlled*) : He put the bridle on the horse before leading it out of the stables. (As a verb — *to control or keep in check*) : She should bridle her tongue.

31. **Canvas** (*coarse cloth of which sails and tents are made*) : Tennis players wear the shoes made of canvas.

Canvass (*to solicit votes, favour etc.*) : His supporters went from door to door canvassing for him.

32. **Casual** (*incidental*) : He made a casual reference to the Buddha while speaking on the need of world peace.

Causal (*denoting cause*) : The causal factors for India's backward economic status were clearly stated by the speaker.

33. **Cemetery** (*burial place*) : As he passed a cemetery he remembered his dead wife.

Symmetry (*harmony*) : The symmetry of the building made us marvel at the architectural skill of its planners.

34. **Capture** (*catch or take into custody; conquer*) : The thief was captured by the police just as he was leaving the station.

Captivate (*to attract*) : The little girl captivated us by her beautiful singing.

35. **Ceremonial** (*relating to ceremonies, formal*) : Visiting heads of state get a ceremonial welcome in every country.

Ceremonious (*showing addiction to ceremony; pettily formal or punctilious*) His ceremonious treatment of even close friends is somewhat ridiculous.

36. **Childish** (*immature ; improper for a grown up person*) : It was childish of Peter to pick a quarrel with the salesman over such a trivial matter.

Childlike (*innocent; like a child*) : His childlike simplicity is not appreciated by his shrewd business partner.

37. **Cite** (*to quote*) : The speaker cited several instances to support his argument.

Sight (*vision; view*) : His sight is growing rather weak. The village was a beautiful sight on Diwali night.

Site (*ground on which building stands or stood or is to stand*) : Being centrally located in the city, this is an ideal site for the hospital.

38. **Coarse** (*1. indecent*) : His coarse jokes irritate many people. (*2. rough*) This cloth is coarse but it is durable.

Course (*1. direction taken*) : The rivers change their course after a mile or so from here.

(*2. part of a meal served at one time*) The dinner consisted of five courses.

39. **Collision** (*striking together: clash*) : The collision between the two buses resulted in several deaths.

Collusion (*secret agreement for committing a crime or fraud*) The watchman must have been in collusion with the thief for such a daring robbery to take place.

40. **Compliment** (*expression of praise*) : She accepts a compliment coolly.

Complement (*that which completes*) : Man and woman should complement each other.

41. **Comprehensive** (*detailed*) The police officer gave a comprehensive report on the dacoity.

Comprehensible (*that which can be understood*) : He bored his listeners as most of what he said was not comprehensible.

42. **Confidant** (*one entrusted with confidences or secrets*) : Only her confidant must be knowing why Reena does not come to college these days.

Confident (*fully assured, bold*) : He is confident of overcoming all the problems and making his business a success.

Confidential (*spoken or written in confidence*) : The matter is confidential and cannot be discussed at the meeting.

43. **Confirm** (*1. establish more firmly*) : The result of the election confirmed the party in power. (*2. corroborate*) : I did not believe Reena's story till her mother confirmed it.

Conform (*adapt oneself to; comply with*) : She was liked by her family as long as she conformed to their wishes, but became unpopular when she asserted her opinion.

44. **Congenial** (*sympathetic; suited*) : The weather was congenial for a picnic.

Congenital (*belonging to one from birth*) : His blindness is congenital and cannot be cured.

45. **Conscience** (*sense of right and wrong*) : The murderer was troubled by his conscience and decided to give himself up to the police.

Conscious (*aware; knowing*) : His is fully conscious of the consequences of such an action.

Conscientious (*scrupulous; obedient to conscience*) : He is a conscientious worker and deserves all praise.

46. **Considerable** (*worth considering; much*) : Asha had to face considerable opposition from her family for wanting to study medicine.

Considerate (*thoughtful for others*) : He was considerate enough to take some fruits for his friend who was ill.

47. **Continual** (*always going on*) : The movement of the sun and the planets is continual. It rained continually for more than five days.

Continuous (*uninterrupted; without any break*) : The continuous chatter of the girls disturbed and annoyed me.

48. **Council** (*assembly or any other body elected or nominated*) : The Council of ministers is responsible to the Legislature.

Counsel (*advice*) : I decided to act upon my father's wise counsel.

49. **Credible** (*believable*) : He lies in such a credible manner that he can get away with anything.

Credulous (*one who believes things easily*) : Reena is too credulous if she believed that tall story.

50. **Custom** (*established practice*) : The customs of tribal societies seem odd to outsiders.

Habit (*settled practice of an individual*) : Arun has got into the bad habit of snapping his fingers while he speaks.

51. **Dairy** (*place supplying milk, cream etc.*) : The Government dairy has a limited supply of milk in summer.

Diary (*daily record*) : Some people enter every boring little thing into their diary.

52. **Decease** (*death*) : It was only two days before his father's decease that Arun arrived in Delhi.

Disease (*sickly condition; sickness*) Modern medicine can cure several diseases which were once incurable.

53. **Decent** (*respectable; proper*) : Arun bought some decent clothes before he went abroad.

Descent (*coining down*) : The car went out of control on its descent from Mussoorie and fell into a ditch.

Dissent (*disagreement*) : There was a lone voice of dissent when the teacher suggested that the class should go for a picnic.

54. **Defect** (*shortcoming*) : The defect of this plan is that too much money will be needed to implement it.

Deficiency (*being incomplete; falling short in quality or quantity*) : It is some deficiency of blood that is making Asha so ill.

55. **Defer** (*postpone*) : The unexpected floods forced us to defer our journey to a later date.

Differ (*disagree*) : My brother thinks girls should not go out to work but I differ with him on this issue.

56. **Deliverance** (*rescue*) : The rains were a deliverance to the farmers who were worried that their crops would fail.

Delivery (*1. distribution of letters, parcels etc.*) The little boy was responsible for the delivery of newspapers every morning (*2. childbirth*) She was admitted to the hospital for the delivery.

57. **Dependent** (*relying*) : Indian farmers are dependent on the rains even now in the age of scientific agriculture.

Dependant (*one who depends on another for support*) : Though he earns a good salary, he cannot save much as he has several dependents to support.

58. **Desert** (*1. sandy plain*) : There are plans to convert the deserts of Rajasthan into fertile agricultural land. (*2. leave*) : She always deserts her friends when they need her help.

Dessert (*a sweet dish at the end of a meal*) : We had ice-cream for dessert.

59. **Discover** (*Find something which already exists but is not known*) : Columbus discovered America after a long and difficult voyage.

Invent (*devise a new thing*) : The Wright brothers invented the aeroplane.

60. **Disinterested** (*impartial*) : It is necessary for a critic of art to be disinterested.

Uninterested (*not interested*) : He was totally uninterested in what was going on in the class.

61. **Draft** (*rough sketch*) : He made many drafts before writing the application.

Draught (*current of air in a room*) : Though all the windows were closed, a cold draught was coming from somewhere.

Drought (*want of rain*) : Indian agriculture suffers either because of floods or due to drought.

62. **Earthen** (*made of earth; baked clay*) : Water stored in and earthen pots is cool.

Earthly (*of the earth, terrestrial*) : The blow of the hammer was enough to end his earthly life.

63. **Economic** (*to do with economics; on a business footing*) : The economic development of a country depends mainly on industrial development.

Economical (*saving; thrifty*) : She can manage a household of five members on a small income because she is economical.

64. **Educational** (*adjective from education*) : The educational institutions today are greatly affected by student unrest.

Educative (*that which has the power of educating*) : The educative value of films should not be underestimated.

65. **Elemental** (*connected with the elements or forces of the physical world*): As he encountered the elemental fury of the storm, Joseph wondered if he would ever reach home safely.

Elementary (*rudimentary*) : His knowledge of electronics is only elementary; he will not be able to repair your TV.

66. **Elicit** (*to draw out*) : The police failed to elicit a confession from the prisoner.

Illicit (*unlicenced*) : The illicit liquor trade has caused many deaths.

Illegal (*contrary to law*) : It is illegal to accept bribes.

67. **Eligible** (*fit to be chosen*) : Arun's qualifications make him eligible to this job.

Illegible (*indistinct*) : This letter is illegible; it must have been written in a hurry.

68. **Elusive** (*escaping from grasp*) : Happiness and contentment are highly elusive on this earth.

Illusive (*deceptive*) : His expensive clothes are illusive, as he is truly speaking, rather poor.

69. **Eminent** (*distinguished*) : The eminent historian gave a very interesting talk on the Indus Valley civilization.

Imminent (*a danger that is about to happen; impending*) : An outbreak of cholera seems imminent in the areas affected by floods.

70. **Enviable** (*worthy of envy*) : Her popularity is enviable.

Envious (*feeling envy*) : The poor are naturally envious of the rich.

71. **Erratic** (*irregular, unpredictable*) : The power supply becomes erratic with the coming of summer.

Erroneous (*mistaken; incorrect*) : He has the erroneous impression that he can pass the examination without studying.

72. **Eruption** (*bursting out*) : The volcanic eruption destroyed several villages.

Irruption (*sudden invasion*) : Frequent irruptions by barbarians destroyed the ancient civilization.

73. **Exalt** (*to place high in rank; praise*) : Mahatma Gandhi has been rightly exalted for his role in the freedom struggle.

Exult (*to rejoice*) : The nation exulted over the victory in the war.

74. **Exceptionable** (*objectionable*) : The exceptionable scenes in the film were censored.

Exceptional (*extraordinary*) : Gandhi was a man of exceptional moral courage.

75. **Exhausting** (*tiring*) : The work was of an exhausting nature, but I managed to do it in time.

Exhaustive (*comprehensive*) : The exhaustive notes on the poem were very useful to the students.

76. **Expedient** (*advisable*) : He found it expedient to talk over the matter with his wife before taking an action.

Expeditious (*quick*) : They have devised some expeditious methods to solve the flood problem.

77. **Expose** (*to unmask*) : As soon as the fingerprints were checked, Don was exposed as the thief.

Espouse (*to support a doctrine, cause*) : The students are ready to espouse the cause of women's freedom.

78. **Extant** (*still existing*) : The students were not sure about the oldest extant animal species.

Extent (*size; degree*) : The extent of damage caused by the earthquake has not yet been assessed.

Extinct (*no longer existing*) : The Great Indian Bustard is in danger of becoming extinct and must be protected.

79. **Facility** (*comfort; ease*) : (1) They were given every facility to make their stay pleasant. (2) She can speak several languages with facility.

Felicity (*happiness*) : They are fortunate to live long in married felicity

80. **Fair** (*1. just*) : His decision was fair. (*2. fair complexioned*) A fair skin is natural and cannot be obtained by using creams and cosmetics. (iii. *periodical market, festival*) They had a good time at the Diwali Fair.

Fare (*1. Charge to be paid for a journey*) : The railway fare from Delhi to Bombay has become very high. (*2. food provided*) : The fare at this hotel is not worth its cost.

81. **Fatal** (*deadly, resulting in death*) : Drunken driving causes many a fatal accident.

Fateful (*producing important results*) : To break the salt law was a fateful decision in the independence struggle.

82. Formally (*ceremoniously*) : The exhibition was formally inaugurated by the Prime Minister.

Formerly (*previously*) : Now tubewells have eased the water supply; formerly, taps remained dry for days together.

83. Foul (*unfair, disgusting*) : It was foul weather for a walk.

Fowl (*bird, like chicken*) : He keeps several fowls on his poultry farm.

84. Gait (*manner of walking*) : The criminal was identified by his peculiar gait.

Gate (*opening in a wall or to a garden*) : She opened the gate and went in.

85. Gentle (*polite; mild*) : She is liked by the children because she is gentle to them.

Genteel (*characteristic of the gentry*) : She puts on airs she thinks herself to be a genteel lady.

86. Graceful (*pleasing*) : She has a graceful walk.

Gracious (*kind*) : He was a gracious man and his servants liked him.

87. Heal (*become healthy again; get cured*) : The doctors told the boy that his broken arm would soon heal.

Heel (*part of foot*) : She felt a terrible pain as a nail went into her heel.

88. Historic (*notable in history*) It was a historic occasion for India when her scientists sent the first satellite into space.

Historical (*relating to history*) : The historical records are kept at the museum.

89. Hoard (*to collect secretly*) : Unscrupulous traders hoard essential commodities in order to increase their prices.

Horde (*crowd*) A horde of football fans rushed out on to the grounds when their favourite team won the match.

90. Honorary (*holding an office without any salary*) He is honorary secretary of the club but does his work well.

Honourable (*worthy of honour*) : He is an honourable man and deserves the praise he has received.

91. Idle (*without work*) : He likes to sit idle while the others work.

Idol (*image*) : A stone idol of god Shiva was stolen and sold abroad for a huge amount.

92. Imaginary (*not real*) : The children were told to write about an imaginary space flight.

Imaginative (*full of imagination*) : The poem is richly imaginative and has won much acclaim.

93. Incite (*instigate*) : Unscrupulous politicians incite the students to become violent.

Insight (*capacity to look deep into something*) : A writer must have insight into human nature if he wants to write well.

94. Inconstant (*not sticking to one thing*) He is an inconstant man and has changed his job for the fourth time in two months.

Inconsistent (*self-contradictory*): Henry is so inconsistent that one cannot rely on his instructions. His claims are inconsistent with the facts.

95. Industrial (*relating to industry*) : A clear-cut industrial policy is essential for the economic progress of any country.

Industrious (*hardworking*) : The industrious boys had no trouble in passing the examination.

96. Ingenious (*skilful, clever*) : Shyam had an ingenious plan to make the painted scenery look realistic.

Ingenuous (*innocent*) : The little boy has an ingenuous look, but he is rather sly.

97. Intense (*extreme*) : The intense heat was more than Neera could bear.

Intensive (*concentrated*) : A month's intensive study was required for Shyam to face the examination with confidence.

98. **Judicial** (*proper to a court of law; characteristic of a judge*) : A judicial inquiry was ordered into the rioting.

Judicious (*having sound judgement*) : Sheela is judicious in the choice of books for children.

99. **Later** (*comparative degree of late*) : Sheela decided to complete her homework first and go to play later.

Latter (*last-mentioned or named*) : Both Arun and Ajay are coming to Delhi but the latter will be coming by plane.

100. **Lay** (i. *arrange, esp. horizontally*) : It was decided to lay the foundation stone of the hospital before the end of this month. (ii. *past tense of lie*): He lay down under the tree to rest.

Lie (*1. have one's body in more or less horizontal position along a surface — of persons or animals: to be at rest—things*): She decided to lie down in the shade of the tree to rest. Meera is carelessly playing while her shoes lie in the garden getting wet in the rain. (*2. falsehood*) : She was ready with a lie when she asked why she came late.

101. **Lightening** (*making lighter*) : The budget, instead of lightening the burden of taxes, has added more levies.

Lightning (*electric flash in the clouds*) : The lightning was followed by peals of thunder.

102. **Literate** (*one who knows how to read and write*) : Many of our villagers get cheated because they are not literate and sign something which they cannot read.

Literary (*pertaining to literature*) : He spends most of his money on buying books as he is a man of literary tastes.

103. **Loathe** (*hate*) : I loathe the sight of dirty dishes.

Loth (*unwilling*) : She was loth to share her food with her friends.

104. **Loose** (*1. not tight*) : She wore loose clothes for comfort. (*2. to set free*): That dog is too dangerous to let loose.

Lose (*be deprived of, cease to possess*) : Pramod will lose all his toys if he is so careless.

105. **Luxuriant** (*rich in growth*) : Most advertisements for hair oil promise their users luxuriant hair

Luxurious (*rich of growth*) : Having won a lottery, he leads a luxurious life.

106. **Masterly** (*excellent*) : He is a masterly player of golf.

Masterful (*dominating*) : He has the masterful nature to manage troublesome boys.

107. **Medal** (*Piece of metal with some inscription awarded on occasions*) : He was given a gold medal for standing first in the college.

Meddle (*interfere*) : Her aunt always meddles with her affairs.

108. **Momentary** (*lasting only a moment*) : There was a momentary silence before the audience burst out in applause.

Momentous (*important*) : Momentous changes have taken place in the country since independence

109. **Moral** (*principles of right or wrong*) : Unless men live according to certain moral values, society will suffer.

Morale (*mental condition which enables persons to keep courage*) : The general's speech boosted the morale of the soldiers.

110. **Necessaries** (*essentials*) : Some people are so poor that they cannot even afford the necessaries of life.

Necessities (*pressing needs*) : The Government should act quickly to meet the necessities of the time.

111. **Negligent** (*careless*) : He is so absorbed in his work that he is quite negligent about his dress.

Negligible (*so little that it can be neglected*) : The rise in temperature is negligible and need cause no worry.

112. **Notable** (*worthy of note; eminent*) : She is a notable writer and is sure to win wide acclaim.

Notorious (*unfavorably-known*) : He is a notorious criminal.

113. Observance (*practice customarily performed*) : The sternest observance of discipline is required if this country is to progress.

Observation (*perception*) : His keen observation of life helped him become a great writer.

114. Official (*relating to office*) : He had to go to Bombay on official work.

Officious (*meddlesome*) : She is disliked by everybody because of her officious manners.

115. Ordinance (*a rule or order*) : The President issued an ordinance banning strikes in essential services.

Ordnance (*military weapons*) : The thieves had stolen some rifles from the ordnance depot.

116. Pail (*bucket*) : We went to fill a pail of water from the public tap.

Pale (*whitish appearance*) *:* He grew pale with fear as the armed robbers came closer.

117. Pair (*two of a kind*) : We bought Neera a new pair of shoes.

Pare (*to cut the outer surface or edge*) *:* She pared her nails

118. Peace (*freedom from disturbance*) : The two warring nations at last arrived at a solution and there was peace.

Piece (*portion*) : She wrote the address on a piece of paper.

119. Persecute (*oppress*) ; The Protestants were persecuted in the reign of Queen Mary in England.

Prosecute (*initiate legal proceedings against*) *:* It was decided to prosecute the thief *as* there was enough evidence against him.

120. Personal (*private*) : As the letter was addressed 'personal', the manager's secretary did not open it.

Personnel (*body of persons*) *:* The personnel working for that company are satisfied by the conditions.

121. Piteous (*fit to excite pity*) *:* The dog's piteous cries made the old woman open the door and let it in.

Pitiable (*deserving pity*) : The beggar was in a pitiable condition.

Pitiful (*full of pity; feeling pity*) *:* She was pitiful towards the weak creatures.

122. Plain (*1. simple, unvarnished*) : I have told you the plain truth. (*2. not attractive*) Kamal may be a plain girl she does not bother much about her dress etc. (*3. level ground*) There was no rain in the plains this year.

Plane (*surface*) : The experiment involved the movement of an object down an inclined plane.

123. Popular (*liked by people*) : Her good humour and cheerfulness make her popular with her colleagues.

Populous (*thickly populated*) The populous areas of the city were greatly affected by the water shortage.

124. Pore (*1. small hole*) : The pores on our skin are very useful. (*2. be absorbed in studying etc.*) He pored over his books late into the night preparing for the examinations.

Pour (*to cause to flow*) : I poured the coffee into two cups.

125. Practicable (*that which can be translated into action*) *:* He is enthusiastic about formulating plans but his ideas are not practicable.

Practical (*pertaining to action or realities*) : He is a practical man and has no patience with dreamers.

126. Pray (*beseech earnestly, especially God*) *:* She prayed for the good health of her children.

Prey (*animal hunted or killed by another for food*) : The deer was an easy prey for the hungry tiger. (*to kill*) The lion preys upon the animals of the forest.

127. Precede (*to go before*) : Seema feels that duty should precede pleasure.

Proceed (*to go on*) : After a brief introduction the lecturer proceeded to give details of the experiment.

128. Prescribe (*refer to*) : The course prescribed for study was rather lengthy.

Proscribe (*prohibit; condemn*) : The Government has proscribed many pornographic books but they are available in some pavement shops.

129. Principal (*chief*) : The principal of the college is a strict disciplinarian.

Principle (*a view or conviction that governs conduct*) : It is against his principles to bribe people to get his work done.

130. Propose (*suggest*) : He proposed that we all go for a picnic by the lake.

Purpose (*object*) : His purpose in going to the city was to look for a job.

131. Punctual (*observant of the appointed time*) : The trains are not punctual during the rainy season.

Punctilious (*extremely carefuls*) : He is punctilious about keeping regular hours.

132. Quiet (*calm; silent*) : The quiet class was suddenly disturbed when a stray dog came into the room.

Quite (*completely*) : It was a long way to walk and Asha was quite tired before half the journey was done.

133. Rain (*condensed moisture of atmosphere falling in separate drops*) : A sudden shower of rain made us run for cover.

Reign (*rule*) : The reign of the Gupta kings is renowned for development in art and culture in Ancient India.

Rein (*curb; means of control*) : Asha should rein her temper if she wants people to like her.

134. Respectable (*worthy of respect*) : He comes from a poor but respectable family.

Respectful (*showing respect*) : Arun is always respectful to his elders.

Respective (*proper to each*) : The students were told to go to their respective classrooms.

135. Right (*1. moral or just*—used of conduct) : He believes in doing the right thing even if it is troublesome. (*2. fair claim; thing one is entitled to*) Every man has the right to freedom in a democracy.

Rite (*ceremony*) : The marriage rites took a long time.

136. Sail (*piece of canvas or other material extended to catch the wind and propel the boat or vessel, travel on water by use of sails*) : The sails of the boat had been torn to shreds in the violent storm.

Sale (*selling*) : The sale of milk products is often banned in the summer because of milk shortage.

137. Sensible (*of good sense*) : She is a sensible girl and will look after the children in her mother's absence.

Sensitive (*easily affected*) : Anita is so sensitive to criticism that the slightest frown will bring tears to her eyes.

138. Sew (*fasten by means of a needle and thread*) : She had to sew the buttons on the shirt before she went out.

Sow (*scatter seed on the ground for the purpose of growth*); : It was time for the farmers to sow wheat. (*adult female hog*) The sow was furious when some children threw sticks and stones at it.

139. Smell (*odour*) : The smell of the soup was appetising.

Smelly (*giving out a bad odour*) : She held her nose as she pushed away the dirty smelly dog.

140. Soar (*to fly high*) : The kite soared in the sky as the boy loosened the string.

Sore (*painful*) : Her sore knee troubled her all through the night.

Sour (*of acid taste*) : The milk turned sour as it had been left out in the heat.

141. Social (*relating to organised society*) Individual right sometimes have to be given up for social good.

Sociable (*friendly*) He is a sociable person and can get on with almost anyone.

142. Sole (*1. one and only*) He is the sole heir to his uncle's property. (*2. lower surface of* *foot)* : As he had walked all the way barefoot his soles were badly cut and bruised.

Soul (*spiritual entity*) : All religions give more importance to the welfare of the soul than to the physical well-being.

143. Spacious (*having space*) : The children could move about freely in the spacious garden.

Specious (*false, though seemingly true*) The lawyer's specious arguments naturally failed to convince the judge.

144. Stationary (*not moving*) : The stationary balloon indicated that there was no wind.

Stationery (*writing material*) : She went to buy some letter paper from the stationery shop.

145. Statue (*image*) : It was decided to set up a stone statue of Gandhi at the Town Hall.

Statute (*written law of a legislative body*) : The statue prohibiting child labour has been of little use.

146. Straight (*direct; not crooked*) : This road leads straight to the station.

Strait (*1. narrow passage of water between the seas or oceans*) : The Straits of Gibraltar is of strategic importance to the British. (*2. distress usually used in the plural*) : He was in bad straits when his father died leaving him penniless.

147. Superficial (*pertaining to the surface; shallow*) : A superficial knowledge of the subject is not enough for a lecturer's job.

Superfluous (*unnecessary; exceeding requirement*) He has written several pages but most of the material is superfluous.

148. Team (*set of players on one side*) : Our school's football team had an easy victory in today's inter-school match.

Teem (*to abound in*) The grounds were teeming with the people who had come to listen to the Prime Minister.

149. Temporal (*worldly; belonging to the present life*) In the Middle Ages the Church had temporal as well as spiritual authority.

Temporary (*lasting only for a time*) : She is taking up a temporary job.

150. Urban (*of the city*) : The urban population has increased by leaps and bounds in the last ten years while the rural population is steadily declining.

Urbane (*smooth, polite*) : His urbane manners make him popular.

151. Vain (*1. fruitless; useless*) : It is vain to go to the museum today as it will be closed. (*2. conceited*) : Aruna is vain about her fair complexion. (*3. empty; trivial*) His claims of being a great athlete are mere vain boasts.

Vein (*1. a blood vessel*) : The veins carry blood back to the heart. (*2. distinctive character or tendency*) He spoke in *a* humorous vein.

Vane (*weather-cock*) : As the vane was not moving we knew that it was a windless day.

152. Veracity (*truthfulness*) : No one questioned the veracity of his statement as he was known to be a man of integrity.

Voracity (*greediness*) : The hungry dog fell to eating with voracity.

153. Virtual (*in effect, not in actual* fact) : Though Aruna is the class monitor, Ashok is the virtual leader of the students.

Virtuous (*possessing virtue; chaste*) : The virtuous man resisted all temptation to become rich by criminal means.

154. Venal (*sold for money; mercenary*) : Once an artist becomes venal his art deteriorates in quality.

Venial (*pardonable*) : Smoking and drinking are his venial faults but his callous neglect of his children is a serious matter.

155. Waive (*not to insist on*) : He is otherwise so well-qualified for the job that his employers waived the condition of nationality in his case.

Wave (*long body of water curling and breaking on the shore*): She liked to sit on the beach and watch the waves playing by the shore.

156. Whether (*if or if not*) : I do not know whether Arun will be coming to office today.

Weather (*atmospheric conditions prevailing at a place and time*) : As the weather was fine that day, we enjoyed the picnic.

Climate (*conditions of temperature, moisture, etc. in a region prevailing for a long time.*) : The climate of bill stations is not suitable for asthmatic people.

MULTIPLE CHOICE QUESTIONS

Directions: *Select the appropriate option to fill in the blanks.*

1. If .... is lost everything is lost.
A. Character B. Characteristics
C. Any one of these D. None of these

2. There is a film .... board in India to censor the films.
A. Censure B. Censor
C. Any one of these D. None of these

3. I have applied for two days .... leave.
A. Casual B. Causal
C. Any one of these D. None of these

4. It is a/an .... to think that honesty does not pay.
A. Error B. Mistake
C. Any one of these D. None of these

5. In the second World .... atom bombs were dropped on Nagasaki and Hiroshima.
A. War B. Battle
C. Any one of these D. None of these

6. Lord Rama went into .... for fourteen years.
A. Banishment B. Exile
C. Any one of these D. None of these

7. India Gate is a war ....
A. Memorable B. Memorial
C. Any one of these D. None of these

8. The .... gate of the building was closed.
A. Main B. Mane
C. Any one of these D. None of these

9. She was awarded a gold .... for bravery.
A. Meddle B. Medal
C. Any one of these D. None of these

10. .... is followed by thunder.
A. Lightning B. Lightening
C. Any one of these D. None of these

11. I have not received any .... from my father for the past two months.
A. Latter B. Letter
C. Any one of these D. None of these

12. Avoid using this .... as it is very narrow.
A. Lain B. Lane
C. Any one of these D. None of these

13. The lawyer quoted many .... in support of his argument.
A. Precedents B. Presidents
C. Any one of these D. None of these

14. The doctor has .... this medicine for my father.
A. Prescribed B. Proscribed
C. Any one of these D. None of these

15. Tresspassers will be ....
A. Persecuted B. Prosecuted
C. Any one of these D. None of these

16. My brother has no .... experience of factory life.
A. Practical B. Practicable
C. Any one of these D. None of these

17. Theory .... practice.
A. Proceeds B. Precedes
C. Any one of these D. None of these

18. I .... the house where my sister was born.
A. Recollect
B. Remember
C. Any one of these
D. None of these

19. The .... of mango trees are very deep.
A. Roots B. Routes
C. Any one of these D. None of these

20. Mohan is .... of his success.
A. Sanguinary B. Sanguine
C. Any one of these D. None of these

21. A .... man like Mr. Malhotra should not have used such words.
A. Sensible B. Sensitive
C. Any one of these D. None of these

22. We sat in the .... of a tree.
A. Shade B. Shadow
C. Any one of these D. None of these

23. My eyes are ....
A. Soar B. Sore
C. Any one of these D. None of these

24. Our new house is very ....
A. Spacious B. Specious
C. Any one of these D. None of these

25. I will tell a .... to those who complete their homework.
A. Storey B. Story
C. Any one of these D. None of these

26. She has not sent a .... to my letter.
A. Reply B. Answer
C. Any one of these D. None of these

27. Shyam is .... to drinking.
A. Devoted B. Addicted
C. Any one of these D. None of these

28. He is the ....boy that stole your pen.
A. Very B. Vary
C. Any one of these D. None of these

29. This child is the .... survivor of this accident.
A. Sole B. Soul
C. Any one of these D. None of these

30. We should not .... others' things.
A. Steel B. Steal
C. Any one of these D. None of these

31. Might is ....
A. Right B. Write
C. Any one of these D. None of these

32. The whole shop was .... to the ground by the fire.
A. Rays B. Razed
C. Any one of these D. None of these

33. The Planning Commission is drawing the next five year ....
A. Plan B. Plane
C. Any one of these D. None of these

34. Rajputs belong to a .... race.
A. Marshal B. Martial
C. Any one of these D. None of these

35. Give me a blade to .... my nails.
A. Pair B. Pare
C. Any one of these D. None of these

36. .... were issued by the court to summon the suspects.
A. Ardours B. Orders
C. Any one of these D. None of these

37. This is a .... problem, you cannot solve it easily.
A. Knotty B. Naughty
C. Any one of these D. None of these

38. Arvind has purchased a new .... of shoes for two hundred rupees.
A. Pare B. Pair
C. Any one of these D. None of these

39. Madhu is full of youthful ....
A. Ardour B. Order
C. Any one of these D. None of these

40. My sister's child is very ....
A. Knotty B. Naughty
C. Any one of these D. None of these

41. Do not be tempted by .... gains.
A. Momentary B. Momentous
C. Any one of these D. None of these

42. About thirty .... lost their lives in an accident at Raniganj colliery.
A. Minors B. Miners
C. Any one of these D. None of these

43. Iron is a very useful ....
A. Metal B. Mettle
C. Any one of these D. None of these

44. I went to the bank and got my .... cashed.
A. Check B. Cheque
C. Any one of these D. None of these

45. We have revised our .... in Hindi.
A. Course B. Corse
C. Any one of these D. None of these

46. Please convey my .... to your brother.
A. Compliments B. Complements
C. Any one of these D. None of these

47. I can work for twelve hours ....
A. Continually B. Continuously
C. Any one of these D. None of these

48. I write my .... daily.
A. Diary B. Dairy
C. Any one of these D. None of these

49. Chicken pox is an infectious ....
A. Decease B. Disease
C. Any one of these D. None of these

50. Vasco da Gama .... the sea route to India in 1498.
A. Invented B. Discovered
C. Any one of these D. None of these

51. The Moon .... from behind a cloud.
A. Immersed B. Emerged
C. Any one of these D. None of these

52. Many Indians .... are settled in Sri Lanka.
A. Emigrants B. Immigrants
C. Any one of these D. None of these

53. We went on an .... to Kashmir.
A. Incursion B. Excursion
C. Any one of these D. None of these

54. Real .... is found only in hard work.
A. Felicity B. Facility
C. Any one of these D. None of these

55. The poor man had to .... his meals.
A. Forego B. Forgo
C. Any one of these D. None of these

56. My final year examination .... on 21st April 1988.
A. Begins B. Commences
C. Any one of these D. None of these

57. Recently there was a bus .... in Patna.
A. Collision B. Collusion
C. Any one of these D. None of these

58. The .... is very fine today.
A. Weather B. Climate
C. Any one of these D. None of these

59. Anand was rewarded for his good ....
A. Character B. Conduct
C. Any one of these D. None of these

60. Everyone made fun of him as his manner of speaking was ....
A. Childlike B. Childish
C. Any one of these D. None of these

61. Lalitha was .... for her objectionable remarks.
A. Censured B. Censored
C. Any one of these D. None of these

62. The judge made a/an .... of judgement.
A. Error B. Blunder
C. Any one of these D. None of these

63. The .... from Kalka to Simla is very steep.
A. Assent B. Ascent
C. Any one of these D. None of these

64. Her remarks were not .... to the occasion.
A. Apposite B. Opposite
C. Any one of these D. None of these

65. He is a very famous ....
A. Artisan B. Artist
C. Any one of these D. None of these

66. The teacher .... her to appear for the paper again.
A. Allowed B. Permitted
C. Any one of these D. None of these

67. You should .... from telling lies.
A. Refrain B. Abstain
C. Any one of these D. None of these

68. I .... that you are innocent, but I am helpless.
A. Admit B. Confers
C. Any one of these D. None of these

69. My brother .... his right to the family property.
A. Waved B. Waived
C. Any one of these D. None of these

70. The .... carry blood in our body.
A. Veins B. Vanes
C. Any one of these D. None of these

71. What .... will you pursue in your life?
A. Vacation B. Vocation
C. Any one of these D. None of these

72. This lake .... with fish.
A. Teems B. Teams
C. Any one of these D. None of these

73. Do not .... at pretty girls.
A. Stair B. Stare
C. Any one of these D. None of these

74. Akbar was a man of deep ....
A. Insight B. Incite
C. Any one of these D. None of these

75. Kanpur is an ....city.
A. Industrious B. Industrial
C. Any one of these D. None of these

76. This is a very .... book.
A. Idle B. Ideal
C. Any one of these D. None of these

77. He has .... much wealth.
A. Hoarded B. Horde
C. Any one of these D. None of these

78. The princess had a very kind ....
A. Hart B. Heart
C. Any one of these D. None of these

79. There is a big .... in air school.
A. Haul B. Hall
C. Any one of these D. None of these

80. We should be determined to achieve our ....
A. Goal B. Gaol
C. Any one of these D. None of these

81. I always .... what I say.
A. Mean B. Mien
C. Any one of these D. None of these

82. We must .... to God daily.
A. Prey B. Pray
C. Any one of these D. None of these

83. The .... is the prettiest of all the flowers.
A. Rose B. Rows
C. Any one of these D. None of these

84. The .... of democracy in India is not little.
A. Roll B. Role
C. Any one of these D. None of these

85. This is not a .... line.
A. Straight B. Strait
C. Any one of these D. None of these

86. To .... is a crime.
A. Gambol B. Gamble
C. Any one of these D. None of these

87. Capt. Singh received .... wounds in the battle field.
A. Fatal B. Fateful
C. Any one of these D. None of these

88. She has a very .... impression of the picture.
A. Feint B. Faint
C. Any one of these D. None of these

89. I found her in ....misery.
A. Abject B. Object
C. Any one of these D. None of these

90. The committee .... a resolution condemning terrorism in the country.
A. Adapted B. Adopted
C. Any one of these D. None of these

91. You .... to do your duty.
A. Ought B. Aught
C. Any one of these D. None of these

92. The accused was released on ....
A. Bale B. Bail
C. Any one of these D. None of these

93. One must not go against the .... of morality.
A. Cannons B. Canons
C. Any one of these D. None of these

94. She had very little time to .... votes.
A. Canvass B. Canvas
C. Any one of these D. None of these

95. Dyanand Saraswati was the .... guide of many people.
A. Spiritual B. Spirited
C. Any one of these D. None of these

96. Aarti should not approve of her .... ways.
A. Wilful B. Willing
C. Any one of these D. None of these

97. Rajesh .... many instances in support of his argument.
A. have B. has
C. Any one of these D. None of these

98. The .... drops on the petals of the rose looked beautiful.
A. due B. dew
C. Any one of these D. None of these

99. Please .... my black shirts red.
A. die B. dye
C. Any one of these D. None of these

100. This is not a .... surface.
A. plain
B. plane
C. Any one of these
D. None of these

ANSWERS

1	2	3	4	5	6	7	8	9	10
B	B	A	A	B	A	B	B	A	B
11	**12**	**13**	**14**	**15**	**16**	**17**	**18**	**19**	**20**
A	B	A	B	B	B	A	B	A	B
21	**22**	**23**	**24**	**25**	**26**	**27**	**28**	**29**	**30**
B	A	B	A	B	B	A	A	B	B
31	**32**	**33**	**34**	**35**	**36**	**37**	**38**	**39**	**40**
B	A	B	A	B	B	A	B	B	A
41	**42**	**43**	**44**	**45**	**46**	**47**	**48**	**49**	**50**
A	B	B	A	A	A	B	B	B	A
51	**52**	**53**	**54**	**55**	**56**	**57**	**58**	**59**	**60**
A	B	A	B	A	B	B	A	B	A
61	**62**	**63**	**64**	**65**	**66**	**67**	**68**	**69**	**70**
A	A	B	A	B	A	B	A	A	B
71	**72**	**73**	**74**	**75**	**76**	**77**	**78**	**79**	**80**
A	B	A	B	A	A	B	A	B	B
81	**82**	**83**	**84**	**85**	**86**	**87**	**88**	**89**	**90**
A	A	B	A	B	B	A	A	B	A
91	**92**	**93**	**94**	**95**	**96**	**97**	**98**	**99**	**100**
A	B	A	B	A	B	A	B	A	B

8 Idioms & Phrases

An idiom is a group of words established by usage as having a meaning different from the individual words.

A phrase is a small group of words standing together as an idiomatic expression.

The use of idioms and phrases makes your expression more effective and powerful.

Learn and practise as many as you can.

A bad egg/a bad penny: A bad character

A bear: A clumsy, rough person

A bear hug: A rough, tight hug

A big shot: An important person, usually someone who is wealthy and influential

A black sheep: A bad character who disgraces his family

A blacklist: A list of people groups, etc. who have done something wrong

A blind date: A social meeting of two persons, usually a boy and a girl who have not met before

A blue-collar job: A factory job

A bolt from the blue: A complete surprise

A bone of contention: Something that causes argument

A bosom friend: A very close, trusted friend

A brain wave: A clever idea; sudden inspiration

A burning question: A matter having to be dealt with at once; an urgent important matter

A cat: A malicious, person. usually referring to females

A chicken-hearted person: A timid, cowardly person

A clean bill of health: A certificate or announcement that someone is healthy

A close-fisted person : Someone who is stingy; a miser

A close shave: A narrow escape from danger, an accident, etc.

A cock-and-bull story: An invented story

A cold war: A serious political struggle between countries which does not actually result in fighting

A confirmed bachelor: A man who has no desire to marry

A country cousin: A person who is simple and inexperienced and not used to city life

A dark horse: A person who competes successfully against another although little is known about him

A dead-end job: A job without prospects; a job that leads to nothing further

A devil: A particularly wicked or mischievous person

A dog: A worthless person; someone who is despised

A dog-eared book: A book where the corners of the pages have been turned down with use

A double agent: A person who works secretly for two opposing sides without either of the sides knowing

A false alarm: A warning of something bad, which does not happen

A fair copy: A neat, legible copy

A fast colour: A colour which does not run out of the material when washed or dried

Fast living: A person who spends too much money in enjoying life

A feather in one's cap: A deserved honour that one is proud of

A fish out of water: A person who feels uncomfortable because he is in a strange place, or among people who are very different from himself

A fishy story: An untrue tale; an unlikely story

A flying visit: A very short visit

A foregone conclusion: A result that is certain, sure

A fox: A crafty, cunning person

Again and again: Repeatedly; continually; very often

A greengrocer: A person who sells fruit and vegetables

A greenhorn: An inexperienced person

A giant: A person who is very large

A Goliath: An extremely large man

A goose: A silly person

A grass widow: A wife who is alone because her husband is away temporarily

A going concern: A successful, thriving business

A golden opportunity: A very good opportunity

A good samaritan: A person who helps a stranger in difficulties

A hand-me-down dress: A dress used by someone after belonging to another

A happy-go-lucky person: Someone who does not think or plan carefully

A hard and fast rule: A rule that cannot be changed; fixed, unchangeable rule

A hard drinker: A person who drinks large quantities of alcohol

A hen party: A party where only women are allowed to be present

A henpecked husband: A husband who is dominated and nagged by his wife

A Hercules: A very strong man

A hit-and-run driver: A driver who drives away after an accident without stopping to find out about damage or injuries

A hushed-up affair: An affair or matter that is kept secret by forcing silence about it

A hot line: A direct telephone line between heads of governments, to be used at times of great difficulty

A jack of all trades: A person who can do many different kinds of work but who may not be good at any of them

A jail bird: A man who has spent a lot of time in prison

A Judas: A mean traitor

A knowing look: A look which suggests that, the person is well-informed of a matter

A man about town: A man who is used to living in the city and associating with well-known fashionable people

A man of means: A rich man

A man of iron: A cruel, hard person

A monkey: A child who is lively and full of mischievous tricks

A much-talked-of affair: Something which is the subject of much discussion

A mule: A very stubborn person

A nine to six job: A job in which the working hours are from nine in the morning to six in evening

A ladies' man: A man who likes to be with women or who likes to please them

A lamb: An innocent harmless person

A last fling: The last opportunity for pleasure or amusement before having to stop

A laughing stock: A person who is unkindly laughed at by everyone

A light-fingered person: A person who is in the habit of stealing small things

A light sleeper: A person who is easily awakened from sleep

A pack of lies: A whole lot of untruths

A package deal: An offer or agreement which includes a number of things all of which must be taken

A package tour: A completely planned holiday at a fixed price arranged by a company

A parasite: A person who lives off others and gives nothing in return

A parrot: A person who learns things off by heart without understanding the real meaning

A passing fancy: A temporary liking for something or someone

A pep talk: A friendly talk to give encouragement to win a game, etc. or to complete something well

A pest: A troublesome person; one who annoys and pesters others

A pet aversion: Something or someone much disliked

A pig: A greedy and dirty person

Apple-pie order: In perfect order

A practical joke: A trick played on a person to make him look silly and to give amusement to others

A raw deal: An unjust or cruel treatment

A red carpet welcome: A special ceremonial welcome to guest

A red-letter day: A notable, fortunate day that will be remembered

A rolling stone: Person who travels around a lot without staying in any one place or job for long

A round the-clock service: A twenty-four hour service

A run-of the-mill job: An ordinary unexciting job

A Samson: A very strong man

A security risk: A person who is a risk to a country's security because of his political activities; one whose loyalty is doubted

A shady character: A person of very doubtful honesty or character

A shark: A greedy and cunning person; one who swindles others

A shot in the dark: A guess which is not supported by arguments; a wild guess

A shot in the arm: Something which acts to bring back a happy state or condition

A short cut: An easier method of doing something or getting somewhere; a quicker, more direct way

A sideline: Work one does apart from one's regular job

A slap in the face: A rebuff

A sleeping partner: A business partner who provides a share of the capital for a venture but does not take an active part in its operation

A slip of the tongue: Something said unintentionally

A small-time business: A business limited in activity and profits

A smash-and-grab robbery: A robbery done quickly, usually by breaking windows or showcases taking away valuables, and running away

A snake in the grass: A cunning, harmful person who pretends to be a friend; a false friend

A snake/serpent: A treacherous, dangerous person

A soft spot: A feeling of special fondness for something or someone

A Solomon: A very wise man

A sore point: A matter which irritates or hurts when it is mentioned

A storm in a teacup: A big fuss made over a small, trivial event

A stone's thorw: A short distance

A spending spree: An outing during which one spends a lot of money

A splitting headache: A very severe and painful headache

A square deal: A fair bargain or fair treatment

A square meal: A meal with adequate good; a satisfying meal

A stag party: A party where only men are allowed to be present

A stay-at-home person: A person who is in the habit of staying at home, and not liking to travel

A sugar daddy: An older man who has a relationship, especially sexual, with a younger woman, providing her with money and presents

A sweeping statement: A statement which is not careful or correct in its details; a generalisation

A tall order: A request which is unreasonably difficult to grant or carry out

A trend-setter: A person who starts a new fashion which becomes popular

A thick-skinned person: A person who is not easily offended

A tight spot/corner: A difficult situation

A well-to-do man/woman: A rich person

A wet blanket: A person who discourages others or prevents them from enjoying what they are doing

A white-collar job: An office job

A white elephant: A worthless possession which the owner wants to get rid of

A wild goose chase: A search for something which has no chance of being successful

A willing horse: A helpful person who often gets all the work to do

A wolf: A greedy and cunning person

A working lunch/dinner: A meal at which the people who attend, discuss business

A working knowledge: Enough practical knowledge to do something

A wizard: A clever and skillful person

An absent-minded person: A forgetful, inattentive person

An Adonis: A very handsome man

An angel: A person who is gentle and kind to others

An ape: A person who foolishly imitates others

An Apollo: A man with a perfect physique or body shape

An armchair critic: A person who critically judges others' work and gives advice, but who has not himself experienced doing the work

An ass/donkey: A stupid person

An easy victim/mark: Somebody who can easily be cheated or treated badly

An elephant: A huge, clumsy, ungainly person

An iron will: A very strong will

An inside job: A theft committed by someone inside a building, i.e., by an employee, not a stranger

An odd-job man: A man who does various types of work, usually manual, for pay

An open secret: Something supposed to be a secret but which in fact is known to everyone

An open and shut case: A case which is easy to settle or solve

An out-of the way place: A place that is distant and far away from people and places

Back and forth/backward: Moving first in one direction and then in the opposite direction and forwards

backstairs influence: Secret and usually unfair influence

Bad blood: Bad feelings or unfriendliness between two persons

Birds of a feather: People of the same kind (often bad) who like each other's company

Black and blue: Badly bruised after a beating/a fall

Blue blood: Royal or noble blood

Broken English: Imperfect, ungrammatical English

Bumper-to-bumper traffic: Cars that are very close together one after another

By hook or by crook: By any means possible

By fits and starts: At irregular intervals

By and by: Soon; before long

By and large: On the whole; in general; all things considered

Castles in the air: Plans which cannot be carried out or which will probably not succeed

Crocodile tears: Pretended sorrow; insincere tears

Elbow room: Space, in which to move and act freely

Every now and then/again: From time to time; at times

Far and near/far and wide: Everywhere

Far and away: Very much

First and foremost: In the first place; firstly

French leave: Absence from work that is taken without permission

Forty winks: A short nap or sleep

Green with envy: Tilled with jealousy

Grey matter: Common sense; brains

Half-hearted: Having no enthusiasm for a particular task

Hard cash: Actual money, not a cheque, etc.

Hard labour: Hard, manual work usually done as a punishment

Here and there: In various places; firstly

Here, there and everywhere: In all possible places; everywhere

High time: At the most important point of time

Hot news: Very recent, important or sensational news

Hot water: Trouble

Hush money: A bribe paid to keep a matter secret from the public

In and out: Sometimes inside and sometimes outside

In a rash moment: Doing something hastily without thinking of the results

In black and white: In writing or print

In someone's black books: Out of favour with someone

In the pink of health: In excellent health

Nowadays: In these times

Now and again: Sometimes; occasionally; not very often

Off and on: From time to time; occasionally

Old hat: No longer fashionable

On and on: Without stopping

Once and for all: Finally; for the last time

Once in a blue moon: Very rarely

One-track mind: A person's mind that is limited and thinks of only one thing at a time

Out and out: Complete, thorough; total

Out and away: By far

Out of the blue: Suddenly; without warning

Over and over again: Again and again; repeatedly

Pin money: A wife's allowance for her personal needs

Plain dealing: Truthfulness and honesty, especially in business

Plain sailing: A plan or action that is simple and free from trouble

Purple with rage: So angry that the face becomes purple

Ready money: Money which is immediately available in coins or notes

Red tape: Official rules which cause delay in settling one's problems

Round and round: Repeatedly moving round

Second best: Next to the best; second in value or importance

Second nature: Some acquired habit or skill which seems perfectly natural to someone; a very firmly fixed habit

Second sight: An ability to foresee future events

Second thoughts: A change of mind, attitude or decision after thinking about the matter

Small talk: Trivial, light conversation on unimportant topics

Strong language: Angry language consisting of many swear words

Take-home pay/wages: The amount a person receives after taxes have been deducted

The green-eyed monster: Jealousy

The green light: The signal to proceed

The red flag: A flag used as a danger signal

The red light: A signal to stop; a danger signal

Through and through: Completely; entirely; in every way

The white flag: A sign that one accepts defeat or surrenders

To act the goat: To behave foolishly

To-and fro: Backwards and forwards; from side to side

To air one's opinion: To express one's feelings in public

To backbite a person: To speak ill of someone

To back chat: To be cheeky; to talk back to someone

To be a bag of bones: To be extremely thin

To be a blockhead: To be an idiot

To be a chip off the old block: A son who is very much like his father in appearance, character, habits, etc

To be at death's door: To be so ill as to be near death

To be a great hand at: To be an expert

To be a sight for sore eyes: Something or someone who appears before another and is very welcome

To be all ears: To be eager to listen

To be armed to the teeth: Fully armed or protected

To be as fit as a fiddle: To be in excellent health

To be at one's wits' end: Completely puzzled

To be at a loss for words: Not knowing what to say; to be speechless

To be at a loose end: To have nothing to do

To be caught red-handed: To be caught in the act of committing a crime

To be close-fisted: To be mean; miserly

To be double-faced: Insincere

To be down in the mouth: To feel depressed and unhappy

To be/feel off colour: To be unwell or rather ill

To be head and shoulders above someone else: To be very much better or superior

To be out of one's mind: To be mad; crazy

To be someone's blue-eyed boy: To be someone's favourite

To be the apple of someone's eye: To be someone's favourite

To bite someone's head off: To speak abruptly or sharply to another

To blackmail someone: To threaten to reveal someone's misdeeds unless he pays money

To burn one's fingers: To get into trouble

To catch someone's eye: To suddenly exchange glances with another

To change hands: To pass from one owner to another

To come off with flying colours: To achieve great success

To dig someone in the ribs: To make unkind remarks or insinuations about another

To eat one's heart out for another: To long for someone who is unattentive

To feel blue/have the blues: To be sad or depressed

To foot the bill: To pay the bill, especially for some social outing

To get on someone's nerves: To irritate someone very greatly

To get something off one's chest: To confess to something

To get the upper hand: To gain mastery over an opponent

To give someone the cold shoulder: To ignore someone; to slight another

To give someone the sharp: To thoroughly scold another person edge of one's tongue

To go on all hands: To crawl on hands and knees

To have a chip on one's shoulder: To bear a grudge against the world/society

To have a finger in every pie: To have many business interests

To have a head like a sieve: To have a very poor memory

To have a high colour: To appear very red in the face

To have a skeleton in the cupboard: To have a guilty secret, especially a family scandal

To have at one's fingertips: To know thoroughly

To have cold feet: To be afraid

To have no backbone: To be a weak, spineless person

To have one's head screwed on: To be very sensible

To have someone under one's thumb: To dominate another

To have the upper hand: To be in command/charge; to be someone in power

To have two left hands: Someone who is clumsy

To hold one's tongue: To keep silent even though there is an urge to talk

To hold up one's head: To be able to look people in the face

To jump out of the frying-pan into the fire: To get out of one bad situation and fall into another worse situation

To jump out of one's skin: To get a sudden fright

To keep a cool head: To keep calm, especially in an emergency

To keep a stiff upper lip: To remain calm and courageous

To keep one's fingers crossed: To hope for luck

To keep one's hair on: To keep cool and patient

To keep one's head above water: To avoid getting into debt or trouble

To keep someone at arm's length: Not too friendly with another

To knock something on the head: To suddenly stop an idea/project

To know something by heart: To be able to say something from memory

To lay hands on someone: To handle someone roughly

To lend a hand: To help

To let the grass grow under one's feet: To be inactive and uninvolved

To live from hand to mouth: To live in hardship with the barest essentials

To lose face: To lose one's reputation/honour

To lose heart: To be discouraged

To lose one's head: To be very angry; to lose control of oneself

To make a clean breast of something: To confess to something; to reveal all

To make neither head nor tail of something: To understand nothing of a particular issue

To pat someone on the back: To give praise and encouragement to another

To pay through the nose for something: To pay an excessively high price for something

To poison someone's mind: To turn someone against another person

To pull one's weight: To do one's share of work

To pull someone's leg: To play a joke on someone

To pull the wool over someone's eyes: To deceive another

To put one's back into it: To work hard

To put one's foot down: To be firm about an issue

To put one's shoulder to the wheel: To work hard and earnestly

To put someone's nose out of joint: To make someone jealous by taking his place as the centre of attraction

To rack one's brains: To try to recall or remember something

To receive with open arms: To welcome warmly

To save face: To save one's honour/reputation/name

To scream blue murder: To complain loudly

To see red: To lose control of oneself in anger

To show a clean pair of heels: To escape by running

To show the white feather: To show signs of cowardice

To show one's true colours: To show what one is really like; to show one's true character

To snap someone's head off: To speak abruptly

To stand on one's own feet: To do things without help; to be independent

To sweep someone off his/her feet: To flatter and woo someone, usually a girl

To take matters into one's own hands: To do something independently without help

To take something to heart: To take something seriously

To take to one's heels: To run away

To throw dust in someone's eyes: To try to deceive someone

To tread in someone's foot steps: To follow the example of another, usually of talent/occupation

To tread on someone's toes: To offend another person

To try one's hand at: To try doing something for the first time

To turn a blind eye: To refuse to see

To turn a deaf ear: To refuse to hear

To turn up one's nose at something: To treat with contempt

To twist someone's arm: To force someone into doing something for you

To wash one's hands of something: To have nothing to do with a particular matter

To be at sixes and sevens: To be in confusion and discord

To be at the end of one's teeter: To be at a loss as to what to do

To be born under a lucky star: To have considerable luck in whatever one does

To be born with a silver spoon in one's mouth: To be born into a rich family

To be dead beat: To be worn out by fatigue

To be in hot water: To be in serious trouble

To be in someone's bad/good books: To be out of/ in favour with someone

To be in the doldrums: To be in low spirits

To be in the same boat: To have the same troubles/ circumstances

To be mad about someone: To like someone very much

To be made of money: To have plenty of money; to be well-off

To be on tenterhooks: To be in a state of suspense and anxiety

To be on the ball: To be alert, up-to-date, prepared

To be on the horns of a dilemma: Not knowing what to do from several courses of action

To be on the rocks: To be in danger of failing, collapse, especially a business, a marriage, etc

To be on top of the world: To be very happy; to be in high spirits

To be out of the woods: To be out of danger, especially a serious illness

To be quick on the uptake: To be alert and quick to do or say something

To be rolling in money: To be rich; to have plenty of money

To be scared to death: To be extremely frightened of something

To be slow on the uptake: Slow to do or say something

To be too big for one's boots: To think very highly of oneself

To bear the brunt of: To bear the main force or strain of some action

To beat about the bush: To be indecisive; not coming to the point

To blow hot and cold: To do one thing at one time and the opposite soon after

To blow one's own trumpet: To boast about one's abilities, achievements etc.

To break the ice: To take the first step; to be the first to begin, especially a conversation

To bring down the house: To cause loud and long applause through one's skill

To bring to light: To disclose, reveal

To build castles in the air: To think of things impossible to realize

To burn the candle at both ends: To use one's energy in two directions at the same time

To burn the midnight oil: To work till late at night

To call a spade a spade: To speak out bluntly and frankly

To clip one's wings: To deprive one of power and/ or freedom

To cook an account: To tamper with/falsify an account

To come down on someone like a: To harshly criticise another ton of bricks

To come of age: To reach adulthood

To come to grief: To meet with danger

To come to light: To become known

To count-sheep: To try various methods to get to sleep

To cry over spilt milk: To be unhappy about something that can no longer be remedied

To curry favour: To seek/win favour by flattery or gifts

To cut off in its prime: To destroy something when it is at its best

To cut one's coat according to: To live within one's income one's cloth

To cut someone down to size: To put someone in his place especially a person who thinks too highly of himself

To do a city/the sights: To visit a city and see its well-known places

To do a thing by fits and starts: To work intermittently on something

To do a thing by hook or by crook: To do something by any means, fair or foul, direct or indirect

To do something on the spur of the moment: To suddenly decide to do something

To drop a brick: To say or do something very tactless and unexpected

To drop a hint: To make veiled and subtle suggestions

To eat like a horse: To eat a lot

To eat one's words: To take back what one has said; to apologise

To egg on: To spur on to further action

To face the music: To meet the worst; to face punishment for doing something wrong

To fall out with someone: To quarrel with someone

To fall through: To fail, especially a plan, project, etc.

To fancy someone/something: To take a great liking to someone/something

To fight shy of: To avoid

To fire someone: To dismiss someone from employment

To flog a dead horse: To try fruitlessly to revive interest in something

To follow the crowd: To follow unthinkingly; to believe or act as most people do

To follow suit : To do the same thing as another person

To gain ground: To make progress in an undertaking

To get away with something: To escape detection despite doing something wrong

To get blood out of stone: To get more than is fair out of someone

To get down to work: To start on the task in hand

To get even with someone: To take revenge of someone

To get hitched: To get married

To get into a flap: To get worried and nervous

To get into hot water: To be in/to get into trouble

To get off scot-free: To escape punishment; to be let off payment

To get out of bed on the wrong side: To start the day in a bad temper

To get the sack: To be dismissed from employment

To get wind of: To hear a rumour of

To get the wind up: To get worried and nervous; to get a fright

To give someone a telling-off: To scold someone

To give someone the slip: To manage to avoid someone who is looking for you

To give the game away: To let out a secret

To give up the ghost: To die; to cease trying

To go a long way: To excel; to go far, especially in a career

To go off at a tangent: To change suddenly to a different course of thought or action

To go like a bomb: To go fast; to function well, especially a vehicle

To go to rack and ruin: To fall into a ruined or disorganised state

To grin and bear it: To make the best of a bad job; to put up with something

To haul someone over the coals: To reprimand someone

To have a bee in one's bonnet: To be strong-minded over certain issues

To have a soft spot for: To be very fond of someone or something

To have an axe to grind: To have a selfish motive for doing something

To have one's knife in someone: To be always finding fault with another person

To hit below the belt: To attack an opponent unfairly

To hit the nail on the head: To do or say exactly the right thing

To jog someone's memory: To remind someone of something

To keep a person in the dark: To keep something hidden from someone

To keep open house: To encourage visitors to come at any time

To keep one's pecker up: To keep one's courage up

To keep one's shirt on: To keep cool and calm in a dispute

To keep the ball rolling: To keep a conversation going

To keep up appearances: To pretend to be well-off and to live in a certain style

To kick the bucket: To die

To kid someone: To tease

To kill two birds with one stone: To accomplish two things with one action

To knock off work: To stop working

To know the ropes: To be thoroughly familiar with a particular situation

To knock someone down with a feather: To surprise someone very much

To kowtow to someone: To act in a very servile manner hoping for favour

To lay down the law: To speak in an authoritative way

To lead someone up the garden path: To deceive someone by hiding the real intention

To leave someone in the lurch: To desert someone in time of difficulties

To let bygones be bygones: To let things that are past and gone remain untouched and forgotten

To let the cat out of the bag: To reveal a secret; to expose a trick

To look like a wet week: To look miserable and depressed

To make a go of something: To try one's best to succeed in something

To make a hash/a mess of something: To fail at a task

To make believe: To pretend

To make both ends meet: To be able to manage on one's income

To make hay while sun shines: To take advantage of an opportunity

To make much ado about nothing: To make a great fuss about something unimportant

To make oneself scarce: To disappear

To nip something in the bud: To stop something before it can develop into something serious

To pass the buck: To pass on the responsibility

To pick holes in something: To find fault with

To pick to pieces: To analyse critically

To pick and choose: To make a careful selection

To play a double game: To do one thing openly and a different thing in secret

To play fast and loose: To disregard one's promises

To play second fiddle: To take a subordinate position

To pooh-pooh an idea: To express contempt for an idea

To pull strings: To use friends in influential positions, or to use one's own influence, to secure favours

To put the cart before the horse: To do the wrong thing first

To put two and two together: To arrive at a conclusion

To put a spoke in one's wheel: To hinder; to obstruct progress

To rain cats and dogs: To rain very heavily

To read between the lines: To detect the hidden meaning

To rule the roost: To domineer over others

To run in the blood: Inherited qualities

To see something through coloured spectacles: To see only the best points about a thing

To see the light: To begin to understand

To sit on the fence: To take neither side in a dispute; to remain neutral

To smell a rat: To become suspicious about something

To steer clear of: To avoid

To take French leave: To be absent from work without permission

To take someone for a ride: To deceive someone

To take the bull by the horns: To meet a difficulty with courage

To take the law into one's own hands: To punish a person, usually by force, witnout his being tried in a law court

To take with a pinch of salt: To accept what someone has said with doubt and misgiving

To talk nineteen to the dozen: To speak a lot

To talk the hind legs of a donkey: To talk a great deal at great length

To tear a strip off someone: To scold harshly

To throw cold water upon: To discourage effort

To turn over a new leaf: To give up one's bad ways, and lead a better life

To turn the tables on someone: To defeat someone who has previously defeated you

To upset the apple cart: To disturb the routine of something

The small hours: The early morning hours just after midnight

The generation gap: The difficulties arising when younger and elder people do not understand each other's way of life

The happy medium: The middle course of doing something when opposite ways are suggested

Tall talk: Boastful talk

Tough luck: Bad luck; hard luck

The naked eye: The eye unaided by any instrument

The writing on the wall: An indication that something bad or difficult is about to happen

The talk of the town: A person or event that is causing great excitement and is the subject of much discussion

Teething troubles: Troubles and difficulties which occur during the early stages of an activity or enterprise, but which will lessen with time

The tricks of the trade: The best and most successful ways of doing good business

The bottom of the ladder: In the least important position

The man in the street: The ordinary, average man

The gift of the gab: A person fluent in speech; a persuasive speaker

The life and soul: The person who is the centre of attaction because he is amusing and lively

The lion's share: The greater part; an unfairly large share

The long arm of the law: The police

The ups and downs: The good and bad times, the happy and sad times

The rank and file: Ordinary people without special positions; the masses

Up and about: On one's feet; up again after an illness

Yellow at heart: Cowardly

MULTIPLE CHOICE QUESTIONS

Directions: *Select the options which express the correct meaning of the given Idioms/Phrases.*

1. **A far cry**
   A. an unfulfilled desire
   B. a very low voice
   C. remote from
   D. a distant place
2. **To feather one's nest**
   A. to provide for one's own comfort
   B. to be proud
   C. to succeed again
   D. to decorate one's house
3. **To fish in troubled waters**
   A. to be in trouble
   B. to make capital out of other's troubles
   C. to be in trouble because of other's fault
   D. to laugh at other's trouble
4. **To follow suit**
   A. to follow the command
   B. to obey the rules
   C. to work in accordance with
   D. to behave in the same manner
5. **To get the hang of a thing**
   A. to understand the implications of something
   B. to get a trace of theft
   C. to find a new resource
   D. to have some indications
6. **To get wind of**
   A. to get news about something much before the event actually takes place
   B. to forget the event that had taken place
   C. to spread a rumour
   D. to have some idea of a conspiration
7. **French leave**
   A. a long leave
   B. a small leave
   C. absence from one's place of work without prior information
   D. to leave the place forever
8. **To steal a march upon**
   A. to outshine somebody
   B. to rob
   C. to move forward
   D. to crush the enemy
9. **A long face**
   A. a sad or mournful countenance
   B. a very shameful defeat
   C. a shameful act
   D. an ugly face
10. **To set one's face against**
    A. to criticise openly
    B. to oppose with determination
    C. a biased disapproval
    D. to show disappointment
11. **To go to pieces**
    A. to tear
    B. to feel disheartened
    C. to be wrecked completely
    D. to dismantle
12. **To have too many irons in the fire**
    A. to be engaged in too many things
    B. to handle more than one work at the same time
    C. to have lot of energy
    D. to have various plans in the mind
13. **To put a spoke in one's wheel**
    A. to obstruct one in his work
    B. to assist one in his work
    C. to interfere one in his work
    D. to increase the strength of a team
14. **On the rack**
    A. in a dilemma
    B. tortured by anxiety
    C. highly curious
    D. to be in a disadvantageous position
15. **To get into hot water**
    A. an acute pain
    B. to be in trouble
    C. to face a short-tempered person
    D. to be in hypertension
16. **Fish and blood**
    A. by extreme means

B. by unlawful ways
C. human nature
D. life-like

17. From hand to mouth
A. to harm and humiliate
B. to be a bankrupt
C. to spend all that is earned
D. to feed someone

18. Hit the nail on the head
A. to take revenge openly
B. to insult on the face
C. to do a wrong thing
D. to do exactly the right thing

19. Put the cart before the horse
A. to reverse the natural order
B. to put obstruction
C. to cause problem for others
D. to stop one's advancement

20. Pay back in one's own coin
A. to save money
B. to treat in the same way as one has been treated
C. to get the return of the investment
D. to give a befitting reply

21. Cats' paw
A. a person who is used as a tool by another person
B. very slowly and quietly
C. very cleverly
D. to share a responsibility

22. To catch a tartar
A. to overcome a serious problem
B. to attack one who turns out to be stronger than is expected
C. to achieve the goal
D. to struggle hard

23. Cheek of jowl
A. very soft
B. close together
C. intimate relationship
D. low in status

24. A chip of the old block
A. a symptom of a serious disease
B. a child of a parent
C. a part of a whole
D. offsprings who display characteristics of their parents

25. To cool one's heels
A. to be kept waiting
B. to give a cold response to somebody
C. to follow somebody
D. to answer all the queries of somebody

26. To cleanse the Augean stables
A. to clean something which has not been cleaned for a long time
B. to wind up a joint business
C. to remove the stains of blood
D. to remove the traces of murder

27. A cry in wilderness
A. The cry of the poors
B. a warning that goes unheeded
C. A speech made by a less important leader
D. A cry out of deep sorrow

28. To cut one's coat according to one's cloth
A. to work according to one's capacity
B. to allot portfolio according to one's capability
C. to live within one's means
D. to live as one desires

29. Chicken hearted
A. coward
B. brave
C. kind
D. mortal

30. To clip one's wings
A. to lessen one's power
B. to defame
C. to dismiss
D. to punish

31. Day in and day out
A. always
B. forever
C. to break a promise done earlier
D. to remain busy always

32. Champ at
A. to pounce at
B. be impassioned
C. be composed
D. be eager or impatient

33. Burn one's fingers
A. to get oneself into trouble
B. to commit a blunder
C. a heavy monetory loss
D. to be in great rage

34. Down in the dumps
A. in a solitary mood
B. in a bad mood
C. to be in an unfavourable situation
D. to decline

35. To beg the question
A. to beg the pardon
B. to request for some extra-time to finish the work
C. unanswerable
D. to assume in the premises somethign which is to be proved

36. To carry the day
A. to be victorious
B. an on-going discussion
C. a memorable day
D. a miserable phase of life

37. At death's door
A. on the point of expiring
B. on the point of gun
C. to show bravery
D. a gradual deterior

38. To pay the debt of nature
A. to die
B. to give birth
C. to safeguard the natural things
D. to avoid environmental pollution

39. To do up
A. to finish off B. to mend
C. to improve D. to make tidy

40. To do away with
A. to break B. to destroy
C. to get rid of D. to forget

41. To come round
A. to agree with another's point of view
B. to come back to the point of origin
C. a circular movement
D. to wander

42. To call to order
A. a command
B. to rebuke for improper or incorrect behaviour
C. to obey an order
D. to show superiority

43. To cover one's tracks
A. to maintain the secrecy
B. to hide one's weaknesses
C. to carefully hide all traces of one's actions
D. to conceal the falsity

44. To throw up one's cards
A. To make a last effort
B. to cease to struggle
C. to end up the game
D. to come out victorious

45. To let the cat out of the bag
A. to disclose a secret
B. to set free
C. a person without a shelter
D. to permit the thief to run away

46. To cave in
A. to interfere B. to prohibit
C. to find a way D. to give way

47. To chuck up
A. to abandon B. to decorate
C. to summarize D. to cut into pieces

48. A dead letter
A. a delayed report
B. a false report
C. something exaggerated
D. something which is null and void

49. To die in harness
A. to die in office
B. to die with great pain
C. a premature death
D. a cruel murder

50. At the drop of a hat
A. without fail
B. without delay
C. against the self-respect
D. against the will

51. To have to do with
A. to be interested in
B. to do something under compulsion
C. work done unenthusiastically
D. to complete

52. To egg on
A. just a beginning
B. to urge on
C. to develop something
D. an initial stage

53. To face the music
A. to face the consequences
B. to get filled with ecstasy
C. to be lucky
D. to lead a happy life

54. To end in smoke
A. all efforts in vain
B. the end of life
C. to come to nothing
D. to end the enmity

55. Eye to eye with
A. agree completely
B. a confrontation
C. full of anger
D. a quarrel between the two persons

56. To eat humble pie
A. to harass a humble person
B. a celebration or a treat without any cause
C. to confess that one is in the wrong
D. food provided to the needy or poor

57. Easy come easy go
A. what is gained without difficulty is spent without much thought
B. anything which is surplus
C. without any difficulty
D. to achieve something without any struggle

58. To eat out one's heart
A. to break one's heart
B. to deceive someone
C. to get deceived
D. to suffer intensely

59. To see with half an eye
A. to see with great ease
B. to dislike
C. to see stealthily
D. to feel jealous

60. A fair-weathered friend
A. A friend always eager to help
B. A friend who deserts one in times of adversity
C. a selfish friend
D. a true friend

61. To fall away from
A. to decline
B. to desert
C. to avoid
D. to leave

62. To fall flat
A. to cause no amusement or interest
B. to lie down
C. to defeat the opponent
D. to plead

63. To have a finger in the pie
A. to be mixed up in any affair
B. to interfere in other's work
C. to have a share in the profit
D. to be a member of an organisation

64. In full cry
A. in full volume
B. in hot pursuit
C. a verbosity
D. manifestation of grief

65. To give a piece of one's mind
A. to rebuke
B. to give an idea
C. to present one's view
D. to judge one's intelligence on the basis of his work or contributions

66. Gift of the gab
A. the ability of verbosity
B. the ability of writing creatively
C. the ability to speak in an impressive manner
D. a man of versatile genius

67. To give the cold shoulder
A. to give support
B. to be indifferent
C. to express anger silently
D. to behave in a cold manner with someone

68. To give devil his due
A. to give an evil person credit for whatever good he has done
B. to punish one who has committed sin
C. an evil person meeting a tragic end
D. to give devil his share

69. To give up the ghost
A. to die
B. to sacrifice
C. to murder
D. to convert from vicious to virtuous

70. To give wide berth to
A. to give more space
B. to keep far away from
C. to appreciate more than what one deserves
D. to maintain a distance

ANSWERS

1	2	3	4	5	6	7	8	9	10
C	A	B	D	A	A	C	A	A	B
11	12	13	14	15	16	17	18	19	20
C	A	A	B	B	C	C	D	A	B
21	22	23	24	25	26	27	28	29	30
A	B	B	D	A	A	B	C	A	A
31	32	33	34	35	36	37	38	39	40
A	D	A	B	D	A	A	A	D	C
41	42	43	44	45	46	47	48	49	50
A	B	C	B	A	D	A	D	A	B
51	52	53	54	55	56	57	58	59	60
A	B	A	C	A	C	A	D	A	B
61	62	63	64	65	66	67	68	69	70
B	A	A	B	A	C	D	A	A	B

9 Word Analogy

Like different people words also have different relationships with each other in comparison to each other. This is called word analogy. Try and master it in the following questions.

MULTIPLE CHOICE QUESTIONS

Directions: *Each question consists of two words which have a certain relationship to each other followed by four pairs of related words. Select the pair which has the same relationship.*

1. Useless : Cheap

A. Late : unpunctual
B. Real : illusive
C. Just : unfair
D. Humble : proud

2. Loyal : Faithful

A. Treacherous : devoted
B. Just : fair
C. Yield : suppress
D. Uncertain : sure

3. Cancel : Confirm

A. Certain : ambiguous
B. Vulgar : crude
C. Reliable : trustworthy
D. Obscure : anonymous

4. Gloomy : Bright

A. Pleasant : delightful
B. Funny : comic
C. Condemn : blame
D. Hard : flexible

5. Modern : Ancient

A. Happy : joyful
B. Service : slavery
C. Mild : harsh
D. assumed : unreal

6. Braggart : Modesty

A. profound : intelligence
B. opinionated : over confident
C. buffoon : dignity
D. arrogant : acuity

7. Posthumous : Death

A. selection : nomination
B. product : factory
C. clay : mould
D. cloudy : sunny

8. Prophet : Foreteller

A. precursor : forerunner
B. pretentious : ambitious
C. prodigy : wonderful
D. teacher : intellectual

9. Indigent : Wealth

A. yelp : cry
B. yearn : desire
C. wrangle : argue
D. emaciated : nourishment

10. Senorita : Woman

A. sophisticated : self assured
B. monologue : discourse

C. semite : jew
D. general : military

11. Wan : Colour
A. copulent : weight
B. insipid : flavour
C. pallid : complexion
D. enigmatic : puzzle

12. Thrust : Spear
A. mangle : iron
B. scabbard : sword
C. bow : arrow
D. fence : epee

13. Indigent : Wealthy
A. angry : rich
B. native : affluent
C. gauche : graceful
D. scholarly : erudite

14. Diva : Opera
A. producer : theatre
B. director : drama
C. conductor : bus
D. thespian : play

15. Army : Logistics
A. business : strategy
B. soldiers : students
C. war : logic
D. team : individual

16. Lunatic : Asylum
A. The poor : palace
B. Soldiers : barracks
C. Flowers : fields
D. Crops : garden

17. Soldier : Rifle
A. Blacksmith : anvil
B. Thief : ladder
C. Watchman : uniform
D. Barber : hair

18. Frog : Tadpoles
A. Man : sons
B. Woman : daughters
C. Cat : kids
D. Elephant : calves

19. Lizards : Reptiles
A. Frogs : amphibians
B. Tree : fruit
C. Earth : moon
D. Man : woman

20. Earthworm : Segments
A. Tree : wood
B. Crocodiles : scales
C. Apple : juice
D. Earth : moisture

21. Pain : Sedative
A. comfort : stimulant
B. grief : consolation
C. trance : narcotic
D. ache : extraction

22. Hope : Aspires
A. love : elevates
B. film : flam
C. fib : lie
D. fake : ordinary

23. Gravity : Pull
A. iron : metal
B. north pole : directions
C. magnetism : attraction
D. dust : desert

24. Light : Blind
A. speech : dumb
B. language : deaf
C. tongue : sound
D. voice : vibration

25. Symphony : Composer
A. Leonardo : music
B. Fresco : painter
C. colours : pallet
D. art : appreciation

26. Mosquito : Malaria
A. Rabid dog : rabies
B. House fly : AIDS
C. Cockroach : influenza
D. Virus : diabetes

27. Fish : Water
A. Man : air
B. Cat : mouse
C. Lion : flesh
D. Tree : roots

28. Impulsive : Cautious
A. Liberty : bondage
B. Tyrant : bully
C. Tremble : quake
D. Vulgar : indecent

29. Weighty : Voluminous
A. Jolly : dismal
B. Loyalty : perfidy
C. Wealth : opulence
D. Odd : normal

30. Innocent : Guilty
A. Kill : produce
B. Suspect : doubt
C. Depress : discourage
D. Contract : condense

31. Dexterous : Clumsy
A. Cheap : worthless
B. Usual : common
C. Zenith : acme
D. True : false

32. Luscious : Sweet
A. Above : below
B. Absolve : penalise
C. Lucrative : profitable
D. Adopt : abandon

33. Fraud : Duplicity
A. Inferior : cheap
B. Delicious : abhorrent
C. Desire : detest
D. Diligent : lackadaisical

34. Weired : Ordinary
A. Vacant : void
B. Vivid : clear
C. Vivid : dim
D. Wicked : unvirtuous

35. Build : Demolish
A. Abide : persist
B. Compel : coax
C. Odious : hateful
D. Claim : demand

36. Lawyer : Court
A. businessman : market
B. chemist : laboratory
C. labourer : factory
D. athlete : olympics

37. Corporeal : Spiritual
A. mesa : plateau
B. moron : savant
C. foreigner : immigrant
D. pedagogue : teacher

38. Ten : Decimal
A. seven : septet
B. four : quartet
C. two : binary
D. five : quince

39. Grain : Salt
A. shard : pottery
B. shred : wood
C. blades : grass
D. chip : glass

40. Fish : Shoal
A. audience : theatre
B. elephant : flock
C. whale : herd
D. shark : school

41. Astringent : Pucker
A. car : engine
B. spark : ignition
C. quell : allay
D. sophisticated : rural

42. Saga : Heroic
A. epigram : pithy
B. tragedy : comedy
C. editorial : newspaper
D. picture : book

43. Obdurate : Flexibility
A. stagger : amaze
B. adamant : submissiveness
C. semite : jew
D. ridicule : scorn

44. Percept : Instructive
A. ribald : decent
B. metaphor : figurative
C. institution : study
D. library : calmness

45. Hermit : Gregarious
A. sanguine : optimistic

B. repose : rest
C. ruthless : merciless
D. ascetic : hedonistic

46. Distance : Mile
A. liquid : litre
B. bushel : corn
C. weight : scale
D. fame : television

47. After : Before
A. first : second
B. present : past
C. contemporary : historic
D. successor : predecessor

48. Mundane : Spiritual
A. common : ghostly
B. worldly : unworldly
C. routine : novel
D. secular : clerical

49. Filter : Water
A. curtail : activity
B. expurgate : book
C. edit : text
D. censor : play

50. Pork : Pig
A. rooster : chicken
B. mutton : sheep
C. steer : beef
D. lobster : crustacean

51. Passionate : Impassive
A. Deter : discourage
B. Folly : stupidity
C. Polite : rude
D. Fanciful : whimsical

52. Gauche : Attractive
A. True : exact
B. Tough : hard
C. Tasteful : palatable
D. Insipid : delicious

53. Existence : Life
A. Silence : noise
B. Risk : shield
C. Enormous : immense
D. Rural : urban

54. Belief : Suspicion
A. Unravel : unweave
B. Profuse : insufficient
C. Urge : spur
D. Use : occupy

55. Violent : Calm
A. Tranquil : peaceful
B. Reticent : quiet
C. Even : smooth
D. Disdain : reverence

ANSWERS

1	2	3	4	5	6	7	8	9	10
A	B	A	D	C	C	A	A	D	B
11	**12**	**13**	**14**	**15**	**16**	**17**	**18**	**19**	**20**
C	D	C	D	A	B	A	D	A	B
21	**22**	**23**	**24**	**25**	**26**	**27**	**28**	**29**	**30**
B	C	C	A	B	A	A	A	C	A
31	**32**	**33**	**34**	**35**	**36**	**37**	**38**	**39**	**40**
D	C	A	C	B	A	B	C	D	D
41	**42**	**43**	**44**	**45**	**46**	**47**	**48**	**49**	**50**
B	A	B	B	D	A	D	B	D	B
51	**52**	**53**	**54**	**55**					
C	D	C	B	D					

10 Parts of Speech

Whatever we speak or state is called speech. Speech comprises sentences which are composed of words. We can divide words into different classes called parts of speech, according to their use. The parts of speech are eight in number as shown in the table given below along with their definitions and examples.

Part of speech	*Definition or Function*	*Examples*
Noun	Name of a person, place, animal, quality or thing	Ram, boy, dog, pen, sun, Delhi, truth, honesty
Pronoun	Used in place of a noun	I, you, he she, they
Articles & Determiners	Points out indefinite and definite nouns	a, an, the, few, some
Adjective	Describes a noun or pronoun	big, honest, wooden, valuable, quiet, deep, soft, narrow
Adverb	Describes a verb, an adjective or another adverb	silently, widely, softly, quietly, very, carefully
Verb	Tells about action or state of something or someone	is, am, was, have, do, like, walk, work, make, throw, tell
Conjuction	Joins words, clauses or sentences	and, but, when, yet, while, else
Preposition	Links a noun or pronoun to another word	at, to, after, on for, under, over, with
Interjection	Expresses sudden feelings or emotions	Ah!, Alas!, oh!, ouch!, hi!, well!, Hurrah!

NOUNS

A word which denotes a person, a thing, an animal or a place is said to be a noun.

There are two noun numbers in English — the *Singular* and the *Plural*.

Singular Numbers : A noun that denotes one person or one thing, is said to be in the Singular number. For example — book, pencil, bird, dog, hen etc. are in singular number.

Plural Number : A noun that denotes more than one person or one thing is said to be in plural number. For example — boys, pens, lions, girls, men etc. are in plural number.

1. Note the change in plurals of the following nouns:

Singular	*Plural*
copy	copies
baby	babies
body	bodies

family	families
fly	flies
city	cities
army	armies
bay	bays
cry	cries
duty	duties
country	countries
diary	diaries
fairy	fairies
spy	spies
storey	storeys
monkey	monkeys

2. The following nouns do not undergo any change in plural form, in general:

Singular	***Plural***
deer	deer
thousand	thousand
hundred	hundred
dozen	dozen
sheep	sheep
pair	pair
score	score
gross	gross

☛ We can write—

(*a*) thousands of men; (*b*) two pairs of shoes; (*c*) dozens of mangoes; (*d*) scores of people etc.

But—

(*a*) two thousand rupees; (*b*) three hundred men; (*c*) five dozen eggs, etc.

3. The following nouns are usually used in plural forms. They take a plural verb after them:

eatables	fetters	surroundings
riches	alms	spectacles
trousers	pants	scissors
premises	thanks	annals
congratulations	goods	shorts
tongs	pains (for troubles)	arms

4. The following are the nouns which are plural in appearance but are usually used in singular number. They are followed by a singular verb:

news	politics	physics
mathematics	economics	ethics
politics	classics	gallows
statistics	athletics	innings
mechanics	summons	mumps

5. Collective nouns often used as plurals:

public	police	cattle
audience	clergy	folk
people	poultry	nation
elite	gentry	glitterati

6. The nouns that are usually used in singular forms:

advice	hair	rice
fuel	alphabet	machinery
offspring	issue	furniture
mischief	stationery	luggage
bedding	information	abuse

7. Material nouns are always used in singular number:

gold	copper	milk
water	silk	wool

☛ They may be used in plural with a different meaning. *e.g.,* copper coins (coppers), chains or fetters (irons), cans made of tin (tins).

GENDERS

The difference in sex is denoted by Gender in grammar. The various genders are as follows:

1. **Masculine Gender :** A noun that denotes a male is said to be of the masculine gender, as man, uncle, ox, boy etc.
2. **Feminine Gender :** A noun that denotes a female is said to be of feminine gender, as woman, aunt, princess, cow etc.
3. **Common Gender :** Nouns which denote both males and females are said to be of the common gender, as friend, cousin, person, parent, baby etc.
4. **Neuter Gender :** A noun that denotes the name of object without life is said to be of neuter gender, as file, table, pencil etc.

PRONOUNS

The repetition of a noun in a sentence or a set of sentences is really boring. So, instead of repeating the noun, we can use a word (for that noun) called the pronoun.

"A pronoun is a word that we use instead of a noun".

Example:

This is *Sachin. He* plays cricket.

☛ *He* is the pronoun used in place of *Sachin.*

Kinds of Pronouns

1. **Personal pronouns :** A pronoun which is used instead of the name of a person is known as a 'Personal Pronoun'. A list of the 'Personal pronouns' is listed below :

   I, my, mine, me, we
   (First Person)
   You, your, yours
   (Second Person)
   He, his, him, she, her, hers, it,
   its, they, their, theirs, them
   (Third Person)

2. **Demonstrative, Indefinite and Distributive Pronouns :**

   (*a*) **Demonstrative Pronouns :** Pronouns used to point out the objects to which they refer are called Demonstrative Pronouns.

   Examples:

   (*i*) *This* is a present from my uncle.
   (*ii*) *These* are merely excuses.
   (*iii*) Bembay mangoes are better than *those* of Bangaluru.

   (*b*) **Indefinite Pronouns :** All pronouns which refer to persons or things in a general way and do not refer to any particular person or thing are called Indefinite Pronouns.

   Examples:

   (*i*) *Somebody* has stolen my watch.
   (*ii*) *Few* escaped unhurt.
   (*iii*) Did you ask *anybody* to come?

   (*c*) **Distributive Pronouns :** Each, either, neither are called distributive pronouns because they refer to persons or things one at a time. For this reason they are always singular and followed by the verb in singular.

   Examples:

   (*i*) *Each* of the men received a reward.
   (*ii*) *These* men received *each* a reward.
   (*iii*) *Either* of you can go.

3. **Relative Pronouns :** A relative pronoun refers or relates to some noun going before, which is called its Antecedent.

   Examples:

   (*i*) I met Hari *who* used to live here.
   (*ii*) I have found the pen *which* I had lost.
   (*iii*) Here is the book *that* you lent me.

4. **Interrogative Pronouns :** These pronouns, are used for asking questions.

   Examples:

   (*i*) *Whose* book is this?
   (*ii*) *What* will all the neighbours say?
   (*iii*) *Which* do you prefer, tea or coffee?

☛ Interrogative pronouns can also be used in asking indirect questions. Consider the following examples:

(*i*) I asked *who* was speaking.
(*ii*) Tell me *what* you have done.
(*iii*) Say *which* you would like best.

Behaviour of the Pronouns

1. If three pronouns are used together in the same sentence they are arranged in the following order :

2	+	3	+	1
↓		↓		↓
Second Person		Third Person		First Person

Examples:

I, you and he must help *that* poor man. (Incorrect)

You, he and I must help *that* poor man. (Correct)

2. When two or more singular nouns are joined by and, the pronoun used for them should be plural.

Examples:
Mohan and Sohan are friends. *They* play football. *They* live at Lajpat Nagar.

3. But if these nouns joined by and refer to the same person or thing, the pronoun used should be singular.

Examples:
(*i*) Delhi, the beautiful city and the capital of India, is famous for *its* historical monuments.
(*ii*) The manager and owner of the firm expressed *his* views on the demands of the workers.

4. When two nouns are used with as well as, the pronoun agrees with the first subject.

Examples:
(*a*) Mohan as well as his friends is doing *his* work.
(*b*) The students as well as their teachers are doing *their* work.

5. When two singular nouns joined by 'and' are preceded by *each* or *every,* the pronoun used must be singular and should agree in gender with the second noun.

Examples:
(*a*) Every man and every woman will do *her* best for the nation.
(*b*) Each boy and each girl went to *her* house.

6. When two nouns are joined by using 'with', the pronoun agrees with the noun coming before 'with'.

Examples:
(*a*) The boy with *his* parents has gone to see a movie.
(*b*) The children with *their* parents have gone to picnic.

7. When two different nouns are joined by either......... or; neither .... nor, the pronoun is used according to the number and gender of the second noun.

Examples:
(*a*) Either your sister or you have done *your* work.
(*b*) Neither the students nor the teacher was in *his* class.

8. The pronoun coming after '*than*' must be in the same case as that coming before '*than*'.

Examples:
(*a*) She plays better than *me.* (Incorrect)
She plays better than *I.* (Correct)
(*b*) His elder brother is more intelligent than *him.* (Incorrect)
His elder brother is more intelligent than *he.* (Correct)

9. 'Many a' always takes a singular pronoun and singular verb.

Example:
Many a soldier has met *his* death in the battle field.

10. 'Who', 'Whose', 'Whom' are used only for persons.

Examples:
(*a*) *Who* is knocking at the door?
(*b*) *Whose* pen is this?
(*c*) *What* do you want?

11. 'Which' is used for things.

Example:
Which game do you like?

MULTIPLE CHOICE QUESTIONS

Directions: *In the following questions choose the correct options to fill in the blanks.*

1. It is a good chance, You must avail .... this opportunity.
A. of B. yourself of
C. for D. from

2. The person who is elected .... my relative.
A. is B. he is
C. his D. him

3. He made ....
A. yours mention
B. mention of you

C. mention for you
D. mention about you

4. .... I know, he is quite faithful.
A. As far as B. So far as
C. So far this D. So far so

5. It is a duty of a person to take .... for his family.
A. pain B. pains
C. pain-killers D. pained

6. The place was so dirty that ..... wished to run away from there.
A. everybody B. anybody
C. few D. some

7. ..... was there to help me.
A. Somebody B. Anything
C. Anybody D. Nobody

8. Is there .... to eat?
A. some B. something
C. any D. few

9. ..... of the students were making a great noise.
A. Anyone B. Somebody
C. Many D. Nobody

10. ..... of the students can solve this sum.
A. Someone B. Anybody
C. Somebody D. None

11. Vivek works harder than ....
A. me B. I
C. her D. his

12. They should help ....
A. the poor people B. the poor
C. the poor persons D. the poor peoples

13. .... are mad.
A. All his sons B. His all sons
C. Sons all his D. All sons his

14. The poor fellow .... to fate.
A. resigned
B. resigned himself
C. resigned itself
D. resigned themselves

15. Nobody will help you but ....
A. I B. me
C. ours D. his

16. She does not love .... husband.
A. his B. her
C. its D. their

17. Let .... work together.
A. him and me B. he and I
C. he and him D. I and me

18. Copper, Silver and Gold ....
A. each will do B. either will do
C. any one will do D. any will do

19. Jessica and Roma are very irregular .... habits.
A. in her B. in their
C. in its D. in every

20. One likes to enjoy .... who was a great poet.
A. The sonnets of Shakespeare
B. Shakespeare's sonnets
C. Sonnets
D. Shakespeare

21. One is supposed to do ....
A. our duty B. their duty
C. one's duty D. his duty

22. Take anything .... you want.
A. that B. which
C. than D. then

23. I cannot tolerate ....
A. separated you
B. your separation
C. separation from you
D. you separated

24. He is .... faithful partner.
A. Yours B. You
C. Your D. Your's

25. Ajay is more smart than ....
A. her B. hers
C. herself D. she

26. ...... of us should try our best to make India a heaven.
A. Any B. Somebody
C. Anybody D. All

27. ...... of us do not know the real meaning of our lives.
A. Any B. Something
C. Several D. Many

28. My .... black.
A. hairs are B. hair is
C. hairs shall D. hair will

29. She saw two .... on the last Sunday.
A. thiefs B. theifs
C. thieves D. theives

30. My sister is a ....
A. bacheloress B. bachelor
C. unmaried D. spinster

31. That is the boy .... everybody loves.
A. whom B. who
C. that D. whose

32. That is the girl .... won the first prize.
A. whom B. who
C. whose D. which

33. That is the man .... purse was lost.
A. who B. whom
C. whose D. their

ANSWERS

1	2	3	4	5	6	7	8	9	10
B	A	B	A	B	A	D	B	C	D
11	**12**	**13**	**14**	**15**	**16**	**17**	**18**	**19**	**20**
B	B	A	B	B	B	A	C	B	A
21	**22**	**23**	**24**	**25**	**26**	**27**	**28**	**29**	**30**
C	A	C	C	D	D	D	B	C	D
31	**32**	**33**							
A	B	C							

ARTICLES

A / AN / THE

'A' and 'an' are Indefinite Articles.
'The' is the Definite Article.
'A' and 'an' modify a noun in a general way.
'The' particularises it. *e.g.,*
Mohan has **a pen.**
The pen which you gave me was expensive.

A / AN

(*i*) 'A' is used before words starting with the sound of a consonant.

(*ii*) 'An' is used before a vowel sound (vowels a, e, i, o, u) *e.g.,*
a book, a cat, a useful thing, a European girl, a university,
but an FDR, an MA, an honest boy, an hour, an owl, an egg, an umbrella, etc.

The use of a/an/the

A cat mews. (*i.e.,* every cat)

The cat of my neighbour mews day and night. (*i.e.,* a particular cat)

He gave me **an** egg. (Here 'an' means 'one')

The use of the

1. 'The' is used before names of rivers, mountains, seas, oceans:
The Himalayas, the Ganga, the Yamuna, the Bay of Bengal, the Indian Ocean, the Nile, the English Channel, *etc.*
2. Names of newspapers and magazines:
The Times of India, the Tribune, The Sun, *etc.*
3. Names of the famous and holy books:
The Guru Granth Sahib, The Gita, The Ramayana, *etc.*
4. Names of creations of nature:
the sun, the earth, the moon, the sky, *etc.*
5. While using Adjectives as Nouns:
The poor should be helped by **the rich.**

6. Sometimes with the Comparative Degree.
 The more you think, **the more** you worry.
7. With the Superlative Degree
 She is **the most intelligent** girl in our school.
8. Before the imaginary lines and directions.
 The Latitude, The Equator, the east, the west, etc.
9. Before the names of musical instruments:
 the violin, the piano, the flute, etc.
10. While using a Proper Noun as a Common Noun:
 Mohan is **the Sachin** of our team.

OMISSION OF ARTICLE 'THE'

1. Before some Nouns used to convey general sense, articles are not used:
 Man is mortal.
2. Before Proper Nouns:
 Rakesh is an intelligent boy.
3. With Abstract Noun:
 Childhood is the prime time of one's life.
 The childhood of Sohan was full of sorrow.
4. With Material Nouns:
 Milk is an essential food.
 The milk of the cow is sweet.
5. Usually no article is used before names of diseases:
 Cancer is a fatal disease.
 However, when we talk about a disease figuratively, we use an article before its name, e.g.
 Corruption is a cancer.
6. Names of games and language:
 I like football.
 I can speak Punjabi, Hindi and English.
7. Gold is a precious metal.

NOTE: As you must have noted above, the definite article 'the', has been used where a noun is particularized.

DOUBLE USE OF ARTICLE 'THE'

Read the following sentences carefully:

1. The poet and novelist has been honoured.
 (The same person is the poet as well as novelist)
2. The poet and the novelist have been honoured.
 (The poet and the novelist are two different persons).
3. I have a black and white dog.
 (that is, one dog)
4. I have a black and a white dogs.
 (that is, two dogs)

MULTIPLE CHOICE QUESTIONS

Directions: *Fill in the blanks with suitable articles.*

1. He looks as foolish as .... ass.
 A. a B. an
 C. the D. No article

2. Did you go to .... prison to visit him?
 A. a B. an
 C. the D. No article

3. I found .... one-rupee note in the market.
 A. a B. an
 C. the D. No article

4. It is a pleasure to meet such .... efficient man.
 A. a B. an
 C. the D. No article

5. The Sanyasi lived in a cave in .... Himalayas.
 A. a B. an
 C. the D. No article

6. There is .... union in our factory.
 A. a B. an
 C. the D. No article

7. He hit his wife on the head with .... umbrella.
 A. a B. an
 C. the D. No article

8. I caught him by .... collar.
 A. a B. an
 C. the D. No article

9. Child is .... father of man.
A. a B. an
C. the D. No article

10. He gazed at .... moon for two hours.
A. a B. an
C. the D. No article

11. Do you know .... boy in white?
A. a B. an
C. the D. No article

12. She is .... girl I am looking for.
A. a B. an
C. the D. No article

13. Have you read .... Mahabharat?
A. a B. an
C. the D. No article

14. ....rich are not always happy.
A. A B. An
C. The D. No article

15. Oranges are sold by .... dozen.
A. a B. an
C. the D. No article

16. Milk is sold by .... litre.
A. a B. an
C. the D. No article

17. .... Amazon is the longest river in the world.
A. A B. An
C. The D. No article

18. .... higher you climb, the colder it gets.
A. A B. An
C. The D. No article

19. She is .... untidy girl.
A. a B. an
C. the D. No article

20. I am .... M.A. is English.
A. a B. an
C. the D. No article

21. I have already spent .... few rupees I had.
A. a B. an
C. the D. No article

22. .... English are very hard-working.
A. A B. An
C. The D. No article

23. April is the fourth month of .... year.
A. a B. an
C. the D. No article

24. Rice is sold by .... kilogram
A. a B. an
C. the D. No article

25. She is .... best of the three girls.
A. a B. an
C. the D. No article

26. .... man in the car is a friend of mine.
A. A B. An
C. The D. No article

27. Brevity is .... soul of wit.
A. a B. an
C. the D. No article

28. .... thing of beauty is a joy for ever.
A. A B. An
C. The D. No article

29. .... little learning is a dangerous thing.
A. A B. An
C. The D. No article

30. .... best sauce for food is hunger.
A. A B. An
C. The D. No article

ANSWERS

1	2	3	4	5	6	7	8	9	10
B	C	A	B	C	A	B	C	C	C
11	**12**	**13**	**14**	**15**	**16**	**17**	**18**	**19**	**20**
C	C	C	C	C	C	C	C	B	B
21	**22**	**23**	**24**	**25**	**26**	**27**	**28**	**29**	**30**
C	C	C	C	C	C	C	A	A	C

ADJECTIVES & ADVERBS

An Adjective is a word which adds something to the meaning of a noun or a pronoun.

Mridula is an *intelligent* girl.

He has a *black* goat.

He is a *brilliant* student.

She is a *clever* girl.

It is a *beautiful* picture.

In the sentences given above, the words in italics are adjectives.

An Adverb is a word which qualifies the meaning of a Verb, an Adjective or another Adverb.

(*i*) He talks *slowly.*

(*ii*) He is a *very* good student.

(*iii*) He talks *very* slowly.

In sentence (*i*), *slowly* qualifies the verb *talks.*

In sentence (*ii*), *very* qualifies the adjective *good.*

In sentence (*iii*), *very* qualifies the adverb *slowly.*

Adjectives have three degrees of comparison :

1. **Positive Degree :** It expresses the common form of an adjective.

   Example:

   Ram is a *tall* boy.

   In the above sentence *tall* is an adjective and expresses the common form.

2. **Comparative Degree :** It expresses the more of the same form.

   Example:

   Ram is *taller* than Mahesh.

   In the above sentence *taller* is an adjective that expresses the more of the common form of the adjective *tall.*

   "When and How to Use" Comparative Degree?

   (*a*) Comparative Degree is used when two persons or two groups of persons or things are compared.

   Examples :

   (*a*) He is *wiser* than his younger brother.

   (*b*) This glass is *cleaner* than the other.

   (*b*) When two different qualities in the same person are compared, more is used instead of 'er' to form the comparative. The formula used in this case should be :

   More + Positive Degree

   She is *fairer* than polite. (Incorrect)

   She is *more fair* than polite. (Correct)

   (*c*) When selection of one out of two persons or things is meant, the degree of comparison is followed by of and *the* is used before it.

   Example:

   Zia is abler of *the* two sisters.

   (*d*) If two comparatives are used in the same sentence to impress upon an idea, both should be preceded by the definite article.

   Examples :

   (*i*) The higher you go, the cooler it is.

   (*ii*) The more we get, the more we desire.

   (*e*) When one person or thing is compared with another of the same kind, other is used after the comparative degree. In such sentences other is normally preceded by any or all.

   Examples:

   (*i*) Kalidas is greater than any dramatist. (Incorrect)

   Kalidas is greater than any other dramatist. (Correct)

   (*ii*) Lead is heavier than all metals. (Incorrect)

   Lead is heavier than all other metals. (Correct)

   (*f*) Senior, junior, superior, inferior, prior, anterior (earlier than) and posterior (later than) are always followed by 'to'.

Examples:

(*i*) Ram is senior *to* Mohan by three years.
(*ii*) That pen is inferior *to* that.
(*iii*) He is junior *to* me in rank.
(*iv*) This event was posterior *to* that.

☛ Never use *than* after the above mentioned adjectives.

Important Information

(*a*) 'Preferable' is also used as an adjective of the comparative degree. As such, it is always followed by *to* and not *a*.

Death is preferable than dishonour. (Incorrect)
Death is preferable *to* dishonour. (Correct)

(*b*) To intensify the Degree of comparison, we use *far* or *much* before the comparative.

Examples:

(*i*) This book is *far* better than that.
(*ii*) His performance was *much* better than Mohan's.

Warning: Always avoid the use of double comparatives.

Don't say: Ram is more cleverer than his younger brother.

Say: Ram is cleverer than his younger brother.

3. **Superlative Degree :** It expresses the most of the common form of an adjective.

Example:
He is the ablest man of the town.

How and when to use the Superlative Degree?

(*a*) The Superlative Degree is used when more than two persons or things are compared.

(*b*) The Superlative Degree is generally preceded by 'the' and followed by 'of' in most of the cases or otherwise.

(*c*) When an adjective of the superlative degree is preceded by a Possessive Adjective or a Noun in the Possessive case, 'the' should not be used before it.

Example:
Which is Kalidas' best play?

It will be a blunder to use 'the' before the Superlative Degree in such cases.

Don't say : Which is Kalidas' the best play.

(*d*) To intensify the degree of comparison, *by far* is used before the superlative degree.

Example:
India is *by far* the most beautiful country of the world.

☛ Always avoid the use of double superlatives.

Don't say : He is the most strongest boy in the class.

Say : He is the strongest boy in the class.

Use of some Important Adjectives

1. (*a*) **'Some'** is used as follows :

(*i*) With countable nouns where it means — a little, a small quantity.
(*ii*) In a question which shows some request.

Examples:

(*i*) There is some water in the bottle.
(*ii*) Some of the students were absent yesterday.
(*iii*) Will you have some milk?
(*iv*) Will you buy some fruit for me?

(*b*) **'Any'** is used as follows :

(*i*) In negative sentences.
(*ii*) In interrogative sentences.
(*iii*) After 'Hardly', 'Scarcely' and 'Barely'.
(*iv*) After 'If'.

Examples:

(*i*) There is not any sugar in the pot.
(*ii*) We haven't any rice in the house.
(*iii*) I have hardly any money.
(*iv*) There are scarcely any plants in this field.
(*v*) If there is any danger, blow the whistle.

2. (*a*) **Older :** Older (and oldest) are used for persons animals and things. But 'Older' and 'Oldest' refer to the persons who do not belong to the same family.

Examples:

(*i*) Radha is older than Shyama.
(*ii*) John is the oldest member of the staff.

(b) **Elder** (and **eldest**) are used in respect of the members of the same family like sons, daughters, brothers, sisters.

Examples:

(i) My elder sister is a lecturer.

(ii) Meenakshi is the eldest of the three sisters.

☛ (i) 'Elder' is not followed by 'than'.

(ii) 'Elder' and 'Eldest' cannot be used for things.

3. (a) **'Few'** is negative and is the opposite of 'Many'. It means 'not many'.

(b) **'A few'** is positive and means 'some at least'. It is the opposite of 'None'.

(c) **'The few'** means 'minority' and suggests 'whether there is'.

Examples:

(i) We have few holidays in school.

(ii) Only a few boys will pass in the examination.

(iii) The few poems that he wrote are very popular.

4. (a) **Further** means 'something additional'.

(b) **Farther** means 'a greater distance'.

Examples:

(i) Further discussion will be held in the office of the principal.

(ii) Amritsar is farther from Delhi than Ambala.

5. (a) **Little** is negative. It means, 'not much', or 'hardly any'.

(b) **A little** is positive. It means 'some quantity'.

(c) **The little** denotes quantity. It means, 'not much but all that is, or whatever quantity there is'.

Examples:

(i) There is little hope of his success.

(ii) He knows a little of everything.

(iii) I have spent the little money I had.

(iv) The little knowledge of Urdu proved very useful to me.

6. (a) **'Much'** expresses 'quantity'.

(b) **'Many'** expresses 'number'.

(c) **'Many a'**—'Singular noun' and 'Singular verb' are used with 'many a'.

Examples:

(i) There is not *much* water in the jug.

(ii) *Many* boys are absent today.

(iii) *Many* a battle has been fought on the soil of India.

7. (a) **'Less'** denotes 'in a small degree'.

(b) **'Fewer'** denotes 'number'.

Examples:

(i) He devotes less time to his studies.

(ii) There are no fewer than ten chairs in this room.

8. (a) **'Each'** is used for a single number of 'two persons' or 'things'.

(b) **'Every'** is used for a single number of 'many persons' or 'things'.

Examples:

(i) Each boy must take part in games.

(ii) There were only two poets. Each poet recited his poem.

(iii) Every man dies in this world.

(iv) Every man is expected to do his duty.

9. (a) **'Either'** means one of the two or both.

(b) **'Neither'** is negative of the either.

Examples:

(i) You may buy either of these two chairs.

(ii) Neither of them could speak on the stage.

10. (a) **'Later'** expresses 'late in time'.

(b) **'Latter'** means 'second in position or order'.

Examples:

(i) My father reached later than I expected.

(ii) The latter position was better than the former.

Use of some Important Adverbs

1. (a) **Also, too, enough:**

(i) He taught English. Also, he edited the school magazine

(ii) He is a writer and also he is a painter.

(iii) He is too obstinate to listen to any reason.

(iv) This is too difficult a piece for the junior students.

(v) Sarla was kind enough to help the poor.
(vi) He is brave enough to face the truth.

☛ 'Too' is used in a negative sense, but enough is used in a positive sense.

(b) **Fairly and rather:** Both suggest the meaning 'moderately'. But, mainly 'fairly' is used with the words that denote a positive meaning and rather is used with the words that denote a negative meaning:

(i) Rita did fairly well in that competition, but her performance was rather poor in sports.
(ii) Mona is fairly rich, but she is rather stingy.

☛ 'Rather' can also be used in a positive sense.

(i) This is a rather interesting job.
(ii) That boy is rather smart.

(c) **Hardly, barely, scarcely:** These words mostly convey the negative suggestions and are almost similar.

(i) I have hardly any strength now.
(ii) There was barely any supply to the township,
(iii) There were scarcely a hundred guests present.

☛ With slight variance in the meaning, the words given above convey the idea of 'very little', 'not enough', 'lack of quantity and number'.

(d) **Yet, Still:** These adverbs can often be used to connect the sentence units:

(i) He has been defeated many times in the contest; still he wants to be a competitor.
(ii) Mona was sick; yet she went on doing her work.

(e) **Alone:**

(i) He alone (none else) is capable of handling that fire.
(ii) He hunted all alone in the forest. (not in any company)

Special Note:

(a) Apart from their conventional positions the adverbs might be used in different positions with different meanings and angles.

(i) He had only four books.
(ii) John only contacted his friend in need.
(iii) He greeted me only.
(iv) Only he greeted me there.

(b) **Inversion:** Some adverbs can be inverted *i.e.* placed in the beginning of the sentence and then be followed by an interrogative form. The most common of these adverb are: so, seldom, never, nowhere, under no circumstances, hardly, scarcely etc.

(i) So big was the bus that it could not enter the narrow lane.
(ii) Hardly had he reached the station when he received the message.

MULTIPLE CHOICE QUESTIONS

Directions: *In the following questions choose the correct options to fill in the blanks.*

1. .... water that was in the jug evaporated.
A. Little B. The little
C. Small D. A small

2. He has not sung .... songs.
A. much B. most
C. more D. many

3. Srishti has searched .... office.
A. whole the B. the whole
C. a whole D. some whole

4. Premchand was .... best and .... famous writer.
A. a, the most B. the, a most
C. the, more D. the, the most

5. William Shakespeare is famous as ....
A. a poet and a dramatist
B. a poet and dramatist

C. the poet and the dramatist
D. a poet and the dramatist

6. She returned .... than I had thought.
A. quickly B. more quicker
C. more quickly D. quicker

7. He is .... foolish person.
A. rather the B. a rather
C. rather a D. rather

8. This pen .... rupees.
A. costs twenty B. twenty costs only
C. costs only twenty D. only costs twenty

9. It is .... pride.
A. nothing else but B. nothing else than
C. else nothing than D. but

10. This tea is .... to drink.
A. too hot B. very hot
C. enough hot D. much hot

11. The girl whom you met is the .... sister of Ravi.
A. eldest B. elder
C. older D. oldest

12. The historical place is ....
A. seeing worth B. worthy of seeing
C. worth seeing D. worthy seeing

13. These flowers smell ....
A. sweet B. sweetly
C. more sweetly D. sweetest

14. .... aspirant cannot pass the entrance examination.
A. Each B. Every
C. All D. No

15. Prem Chand .... second Shakespeare.
A. is a B. is
C. is the D. is an

16. What does the .... leader suggest?
A. other B. another
C. others D. anothers

17. He .... money.
A. has few B. have few
C. has little D. have little

18. The .... boys are rewarded.
A. first two B. two first
C. firsts two D. two's first

19. He is .... brave.
A. stronger than B. stronger then
C. more strong then D. more strong than

20. No sooner said ....
A. so done B. and done
C. then done D. but done

21. .... student in the class got prizes.
A. Each and every B. Every and each
C. Every D. Never

22. It is .... picture than the one we saw last Monday.
A. interesting B. much interesting
C. more interesting D. most interesting

23. She is clever ....
A. that her mother is B. as her mother is
C. to her mother is D. than her mother is

24. They will get ....
A. Red, green and black paper
B. Red, green black paper
C. Red and green and black paper
D. Red green black paper

25. Health is .... wealth.
A. preferable to
B. more preferable than
C. more preferable to
D. most preferable then

ANSWERS

1	2	3	4	5	6	7	8	9	10
B	D	B	D	B	C	C	C	A	A
11	12	13	14	15	16	17	18	19	20
A	C	A	B	A	A	C	A	D	C
21	22	23	24	25					
C	C	C	A	A					

DETERMINERS

Determiners are actually Adjectives. They are always followed by nouns.

Determiners are of the following kinds:

1. **Demonstrative Determiners**
this, that, these, those
2. **Possessive Determiners**
my, our, your, his, her, its, their
3. **Quantitative Determiners**
some, any, much, enough, sufficient, whole, a little, the little, little, all, both
4. **Numerical Determiners**
a few, some, few, the few, any, several, many, no, etc.
One, two, three ... (Cardinals)
First, second, third ... (Ordinals)
5. **Distributive Determiners**
either, neither
6. **Articles**
Indefinite: a, an
Definite: the

MULTIPLE CHOICE QUESTIONS

Directions: *In the following questions choose the correct options to fill in the blanks.*

1. My brother is .... MBA.
A. a B. an
C. the D. any
2. Have you got .... cheese?
A. some B. many
C. a few D. few
3. No, I have not got .... cheese.
A. many B. few
C. any D. some
4. There is only .... milk left in the bottle.
A. enough B. few
C. much D. a little
5. There is .... hope of his recovery.
A. any B. little
C. many D. few
6. .... water in the jug has been drunk by Mohan.
A. The little B. The few
C. A few D. Few
7. I shall play .... piano at the party.
A. some B. any
C. the D. few
8. .... labourers were found dead in the mine.
A. Any B. Fewer
C. Many D. Less
9. Could I borrow .... umbrella?
A. our B. your
C. yours D. my
10. My brother is standing in the .... row.
A. any B. many
C. some D. first
11. Give me .... rice.
A. some B. few
C. a few D. any
12. .... sheep grazing on the slope of the hill had gone away.
A. Any B. The few
C. This D. Much
13. Have you got .... magazines to read?
A. all B. much
C. some D. little
14. I have ...... money that I want to spend on shares.
A. any B. much
C. less D. some
15. There is .... owl on the branch of the tree.
A. a B. the
C. an D. some
16. .... dogs were barking at the strangers.
A. Some B. Any
C. Much D. Less

17. The girl bought her father .... juice.
A. few B. some
C. any D. many

18. You should take .... honey everyday.
A. any B. many
C. a little D. a few

19. .... boy was punished by the teacher.
A. Either B. All
C. Any D. Many

20. .... girl was asked to join the army.
A. None B. Neither
C. All D. Any

ANSWERS

1	2	3	4	5	6	7	8	9	10
B	A	C	D	B	A	C	C	B	D
11	**12**	**13**	**14**	**15**	**16**	**17**	**18**	**19**	**20**
A	B	C	D	C	A	B	C	A	B

VERBS

A verb is a word that tells something about the action or state of or happenning to a person or thing.

A verb tells the following:

1. What a person or thing does.

Examples:

(*i*) Sachin goes to school daily.

(*ii*) The bell *rang* loudly.

(*iii*) Many birds fly in the sky.

(*iv*) She *sang* a song.

2. What a person or thing is.

Examples:

(*i*) India *is* the biggest democracy in the world.

(*ii*) Ram Mehar *is* very rich.

(*iii*) They *are* happy.

3. What is done to a person or thing.

Examples:

(*i*) You *are liked* by all.

(*ii*) Two thieves *were arrested*.

(*iii*) Four students *were punished* by the teacher.

4. What happens to a person or thing.

Examples:

(*i*) His maternal uncle *died* last week.

(*ii*) Two ships *sank* yesterday.

(*iii*) Leaves *turn* yellow in autumn.

5. What a person or thing has, had, and so on.

Examples:

(*i*) I *have* a new car.

(*ii*) He *had* a scooter last year.

(*iii*) He *has* several cows and goats.

It goes without saying that a verb is the most important part of a sentence. No sentence is complete without a Verb.

Important Information

1. If two or more singular nouns are joined by 'and' the verb used will be plural.

Example:

(*i*) He and I were going to the market.

(*ii*) Ram and Mohan are friends.

2. If two singular nouns joined by 'and' points out to the same thing or person, the verb used must be singular.

Example:

(*i*) Rice and curry is the favourite food of the Punjabis.

(*ii*) The Collector and District Magistrate is away.

3. In case two subjects are joined by 'as well as' the verb agrees with the first subject.

Example:

(*i*) Kanta as well as her children is playing.

(*ii*) Children as well as their mother are playing.

In the case of first sentence the verb (is) agrees with Kanta and in the case of second sentence the verb (are) agrees with the children.

4. 'Neither', 'Either', 'Every', 'Each', 'Everyone', and 'Many a' are followed by a singular verb.

Example:

(*i*) Either of the plans is to be adopted.

(*ii*) Neither of the two brothers is sure to pass.

(*iii*) Every student is expected to be obedient.

(*iv*) Everyone of them desires this.

(*v*) Many a person is drowned in the sea.

5. If two subjects are joined by 'Either .... or' / 'Neither .... nor', the verb agrees with the subject near to it.

Example:

(*i*) Either my brother or I am to do this work.

(*ii*) Neither he nor they are prepared to do this work.

6. 'A great many' is always followed by a 'plural noun' and a 'plural verb'. For example : A great many students have been declared successful.

7. Similarly if two subjects are joined by 'with', 'together with', 'no less than', in addition to 'and not', etc. the verb agrees with the first subject.

Example:

(*i*) The boy with his parents has arrived.

(*ii*) He, no less than I, is to blame.

8. Nouns, plural in form, but singular in meaning, take a singular verb.

Example:

This news was broadcast from television yesterday.

MULTIPLE CHOICE QUESTIONS

Directions: *In the following questions choose the correct options to fill in the blanks.*

1. They each .... a book.
A. have B. are
C. has D. is

2. He and I .... close friends.
A. is B. am
C. was D. are

3. She as well as I .... guilty.
A. is B. are
C. am D. must be

4. Purushottam .... not read more on this chapter.
A. needs B. has been need
C. need D. had been need

5. He came .... to his aunt.
A. run B. running
C. to run D. in run

6. The bus with all its passengers .... lost.
A. were B. was
C. are D. would

7. You as well as I .... responsible for this work.
A. am B. are
C. was D. is

8. Raghava like all his companions .... a spoiled child.
A. are B. were
C. is D. will be

9. Pen and ink .... required for me.
A. are B. were
C. is D. has required

10. Every girl and every boy .... attended the seminar.
A. have B. has
C. is D. are

11. She dislikes .... meat.
A. eat to B. to eat
C. eating D. to eating

12. He likes..........
A. sing to B. singing
C. to sing D. to singing

13. We are ready .... the match.
A. play to B. to playing
C. playing D. to play

14. .... is injurious to health.
A. Smoking B. To smoke
C. To smoking D. Smoke to

15. He loves .... raw vegetables.
A. eaten B. eating
C. to eating D. eat to

16. Not only she but all her sisters ...... been married.
A. has B. have
C. is D. are

17. There .... nothing but miseries in life.
A. is B. are
C. were D. will be

18. Neither prose nor poem .... given.
A. were B. was
C. has D. have

19. Either he or I .... wrong.
A. is B. are
C. am D. were

20. Either Sulekha or Rekha .... coming here.
A. are B. is
C. were D. have

21. .... the child or his parents to blame?
A. Is B. Are
C. Were D. Has

22. You and I .... neighbours.
A. am B. are
C. was D. has

23. The house with all its belongings ..... sold away.
A. were B. are
C. was D. must

24. Either water or juice .... required.
A. is B. are
C. were D. has

25. There were not as many tables as .... required.
A. was B. were
C. is D. are

26. He seemed .... finished his homework.
A. have to B. to have
C. having D. to having

ANSWERS

1	2	3	4	5	6	7	8	9	10
A	D	A	C	B	B	B	C	C	B
11	**12**	**13**	**14**	**15**	**16**	**17**	**18**	**19**	**20**
C	B	D	A	B	B	A	B	C	B
21	**22**	**23**	**24**	**25**	**26**				
A	B	C	A	B	B				

CONJUNCTIONS

A conjunction is a word which connects words, clauses or sentences.

Look at the following sentences.

(*i*) He bought apples *and* mangoes.

(*ii*) God made the country *and* man made the town.

(*iii*) The door was open *but* there was no one in the house.

(*iv*) He knows that I am here *and* that I want to see him.

In the sentence (*i*), *and* connects two words—*apples* and *mangoes.*

In the sentence (*ii*), *and* connects two sentences—*God made the country* and *man made the town.*

In the sentence (*iii*), *but* connects two sentences— *The door was open* and *there was no one in the house.*

In the sentence (*iv*), *and* connects two clauses—*that I am here* and *that I want to see him.*

The main coordinating conjunctions are:

and, but, for, or, nor, also, either ..... or, neither ..... nor.

There are some conjunctions which are used in pairs. They are:

either .... or, ... neither .... nor, both .... and, though .... yet, whether .... or, not only .... but also.

Example: *Either* take it *or* leave it.

It is *neither* useful *nor* ornamental.

They *both* like *and* respect me.

Though he is suffering from high fever, *yet* he does not cry.

He does not care *whether* you go *or* stay.

He is *not only* doltish, *but also* obstinate.

The conjunctions which are used in pairs in this way, are called correlative conjunctions, or merely correlatives.

Use of Important Conjunctions

1. **As soon as:** As soon as denotes simultaneous time.

   Example: As soon as he saw his enemy, he took to his heels.

2. **No sooner .... than :**
   (*a*) 'No sooner' is always followed by 'than'.
   (*b*) Please remember that 'No sooner' is always followed by do/does/did. As such only first form of the verb should be used after the subject.

   Example:

   No sooner did he see his enemy than he took to his heels.

3. **Hardly:** 'Hardly' is followed by 'when'.

   Examples:

   (*i*) Hardly had I left the house when it started raining.
   (*ii*) We had hardly come into the room when his father began chastising him.

☛ A. 'Hardly' is never followed by 'than'.

B. 'Scarcely' can also be used in the sense and manner of 'Hardly'.

4. **Lest:** Lest is used in the sense of 'so that .... not'. It is always followed by 'should'. Lest is negative in sense. Hence 'not' should never be used with it.

   Example:

   Work hard lest you should fail.

☛ 'Lest' is always followed by 'should' and not 'may'.

5. **Unless:** Unless expresses condition. It is also used in the negative sense. Use of 'not' is not allowed with 'unless' because 'unless' is already in the negative sense.

   Example:

   Unless you labour hard you will not pass.

6. **Until:** 'Until' expresses time. It means 'till not'.

   Example:

   Wait here until I return.

☛ Until is in the negative sense. So 'not' should not be used with it.

Example :

Wait here until I do not return. (Incorrect)

Wait here until I return. (Correct)

7. **As well as:** When two subjects are joined by 'as well as', the verb always agrees with the first subject.

   Examples:

   (*i*) The teacher as well as students is playing.
   (*ii*) Students as well as the teacher are playing.

☛ 'Both' and 'as well as' cannot be used together in the same sentence.

Examples:

Both Sita as well as Kanta are beautiful. (Incorrect)

Sita as well as Kanta is beautiful. (Correct)

Both Sita and Kanta are beautiful. (Correct)

8. **As if:** 'As if' is used in the sense of pretension. While using 'as if' in a sentence, we should see that even the third person singular subject gets 'were'.

Example:
He talks as if he were mad.

9. Till: Till expresses time. Till is always used in the affirmative.

Example:
We did not come back till sunset.

10. Rather than: 'Rather than' is used in the sense of 'preference'. 'Rather' is always followed by 'than'.

Example:
I would rather die than submit.

11. As long as/so long as: Both express time during which an action or event takes place.

Example:
As long as there is life, there is hope.

12. However: It is both a subordinate and co-ordinate clause.

Examples:
(*a*) Mala worked hard, she however, failed.
(*b*) However hard he may work, he cannot pass.

13. Such as: 'Such as' gives us the sense of 'like'. Such is always followed by 'as'.

Example:
Life is such a puzzle as cannot be solved.

MULTIPLE CHOICE QUESTIONS

Directions: *In the following questions choose the correct options to fill in the blanks.*

1. Hardly had he left .... his brother came.
A. then B. than
C. when D. that

2. I would rather have a copy .... a book.
A. then B. than
C. when D. that

3. He is no other .... my friend.
A. then B. than
C. when D. but

4. He saw a snake ....he awoke.
A. then B. when
C. than D. No word needed

5. Ten years have passed .... my grandmother died.
A. since B. when
C. then D. than

6. She is .... good .... bad.
A. either, not B. neither, or
C. neither, nor D. neither, than

7. The cellphone is both cheap .... best.
A. than B. and
C. then D. or

8. No sooner did the rogue see the police .... he disappeared.
A. then B. than
C. so D. because

9. Srishti will go .... Sanju goes.
A. if B. than
C. then D. although

10. She is wise .... timid.
A. and B. yet
C. but D. however

11. Neither he .... his friend is good.
A. or B. and
C. but D. nor

12. The officer asked the peon .... why he was late.
A. that B. if
C. but D. No word needed

13. Both Ajay .... Vijay are intelligent.
A. or B. nor
C. and D. No word needed

14. No Sooner did the thief see the public .... he ran away.
A. then B. and
C. but D. than

15. Abhinav .... his brothers was going to Mumbai.
A. but B. yet
C. No word needed D. together with

16. He behaves .... he were the captain of the team.
A. as if B. as
C. No word needed D. that

17. Either Rupali .... Sonali is going to attend the meeting.
A. and B. but
C. nor D. or

18. Neither Nirmal .... Ashwinee is going to listen the speech.
A. and B. but
C. nor D. or

19. Ravi .... Prakash are going to Kolkata.
A. or B. nor
C. but D. and

20. Rice .... curry is my usual breakfast.
A. and B. but
C. then D. than

21. Make hay .... the sun shines.
A. though B. while
C. after D. before

22. He is so weak .... he cannot walk.
A. but B. that
C. then D. so

23. Although he is rich, ... he is unhappy.
A. but B. yet
C. so D. still

24. Wait here .... I come back.
A. till B. until
C. before D. after

25. He is my friend .... I shall help him.
A. so B. hence
C. that is why D. therefore

26. He must go away .... he will be beaten.
A. otherwise B. and
C. or D. else

27. God loves good men .... good men love God.
A. and B. or
C. that D. those

28. He was late .... he was not punished.
A. but B. yet
C. still D. therefore

29. Walk slowly ...., you may fall.
A. and B. or
C. so D. otherwise

30. Work hard, ... you will fail.
A. and B. or
C. otherwise D. else

ANSWERS

1	2	3	4	5	6	7	8	9	10
C	B	B	B	A	C	B	B	A	C
11	**12**	**13**	**14**	**15**	**16**	**17**	**18**	**19**	**20**
D	D	C	D	D	A	D	C	D	A
21	**22**	**23**	**24**	**25**	**26**	**27**	**28**	**29**	**30**
B	B	B	A	B	C	A	C	D	D

PREPOSITIONS

A preposition is a word placed before a noun or a pronoun to show the relationship between things, people or events. It expresses relationship in space, position, direction, time, place, method, purpose or result.

Usage:

1. A preposition is usually placed before a noun or noun-equivalent it governs.
e.g. She died of AIDS.

2. The preposition is always placed at the end when the object is the Relative pronoun 'that'; as -

e.g. Here is the book that you asked for.

He snatched the paper that I was writing on.

3. For the sake of emphasis the object governed by the preposition is placed first/before the preposition;

as - *e.g.* This I aimed at.

His acheivement is known all the world over.

ERRORS IN USE OF PREPOSITIONS

Preposition of Time:

1. At is used (*a*) with a definite point of time (*b*) with festivals.

e.g. I go to my office at 9.30 a.m.

He will come at Christmas.

2. **In** is used: (*a*) with a specific time, period, month, year, season,

e.g. I talk in the morning.

In winter the weather is cold.

Note: 'At' is used with noon.

e.g. He comes at noon for lunch.

(*b*) With the future tense referring to the period in which action may take place:

e.g. Inflation will rise in future.

3. **On** is used with days and dates.

e.g. The Annual function is on Saturday.

My Birthday is on twenty-seventh July.

4. **By** determines the time by which anything is to be done; done before not later;

e.g. Application should reach this office by 5th June.

Work will be completed by Monday.

5. **Before** This implies 'earlier than';

e.g. Children must reach school before the bell rings.

6. **From** It indicates the time of beginning.

e.g. I am on leave from 10th April.

She is dumb from birth.

7. **Since** expresses a specified time in the past up to the present.

e.g. He has taken up this job last year and has been here ever since.

I am waiting for him since yesterday.

8. **For** has three implications:

(*a*) Firstly it expresses a period of time or say duration

e.g. He worked in this office for eight years.

(*b*) Secondly it refers to the specified time when something is intended to happen;

e.g. The appointment is for 7.30 p.m

(*c*) Thirdly it indicates the occasion when something happens.

e.g. I am going college for the first time.

PREPOSITIONS OF POSITION

1. **At** refers to an exact point.

e.g. He is going to meet him at Mcdonald Restaurant.

She is at a meeting.

2. **In** implies inside; within the shape or area of.

e.g. We live in India.

He was hit in the chest.

3. **Between** is used for two persons or two things.

e.g. Equator lies between the Tropic of Cancer and Tropic of Capricorn.

4. **Beside** shows a position next to.

e.g. Whenever I travel, I keep my costly luggage beside me.

5. **Besides** means in addition to.

e.g. Besides these flowers, we need some decoration materials too.

6. **Below** shows the position at a lower level.

e.g. The temperature in Delhi remained below 5°C all day.

7. **Beneath** means in a lower position

e.g. Several dead bodies are still lying beneath the debris caused by earthquake.

8. **Among** is used with more than two persons or things but before the word which starts with a consonant letter.
e.g. He loves to sit among the children and narrate stories.
9. **Amongst** is used with more than two persons or things but before the word which starts with a vowel letter.
e.g. Divide the chocolates amongst us.
10. **Over** is used for vertically above.
e.g. A white cloth was spread over the dead body.
There is a fan over the bed.
11. **Within** shows the position near by or approachable.
e.g. Within the school campus, there is a swimming pool.
12. **Onto** means upon the surface.
e.g. The child enjoyed jumping onto the sofa.

PREPOSITION OF DIRECTION

1. **To** is used to express motion from one place to another.
e.g. We walked to the hills and back.
2. **Towards** refers to direction in which the progress is being made.
e.g. While performing on the stage one should face towards the audience.
3. **Into** denotes motion towards the inside of something.
e.g. He immediately dived into the water and saved the child.
4. **At** refers to aim.
e.g. He aimed at the bird on window.
5. **For** denotes direction.
e.g. I will leave for Bombay tomorrow.
6. **Against** shows pressure.
e.g. Place the ladder against the wall.
7. **Off** refers to separation.
e.g. He slipped off the scooter.
8. **From** refers to the point of departure.
e.g. He borrowed the money from his sister.

OTHER USES OF PREPOSITIONS

1. **About** shows nearness.
e.g. His father is about to retire.
2. **Along** is used to express the position from one end to or towards the other end; or parallel with the length of something.
e.g. We walked along the river bank.
3. **Across** is used in three different meaning
Firstly, it refers to something extending from one side to the other.
e.g. The railway bridge is to be constructed across the river.
Secondly, to express from one side to the other side of something.
e.g. He rowed across the Chilka lake.
Thirdly, to express something that intersects or cross.
e.g. On the death of her only son the mother cried with her arms across the chest.

MULTIPLE CHOICE QUESTIONS

Directions: *Fill in the blanks with suitable prepositions.*

1. Children should be able to adopt ..... harsh weather conditions.
A. to B. with
C. in D. onto
2. The boat which was rowed with only one oar went ..... in circles, only when it was rowed with both the oars, it moved.
A. around B. round
C. away D. about
3. The Sergeant was returning from a New Year eve dinner with friends when he chanced ..... five drunken passengers ..... a taxi harassing girl.
A. upon, in B. against, in
C. at, inside D. on. inside

4. In most parts of the city there were huge traffic jams with vehicles backed up ..... miles.
A. to B. at
C. through D. for

5. The huge surge in foreign exchange reserves ..... the current financial year should be a cause ..... concern to the policymakers.
A. of, for B. of, of
C. in, for D. in, of

6. Celebrations transform our life of routine and boredom .... rejuvenation and rejoicing.
A. towards B. unto
C. into D. to

7. Miserly people are incapable of trusting life and that's why life does not open its treasures ..... them.
A. to B. for
C. within D. towards

8. There are so many people of Indian origin settled ..... the globe, from different professions.
A. throughout B. across
C. round D. wide

9. Fluctuations in business fortunes is another reason for companies going in .... a floating workforce.
A. to B. towards
C. through D. for

10. She hopes to be a teacher but her real talent lies in wielding the brush .... aplomb.
A. in B. with
C. beyond D. into

11. Thousands of young patriotic Indians responded to Vivekananda's clarion call and jumped whole-heartedly ...... the freedom struggle.
A. for B. to
C. in D. into

12. Today, the youth are so self-centered, they are not bothered ..... the poverty around them.
A. about B. with
C. to D. for

13. Many NRIs are looking ..... investing in India like buying homes.
A. for B. to
C. into D. at

14. The new Science and Technology Policy rightly reeks to put in place simplified administrative and financial procedures that will hopefully breathe fresh life........Indian science.
A. within B. in
C. into D. for

15. She is not the only artist to have faced threats from underworld but she is the only one brave to talk ..... them.
A. about B. on
C. relating D. upon

16. Life would be fun without any restraint imposed ..... belonging to one religion.
A. for B. by
C. at D. on

17. There has been a large accession of books .... the library.
A. at B. to
C. for D. in

18. His aggressive way of dealing ..... people will make many misconotrue his actions.
A. of B. at
C. with D. in

19. He felt it to be an insult .... his pride when I did not believe his words.
A. in B. at
C. on D. to

20. The new hospital provides ample amenities ..... the patients.
A. for B. to
C. through D. towards

21. Literature cannot close its eyes ..... the ambient society.
A. upon B. on
C. against D. to

22. The monetary help that he rendered .... the most appropriate moment was really appreciable.
A. in B. at
C. to D. into

23. He had no option but to resign from the office after the defamation heaped ..... him.
A. against B. on
C. upon D. around

24. His habit of interfering made him extremely unpopular ..... his colleagues.
A. in B. against
C. on D. at

25. His ignoble tastes are ..... variance with his elevated social status.
A. in B. against
C. on D. at

26. It is difficult for an over-scrupulous person to live ..... coarse people.
A. in B. amongst
C. around D. between

27. After the earthquake, the whole city appeared to be .... a shambles.
A. at B. in
C. on D. upon

28. ...... circumstances compelled him, the lazy refused to work for his living.
A. Till B. Until
C. Since D. After

29. A shocked nation was trying to come to terms ..... the sudden death of the Prime Minister.
A. on B. at
C. with D. after

30. .... his passing away, the nation has lost a great patriot who made an outstanding contribution to public life.
A. With B. On
C. In D. After

ANSWERS

1	2	3	4	5	6	7	8	9	10
A	D	A	D	C	C	A	B	D	B
11	12	13	14	15	16	17	18	19	20
D	A	D	C	A	B	B	C	D	B
21	22	23	24	25	26	27	28	29	30
A	B	C	D	D	B	B	B	C	C

INTERJECTIONS

An *interjection* is a word which expresses a sudden feeling for emotion. It must be borne in mind that an interjection has no grammatical relation with any other word in a sentence.

It is a convention that an interjection is followed by the exclamation mark(!).

An interjection usually expresses *joy, grief, surprise, anger, contempt, alarm, attention,* approval, disapproval , etc.

Important interjections and the emotions they express are named below:

Joy : *Hurrah! Ha! Ha!*
Grief : *Alas! Ah!*
Surprise : *Oh! What!*
Approval : *Bravo! Hear! Hear! Well done!*
Calling : *Hello! Hi! Hey!*
Contempt : *Fie! Pooh!*

Observe the following sentences

Hurrah! We have won the match.

Alas! It is a sad day for us. We have lost the game.

Hush! Don't make a noise. The baby is sleeping.

Hello! What are you doing there?
Who is there?

Oh! I got such a fright.

Ah! I should have been there. What a sorry plight.

Hark! Don't you hear a sound?

What! So early.

The following interjection phrases are in common use:

Ah me!	Good God!
For shame!	Hold on!
Well done!	Off with you!
Good Grace!	Dear me!
Good heavens!	

Other parts of speech are also sometimes used as interjections. Some examples are given below:

Noun	: A horse! A horse! My kingdom for a horse!
Pronoun	: What a lame excuse! What a beautiful sight it is!
Verb	: Would that I were young again!
Adverb	: How lovely the flowers are!
Conjunction	: If I could only see her once again!
Infinitive	: To think of him as a friend!

MULTIPLE CHOICE QUESTIONS

Directions: *Tick the correct interjection to be applied to the given sentences.*

1. .... A soldier and afraid of death.
A. Hurrah! B. Bravo!
C. Fie on you! D. Pshaw!

2. .... He didn't accept your proposal.
A. Oh! B. What!
C. Hark! D. Good Heavens!

3. .... The cuckoo is singing.
A. Hark! B. What!
C. Oh! D. Hurrah!

4. .... What do I see here?
A. Good heavens! B. What!
C. Ha! Ha! D. Hush!

5. .... Well done.
A. What! B. Oh!
C. Bravo! D. Hurrah!

6. .... What do you talk of him?
A. Chi! Chi! B. Alas!
C. Well! D. Hark!

7. .... What next?
A. Hush! B. Well!
C. Hurrah! D. Hark!

8. .... The meeting is going on.
A. What! B. Oh!
C. Hurrah! D. Hush!

9. .... We have won the match.
A. Chi-Chi! B. Fie! Fie
C. Hurrah! D. Phew!

10. .... He is no more.
A. Hush! B. Alas!
C. Hark! D. Pooh!

11. .... How good of you.
A. Oh!
B. Hush!
C. Good Heavens!
D. Bravo!

12. .... You took so much trouble for us.
A. What! B. Oh!
C. Phew! D. Well!

ANSWERS

1	2	3	4	5	6	7	8	9	10
C	B	A	A	C	A	B	D	C	B
11	**12**								
A	B								

11 Modals

Modals are actually helping verbs. They help the finite verbs in framing sentences:

She **was** cooking food.

I **shall** guide you.

Kinds of Modals

Modals are of two kinds:

A. Primary Modals

B. Auxiliary Modals

A. Primary Modals

Primary modals work both as Helping Verbs and Finite Verbs.

Be = is, am, are, was, were, being, been

Have = has, have, had, having

Do = do, does, did, done, doing

(*a*) **Usage of be/have/do as Helping verbs:**

She **is** making a cane basket.

I **have** finished my homework.

She **does** know French.

(*b*) **Usage of be/have/do as Finite verbs:**

She **was** happy.

I **have** an expensive pen.

She **is doing** her homework.

B. Auxiliary Modals

Shall, should, will, would, can, could, may, might, must, ought to, used to, have to, had to, dare, daren't, need needn't, mustn't are modal Auxiliaries.

Shall

'Shall' is used in the following ways:

(*a*) **With first Person Pronouns (I/we)**

I shall lend you my book.

We shall go to school together.

(*b*) **to express a suggestion**

Shall we go out for a walk?

Shall we meet the officer tomorrow?

Sometimes 'Shall' is used with Second and Third Person Pronouns as under:

(*a*) **to express a command**

You shall not tell a lie.

You shall not disturb us.

(*b*) **to express prohibition**

You shall not smoke here.

You shall not drink here.

(*c*) **to express a legal obligation**

You shall submit your sales tax return before the end of this month.

Should

'Should' is used in the following ways:

(*a*) **As Past Tense of 'shall'**

She said that she **should** settle in America.

(*b*) **to express duty and obligation**

You should do your duty honestly.

(*c*) **to express advice**

You should reach the station before time.

(*d*) **to express guess**
It should be 9 o'clock now.

(*e*) 'Should' is used with lest to express purpose.
Walk fast lest you should miss the train.

Will

'Will' is used in the following ways:

(*a*) **With Second and Third person Pronouns:**
You will dance at the party.
He will sing a song.

(*b*) **to express (Invitation/offer)**
Will you dine with me tonight?

(*c*) **to express an order**
Will you shut your big mouth?

(*d*) **to express probability**
He will come to see me tomorrow.

Sometimes 'Will' is used with 'I'

(*a*) **Determination**
I will win the first position.

(*b*) **A threat**
I will punish you.

(*c*) **A promise**
I will lend you Rs. 500/- tomorrow.

Would

'Would' is used in the following ways:

(*a*) **As Past Tense of 'will'**
He said that they would be attending the meeting the next day.

(*b*) **to express a desire or wish**
Would that I were a king!

(*c*) **to express a polite invitation**
Would you like some biscuits?

(*d*) **The usage of would in conditional sentences**
You would get good marks if you worked hard.
You would have won the race if you had run fast.

(*e*) **to express a piece of advice**
I would not meet him if I were you.

Can

'Can' is used in the following ways:

(*a*) **to express ability**
He can speak English fluently.

(*b*) **to grant permission**
You can go now.

(*c*) **to express impossibility**
Who can defeat his fate?

(*d*) **to make a request**
Can I use your motorbike?

Could

'Could' is used in the following ways:

(*a*) **As Past Tense of 'can'**
She said that she could see the sun rising.

(*b*) **to express past ability**
I could sing and dance when I was young.

(*c*) **to express a request**
Could I use your phone?

May

'May' is used in the following ways:

(*a*) **to express a request**
May I use your bicycle?

(*b*) **to seek and allow permission**
May I come in, sir?
Yes, you may.

(*c*) **to express possibility**
It may rain tonight.

(*d*) **In optative sentences**
May you live long!

Might

'Might' is used in the following ways:

(*a*) **As past tense of 'may'**
She said that her brother might come back home.

(*b*) **to express less possibility**
It might rain tonight.

(*c*) **to give and seek permission**
Might I come in, sir?
You might go home now.

Must

'Must' is used in the following ways:

(*a*) **to express duty**
You must serve your motherland.

(*b*) **to express obligation**
We must obey our elders.

(*c*) **to express advice**

You must take an umbrella before going to office.

(*d*) **to express probability**

'Must' expresses a stronger probability than may.

It must rain tonight.

Ought to

'Ought to' is used in the following ways:

(*a*) **to express obligation**

We ought to respect our teachers.

(*b*) **to express advice**

You ought to help the poor.

Used to

'Used to' is used in the following ways:

(*a*) **to express past habits**

He used to smoke.

(*b*) **to express past existence of something**

There used to be a five star hotel in this city.

Have to

'Have to' expresses compulsion in the present tense.

You have to sign the documents.

Had to

'Had to' expresses compulsion in the past time.

She had to join the office again.

Dare

'Dare' is used as a Modal only in Interrogative sentences.

How dare you touch my bag?

Dare not (Daren't)

'Dare not (Daren't)' is used in negative sentences.

She daren't complain against me.

Need

'Need' expresses an obligation/compulsion. It is used in Interrogative Sentences.

Need I say more?

Need not (Needn't)

'Need not (Needn't)' is used in negative sentences.

You needn't come here again.

Must not (Mustn't)

'Must not (Mustn't)' is the negative form of must.

You mustn't follow us.

MULTIPLE CHOICE QUESTIONS

Directions: *In the following questions choose the correct options to fill in the blanks:*

1. You .... not bring the child here.

A. have B. had
C. need D. would

2. ..... you live long!

A. Will B. May
C. Shall D. Can

3. ..... God help you!

A. Can B. Will
C. May D. Shall

4. ..... that I were a leader!

A. Would B. Should
C. Could D. Will

5. It ...... be ten o'clock now.

A. could B. would
C. should D. will

6. He ..... have reached the station by now.

A. shall B. will
C. would D. should

7. Being a receptionist, she will .... type a letter.

A. has to B. have to
C. need to D. must

8. The birds ...... fly high in the sky.

A. may
B. should
C. can
D. would

9. ...... I open the main gate?
A. Should B. Would
C. Could D. Must

10. If you played well, we ...... win the match.
A. would B. should
C. must D. need

11. I think you .... not mind my reciting the poem loudly.
A. should B. could
C. may D. would

12. ..... I sit here for some time?
A. Can B. Shall
C. Will D. Must

13. You ...... take the child to an intelligent doctor.
A. shall B. will
C. ought to D. would

14. She ...... smoke in those days.
A. used to B. could
C. would D. had to

15. If I were you I ... not attend the meeting.
A. can B. would
C. could D. should

16. You .... submit your file to the authorities within a week.
A. have B. had
C. should D. would

17. ...... I use your phone?
A. Have B. Could
C. Would D. Had

18. ..... you give me your pen?
A. May B. Can
C. Must D. Dare

19. There ...... be an hospital at this place.
A. have to B. may
C. used to D. might

20. He ...... read and write when he was young.
A. would B. could
C. should D. can

21. He said that he ..... sing a song at the party.
A. should B. would
C. can D. will

22. She asked if he ...... help her.
A. should B. can
C. must D. would

23. We .... respect our elders.
A. need to B. have to
C. ought to D. had to

24. Nothing .... be done under such circumstances.
A. can B. used to
C. must D. have to

25. She ..... not ask about it.
A. has B. have
C. had D. dare

26. ...... that I were an actor!
A. Would B. Should
C. Could D. Will

27. Had you made one more effort you ...... have won the race.
A. will B. may
C. would D. shall

28. I ...... solve any sum.
A. may B. am
C. must D. can

29. ...... I smoke here?
A. Can B. Will
C. Could D. Must

30. The passengers .... keep watch on their luggage.
A. has B. have
C. should D. had

31. Work hard lest you .... fail.
A. should B. may
C. can D. must

32. .... I come in, madam?
A. Can B. May
C. Will D. Must

33. It ...... rain tonight.
A. shall B. will
C. may D. can

34. You ...... love your countrymen.
A. need to B. have to
C. had to D. ought to

35. .... you like some pastries?
A. Should B. Would
C. Could D. Will

36. You .... smoke here.
A. shall not B. will not
C. would not D. would not

37. .... I say more about it?
A. Need B. Ought
C. Should D. Dare

38. You .... leave these premises without my permission.
A. mustn't B. ought not to
C. may not D. may not

39. You .... pay full attention to your teacher.
A. should B. can
C. may D. would

40. .... that I were a billionaire!
A. Could B. Should
C. Would D. Ought

41. .... you like some biscuits?
A. Would B. Should
C. Could D. Will

42. .... I open the door?
A. Would B. Should
C. Could D. Might

43. You .... do some jogging in the morning to maintain your figure.
A. could B. might
C. should D. would

44. .... I go now or would you like to give me some more instructions?
A. Should B. Would
C. Could D. Might

45. .... you come across stale bread, you must ring me up. I .... try to ascertain who is not working honestly in my company.
A. Would, should B. Could, should
C. Could, would D. Should, would

46. You .... drive slow because there is a school ahead.
A. would B. could
C. should D. may

47. I .... like to check your blood pressure and once again I advise you to reduce the intake of salt.
A. should B. would
C. could D. shall

48. I .... not tell him about it if I were you.
A. should B. could
C. may D. would

49. .... you mind not drinking here? It is a hospital.
A. Would B. Could
C. Should D. Wouldn't

50. What .... he say to you if you didn't obey him?
A. should B. shall
C. would D. will

ANSWERS

1	2	3	4	5	6	7	8	9	10
C	B	C	A	C	B	B	C	A	A
11	**12**	**13**	**14**	**15**	**16**	**17**	**18**	**19**	**20**
D	A	C	A	B	A	B	B	C	B
21	**22**	**23**	**24**	**25**	**26**	**27**	**28**	**29**	**30**
B	D	C	A	D	A	C	D	A	C
31	**32**	**33**	**34**	**35**	**36**	**37**	**38**	**39**	**40**
A	B	C	D	B	A	A	A	A	C
41	**42**	**43**	**44**	**45**	**46**	**47**	**48**	**49**	**50**
A	B	C	A	D	C	B	D	A	C

12 Fill in the Blanks

Fill in the blanks is such an exercise that begins from the primary schooling and continues till the highest competitive examinations. With regular practice one can master it easily.

MULTIPLE CHOICE QUESTIONS

Directions: *Pick out the most effective word(s) from the given words to fill in the blanks to make the sentence meaningfully complete.*

1. While the contest in Kashmir has international ....., the outcome in Gujarat will be of enormous significance at the national level.
A. ravening B. ramifications
C. reconnaissance D. renunciation

2. No amount of post facto sophistry can conceal the ..... and inflammable crudity of this exhortation.
A. cruel B. shameful
C. horrible D. horrendous

3. There were ..... voices coming out from the amalgam.
A. discordant B. sneering
C. impalpable D. disquisite

4. Online learning can also offer a ..... of exciting and technology driven courses.
A. spectrum B. spume
C. spate D. stolidity

5. Work experience does carry some weight, the extent of which is a matter of ..... .
A. erudition B. decision
C. determination D. conjecture

6. The curricula of education has to respond and reshape with ..... modification according to the needs and aspirations of the dynamic society.
A. ambient B. alliterate
C. allotropic D. ample

7. It may look ..... to pronounce but this is the reality that the situation is that of the largest concentration illiterate population is an existence.
A. surprising B. contradictory
C. paradoxical D. contrary

8. If we take the global, developmental ....., education is not only a master key but also acts as a catalyst in the positive direction.
A. context B. pretext
C. progress D. continuum

9. It is mainly the utmost utilization of knowledge which emanates from the deep-delved ..... in every human being.
A. acquisition B. core
C. mind D. self

10. The book is a rare ..... of facts and figures illustrating every aspect of education.
A. chronicle B. compendium
C. combination D. presentation

11. The ..... reason behind the terrorist attack on the temple is obvious.
A. devious B. diabolical
C. factual D. original

12. He had the ..... to reject plans.
A. disquisition B. gibe
C. gumption D. grudge

13. Unable to ..... the election process in Kashmir, the terrorists have spread out all over India.
A. scrounge B. scruff
C. scuttle D. scuffle

14. Their hopes of a communal ..... is not going to come true.
A. conflagration B. plenipotentiary
C. podium D. coterie

15. Fundamentalism refers to an ideology which takes certain articles of faith to be ....., beyond question.
A. inviolable B. invulnerable
C. irrefragable D. ineverent

16. The separation of Church and State has its origins in the vicious and ..... 16th century sectarian wars within European Christianity.
A. debacle B. debilitating
C. debase D. dastard

17. It's time to look beyond the simplistic ..... between secularism and fundamentalism.
A. dichotomy B. disarray
C. diabolical D. fetid

18. When unemployment is rampant, the future is ..... and fraught with worry, depression and frustration.
A. fluster B. foible
C. occlude D. ominous

19. We are worried by the ..... tendencies prevailing in our social and political life.
A. flotsam B. fissiparous
C. perfidy D. aphoristic

20. The intellectual experience had culminated new methodology in ..... .
A. assuage B. value
C. pedagogy D. pedantic

21. Human rights awareness is ignited to propagate in conflagration which could ..... down to the masses.
A. perfidy B. kindle
C. percolate D. exude

22. It is no use living a wretched life, where human dignity is an ..... .
A. abyss B. abhor
C. abnegation D. chastise

23. Upheavals and ..... de-humanisation are the paralytic traumas which degrade and nullify glamorisation of the human values.
A. profligate B. entropic
C. obdurate D. intransigence

24. The driver tried to ..... the fears of the passenger by announcing that the accident has been prevented.
A. overcome B. remove
C. eradicate D. allay

25. ..... should be removed among the people and equal chances should be given to those who have been denied equality so long.
A. Distinction B. Diaphanous
C. Differences D. Disparities

26. It is uncertainty and ..... of purpose which create defects in our present system of education.
A. confusion B. ambivalence
C. vagueness D. doubt

27. The golden jubilee of the Independence of India is being celebrated in an ..... and jubilant manner.
A. joyful B. pleasant
C. ecstatic D. eclat

28. Education has become capable of meeting all the changes of the ..... society by broadening the new paths of learning.
A. dynamic B. growing
C. developing D. modern

29. The world and inevitably India, are in the ..... of major economic and technological changes.
A. gulf B. tendentious
C. insularity D. throes

30. ..... officer finally surrendered before the court yesterday, after being on the run for two months.
A. Crustacean B. Complacent
C. Fugitive D. Beguile

31. Gujarat riots have attracted national and international ..... .
A. opprobrium B. opossum
C. repugnance D. reconnoitre

32. The political and administrative leadership may have been determined to prevent any mischief makers from running ..... .
A. gauche B. amok
C. cathartic D. berserk

33. After her long illness she is suffering from general ..... .
A. fawning B. debility
C. lethargic D. inchoate

34. They are so poor that they have to .....
A. slack B. slander
C. skimp D. bicker

35. ..... about in the corridors.
A. fecund B. droll
C. carp D. skulk

36. The Queen's request was .... to a command.
A. tantamount B. tenet
C. nexus D. nascent

37. We cannot ..... base metals into gold.
A. transmute B. trek
C. sodden D. impede

38. ..... an official tour to Switzerland.
A. Warble B. Wane
C. Wangle D. Warren

39. His inattention in the classroom is a clear ..... of failure.
A. pristine B. propriety
C. prognosis D. prognostic

40. I find singing ..... challenging.
A. intrinsically B. incredibly
C. extrinsically D. preposterously

41. Educating people to think your way is ....
A. prodigious B. presumptuous
C. sagacious D. unpretentious

42. The birth of United Nations Organisation in 1945 was a ..... device to achieve specific objectives in the realm of world order.
A. subjugate B. precarious
C. pragmatic D. unabated

43. Inefficiency and delaying habits are the ..... of Indian offices.
A. averse B. assuagement
C. banal D. bane

44. It is a most ..... situation for a young person to find a place under the sun and lead a comfortable though hard-working life.
A. exhilarating B. barbarous
C. bucolic D. cantankerous

45. The hot weather created a feeling of ..... and encouraged drowsiness.
A. uninterested B. lethargic
C. lassitude D. exhaustion

46. One prefers to be alone than to be in his company because of his ..... temper.
A. stoic B. smattering
C. sleight D. irascible

47. The boss scolded him in a ..... voice.
A. preposterous B. loud
C. suave D. strident

48. The ..... provided by the government to those affected by the flood were not sufficient.
A. ensconce B. victuals
C. baroque D. accrue

49. Zakir Hussain is a tabla .....
A. abettor B. adroit
C. virago D. virtuoso

50. He took ..... at his remarks and resigned immediately.
A. umbrage B. surly
C. unseemly D. valour

51. The more your action and thought are allied and ..... the happier you grow.
A. diverged
B. unravelled
C. integrated
D. invincible

52. Many of the advances of civilisation have been conceived by young people just on the ..... of adulthood.
A. boundary B. threshold
C. peak D. horizon

53. Wheat ..... carbohydrates, vitamins, proteins and dietary fibre in our daily diet.
A. has B. gives
C. yields D. provides

54. The cinema ..... a welcome escape from cramped and dull city life and the Indians are avid movie-goers.
A. depicts B. highlights
C. follows D. offers

55. This machine is difficult to build ..... easy to maintain.
A. but B. and
C. for D. if

56. Farida sings very well and ..... does Salim.
A. even B. too
C. also D. so

57. Government buildings are .... on the Republic Day.
A. enlightened B. lightened
C. illuminated D. glowed

58. Sonika is quite intelligent but rather ..... .
A. idealistic B. generous
C. lazy D. optimistic

59. You've only three months more to complete the course. Don't give ..... now.
A. out B. away
C. up D. off

60. About twenty clerks were made ..... when the bank introduced computers.
A. dispensable B. redundant
C. expendable D. obsolete

61. To err is ..... to forgive divine.
A. beastly B. human
C. inhuman D. natural

62. God is .....
A. graceful B. gracious
C. grateful D. greatful

63. The king ..... the rebel.
A. excused B. forgave
C. pardoned D. none of these

64. The boy was cured ..... typhoid.
A. from B. of
C. for D. through

65. Jawaharlal spent his childhood ..... Anand Bhawan.
A. at B. in
C. on D. across

66. The boy fell ..... the bicycle.
A. of B. off
C. from D. under

67. Affix a revenue stamp and put your signature ..... it.
A. on B. upon
C. above D. over

68. The answer was written ..... blue ink.
A. with B. by
C. in D. on

69. The park ..... as far as the river.
A. extends B. advances
C. enlarges D. emerges

70. My father ..... down for a nap.
A. lay B. laid
C. lain D. lie

71. I put ..... the light and slept.
A. up B. down
C. in D. out

72. I shall call ..... you tomorrow.
A. at B. on
C. with D. by

73. West Bengal ..... plentiful rainfall and is consequently a very green part of the country.
A. misses B. receives
C. expects D. regrets

74. If you work beyond your capacity, you will naturally feel .....
A. drowsy B. tired
C. confident D. giddy

75. I have read one novel by Premchand. I want to read ..... novel by him.
A. other B. another
C. all D. few

76. Fate smiles ..... those who untiringly grapple with stark realities of life.
A. with B. over
C. on D. round

77. Those who persist in their endeavour at long last triumph ..... the odds of life.
A. over B. on
C. upon D. about

78. The parliament invested the new organisation ..... judicial authority.
A. by B. with
C. from D. through

79. She has an aversion ..... taking even onion and garlic.
A. with B. at
C. against D. to

80. Brothers must live in harmony. They must never fall .....
A. off B. out
C. apart D. away

81. The man came in a van to ..... the television set.
A. mend B. reform
C. correct D. alter

82. He was accused .... stealing his aunt's necklace.
A. for B. with
C. of D. on

83. Indeed, all over the world, more and more people are ..... coffee.
A. wanting B. drinking
C. liking D. partaking

84. He felt no ..... as he plunged the knife into her back.
A. qualms B. scruple
C. conscience D. morals

85. A sanguine outlook is associated with the .....
A. rationalist B. socialist
C. philanthropist D. optimist

86. True brevity ..... in saying only what needs to be said.
A. consists B. depicts
C. portrays D. resides

87. He became enamoured ..... her grace when he first saw her dance.
A. with B. of
C. buy D. in

88. We shall not be able to use your alibi in court unless we can find someone to ..... your statements.
A. corroborate B. avouch
C. verify D. approve

89. In a little-publicised deal, Pepsi, Cola has ..... the entire soft drink market in Afghanistan.
A. occupied B. conquered
C. swallowed D. captured

90. If negotiations are to prove fruitful, there must not only be sincerity on each side, but there must also be ..... in the sincerity of the other side.
A. faith B. belief
C. substance D. certainty

91. My first lesson ..... forgiveness came from my father
A. upon B. about
C. in D. on

92. He knew everything better than anybody else, and it was an affront to his ..... vanity that you should disagree with him.
A. overstrung B. overweening
C. overwhelming D. overwrought

93. He passed the examination in the first class because he .....
A. was hard working for it
B. worked hardly for it
C. had worked hard for it
D. was working hard for it

94. The American ..... presented his credentials to the President of India.
A. adviser B. ambassador
C. delegate D. representative

95. Man does not live by ..... alone.
A. food B. bread
C. meals D. diet

96. You cannot devise a method which ..... all possibility of error.
A. excludes B. includes
C. avoids D. ignores

97. When the morning ..... the murder was discovered.

A. occurred B. arrived
C. came D. happened

98. My uncle decided to take ..... and my sister to the market.

A. I B. mine
C. me D. myself

99. Hardly had he arrived ..... it started raining.

A. before B. when
C. than D. after

100. It is fourteen years since I ..... him.

A. have seen
B. had seen
C. saw
D. see

ANSWERS

1	2	3	4	5	6	7	8	9	10
B	D	A	A	D	C	C	D	A	B
11	**12**	**13**	**14**	**15**	**16**	**17**	**18**	**19**	**20**
B	C	C	A	A	B	A	D	B	C
21	**22**	**23**	**24**	**25**	**26**	**27**	**28**	**29**	**30**
C	A	B	D	D	B	C	A	D	C
31	**32**	**33**	**34**	**35**	**36**	**37**	**38**	**39**	**40**
A	B	B	C	D	A	A	C	D	B
41	**42**	**43**	**44**	**45**	**46**	**47**	**48**	**49**	**50**
B	C	D	A	C	D	D	B	B	A
51	**52**	**53**	**54**	**55**	**56**	**57**	**58**	**59**	**60**
C	B	D	D	A	D	C	C	C	B
61	**62**	**63**	**64**	**65**	**66**	**67**	**68**	**69**	**70**
B	B	C	B	A	B	A	C	A	A
71	**72**	**73**	**74**	**75**	**76**	**77**	**78**	**79**	**80**
D	C	B	B	B	C	A	B	D	B
81	**82**	**83**	**84**	**85**	**86**	**87**	**88**	**89**	**90**
A	C	B	A	D	A	B	A	D	A
91	**92**	**93**	**94**	**95**	**96**	**97**	**98**	**99**	**100**
D	A	C	B	B	A	C	C	B	C

13 Clauses

THE CLAUSE AND THE SENTENCE

1. **The Sentence** is a group of words that makes complete sense. As such it contains a subject and a predicate containing a finite verb. Sometimes, it has one or more objects. It is independent and grammatically self-contained.
2. **The Clause** is a part of the predicate and has a finite verb. It also has a subject but it is dependent on the Principal (or the main) clause.

KINDS OF CLAUSES

The following are the kinds of clauses:

1. Principal clause
2. Coordinate clause
3. Subordinate clause

There are three kinds of subordinate clauses:

I. Adjective clause
II. Adverb clause
III. Noun clause

I. Adjective Clause

A clause which acts as an adjective is known as Adjectives clause. Most often it can replace an adjective or adjective phrase e.g.

(i) Mrs Sharma has a **black** purse. (Adjective)
(ii) Mrs Sharma has a purse of **black colour.** (Adjective Phrase)
(iii) Mrs Sharma has a purse **which is black in colour**. (Adjective clause)

In sentence no. (i) 'black is an adjective and in sentence no. (ii) 'of black colour' is an adjective phrase. Both of these can be replaced with an adjective clause 'which is black in colour.'

All Relative clauses are the examples of the adjective clauses.

A clause which follows a Noun or Pronoun is known as an Adjective clause. The said Noun or Pronoun is called 'Antecedent'.

Relative clauses are made by the Relative Pronouns and Relative Adverbs.

Relative Pronouns which make Adjective clauses

who whose whom which that, as what, whatsoever

Relative Adverbs which make Adjective clauses

when, why, how, whenever, where, wherever

II. Adverb Clause

An Adverb clause is the clause which does the function of an Adverb. Most often it replaces an Adverb or an Adverb Phrase. It may modify a verb, an adjective or another adverb, e.g.

(i) Amar is taller **than you** (are).
(ii) **As soon as the boy saw the snake**, he cried loudly.
(iii) If you work hard, you'll get good marks.

Classification of Adverb Clauses

Adverbs clauses can be classified as under:

I. Adverb clauses of Place.
II. Adverb clauses of Time.
III. Adverb clauses of Manner.
IV. Adverb clauses of Comparison.
V. Adverb clauses of Condition.

VI. Adverb clauses of Cause or Reason.
VII. Adverb clauses of Purpose.
VIII. Adverb clauses of Result or Consequences.
IX. Adverb clauses of Extent or Degree.
X. Adverb clauses of Contrast or Concession.

I. Adverb Clauses of Place

A clause which shows the place of an action is know as Adverb Clause of Place.

(i) This is the place **where** I found a coin.
(ii) I'll follow you **wherever** you go.

II. Adverb clauses of Time

A clause which is related to time is called an Adverb clause of Time.

(i) Stay here until I come back.
(ii) I was reading my book when somebody called out my name.

III. Adverb Clauses of Manner

The clause which indicates the manner of an action is known as the Adverb clause of Manner.

(i) Do as you are instructed.
(ii) He talks as if he were a prince.

IV. Adverb Clauses of Comparison

The clause which indicates the comparison is known as the Adverb clause of comparison.

(i) She is fatter than you.
(ii) He is as wise as he.

V. Adverb Clauses of Condition

A clause which indicates the condition imposed on the action of the verb is called the Adverb Clause of condition.

(i) If you work hard you may get good marks.
(ii) In case you need my help, please call me out loudly.

VI. Adverb Clauses of Cause or Reason

The clause which indicates the cause or reason of an action is known as the Adverb Clause of Cause or Reason.

(i) He could not run fast because he was injured.
(ii) I do not like him as he lacks in manners.

VII. Adverb Clauses of Purpose

The clause which indicates the purpose of an action is known as the Adverb clause of Purpose.

(i) Walk carefully lest you should fall.
(ii) She cried loudly so that she might be heard.

VIII. Adverb Clauses of Result or Consequence

The clause which indicates the result or consequence of an action is known as Adverb Clause of Result or Consequence.

(i) She is so weak in studys that she cannot read anybook.
(ii) He runs so fast that you cannot catch him.

IX. Adverb Clauses of Extent or Degree

The clause which indicates the extent or degree of an action is known as the Adverb Clause of Extent or Degree.

(i) As far as I know, he is a good man.
(ii) The more, the marrier.

X. Adverbs Clauses of contrast or concession

(i) Although he ran fast, he could not catch the train.
(ii) Howsoever busy he may be, he'll attend to you.

III. Noun Clauses

The clause which does the function of a Noun is known as a Noun Clause.The Noun Clause can act in the following ways:

1. As Subject to a verb.
2. As Object to a participle.
3. As Object to an infinitive.
4. As Object to a preposition.
5. As Object to a verb.
6. As Complement to a verb.
7. Case in Apposition to a noun or pronoun.

1. As the Subject to a verb

(i) **Why you are crying** we fail to understand.
(ii) **Where he will go,** nobody cares.
(iii) **How he earned money** is known to all.
(iv) **When he will wake up** is not sure.

2. As Object to a participle

(i) **Knowing that his father will not rebuke him,** he starts disturbing his sister.

(*ii*) **Finding that the necklace lying on the ground** was of gold, he picked it up.

(*iii*) **Saying that he did not know French** he started singing English songs.

(*iv*) They started playing in the ground thinking that nobody will object to it.

3. As Object to an infinitive

(*i*) I would like to know **whether you are going** to the USA or Russia.

(*ii*) He wants to say whether his brother will come back or not.

(*iii*) She wants to inform why she did not attend the meeting.

4. As Object to a preposition

(*i*) He stuck to **what he believed.**

(*ii*) Listen to **what she says.**

(*iii*) She Objected to what you said.

5. As Object to a verb

(*i*) I do not understand **why he behaves like this.**

6. As complement to a verb

(*i*) His fear is that he will be asked about the murder.

(*ii*) It seems that he would catch the train.

7. Case in Apposition to a noun or a pronoun

(*i*) The fact that he is honest is known to all.

(*ii*) The reason why he failed in the examination is not far to seek.

MULTIPLE CHOICE QUESTIONS

Directions: *Tick the correct alternative for each of the following italicised clauses:*

1. She heard someone singing around *when she was washing clothes.*
A. Noun clause B. Adjective clause
C. Adverb clause D. None of these

2. This is the girl *whose uncle is the personal assistant to the PM.*
A. Adverb Clause B. Adjective Clause
C. Noun Clause D. None of these

3. Do *as you are instructed.*
A. Adverb Clause B. Adjective Clause
C. Noun clause D. None of these

4. He does not know *where his brother has gone.*
A. Noun Clause B. Adverb Clause
C. Adjective Clause D. None of these

5. It is still unknown *why he behaved rudely at the party.*
A. Adjective clause B. Adverb Clause
C. Noun Clause D. None of these

6. I do not know the time *when he gets up* in the morning.
A. Adjective Clause B. Adverb Clause
C. Noun Clause D. None of these

7. I like her *because she is honest.*
A. Adverb Clause B. Adjective Clause
C. Noun Clause D. None of these

8. The boy *who stood first in our class* was given a prize by the Principal.
A. Adjective Clause B. Noun clause
C. Adverb clause D. None of these

9. If *you want to earn a lot of money*, start learning assembling computer.
A. Adjective clause B. Adverb clause
C. Noun clause D. None of these

10. Wait here *until I come back.*
A. Adjective clause B. Noun clause
C. Adverb clause D. None of these

11. She is not *what she seems.*
A. Noun clause B. Adjective clause
C. Adverb clause D. None of these

12. I want to know *where you have put my watch.*
A. Adverb Clause B. Adjective Clause
C. Noun Clause D. None of these

13. It is known to all of us *that he is a stupid fellow.*
A. Adjective Clause B. Adverb Clause
C. Noun clause D. None of these

14. I went to my father finding *that none of us could open that box.*
A. Adverb Clause B. Noun Clause
C. Adjective Clause D. None of these

15. She came back *before it was morning.*
A. Adjective clause B. Adverb Clause
C. Noun Clause D. None of these

16. We looked *where mush-rooms were growing.*
A. Adjective Clause B. Noun Clause
C. Adverb Clause D. None of these

17. *Where there is a will* there is a way.
A. Adverb Clause B. Adjective Clause
C. Noun Clause D. None of these

18. You may go *wherever you like.*
A. Adjective Clause B. Noun clause
C. Adverb clause D. None of these

19. *As soon as the thief saw a policeman,* he ran away.
A. Adjective clause B. Adverb clause
C. Noun clause D. None of these

20. Wait here *until I come.*
A. Adjective clause B. Noun clause
C. Adverb clause D. None of these

21. He walked out of the house *when the rain stopped.*
A. Noun clause B. Adjective clause
C. Adverb clause D. None of these

22. Her brother danced *while she sang.*
A. Adverb Clause B. Adjective Clause
C. Noun Clause D. None of these

23. You must listen to me *whenever you have finished your home work.*
A. Adjective Clause B. Adverb Clause
C. Noun clause D. None of these

24. We had returned home *before the storm started.*
A. Noun Clause B. Adverb Clause
C. Adjective Clause D. None of these

25. *As long as I'm here* you needn't get afraid of anybody.
A. Adjective clause B. Noun Clause
C. Adverb Clause D. None of these

26. I haven't seen him since I *met him five years ago.*
A. Adverb Clause B. Adjective Clause
C. Noun Clause D. None of these

27. *Just as I was getting out of my car,* I saw a monkey jumping over the wall of the orchard.
A. Adjective Clause B. Adverb Clause
C. Noun Clause D. None of these

28. *As I went out into the courtyard of my house,* I saw a snake in the grass.
A. Adjective Clause B. Noun clause
C. Adverb clause D. None of these

29. She was happy *because she had won a jackpot.*
A. Adjective clause B. Adverb clause
C. Noun clause D. None of these

30. *Since/As you are not going to office,* let's play hockey.
A. Adjective clause B. Noun clause
C. Adverb clause D. None of these

31. I take antihypertensive drugs *that my blood pressure may remain in control.*
A. Noun clause B. Adjective clause
C. Adverb clause D. None of these

32. He is running fast *so that he may catch the train.*
A. Adverb Clause B. Adjective Clause
C. Noun Clause D. None of these

33. Walk fast *lest you should miss the train.*
A. Adjective Clause B. Adverb Clause
C. Noun clause D. None of these

34. I don't let him run a race *in case he is ill.*
A. Noun Clause B. Adverb Clause
C. Adjective Clause D. None of these

35. We've arranged her a tutor *in order that Mshe may continue her studies.*
A. Adjective clause B. Noun Clause
C. Adverb Clause D. None of these

36. He walks *as if or as though he were a king.*
A. Adjective Clause B. Adverb Clause
C. Noun Clause D. None of these

37. Do *as I tell you.*
A. Adverb Clause B. Adjective Clause
C. Noun Clause D. None of these

38. He can do *as he wishes.*
A. Adjective Clause B. Noun clause
C. Adverb clause D. None of these

39. He *is wiser than you.*
A. Adjective clause B. Adverb clause
C. Noun clause D. None of these

40. She will work *as fast as she can.*
A. Adjective clause B. Noun clause
C. Adverb clause D. None of these

41. He likes to sit calmly *rather than work.*
A. Adverb clause B. Adjective clause
C. Noun clause D. None of these

42. *Although he had worked* hard, he failed in the examination.
A. Noun Clause B. Adjective Clause
C. Adverb Clause D. None of these

43. *Even if/even though/although you don't like him,* you should greet him in the party.
A. Adjective Clause B. Adverb Clause
C. Noun clause D. None of these

44. *However hard you work* you'll not (or won't) get success.
A. Adverb Clause
B. Noun Clause
C. Adjective Clause
D. None of these

45. *If you call him,* he will come to see you.
A. Adjective clause B. Adverb Clause
C. Noun Clause D. None of these

46. *If the weather is not good,* the flight may be cancelled.
A. Adjective Clause B. Noun Clause
C. Adverb Clause D. None of these

47. If *I had the magazine Sun,* I would show you the picture of Madonna in it.
A. Adverb Clause B. Adjective Clause
C. Noun Clause D. None of these

48. *If anybody threatened me,* I would call the police.
A. Adjective Clause B. Noun clause
C. Adverb clause D. None of these

49. I would not tell him this *if I were you.*
A. Adjective clause B. Adverb clause
C. Noun clause D. None of these

50. You would have won the race *if you had run fast.*
A. Adverb clause B. Noun clause
C. Adjective clause D. None of these

ANSWERS

1	2	3	4	5	6	7	8	9	10
C	B	A	A	C	A	A	A	B	C
11	**12**	**13**	**14**	**15**	**16**	**17**	**18**	**19**	**20**
A	C	C	B	B	C	A	C	B	C
21	**22**	**23**	**24**	**25**	**26**	**27**	**28**	**29**	**30**
C	A	B	B	C	A	B	C	B	C
31	**32**	**33**	**34**	**35**	**36**	**37**	**38**	**39**	**40**
C	A	B	B	C	B	A	C	B	C
41	**42**	**43**	**44**	**45**	**46**	**47**	**48**	**49**	**50**
A	C	B	A	B	C	A	C	B	A

14 Narration

Direct Speech and Indirect Speech

The words spoken by a speaker are in Direct Speech.

The words spoken by somebody and expressed by someone else with some modification are known as Indirect Speech.

(*a*) Rohit says to me, "You do not understand me."

(*b*) Rohit tells me that I do not understand him.

The sentence (*a*) shows the words spoken by Rohit. So, it is a sentence of direct speech.

The sentence (*b*) shows the words spoken by Rohit and they have been reported with certain modification. So, it is a sentence of Indirect Speech.

Important Rules Regarding the change of Direct Speech into Indirect Speech

1. In a sentence of direct speech the verb outside the inverted commas is known as the Reporting Verb.
2. The words inside the inverted commas are known as Direct Speech.
3. When the sentence is indirect speech, it won't take a sign of exclamation or a sign of interrogation.
4. The Reporting Verb can be given in Present, Past or Future Tense.
5. When the Reporting Verb is in Present or Future Tense, there will be no change in the tense of direct speech while converting it into indirect speech.
6. When the Reporting Verb is in Past Tense the tense of direct speech will be changed while converting it into Indirect Speech.
7. The following adverbs and possessives should be changed as given:
   (*i*) This into that
   (*ii*) These into those
   (*iii*) Here into there
   (*iv*) Now into then
   (*v*) Today into that day
   (*vi*) Last night into the previous night
   (*vii*) Tomorrow into the next day
   (*viii*) The next day/week into the following day/week
   (*ix*) Hence into thence.

Change of Tense

Reporting Verb	*Reporting Speech*	*Change of Tense*
Present Tense	Any Tense	No change
Future Tense	Any Tense	No change
Past Tense	Present/ Future Tense	Change into corresponding Past Tense
Past Tense	Past Indefinite Tense	Change into Past Perfect Tense
Past Tense	Past Continuous Tense	Change into Past Perfect Continuous Tense

Reporting Verb	*Reporting Speech*	*Change of Tense*
Past Tense	Past Pefect/ Perfect Continuous Tense	No change
Past Tense	Universal Truth	No change
Past Tense	Proverb	No change

Transformation Based on Special Rules

1. Rule Related to Interrogative Sentence

- If the answer of an interrogative sentence is possible in yes-no manner.

Illustration.

M.S. Dhoni told Rahul Dravid, "Will you help me?"

M.S. Dhoni asked Rahul Dravid whether he would help him.

☛ The answer of Reporting Verb is possible in yes-no manner.

Rule of Transformation from Direct to Indirect speech

Step I : Change R.V. into ask.

Step II : In place of comma use 'if/whether'.

Step III : Change interrogative sentence into assertive sentence.

- If the answer of an interrogative sentence is not possible in yes-no manner.

Illustration:

Rahul Dravid told Dhoni, "What do you want?"

Rahul Dravid asked Dhoni what he wanted.

☛ Only in Step II, you have to avoid comma and inverted comma and rest will be same as mentioned above.

2. Rule related to Imperative Sentence

- Imperative sentence is a sentence which shows Order/Advice/Request

Illustration:

My father said to me, "Go there".

My father ordered me to go there.

Rule of Transformation from Direct to Indirect Speech

Step I : Change R.V. as per meaning/sense of R.S. into order/request/advise.

Step II : In place of comma, use 'to'.

Step III : Rest portion will be same.

3. Rule related to Optative Sentence

- Optative sentence is a sentence which exposes the feeling of bless/curse/pray/wish.

Illustration:

Mother said to me, "May you live long!"

Mother blessed me that I might live long.

Rule of Transformation from Direct to Indirect Speech

Step I : Change R.V. as per meaning/sense of R.S. into bless/curse/pray/wish.

Step II : In place of comma, use 'that'.

Step III : Change optative sentence into assertive sentence.

4. Rule related to Exclamatory Sentence

- Exclamatory sentence is a sentence which takes note of exclamatory (!) mark in that sentence showing inner feeling.

Illustration:

She said, "Alas! I am ruined".

She exclaimed with sorrow that she was ruined.

Rule of Transformation from Direct to Indirect Speech

Step I : Change R.V. as per meaning/sense of R.S. into exclaim/exclaims/exclaimed/will or shall exclaim + joy/sorrow/anger/surprise/applause/contempt.

Step II : Change comma into that.

Step III : Change note of exclamation (!) into full (.)

Step IV : Change exclamatory sentence into assertive sentence.

MULTIPLE CHOICE QUESTIONS

Directions (Qs. 1 to 5): *A sentence correctly changed into indirect narration is followed by four sentencs in the direct narration. Pick out from the alternative one which, when changed into indirect narration will be the same as the indirect sentence preceding the alternatives.*

1. The driver asked the mechanic if he would repair his car.
A. "Repair the car," the driver ordered the mechanic.
B. "Please repair the car," the driver asked the mechanic.
C. "O, please repair the car," the driver asked the mechanic.
D. "Will you repair my car?" the driver asked the mechanic.

2. She thanked me and asked me not to disturb her.
A. "Thank you. Do not disturb me," she said.
B. "Dear friend than you, do not disturb," she said.
C. "Disturb not, thank you," she said.
D. "Thank you, please ask not to disturb," she said.

3. In a tone of anger she asked her boy-friend why he had come.
A. "You fool, why have you come," she said.
B. "Oh, why have you come," said she.
C. "You damned! Why have you come?" she said.
D. "You, you, O you why have you come," she said.

4. Calling him a coward, the girl asked him to come out.
A. "Come out, you coward!" said the girl.
B. "Come out," said the girl to the coward.
C. The girl said, "Alas coward come."
D. The girl said, "Come out".

5. He called her a naughty girl.
A. "Oh! naughty girl," said he.
B. "You naughty girl!" said he.
C. He said, "naughty girl."
D. "Naughty," boy said to her.

Directions (Qs. 6 to 30): *Each sentence in direct speech is followed by four options in indirect speech, only one is correct. Spot the correct answer.*

6. She said, "Shall I thread the needle?"
A. She asked if she should thread the needle.
B. She asked if she shall thread the needle.
C. She requested if she should thread the needle.
D. She says that if she would thread the needle.

7. We said, "What a place it is!"
A. We said that it was a very fine place.
B. We said that is a very fine place.
C. We said that the place is fine.
D. We exclaimed with joy that the place was very fine.

8. My father said, "The earth is round".
A. My father said that the earth was round.
B. My father says that the earth is round.
C. My father said that the earth is round
D. My father ordered that the earth is round.

9. The teacher said, "Don't make a noise".
A. The teacher says to us not to make a noise.
B. The teacher asked us not to make a noise.
C. The teacher requested us not to make a noise.
D. The teacher asked us not to made a noise.

10. He said, "Bring a chair at once".
A. He ordered to bring a chair at once.
B. He requested to bring a chair at once.
C. He told to bring a chair at once.
D. He says to bring a chair at once.

11. She said to me, "Keep quite and listen to my words".
A. She requested me to keep quite and listen to her words.
B. She ordered me to keep quite and listen to her words.
C. She entreated me to keep quite and listen to her words.
D. She told me to keep quite and listen to her words.

12. My brother said to me, "What are you doing here?"

A. My brother asked me that what I was doing there.

B. My brother asked me what I was doing there.

C. My brother asked me that what was I doing there.

D. My brother asked me what I was doing here.

13. Ravi said, "My father lived in this city two years ago."

A. Ravi said that his father had lived in that city two years before.

B. Ravi said that his father had lived in that city two years ago.

C. Ravi told that his father had lived in that city ago two years.

D. Ravi asked that his father had lived in that city before two years.

14. My brother said to me, "When I was young, I used to play cricket".

A. My brother told me that when I was young, I used to play cricket.

B. My brother told me that when I was young, I used to play cricket.

C. My brother told me that when he was young, I used to play cricket.

D. My brother told me that when he was young, he used to play cricket.

15. The student said, "Sir, I am not guilty".

A. The student said with respect that he was not guilty.

B. The student pleaded that he was not guilty.

C. The student pleaded with respect that he was not guilty.

D. The student said respectfully that he was not guilty.

16. I said to my sister, "Please, give me more money".

A. I requested my sister to give me more money.

B. I ordered my sister to give me more money.

C. I advised my sister to gave me more money.

D. I requested my sister to give her more money.

17. Baby said, "I will go".

A. Baby said that she will go.

B. Baby said that she could go.

C. Baby say that she will go.

D. Baby said that she would go.

18. The teacher says, "Two and two makes four".

A. The teacher says that two and two made four.

B. The teacher wishes that two and two makes four.

C. The teacher advises that two and two makes four.

D. The teacher says that two and two makes four.

19. He told me, "Shall I go to the picture?"

A. He asked that he should go to the picture.

B. He asked me if he shall go to the picture.

C. He asked me if he should go to the picture.

D. He requested me to go to the picture.

20. I told Ravi, "Do have a cup of tea".

A. I ordered Ravi to have a cup of tea.

B. I advised Ravi to had a cup of tea.

C. I requested Ravi to have a cup of tea.

D. I said Ravi to have a cup of cold tea.

21. Mohini said to me, "Trust in God."
Mohini advised me:

A. that I should trust in God.

B. should trust in God.

C. trusted in God.

D. to trust in God.

22. I said to him, "Let us go to school."
I told him:

A. we would go to school.

B. we shall go to school.

C. that we would go to school.

D. that we should go to school.

23. Rajni said, "May God bless you?"
Rajni:

A. exclaimed with wish that God might bless me.

B. expressed a wish that God might bless me.

C. asked God to bless me.

D. shouted with joy to bless me.

24. My mother said to me, "Do not have so many friends."
My mother forbade me:
A. to have so many friends.
B. not to have so many friends.
C. to have been so many friends.
D. to possess so many friends.

25. Ram said, "Pay attention to me."
Ram asked:
A. pay attention to him.
B. paid attention to him.
C. having paid attention to him.
D. to pay attention to him.

26. She said, "I am an early-riser".
A. She regretted that she was an early-riser.
B. She said that she is an early-riser.
C. She said that she was an early-riser.
D. She regretted that she is an early-riser.

27. The police officer said to the criminal, "Speak as I tell you".
A. The police officer directed the criminal to speak as he told him.
B. The police officer told the criminal to speak as he told him.
C. The police officer advised the criminal to speak as he told him.
D. The police officer requested the criminal to speak as he told him.

28. The preacher said to me, "May God help you!"
A. The preacher prayed that God might help me.
B. The preacher prayed that God might help him.
C. The preacher requested that God might help me.
D. The preacher requested the God might help them.

29. She said to me, "Happy Diwali!"
A. She blessed me a happy Diwali.
B. She wished me a happy Diwali.
C. She prayed a happy Diwali.
D. She said to me a very happy Diwali.

30. He said, "Shall I open the gate?"
A. He asked that he should open the gate.
B. He asked if he should open the gate.
C. He ordered that he should open the gate.
D. He requested that he should open the gate.

ANSWERS

1	2	3	4	5	6	7	8	9	10
D	A	C	A	B	A	D	C	B	A
11	**12**	**13**	**14**	**15**	**16**	**17**	**18**	**19**	**20**
B	B	A	D	C	A	D	D	C	C
21	**22**	**23**	**24**	**25**	**26**	**27**	**28**	**29**	**30**
A	D	B	A	D	C	A	A	B	B

15 Agreement of Subjects & Verbs

It is very important that the verb in a sentence should obey the subject, otherwise the sentence will be considered wrong.

1. When the Subject is a Singular Noun

A singular noun takes a singular verb.

(*i*) Mohit **makes** a noise in the class.

(*ii*) The child is **crying** for a cake.

2. When two singular nouns are joined with 'and'

When two singular nouns are joined with 'and' and they refer to two different persons, the plural verb should be used, *e.g.,*

(*i*) The novelist and the poet **were** honoured by the government.

(*ii*) The black and the white dogs **bark** at the strangers.

☛ Article 'the' is used with both the subjects.

If article is used only once, the singular verb should be used.

(*i*) The painter and singer is going abroad.

(*ii*) The white and black dog has a bushy tail.

3. When the subjects together give a single idea, singular verb is used.

(*i*) Slow and steady wins the race.

(*ii*) Rice and curry is my favourite dish.

4. A collective noun takes a singular verb when it acts as a whole, but it takes a plural verb when the individual, of which it is composed are considered separately.

(*i*) The committee was unanimous on imposing the new law.

(*ii*) The committee have given their separate opinions in the matter.

5. When the subjects are joined by neither . . . nor, either . . . or, and 'or', the verb should obey the last subject.

(*i*) Rakesh or his friends have been selected for the match.

(*ii*) His friends or Rakesh has been selected for the match.

(*iii*) Neither Rohit nor his brothers are going abroad.

(*iv*) Neither his brothers nor Rohit is going abroad.

(*v*) Either SOHAN or his sisters were dancing at the function.

(*vi*) Either his sisters or Sohan was dancing at the function.

6. Either, neither, either of, neither of, take singular verb.

(*i*) Either boy was honest.

(*ii*) Neither girl was allowed to leave the premises.

(*iii*) Either of the boys was ready to help the old man.

(*iv*) Neither of the girls was asked to join the extra classes.

7. Some nouns are always used as plurals so, they take plural verbs.

(*i*) Where are your glasses?

(*ii*) His pants are attractive.
(*iii*) Cattle are grazing in the field.
(*iv*) Whose scissors are these?

8. Some nouns are always used as singulars, so, they take singular verbs.
(*i*) What is the latest news?
(*ii*) The furniture in the house is of a poor quality.
(*iii*) Mumps is not a fatal disease.
(*iv*) Physics is a tough subject.

9. Nouns formed by alongwith, as well as, together with, accompanied by, etc., take verb according to the first subject.
(*i*) I, as well as you, am to blame.
(*ii*) You, as well as I, are going to see a movie.
(*iii*) John, accompanied by his parents, is going to visit the Taj.
(*iv*) His parents, accompanied by John, are going to visit the Taj.
(*v*) His brothers, together with Vivek, are ready to whitewash the fence.

10. To indicate something hypothetical or not factually true, plural verb 'were' with *as if* is used.
(*i*) He talks as if he were a king.
(*ii*) She dresses herself as if she were a princess.

MULTIPLE CHOICE QUESTIONS

Directions: *In the following questions, a sentence is given followed by four options. Select the option that replaces the given sentence or its part correctly.*

1. Slow and steady win the race.
A. Slowly and steady wins the race.
B. Slow and steadily wins the race.
C. Slow and steady wins the race.
D. None of these.

2. These news were broadcasted on Radio BBC.
A. These news were broadcast on Radio BBC.
B. This news was broadcast on Radio BBC.
C. This news was broadcasted on Radio BBC.
D. None of these.

3. Every boy and girl were given a prize.
A. Every boy and girl were given prizes.
B. Every boy and girl was given prizes.
C. Every boy and girl was given a prize.
D. None of these.

4. Everyone of them were clapping at the performance of the clown.
A. Everyone of them were clapping at the performance of the clowns.
B. Everyone of them was clapping at the performance of the clowns.
C. Everyone of them was clapping at the performances about the clowns.
D. None of these.

5. Law and order are to be maintained at all costs.
A. Law and orders are to be maintained at all costs.
B. Law and order is to be maintained at all costs.
C. Laws and orders are to be maintained at all costs.
D. None of these.

6. Five hundred rupees are a long sum.
A. Five hundred rupee is a long sum.
B. Five hundred rupee is a big sum.
C. Five hundred rupees is a big sum.
D. None of these.

7. Mohit, not his friends are to blame.
A. Mohit, not his friends is to blame.
B. Mohit, not his friend are to blame.
C. Mohit, not his friends is on to blame.
D. None of these.

8. I as well as you are to blame.
A. I as well as you, is to blame.
B. I as well as you are to blames.
C. I, as well as you, am to blame.
D. None of these.

9. The patient died before the doctor came.
A. The patient died before the doctor had come.

B. The patient had died before the doctor came.

C. The patient had died before the doctor had come.

D. None of these.

10. I knew that he will not respect his elders.

A. I knew that he would not respect his elders.

B. I knew that he shall not respect his elders.

C. I knew that he will not be respect his elders.

D. None of these.

11. He is one of the greatest player who has participated in one day cricket matches.

A. He is one of the greatest players who has ....

B. He is one of the greatest players who have ....

C. He is one of the greatest player who have ....

D. None of these.

12. He behaves as if he is king.

A. He behaves as if he are a king.

B. He behaves as if he are kings.

C. He behaves as if he were a king.

D. None of these.

13. He laughed as if he were mad.

A. He laughed as if he was mad.

B. He laughed as if he had been mad.

C. He laughed as if he are mad.

D. None of these.

14. The white and the black dog is dead.

A. The white and black dog are dead.

B. The white and the black dog are dead.

C. The white and black dogs are dead.

D. None of these.

15. The painter and poet are dead.

A. The painter and the poet is dead.

B. The painter and poets are dead.

C. The painter and poet is dead.

D. None of these.

16. The committee has announced their decision.

A. The committees has announced their decision.

B. The committee has announced its decision.

C. The committee have announced its decision.

D. None of these.

17. I wish I am a millionaire.

A. I wish I was a millionaire.

B. I wish I are a millionaire.

C. I wish I were a millionaire.

D. None of these.

18. A large number of students is absent.

A. A large numbers of students is absent.

B. A large number of students are absent.

C. A large number of student is absent.

D. None of these.

19. Walking on the road, I met one of my old friends.

A. When I was walking on the road, I met one of my old friend.

B. When I was walking on the road, I met one of my old friends.

C. Walking on the road, I met one of my friend.

D. None of these.

20. Our only guide were the stars.

A. Our only guide were the star.

B. Our only guides was the star.

C. Our only guide was the stars.

D. None of these.

21. Renu is living in this house since 2012.

A. Renu is living in this house for 2012.

B. Renu has been living in this house for 2012.

C. Renu has been living in this house since 2012.

D. None of these.

22. Better you had not to gone there.

A. Better you had not went there.

B. Better you had not gone there.

C. Better had you not to go there.

D. None of these.

23. You did not do so, nor he did.

A. You did not do so, he nor did.

B. You did not do so, nor did he.

C. You did not do so, he did nor.

D. None of these.

24. Hardly I had opened the window when a stream of cool breeze started rushing in.
A. Hardly I had opened the window then.........
B. Hardly had I opened the window when.........
C. Hardly had I opened the window then.........
D. None of these.

25. No sooner he did open the window, when the cool breeze started rushing in.
A. No sooner did he open the window then ....
B. No sooner did he open the window when ....
C. No sooner he did open the window than ....
D. None of these.

26. Neither she laughed nor I did.
A. Neither she laughed nor did I.
B. Neither she laughed did nor I.
C. Neither she laughed I did nor.
D. None of these.

27. Deepak alongwith his aunts were present in the party.
A. Deepak alongwith his aunts were present in the parties.
B. Deepak alongwith his aunts was present in the party.
C. Deepak alongwith his aunt were present in the party.
D. None of these.

28. Many a girls have gone to see the movie.
A. Many a girl have gone to see the movie.
B. Many a girls has went to see the movies.
C. Many a girl has gone to see the movie.
D. None of these.

29. Sohan, like Mohan, are good singers.
A. Sohan, like Mohan, is a good singer.
B. Sohan, like Mohan, is a good singers.
C. Sohan, like Mohan, are a good singer.
D. None of these.

30. The train arrived before I reached the station.
A. The train arrived before I had reached the station.
B. The train arrived before I have reached the station.
C. The train had arrived before I reached the station.
D. None of these.

31. Either he or she has done his work.
A. Either he or she has done their work.
B. Either he or she has done her work.
C. Either he or she has done their work.
D. None of these.

32. A hundred miles are a high distance.
A. A hundred miles are a big distance.
B. A hundred miles are a long distance.
C. A hundred miles is a long distance.
D. None of these.

33. 'A Tale of Two Cities' were written by Charles Dickens.
A. 'A Tale of Two Cities' was written by Charles Dickens.
B. 'A Tale of Two Cities' is wrote by Charles Dickens.
C. 'A Tale of Two Cities' are wrote by Charles Dickens.
D. None of these.

34. Many a boys were playing in the garden.
A. Many a boy were playing in the garden.
B. Many a boys was playing in the garden.
C. Many a boy was playing in the garden.
D. None of these.

35. A bandit besides his gangsters were nabbed by the police.
A. A bandit besides his gangster were nabbed by the police.
B. A bandit besides his gangsters was nabbed by the police.
C. A bandits besides his gangsters was nabbed by the police.
D. None of these.

36. The bell went when I reached the school.
A. The bell went when I had reached the school.
B. The bell had gone when I have reached the school.
C. The bell had gone when I reached the school.
D. None of these.

37. My teacher told me that the earth revolved round the sun.

A. My teacher told me that the earth was revolving round the sun.
B. My teacher told me that the earth revolves round the sun.
C. My teacher told me that the earth had revolved round the sun.
D. None of these.

38. Rice and curry are the favourite food of my brother.

A. Rice and curry is the favourite food...
B. Rice and curry are the favourite foods...
C. Rice and curry is the favourite foods...
D. None of these.

39. The Principal together with his staff were on a tour to the Himalayas.

A. The Principal together with his staffs were...
B. The Principal together with his staffs was...
C. The Principal together with his staff was...
D. None of these.

40. Neither Ravi nor his friends was present in the class.

A. Neither Ravi nor his friend were present in the class.
B. Neither Ravi nor his friends was present in the classes.
C. Neither Ravi nor his friends were present in the class.
D. None of these.

41. None of the ten pens are yours.

A. None of the ten pen are yours.
B. None of the ten pens is yours.
C. None of the ten pens are your.
D. None of these.

42. The captain with all his players are in the playground.

A. The captain with all his player are in the playgrounds.
B. The captain with all his player is in the playgrounds.
C. The captain with all his players is in the playground.
D. None of these.

ANSWERS

1	2	3	4	5	6	7	8	9	10
C	B	B	B	A	B	C	B	B	C
11	**12**	**13**	**14**	**15**	**16**	**17**	**18**	**19**	**20**
C	B	C	B	B	B	C	A	C	B
21	**22**	**23**	**24**	**25**	**26**	**27**	**28**	**29**	**30**
A	B	C	A	C	C	A	C	B	A
31	**32**	**33**	**34**	**35**	**36**	**37**	**38**	**39**	**40**
C	B	A	C	C	B	C	B	B	C
41	**42**								
B	C								

16 Transformation of Sentences

A sentence may be written in many different ways conveying the same meaning. This is called transformation of sentences. Practise various methods of transformation given below:

REMOVING 'TOO'

By replacing 'too' with 'so that'

1. He is too weak to walk.
   He is so weak that he cannot walk.
2. The book was too tough to comprehend.
   The book was so tough that it could not be comprehended.

☛ Sentence No. 1 is in the Present Tense so in it 'cannot' has been used; Sentence No. 2 is in the Past Tense, so, in it 'could not' has been used.

INTERCHANGE OF DEGREE OF COMPARISON

Degree of Comparison of Adjectives

Read the following sentences:

1. She is as clever as a fox. (Positive)
   A fox is not cleverer than her. (Comparative)

☛ In Positive Degree as is used but in Comparative Degree a Negative sentence is used. If the negative has been used with the Positive Degree, it will be removed from the comparative degree.

2. He is not so weak as his brother. (Positive)
   He is stronger than his brother. (Comparative)
3. Shimla is the coldest tourist spot in India. (Superlative)
   Shimla is colder than any other tourist spot in India. (Comparative)
   No other tourist spot is as cold as Shimla. (Positive)
4. Rohit is one of the most intelligent boys in our class. (Superlative)
   Rohit is more intelligent than most other boys in our class. (Comparative)
   Very few boys in our class are so intelligent as Rohit. (Positive)

5. Gold is not the most expensive metal. (Superlative)
   A few metals are more expensive than gold. (Comparative)
   Some metals are at least as expensive as gold. (Positive)
6. Lead is the heaviest of all metals. (Superlative)
   Lead is heavier than any other metal. (Comparative)
   No other metal is so heavy as lead. (Positive)

CHANGING IMPERATIVE SENTENCES INTO ASSERTIVE

Read the following sentences:

1. Walk fast. (Imperative)
   You are ordered to walk fast. (Affirmative)
2. Let us take a cup of tea. (Imperative)
   It is proposed that we should take a cup of tea. (Affirmative)
3. Please bring me a glass of water. (Imperative)
   You are requested to bring me a glass of water. (Affirmative)
4. Work hard. (Imperative)
   You are advised to work hard. (Affirmative)
5. Don't smoke. (Negative imperative)
   You are forbidden to smoke. (Assertive)

INTERCHANGE OF AFFIRMATIVE AND NEGATIVE SENTENCES

Read the following sentences:

1. He runs slow. (Affirmative)
   He does not run fast. (Negative)
2. He loves himself the most. (Affirmative)
   He does not love anybody more than himself. (Negative)
3. Mr Sharma is a busy man. (Affirmative)
   Mr Sharma is not an idle man. (Negative)
4. She is as brilliant as you. (Affirmative)
   You are not more brilliant than her. (Negative)
5. He spoke angrily. (Affirmative)
   He did not speak calmly. (Negative)

INTERCHANGE OF INTERROGATIVE AND ASSERTIVE SENTENCES

Read the following sentences:

1. Why to speak ill of anybody? (Interrogative)
   We should not speak ill of anybody. (Assertive)
2. Who can win his fate? (Interrogative)
   No one can win his fate. (Assertive)
3. Where will you find such beautiful shoes? (Interrogative)
   You will not find such beautiful shoes anywhere. (Assertive)

4. How can he die without paying my debt? (Interrogative)
   He cannot die without paying my debt. (Assertive)
5. When will he learn manners? (Interrogative)
   He will never learn manners. (Assertive)
6. What can be done now? (Interrogative)
   Nothing can be done now. (Assertive)

INTERCHANGE OF EXCLAMATORY AND ASSERTIVE SENTENCES

Read the following sentences:

1. What a beautiful flower it is! (Exclamatory)
   It is a very beautiful flower. (Assertive)
2. How beautiful the Taj is! (Exclamatory)
   I am surprised that the Taj is very beautiful. (Assertive)
3. O for a one-rupee coin! (Exclamatory)
   A one-rupee coin is urgently desired. (Assertive)
4. Would that I were rich! (Exclamatory)
   I wish that I were rich. (Assertive)
5. O that I were rich! (Exclamatory)
   I wish that I were rich! (Assertive)

INTERCHANGE OF PARTS OF SPEECH

Read the following sentences:

1. This way you will **minimize** the risk. (Verb)
   This way you will bring the risk to the **minimum level**. (Adjective)
2. She fought **courageously**. (Adverb)
   She showed a great **courage** in the fight. (Noun)
3. She does not speak the **truth**. (Noun)
   She is not **truthful**. (Adjective)
4. He fought **bravely**. (Adverb)
   He fought with **bravery**. (Noun)
5. He **ran** fast. (Verb)
   He ran a fast **race**. (Noun)
6. He showed **generosity** towards his opponent. (Noun)
   He was **generous** towards his opponent. (Adjective)

CHANGING OF SIMPLE SENTENCES INTO COMPOUND ONES

Read the following sentences:

1. Besides being abused he was charged with misbehaving with others. (Simple)
   He was not only abused but also charged with misbehaving with others. (Compound)
2. You must run fast to catch the bus. (Simple)
   Run fast or you may miss the bus. (Compound)

3. Having finished her kitchen work, Mrs Sharma sat against the T.V. set. (Simple)
   Mrs Sharma finished her kitchen work and sat against the T.V. set. (Compound)
4. In spite of bitter cold, they managed to climb the hill. (Simple)
   It was bitter cold, yet they managed to climb the hill. (Compound)
5. In spite of being strong, he dare not oppose his opponents. (Simple)
   He is strong but still he dare not oppose his opponents. (Compound)

CHANGING OF SIMPLE SENTENCES INTO COMPLEX ONES

Read the following sentences:

1. In spite of being on crutches, he managed to catch the thief. (Simple)
   Though he was on crutches, he caught the thief. (Complex)
2. She is too weak in mathematics to solve even a simple sum. (Simple)
   She is so weak in mathematics that she cannot solve even a simple sum. (Complex)
3. The girl in all black is my classmate. (Simple)
   The girl, who is in all black, is my classmate. (Complex)
4. Because of/Owing to his negligence he lost his credibility. (Simple)
   He lost his credibility because he was negligent. (Complex)
5. He was happy at having been able to make an impressive speech. (Simple)
   He was happy that he was able to make an impressive speech. (Complex)
6. Put the ring at the place of your finding. (Simple)
   Put the ring where you found it. (Complex)

CHANGING OF COMPOUND SENTENCES INTO COMPLEX SENTENCES

Read the following sentences:

1. He is intelligent, but he is unkind. (Compound)
   Although he is intelligent, he is unkind. (Complex)
2. Buy a ticket or you cannot go insidc the hall. (Compound)
   You cannot go inside the hall unless you buy a ticket. (Complex)
3. He could not attend the meeting, for he was ill. (Compound)
   He could not attend the meeting because he was ill. (Complex)
4. Work hard or you won't be able to earn a lot. (Compound)
   If you don't work hard, you cannot earn a lot. (Complex)
5. It was fog all around, yet he managed to cross the uneven stretch of land. (Compound)
   Although it was fog all around, he managed to cross the uneven stretch of land. (Complex)

ACTIVE & PASSIVE VOICE

Sentences containing a transitive verb can usually be written in Active as well as Passive voice. When the subject acts upon the object the sentence is written in Active voice. When the subject is acted upon, the sentence is written in Passive voice.

1. Do you read a book? (Active)
   Is a book read by you? (Passive)

2. He flies an aeroplane. (Active)
An aeroplane is flown by him. (Passive)
3. She is unfolding the bed sheet. (Active)
The bed sheet is being unfolded by her. (Passive)
4. Are the boys singing songs? (Active)
Are songs being sung by the boys? (Passive)
5. Mohit has forwarded your request. (Active)
Your request has been forwarded by Mohit. (Passive)
6. Have you ever seen the Taj? (Active)
Has the Taj ever been seen by you? (Passive)
7. He freed all the slaves. (Active)
All the slaves were freed by him. (Passive)
8. Did the dog bite the stranger? (Active)
Was the stranger bitten by the dog? (Passive)
9. Ajeet was helping his relatives. (Active)
His relatives were being helped by Ajeet. (Passive)
10. Was Karan grazing the horses? (Active)
Were the horses being grazed by Karan? (Passive)
11. She had gained great flesh. (Active)
Great flesh had been gained by her. (Passive)
12. Had you gripped the knob on the door? (Active)
Had the knob on the door been gripped by you? (Passive)
13. I'll hit him hard. (Active)
He will be hit hard by me. (Passive)
14. Will you imitate your brother? (Active)
Will your brother be imitated by you? (Passive)
15. You will have opened the envelope? (Active)
The envelope will have been opened by you. (Passive)
16. Will she have printed her name on the title page? (Active)
Will her name have been printed on the title page by her? (Passive)

USE OF TIME-CLAUSES

As soon as
No sooner did .... than
Hardly had .... when
Scarcely had .... when or before

These sentences are used to express two actions taking place immediately one after the other.

1. As soon as the cat saw the dog, it started to run.
2. No sooner did the cat see the dog than it started to run.
3. Hardly had the cat seen the dog when it started to run.
4. Scarcely had the cat seen the dog when it started to run.

MULTIPLE CHOICE QUESTIONS

Directions (Qs. 1-20): *In the following questions, one out of the given four alternatives is the correct transformation of the given statement, pick that one.*

1. You should give full information.
This statement can be converted into negative as—
A. Everybody should not give full information.
B. Nobody is allowed to give full information.
C. You should not hide anything.
D. You should not give full information only.

2. You dare not speak against me in public.
This statement can be converted into Interrogative as—
A. Dare you speak against me in public?
B. Is it proper for you to speak against me in public?
C. Can anybody speak against somebody in public?
D. Speaking against anybody in public is nobody's business.

3. A sailor should not be afraid of water.
This statement can be converted into Exclamatory as—
A. Should a sailor be afraid of water?
B. A sailor and afraid of water!
C. How afraid of water a sailor is!
D. A sailor cannot be afraid of water.

4. Oh! What an interesting book that was.
This statement can be converted into assertive as—
A. What an interesting book it was!
B. It was a very interesting book.
C. A very interesting book was read by me.
D. It was not an interesting book at all.

5. What can be done now?
This interrogative sentence can be converted into an assertive one as—
A. Nothing can be done now.
B. You can do everything now.
C. They can do something now.
D. Something can be done now.

6. It is useless to give any advice to an obstinate person.
This statement can be converted into negative as—
A. It is useless to ask an obstinate person not to seek advice.
B. It is of no use giving advice to an obstinate person.
C. An obstinate person does not like the person who gives him any advice.
D. Some people do not make any use of advice given to obstinate persons.

7. Good people do not hate others.
This statement can be converted into interrogative as—
A. Do good people never hate others?
B. Why do not good people hate others?
C. When do good people say that they hate others.
D. Do good people hate others?

8. Isolation is very horrible for a child.
This statement can be converted into exclamatory as—
A. How horrible for a child isolation is !
B. How for a child isolation is horrible !
C. How horrible is for a child isolation !
D. How isolation is horrible for a child !

9. What a lame excuse !
This statement can be converted into assertive as—
A. A lame excuse it is.
B. How lame this excuse is.
C. Why do you make a lame excuse?
D. It is a very lame excuse.

10. True friends help each other not just once or twice.
This statement can be converted into affirmative as—
A. True friends help each other several times.
B. True friends help each other even unasked.
C. True friends help each other if they can.
D. True friends are helpful to each other.

11. You must be present in the meeting.
This statement can be converted into Negative as—
A. Nobody should be absent from the meeting.
B. You must not be absent from the meeting.
C. Anybody cannot be absent from the meeting.
D. You must not walk out of the meeting.

12. It is a beautiful bird.
This statement can be converted into Exclamatory as—
A. Is it a beautiful bird?
B. How is it a beautiful bird?
C. Who says it is not a beautiful bird?
D. What a beautiful bird it is!

13. It does not matter if we lose the match.
This statement can be converted into Interrogative as—
A. What does it matter if we lose the match?
B. Does it not matter if we lose the match?
C. Who says it does not matter if we lose the match?
D. How can we lose the match?

14. How happy I am!
This statement can be converted into Assertive as—
A. Am I happy?
B. I cannot say I am happy.
C. I am very happy.
D. How is it that I am happy?

15. There is none who cannot buy a bicycle.
This statement can be converted into Affirmative as—
A. Nobody can buy a bicycle.
B. Any one can buy a bicycle.
C. Some people cannot buy a bicycle.
D. It is useless to buy a bicycle.

16. You are forbidden to pluck flowers.
This statement can be converted into negative as—
A. You should not pluck flowers.
B. You are allowed to pluck flowers.
C. You are not allowed to pluck all the flowers.
D. You should give up the habit of plucking flowers.

17. He will definitely come here.
This statement can be converted into interrogative as—
A. When will he come here?
B. With whom will he come here?
C. How will he come here?
D. Will he not come here?

18. What a comfortable life he leads!
This sentence can be converted into an assertive sentence as—
A. I do not understand why he leads a comfortable life.
B. He leads a very comfortable life.
C. How does he lead a comfortable life.
D. Nobody knows how his life has become comfortable.

19. You should not absent yourself from the class any day.
This negative sentence can be converted into an affirmative one as—
A. You should be present in the class every day.
B. You should absent yourself from the class only rarely.
C. It is improper for you to be absent from the class.
D. You can come to the class any day you like.

20. What is the cause for worry?
This interrogative sentence can be converted into an assertive sentence as—
A. There is some cause for worry.
B. There is not much cause for worry.
C. There is no cause for worry.
D. Never think of a cause for worry.

Directions (Qs. 21-30): *In these questions, the sentences have been given in Active/Passive voice. From the given options, choose the one which best expresses the given sentence in Passive/Active voice.*

21. We chose him our leader.
A. He was chosen our leader.
B. He has been chosen our leader.
C. He had chosen our leader.
D. He have been chosen our leader.

22. Who made a maiden century?
A. By whose was a maiden century made?
B. By whom was a maiden century make?
C. By whom was a maiden century made?
D. By whom had a maiden century made?

23. I may help her in her project.
A. She might be helped by me in her project.
B. She may be helped by me in her project.
C. She might be helped in her project by me.
D. In her project, she may be help by me.

24. Take medicine in time.
A. Medicine should be taken in time.
B. Medicine will be taken in time.
C. Medicine will be took in time.
D. Medicine shall take in time.

25. I am solving the questions.
A. The questions are being solved by me.
B. The questions have been solved by me.
C. The questions are to be solved by me.
D. The question are solved by me.

26. May I take this pen?
A. May this pen will be taken by me?
B. May this pen shall be taken by me?
C. May this pen should be taken by me?
D. May this pen be taken by me?

27. Can we send it by air?
A. Can this be sent by air?
B. Can it be sent by air?
C. Can it go by air?
D. Can it be send by air?

28. Who wrote this book?
A. By whom was this book written?
B. By whom is this book written?
C. By whom was this book being written?
D. By whom is this book being written?

29. What did you buy?
A. What is bought by you?
B. What is being bought by you?
C. What was bought by you?
D. What was being bought by you?

30. Whom do you want?
A. Who is wanted by you?
B. Who is being wanted by you?
C. You are wanted by whom?
D. You are being wanted by whom?

Directions (Qs. 31-40): *Select the correct transformation of the given sentences.*

31. She is too proud to listen to you.
A. She is very proud to listen to you.
B. She feels too proud to listen to you.
C. She is so proud listening to you.
D. She is so proud that she will not listen to you.

32. He ran so slowly that he could not catch the train.
A. He ran so slowly to catch the train.
B. He ran very slowly to catch the train.
C. He ran too slowly to catch the train.
D. He ran too slow to catch the train.

33. I like him because he is good person.
A. He is a good person. I like him.
B. He is a good person for which I like him.
C. He is a good person as I like him.
D. He is a good person for I like him.

34. In spite of working hard, he failed.
A. He worked hard but he failed.
B. He worked hard as he failed.
C. He worked hard so he failed.
D. He worked hard for which he failed.

35. Unless you work hard, you cannot pass.
A. If you work hard, you cannot pass.
B. Work hard if you cannot pass.
C. You cannot pass without working hard.
D. You should work hard, you can pass.

36. As soon as the thief saw the policeman, he started to run fast.
A. No sooner did the thief see the policeman when he started to run fast.
B. No sooner did the thief see the policeman than he started to run fast.
C. No sooner did the thief saw the policeman when he started to run fast.
D. No sooner did the thief saw the policeman than he started to run fast.

37. No sooner did I walk out of the house than it began to rain.
A. Hardly did I walked out of the house when it began to rain.
B. Hardly had I walked out of the house than it began to rain.
C. Hardly had I walked out of the house then it began to rain.
D. Hardly had I walked out of the house when it began to rain.

38. Hardly had the passenger boarded the bus when it punctured.
A. Scarcely had the passenger boarded the bus than it punctured.
B. Scarcely had the passenger boarded the bus then it punctured.
C. Scarcely had the passenger boarded the bus when it punctured.
D. Scarcely had the passenger boarded the bus but it punctured.

39. Scarcely had the ship berthed in America when it began to blow hard.
A. No sooner did the ship berth in America than it began to blow hard.
B. As soon as the ship berthed in America then it began to blow hard.
C. Hardly had the ship berthed in America then it began to blow hard.
D. Scarcely had the ship berthed in America then it began to blow hard.

40. No sooner did she alight from the train than the guard whistled.
A. Scarcely had she alighted from the train then the guard whistled.
B. Scarcely had she alighted from the train than the guard whistled.
C. Scarcely had she alighted from the train when the guard whistled.
D. Scarcely did she alight from the train when the guard whistled.

ANSWERS

1	2	3	4	5	6	7	8	9	10
C	A	B	B	A	B	D	A	D	A
11	**12**	**13**	**14**	**15**	**16**	**17**	**18**	**19**	**20**
B	D	A	C	B	A	D	B	A	C
21	**22**	**23**	**24**	**25**	**26**	**27**	**28**	**29**	**30**
A	C	B	A	A	D	B	A	C	A
31	**32**	**33**	**34**	**35**	**36**	**37**	**38**	**39**	**40**
D	C	B	A	C	B	D	C	A	C

17 Tenses

Tense indicates a point in time or period of time in the past, present, or future tense.

Tense is related to the verb. The verb may consist of a single word, or a main verb and one or more auxiliary words.

A. The verb can indicate a state of being (What the subject is) or location.
   Bhaskar is intelligent.
   Mahesh is at work.

B. A verb can indicate what the subject is like or becomes.
   That child **seems** frightened.

C. A verb can indicate an action. (What the subject is doing).
   The students **will finish** in time.

There are normally three forms of the verb, say, V_1, V_2, V_3 and for convenience a fourth form V_4 as verb+ing may be assumed.

Forms of Verb

V_1	V_2	V_3	V_4
Write	Wrote	Written	Writing
Read	Read	Read	Reading
Go	Went	Gone	Going
...	...	...	...

A Comparative Chart Regarding Tenses and Verbs

Simple Present	**Simple Past**	**Simple Future**
V_1	V_2	shall/will + V_1
Present Continuous	**Past Continuous**	**Future Continuous**
is/am/are + V_4	was/were + V_4	shall/will + be + V_4
Present Perfect	**Past Perfect**	**Future Perfect**
has/have + V_3	had + V_3	shall/will + have + V_3
Present Perfect Cont.	**Past Perfect Cont.**	**Future Perfect Cont.**
has/have + been + V_4	had + been + V_4	shall/will + have been + V_4

SIMPLE PRESENT:

A. A present state of affairs.	A. My sister lives in Shri Nagar.
B. A general fact.	B. The sun rises in the east.
C. Habitual actions.	C. I listen to the radio in the mornings.
D. Future time-tables.	D. My flight leaves at 10:00.

PRESENT CONTINUOUS:

A. A specific action that is occurring.	A. Arvind is watching TV (right now).
B. A general activity that takes place.	B. These days, I'm taking it easy.
C. Future arrangements.	C. I'm inviting Hari to the party on Friday.

SIMPLE PAST:

A. An action that began and ended at a particular time in the past.	A. The mail came early this Morning.
B. An action that occurred over a period of time but was completed in the past.	B. Dad worked in advertising in the past.
C. An activity that took place regularly in the past.	C. We jogged every morning before class.

PAST CONTINUOUS:

A. Interrupted Actions.	A. I was sewing when the telephone rang.
B. A continuous state over a period of timc but was completed in the past.	B. She was looking very ill. I was meeting lots of people at that time.
C. Events planned in the past.	C. Neetu was leaving for Kashmir but had to make a last minute change
D. Expressing a future intent.	D. Jyoti is going to bring her sister tonight.
E. Predicting an event.	E. You are going to pass the test. Don't worry.

SIMPLE FUTURE:

A. Making a future decision.	A. I will call you after lunch.
B. Predicting a future event.	B. You will pass the test. Don't worry.
C. Indicating willingness to do something.	C. If I don't feel better soon, I will go to the doctor.

FUTURE CONTINUOUS:

A. An action that will be going at a particular time in the future.	A. At noon tomorrow, I will be taking the children to their piano lessons.
B. Future actions which have already been decided.	B. I will be wearing my black dress the dinner.

PRESENT PERFECT:

A. An action that happened at an unspecified time.	A. She has never climbed a mountain. I'm sorry. I have forgotten your Name.
B. An action that has recently occurred.	B. He's just gone to sleep.
C. An action that began in the past and continues up to the present (often used with "for" or "since").	C. Jack has lived in Jammu all his life. I have been here since Monday. He has known her for two weeks.
D. An action that happened repeatedly before now.	D. We have flown across the Pacific four times. I've failed my driver's test twice.

PRESENT PERFECT CONTINUOUS:

A. An action that began in the past and has just recently ended.
A. Have you been ringing the Bell?

B. An action that began in the past and continues in the present.
B. Lokesh has been studying for two hours.

C. An action repeated over a period of time in the past and continuing in present.
C. Suresh has been smoking since he was fifteen.

PAST PERFECT:

A. An action that occurred before another past action.
A. Tarun had left hours before we got there.

B. An action that was expected to occur in the past.
B. I had hoped to know about the job before now.

PAST PERFECT CONTINUOUS:

A. An action that occurred before another past action.
A. His eyes hurt because he had been Reading for eight hours.

B. An action that was expected to occur in the past.
B. I had been expecting a change in his attitude.

FUTURE PERFECT:

A. An action that will be completed before a particular time in the future.
A. By next July, my parents will have been married for fifty years.

FUTURE PERFECT CONTINUOUS:

A. Emphasizing the length of time that has occurred before a specific time in the future.
A. By May, my father will have been working at the same job for thirty years.

MULTIPLE CHOICE QUESTIONS

Directions (Qs. 1-25): *Fill in the blanks with correct present tense forms of the verbs given in brackets.*

1. They .... (live) in Shri Nagar for five years.
   A. are living B. were living
   C. has been living D. have been living
2. At the moment the child .... (play) in the garden.
   A. playing B. plays
   C. is playing D. has been playing
3. I .... (tell) you already about it.
   A. told B. have told
   C. tells D. am telling
4. If you .... (study) hard, you will secure a first division.
   A. studied B. study
   C. have studies D. are study
5. She ....(pass) the post office on her way to school every day.
   A. is passing B. has been passing
   C. passes D. passed
6. He .... (read) since morning.
   A. have been reading
   B. has been reading
   C. is reading
   D. had been reading
7. This pen .... (cost) me ten rupees.
   A. costs B. costing
   C. has cost D. costed

8. He .... (wait) for me since morning.
A. has been waiting B. have been waiting
C. had been waiting D. is waiting

9. The sun .... (shine) by day.
A. shining B. has been shining
C. shines D. is shining

10. The bell .... (ring) just now.
A. rings B. ringing
C. rung D. has rung

11. She .... (attend) college since 4th July.
A. has been attending B. attends
C. is attending D. attended

12. Why .... (you come) late every day?
A. do you come B. did you come
C. have you come D. did you come

13. When he .... (meet) you, he will love you.
A. will meet B. is meeting
C. meets D. has met

14. It .... (not rain) now.
A. does not rain B. did not rain
C. has not rained D. is not raining

15. I .... (not yet give) up hope.
A. have not yet given B. do not yet given
C. did not yet give D. am not giving

16. If you .... (be) hungry, you can eat.
A. being B. are
C. have been D. will be

17. The earth .... (move) round the sun.
A. is moving B. has been moving
C. moves D. moving

18. The sun .... (rise) in the east and .... (set) in the west.
A. rising, is setting
B. rises, sets
C. rising, setting
D. has been rising, has been setting

19. He .... (suffer) from malaria since day before yesterday.
A. has been suffering B. have been suffering
C. suffers D. is suffering

20. It .... (rain) all the year round here.
A. has rained B. is raining
C. rains D. has been raining

21. He .... (write) to me every month.
A. is writing B. writes
C. has been writing D. has been writing

22. Where .... he .... (go) to play in the evening?
A. did, go B. has, gone
C. does, go D. does, going

23. This servant .... (work) with us for ten years.
A. works B. has been working
C. is working D. does work

24. What time .... you .... (reach) home in the evening?
A. do, reach B. does, reach
C. did, reached D. have, reached

25. How .... you .... (get) on with your studies?
A. is, get B. do, get
C. is, getting D. have, got

Directions (Qs. 26-45): ***Fill in the blanks with correct past tense forms of the verbs given in brackets.***

26. He .... (buy) a car one month ago.
A. bought B. has bought
C. has been buying D. had been buying

27. She .... (leave) for Jammu yesterday.
A. leaves B. is leaving
C. has been leaving D. left

28. He .... (teach) in this college for five years.
A. teaches B. is teaching
C. taught D. has been teaching

29. I .... (write) to her last week.
A. wrote B. have been writing
C. had been writing D. written

30. He .... (be) weak in English in the beginning.
A. being B. been
C. was D. had been

31. People .... (vote) them out in the recent elections.
A. were voting B. haven been voting
C. voted D. have voted

32. I .... (have) my breakfast at 8.30 a.m. yesterday.
A. am having B. was having
C. will be having D. have been doing

33. I .... (write) a letter when she knocked at the door.
A. wrote B. had writing
C. have written D. was writing

34. We .... (bathe) in the river when it was raining.
A. were bathing B. have been bathing
C. are bathing D. did bath

35. He .... (watch) television when I came in.
A. watched B. was watching
C. had watched D. has been watching

36. He .... (tell) me that he had never met you.
A. is telling B. did tell
C. told D. has told

37. Whe .... (arrive) before I came.
A. was arriving B. is arriving
C. had arrived D. has been arriving

38. He .... (arrive) here only last night.
A. has arrived B. arrived
C. had arrived D. was arriving

39. If you .... (work hard), you would have passed.
A. have worked hard
B. had worked hard
C. have been working hard
D. worked hard

40. She .... (come) to see me yesterday.
A. came B. has came
C. had came D. had been coming

41. When I reached his home, he .... (sleep).
A. has slept B. had sleep
C. was sleeping D. slept

42. When he left this morning, the sun .... (shine).
A. shines B. has shone
C. had shone D. was shining

43. Madhu .... (not attend) the office yesterday.
A. was not attending B. did not attend
C. was not attend D. had not attend

44. Last year, it .... (not rain) heavily.
A. did not rain B. had not rain
C. has not rian D. was not rain

45. I .... (write) to him yesterday.
A. has written B. and written
C. wrote D. have been writing

Directions (Qs. 46-50): *Fill in the blanks with correct future tense forms of the verbs given in brackets.*

46. I don't think we .... (meet) again.
A. are meeting B. will be meeting
C. will meet D. can meet

47. He .... (be) here early next month.
A. was B. has been
C. had been D. will be

48. If I go to school late, the teacher .... (punish) me.
A. is punishing B. punishing
C. will punish D. shall punish

49. If you study hard, you .... (get) a first class.
A. are getting B. will get
C. will be getting D. shall get

50. He .... (leave) for Shri Nagar next week.
A. will leave B. shall leave
C. going to leave D. will be leaving

ANSWERS

1	2	3	4	5	6	7	8	9	10
D	C	B	B	C	B	C	A	C	D
11	12	13	14	15	16	17	18	19	20
A	A	C	D	A	B	C	B	A	A
21	22	23	24	25	26	27	28	29	30
B	C	B	A	B	A	D	C	A	C
31	32	33	34	35	36	37	38	39	40
C	B	D	A	B	C	C	B	B	A
41	42	43	44	45	46	47	48	49	50
C	D	B	A	C	C	D	C	B	A

18 Figures of Speech

It is a common saying that a picture is worth a thousand words. Same goes with the figures of speech as they elaborate the meaning of words.

FIGURATIVE LANGUAGE

One meaning of "figure" is "drawing" or "image" or "picture". Figurative language creates figures (pictures) in the mind of the reader or listener. These pictures help convey the meaning faster and more vividly than words alone.

We use figures of speech in "figurative language" to add colour and interest, and to awaken the imagination. Figurative language is everywhere, from classical works like Shakespeare or the Bible, to every day speech, pop music and television commercials. It makes the reader or listener use their imagination and understand much more than the plain words.

Figurative language is the opposite of literal language. Literal language means exactly what it says. Figurative language means something different to (and usually more than) what it says on the surface. *e.g.*,

- He ran fast. (literal)
- He ran like the wind. (figurative)

In the above example "like the wind" is a figure of speech (in this case, simile). It is important to recognize the difference between literal and figurative language. There are many figures of speech that are commonly used and which you can learn by heart. At other times, writers and speakers may invent their own figures of speech. If you do not recognize them as figures of speech and think that they are literal, you will find it difficult to understand the language.

In this chapter we will discuss four common types of figures of speech :

- Simile
- Metaphor
- Hyperbole
- Oxymoron

Simile

A simile is a figure of speech that says that one thing is like another different thing. We can use similes to make descriptions more emphatic or vivid.

We often use the words *as....as* and like with similes.

Common patterns for similes, with example sentences, are :

- Something AS *adjective* AS *something*
  His skin was as cold as ice.
  It felt as hard as rock.
  She looked as gentle as a lamb.
- Something LIKE something
  My love is like a red, red rose.
  These cookies taste like garbage.
  He had a temper (that was) like a volcano.

- Something LIKE something
  He eats like a pig.
  He smokes like a chimney.
  They fought like cats and dogs.

Here are some more examples of well known similes :

AS *adjective* AS *something*	Meaning
as blind as a bat	completely blind
as cold as ice	very cold
as flat as a pancake	completely flat
as gentle as a lamb	very gentle
as light as a feather	very light
as old as the hills	very old
as sharp as a knife	very sharp
as strong as a bull	very strong
as white as snow	pure white
as wise as an owl	very wise

LIKE *something*	Possible meaning (depending on context)
like a rose	beautiful
like a volcano	explosive
like garbage	disgusting
like an animal	inhuman
like spaghetti	entangled
like dewdrops	sweet and pure
like golddust	precious
like a tip	very untidy (tip = garbage dump)
like a dream	wonderful, incredible
like stars	bright and beautiful

LIKE something	Meaning
to drink like a fish	to drink a lot
to eat like a bird	to eat very little
to eat like a horse	to eat a lot
to eat like a pig	to eat impolitely
to fight like cats and dogs	to fight fiercely
to sing like an angel	to sing beautifully
to sleep like a log	to sleep well and soundly
to smoke like a chimney	to smoke heavily, all the time
to soar like an eagle	to fly high and free
to work like a dog	to work very hard

Note that with the AS...AS pattern, the first AS is sometimes suppressed, for example :

His skin was cold as ice.

The above patterns of simile are the most common, but there are others made with adverbs or words such as than and as if, for example :

- He ran as fast as the wind.
- He is larger than life.
- They ran as if for their lives.

Similes can include other figures of speech. For example. "He ran like greased lightning" is a simile that includes hyperbole (greased lightning).

Similes often make use of irony or sarcasm. In such cases they may even mean the opposite of the adjective used. Look at these examples :

- His explanation was as clear as mud. (not clear at all since mud is opaque)
- The film was about as interesting watching a copy of Windows download. (long and boring)
- Watching the show was like watching paint dry. (very boring)

Similes are often found (and they sometimes originate) in poetry and other literature. Here are a few examples :

- A woman without a man is like a fish without a bicycle—Irina Dunn
- Dawn breaks open like a wound that bleeds afresh—Wilfred Owen
- Death has many times invited me : it was like the salt invisible in the waves—Pablo Neruda

- Guiltless forever, like a tree—Robert Browning
- Happy as pigs in mud—David Eddings
- How like the winter hath my absence been—William Shakespeare
- As idle as a painted ship upon a painted ocean—Samuel Taylor Coleridge
- Jubilant as a flag unfurled—Dorothy Parker
- So are you to my thoughts as food to life—William Shakespeare
- Yellow butterflies flickered along the shade like flecks of sun—William Faulkner

Metaphor

A metaphor is a figure of speech that says that one thing is another different thing. This allows us to use fewer words and forces the reader or listener to find the similarities.

The word metaphor comes from the Greek word *metapherin* (meaning "transfer").

The simplest form of metaphor is : "The [first thing] is a [second thing]."

Look at this example :

Her home was a prison.

In the above sentence, we understand immediately that her home had some of the characteristics of a prison. Mainly, we imagine, she could not leave her home. She was trapped inside. Why it was a prison we do not know, but that would be clear from the context—perhaps her husband forced her to stay at home, perhaps she was afraid of the outside. We don't know, but the rest of the story would tell us. What is important here is that in five simple words we understand a lot about her environment, how she felt and how she behaved. In this sentence, "prison" is a metaphor.

Look at another example :

George is a sheep.

What is one characteristic of sheep? They follow each other. So we can imagine that George is a follower, not a leader. In this sentence "sheep" is a metaphor.

Metaphors are very common in everyday language. But poets also like to use metaphors.

Look at these examples of metaphors with sample sentences and meanings :

Metaphor example	Metaphorical sense	Original sense
I'm not an angel, but I wouldn't a behave like that.	exemplary person	a spiritual being believed to be messenger of God
America is a melting pot.	place where different peoples, styles and cultures are mixed together	a container in which metals or other materials are melted and mixed
John is a real pig when he eats.	greedy person	a four-legged animal kept for meat (pork)
My father is a rock.	very strong or reliable person	a hard, mineral material made of stone
How could she marry a snake like that!	traitor	a long, limbless reptile (e.g., cobra, python, viper)
The policeman let him off with a yellow card.	warning	(in soccer) a yellow card that the referee shows to players when cautioning them

All the above metaphors (the simplest form) are nouns. But there are other ways of making metaphors, for example with verbs or adjectives. Here are some examples :

Metaphor example	Original sense of the word (example)
The committee **shot** ideas **down** one by one.	Anti-aircraft guns that shoot down planes.
The private detective **dug** up enough evidence to convince the police to act.	Dugs like to bury bones and dig them up later.
He **broke into** her conversation	Burglars break into buildings.
The new movie was very popular. People **flocked** to see it.	Birds flock together before they migrate.
His head was **spinning** with ideas.	Some computer hard drives spin at over 10,000 revolutions per minute.
Reading that book **kindled** my interest in branches when you kindle a camp fire.	You need to start with twigs and small politics.
Tim lost his job after a **heated** argument with his boss.	We have a heated swimming pool.
The new car's **sexy** design increased sales for the company.	Some women think that lipstick makes them look sexy.
He was dressed rather vulgarly in a **loud** checked suit.	I can't hear you because the radio is too loud.
It wasn't long before their relauonship turned **sour**.	Sour food has an acid taste like lemon or vinegar.

Difference Between Metaphor and Simile

Both similes and metaphors link one thing to another. A simile usually uses "as" or "like". A metaphor is a condensed simile, a shortcut to meaning, which omits "as" or "like". A metaphor creates a relationship directly and leaves more to the imagination. With simile, A is like B. With metaphor, *A* is *B*.

Simile	Metaphor
Your eyes are like sun.	You are my the sunshine.
He eats like a pig.	He is a pig.
He lives like a pig.	He is a pig.

Dead Metaphors

In the phrase "to grasp the concept" the physical action "to grasp" is used as a metaphor for "to understand" (which is non-physical). But this phrase has been used so often that most English speakers do not have an image of the physical action in their mind. This metaphor is a "dead metaphor".

Mixed Metaphors

The awkward use of two or more different metaphors at the same time is normally best avoided. It creates conflicting images in the reader or listener's mind, reduces each metaphor's impact, and generally causes confusion. Look at this example :

America is a **melting pot** where new ideas are **kindled**.

Hyperbole

Hyperbole is a figure of speech that uses an exaggerated or extravagant to create a strong emotional response. As a figure of speech it is not intended to be taken literally. Hyperbole is frequently used for humour. Examples of hyperbole are :

- They ran like greased lightning.
- He's got tons of money.
- Her brain is the size of a pea.
- He is older than the hills.
- I will die if she asks me to dance.
- She is as big as an elephant!
- I'm so hungry I could eat a horse.
- I have told you a million times not to lie!

The media and the advertising industry often use hyperbole (which may then be described as hyper or media hype).

Oxymoron

An oxymoron is a figure of speech that deliberately uses two contradictory ideas. This contradiction creates a paradoxical image in the reader or listener's mind that generates a new concept or meaning for the whole. Some typical oxymorons are :

- a living death
- sometimes you have to be cruel to be kind
- a deafening silence
- bitter-sweet
- The Sounds of Silence (song title)
- make haste slowly
- he was conspicuous by his absence

Pseudo Oxymorons

In the standard meaning of oxymoron the contradiction is deliberate. However, in popular usage oxymoron is sometimes used to mean "contradiction in terms", where the contradiction is unintentional. Such expressions, unlike real oxymorons, are commonly used without any sense of paradox in everyday language, for example :

- anecdotal evidence
- friendly fire
- pretty ugly

A common attempt at humour is to describe a certain phrase as an oxymoron, implying that the two parts of the phrase are mutually exclusive and that consequently the phrase as a whole must be nonsensical :

- airline food
- American culture
- eco-tourism
- Microsoft security
- military intelligence

The following are the other major Figures of Speech :

1. **Personification**—In Personification inanimate objects and abstract notions are spoken of as having life or intelligence.

   Example: 1. Laughter holding both her sides.
   2. Death lays his icy hand on kings.

2. **Onomatopoeia**—Onomatopoeia is that artifice of language by which the sound of words is made to suggest or echo the sense.

   Example: 1. The murmurous haunt of flies on summer eves.
   2. Murmuring of innumerable bees.

3. **Apostrophe**—An Apostrophe is a direct address to the dead, to the absent, or to a personified object or idea.

   Example: 1. O death! where is thy sting? o grave! where is thy victory?
   2. Milton! thou should'st be living at this hour.

4. **Alliteration**—Alliteration consists in the repetition of the same sound or syllable at the beginning of two or more words.

   Example: 1. How high his honour his haughty head!
   2. A reeling road, a rolling road, that rambles round the shire.

5. **Irony**—Irony is a mode of speech in which the real meaning is exactly the opposite of that which is literally conveyed.

   Example: 1. The atrocious crime of being a young man, which the honourable gentleman has, with such spirit and decency, charged upon me. I shall neither attempt to palliate nor deny.

2. No doubt but ye are the people, and wisdom shall die with you.

6. Pun—This consists in a play on the various meanings of a word, and is seldom used except as a joke.

Example: 1. An ambassador is an honest man who *lies* abroad for the good of his country.

2. Is life worth living ?–It depends upon the *liver*.

7. Metonymy—In Metonymy an object is designated by the name of something which is generally associated with it.

Example: 1. The laurel, for success.

2. Bluejackets, for sailors.

8. Synecdoche—In Synecdoche a part is used to designate the whole, or the whole to designate a part.

Example: 1. Uneasy lies the *head* that wears a crown.

2. Give us this day our daily *bread* (*i.e.*, food).

9. Antithesis—In Antithesis a striking opposition or contrast of words or sentiments is made in the same sentence. It is employed to secure emphasis.

Example: 1. Give every man thy ear, but few thy voice.

2. Many are called, but few are chosen.

10. Transferred Epithet—In this figure an epithet is tranferred from its proper word to another that is closely associated with it in the sentence.

Example: 1. He passed a *sleepless* night.

2. A lackey presented an *obsequious* cup of coffee.

MULTIPLE CHOICE QUESTIONS

Directions (Qs. 1 to 30) : *In each of the following sentences or verses a Figure of Speech has been used. You have to choose the correct Figure of Speech out of the four choices given under each :*

1. Rivers of blood flowed on the battlefield :
A. Simile B. Metaphor
C. Hyperbole D. Alliteration

2. Camel is the ship of the desert :
A. Metaphor B. Simile
C. Pun D. Personification

3. 'O my love's like a red, red rose, that's newly sprung in June':
A. Alliteration B. Metaphor
C. Simile D. Hyperbole

4. "Opportunity knocks at the door but once."
A. Hyperbole
B. Metaphor
C. Antithesis
D. Personification

5. "Death lays his icy hand on Kings" :
A. Personification B. Antithesis
C. Metaphor D. Oxymoron

6. "The murmurous haunt of flies on summer eves."
A. Hyperbole B. Alliteration
C. Onomatopoeia D. Personification

7. "Milton! thou should'st be living at this hour."
A. Personification B. Apostrophe
C. Alliteration D. Irony

8. How high his honour holds his haughty head!
A. Oxymoron B. Personification
C. Alliteration D. Irony

9. "Yet Brutus says he was ambitious. And Brutus is an honourable man."
A. Irony B. Oxymoron
C. Apostrophe D. Pun

10. Is life worth living? That depends upon the liver.
A. Pun B. Alliteration
C. Irony D. Metaphor

11. "Thy soul was like a star, and dwelt apart."
A. Metaphor B. Personification
C. Simile D. Onomatopoeia

12. He can devour mountains of food, and drink rivers of whisky.
A. Onomatopoeia B. Hyperbole
C. Metaphor D. Personification

13. "There Honour comes a pilgrim grey" :
A. Metaphor
B. Apostrophe
C. Personification
D. Onomatopoeia

14. An ambassador is a man who lies abroad for the good of his country :
A. Metonymy B. Personification
C. Pun D. Irony

15. "Husbands had she five on the holy altar" :
A. Hyperbole B. Metaphor
C. Irony D. Pun

16. His honour rooted in dishonour stood :
A. Antithesis B. Oxymoron
C. Irony D. Personification

17. "Sceptre and crown must tumble down."
A. Metonymy B. Antithesis
C. Irony D. Oxymoron

18. A lie has no legs :
A. Apostrophe B. Pun
C. Personification D. Irony

19. Youth is full of pleasure; Age is full of care :
A. Antithesis B. Pun
C. Metaphor D. Personification

20. The righteous shall flourish as the palm trees :
A. Simile
B. Transferred Epithet
C. Antithesis
D. Synecdoche

21. The pen is mightier than the sword.
A. Simile B. Metaphor
C. Metonymy D. Irony

22. A reeling road, a rolling road, that rambles round the shire.
A. Alliteration B. Metonymy
C. Personification D. Apostrophe

23. "The ploughman homeward plods his weary way."
A. Oxymoron
B. Synecdoche
C. Transferred Epithet
D. Pun

24. To err is human, to forgive divine :
A. Oxymoron
B. Antithesis
C. Transferred Epithet
D. Pun

25. He passed a sleepless night :
A. Transferred Epithet
B. Antithesis
C. Synecdoche
D. Oxymoron

26. The best brains assembled there :
A. Oxymoron B. Synecdoche
C. Irony D. Pun

27. I have many mouths to feed :
A. Synecdoche B. Irony
C. Pun D. Oxymoron

28. Man proposes, God disposes :
A. Synecdoche B. Antithesis
C. Pun D. Irony

29. O Death! Where is thy sting?
A. Metaphor B. Oxymoron
C. Personification D. Apostrophe

30. "Life is a tale told by an idiot,
Full of sound and fury ...."
A. Simile B. Personification
C. Metaphor D. Apostrophe

Directions (Qs. 31 to 50) : *Select the correct option for each of the following questions.*

31. What Figure of Speech is used when a statement is made emphatic by over statement?
A. Apostrophe B. Hyperbole
C. Personification D. Antithesis

32. What Figure of Speech is used when two contradictory qualities are predicted at once of the same thing?
A. Antithesis B. Onomatopoeia
C. Oxymoron D. Hyperbole

33. In which Figure of Speech the sense is conveyed by the sound of words?
A. Metonymy B. Synecdoche
C. Alliteration D. Onomatopoeia

34. In which Figure of Speech is there a play on the various meanings of a word?
A. Pun
B. Metaphor
C. Transferred Epithet
D. Irony

35. Which Figure of Speech is produced when the same sound is repeated more than twice at the beginning of a word?
A. Onomatopoeia B. Alliteration
C. Metonymy D. Synecdoche

36. Which of the following is an example of Onomatopoeia?
A. Sweet-bitter tears flowed from her eyes
B. The beetle wheels his droning flight
C. A load of learning lumbering in his head
D. Fair is that fair does

37. Which of the following is an example of Oxymoron?
A. There is kind cruelty in the surgeon's knife
B. Ruin seize thee, ruthless king!
C. And Brutus is an honourable man!
D. Kalidas is the Shakespeare of India

38. Which of the following is an example of Antithesis?
A. Who is to blame but you!
B. Fair is foul, and foul is fair!
C. As you sow, so will you reap
D. Forget me not!

39. Which of the following is an example of Apostrophe?
A. Barking dogs seldom bite
B. My misfortune is your fortune
C. O Solitude! Where are thy charms?
D. I am the monarch of all I survey

40. Which of the following is an example of Alliteration?
A. Sweet are the uses of adversity!
B. Thus idly busy rolls their world away
C. He is the heir apparent
D. With beaded bubbles winking at the brim

41. Recognize the figure of speech in the following statement.
He is the Newton of our class.
A. Simile B. Hyperbole
C. Metaphor D. Climax

42. Which of the following statements shows oxymoron:
A. He is leading a busy life.
B. He is leading a highly busy-idle life.
C. He is leading an idle life.
D. How happy I am!

43. Recognize the figure of speech in the following:
The Child is father of the Man.
A. alliteration B. hyperbole
C. paradox D. metaphor

44. Which of the following shows Metonymy:
A. Have you read the whole of George Eliot?
B. Which building in Delhi do you like most?
C. Whose acting do you like most among the Bollywood actors?
D. Why are day and night equal on 21 March?

45. Recognize the figure of speech in the following statement.
I wandered lonely as a cloud.
A. Simile B. Metaphor
C. Alliteration D. Hyperbole

46. Which of the following phrases shows onomatopoeia:
A. living like a king.
B. looking beyond the horizon.
C. burning the candle at both ends.
D. murmuring of innumerable bees.

47. Recognize the figure of speech in the following:
Five miles meandering in mazy motion.
A. oxymoron B. climax
C. anticlimax D. alliteration

48. Which of the following shows 'climax':
A. I walk, I jump, I dance.
B. I run, I walk, I sit.
C. He lies, runs and sits.
D. She thinks, writes and observes.

49. Recognize the figure of speech in the following:
Lightly, O lightly, they bear her along.
A. Hyperbole B. Onomatopoeia
C. Climax D. Repetition

50. Which of the following shows 'Hyperbole':
A. You will have to speak for a hundred thousand years to describe her beauty.
B. Love begets love.
C. Better alone than in bad company.
D. Nothing can be decided by war.

ANSWERS

1	2	3	4	5	6	7	8	9	10
C	A	C	D	A	C	B	C	A	A
11	**12**	**13**	**14**	**15**	**16**	**17**	**18**	**19**	**20**
C	B	C	C	C	B	A	C	A	A
21	**22**	**23**	**24**	**25**	**26**	**27**	**28**	**29**	**30**
C	A	C	B	A	B	A	B	D	C
31	**32**	**33**	**34**	**35**	**36**	**37**	**38**	**39**	**40**
B	C	D	A	B	B	A	B	C	D
41	**42**	**43**	**44**	**45**	**46**	**47**	**48**	**49**	**50**
C	B	C	A	A	D	D	A	D	A

English Literature

1 Classification and Forms of English Literature

Literature plays a very significant role in human life. It is considered to be the mirror of the society which reflects the image of the time in which it was created. It is a medium of expressing thoughts and ideas for the writer. It is one of the most ancient forms of entertainment in the history of mankind. At the beginning when there was no written form of language, literature was composed in the form of poetry and preserved through the words of mouth. In the history of literature, poetry is the most ancient form of literature. Then it developed into various other forms like drama, novel, and short story.

CLASSIFICATION & FORMS

Literature can be classified and sub-classified in various forms as:

1. Drama
2. Prose
3. Poetry
4. Novel

Drama

The following are the Major Forms of Drama :

1. Miracles & Mystery Plays, Morality Plays and Interludes
2. Heroic, Revenge, Shakespearean, Sentimental, Tragedies & Melodramas
3. Comedies
   - Classical Comedies
   - Tragi-Comedies
   - Romantic Comedies
   - Comedy of Humour
   - Comedy of Manners
   - The Farce
   - The Masque
4. The Poetic Play
5. The Dramatic Monologue
6. The Problem Play
7. The One-Act Play

Prose

The following are the Major Forms of Prose :

1. Long Prose-Works
2. The Essay
3. The Periodical Journals
4. The Biography
5. The Autobiography
6. The Memoirs

Poetry

Poetry and its Major Forms are these :

1. The Epic
2. The Mock Epic
3. The Sonnet
4. The Ode
5. The Lyric
6. The Idyll
7. The Pastoral
8. The Elegy
9. The Pastoral Elegy
10. The Ballad
11. The Satire

Novel

The following are the Major Forms of the Novel :

1. The Prose Romances
2. The Travelogues
3. The Gothic Novel
4. The Picaresque Novel
5. The Epistolary Novel
6. The Domestic Novel
7. The Historical Novel
8. The Regional Novel
9. The Prophetic Novel
10. The Psychological Novel
11. The Short Story

DRAMA

The term 'drama' originates from Greek language, which means 'to do'. In a drama, we come across objective representation of the conflicts, actions, events and crisis from the lives of the concerned characters. Drama is the specific mode of fiction represented in performance. It is primarily a performing art. It is the most powerful literary expression as action is presented on the stage, engaging the audio-visual faculties of the audience.

Drama is an ancient form of literature having a long history of more than 2500 years. Historically speaking following are the stages in the development of drama:

Greek Drama

History of literature shows the origin of drama in Greece in 6th century B.C. In ancient Greece dramatic competitions were held to celebrate the festival of God Dionysus. The dramatists participating in this competition were required to present a tetralogy of plays consisting of three tragedies and a satyr play. The plays performed in this period were tragedy, comedy and the satyr play. Aeschylus, Sophocles, Euripides, Aristophanes and Menander are the best-known dramatists of Ancient times.

Roman Drama

Greek drama came in contact with the Romans after the Roman Empire expanded into Greece territories in the 3rd century B.C. Roman dramatists of this period like Andronicus and Naevius took drama all over Europe. During the 2nd century B.C. it had become one of the chief means of entertainment with many men of letters practicing it. The comedies written by Plautus and Terence became very popular, many of which have survived. The Roman tragedian, Seneca popularized tragedy so much so that it is called Senecan tragedy.

Medieval Drama

The drama of the Middle Ages dealt with Bible stories and allegorical mysteries. It was being written in the regional languages of the times. To help the laymen understand the teachings of the religion, the clergymen used to perform the incidents from Bible in dramatic form. The plays of this period are called Mystery and Miracle plays.

Elizabethan Drama

With the construction of Globe Theatre in London, drama as a major form of literature flourished in England. The main practitioners of this form in 16th and 17th century are Ben Jonson, Shakespeare and Christopher Marlowe. The plays of this period were written on the themes like ancient history and Greek and Roman mythology, and contemporary socio-political issues.

Modern Drama

Henrik Ibsen and Bertolt Brecht dominate the modern drama of 19th and 20th Century respectively. Ibsen started a new kind of drama by making an ordinary housewife as the heroine of his play, 'A Doll's House'. Anton Chekhov, Eugene O'Neill, Luigi Pirandello, Samuel Beckett, Harold Pinter, John Osborne and George Bernard Shaw are the important dramatists of this period.

Indian Classical Drama

Indian Classical drama originated from the Rig-Veda. The plots of these plays were based on the stories taken from the great Sanskrit epics, *The Ramayana* and *The Mahabharata*. Our ancient writer, Bharata penned the theory of writing a play in his book '*Natya Shastra*'. Bhasa, Kalidasa, Sudraka, Asvaghosa and Harsha are the famous Sanskrit playwrights.

MAJOR FORMS OF DRAMA

1. Miracles & Mystery Plays, Morality Plays and Interludes
2. Heroic, Revenge, Shakespearean & Sentimental Tragedies & Melodramas
3. Comedies
   - Classical Comedies
   - Tragi-Comedies
   - Romantic Comedies
   - Comedy of Humour
   - Comedy of Manners
   - The Farce
   - The Masque
4. The Poetic Play
5. The Dramatic Monologue
6. The Problem Play
7. The One-Act Play

MIRACLE & MYSTERY PLAYS, MORALITY PLAYS AND INTERLUDES

These are all types of late-medieval drama, written in a variety of verse forms.

Miracle & Mystery Plays

The miracle play had as its subject either a story from the Bible, or else the life and martyrdom of a saint. In the usage of some historians, however, "miracle play" denotes only dramas based on saints' lives, and the term mystery play is applied to dramas based on the Bible.

"Mystery" is used in the archaic sense (probably derived from the Latin *ministerium*, "work," "occupation") of the "trade" conducted by each of the medieval guilds which sponsored these plays.

The plays representing biblical narratives originated within the church in about the tenth century, in dramatizations of brief parts of the Latin liturgical service, called tropes, especially the "*Quem quaeritis*" ("Whom are you seeking") trope portraying the visit of the three Marys to the tomb of Christ. Gradually these evolved into complete plays which were written in English instead of in Latin, produced under the auspices of the various trade guilds, and acted on stages set outside the church. The miracle plays written in England are unknown authorship. In the fourteenth century there developed in cities such as York and Chester the practice, on the feast of Corpus Christi (sixty days after Easter), of putting on great "cycles" of such plays, representing crucial events in the biblical history of mankind from the Creation and Fall of man, through the Nativity, Crucifixion, and Resurrection of Christ, to the Last Judgement. The precise way that the plays were staged is a matter of scholarly debate, but it is widely agreed that each scene was played on a separate "pageant wagon" which was drawn, in sequence, to one after another fixed station in a city, at each of which some parts of the cycle were enacted. The biblical texts were greatly expanded in these plays, and the unknown authors added scenes, comic as well as serious, of their own invention. For examples of the variety, vitality, and power of these dramas, see the Wakefield "Noah" and "Second Shepherd's Play," and the Brome "Abraham and Isaac."

Morality Plays

Morality plays were dramatized *allegories* of a representative Christian life in the plot form of a quest for salvation, in which the crucial events are temptations, sinning, and the climactic confrontation with death. The usual protagonist represents Mankind, or Everyman; among the other characters are personifications of virtues, vices, and Death, as well as angles and demons who contest for the prize of the soul of Mankind. A character known as the Vice often played the role of the tempter in a fashion both sinister and comic; he is regarded by some literary historians as a precursor both of the cynical, ironic villain and of some of the comic figures in Elizabethan drama, including Shakespeare's *Falstaff*. The best-known morality play is the fifteenth-century *Everyman*, which is still given an occasional performance; other notable examples, written in the same century, are *The Castle of Perseverance and Mankind.*

Interludes

Interlude (Latin, "between the play") is a term applied to a variety of short stage entertainments, such as secular farces and witty dialogues with a religious or political point. In the late fifteenth and early sixteenth centuries, these little dramas were performed by bands of professional actors; it is believed that they were often put on between the courses of a feast or between the acts of a longer play. Among the better-known interludes are John Heywood's farces of the first half of the sixteenth century, especially The Four PP (that is, the Palmer, the Pardoner, the 'Pothecary, and the Peddler, who engage in a lying contest), and *Johan the Husband, Tyb His Wife, and Sir John the Priest*.

Until the middle of the twentieth century, concern with medieval drama was scholarly rather than critical. Since that time a number of studies have dealt with the relationships of the texts to the religious and secular culture of medieval Europe, and have stressed the artistic excellence and power of the plays themselves.

THE TRAGEDY

The history of drama shows that tragedy originated in religious festival of the Greek God, Dionysus in 6th century B.C. Etymologically the word 'tragedy' is derived from Greek word 'tragodi' meaning 'a goat song' It came to be used for plays probably because of the practice of sacrificing a goat during the festival of Dionysus. The other reason may be that the winner of the dramatic contest was given a goat as the award. To participate in the dramatic contest, the contestants were required to present a tetralogy of plays consisting of three tragedies and a satyr play. In ancient Greek literature the concept of tragedy is different from the modern concept. The modern tragedy is usually considered to as a play with unhappy ending. However, many of the Greek tragedies end on a happy note.

Tragedy is defined as "the imitation of an action, serious, complete and of a certain magnitude, in a language beautified in different parts with different kinds of embellishment, through action and not narration, and through scenes of pity and fear bringing about the catharsis of these or such like emotions".

Plato considers 'imitation' to be an act of mimicry. But Aristotle has given a new meaning to this term. For him imitation does not mean servile copying but an imaginative recreation. Aristotle says that imitation is the basic principle of all fine arts. Tragedy is distinguished from other fine arts according to the object, medium and manner of imitation. On the basis of objects of imitation, tragedy is distinguished from comedy. Tragedy imitates serious actions whereas comedy imitates the non-serious. So far as the medium of imitation is concerned, tragedy is distinguished from the lyric, as tragedy uses several kinds of embellishments. Tragedy is differentiated from epic on the basis of its manner of imitation, as tragedy represents through action whereas epic narrates.

Aristotle has used the term 'magnitude' for the length of the action of a tragedy. In this respect, usually the tragedy is compared with the human body. As too short or too tall human body does not look beautiful, similarly, too short or too long tragedy is not good. As a tragedy is performed on the stage within two or three hours, the dramatic action should not be too long as the audience will forget about the beginning before the dramatic action reaches to its end. It should not also be too short as it would not allow the writer to develop the essential aspects of the plot and characters.

Any dramatic action must have a beginning, middle and an end. A good beginning is the one which is not dependent on any of the previous situation and from which further action flows out. A good middle arises out of the events which have gone before and leads the action towards its logical and convincing conclusion. A good end is the natural outcome of whatever has gone before without leading the action any further.

The function of tragedy, like any other work of literature, is to 'delight' or to 'please'. While speaking about the function of a tragedy, Aristotle has used the term 'catharses'. But Aristotle has not defined 'catharsis' and so there are endless debates on the exact meaning of the term. Some scholars consider that 'catharsis' means purgation. According to the theory of purgation, the spectators in the theatre are relieved or cleansed or purged of the harmful emotions of pity and fear. According to the other group of scholars Catharsis is the resolution of dramatic tension, within the plot. It means in his play, the dramatist represents the incidents which arouse the emotions of pity and fear for the fate of the protagonist. During the course of the action, the dramatist resolves the conflicts which help him to take the action to its logical conclusion along with creating the emotions of pity and fear.

TYPES OF TRAGEDY

1. Heroic Tragedy
2. Revenge Tragedy
3. Shakespearean Tragedy
4. Sentimental Tragedy
5. Melodrama

Heroic Tragedy

The Heroic Tragedy is also known as the Restoration Tragedy. The influence of French romance and drama produced its first important result in the form of the heroic play.

The Heroic Tragedy is artificial. Its emotions are unreal. It mainly deals with conflict between love and honour.

John Dryden was the principal writer of the Heroic Tragedy. His famous tragedies are *Tyannic Love, Conquest of Granada* and *All for Love.* In Dryden's heroic plays we find a hero of superhuman powers and with superhuman ideals; there is a heroine of unsurpassed beauty and constancy; there is an inner conflict in the minds of several characters between love and honour; and there is a striving story of fighting and martial enthusiasm, filled with intense dramatic interest. *All For Love* is the finest tragedy of this period.

Another playwright was Thomas Otway. He wrote *Alcibiades, Don Carlos, The Orphan* and *Venice Preserved.*

Revenge Tragedy

The Revenge Tragedy genre of English literature generally refers to a body of dramatic works written from the mid-1580s to the early 1640s, from the Elizabethan to the Caroline period. Typically, these works feature such themes and devices as a wronged revenge-seeker, ghosts, madness, delay, sinister intrigue, a play-within-the-play, torture, multiple murders, and the realistic depiction of bloody violence on stage. Nearly all of the major playwrights of the time contributed to this class of drama, including Thomas Kyd, William Shakespeare, John Marston, George Chapman, Cyril Tourneur, Thomas Middleton, John Webster, James Shirley, and John Ford. Most literary scholars have credited Kyd with initiating the dramatic archetype with his *The Spanish Tragedy* (1585–90) and the so-called *Ur-Hamlet*—a drama no longer extant but which is believed to have been written before 1589, and upon which Shakespeare likely based his great tragedy—and have credited Shakespeare with bringing the genre to its artistic maturity with *Hamlet* (c. 1600-01). Critics have maintained that revenge tragedy was a markedly dynamic genre, observing that while Kyd invented the basic formula, his successors added ingenious new layers of dramatic suspense, characterization, symbolism, and ideological representation to the theatrical form.

Shakespearean Tragedy

Shakespeare wrote tragedies from the beginning of his career. One of his earliest plays was the Roman tragedy *Titus Andronicus*, which he followed a few years later with *Romeo and Juliet.* However, his most admired tragedies were written in a seven-year period between 1601 and 1608. These includes his four major tragedies *Hamlet, Othello, King Lear* and *Macbeth*, along with *Antony & Cleopatra, Coriolanus, Cymbeline, Julius Caesar* and the lesser-known *Timon of Athens* and *Troilus* and *Cressida.*

Shakespearean Tragedy is fundamentally serious, involving the downfall of a heroic figure. The themes are lofty: passion *(Romeo and Juliet)*, revenge *(Hamlet)*, ambition *(Macbeth)* and jealousy *(Othello)*.

Unique elements of tragedy are the tragic hero who is an articulate, social authority, someone who is "important" within his society, this hero has at least one weakness or fault—a tragic flaw—which during the course of the drama grows until it overcomes his virtues and leads to his downfall and the destruction of his world; and chorus borrowed from Greek tragedy in which dancers/singers appear at intervals within the play to comment on the action—express objective judgement on the proceedings.

Sentimental Tragedy

While sentiment, in its modern sense, may be found in all forms of drama and theatre, Sentimental Drama was a specifically 18th century European form in which, as Oliver Goldsmith put it, "the virtues of private life are exhibited, rather than the vices exposed". "Sentiment" at this period meant "feeling" or "sensibility". While many of the plays were nominally comic, the characters tended to be dull and priggish, the plots bathetic and the language stilted. Despite this, it was popular with the rising middle-class audience, especially in Germany, France and Britain, because it tended to treat them seriously in ways which neither comedy nor tragedy did. For all its dramatic ineptness (at least from today's perspective) it is important in theatre-historical terms, as it marks an important stage in the development of serious prose drama.

In the English language, the most famous and most successful tragedies are those by William Shakespeare and his Elizabethan contemporaries.

A contemporary of Shakespeare, Christopher Marlowe, also wrote examples of tragedy in English, notably:

The Tragical History of Doctor Faustus; and *Tamburlaine*

John Webster also wrote famous plays of the genre: *The Duchess of Malfi* and *The White Devil*.

The Melodrama

Though the term "melodrama" is sometimes applied to the dramatic productions of a certain period, it also often designates a certain kind of literary structure.

Melodrama is the fantasy of a world that operates according to our heart's desires in contrast to the other formula types that are fantasies of particular actions or states of being that counter some of our deepest fears or concentrate on particular wishes for victory or love or knowledge. Therefore, melodrama can contain all the other fantasies and often does. In fact, its chief characteristic is the combination of a number of actions and settings in order to build up the sense of a whole world bearing out the audience's traditional patterns of right and wrong, good and evil.

One thing possessed in common by these otherwise very different sorts of stories is the quality that has traditionally been understood as the hallmark of melodrama: the drama of intensified effects (i.e., music, "melos") added to the play to increase its emotional power and intensify its hold on the audience. Therefore, the idea of melodrama has come to be associated with violence and sensationalism— "the plot revolves around malevolent intrigue and violent action, while credibility both of character and plot is sacrificed for violent effect and emotional opportunism." This is undoubtedly one major characteristic of melodrama, but the quest for intensified narrative or dramatic effects is characteristic of the entire range of formulaic types. Particular formulas come into existence and flourish at least in part because they invent heightened narrative or dramatic patterns. In this sense all formulaic stories are melodramatic, and we might look at the various formulaic types—adventure, romance, and mystery—as simply specialized forms of melodrama. Indeed, many of the modern specialized formulas such as the classical detective story, the spy story, the hard-boiled detective story, and the gothic romance did evolve historically from the broader melodramatic forms of the early nineteenth century.

The specific formulas that depend on the basic moral fantasy of melodrama are many and various. Some of the more important contemporary examples are the best-selling panoramic social novel such as those written by Irving Wallace, Harold Robbins, and Jacqueline Susann, the historical spectacle such as *Gone with the Wind,* the soap opera, the gangster saga, the professional drama such as the doctor, lawyer, or teacher story, and many others. Though extremely various in the cultural materials they employ, all these formulas are shaped by the basic qualities of melodrama: the heightening of feeling and moral conflict and multiple lines of action that work together to create a sense of the rightness of the world order.

Some important examples of melodramas are:

John Fletcher's *The Maid's Tragedy;* John Webster's *The White Devil;* John Ford's *The Broken Heart;* Thomas Heywood's *A Woman Killed with Kindness;* Francis Beaumont's *A King and No King*..

THE COMEDY

Comedy may be considered to be a representation of the character of a lower type. Here 'lower' means 'ridiculous.' By presenting the character in a ridiculous manner, the writer of a comedy aims at producing laughter. Though the genre of comedy is practiced since the ancient times with the practitioners like Aristophanes and Plautus, the scholars have not paid enough attention towards the serious study of its nature and function. While speaking about the function of comedy, George Meredith says that comedy appeals to the intelligence pure and simple and aims not at our ribs or armpits but at our heads. It means, it is the business of a comedy writer to look on what ails the world. He observes his environment minutely and fids out its follies and exposes them. But while exposing those follies, the purpose of the writer is to 'correct' or 'reform' those follies. Some scholars are of the opinion that the function of a comedy is not 'to reform' or 'to correct' the follies of the world bur to provide light-hearted mirth. But while creating mirth, the comedian encourages the audience to laugh with not laugh at the follies of the world. Such kind of play is purely meant for the entertainment of the audience.

Comedies are of following types:

1. Classical Comedies
2. Tragi-Comedies
3. Romantic Comedies
4. Comedy of Humour
5. Comedy of Manners
6. The Farce
7. The Masque

The Classical Comedy

This type of comedy is written as per the rules laid down by the ancient Greek and Roman masters. The function of such a comedy is 'corrective' or 'reformative'. In this comedy some human folly is exposed and ridiculed. It follows the rules of three unities—unity of time, place and action. The writer of this comedy strictly avoids the mingling of comic with tragic.

The Tragi-Comedy

In understanding about tragi-comedy, one finds oneself in the position of the proverbial blind philosophers attempting to identify an elephant. The individual who gets hold of its trunk thinks it is a snake, he who grasps its tail supposes it a rope, while she who clasps one of its legs believes it to be a tree. A.E. Housman commented in the essay "the legitimate meanings of the word poetry were themselves so many as to embarrass the discussion of its nature." The same is true to a lesser degree of the word *tragi-comedy*. The nature of tragicomedy is difficult to define because its name has been used so variously since Plautus first coined the term as a joke in his *Amphitryon* and because the dramatic genre tragi-comedy can comprise so many different modes (romantic, satiric, pastoral, melodramatic, and so on, as well as, indispensably, tragic and comic).

This play is a combination of the elements of both the comedy and the tragedy. Naturally, the play ends on a happy note for some characters and on a sad note for the others. Shakespeare is a famous practitioner of this kind of play. Though Aristotle had opposed the mingling of the tragic with the comic, scholars like John Dryden and Dr. Samuel Johnson have defended this type of play by saying that it is nearer to the human life. These critics argue that as the life itself is a combination of happy and sad events there is no harm in combining them in plays. Shakespeare's well-known tragi-comedies are *The Winter's Tale, The Merchant of Venice* and *The Tempest*.

The study of genre, despite recurring critical objections, continues to be indispensable to the study of drama in particular. Genre is not simply a matter of definition or classification. Rather, genre communicates; genre enables comprehension and conditions response. As Tzvetan Todorov explains, "It is because genres exist as an institution that they function as 'horizons of expectation' for readers and as 'models of writing' for authors." And Marco De Marinis, writing of performance, similarly observes, "By supplying the receiver with intertextual schemas and systems of expectation, *genre* (in its widely accepted analytical and descriptive meaning as a 'class of texts with specific co-textual and/or contextual traits in common') plays a crucial role in the process of textual comprehension and interpretation."

Dramatic genres in particular are modes of perception, conveying attitudes to human experience, as much as they are formal categories.

Although tragi-comedy is an especially slippery genre, there is actually a good deal of critical agreement (among those critics who recognize it as a genre at all) as to which plays constitute its major achievements. Differences of opinion arise inevitably and properly at the edges of the genre. The familiar. central examples of the genre range from *Il Pastor Fido, The Malcontent, Measure for Measure, The Winter's Tale, A King and No King,* and *A Wife for a Month* to *The Wild Duck, The Cherry Orchard, The Playboy of the Western World, The Killer, Waiting for Godot, and No Man's Land.* Within each of these two groups, however, the plays seem in many respects quite unlike one another, and the modern tragi-comedies appear superficially to have little in common with those written in the sixteenth and early seventeenth centuries.

The Romantic Comedy

Romantic comedy is a popular genre that depicts burgeoning romance in human terms, and focuses on the foibles of those who are falling in love.

Comedy as a whole has rarely been seen as being as critically respectable as other genres; perhaps it is rather a self-defeating paradox to ask for it to be taken seriously. Even Shakespeare's comedies seem to be critically overshadowed by the tragedies, perhaps diminished by the foregrounding of characters who are not heroic or noble, and themes that concern issues that can be found in everyday life, such as love and relationships, rather than elemental issues of life, death, good and evil. The most respected romcoms are those associated with artistic figures that are respected as auteurs.

Romantic comedy has proved to be one of the most enduring genres. It has certainly undergone some ebbs and flows in its popularity, but, as with all the major genres, it proves perennially resilient. Audiences still enjoy the blueprint of the romantic comedy, with all its traditional ingredients. Every year sees the release of new romantic comedies, which are strongly in the mould of the earliest examples in history. We want to see the same characters, the same situations, the same narrative trajectory, the same settings and dialogue, with new stars that speak to new generations, yet tell the same story.

Romantic comedy does not follow the rules of writing a comedy laid down by the ancient classical writers. The writer freely mingles the comic with the tragic. The unities of time, place and action are modified as per the requirements of the plot. The aim of such a comedy is 'to produce innocent, good-natured laughter, thereby entertaining the audience without trying to teach anything.

Shakespearean Comedy

Shakespeare is a great writer of comedies. His comedies are called romantic or sunny comedies. With the help of his creative imagination, Shakespeare creates a brilliant world of romance which is far away from the drab realities of the everyday life. These comedies are usually set in some distant, far-off places, where the inhabitants have no other business but that of love-making. The lovers of a Shakespearean comedy fall in love at first sight and get married at the end. But the course of their love is always full of difficulties. There are made a lot of misunderstandings, family feuds, tears and sighs. Shakespeare forces his lovers to face these difficulties in order to test their love for each other. But ultimately, these lovers are helped to overcome these difficulties but the intervention of Goddess Fortune. Then comes the Goddess

Marriage who unites the lovers in the bond of marriage followed by music, dance and merry-making.

The Comedy of Humours

A type of comedy developed by Ben Jonson, the Elizabethan playwright, based on the ancient physiological theory of the "four humours" that was still current in Jonson's time. The humours were held to be the four primary fluids—blood, phlegm, choler (or yellow bile), and melancholy (or black bile)—whose "temperament" (mixture) was held to determine a person's both physical condition and type of character. An imbalance of one or another humour in a temperament was said to produce four kinds of disposition, whose names have survived the underlying theory: sanguine (from the Latin "sanguis," blood), phlegmatic, choleric, and melancholic. In Jonshon's comedy of humours each of the major characters has a preponderant humour that gives him a characteristic distortion or eccentricity of disposition. Jonson expounds his theory in the "induction" to his play *Every Man in His Humour* (1598) and exemplifies the mode in his later comedies; often he identifies the ruling disposition of a humours character by his or her name: "Zeal-of-the-land Busy," "Dame Purecraft," "Wellbred." The Jonsonian type of humours character appears in plays by other Elizabethans, and remained influential in the *comedies of manners* by William Wycherley, Sir George Etheredge, William Congreve, and other dramatists of the English Restoration, 1660–1700.

The characters in a Comedy of Humour represent some 'humour'. The actions and behaviour of the characters are governed by some kind of passion. As the characters represent some typical trait, there is a lack of individuality in them. Rather they become stereotypes. Generally, these characters are taken from low life. The purpose of the writer of such a comedy is to satirize the follies of the characters and correct them.

The Comedy of Manners

A kind of comedy representing the complex and sophisticated code of behaviour current in fashionable circles of society, where appearances count for more than true moral character. Its plot usually revolves around intrigues of lust and greed, the self-interested cynicism of the characters being masked by decorous pretence. Unlike satire, the comedy of manners tends to reward its cleverly unscrupulous characters rather than punish their immorality. Its humour relies chiefly upon elegant verbal wit and repartee. In England, the comedy of manners flourished as the dominant form of Restoration comedy in the works of Sir George Etherege, William Wycherley (notably *The Country Wife*, 1675), and William Congreve; it was revived in a more subdued form in the 1770s by Goldsmith and Sheridan, and later by Oscar Wilde. Modern examples of the comedy of manners include Noël Coward's Design for living (1932) and Joe Orton's *Loot* (1965).

The Comedy of Manners is also called Restoration Comedy. It focuses upon the mannerism of the upper classes of the society. The characters of this comedy belong to the upper class. Here the dramatist represents a fashionable men and women, with their manners, love-intrigues, scandals and affectations. These comedies attempt to imitate everything refined. So anything coarse or low is strictly avoided.

The language of such a comedy is very witty and refined. The focus of the dramatist is not on the 'individuality' of the character but on its manners, so the characters become lifeless. This type of comedy was very famous during the Restoration period with the writers like William Congreve, William Wycherley and Oliver Goldsmith practicing it.

The Farce

This was another popular form of theatre in France (and England) in the 19th century. Farce consists of unsubtle physical and verbal comedy. It flourishes in a moral community because it is anarchical, relying on overturning widely accepted values. The chief characteristics of farce are sexual misadventure, flirtation, verbal abuse and comic despair, which frequently lead to instant decisions and spontaneous action.

The most prolific and famous French farce writers were Feydeau (1862–1921) and Labiche (1815–1888). Labiche wrote nearly sixty plays and helped write about 100 others. Not surprisingly, the plays lack originality and concentrate on reworking old jokes. His most famous is *An Italian Straw Hat* (1851).

Feydeau was the originator of bedroom farces, the descendants of which can still be seen occasionally in London today.

Feydeau's middle period plays are the archetype of French farce. The principal characters are Parisian bourgeois, their major driving force is extra-connubial lust, and the basic source of the humour is their ever more desperate attempts to avoid being found out. Although no respectable married woman is ever seduced by her husband's best friend, it is not for want of trying on either side. The plots seem to have been constructed by a mad watchmaker, but the status quo is always restored at the end.

A farce is a comedy that focuses on physical humour. The dramatist aims at creating hilarious laughter by representing absurd characters and situations on the stage. To create his characters and situations, the dramatist makes use of exaggeration and extravagance. Exaggerated characters and situations, improbable coincidences, mistaken identities and miscommunication are the common techniques used by the writers to make his plot more complicated. All these instruments enable the dramatist to entertain his audience in the most direct way.

The Masque

Form of dramatic entertainment popular with the French and English aristocracy of the sixteenth and seventeenth centuries. Developed in Renaissance Italy, the masque was probably an evolution of primitive folk rituals. When adopted by court circles, it became a lavish spectacle, usually based on a mythological theme and involving elaborate costumes and stage machinery. Essentially it was a theatrical performance by a group of disguised guests (hence the name) who, arriving at a banquet, offered the host an entertainment of dances, poetry and music.

The characters in a masque wear some masks on their faces. Initially, a masque was a series of dances, illustrating some story, but afterwards it developed into a play. The writer of a masque chooses his characters and story from mythology. These masques were written to be performed on some private occasions by a limited number of characters. There is abundant use of music, dance, costly costumes and elaborate scenery.

The masque first appeared in the fifteenth century when Lorenzo de' Medici adapted the seasonal revels of the Florentines into sophisticated displays of art and poetry for the delight of his guests. In the French court these displays evolved into the *ballet de cour* and *the mascarade*. A form of the masque was brought to England in 1512 by Henry VIII, who liked to disguise himself as a player and pretend to be an uninvited guest at his own parties. Henry's daughter Elizabeth added the spoken introduction, which, with the inclusion of speeches and elements of court drama, was developed into a unified dramatic performance in the hands of Ben Jonson, who became court poet of the Stuarts in 1603. Until his time the main feature of the masque was the dance and revel, which the audience was invited to join. Under Jonson's influence the masque became a literary form, a dramatic poem of classical scholarship. Jonson also introduced the antimasque, so called because it preceded the main masque and because it included grotesque or comic elements in contrast, yet relevant, to the serious main masque. Jonson's influence was eventually eclipsed by his sometime collaborator and rival Inigo Jones, the architect and scenic designer, to whom theatrical spectacle was more important than literary content. It was Jones who thought of placing the layers on a raised stage and who eventually, by his attention to spectacle rather than content, effected the deterioration of the masque as a dramatic form.

A courtly rather than a popular entertainment, the masque disappeared with the Puritan revolution of the 1640s. When the theatres reopened in 1660, however, scenic designers, playwrights, and actors took their principal inspiration not from the Elizabethan stage but from the masques of the court festivals.

THE POETIC PLAY

Poetic drama is not merely a drama which is written in verse, because prose may also be its effective medium. It is, in fact, a blending of the poetic and dramatic elements in a fruitful union. Here poetry is an integral part of the play, twined with plot, character and their interplay, not an element of isolated beauty or lyricism for its own sake, as is the case with splendid lyricism in some parts of Marlowe's *Dr. Faustus*, for example. At the same time the dramatic elements must be capable of sustaining the poetic grace and intensity. It means its themes and characters should be poetically convinced and should be larger than the average humanity and humdrum monotony of daily life, the passions and emotions permeating them should be naturally productive of the poetic expression, calculated to lift the mind of the spectator above the sphere of our ordinary joys and sorrows and send the penetrating gaze of his inner vision far down below the surface of life to the very springs of human action and human drives. Moreover, drama being so intimately bound up with the stage condition and the historic skill its practitioner must combine mastery over the poetic resources, with a real understanding of the peculiar needs and modes of the dramatic representation in the theatre. The history of the poetic drama in England is littered with the frozen anatomies of poetic plays written by the distinguished poets of the nineteenth century who failed to subordinate poetry to the general dramatic spirit and adapt the plays to the conditions and requirements of the stage.

Poetic drama reached its glorious peak in Elizabethan England when the general conditions of society and richness of language combined with the whole nation's insatiable craving for amusement and edification and the writer's intimacy with the theater to make the stage a national institution. But the glory did not last long and its decline was precipitated by the victory of the puritan fanaticism which sounded its death-knell. When it was revived again in the Restoration era, the conditions had changed and the heroic tragedy in rhyming couplet was simply the fury and the violence of its ghost. A sort of artificial respiration was given to it is the blank-verse tragedies which followed. They, however, failed to sustain its life and with one flash of life in Otway's *Venice Preserved* it gave up the ghost.

The nineteenth century efforts by the great poets were splendid failures on the big commercial stage, for which the writers themselves were partly to blame because they could not rise above the slavish imitation and adaptation of the Elizabethan blank-verse tragedy to re-orient the poetic drama to changed conditions of society and the taste and sensibility of the spectators. This was the condition when the present century opened with the prospect of a great dramatic Renaissance.

THE DRAMATIC MONOLOGUE

In theatre, a monologue (or monolog) is a speech presented by a single character, most often to express their thoughts aloud, though sometimes also to directly address another character or the audience. Monologues are common across the range of dramatic media (plays, films, etc.) as well as in non-dramatic media such as poetry. Monologues share much in common with several other literary devices including soliloquies, apostrophes, and asides. There are, however, distinctions between each of these devices.

One of the most important influences on the development of the dramatic monologue is the Romantic poets. The long, personal lyrics typical of the Romantic period are not dramatic monologues, in the sense that they do not, for the most part, imply a concentrated narrative. However, poems such as William Wordsworth's *Tintern Abbey* and Percy Bysshe Shelley's Mont Blanc, to name two famous examples, offered a model of close psychological observation and philosophical or pseudo-philosophical inquiry described in a specific setting.

The novel and plays have also been important influences on the dramatic monologue, particularly as a means of characterization. Dramatic monologues are a way of expressing the views of a character and offering the audience greater insight into that character's feelings. Dramatic monologues can also be used in novels to tell stories, as in Mary Shelley's Frankenstein, and to implicate the audience in moral judgments, as in Albert Camus' *The Fall* and Mohsin Hamid's *The Reluctant Fundamentalist*.

Monologues are also linked with soliliquys—such as in *Macbeth,* when Lady Macbeth reads a letter to herself and then speaks her thoughts as though she is thinking.

The Victorian Period

The Victorian period represented the high point of the dramatic monologue in English poetry.

Alfred, Lord Tennyson's *Ulysses,* published in 1842, has been called the first true dramatic monologue. After *Ulysses,* Tennyson's most famous efforts in this vein are *Tithonus, The Lotos-Eaters,* and *St. Simon Stylites,* all from the 1842 poems; later monologues appear in other volumes, notably *Idylls of the King*.

Matthew Arnold's *Dover Beach* and Stanzas from the *Grand Chartreuse* are famous, semi-autobiographical monologues. The former, usually regarded as the supreme expression of the growing skepticism of the mid-Victorian period, was published along with the later in 1867's *New Poems*.

Robert Browning is usually credited with perfecting the form; certainly, Browning is the poet who, above all, produced his finest and most famous work in this form. While *My Last Duchess* is the most famous of his monologues, the form dominated his writing career. Fra Lippo Lippi, Caliban upon Setebos, Soliloquy of the Spanish Cloister and Porphyria's Lover, as well as the other poems in *Men and Women* are just a handful of Browning's monologues.

Other Victorian poets also used the form. Dante Gabriel Rossetti wrote several, including *Jenny* and *The Blessed Damozel;* Christina Rossetti wrote a number, including *The Convent Threshold.* Algernon Charles Swinburne's *Hymn to Proserpine* has been called a dramatic monologue vaguely reminiscent of Browning's work.

THE PROBLEM PLAY

The "problem play" idea has sometimes helpfully, sometimes dubiously informed discussion of Shakespeare's plays, and though, along with much genre criticism, it has gone out of fashion now, it has figured periodically in the scholarship that helps us understand how the plays work technically. Problem play as a term has aroused debate because in some ways it may seem to solve nothing: it leaves us with only a question about a play's genre, not with even a tentative guideline for reading such as we get from calling a work comedy or tragedy.

As Harold Goddard wrote, we can find "nothing to indicate that Shakespeare's imagination ever allowed itself to be shackled by such prescriptions or definitions"; one of the few points that caused audiences of his own time to question his skills, his freedom with respect to Classical "rules" or transgressing genre expectations, allowed him to create plays that beg irresolution and thus continued meditation from his audiences.

The term problem play comes from F.S. Boas in Shakespeare and His Predecessors in 1896 (printed in the U.S. in New York by Charles Scribner's Sons, 1900): Boas used it to label those plays (such as *Measure for Measure, All's Well That Ends Well,* and *The Merchant of Venice*) that foreground perhaps unsolvable moral problems. More recently critics have used the term to indicate plays that defy easy categorization by genre, or literary type. Genre, a term that applies largely to the form and partly to the content of an artistic work (as in comedy, tragedy, epic, or novel), has much to do with how we read or view a work: if we attend a comedy or tragedy, we go with expectations about how we will find the work presented and how it will end. So criticism had already problematized problem play itself, since different critics have used it with different notions in mind. But it remains useful, because it directs our attention to an immediate interpretive difficulty that we experience as soon as we study particular plays. The idea of the problem play applies to nearly all of Shakespeare's plays: what we call them does make a difference in how we read and interpret and play them, since labels (like titles) guide audience expectations and invoke interpretive strategies.

THE ONE-ACT PLAY

In October 1909, when Strindberg wrote a brief preface to then unpublished *Författaren* (The Author), the fourth volume of his autobiography *Tjänstekvinnans son* (1886), he listed among his most important (viktigaste) works the one-act plays of the early 1890s as "one-actors out of cynical life." The item included The First Warning, Debit and Credit, Facing Death, Mother Love, Playing with Fire, and The Bond. He might just as well have included three one-act plays from the late 1880s: *The Stronger, Pariah,* and *Simoon.* All nine are short, stageworthy one-act plays; all were designed for production in experimental theaters; and all are interpretations of human situations from a cynical point of view.

Strindberg's hope of having a theater in which his plays would be produced seemed to have a chance of realization in the late 1880s in Copenhagen but did not materialize until the Intimate Theater opened in Stockholm in 1907. He had written his great plays *The Father* (1887), *Lady Julie* (1888), and *Creditors* (1888)—deliberately as what might very well be segments of actual life with increasing emphasis on universal themes, avoidance of distracting factors such as intermissions, and simplification of staging. The one-act plays listed above are essentially further extensions of his "attempts to transform drama into a form suitable for the time". They deal, moreover, with universal and timeless themes. The very brevity of these plays precludes examination in appreciable depth as in the longer plays of 1887 and 1888, but they have enough detail to provide audience and reader with material for creative participation and involvement. In each there is enough irritating matter to arouse reaction and to stimulate discussion.

The human situations presented are surely typical: people's willingness to claim credit for a fellow human being's success, a mother's manipulation of her daughter's life, a wife's indifference to her mate except when others obviously want him, denigration of a mate for one's own purposes, indifference to and rationalization of one's sins, playing with one's own and other's emotions, and the unhesitating destruction of a fellow human being at least partly in the name of religion.

PROSE

Prose or Non-Fiction writing that presents and explains ideas or that tells about real people, places, objects, or events. It is an account or representation of a subject which is presented as fact. This presentation may be accurate or not; that is, it can give either a true or a false account of the subject in question. However, it is generally assumed that the authors of such accounts believe them to be truthful at the time of their composition. Autobiographies, biographies, essays, reports, letters, memos, and newspaper articles are all types of non-fiction.

Characteristics of Prose

Works of Prose differ from works of fiction in several ways.

- The people, events, places, and ideas presented in Prose are real, not invented.
- Prose is narrated by an author who is a real person.
- It presents facts, describes true-life experience, or discusses ideas.
- Prose is written for a specific audience, or group of readers. In addition, it addresses a clear purpose, or reason for writing. The audience and purpose influence the type of information a writer includes.
- Tone, that is author's attitude toward the subject or reader, is displayed through the writer's word choice and style.

The writer contributes more than informal to non-fiction.

- Style is the particular way in which a writer uses language. Style reflects an author's personality. Factors that contribute to an author's style include level of formality, use of figurative language, diction or word choice, sentence patterns, and methods of organization.

- Tone is the author's attitude toward both the subject and readers or listeners. In conversations, you can hear a speaker's tone in the way words and phrases are spoken. When reading, you can "hear" tone in an author's choice of words and details. The tone of a literary work can often be described with a single word such as: pompous, playful, serious, personal, sarcastic, or friendly.
- Perspective is the viewpoint or opinion an author expresses about the subject, either directly or indirectly. Bias occurs when a writer makes a one-sided presentation (for example, by ignoring relevant facts or by using emotional language that unfairly sways readers' or listeners' feelings).
- Purpose is the author's reason for writing. Common purposes are to inform, to persuade, to honour, to entertain, to explain, and to warn.

Types of Prose

There are four main types, or modes, of Prose that are defined by their purposes.

- Narrative Prose tells stories of real-life events. Examples include autobiographies and memoirs. Some narrative Prose is reflective writing, which shares the writer's thoughts and feelings about a personal experience, an idea, or a concern. Examples include reflective essays, personal essays, and journals.
- Expository Prose informs or explains. Examples include analytical essays and research reports.
- Persuasive Prose presents reasons and evidence to convince the reader to act or think in a certain way. Examples include editorials and political speeches.
- Descriptive Prose uses details related to the senses to create mental images for the reader. Examples include character sketches and scientific observations.

MAJOR FORMS OF PROSE

The following are the Major Forms of Prose :

1. Long Prose-Works
2. The Essay
3. The Periodical Journals
4. The Biography
5. The Autobiography
6. The Memoirs

LONG PROSE-WORKS

In its ordinary and practical sense, Prose is the sustained use of language as we ordinary speak it. Prose is different from verse in the sense that it is not split up into meter or stanza forms like the verse. However, the lack of meter does not mean that prose has no art or aesthetic sense. The writing of distinguished prose has as much art as the writing of distinguished verse. In all literatures, written prose developed much later than written verse. Good prose has high aesthetic value, and it can fully make use of all figures of speech. Good prose can also have high poetic cadence too, as the prose of the Bible.

Many forms of literature are normally written in prose only. They include long social, religious, scientific, or metaphysical treatises, essays, prose romances, novels, short stories, biographies, autobiographies, memoirs, travelogues, adventures and literary criticism.

Many great authors wrote long prose-works even before the Age of Chaucer. They included long religious, metaphysical, political, and biographical treatises and prose-romances. The trend has come down ever since to the present day.

Some Examples of the great prose-works are:

Chaucer's : *The Treatise on the Astrolabe,*

Wyclif's : *The Bible,*

and Walter Pater's : *Renaissance*

THE ESSAY

An essay is generally a short piece of writing written from an author's personal point of view, but the definition is vague, overlapping with those of an article, a pamphlet and a short story.

Essays can consist of a number of elements, including: literary criticism, political manifestos, learned arguments, observations of daily life, recollections, and reflections of the author. Almost all modern essays are written in prose, but works in verse have been dubbed essays (e.g. Alexander Pope's *An Essay on Criticism* and *An Essay on Man*). While brevity usually defines an essay, voluminous works like John Locke's *An Essay Concerning Human Understanding* and Thomas Malthus's *An Essay on the Principle of Population* are counter examples.

THE PERIODICAL JOURNALS

A journal has several related meanings: a daily record of events or business; a private journal is usually referred to as a diary, a newspaper or other periodical, in the literal sense of one published each day many publications issued at stated intervals, such as magazines, or scholarly journals, academic journals, or the record of the transactions of a society, are often called journals. Although journal is sometimes used as a synonym for "magazine" in academic use, a journal refers to a serious, scholarly publication that is peer-reviewed. A non-scholarly magazine written for an educated audience about an industry or an area of professional activity is usually called a professional magazine.

The word "journalist", for one whose business is writing for the public press and nowadays also other media, has been in use since the end of the 17th century.

THE BIOGRAPHY

A biography or simply bio is a detailed description or account of a person's life. It entails more than basic facts like education, work, relationships, and death—a biography also portrays a subject's experience of these events. Unlike a profile or curriculum vitae (résumé), a biography presents a subject's life story, highlighting various aspects of his or her life, including intimate details of experience, and may include an analysis of the subject's personality.

Biographical works are usually non-fiction, but fiction can also be used to portray a person's life. One in-depth form of biographical coverage is called legacy writing. Works in diverse media—from literature to film—form the genre known as biography.

An authorized biography is written with the permission, cooperation, and at times, participation of a subject or a subject's heirs.

THE AUTOBIOGRAPHY

An autobiography is a written account of the life of a person written by that person. An autobiography is written by the person themselves or sometimes with the assistance of a collaborator or ghostwriter.

THE MEMOIRS

Memoir (from French: *mémoire: memoria*, meaning memory or reminiscence), is a literary non-fiction genre. More specifically, it is a collection of memories that an individual writes about moments or events, both public or private that took place in the author's life. The assertions made in the work are understood to be factual. While memoir has historically been defined as a subcategory of autobiography since the late 20th century, the genre is differentiated in form, presenting a narrowed focus. Like most autobiographies, memoirs are written from the first-person point of view. An autobiography tells the story of a life, while memoir tells a story from a life, such as touchstone events and turning points from the author's life. The author of a memoir may be referred to as a memoirist.

POETRY

A poem is a literary composition that is given intensity by particular attention to diction (sometimes involving rhyme), rhythm, and imagery. Poems, collectively are called poetry.

As writing poetry is an art, reading poetry also is an art. We cannot enjoy reading anything without understanding it. And understanding poetry requires a special taste and aesthetic sense. Poetry is the language of heart. It flows from heart to heart.

MAJOR FORMS OF POETRY

Poetry and its Major Forms are these :

1. The Epic
2. The Mock Epic
3. The Sonnet
4. The Ode
5. The Lyric
6. The Idyll
7. The Pastoral
8. The Elegy
9. The Pastoral Elegy
10. The Ballad
11. The Satire

THE EPIC

An epic (from the Ancient Greek adjective "word, story, poem" is a lengthy narrative poem, ordinarily concerning a serious subject containing details of heroic deeds and events significant to a culture or nation. Oral poetry may qualify as an epic, and Albert Lord and Milman Parry have argued that classical epics were fundamentally an oral poetic form. Nonetheless, epics have been written down at least since the works of Virgil, Dante Alighieri, and John Milton. Many probably would not have survived if not written down. The first epics are known as primary, or original, epics. One such epic is the Old English story Beowulf. Epics that attempt to imitate these like Milton's *Paradise Lost* are known as literary, or secondary, epics. Another type of epic poetry is epyllion (plural: epyllia), which is a brief narrative poem with a romantic or mythological theme. The term, which means 'little epic', came into use in the nineteenth century. It refers primarily to the erudite, shorter hexameter poems of the Hellenistic period and the similar works composed at Rome from the age of the neoterics; to a lesser degree, the term incl· 'es some poems of the English Renaissance, particularly those influenced by Ovid. The most famous example of classical epyllion is perhaps *Catullus 64.*

In the East, the most famous works of epic poetry are the *Ramayana* and *Mahabharata*, with the *Iliad* and the *Odyssey*, which form part of the Western canon, fulfilling the same function in the Western world.

Oral epics or world folk epics

The first epics were products of preliterate societies and oral poetic traditions. In these traditions, poetry is transmitted to the audience and from performer to performer by purely oral means.

Early twentieth-century study of living oral epic traditions in the Balkans by Milman Parry and Albert Lord demonstrated the paratactic model used for composing these poems. What they demonstrated was that oral epics tend to be constructed in short episodes, each of equal status, interest and importance. This facilitates memorization, as the poet is recalling each episode in turn and using the completed episodes to recreate the entire epic as he performs it.

THE MOCK EPIC

A poem which deals with slight and trivial subjects but employs the elevated and dignified conventions of epic poetry. Thus, such a poem becomes a satire, a mockery, a burlesque at the inconsistency of the subject to its representation. The characteristic conventions of the epic poetry, such as invocations, epic similes, grand and elevated language, battles and supernatural machinery, are comically used in mock-epic, which make the trivial subject ridiculous. A few well-known examples are Alexander Pope's *Rape of the Lock*, Jonathan Swift's *Battle of the Books*, Pope's *The Dunciad*, Chaucer's *The Nun's Priest's Tale* and Boileau's" *Le Lutrin* (French).

THE SONNET

A sonnet is a form of poetry that originated in Europe, mainly Italy: the Sicilian poet Giacomo da Lentini is credited with its invention. They commonly contain 14 lines. The term "sonnet" derives only from the Occitan word *sonet* and the Italian word *sonetto*, both meaning "little song" or "little sound". By the thirteenth century, it signified a poem of fourteen lines that follows a strict rhyme scheme and specific structure. Conventions associated with the sonnet have evolved over its history. Writers of sonnets are sometimes called "sonneteers," although the term can be used derisively. One of the best-known sonnet writers is William Shakespeare, who wrote 154 of them (not including those that appear in his plays). A Shakespearean, or English sonnet consists of 14 lines, each line containing ten syllables and written in iambic pentameter, in which a pattern of an unstressed syllable followed by a stressed syllable is repeated five times. The rhyme scheme in a Shakespearean sonnet is a-b-a-b, c-d-c-d, e-f-e-f, g-g; the last two lines are a rhyming couplet.

Traditionally, English poets employ iambic pentameter when writing sonnets, but not all English sonnets have the same metrical structure: the first sonnet in Sir Philip Sidney's sequence *Astrophel and Stella*, for example, has 12 syllables: it is iambic hexameters, albeit with a turned first foot in several lines. In the Romance languages, the hendecasyllable and Alexandrine are the most widely used metres.

THE ODE

Ode (from the Ancient Greek is a type of lyrical verse. A classic ode is structured in three major parts: the strophe, the antistrophe, and the epode. Different forms such as the homostrophic ode and the irregular ode also exist. It is an elaborately structured poem praising or glorifying an event or individual, describing nature intellectually as well as emotionally.

Greek odes were originally poetic pieces accompanied by symphonic orchestras. As time passed on, they gradually became known as personal lyrical compositions whether sung (with or without musical instruments) or merely recited (always with accompaniment). For some, the primary instrument of choice was either the aulos or the lyre (the latter of which was the most revered instrument to the Ancient Greeks). The written ode, as it was practiced by the Romans, returned to the lyrical form of the Lesbian lyricists.

There are three typical forms of odes: the Pindaric, Horatian, and irregular. Pindaric odes follow the form and style of Pindar. Horatian odes follow conventions of Horace; the odes of Horace deliberately imitated the Greek lyricists such as Alcaeus and Anacreon. Odes by Catullus, as well as other poetry of Catullus, was particularly inspired by Sappho. Irregular odes are rhyming, but they do not employ the three-part form of the Pindaric ode nor the two- or four-line stanza of the Horatian ode.

English ode

An ode is typically a lyrical verse written in praise of, or dedicated to someone or something which captures the poet's interest or serves as an inspiration for the ode.

The initial model for English odes was Horace, who used the form to write meditative lyrics on various themes. The earliest odes in the English language, using the word in its strict form, were the Epithalamium and Prothalamium of Edmund Spenser.

In the 17th century the most important original odes in English are those of Abraham Cowley and Andrew Marvell. Marvell, in his Horatian Ode upon Cromwell's Return from Ireland uses a regular form (two four-foot lines followed by two three-foot lines) modelled on Horace, while Cowley wrote *"Pindarique"* odes which had irregular patterns of line lengths and rhyme schemes, though they were iambic. The principle of Cowley's *Pindariques* was based on a misunderstanding of Pindar's metrical practice but was widely imitated nonetheless, with notable success by John Dryden. With Pindar's metre being better understood in the 18th century, the fashion for Pindaric odes faded, though there are notable actual Pindaric odes by Thomas Gray, *The Progress of Poesy* and *The Bard.*

The Pindarick of Cowley was revived around 1800 by William Wordsworth for one of his very finest poems, the Intimations of Immortality ode; irregular odes were also written by Samuel Taylor Coleridge, John Keats, and Percy Bysshe Shelley who wrote odes with regular stanza patterns. Shelley's *Ode to the West Wind*, written in fourteen line terza rima stanzas, is a major poem in the form, but perhaps the greatest odes of the 19th century were Keats's *Five Great Odes* of 1819 which included *Ode to a Nightingale, Ode on Melancholy, Ode on a Grecian Urn, Ode to Psyche*, and *To Autumn*. After Keats, there have been comparatively few major odes in English. One major exception is the fourth verse of the poem *For the Fallen* by Laurence Binyon which is often known as *"The Ode to the Fallen"* or more simply as *"The Ode"*.

W.H. Auden also wrote *'Ode'*, one of his most popular poems from his earlier career when based in London, in opposition to people's ignorance over the reality of war. In interview Auden once stated that he had intended to title the poem *My Silver Age* in mockery of the supposedly imperial Golden age, however chose *'Ode'* as it seemed to provide a more sensitive exploration of warfare.

The English ode's most common rhyme scheme is ABABCDECDE.

THE LYRIC

Is a genre of poetry that expresses personal and emotional feelings. In the ancient world, lyric poems were sung, accompanied by a lyre a musical instrument. Lyric poems do not have to rhyme, and today do not need to be set to music or a beat. Aristotle, in *Poetics*, mentions lyric poetry (kitharistike played to the cithara, a type of lyre) along with drama, epic poetry, dancing, painting and other forms of mimesis. The lyric poem, dating from the Romantic era, does have some thematic antecedents in ancient Greek and Roman verse, but the ancient definition was based on metrical criteria, and in archaic and classical Greek culture presupposed live performance accompanied by a stringed instrument.

Although arguably the most popular form of lyric poetry in the Western tradition is the 14-line sonnet, either in its Petrarchan or its Shakespearean form, lyric poetry appears in a variety of forms. Other forms of the lyric include ballades, villanelles, odes, pastourelle and canzone.

Ancient Hebrew poetry relied on repetition, alliteration, and chiasmus for many of its effects. Ancient Greek and Roman lyric poetry was composed in strophes. Pindar's epinician odes, where strophe and antistrophe are followed by an epode, represent an expansion of the same basic principle. The Greeks distinguished, however, between lyric monody (e.g. Sappho, Anacreon) and choral lyric (e.g. Pindar, Bacchylides). In all such poetry the fundamental formal feature is the repetition of a metrical pattern larger than a verse or distich. In some cases (although not in antiquity), form and theme are wed in the conception of a genre, as in the medieval alva or aubade, a dawn song in which lovers must part after a night of love, often with the watchman's refrain telling them it is time to go. A common feature of some lyric forms is the refrain of one or more verses that end each strophe. The refrain is repeated throughout the poem, either exactly or with variation. In the medieval Galician-Portuguese *cantigas de amigo*, thought to reflect an old oral tradition, 90% of the texts have a refrain.

Lyric in European literature of the medieval or Renaissance period means a poem written so that it could be set to music—whether or not it is. A poem's particular structure, function or theme is not specified by the term. The lyric poetry of Europe in this period was created largely without reference to the classical past, by the pioneers of courtly poetry and courtly love. The troubadours, travelling composers and performers of songs, began to flourish towards the end of the 11th century and were often imitated in successive centuries. Trouveres were poet-composers who were roughly contemporary with and influenced by the troubadours but who composed their works in the northern dialects of France. The first known trouvere was Chretien de Troyes (1160s-80s). The dominant form of German lyric poetry in the period was the Minnesang, "a love lyric based essentially on a fictitious relationship between a knight and his high-born lady". Initially imitating the lyrics of the French troubadours and trouveres, Minnesang soon established a distinctive tradition. There is also a large body of medieval Galician-Portuguese lyric.

Hebrew singer-poets of the Middle Ages include: Yehuda Halevi, Solomon ibn Gabirol and Abraham ibn Ezra.

In Italy, Petrarch developed the sonnet form pioneered by Giacomo da Lentini, which Dante used in his Vita Nuova. In 1327, according to the poet, the sight of a woman called Laura in the church of Sainte-Claire d'Avignon awoke in him a lasting passion, celebrated in the Rime sparse ("Scattered rhymes"). Later, Renaissance poets who copied Petrarch's style named this collection of 366 poems Il Canzoniere ("Song Book"). Laura is in many ways both the culmination of medieval courtly love poetry and the beginning of Renaissance love lyric.

The eighteenth and early nineteenth centuries constitute the period of the rise of Russian lyric poetry, exemplified by Aleksandr Pushkin. The Swedish "Phosphorists" were influenced by the Romantic movement and their chief poet, Per Daniel Amadeus Atterbom produced many lyric poems. Italian lyric poets of the period include Ugo Foscolo, Giacomo Leopardi, Giovanni Pascoli and Gabriele D'Annunzio. Japanese lyric poets include Taneda Santoka, Masaoka Shiki and Ishikawa Takuboku. Spanish lyric poets include Gustavo Adolfo Becquer, Rosalia de Castro and Jose de Espronceda.

THE IDYLL

A composition in verse or prose which describes scenes and incidents of country life which are simple, charming and appealing due to their idealised innocence and contentment. An idyll is a pastoral poem, and an ancient example is *Theocritus's Idylls* (in 3rd century B.C.) which describes the country life, and the charming rustic life of the Sicilians. John G. Whittler's *Maud Muller* is yet another example of an idyll.

THE PASTORAL

The originator of the pastoral was the Greek poet Theocritus, who in the third century BC wrote poems representing the life of Sicilian shepherds. ("Pastor" is Latin for "shepherd.") Virgil later imitated Theocritus in his Latin *Edogues*, and in doing so established the enduring model for the traditional pastoral a deliberately conventional poem expressing an urban poet's nostalgic image of the supposed peace and simplicity of the life of shepherds and other rural folk in an idealized natural setting. The conventions that hundreds of later poets imitated from Virgil's imitations of Theocritus include a shepherd reclining under a spreading beech tree and meditating on the rural muse, or piping as though he would ne'er grow old, or engaging in a friendly singing contest, or expressing his good or bad fortune in a love affair, or grieving over the death of a fellow shepherd. From this last type developed the pastoral elegy, which persisted long after the other traditional types had lost their popularity. Other terms often used synonymously with pastoral are idyll, from the title of Theocritus' pastorals; eclogue (literally, "a selection"), from the title of Virgil's pastorals; and bucolic poetry, from the Greek word for "herdsman."

Classical poets often described the pastoral life as possessing features of the mythical golden age. Christian pastoralists conjoined the golden age of pagan fable with the Garden of Eden in the Bible, and also exploited the religious symbolism of "shepherd" (applied to the ecclesiastical or parish "pastor," and to the figure of Christ as the Good Shepherd) to give many pastoral poems a Christian range of reference. In the Renaissance the traditional pastoral was also adapted to diverse satirical and allegorical uses. Edmund Spenser's *Shepherd's Calendar* (1579), which popularized the mode in English poetry, included most of the varieties of pastoral poems current in that period.

Such was the attraction of the pastoral dream that Renaissance writers incorporated it into various other literary forms. Sir Philip Sidney's *Arcadia* (1581–84) was a long pastoral romance written in an elaborately artful prose. (*Arcadia* was a mountainous region of Greece which Virgil substituted for Theocritus' Sicily as his idealized pastoral milieu.) There was also the pastoral lyric (Christopher Marlowe's *"The Passionate Shepherd to His Love"*), and the pastoral drama. John Fletcher's *The Faithful Shepherdess* is an example of this last type, and Shakespeare's *As You Like It*, based on the contemporary pastoral romance *Rosalynde* by Thomas Lodge, is set in the forest of Arden, a green refuge from the troubles and complications of ordinary life where enmities are reconciled, problems resolved, and the course of true love made to run smooth.

The last important series of traditional pastorals, and an extreme instance of their calculated and graceful display of high artifice, was Alexander Pope's *Pastorals* (1709). Five years later John Gay, in his Shepherd's Week, wrote a parody of the type by applying its elegant formulas to the crudity of actual rustic manners and language; by doing so, he inadvertently showed later poets the way to the seriously realistic treatment of rural life. In 1783 George Crabbe published *The Village* specifically in order to paint the cot. *As Truth* will paint it and as bards will not.

How far the term then lost its traditional application to a poetry of aristocratic artifice is indicated by Wordsworth's title for his realistic rendering of a rural tragedy in 1800: *"Michael, A Pastoral Poem"*.

THE ELEGY

A lament or a meditative poem, often written on the occasion of a death or other solemn event or theme. Although an elegy may appear as a discrete section in a larger work (as in the oration at the funeral of Beowulf), it is usually a complete poem in a formal style. A famous example is Thomas Gray's *"Elegy Written in a Country Churchyard"* (1751), whose thirty-two stanzas ruminate upon the passing of time and souls:

Can storied urn or animated bust
  Back to its mansion call the fleeting breath?
Can Honor's voice provoke the silent dust,
  Or Flattery soothe the dull cold ear of Death?

Perhaps in this neglected spot is laid
  Some heart once pregnant with celestial fire;
Hands that the rod of empire might have swayed,
  Or waked to ecstasy the living lyre.

THE PASTORAL ELEGY

One kind of elegy that is especially important in English literary history is the pastoral elegy, whose highlights include John Milton's *"Lycidas"* (1637) and Percy Bysshe Shelley's *"Adonais"* (an elegy for the dead John Keats, 1821). Pastoral elegies combine pastoral themes and images—nature deities, seasonal vegetation—with a memorialization of a deceased friend or comrade.

THE BALLAD

A ballad is a form of verse, often a narrative set to music. Ballads were particularly characteristic of the popular poetry and song of the British Isles from the later medieval period until the 19th century and used extensively across Europe and later the Americas, Australia and North Africa. Many ballads were written and sold as single sheet broadsides. The form was often used by poets and composers from the 18th century onwards to produce lyrical ballads. In the later 19th century it took on the meaning of a slow form of popular love song and the term is now often used as synonymous with any love song, particularly the pop or rock power ballad.

Most northern and west European ballads are written in ballad stanzas or quatrains (four-line stanzas) of alternating lines of iambic (an unstressed followed by a stressed syllable) tetrameter (eight syllables) and iambic trimeter (six syllables), known as ballad meter. Usually, only the second and fourth line of a quatrain are rhymed (in the scheme a, b, c, b), which has been taken to suggest that, originally, ballads consisted of couplets (two lines) of rhymed verse, each of 14 syllables. As can be seen in this stanza from *'Lord Thomas and Fair Annet'*:

The horse| fair Ann|et rode| upon|
He amb|led like| the wind|,
With sil|ver he| was shod| before,
With burn|ing gold| behind|.

However, there is considerable variation on this pattern in almost every respect, including length, number of lines and rhyming scheme, making the strict definition of a ballad extremely difficult. In southern and eastern Europe, and in countries that derive their tradition from them, ballad structure differs significantly, like Spanish romances, which are octosyllabic and use consonance rather than rhyme.

In all traditions most ballads are narrative in nature, with a self-contained story, often concise and relying on imagery, rather than description, which can be tragic, historical, romantic or comic. Another common feature of ballads is repetition, sometimes of fourth lines in succeeding stanzas, as a refrain, sometimes of third and fourth lines of a stanza and sometimes of entire stanzas.

THE SATIRE

Satire can be described as the literary art of diminishing or derogating a subject by making it ridiculous and evoking toward it attitudes of amusement, contempt, scorn, or indignation. It differs from the *comic* in that comedy evokes laughter mainly as an end in itself, while satire derides; that is, it uses laughter as a weapon, and against a butt that exists outside the work itself. That butt may be an individual (in "personal satire"), or a type of person, a class, an institution, a nation, or even (as in the Earl of Rochester's *"A Satyr against Mankind,"* 1675, and much of Jonathan Swift's *Gulliver's Travels*, 1726, especially Book IV) the entire human race. The distinction between the comic and the satiric, however, is sharp only at its extremes. Shakespeare's *Falstaff* is mainly a comic creation, presented primarily for our enjoyment; the puritanical Malvolio in Shakespeare's *Twelfth Night* is for the most part comic but has aspects of satire directed against the type of the fatuous and hypocritical Puritan; Ben Jonson's *Volpone* (1607) clearly satirizes the type of person whose cleverness—or stupidity—is put at the service of his cupidity; and John Dryden's *MacFlecknoe* (1682), while representing a permanent type of the pretentious poetaster, satirized specifically the living author Thomas Shadwell.

Satire has usually been justified, by those who practice it, as a corrective of human vice and folly; Alexander Pope, for example, remarked that "those who are ashamed of nothing else are so of being ridiculous." Its frequent claim (not always borne out in the practice) has been to ridicule the failing rather than the individual, and to limit its ridicule to corrigible faults, excluding those for which a person is not responsible. As Swift said, speaking of himself in his ironic *"Verses on the Death of Dr. Swift"* (1739):

> Yet malice never was his aim;
> He lashed the vice, but spared the name....
> His satire points at no defect,
> But what all mortals may correct....
> He spared a hump, or crooked nose,
> Whose owners set not up for beaux.

Satire occurs as an incidental element within many works whose overall mode is not satiric—in a certain character or situation, or in an interpolated passage of ironic commentary on some aspect of the human condition or of contemporary society. But for some literary writings, verse or prose, the attempt to diminish a subject by ridicule is the organizing principle of the whole, and these works constitute the formal genre labeled.

NOVEL

A novel is a book of long narrative in literary prose. The genre has historical roots both in the fields of the medieval and early modern romance and in the tradition of the novella. The latter supplied the present generic term in the late 18th century.

Further definition of the genre is historically difficult. The construction of the narrative, the plot, the way reality is created in the works of fiction, the fascination of the character study, and the use of language are usually discussed to show a novel's artistic merits. Most of these requirements were introduced in the 16th and 17th centuries, in order to give fiction a justification outside the field of factual history. The individualism of the presentation makes the personal memoir and the autobiography the two closest relatives among the genres of modern histories.

MAJOR FORMS OF NOVEL

The following are the Major Forms of the Novel :

1. The Prose Romances
2. The Travelogues
3. The Gothic Novel
4. The Picaresque Novel
5. The Epistolary Novel
6. The Domestic Novel
7. The Historical Novel
8. The Regional Novel
9. The Prophetic Novel
10. The Psychological Novel
11. The Short Story

THE PROSE ROMANCES

Romances in verse were written much earlier than the Romances in prose. Prose Romances are the earliest form of the novel. They are simply fantasies in which the authors make the fullest use of their imagination and fancy and create an ideal world which bears little or no semblance with real life. The earliest of them is the famous *Morte d' Arthur*, the legends retold by Sir Thomas Malory in prose. This takes us back to the legendary world of knighthood and chivalry. The other sixteenth century prose romances are Lyly's *Euphues* in two parts and Sidney's *Arcadia*, a pastoral romance, conceiving a dream-land of pre fancy. Lodge's *Rosalynde* is a love-romance, so is also Robert Greene's *Pandosto*, Bacon's *The New Atlantis* is also a prose romance.

THE TRAVELOGUES

The novel proper started in a limited sense with Travelogues. The travelogues are travel-stories relating the adventures of the travelers or voyagers in unknown and unchartered seas. They often land on uninhabited islands or some islands inhabited by strange creatures. The earliest of them is Daniel Defoe's *Robinson Crusoe*. Robinson Crusoe lands on an uninhabited island and somehow managers to live there for several years, until he is rescued from there by a lucky chance by a passing ship of his own country. Another famous travelogue is Jonathan Swift's *Gulliver's Travels*. In this romance Gulliver lands on several islands inhabited by such strange creatures as the Lilliputians, Houynhnms, Brobdingnags, and Yahoos. However, Swift's episodes in these adventures have very pungent satire on contemporary political situations.

THE GOTHIC NOVEL

Derived from the word 'Goths' used for a Germanic tribe, the Gothic novel has supernatural elements like ghosts, haunted houses, etc. which induces horror, apprehension and insecurity. Examples – Horace Walpole's *Castle of Otranto, a Gothic Story*, Ann Radcliff's *The Mysteries of Udolpho*, etc.

THE PICARESQUE NOVEL

The picaresque novel (Spanish: "picaresca," from "picaro," for "rogue" or "rascal") is a popular sub-genre of prose fiction which is usually satirical and depicts, in realistic and often humorous detail, the adventures of a roguish hero of low social class who lives by his wits in a corrupt society. This style of novel originated in sixteenth century Spain and flourished throughout Europe in the seventeenth and eighteenth centuries. It continues to influence modern literature.

The word picaro starts to first appear in Spain with the current meaning in 1545. The word picaro does not appear in *Lazarillo de Tormes* (1554), the novella credited with founding the genre. The expression picaresque novel was coined in 1810.

The character type of Lazarillo, which determines the story and the so-called picaresque novel genre, has been shaped from characterization elements already present in Roman literature. With Petronius' *Satyricon*, Lazarillo takes some of the traits of the central figure of Encolpius, a former gladiator. but it is unlikely that the author had access to Petronius' work; from the comedies of Plautus, it borrows from the figure of the parasite and the supple slave; other traits are taken from Apuleius's *The Golden Ass*. *The Golden Ass* and *Satyricon* were particularly revived and widely read in renaissance Europe, and are rare surviving samples of a mostly lost genre, which was highly popular in the classical world, known as *"Milesian tales"*.

Arabic literature, which was read widely in Spain in the time of Al-Andalus and possessed a literary tradition with similar themes, is another possible formative influence on the picaresque style. *Al-Hamadhani* (d.1008) of Hamadhan (Iran) is credited with inventing the literary genre of maqamat in which a wandering vagabond makes his living on the gifts his listeners give him following his extemporaneous displays of rhetoric, erudition, or verse, often done with a trickster's touch *Ibn al-Astarkuwi* or *al-Ashtarkuni* (d.1134) also wrote in the genre maqamat, comparable to later European picaresque novels. While elements of Chaucer and Boccaccio have a picaresque feel and are likely to have contributed to the style, the modern picaresque begins with Lazarillo de Tormes, which was published anonymously in Antwerp and Spain in 1554. It is variously considered either the first picaresque novel or at least the antecedent of the genre. The title character, Lazarillo, is a picaro who must live by his wits in an impoverished country full of hypocrisy.

The autobiography of Benvenuto Cellini, written in Florence beginning in 1558, also has much in common with the picaresque. Another early example is Mateo Aleman's *Guzman de Alfarache* (1599), characterized by religiosity.

Francisco de Quevedo's *El buscon* (1604 according to Francisco Rico; the exact date is uncertain, yet it was certainly a very early work) is considered the masterpiece of the subgenre by A.A. Parker, because of his baroque style and the study of the delinquent psychology. However, a more recent school of thought, led by Francisco Rico, rejects Parker's view, contending instead that the protagonist, Pablos, is a highly unrealistic character, simply a means for Quevedo to launch classist, racist and sexist attacks. Moreover, argues Rico, the structure of the novel is radically different from previous works of the picaresque genre: Quevedo uses the conventions of the picaresque as a mere vehicle to show off his abilities with conceit and rhetoric, rather than to construct a satirical critique of Spanish Golden Age society.

Indeed, in order to understand the historical context that led to the development of these paradigmatic picaresque novels in Spain during the sixteenth and seventeenth centuries, it is essential to take into consideration the circumstances surrounding the lives of conversos, whose ancestors had been Jewish, and whose New Christian faith was subjected to close scrutiny and mistrust. In other European countries, these Spanish novels were read and imitated. In Germany, Grimmelshausen wrote *Simplicius Simplicissimus* (1669), the most important of non-Spanish picaresque novels. It describes the devastation caused by the Thirty Years' War. In Le Sage's *Gil Blas* (1715) is a classic example of the genre, which in France had declined into an aristocratic adventure. In Britain, the body of Tobias Smollett's work, and Daniel Defoe's *Moll Flanders* (1722) are considered picaresque, but they lack the sense of religious redemption of delinquency that was very important in Spanish and German novels. The triumph of *Moll Flanders* is more economic than moral.

The classic Chinese novel *Journey to the West* is considered to have considerable picaresque elements. Having been written in 1590, it is contemporary with much of the above - but is unlikely to have been directly influenced by the European genre.

THE EPISTOLARY NOVEL

An epistolary novel is a novel written as a series of documents. The usual form is letters, although diary entries, newspaper clippings and other documents are sometimes used. Recently, electronic "documents" such as recordings and radio, blogs, and e-mails have also come into use. The word epistolary is derived through Latin from the Greek word *epistole*, meaning a letter.

The epistolary form can add greater realism to a story, because it mimics the workings of real life. It is thus able to demonstrate differing points of view without recourse to the device of an omniscient narrator.

There are two theories on the genesis of the epistolary novel. The first claims that the genre originated from novels with inserted letters, in which the portion containing the third person narrative in between the letters was gradually reduced. The other theory claims that the epistolary novel arose from miscellanies of letters and poetry: some of the letters were tied together into a (mostly amorous) plot. Both claims have some validity. The first truly epistolary novel, the Spanish *"Prison of Love" (Carcel de amor)* (c.1485) by Diego de San Pedro, belongs to a tradition of novels in which a large number of inserted letters already dominated the narrative. Other well-known examples of early epistolary novels are closely related to the tradition of letter-books and miscellanies of letters. Within the successive editions of Edme Boursault's *Letters of Respect, Gratitude and Love (Lettres de respect, d'obligation et d 'amour)* (1669), a group of letters written to a girl named Babet was expanded and became more and more distinct from the other letters, until it formed a small epistolary novel entitled *Letters to Babet (Lettres a Babet)*. The immensely famous Letters of a Portuguese Nun *(Lettres portugaises)* (1669) generally attributed to Gabriel-Joseph de La Vergne, comte de Guilleragues, though a small minority still regard Marianna Alcoforado as the author, is claimed to be intended to be part of a miscellany of Guilleragues prose and poetry. The founder of the epistolary novel in English is said by many to be James Howell (1594–1666) with *"Familiar Letters"*, who writes of prison, foreign adventure, and the love of women.

The first novel to expose the complex play that the genre allows was Aphra Behn's *Love-Letters Between a Nobleman and His Sister* (1684), which appeared in three successive volumes in 1684, 1685, and 1687. The novel shows the genre's results of changing perspectives: individual points were presented by the individual characters, and the central voice of the author and moral evaluation disappeared (at least in the first volume; her further volumes introduced a narrator). Behn furthermore explored a realm of intrigue with letters that fall into the wrong hands, with faked letters, with letters withheld by protagonists, and even more complex interaction.

The epistolary novel as a genre became popular in the 18th century in the works of such authors as Samuel Richardson, with his immensely successful novels *Pamela* (1740) and *Clarissa* (1749). In France, there was *Lettres persanes* (1721) by Montesquieu, followed by *Julie, ou la nouvelle Heloise* (1761) by Jean-Jacques Rousseau, and Laclos' *Les Liaisons dangereuses* (1782), which used the epistolary form to great dramatic effect, because the sequence of events was not always related directly or explicitly. In Germany, there was Johann Wolfgang von Goethe's *Die Leiden des jungen Werthers* (1774) *(The Sorrows of Young Werther)* and Friedrich Holderlin's *Hyperion*. The first North American novel, *The History of Emily Montague* (1769) by Frances Brooke was written in epistolary form.

Starting in the 18th century, the epistolary form was subject to much ridicule, resulting in a number of savage burlesques. The most notable example of these was Henry Fielding's *Shamela* (1741), written as a parody of Pamela. In it, the female narrator can be found wielding a pen and scribbling her diary entries under the most dramatic and unlikely of circumstances.

The epistolary novel slowly fell out of use in the late 18th century. Although Jane Austen tried her hand at the epistolary in juvenile writings and her novella *Lady Susan*, she abandoned this structure for her later work. It is thought that her lost novel *"First Impressions"*, which was redrafted to become *Pride and Prejudice*, may have been epistolary: *Pride and Prejudice* contains an unusual number of letters quoted in full and some play a critical role in the plot.

The epistolary form nonetheless saw continued use, surviving in exceptions or in fragments in nineteenth-century novels. In Honore de Balzac's novel *Letters of Two Brides*, two women who became friends during their education at a convent correspond over a 17 year period, exchanging letters describing their lives. Mary Shelley employs the epistolary form in her novel *Frankenstein* (1818). Shelley uses the letters as one of a variety of framing devices, as the story is presented through the letters of a sea captain and scientific explorer attempting to reach the north pole who encounters Victor Frankenstein and records the dying man's narrative and confessions. In the late 19th century, Bram Stoker released one of the most widely recognized and successful novels in the epistolary form to date, *Dracula*. Printed in 1897, the novel is compiled entirely of letters, diary entries, newspaper clippings, telegrams, doctor's notes, ship's logs, and the like, which Stoker adroitly employs to balance believability and dramatic tension.

There are three types of epistolary novels: monologic (giving the letters of only one character, like *Letters of a Portuguese Nun*), dialogic (giving the letters of two characters, like *Mme Marie Jeanne Riccoboni's Letters of Fanni Butlerd* (1757), and polylogic (with three or more letter-writing characters). In addition, a crucial element in polylogic epistolary novels like *Clarissa*, and *Dangerous Liaisons* is the dramatic device of 'discrepant awareness': the simultaneous but separate correspondences of the heroines and the villains creating dramatic tension.

THE DOMESTIC NOVEL

The Domestic Novels as their title suggests, present the day-to-day life of the average of middle-class families. The life-patterns of the members of a family and their relations with their friends and neighbours are artistically presented in these novels. The festivals and festivities, functions and celebrations, birthdays, nuptials, and marriages are graphically described in these novels. Jane Austen is the most important writer of the domestic novels. Her *Pride and Prejudice, Sense and Sensibility* and *Emma* are the best examples of domestic novels.

THE HISTORICAL NOVEL

A novel that has as its setting a usually significant period of history and that attempts to convey the spirit, manners, and social conditions of a past age with realistic detail and fidelity (which is in some cases only apparent fidelity) to historical fact. The work may deal with actual historical personages...or it may contain a mixture of fictional and historical characters.

An early example of historical prose fiction is Luo Guanzhong's *14th century Romance of the Three Kingdoms*, which covers one of the most important periods of Chinese history and left a lasting impact on Chinese culture.

The historical novel was further popularized in the 19th century by writers classified as Romantics. Many regard Sir Walter Scott as the first to write historical novels. Gyorgy Lukacs, in his *The Historical Novel*, argues that Scott is the first fiction writer who saw history not just as a convenient frame in which to stage a contemporary narrative, but rather as a distinct social and cultural setting. His novels of Scottish history such as *Waverley* (1814) and *Rob Roy* (1817) focus upon a middling character who sits at the intersection of various social groups in order to explore the development of society through conflict. His *Ivanhoe* (1820) gains credit for renewing interest in the Middle Ages. Victor Hugo's *The Hunchback of Notre Dame* (1831) furnishes another 19th century example of the romantic-historical novel as does Leo Tolstoy's *War and Peace*. In the United States, James Fenimore Cooper was a prominent author of historical novels. In French literature, the most prominent inheritor of Scott's style of the historical novel was *Balzac*.

Though the genre has evolved since its inception, the historical novel remains popular with authors and readers to this day; bestsellers include Patrick O'Brian's *Aubrey–Maturin* series, Ken Follett's *Pillars of the Earth*, and Neal Stephenson's *Baroque Cycle*. A striking development in British/ Irish writing in the past 25 years has been the renewed interest in the First World War. Works include William Boyd's *An Ice-Cream War*; Sebastian Faulks' *Birdsong* and *The Girl at the Lion d'Or* (concerned with the War's consequences); Pat Barker's *Regeneration Trilogy* and Sebastian Barry's *A Long Long Way*.

Many early historical novels played an important role in the rise of European popular interest in the history of the Middle Ages. Hugo's *Hunchback* often receives credit for fueling the movement to preserve the Gothic architecture of France, leading to the establishment of the Monuments historiques, the French governmental authority for historic preservation.

The genre of the historical novel has also permitted some authors, such as the Polish novelist Boleslaw Prus in his sole historical novel, *Pharaoh*, to distance themselves from their own time and place to gain perspective on society and on the human condition, or to escape the depredations of the censor.

In some historical novels, major historic events take place mostly off-stage, while the fictional characters inhabit the world where those events occur. Robert Louis Stevenson's *Kidnapped* recounts mostly private adventures set against the backdrop of the Jacobite troubles in Scotland. Charles Dickens's *Barnaby Rudge* is set amid the Gordon Riots, and *A Tale of Two Cities* in the French Revolution.

In some works, the accuracy of the historical elements has been questioned, as in Alexandre Dumas' *Queen Margot*. Postmodern novelists such as John Barth and Thomas Pynchon operate with even more freedom, mixing historical characters and settings with invented history and fantasy, as in the novels *The Sot-Weed Factor* and *Mason & Dixon* respectively. A few writers create historical fiction without fictional characters. One example is *I, Claudius*, by 20th century writer Robert Graves; another is the *Masters of Rome* series by Colleen McCullough.

THE REGIONAL NOVEL

This type of novel is set in a particular geographical section and deals with the living and culture of that area. Examples are: Thomas Hardy's *Wessex*, R.K.Narayan's *Malgudi*, etc.

These are the common types of novel. Apart from these there are many more varieties that excel in creating the literature of the time and making the essence of novel more dedicated and authentic in the present scenario.

THE PROPHETIC NOVEL

The Prophetic novels try to forecast what the future would be like. These novels do not claim to be absolutely correct or authentic. They only give us a tentative picture of the future on the basis of the tendencies prevailing in the present. Aidous Huxley in the Brave New World envisaged in 1932 a future in which the entire populace would be mentally conditioned by the totalitarian despots.

THE PSYCHOLOGICAL NOVEL

A Psychological fiction is a specific sub-genre of the wide ranging thriller genre. This genre often incorporates elements from the mystery genre in addition to the typical traits of the thriller genre. Usually thrillers focus on plot over fictional characters, emphasizing on intense physical action over the character's psyche. Psychological thrillers tend to reverse this formula to a certain degree, emphasizing the characters just as much if not more so than the plot. psychological novel, also called psychological realism, is a work of prose fiction which places more than the usual amount of emphasis on interior characterization, and on the motives, circumstances, and internal action which springs from, and develops, external action. The psychological novel is not content to state what happens but goes on to explain the motivation of this action. In this type of writing character and characterization are more than usually important, and they often delve deeper into the mind of a character than novels of other genres. The psychological novel can be called a novel of the "inner man," so to say. In some cases, the stream of consciousness technique, as well as interior monologues, may be employed to better illustrate the inner workings of the human mind at work. Flashbacks may also be featured. While these three textual techniques are also prevalent in "modernism," there is no deliberate effort to fragment the prose or compel the reader to interpret the text.

The Tale of Genji, written in 11th century Japan, has often been considered the first psychological novel. In the west, the origins of the psychological novel can be traced as far back as Giovanni Boccaccio's 1344 *Elegia di Madonna Fiammetta;* that is before the term psychology was coined.

THE SHORT STORY

A short story is a work of fiction that is usually written in prose, often in narrative format. A short story usually deals with a few characters and often concentrates on the creation of the mood rather than the plot.

The short story format tends to be more pointed than longer works of fiction, such as novellas (in the 20th and 21st century sense) and novels. Short story definitions based on length differ somewhat, even among professional writers, in part because of the fragmentation of the medium into genres. Since the short story format includes a wide range of genres and styles, the actual length is determined by the individual author's preference (or the story's actual needs in terms of creative trajectory or story arc) and the submission guidelines relevant to the story's actual market. Guidelines vary greatly among publishers.

Many short story writers define their work through a combination of creative, personal expression, and artistic integrity. They attempt to resist categorization by genre as well as definition by numbers, finding such approaches limiting and counter-intuitive to artistic form and reasoning. As a result, definitions of the short story based on length splinter even more when the writing process is taken into consideration.

A short story is often judged by its ability to provide a complete or satisfying treatment of its characters and subject. Fiction, such as novellas (in the 20th and 21st century sense) and novels. Short story definitions based on length differ somewhat, even among professional writers, in part because of the fragmentation of the medium into genres. Since the short story format includes a wide range of genres and styles, the actual length is determined by the individual author's preference (or the story's actual needs in terms of creative trajectory or story arc) and the submission guidelines relevant to the story's actual market. Guidelines vary greatly among publishers.

Many short story writers define their work through a combination of creative, personal expression, and artistic integrity. They attempt to resist categorization by genre as well as definition by numbers, finding such approaches limiting and counter-intuitive to artistic form and reasoning. As a result, definitions of the short story based on length splinter even more when the writing process is taken into consideration.

MULTIPLE CHOICE QUESTIONS

1. One of the following dramatists has written only tragedies. He is—
   A. Ben Jonson B. John Webster
   C. Marlowe D. John Ford
2. How many constituent parts are there in a Tragedy according to Aristotle?
   A. Five B. Six
   C. Four D. Three
3. At what stage of the plot in a play does the Epilogue appear?
   A. At the end of the play
   B. At any stage where its presence is felt necessary
   C. In the beginning of the play
   D. At the end of the third act
4. There were four famous theatrical Cycles enacting the Morality Plays. Which one of the following four names given below is wrong?
   A. Towneley Cycle B. Chester Cycle
   C. York Cycle D. Charles Cycle
5. Biblical themes were enacted in—
   A. The Miracle plays B. The Mystery plays
   C. The Interludes D. The Morality plays
6. Why were the *Interludes* introduced?
   A. They pleased the common class of the spectators
   B. They provided comic relief
   C. They had better theatrical effect
   D. They dealt with the real problems of life

7. The *Mystery Plays* deal with—
A. Heaven and Hell
B. Moral values
C. Biblical Themes
D. The life and deeds of the saints

8. Who is the author of *The Spanish Tragedy*?
A. Christopher Marlowe
B. Thomas Kyd
C. Robert Greene
D. George Peele

9. Which of the following plays is written by George Peele?
A. *Titus Andronicus*
B. *Jocasta*
C. *The Spanish Tragedy*
D. *The Wounds of Civil War*

10. What is the function of the *Chorus* in a play?
A. The Chorus is a band of singers who sing
B. The Chorus comes to declare the ending of an Act
C. The Chorus explains the past and the future events in the play
D. The Chorus represents the views of the dramatist

11. Which is supposed to be the first regular tragedy in English?
A. *Morte de Arthur*
B. *Gorboduc*
C. *Troylus and Cryseyde*
D. *Roister Doister*

12. The first tragedy *Gorboduc* was later given the title—
A. *Corpus Christi*
B. *Ferrex and Porrex*
C. *Gammer Gurton's Needle*
D. *Endymion*

13. What is meant by 'Catastrophe'?
A. The ending of a tragi-comedy
B. The ending of a tragedy
C. The ending of a farce
D. The ending of a comedy

14. Which one of the following types of the plays is not meant for acting?
A. A Closet play B. A Chronicle play
C. A Masque D. A Romance

15. The *Resurrection of Lazarus* was a very popular play in the fifteenth century. It was a—
A. Morality Play B. Mystery Play
C. Miracle Play D. An Interlude

16. Which of the following is the oldest form of literature?
A. Drama B. Novel
C. Poetry D. Prose

17. The term 'drama' originates from which language?
A. English B. Arabic
C. Sanskrit D. Greek

18. 'Drama' originated in ______.
A. Greece B. Rome
C. London D. India

19. Which one of these is not a type of drama?
A. The Tragedy B. The Farce
C. The Masque D. The Ballad

20. Which one of these is a type of drama?
A. The Epic B. The Ode
C. The Farce D. The Satire

21. Which one is not a major form of novel?
A. The Travelogue B. Gothic
C. Picaresque D. The Tragedy

22. Interlude is a type of ______.
A. Novel B. Poetry form
C. Prose form D. Drama

23. A sonnet is a form of ______.
A. Poetry B. Drama
C. Novel D. Prose

24. Shakespearan sonnet contains ______ lines.
A. four B. six
C. twelve D. fourteen

25. An ode is a ______.
A. Drama B. Novel
C. Poetry D. Prose

26. In which year was the *Globe Theatre* built?
A. 1588 B. 1594
C. 1598 D. 1599

27. Who is the author of *The Spanish Tragedy*?
A. Thomas Lodge B. Thomas Kyd
C. George Peele D. Robert Greene

28. A *'Soliloquy'* is defined as the 'loud thinking' of a character. Who can hear this 'loud thinking'?
A. The heroine of the play
B. The whole audience
C. The character himself
D. The characters present on the stage

29. What is meant by *'Denouement'*?
A. The ending of a comedy
B. The ending of a romance
C. The ending of a tragedy
D. The ending of a historical play

30. What is the most significant feature of the *Morality Plays*?
A. They present biblical figures
B. They symbolise Christian moral values
C. They present saints and sages
D. They present Vices and Virtues as personified figures

31. A ballad is a form of ______.
A. Prose B. Poetry
C. Novel D. Drama

32. A satire is a form of ______.
A. Poetry B. Prose
C. Drama D. Novel

33. Which one is a form of novel?
A. The Prophetic B. The Farce
C. The Masque D. The Elegy

34. Which one is not a form of novel?
A. Epistolary B. Regional
C. Pastoral D. Psychological

35. The elegy is a form of ______.
A. Drama B. Prose
C. Poetry D. Novel

36. John Heywood's *Interlude* entitled 4PP (or 4P's) caricatures four professionals whose professions begins with P. In the four professionals listed below, which one is wrong?
A. The Piper B. The Palmer
C. The Pedlar D. The Pardoner

37. How many Dramatic Unities were recommended by the Greeks?
A. One central unity
B. No number fixed
C. Three dramatic unities
D. Two dramatic unities

38. In which one of the following plays the *Epilogue* appears?
A. *Dr. Faustus*
B. *Midsummer Night's Dream*
C. *Hamlet*
D. *As You Like it*

39. The *Miracle Plays* principally deal with the miracles performed by—
A. Supernatural powers
B. Personified Vices and Virtues
C. Saints and Sages
D. Magic

40. Virtues and Vices are personified in—
A. The Moralities B. The Miracles
C. The Interludes D. The Mysteries

ANSWERS

1	2	3	4	5	6	7	8	9	10
C	B	A	D	B	B	C	B	A	C
11	**12**	**13**	**14**	**15**	**16**	**17**	**18**	**19**	**20**
B	B	B	A	C	C	D	A	D	C
21	**22**	**23**	**24**	**25**	**26**	**27**	**28**	**29**	**30**
D	D	A	D	C	D	B	B	A	D
31	**32**	**33**	**34**	**35**	**36**	**37**	**38**	**39**	**40**
B	A	A	C	C	A	C	D	C	A

2 Great Era of English Literature

THE OLD ENGLISH ERA

ANGLO-SAXON PERIOD (450-1050)

Beowulf is probably the oldest epic of the Teutonic world. It is believed to be belonging to the first half of the sixth century.

It is one of the most important Pre-Christian poems in English. It is an epic poem of heroism, full of sadness, that mentions the transience of life. It narrates three stories instead of one, as is the common case in an epic. Its authorship is unknown, but its setting is Denmark and southern Sweden. The poem seems to have been composed in ballad-form by an ancestor of the Anglo-Saxons in Scandinavia, but recast into an epic later by a Christian poet of Northumbria. The setting of the poem is pagan or heathen for its overwhelming sadness with only an insignificant touch of Christian philosophy in the emptiness of life. There is no mention of Great Britain which the Anglo-Saxon invaders had made their home. It is a romance which opens with a Prologue which explains the mysterious origin of the hero like the apparition of Arthur in the British cycle.

Some important works of the Anglo-Saxon period (Pre-Christian Era).

Some important works of the Anglo-Saxon period are: *The Ruined Burg, The Lover's Message. The Maiden's Complaint, The Wanderer* and *the Seafarer.*

'The Wanderer is also known as *'Widsith'*. The work is based on the wandering life of the gleeman.

Belonging to this period, we also have *"Deor's Lament"*, which, according to Long is, "much more poetic than *'Widsith,'* and is the one perfect lyric of the Anglo-Saxon period."

In the *Seafarer*, we have glimpses of hard sea life along with the call of the sea, which we, in our times, find more pronouncedly, but perhaps less picturesquely, in Masefield's *"Sea-Fever"*.

Some Christian writers of the Anglo-Saxon period.

Whereas the pagan literature of the Anglo-Saxon period was chiefly in the form of oral legends which they had brought with them from the foreign lands which they previously inhabited, the Christian writing mainly came into existence as a result of the teachings of the monks who had come under the influence of two schools—the Augustinian School (from Rome) and Northumbrian School (from Ireland).

While the former, did not produce much lasting works, the latter produced a number of good and great writers, *e.g.,* **The Venerable Bede (673-735), Caedmon (seventh century)** and **Cynewulf (eighth century)**.

Besides the poets mentioned above, we have **Alfred (848-90)** who is chiefly known as a translator.

ANGLO-NORMAN PERIOD (1066-1350)

Some important works of the Anglo-Norman period.

One important work of this period is *Geoffrey's "Historic Regum Britanniae"* (1137) commonly known as *"History"*. Geoffrey is believed to have died in 1154.

Geoffrey's work which became immensely popular in his own life, is a mixture of pagan and Christian legends and is based more on lies than on real historical events.

However, the said work has its literary value for its poetry and romance pertaining to king Arthur and his Knights, and hence, it became a source of inspiration and scintillating subject matter for such illustrious authors as Malory, Shakespeare and Tennyson.

Geoffrey's work was in Latin verse. Thereafter appeared *"Layman's Brut"* (c. 1200) which has its main interest in giving Arthur's legends in (Anglo-Saxon) English itself.

Then there appeared what are known as *"Metrical Romances"* which were based on the "matter" of France, Rome and Britain.

While in the *Matter of France,* **Charlemagne's** exploits dominated and in the *Matter of Rome* Alexander's adventures and the war of Troy were the main subjects, in the *Matter of Britain*, exploits of Arthur and his knights of the Round Table were chief subject matter. There were a number of cycles pertaining to the knights of Arthur, among them being **Sir Gawain (1350)** *Quest of the Holy Grail, Death of Arthur, Merlin, etc.*

Besides the above, other works of the period included ballads, lyrics and such poems as the *Owl and the Nightingale, Ormulum, Cursor Mundi (1320), The Pearl, Patience, Cleanness, etc.* Also **Roger Bacon's** *"Opus Majus"* appeared in 1267.

THE AGE OF CHAUCER (1340-1400)

The Hundred years war between England and France had already started in 1338 when **Chaucer** was born in **1340**.

In the earlier years of the war, England was all-powerful and under Edward III it won victories over France at Sluys in 1340 and Crecy in 1346, culminating in the capture of Calais in 1347.

Another thumping victory was won by the Black Prince, Edward III's son in 1356 by defeating the French at Poitiers.

As a result of the English victories, the English foreign trade began to flourish, particularly in the export of wool to Flanders, which filled the coffers of the English king and the people also became richer, as we notice conspicuously in **Chaucer's** *Canterbury Tales* when we consider the lot of so many actors, particularly those belonging to landed aristocracy.

This picture is also graphically depicted in **Trevelyan's** *British History of Six Centuries.*

It was unfortunate for England that in the moment of its glory it was overtaken by plague, the Black Death which took a heavy toll of life all over Europe in 1348-49.

As a result of the Black Death, most of the labourers who escaped death, left the country, and this caused an intense scarcity of the availability of essential commodities at cheap rates. To meet this menace, the Parliament tried to force the labourers to accept the same wages as they were getting before the Black Death, and it all finally precipitated into the well-known Peasants' Revolt during the reign of Richard II.

In spite of the passage of certain statutes purported to safeguard the English clergy against the undue domination of the Pope, the low simmering of wrath among the clergymen for several reasons, there emerged in the "Lollards Movement" under the leadership of the redoubtable Wyclif.

Another prominent feature, this one in the literary world, was the slow advent of the spirit of New Learning from Italy and drastic changes in the structure of the English language which had already been continuing as the inevitable outcome of the Norman conquest at Hastings in 1066.

These were the general conditions in which the most significant writers of the age—**Chaucer, Langland, Dunbar,** etc. lived and flourished, thus heralding a new age slowly, but boldly and surely.

MAJOR AUTHORS AND THEIR WORKS OF CHAUCER'S AGE

Wyclif (1320-1384)

The Bible

Geoffrey Chaucer (1340-1400)

The Boke of the Duchesse
The Romaunt of the Rose
The House of Fame
Troylus Cryseyde
The Canterbury Tales
Legends of Good Women
The Parliament of Fouls

William Langland (1330-1400)

Piers the Piowman (A Vision)
A Treatise on the Astrolabe

John Gower (1332-1408)

Confessio Amantis Vox Clamantis
Speculm Meditantis

Thomas Occleve (1370-1450)

The Governail of Princes
Occleve's Complaint
La Mala Regle
The Complaint of Our Lady

John Barbour (1316-1395)

Bruce

John Lydgate (1370-1451)

Falles of Princes
The Temple of Glass
Story of Thebes
London Lickpenny

King James I of Scotland (1394-1437)

The King's Quair
Pebis to the Play
Christis Kirk on the Green

Sir John Maundevill (14th Century)

The Travels of Sir John Maundevill

John Skelton (1460-1529)

Garland of Laurell
Dirge on Edward IV
Magnificence

William Dunbar (1465-1530)

The Thistle and the Rose
Dance of the Seven Deadly Sins

Gowain Douglas (1474-1522)

The Palace of Honour
King Hart
Conscience

Alexander Barclay (1475-1522)

Ship of Fools
Certayne Ecloges

Sir Thomas More (1478-1535)

Utopia (English Version)

William Tyndale (1485-1536)

New Testament

Sir David Lyndsay (1490-1555)

The Dreme
Meldrum
Estaits

Robert Henryson (15th Century)

Morall Fabillis of Esope
The Testament of Cressied
Orpheus and Eurydice

Sir Thomas Malory (15th Century)

Morte d' Arthur

Nicholas Udall (1505-1556)

Roister Doister

Roger Ascham (1515-1568)

The Scholemaster

Stephen Hawes (?-1523)

The Passetyme of Pleasure
The Examle of Virtue
A Joyfull Medytacyon

Thomas Sackville and Thomas Norton : (1536-1608) (1532-1584)

Gorboduc

John Still (1543-1608)

Gammer Gurton's Needle

John Heywood (1564-1627)

Four P's

THE SEVENTEENTH CENTURY

THE RENAISSANCE (1578-1625)

The Renaissance of English Literature coincides with the Age of Queen Elizabeth I. Hence, in the history of English literature, this period is also called as the *Elizabethan Age*. The inspiration for the great works of this period came from the prolific translations into English of works of ancient Rome and Greece. Thus, **Plutarch's** *Lives* was translated by **Sir Thomas North (1579)** from the French version. Montaigne's Essays was translated by **John Florio (1603)**. In verse, **Ovid's** *Metamorphoses* was translated by **Arthur Golding (1565, 1567)**. Among other works of foreign origin translated into English were Ariosto's *Orlando Furioso* by **Harrington (1591)**, and Homer's *Iliad* by **George Chapman (1598)**.

The rising English stage and the English novel borrowed from Boccaccio, Cinthio, Bandello and Straparola — the Italians. Attracted though England was to Italian art, it resisted the evil influences of debauchery, crime and passions that the Italian spirit represented. Yet, the time was ripe in England for the full development of every art and literary form. Renaissance means *a flowering again of art and culture*. It inculcated a sense of wonder in things. England also wanted to rival Spain, France and Portugal in her navigational triumphs. Thus in 1578, Sir Francis Drake circumnavigated the world, and in 1588, the English navy destroyed the Armada. The same spirit of adventure moved literature. In *Apologie for Poetrie*, Sidney described the poet — of all sciences 'the monarch'. Poets were encouraged to innovate new styles and rhythms.

Poetry

Three great men of letters led the Renaissance in England — Spenser, Sidney and Lyly.

Edmund Spenser (1552-1599) wrote the *Shepheardes Calendar* (1579)—an allegory. The union of line and metre is varied and rich. In *Hymnes In honour of Love and Beautie*, he sets forth his philosophy, the conflict in his mind between paganism and Christianity. He also wrote a satire named, *Mother Hubberd's Tale* to denounce the neglect of arts and letters. His pastoral, *Colin Clout's Come Home Again* describes his stay in London in 1589. His *Amoretti* (1595) are sonnets on love and his *Epithalamion* is an ode, but his masterpiece is the *Faerie Queene* (1589, 1595), an allegory in which characters represent virtues and vices. In it his lyrical quality and colour-effects are at their best. The *Faerie Queene* is Queen Elizabeth. The nine-line stanza he used is now called the *Spenserian stanza*.

Sir Philip Sidney (1554-1586) was a scholar, knight and courtier. In 1580 he wrote *Arcadia* which has a blend of pastoral and heroic elements. It is a romance of chivalry and love. The language is characterized by *pathetic fallacy* — endowing inanimate objects with feelings and sensations. William Shakespeare borrowed from this style. His other poem, *Astrophel and Stella* (1591) describes his lost love for the daughter of an Earl. His *Apologie for Poetrie* (1595) written in an unaffected prose, is a plea for poetry.

John Lyly (1554-1606) invented an artistic, flowery style called *euphuism* through his famous romance, *Euphues, the Anatomy of Wit* (1579). This style was adopted by the refined people of the Court. The style is characterized by the use of alliteration and antithesis, fantastic metaphors and similes based on mythology, and natural history of flora and fauna.

The works of these three trail-blazed many poets and sonneteers like Samuel Daniel, Michael Drayton, Thomas Watson, Henry Constable and Thomas Lodge. Notable works from 1590 to 1603 were **Samuel Daniel's (1562-1619)** *The Civil Wars* (1595) describing the *War of the Roses*, **Michael Drayton's (1563-1631)** *Idea, the Shepherd's Garland, The Baron's Wars, England's Heroicall Epistles* (1603) and *Poly-Olbion*, a long description of England in 15,000 alexandrines or lines of twelve syllables. England came to be known as *"a nest of* *singing birds"* because of the great number of lyrics and poems written in this period. **Thomas Campion (1567-1620)** published an anthology called *Two Books of Ayres* (1612). Many of the best poems are found in plays by Ben Jonson, Thomas Dekker, Beaumont and Fletcher, and Webster. But those of William Shakespeare are probably the most beautiful. In his *Sonnets*, he describes his love for a married woman who betrays him. Other poems of this period are Marlowe's Hero and Leander (1598), Shakespeare's *Venus and Adonis* (1593) and *The Rape of Lucrece* (1594).

After Elizabeth's reign, in James I rule, poetry became religious and didactic. The Protestant spirit dominated the literary works. The poems of George Wither, William Browne, the Fletcher brothers and William Drummond show the influence of Spenser still.

Ben Jonson (1573-1637) was the greatest humanist of the time. He was mainly a playwright but wrote poems also. His poetry is found in collections like *Epigrams* and *The Forest* (1616) and *The Underwoods* (1640). He was a satirist and neo-classicist being influenced by the Latin classics.

John Donne's (1573-1631) poetry is revolutionary. He disobeys the laws of rhythm and uses a device called the metaphysical conceit in which strangely opposite ideas are juxtaposed.

Prose

Much of the prose of the period is poetical, influenced by euphuism. Robert Greene, Thomas Lodge, Thomas Nashe, Thomas Deloney, and Thomas Dekker are the major writers. **Robert Greene's (1558-1592)** works include *Mamilia* and *Menaphon* and **Thomas Lodge's (1558-1625)** include *Rosalynde: Euphues Golden Legacie* (1590). **Thomas Nashe (1567-1601)** wrote pamphlets like The *Anatomie of Absurdities* and *The Terrors of the Night*. **Thomas Dekker's (1572-1632)** *The Gils Horne booke* is famous for its picturesque prose. Most of the poets and prose writers of this period were also dramatists. Shakespeare used prose for homely and humorous scenes and verse for tragic ones.

Many writers of the English Renaissance were inspired by the literary criticism of the Continent to write some themselves. Stephen Gosson's *The Schoole of Abuse* (1579) and *Sidney's Apologie for Poetrie* are good examples. Sidney eulogizes the poet as a law-giver. The period also saw works of religious prose. **Richard Hooker's (1554-1600)** pamphlet on the Marlin Marprelate controversy is a famous one. Hooker's *Of the Laws of Ecclesiastical Polity* (1594) is a masterpiece of English prose. The most seminal work of the period is the authorized version of the Bible published in 1611. The work was commissioned by James I. A beautiful prose minus archaism is used by the revisers. The diction was to influence the English language very deeply. It is the language of daily speech, yet fresh and lofty.

Side by side with religious literature, secular and philosophical literature, mostly written by **Francis Bacon (1561-1626)**, came out. He had taken all knowledge as his province and elaborated his doctrines in his *Novum Organum* (1620). His ideas influenced the formation of *The Royal Society for Improving Natural Knowledge* in 1645. His most popular work is his *Essays* written on diverse topics in a terse, epigrammatic style. The English writers quote copiously from Bacon today. His sentences are household terms. Take for example, "*He that hath wife and children hath given hostages to fortune*". "*Some books are to be tasted, others to be swallowed and some few to be chewed and digested*".

Another great prose-writer of the period was **Robert Burton (1577-1640)** whose *The Anatomy of Melancholy* (1621) is full of pedantry. He borrowed from numerous sources and is full of melancholy and jests; his style abounds in synonyms and epithets.

Drama

Drama thrived in the Renaissance. Foreign influence, especially of Italy, predominated. Plays were written so that the public would enjoy them and applaud the stage. There was a great variety of plays written — pure tragedy, tragi-comedy, historical drama, romantic comedy, comedy of errors, farce, pastoral, etc. The stage was a simple structure, circular in form with a courtyard open to the sky. A platform projected into the courtyard. Boys played the female roles. The public consisted of groundlings and courtiers on galleries. The unities of time, place and action were disregarded. Farce and tragedy were found in succession.

Several mythological allegories were acted before the court. **John Lyly's** euphuistic romances like *Campaspe* (1584), *Sapho and Phao, Endymion* (1592), *Midas* were praises of the queen. **George Peele (1558-1598)** wrote *The Araygnement of Paris* (1584) and *The Old Wives' Tale*. There were violent plays like **Thomas Kyd's (1558-1594)** The *Spanish Tragedie* (1585) and **Christopher Marlowe's (1564-1593)** *Tamburlaine, the Great* (1587) and *Doctor Faustus* (1592). *Doctor Faustus* is an allegory on the Renaissance love of power. It shows how Doctor Faustus, the scientist, sells his soul to the devil for twenty-four years of full power to satisfy every desire. In the end his agony increases as the devil approaches to claim his soul. Marlowe also wrote *The Jew of Malta*, which shows the unbridled love for wealth, and the historical play Edward II. Marlowe crafted the blank verse (mighty line as Shakespeare called it and used). This was suited to the fiery speeches of his characters.

The towering genius of the age was certainly **William Shakespeare (1564-1616)**. He was versatile and wrote about 36 plays and 144 sonnets. "Shakespeare was not of an age but for all times" and "Poets are born not made", wrote Ben Jonson about him. He created a gallery of nearly 800 characters who typify personalities found through human history. Julius Caesar's pride and ambition, Macbeth's unbridled ambition, King Lear's dotedness, and Othello's susceptibility to suspicion against his wife — are tragic flaws that govern men even today.

Shakespeare was not educated except for a few years at a grammar school. He had 'little Latin and less Greek' and read books in translation from Latin and Greek. He adapted the stories into a World entirely his own, instinct with life and vibrancy. Shakespeare began his career by acting for the stage. Then he wrote plays and staged them, mainly to seek court patronage. His great success made him the envy of his contemporaries like Robert Greene. In his tragedies he depicts the fall of great men owing to a tragic flaw in their character. Although they had the will to change their destiny, a fate controlled them. He used the beliefs of his time like the supernatural powers and phenomena to capture the interest of his audience. Some of his historical plays are *Richard II* (1596) and *King John* (1595). Among the romantic comedies *As You Like It* (1600), *The Merchant of Venice* (1596) and *Twelfth Night* (1601) are popular. *A Midsummer Night's Dream* (1595) is a fairy play. *Romeo and Juliet* (1594) is a tragicomedy. He used prose and blank verse.

His *Henry IV* (I & 2) (1597, 1598) contain much more blank verse than his other plays. In depth of psychological insight, and power of style *Hamlet* (1601), one of Shakespeare's great tragedies, stands supreme. *The Tempest* (161I) is one of his last plays which shows the dramatist's mellowed maturity.

Even after 400 years, Shakespeare's plays are very popular, being translated into almost every important language. *"Age cannot wither her nor custom stale her infinite variety"*; Shakespeare described Cleopatra in these words. The same may be said about his plays also.

Ben Jonson was Shakespeare's antithesis. He borrowed the style of the classics and was very erudite. He carefully studied society and wrote about it. He took the different 'humours' or dominating characteristics of men and satirized them in *Every Man in his Humour* (1598) and *Every Man out of his Humour* (1599), *Volpone, or the Fox* (1605) and *The Alchemist* (1605). He also wrote the historical tragedies, *Sejanus His Fall* (1603) and *Catiline His Conspiracy* (1611). The plays are very true to history. John Marston, Thomas Dekker, Thomas Heywood and Middleton were other playwrights of the age. John Webster (1580-1625) is famous for horror plays like *The White Devil* (1609-1612) and *The Duchess of Malfi* (1613-1614).

MAJOR AUTHORS AND THEIR WORKS

Edmund Spenser (1552-1599)

The Faerie Queene
The Shepheardes Calendar
Amoretti
Epithalamion
Prothalamion
Mother Hubberd's Tale
The Ruins of Time
The Tears of the Muses
Astrophel

Phillip Sidney (1554-1586)

Arcadia
Astrophel and Stella
An Apologie for Poetrie

Ben Jonson (1573-1637)

Every Man in His Humour
Every Man Out of His Humour
Volpone Or the Fox
Cynthia's Revels
The Alchemist
Bartholomew Fayre
Epicaene or the Silent Women
Sejanus His Fall
Catline His Conspiracy
The Poetaster
The Devil as an Ass
The Masque of Beauty

Samuel Daniel (1562-1619)

Delia
Civil Wars between the Two Houses of Lancaster and York

Michael Drayton (1563-1631)

The Battle of Agincourt
England's heroic Epistles
The Barons' Wars
Polyolbion

William Shakespeare (1564-1616)

The Two Gentlement of Verona
The Merry Wives of Windsor
Measure for Measure
The Comedy of Errors
Love's Labour's Lost
The Taming of the Shrew
All's Well that Ends Well
A Midsummer Night's Dream
The Merchant of Venice
Much Ado About Nothing
As You Like it
Twelfth Night
Romeo and Juliet
Macbeth
Hamlet
King Lear
Othello
Antony and Cleopatra
Julius Caesar
Timon of Athens
Coriolanus
Titus Andronicus
Troilus and Cressida
King John
King Richard the Second
King Henry the Fourth-Part First
King Henry the Fourth-Second Part
King Henry the Fifth
King Henry the Sixth-First Part
King Henry the Sixth-Second Part
King Henry the Sixth-Third Part
King Richard the Third
King Henry the Eighth
Cymbeline
Pericles
The Winter's Tale
The Tempest
Venus and Adonis and Rape of Lucrece (Narrative Poems)
Sonnets (154 in number).

Christopher Marlowe (1564-1593)

Tamburlaine the Great

Edward II

Doctor Faustus

The Jew of Malta

The Tragedy of Dido, Queen of Carthage.

George Peele (1558-1597)

The Araygnement of Paris

The Famous Chronicle of King Edward I

Robert Greene (1560-1592)

Frier Bacon and Frier Bungey

Orlando Furioso

Pandosto

Thomas Nashe (1567-1601)

The Unfortunate Traveller Or The Life of Jack Wilton

Thomas Lodge (1558-1625)

The Wounds of Civil War

Rosalynde

Thomas Kyd (1557-1595)

The Spanish Tragedy

John Lyly (1554-1606)

Euphues, The Anatomy of Wit

Euphues and His England

Endymion

Francis Bacon (1561-1626)

Essays

The Advancement of Learning

The New Atlantis

Novum Organum

John Webster (1580-1625)

The White Devil

The Duchess of Malfi

The Devil's Law Case.

Thomas Heywood (1575-1650)

A Woman Killed with Kindness

The English Traveller

The Captives

Robert Burton (1577-1640)

The Anatomy of Melancholy

Sir Thomas Browne (1605-1682)

Religio Medici

Vulgar Errors

Hydrotaphia or Urne Búrriale

Christian Morals

Thomas Hobbes (1588-1679)

Leviathan

Jeremy Taylor (1613-1667)

The Liberty of Prophesying

Holy Living

Holy Dying

END OF THE RENAISSANCE (1625-1660)

Prose

Puritanism set the trend for the literature during the reign of Charles I. The Bible was the guiding spirit which may be best seen in Milton's works. The zealous Calvinists enforced Presbyterianism. The passionate curiosity for life which characterized the Renaissance gave place to a search for salvation. **Sir Thomas Browne (1605-1682)** was a scientist, but in his *Pseudodoxia Epidemica or Vulgar Errors* (1646), we see his belief in miracles. His *Religio Medici* (1642) speaks of the vanity of earthly life. **George Herbert's (1596-1633)** *The Country Parson* and **Jeremy Taylor's (1613-1667)** *Holy Living* (1650) and *Holy Dying* (1651) are sermons championing religious freedom. **John Milton (1608-1674)**, who is famous as a poet, wrote numerous pamphlets in favour of divorce which are models of beautiful prose. His *Areopagitica* (1644) is a speech for the liberty of unlicensed writing.

Another great prose-writer was **Thomas Hobbes (1588-1679)** whose *Leviathan* (1651) is a famous work. He was an empiricist and realist and believed that sensations and ideas are caused by physical reasons. Numerous works of ethics, sociology and history were written. *The History of the Rebellion* *and Civil Wars in England* was written by **Edward Hyde (1609-1674). Izaac Walton (1593-1683)** wrote the biographies of John Donne and George Herbert. *The Compleat Angler* (1653) is his famous work on the post-Civil War scene and contains descriptions of the English countryside.

Poetry

Two types of poets existed then — the Cavaliers, who were the Royalists, and the religious or Metaphysical poets. Thomas Carew, Sir John Suckling, John Cleveland, Robert Herrick were Cavalier poets who displayed epicurean tastes. Imagination and sensuous imagery predominate their poems. Among the religious poets, Herbert, Crashaw, Vaughan and Marvell stand out. They were mystics. **George Herbert's (1593-1633)** style is simple and expresses Christian piety in his anthology The Temple (1633). His poems *The Pulley and Love* are very popular. **Richard Crashaw (1613-1649)** used fantastic conceits; e.g. he describes the maudlin St Mary Magdalene's eyes as "walking baths, compedious oceans", **Henry Vaughan (1622-1695)** was a mystic and his poem The Retreat is a nostalgic longing for the blissful heavenly state of childhood.

John Milton's greatest achievement was his *Paradise Lost* (1667). In theme it deals with the fall of man. In form, it follows the strict unity of the classical epic. His other poems are *L'Allegro* (1632), *Il Penseroso* (1632), *Comus* (1634), *Lycidas* (1637), *Samson Agonistes* (1671), etc.

RESTORATION LITERATURE (1620-1734)

Prose

In 1660, Charles II returned to the throne and the Puritan republic ended. The year is also marked as the beginning of the modern literature. **John Bunyan's (1628-1688)** works, *Grace Abounding* (1666) and *The Pilgrim's Progress* (1678) are the last surviving works of Puritan faith. The Pilgrim's Progress is an allegory describing the trials and tribulations on the way to salvation as faced by a Christian. Bunyan's prose is a blend of common speech and the grandeur of the revised Bible.

The scientific spirit took over the reign. The Royal Society of London for the Improvement of Natural Knowledge, to which Bacon and William Harvey (who discovered the circulation of blood) had contributed, now had many learned men. **Sir Isaac Newton** published Principia in 1687. He discovered the laws of gravity, of the diffraction of white light and the theory of fluxions.

John Locke (1632-1704) propounded a new philosophy of commonsense and intelligent reasoning in his *An Essay Concerning Human Understanding* (1690). It lays stress on development of character. It was to influence the English thought. Voltaire was one of his French disciples.

Poetry

Restoration literature was derived from pre-Commonwealth national literature and was a reaction against Puritan oppression. It rejected severe moral codes of conduct and was chiefly satiric in nature. **Samuel Butler's (1612-1680)** poem, *Hudibras* published in three parts (1663, 1664 & 1678), is a typical work of this period. It is inspired by *Don Quixote*. He satirizes Sir Hudibras as a grotesque Presbyterian with a squire called Ralpho. It lays bare all the human follies in octosyllabic couplets. Many court poets like **Andrew Marvell (1621-1678)** and **John Oldham (1653-1683)** were veterans of the Republican era and satirize the follies of the new age.

The great poet of the period was **John Dryden (1631-1700)**. He excelled in almost every kind of composition. He wrote a series of heroic stanzas in honour of Cromwell on his death. He was a disciple of the metaphysical poets displaying their far-fetched images and conceits. In *Astraea Redux* (1660), he celebrated the return of Charles II and in *Annus Mirabilis* (1667) he commemorated the Great Fire of London and the war with Holland. He was a staunch Tory and his famous satires are *Absalom and Achitophel* (1681), *The Medal and Mac-Flecknoe*. In this last work he satirizes Shadwell, the Whig poet. *The Hind and the Panther* (1687) is an allegory on Catholicism and Anglicanism. Dryden also translated the classics, chiefly Persuis and Juvenal. He turned Virgil's *Aeneid* into brilliant couplets. His *Alexander's Feast* is an ode in honour of St. Cecilia.

Drama

The dramatic works of the Restoration were licentious and full of cynicism. They regarded the moral code of the Puritans as a matter of ridicule. Scenery now played an important part on the stage and actresses, not boys, played the female roles. The theatre was regarded as a place of vice and evil. Shakespeare's plays were rewritten and his tragedies like *Romeo and Juliet* given happy endings. French influence dominated and extraordinary superhuman feats were described. Heroes were presented as ideals and were made to give pompous speeches.

Dryden wrote many plays like *Aureng-zebe* or *The Great Mogul* (1675) and The Conquest of Granada (1669, 1670) which abound in rhetoric.

The tragedians were **Thomas Otway (1651-1685)**, Nathaniel Lee (1653-1692) and **Nicholas Rowe (1674-1718)**. The comedy of this period reflects the gay intrigues of the society. Caricature and farce were used and obscenity also touched it. The main aim was to amuse. **Sir George Etheredge (1635-1691)** was an innovator and **William Wycherley (1640-1715)** was a moralist playwright. **William Congreve (1670-1729)** wrote a series of masterpieces including *The Way of the World* (1700). **John Vanbrugh** (1664-1726) and **George Farquhar (1678-1707)** were other comedy writers of the period.

Criticism

Dryden was the first English critic. *The Essay of Dramatick Poesie* (1668) is his longest single prose work and a major piece of English literary criticism. It is in the form of a discussion between four characters, one of whom is Dryden himself. It deals with topics related to theatre and evaluates the works of the Elizabethan dramatists, especially of Shakespeare.

The Diarists of the Restoration Period

One of the sources of information and genres of prose writing during the Restoration were diaries. The important names are those of John Evelyn, Samuel Pepys and Roger North. **John Evelyn (1620-1706)** was a rich man who had cultured tastes. He was a member of the Royal Society and had wide interests in diverse fields like gardening, forestry, navigation and architecture. His *Diary* which was written almost throughout his lifetime throws a floodlight on the major social and national events of the time like the Galley Slaves and the Great Fire. It is written in a plain, graphic style. **Samuel Pepys (1633-1703)** had a chequered career. Coming from the middle classes, he joined the civil services and rose to be the secretary of the Admiralty. He also became the President of the Royal Society and a member of Parliament. His famous *Diary*, covering a period of ten years, is in the form of confessions. It was written in laconic sentences like the messages of a telegram and was in a sort of code which was deciphered only in 1825. The diary shows him to be a man of versatile interests like music, science and literature. But the most controversial aspect is the detailed confessions of his life. Nobody seemed to guess he was a libertine, a morally debauched character who could stoop to low means. When we read the diary, it seems he is writing of another person. **Roger North** belonged to an elite family. He was a Tory gentleman and was engaged in the politics of the times. His famous work is *North's Lives of the Norths* containing biographies of three relatives and an autobiography. His pen pictures and anecdotes are in colloquial style.

MAJOR AUTHORS AND THEIR WORKS

Robert Herrick (1591-1574)

Noble Numbers

Hesperides

Thomas Carew (1598-1639)

Poems

'He that loves a rosy cheek'

Sir John Suckling (1660-1642)

'Ballad upon a Wedding'

'Why so pale and wan, Fond Lover'?

Andrew Marvell (1621-1678)

'To His Coy Mistress'

'The Rehearsal Transprosed'

'Ode upon Cromwell's Return from Ireland'

New Letters (a Prose Work)

George Herbert (1593-1633)

The Temple

Affliction

Easter Wings

The Collar

Man

Richard Crashaw (1613-1649)

Carmen Deo Nostro

The Infant Morturs

Steps to the Temple

John Milton (1608-1674)

Paradise Lost (in twelve Books)

Paradise Regained

Comus

Lycidas

Samson Agonistes

L'Allegro

Ill Penseroso

Areopagitica (Prose Work)

Ode on the Morning of Christ's Nativity

Sonnets (including) :

'On His Blindness'

'On the Late Massacre in Piedmont'

'When the Assault was Intended to the City'

'On His Having Arrived at the Age of Twenty-three'

A large number of Tracts and Pamphlets in support of the Parliament

John Donne (1573-1631)

Songs and Sonnets

Aires and Angels

A Nocturnall upon Lucies Day

A Valediction : Forbidding Mourning

The Extasie

Devotions (Sermon in Prose)

Ignatius His Enclave (a Prose Work)

Of the Progress of the Soul

Death's Duell

Abraham Cowley (1618-1667)

Pyramus and Thisbe

The Mistress

The Davideis

Pindarique Odes

Constantia and Philetus

Discourse by Way of Vision

Concerning the Government of Cromwell (a Prose Work)

Henry Vaughan (1622-1695)

Poems

Regeneration

The Retreat

Olor Iscanus

Thalia Redivia

Silex Scintillans

John Dryden (1631-1700)

(i) *Heroic Stanzas on the Death of Oliver Cromwell*

Astraea Redux (on the Restoration of Charles II)

Absalom and Achitophel

Religio Laici

The Hind and the Panther

The Fables

Annus Mirabilis

The Medal

Mac Flecknoe

Alexander's Feast

Prefaces to His Plays (in Prose)

An Essay of Dramatic Poesy

(ii) *Dryden's Plays*

Tyrannic Love
Conquest of Granada
All for love
The Rival Ladies
The Indian Emperor
Aureng-Zeb
Don Sebastian
Cleomenes
Love Triumphant

John Vanbrugh (1664-1726)
The Relapse
The Provoked Wife
The Confederacy

George Farquhar (1678-1707)
The Recruiting Officer
The Beaux Stratagem

Thomas Otway (1652-1685)
Orphan
Venice Preserved
Don Carlos
Alcibiades

Nathaniel Lee (1653-1692)
Nero
The Rival Queens
Sophonisba

John Bunyan (1628-1688)
The Pilgrim's Progress
Grace Abounding
The Life and Death of Mr. Badman
The Holy War

John Locke (1632-1704)
Essay on the Human Understanding
Treatise on Government
Thoughts on Education

John Evelyn (1620-1706)
Diary

Samuel Pepys (1633-1703)
Diary

MULTIPLE CHOICE QUESTIONS

1. *The Shoemaker's Holiday* is a play written by:
A. Shakespeare
B. Marlowe
C. Thomas Dekker
D. Marston

2. Ben Jonson's *The Poetaster* is a satire on:
A. Marston and Dekker
B. Marlowe
C. Kyd
D. Greene

3. The main theme of Webster's plays is his:
A. humour
B. satire
C. preoccupation with death
D. social life

4. Marlowe, Kyd, Lyly and Greene were known as:
A. Humorists
B. University Wits
C. The Rivals of Shakespeare
D. The Decadents

5. The person who collaborated with Beaumont for many plays was:
A. Fletcher B. Shakespeare
C. Marston D. Greene

6. *Leviathan* is written by:
A. Milton B. Marvel
C. Thomas Hobbes D. Farquhar

7. *The Pilgrim's Progress* by John Bunyan is a/an:
A. book of philosophy
B. treatise on education
C. masque
D. allegory

8. Samuel Butler's satire on Puritanism is:
A. *Hudibras* B. *Way of the World*
C. *Utopia* D. *Paradise Lost*

9. John Evelyn's *Diary* is famous for:
A. describing major social events of his times
B. describing personal experiences
C. scholarly research
D. noting facts and figures

10. Samuel Pepys' *Diary* is mainly:
A. social B. confessional
C. descriptive D. argumentative

11. Who wrote the *Faerie Queene?*
A. John Lyly B. Edmund Spenser
C. Ben Jonson D. Shakespeare

12. What is the nine-line stanza used in the *Faerie Queene* called?
A. Alexandrine B. Shakespearean
C. Spenserian D. Petrarchan

13. *The Anatomy of Melancholy* is written by:
A. Robert Burton B. John Dryden
C. Thomas Dekker D. Milton

14. *Doctor Faustus* is a story of:
A. a scientist
B. revenge
C. the Renaissance love of power
D. a greedy Jew

15. Marlowe invented:
A. sprung rhythm B. sonnet
C. allegory D. blank verse

16. Herrick, Carew, Suckling and Lovelace were collectively called:
A. Metaphysical Poets
B. Religious Poets
C. Puritans
D. Cavalier Poets

17. The *Horatian Ode* by Andrew Marvel is addressed to:
A. Cromwell B. Charles II
C. Queen Elizabeth D. Shakespeare

18. *Comus* by Milton is a/an:
A. masque B. ode
C. epic D. lyric

19. *Lycidas* is an elegy by Milton on:
A. Arthur Hallam B. Edward King
C. Cromwell D. Ben Jonson

20. *The Compleat Angler* is written by:
A. Milton B. Robert Burton
C. Izaak Walton D. Thomas Fuller

21. *Romeo and Juliet* is a:
A. tragedy B. comedy
C. tragi-comedy D. history

22. *Every Man in His Humour* is written by:
A. Ben Jonson B. Dryden
C. John Donne D. Marston

23. Dryden wrote:
A. *Sejanus*
B. *The Compleat Angler*
C. *Aureng-zebe*
D. *Principia*

24. The song *Drink to me only with thine eyes* is written by:
A. Lyly B. Ben Jonson
C. Shakespeare D. Spenser

25. The Puritan Parliament closed the theatres in:
A. 1638 B. 1632
B. 1606 D. 1642

ANSWERS

1	2	3	4	5	6	7	8	9	10
C	A	C	B	A	C	D	A	A	B
11	**12**	**13**	**14**	**15**	**16**	**17**	**18**	**19**	**20**
B	C	A	C	D	D	A	A	B	C
21	**22**	**23**	**24**	**25**					
C	A	C	B	D					

THE EIGHTEENTH CENTURY

THE AUGUSTAN AGE (1700-1740)

In general, the eighteenth century was the age of understanding and enlightenment. The emphasis was on the advancement of the human mind. Sensibility was the guiding principle. This age borrowed the humour and poetic technique of the previous century.

This age is generally called *The Augustan Age* or *The Age of Queen Anne* because the queen patronized the men of letters. The period is also known as the Classical Age. It was an age of tolerance and harmony and was guided by reason. Dryden still wrote and was a contemporary of French authors Corneille, Racine and Moliere. Many English works were translated by the French. Poetry was still for aristocrats and the courts, but prose spread among the common public. People demanded instructions and information and practical hints for living. This led writers to use a simple style to be comprehensible to all.

Poetry

Matthew Prior (1664-1721) began by writing a parody of The Hind and the Panther in which he expounded his opinions on politics. **Sir Samuel Garth (1661-1791)** and **Joseph Addison (1672-1719)** used the heroic couplet of Dryden. Addison described Marlborough's victory at Blenheim in his poem *The Campaign* (1704). But the poetical luminary of the period was **Alexander Pope (1688-1744)**. He polished Dryden's couplet and used it as a weapon of satire, like in the famous *An Essay on Man* (1732-1734). His *An Essay on Criticism* (1711) and *The Rape of the Lock* (1712, 1714) are other great works. The latter is in mock-heroic style and describes the anger of a lady whose lock of hair had been cut off. Pope also translated the Iliad. He wrote *The Dunciad* (1728) to castigate bad poets. His *Imitations of Horace* (1733-1737) is highly admired even today.

Jonathan Swift, usually known as a prose writer, also showed a gift or versification like in his poem *On the Death of Dr. Swift*. **John Gay (1685-1732)** was popular for his fables like *The Hare with Many Friends* and his songs in *The Beggar's Opera*. **Edward Young's (1683-1765)** *The Commaint, or Night Thoughts on Life, Death, and Immortality* (1742), is a poet's delight in meditation underlining the vanity of all earthly glory.

Prose

This period saw an increasing demand for the circulation of facts and ideas among the public. **Daniel Defoe (1659-1731)** was a trail-blazer as a Journalist and his popular works are *The True-Born Englishman* (1701) and *The Shortest Way with the Dissenters* (1702). Defoe wrote the first English novel *Robinson Crusoe* (1719), which is a children's classic or collection of adventure stories. He cultivated the art of reporting and presented his stories as historical narratives which are precise and practical.

Steele, Addison, Swift, Arbuthnot were the other great prose-writers of the time. They introduced a style adorned by figures of speech. The periodicals of Steele and Addison contain essays which deal with practical moral questions and reflect the morals of the time.

Richard Steele (1672-1729) led a dissipated life and was full of remorse for it. He extols the Bible as a guide in life in his work *The Christian Hero*. He launched the journal *The Tatler* in 1709. **Joseph Addison** propagated rational and moderate ideas. He collaborated with Steele on *The Tatler*. Steele then founded *The Spectator* in 1711 and Addison again collaborated. Here they were merely the spectators of the society and its foibles. It epitomizes the whole nation. The character of Sir Roger de Coverley is a masterpiece, a comic personality with eccentricities. Other characters, Sir Andrew Freeport. Will Honeycomb, Captain Sentry capture the imagination of the readers.

Jonathan Swift (1667-1745) enjoyed ridicule rather than correction. He lays bare all the vices of man as something that are beyond correction. He ridiculed the modern authors in his The *Battle of the Books* (1704) and attacked the Papists and Presbyterians in *The Tale of a Tub* (1704). His most popular work is a children's classic, *Gulliver's Travels* (1726), which is also a satire on politics, religions, science and nature of man.

John Arbuthnot (1667-1735) was another humanist and man of wit and is known for his *The History of John Bull* (1712), an amusing allegory on the politics of the time.

During this period a number of deists like Locke, Collins and Tindal propounded a philosophy advocating reasoning rather than superstitious beliefs as advocated by orthodox Christians. Earl of Shaftesbury (1671-1713), Lord Bolingbroke (1678-1751) and Mandeville were other rationalists of the time who wrote many prose works.

THE AGE OF TRANSITION (1740-1800)

Like all other periods of transition, this age was also disturbed and confused. Two movements can be clearly observed in the writings of the time: (*i*) the allegiance to the old order of classicism, and (*ii*) the search after the new order of Romanticism. The period was marked by new learning, new philosophy, growth of historical research and new realism.

This period is also known as the *Age of Johnson* because **Samuel Johnson (1709-1784)**, the greatest English man of letters, flourished during this period. Samuel Johnson was a versatile man of letters translator, journalist, commentator, critic, novelist, biographer and poet. He created two satirical poems, *London* (1738) and *The Vanity of Human Wishes* (1749). He had a supple style and describes his personal reflections in his essays *The Rambler* (1750-1752) and *The Idler* (1758-1760). His *Dictionary of English Language* (1747-1755) shows remarkable precision in definition and a feeling for the correct use of words. Besides the novel *Rasselas, Prince of Abyssinia* (1759) his best works are biographical and literary studies and his edition of *Shakespeare* (1765). His *Lives of the Poets* (1777-1781) is a biographical work. His admirer James Boswell's famous biography of Johnson has made him immortal. He is described here in candid details. His prejudices, excellences and demerits are all laid bare.

Poetry

Poetry showed the influence of Dryden and Pope. It was mainly didactic and satirical and the couplet still was the major form.

Oliver Goldsmith's (1728-1774) *Deserted Village* (1770) is a masterpiece of the period. **James Thomson's (1700-1748)** *The Seasons* (1730) is a praise of the beauties of Nature in all her diversity. Other noteworthy poems of the period are **William Collins' (1721-1759)** *Ode to Evening*, a delightful lyric, and **Thomas Gray's (1716-1771)** *Elegy Written in a Country Churchyard* (1751).

A general belief in human liberty was seen as the French Revolution proceeded. **William Cowper** (1731-1800) who wrote *The Ballad of John Gilpin,* **George Crabbe (1754-1832)**, the Scotsman **Robert Burns (1759-1796)** and the mystic **William Blake (1757-1827)** echoed the sentiments of the period. Burns was a farmer and wrote in original racy dialect thus causing a break from convention. Blake was a visionary and his poems are collected in *Songs of Innocence* (1789) and *Songs of Experience* (1794). In *The Tyger,* he uses the Lamb as a symbol of innocence and of Jesus, and the Tiger as the symbol of evil in the world, of the evil seen in the French Revolution where thousands were sent to the guillotine.

Novel

The period saw the development of the novel. A series of masterpieces came out. In the novel, the author could describe events in detail. Defoe's novels so far were based on strange subjects. Now they concentrated on commonplace events of family life and society. Adventure of earlier novels gave place to character portrayal. The novels were very long and filled with minute details. **Samuel Richardson (1689-1761)** wrote *Pamela, or Virtue Rewarded* (1740) and *Clarissa Harlowe* (1747-

1748). **Henry Fielding (1707-1754)** is famous for *Joseph Andrews* (1742) and *Tom Jones* (1749), **Tobias Smollet (1721-1771)** wrote *The Adventures of Roderick Random* (1748) and *The Expedition of Humphry Clinker* (1771), **Laurence Sterne (1713-1768)** wrote *Tristram Shandy* (1760), and **Oliver Goldsmith** *The Vicar of Wakefield* (1766).

Letter

There were famous letter writers also, like **Lord Chesterfield (1694-1773). Horace Walpole (1719-1797), Thomas Gray and Richardson**. Frequently, a series of letters was bound into book-form. Collections of this kind were the letters of **Lady Mary Wortley Montagu (1689-1762)**, written to Pope from Constantinople, and of Thomas Gray, from the Lake District. Chesterfield's letters to his son contain comments on political and social matters. Richardson's *Pamela* is entirely in letter-form.

Drama

The century was the age of the great novels. Drama lost originality and talent. People saw Shakespeare's plays enacted, but what attracted them was the genius of the actors. However, there were a few good plays written. For instance, Johnson's *Irene* (1749), Fielding's *The Miser*, Goldsmith's anti-sentimental comedy *She Stoops to Conquer* (1773), and Sheridan's *The School for Scandal* (1777) and *The Rivals* (1775).

Historical Work

Towards the last part of the century the history of England was rocked by many revolutionary changes the impact of which were felt in English literature. Till the mid-18th century Victorian England reigned supreme. She was mistress of the seas and her imperial rule covered many colonies. In 1776, America declared her independence and the British Parliament was divided on the issue. Many Britishers favoured the American claims. In 1789, the French Revolution broke out and here too the Britishers were divided into two camps. Inspired by the writings of Rousseau, many believed the Revolution was being fought for the right causes. The Parliament resounded with the speeches of the famous. Some even accused Warren Hastings for his extortion policies in India and some others were against slave-trade.

Treatises on philosophy by **David Hume (1711-1776)** and histories by **William Robertson (1721-1793)** and political economy (*Wealth of Nations*) by **Adam Smith (1723-1790)** came out.

Edmund Burke (1729-1797) read law and began writing to propound his views on human feelings and emotions. His language is as oratorical in Parliament at the trial of Warren Hastings as in his famous writing *A Philosophical Inquiry into the Origin of our Ideas of the Sublime and the Beautiful* (1756).

Other orators who expressed themselves in writing were Tom Paine, Godwin and Jeremy Bentham. **William Godwin (1756-1836)** advocated the elimination of government in *Enquiry Concerning Political Justice* (1793). He proscribed law, marriage, gratitude, everything that limited liberty. His monumental work is *The Decline and Fall of the Roman Empire* (1776-1788) in which he describes the growth of Christianity and his belief in reason rather than the divine. At the same time **William Paley (1743-1805)** wrote *A View of the Evidences of Christianity* (1794) to prove the existence of miracles by logic.

MAJOR AUTHORS AND THEIR WORKS

Alexander Pope (1688-1744)

Pastorals

An Essay on Criticism

Windsor Forest

The Rape of the Lock

Dunciad

Translation of Iliad and Odyssey

To Lord Bathrust

On the Use of the Riches

An Essay on Man

Epistle to Dr. Arbuthnot

Of the Knowledge and Characters of Men

Of the Characters of Women

The Messiah
Satires and Epistles of Horace Imitated

Matthew Prior (1664-1721)
Solomon on the Vanity of the World
Alma : or the Progress of the Mind
The Town and Country Mouse

John Gay (1685-1732)
Fables
The Shepherd's Week
The Rural Sports
Trivia
The Beggar's Opera
The Streets of London

Edward Young (1683-1765)
Night Thoughts

Dr. Samuel Johnson (1709-1784)
The Vanity of Human Wishes
London
The Lives of the Poets
Preface to Shakespeare
Dictionary of the English Language
A Journey to the Western Islands of Scotland
The Rambler
Rasselas
Prince of Abyssinia
The Life of Savage
The Adventurer
The Idler

Daniel Defoe (1661-1731)
Robinson Crusoe
Mall Flanders
Colonel Jack
The Memoirs of a Cavalier
Captain Singleton
Journal of the Plague Year
Roxana

Jonathan Swift (1667-1745)
The Battle of the Books
A Tale of a Tub
Gulliver's Travels
Journal to Stella
The Drapier's Letters
Cadenus and Vanessa

Joseph Addison (1672-1719)
The Spectator
The Campaign
Public Credit
The Vision of Mirza
Cato
Rosamond
The Drummer

Richard Steele (1672-1729)
The Tatler
The Guardian
The Funeral
The Lying Lover
The Tender Husband
The Conscious Lover

Thomas Gray (1716-1771)
Elegy Written in a Country Churchyard
On a Distant Prospect of Eton College
On the Death of a Favourite Cat
The Bard
The Progress of Poesy
The Fatal Sisters
The Descent of Odin

MULTIPLE CHOICE QUESTIONS

1. The novel written in epistolary or letter form is:
A. *Joseph Andrews*
B. *Pamela*
C. *Vicar of Wakefield*
D. *Tom Jones*

2. Johnson's biographer was:
A. Boswell
B. Irene
C. Swift
D. Edmund Burke

3. A play which describes heroes as virtues personified and is full of pompous speeches is:
   A. Heroic play
   B. Sentimental Comedy
   C. Anti-Sentimental Comedy
   D. Tragi-Comedy
4. Edmund Burke was:
   A. poet and scholar B. playwright
   C. orator and writer D. lexicographer
5. *The Decline and Pall of the Roman Empire* is written by:
   A. Paley B. Smith
   C. Johnson D. Godwin
6. John Gay is famous for a musical drama named:
   A. *The Beggar's Opera*
   B. *Polly*
   C. *The Secretary*
   D. *Fables*
7. *The Ballad of John Gilpin* is written by:
   A. Thomas Gray B. William Cowper
   C. William Blake D. Robert Burns
8. The son of a British Prime Minister is famous for his letters and *The Castle of Otranto*, a gruesome play. His (the son's) name was:
   A. Robert Walpole B. Horace Walpole
   C. William Pitt D. Churchill
9. *Wealth of Nations* is written by:
   A. Joshua Reynolds B. Adam Smith
   C. Godwin D. David Hume
10. Sheridan was a:
    A. poet B. dramatist
    C. novelist D. musician
11. *The Hind and the Panther* is a parody about:
    A. religion
    B. society
    C. politics
    D. human beings in general
12. Which poem is in mock-heroic style?
    A. *The Rape of the Lock*
    B. *The Christian Hero*
    C. *On the Death of Dr. Swift*
    D. *The Hare with Many Friends*
13. Who was the first journalist of the age?
    A. Dryden B. Daniel Defoe
    C. Swift D. Arbuthnot
14. Who wrote the first English dictionary?
    A. Goldsmith B. Boswell
    C. Webster D. Samuel Johnson
15. Lord Chesterfield is famous as a:
    A. Novelist B. Letter-writer
    C. Playwright D. Poet
16. *The Rivals* is a play by:
    A. Sheridan B. Goldsmith
    C. Johnson D. David Garrick
17. *Origin of our Ideas of the Sublime and the Beautiful* is an essay by:
    A. Edmund Burke B. Godwin
    C. Thomas Paine D. Hume
18. The greatest Scottish poet of the 18th century is:
    A. Robert Burns B. Waltor Scott
    C. William Cowper D. John Gay
19. The lines, *"O My luve's like a red, red rose,/That's newly sprung in June;...."* are attributed to:
    A. William Blake B. Fergusson
    C. Robert Burns D. Macpherson
20. Who was known as the "Man of Feeling" after his sentimental novel *The Man of Feeling*?
    A. Francis Burney B. Ann Rediliffe
    C. Matthew Lewis D. Henry Mackenzie
21. The main reason why papers came out in Queen Anne's time was:
    A. People were hungry for information about current events
    B. People wanted to contact businessmen
    C. People wanted to improve their writing style
    D. People liked sensational fiction stories
22. The characters Sir Andrew Freeport, Captain Sentry and Sir Roger are featured in:
    A. *The Tatler*
    B. *The London Gazette*
    C. *The Spectator*
    D. *The Review*

23. The countries that influenced British literature and art in the 18th century were:
A. Germany and Holland
B. Sweden and Norway
C. Austria and France
D. France and Italy

24. The religious revival of the 18th century started by John and Charles Weslay was known as:
A. Methodism
B. Deism
C. Presbyterianism
D. Evangelism

25. *The Hind and the Panther Transvers'd to the Story of the Country and City Mouse* is a poem by:
A. Dryden
B. Matthew Prior
C. Pope
D. John Gay

ANSWERS

1	2	3	4	5	6	7	8	9	10
B	A	B	C	D	A	B	B	B	B
11	**12**	**13**	**14**	**15**	**16**	**17**	**18**	**19**	**20**
C	A	B	D	B	A	A	A	C	D
21	**22**	**23**	**24**	**25**					
A	C	D	A	B					

THE NINETEENTH CENTURY

THE ROMANTIC AGE (1798-1830)

The eighteenth century literature of England was inspired by reason, but the nineteenth century was the age of imagination. The Preface to the *Lyrical Ballads* by William Wordsworth and Samuel Taylor Coleridge in 1798, heralds the period of English Romanticism. The authors of this work were disgusted with the excesses of the French Revolution, they condemned the Rationalist Movement. England turned away from the literature of France and transferred her sympathies to Germany. The philosophical doctrine of Romanticism was inspired by Germany. Romanticism was essentially poetic. Although poles apart in their political beliefs, Wordsworth and Shelley both considered the poet as the guide, prophet and seer of mankind.

Poetry

For the great Romantics — Wordsworth, Shelley, Keats, Byron — the study of the wondrous world of feelings, senses, instincts, of Man' relation to Nature, were of prime importance. Romanticism is shot with *metaphysics*. As M. Lanson puts it, *tout traverse de frissons metaphysique* Alexander Pope had used poetry to depict the thoughts of the philosophers in his *Essay on Man*. The Romantics, dedicated to Romantic imagination — *the esemplastic imagination* as Coleridge called it — were convinced that what was revealed to their poetic intuitions, was right, the Truth. Mysterious forces divine in origin moved the earth, not cold rationalist cause and effect. Pope's couplet was dull and too precise governed by convention. The Romantics sought a lyrical form using unusual images and association of words. They found models for these in the Renaissance and the old popular poetry.

William Wordsworth (1770-1850) is aptly called the "High Priest of Nature". He saw Nature as the *'Stern Daughter of the voice of God'*, man's conscience whose balmy presence never disappointed. He was born in 1770 in the picturesque Lake District of England. Here he spent happy years of his childhood in communion with God and Nature. After study at Cambridge, he went to France in 1791 and was enthused by the cause of the Revolution. But when the Reign of Terror came and thousands died at the guillotine, his fine sensibilities, his search for human equality and peace received a rude shock. He engaged himself in the philosophy of William Godwin for sometime. Finding no solution to the problem of human pain, he finally turned to the study of Nature. In the poems of the Lyrical Ballads he describes the mundane happenings of country life, the activities of humble people. He used their common dialect with its flawed grammar as his style. He decries the coming of the industrial era which mechanized English life. With no ornament, his poetry draws its power from the intensity of his feelings and imagination, In The Prelude (1805), a long poem, Wordsworth set out to look back and retrospect on his life. He follows the growth, the turnings of his poetic genius since childhood, ruminates on his errors and recalls the corrective lessons of Nature. In his great moral poem, The Excursion (1814), he uses a philosophy to refute the pessimism that the Revolution had brought.

Samuel Taylor Coleridge (1772-1834) was Wordsworth's "Spirits Brother". He was guided by the same philosophy of the imagination. While Wordsworth's imagination gave him a special vision of the common things of rustic life, Coleridge stirred up the supernatural. To appreciate his poetry peopled with strange, translunary beings like *The Ancient Mariner,* one needs *'that willing suspension of disbelief that constitutes poetic faith'*. In *The Rime of the Ancient Mariner*, Coleridge describes the strange adventures of a sailor in a ship. Having killed an albatross, the mariner suffers from hallucinations. The poem, with strange rhythm and cadences, creates a wondrous world. Coleridge was a master of lyrical style. His other famous poems are *Christabel* (1816), and *Kubla Khan* (1816). *Kubla Khan* was written as a result of an opium dream and described the wonderful, strange palace of the Chinese king, Kubla Khan. Coleridge certainly fulfils the meaning of *'Renaissance'* as *'a renascence of wonder'*.

Robert Southey (1774-1843) wrote poetry based on outlandish settings and myths like *Thalaba, the Destroyer* (1801), *The Curse of Kehama* (1810), and *Roderick, the Last of the Goths* (1814). His descriptions are rich and graphic and he uses a great variety of verse forms. He wrote a number of poems in ballad form.

Walter Scott (1771-1832) also had an interest in ballad poetry. He translated the *Lenore* from German (1796). His *The Minstrelsy of the Scottish Border* (1802) shows a great romantic interest in the Middle Ages and the days of chivalry.

The second generation of great Romantic poets include Shelley, Keats and Byron.

Percy Bysshe Shelley (1792-1822) gave up his title and wealth to write poetry. His aim was to awaken mankind to the millenium, the coming future, which would remove human anguish and sorrow. His famous ode, *Ode to the West Wind* is an impassioned exhortation — *Make me thy lyre eu'n as the forest is ...... If Winter comes, can Spring be far behind?* He came under the influence of William Godwin, the philosopher. He proclaimed himself an atheist at the age of 21. His works include *Queen Mab* (1813), *Prometheus Unbound* (1818-1819), which shows human revolt against false gods, *To a Skylark, Adonais* (1821), which is an elegy to Keats, and The Cenci (1819). Shelley's style is a mixture of abstractions and visual images.

John Keats (1795-1821) was the most sensuous of the great Romantic poets. As we read his poems, richly laden with imagery and associations, all the senses are stirred up the visual, olfactory, auditory and tactile. It is said he tasted pepper in wine to describe certain lines. His famous odes are *To a Nightingale, To Autumn* and *On a Grecian Urn.*

Lord George Gordon Byron (1788-1824) was a wealthy nobleman who shunned the popular beliefs of his times. He was notorious as a dilletante. At the age of 19, he wrote Hours of Idleness (1807). With the publication of *Childe Harold's Pilgrimage* (1812) he became famous. Childe Harold was Byron himself, the figure of the disillusioned man, the hero fed up of pleasures and debauches. He lives an outlawed life and is rebellious in spirit. He took on more incarnations in his poems, *The Giaour* (1813), *The Corsair* (1814), *The Siege of Corinth* (1815). In these he displayed his own passions and eccentricities. In 1816, divorced from his wife, he retired to Switzerland and then to Italy. He wrote a number of plays — *Manfred* (1817), *Cain* (1821) and *The Deformed Transformed* (1824). The crowning work was his lyrical, satirical *Don Juan* (1819-1823). He went to Greece to fight for its independence, but died of illness. His satire is political, against England and also against English hypocrisy and cant. His licentious descriptions caused scandals. Don Juan, his magnum opus, is written in ottava rima or eight-line stanzas and is full of wit and mockery.

Thomas Moore (1779-1852), Thomas Campbell (1777-1844), Samuel Rogers (1763-1855), James Hogg (1770-1835), Walter Savage Landor (1775-1864) and **Leigh Hunt (1784-1859)** were other poets of the time.

Novel

Novels of terror and mystery prospered from 1800 to 1830. **Matthew Gregory Lewis** (1775-1818) wrote *Tales of Terror* (1800) and *Tales of Wonder* (1801). **Charles Lamb's (1775-1834)** *Tales from Shakespeare* (1807) is very popular even today. *Mrs Shelley,* the poet's wife, wrote the classic *Frankenstein* in which a scientist creates a monster that turns on its creator and destroys his most beloved ones. It is a novel of prophetic fear. **Miss Mary Mitford** wrote on country life and **Maria Edgeworth (1767-1849)** brought out educational novels like Belinda (1801) and *Tales of Fashionable Life* — novels for children.

Jane Austen (1775-1817) produced half a dozen novels which are drawing-room comedies of life. They study the passion and distress of young ladies and the life of country-folk. The novels — *Pride and Prejudice* (1813), *Sense and Sensibility* (1811), *Emma* (1816), *Persuasion* (1818), *Mansfield Park* (1814), *Northanger Abbey* (1818) — are realistic and witty, full of bracing dialogue.

Walter Scott was Scotland's greatest novelist recreating the past of his country's myths and ballads with rich humour. *Waverly* (1814), *Guy Mannering* (1815), *The Heart of Midlothian* (1818) contain history and direct observation. In *Ivanhoe* (1820), he describes the history of England in the days of the legendary Richard, the Lion Heart. *Kenilworth* (1821), *Quentin Dunward* (1823) were his other famous historical novels. He imbued the Romantic era with a love for the Middle Ages.

Prose/Criticism

The Romantic Age saw a number of reviewers and critics like **Jeremy Bentham (1748-1832)**, who expounded utilitarian doctrines, **Sydney Smith (1771-1845)**, and **William Cobbett (1762-1835)**. Coleridge, the poet, interpreted the doctrines of Kant and Schelling which show the distinction between pure reason and practical reason.

Lamb, Hazlitt, De Quincey and Leigh Hunt were Romantic critics of literature. **Charles Lamb's** essays on Shakespeare's tragedies state that we cannot do justice to them by staging them since the passions which are to be felt in their intensity are torn to tatters by the gimmickry of the actors. **William Hazlitt's (1778-1830)** criticism of some of Shakespeare's characters like Falstaff — *he laughs three inches below the flesh* — is a masterpiece. Coleridge's famous work of criticism, *Biographia Literaria* (1817), marvellously analyses Wordsworth's poetry. The Romantics believed that Shakespeare's art was organic like a work of Nature and *"esemplastic"* — able to blend different elements by imagination. **Thomas De Quincey's (1785-1859)** style is penetrating and incisive when criticizing the poets in *The Confessions of an English Opium Eater* (1821).

MAJOR AUTHORS AND THEIR WORKS

William Wordsworth (1770-1850)

The Lyrical Ballads
The Prelude
The Excursion
Tintern Abbey
Ode on Intimations of Immortality
Michael
The Solitary Reaper
Loadamia

Ode to Duty
To Milton
The Leech-Gatherer
Upon Westminster Abbey
The Rainbow
We Are Seven
The World Is Too Much with Us
To the Cuckoo
The Daffodils
Lucy Gray
Simon Lee
Early Spring
Strange Fits of Passion Have I Known

Walter Scott (1771-1832)
The Bride of Lammermoor
Ivanhoe
Quentin Durward
The Heart of midlothian
Old Mortality
The Antiquity
Guy Mannering
Waverly
Rob Roy
Kenilworth
Red Gauntlet
The Black Dwarf
The Monastery
The Abbot
The Pirate
The Fortunes of Night
The Betrothed
The Talisman
Woodstock
Lives of the Novelists
Life of Napoleon
Tales of Grandfather
The Lay of the Last Minstrel
The Minstrelsy of the Scottish Border
Marmion
The Lady of the Lake
Rockeby

Robert Southey (1774-1843)
Joan of Arc
Wat Tyler
After Blenheim
The Holly Tree
The Scholar
A Vision of Judgement
Madoc
Life of Nelson
Thalaba the Destroyer
Roderick
The Curse of Kehama

S.T. Coleridge (1772-1834)
Biographia Literaria
Table Talk
Aids to Reflection
Christabel
Kubla Khan
The Rime of the Ancient Mariner
France : An Ode
Destiny of Nations
Frost at Midnight
Dejection : An Ode
Youth and Age
Religious Musings

Lord Byron (1788-1824)
Childe Harold's Pilgrimage
Don Juan
The Bride of Abydos
Manfred
The Giaour
Hours of Idleness
The Vision of Judgement
The Prisoner of Chillon
Lara
Marino Faliero
English Bards and Scotch Reviewers
The Siege of Corinth
The Corsair
Cain

P.B. Shelley (1792-1822)
On the Necessity of Atheism
The Revolt of Islam
Prometheus Unbound
The Mask of Anarchy
Hellas
The Cenci
The Witch of Atlas
The Indian Serenade
Ozymandias of Egypt
Epipsychidion
Alaster
Queen Mab
Adonais
Ode to the West Wind
The Cloud
Ode to a Skylark
O World! O Life! O Time!
Defence of Poetry (a Prose Work)
To Night
The Sensitive Plant
A Lament

John Keats (1795-1821)
Endymion
Lamia
Hyperion
The Eve of St. Agnes
Isabella
The Eve of St. Mark
La Belle Dame Sans Merci
Ode to a Nightingale
Ode to Autumn
Ode On a Grecian Urn
Ode to Psyche
On Melancholy
On First Looking into Chapman's Homer
Bright Star

Jane Austen (1775-1871)
Sense and Sensibility
Pride and Prejudice
Mansfield Park
Emma
Persuasion
Northanger Abbey

Charles Lamb (1775-1834)
Essays of Elia
The Last Essays of Elia
John Woodvil
Tales from Shakespeare
Specimens of English Dramatic Poets
The English Comic Writers
The Old Familiar Faces

William Hazlitt (1778-1830)
Characters of Shakespeare's Plays
The English Poets
The English Comic Writers
The Dramatic Literature of the Age of Elizabeth
The Round Table : A Collection of Essays
Table Talk on Men and Manners
The Spirit of the Age

Thomas De Quincey (1785-1859)
Confessions of an English Opium Eater
Joan of Arc
English Mail Coach
Dream Fugue
Murder Considered as One of the Fine Arts
Suspiria de Profundis

Samuel Rogers (1763-1855)
Pleasures of Memory
Italy

James Hogg (1770-1835)
Kilmeny
The Queen's Wake

Thomas Campbell
Pleasures of Hope
Theodoric
Gertrude of Wyoming
Lachiel
Lord Ullin's Daughter
The Last Man
Ye Mariners of England

Hohenlinden
The Battle of Baltic

Thomas Moore (1779-1852)
Lalla Rookh
Irish Melodies

Leigh Hunt (1784-1859)
Story of Rimini
Autobiography

Walter Savage Landor (1775-1864)
Gebir
Hellenics
Imaginary Conversations
The Citations of William Shakespeare
Pericles and Aspasia

THE VICTORIAN ERA (1830-1880)

During this era, the conflict between religion and science, mysticism and rationalism, became intense. There were those who, influenced by Darwin's theory of evolution as expounded in his *On the Origin of Species,* lost their faith in the biblical explanation of man's descent from Adam and Eve. They wanted to shun dogma and accept the scientific spirit. Others lamented the loss of faith and the rising consumer values. Mathew Arnold in his poem *Dover Beach* writes:

"The Sea of Faith was once too at the full.....
But now I only hear its long withdrawing melancholy roar......"

Prose

Carlyle and Ruskin echoed the prophecies of the Romantic era in their prose works. **Thomas Carlyle (1795-1881)**, the Scotsman, abandoned orthodoxy and came under the influence of the German writers Schiller, Novalis, Richter and Goethe. His work *Sartor Resartus* (1833-1834) is a sort of allegory based on a German professor who has written a treatise on clothes. He penetrates through the clothes to the essence of the man's being. Carlyle was also a historian. His historical works are *The French Revolution* (1837) and *The History of Frederich II of Prussia, called frederik the Great* (1858-1865). These are satirical and prophetic, expounding how man and society are organized. He was against materialism and praised the Magi and prophets of the past. He advocates strength and power.

John Ruskin (1819-1900) was indignant about the ugliness of existence brought in by industrialism and the machine. *Unto This Last* (1860), which influenced Gandhiji's economic theories, describes his disgust for soulless labour. He was a student of arts. *Modern Painters* (1843, 1860) is about landscape painters like Turner. He also wrote *The Seven Lamps of Architecture* (1849) and *The Stones of Venice* (1851-1853), praising Gothic art.

Matthew Arnold (1822-1888), the poet, wanted his countrymen to inculcate classical qualities to become harmonious in morals and in creative works. The English must break away from their insular moorings by imbibing the teachings of Greece and the French. He is *the detector-general of the intellectual failings of his own nation.* Poetry, according to him, is important in character formation, and culture is *"the minister of the sweetness and light essential to the perfect character"*. His works include *On translating Homer, The Study of Celtic Literature and Essays in Criticism* (1865, 1889). He wrote St. Paul and Protestantism advocating that dogma should be removed from Christianity and it should adjust itself to the findings of science.

A number of philosophers, historians and scholars wrote in this period. Charles Darwin's theory of evolution dramatically affected human thought. **John Stuart Mill (1806-1873)** expounded the processes of logic and political economy. **Herbert Spencer (1820-1903)** and **Thomas Henry Huxley (1825-1895)** were scientists. **Thomas Babington Macaulay (1800-1859)** was a poet, essayist and historian who advocated English education in India. The Oxford Movement gave rise to religious writers like **John Keble (1792-1866)** and **John Henry Newman (1801-1890)**. Newman's famous work is *Apologia pro Vita Sua* (1864) in which he explains why he had converted to the Roman Church.

Novel

The transition from Walter Scott's novels to Charles Dicken's first novel in 1836 is a great one. When Queen Victoria ascended the throne, **Frederick Marryat (1792-1848)** produced sea-stories; **Edward Bulwer Lytton (1803-1873)** wrote about Byronic heroes, attractive criminals and historical novels like *The Last Days of Pompeii* (1834); **Benjamin Disraeli** (1804-1881), the Prime Minister of England, wrote *Coningsby: or The New Generation* (1844) and *Sybil: or The Two Nations* (1845) to show that the aristocrats of the society had a duty towards the unfortunate ones. In Disraeli's novels, one finds the politics of Queen Victoria's reign.

Perhaps the greatest Victorian novelist is **Charles Dickens (1812-1870)**, whose identification with the underdog in society was unmatched by any writer. One reason for this is his own troubled childhood led in penury under the shadow of a father who was in debtor's prison. The part of his life comes through vividly in his novel *David Copperfield* (1849-1850) which is also an indictment of the cruel, unimaginative schools of his times. He was a master craftsman in character delineation. A host of characters and their dialogues have become household in the English-speaking world. Thus the incorrigible optimist Micawber, Geakle, Pickwick, Fagin and others are types of characters that may be seen all around us anywhere. Dickens had a forgiving sense of humour. He never let bitterness creep into his recreations of painful events of the past. Among his famous novels are: *Pickwick Papers* (1836; in the picaresque style), *Barnaby Rudge* (1841) and *A Tale of Two Cities* (1859; based on the French Revolution), *Oliver Twist* (1837) and *Hard Times* (1854); novels exposing social conditions. He has a picturesque style and concrete imagination.

William Makepeace Thackeray (1811-1863) made a penetrating analysis of upper middle class and aristocratic society. He was a master of irony. In *The Book of Snobs* (1849), he ridicules the tendency to fawn on nobility and to imitate their manners. *Vanity Fair* (1847-1848), *History of Pendennis* (1848-1850), *The Newcomes* (1853-1855), *The History of Henry Esmond* (1852) and *The Virginians* (1857-1859) are pictures of contemporary life in which he depicts human eccentricities and follies. He was adept at reproducing jargon and idiolects.

The Romantic spirit was still alive in the works of the Bronte sisters. **Charlotte Bronte (1816-1855)** wrote *Jane Eyre* (1847), the story of a governess in a terrifying house. Her sister **Emily Bronte (1818-1848)** wrote *The Wuthering Heights* (1847), set in a wild landscape. Powerful passions and characters have made this one of the greatest novels of all times.

George Eliot (1819-1880), a pen-name for Mary Ann Evans, wrote Adam Bede (1859), the story of a girl who was forced to murder her own baby. *The Mill on the Floss* (1860) and *Romola* (1863) are other novels by her. In *Middlemarch, a Study of Provincial Life* (1871-1872), the novelist builds up, from the lives of a great number of deeply studied characters, the complex picture of the life of a small town.

Poetry

The poetry of this period still shows the influence of the Romantic Era. **Alfred, Lord Tennyson (1809-1892)** was an eclectic, selecting the best of his forerunners. He was first interested in style and metre, but later on ideas started interesting him. A great many poems by him are flawlessly beautiful. If *The Lotus Eaters* is softly languorous, *Ulysses* has a striking severity. Tennyson also experienced the intellectual crisis of his times and shared its anxieties. For instance, *The Princess* (1847) is occupied with the question of feminism. *In Memoriam* (1850) is one of his most beautiful poems. It is an elegy on the premature death of his friend Arthur Hallam. It concerns itself with the belief in immortality, the conflict between the hopes of Christianity and the rationalism of science. It is composed of octosyllabic quatrains. He shows a type of Byronic revolt in Locksley Hall (1886) and Maud (1855). In *Idylls of the King* (1859, 1869, 1889) he took Arthurian legends as his theme.

Robert Browning (1812-1889) was famous for using the technique of dramatic monologue in his poems. Through the protagonists of his poems he gives vent to his feelings, passions and aspirations. Thus in *Paracelsus* (1835), he describes the highly ambitious hero who wanted to transform man's life. We find here Browning's views on truth and philosophy. His other poems include *Sordello* (1840), *Pippa Passes* (1841), *My Last Duchess, Porphyria's Lover* and his masterpiece, *The Ring and the Book* (1868-1869). In his works we find an excess of thought and a rare vocabulary. He uses blank verse dexterously. His brusque speech, broken syntax and uneven rhythm are in contrast to Tennyson's. As Pound and Eliot have said, Browning brought verse nearer to modern colloquial speech. Browning's characters are remote in time and culture. Some of these are Rabbi Ben Ezra, Fra Lippo Lippi and Andrea del Sarto. In *The Ring and the Book* he takes as his subject an Italian crime and explores the minds of all his characters. He strikes a note of hope in his poems. The lines *"God's in his heaven/And all's well with the world"* lay bare his beliefs. But in general, Browning is considered a difficult poet.

Matthew Arnold (1822-1888) was a reflective poet with a melancholic bent. A deep brooding pensiveness informs his poetry. Dover Beach shows his concern with the loss of faith in a world of science. His epic poem *Sohrab and Rustum, Tristram and Iseult, The Scholar Gypsy* are other famous works.

Dante Gabriel Rossetti, William Morris and Algernon Charles Swinburne together are known as the Pre-Raphaelite poets. They affected Raphael, the Renaissance painter, in their desire to paint sonorous wordpictures which may not have much content to conveyor any philosophy to reveal. It was in accordance with the aestheticism of Ruskin. In fact Rossetti and Morris were painters as well as poets. They worshipped beauty like John Keats did. Robert Buchanan attacked these poets as belonging to *the fleshly school of poetry.*

Dante Gabriel Rossetti (1828-1882) translated the Italian poet Dante's *Vita Nuova*. His *The Blessed Damozel* is an exquisite poem and his best sonnets are contained in *The House of Life* in which he extols his young and beautiful wife. They are full of rich sounds and images and mystic symbols. Rossetti was inspired by the ballads of the Middle Ages. Like the primitive Italian painters, he uses rich colours and depicts warm sensuous feelings.

William Morris (1834-1896) was enchanted by Gothic art of the Middle Ages. His poems drew inspiration from those of Froissart, Chaucer and Malory. He borrowed stories from Scandinavia and Iceland. His poems are like frescoes and are very lyrical in quality. The famous ones are *The Earthly Paradise* (1868-1870) and *The Life and Death of Jason* (1867). These works show rhythm and use of archaism. He strove to bring civilization back to art from the utilitarian industrialization.

Algernon Charles Swinburne (1837-1909) was a prodigy. He was a musician, and a sonority of rhymes filled his poetry. He took romantic themes like revolt against society, hatred of monarchy and struggle against traditional morality. His *Atalanta in Calydon* (1865) is his masterpiece and is known for its choral passages.

To these poets of the Victorian Age must be added the name of **Edward Fitzgerald (1809-1883)** whose **The Rubaiyat of Omar Khayyam (1859)** is a classic.

MAJOR AUTHORS AND THEIR WORKS

Alfred Lord Tennyson (1809-1892)

The Princess
In Memoriam
Maud
Enoch Arden
Idylls of the King
Queen Mary
Harold
Backet
Akbar's Tomb
Crossing the Bar
Locksley Hall
Locksley Hall Sixty Years After
Dora
Poems by Two Brothers
The Falcon

The Cup
Poems Chiefly Lyrical
Ulysses
Poems Chiefly Lyrical
Ulysses
The Lotos-Eaters
The Death of Oenone and Other Poems

Robert Browning (1812-1889)

Pauline
Paracelsus
Strafford
Sordello
Bells and Pomegranates
Christmas Eve and Easter Day
Men and Women
Dramatis Personae
The King and the Book
Asolando
Pippa Passes
Fra Lippo Lippi
Andrea del Sarto
King Victor and King Charles
Dramatic Lyrics
Dramatic Romances and Lyrics

Matthew Arnold (1822-1888)

Sohrab and Rustum
Tristram and Iseult
Balder Dead
Empedocles on Etna
Stanzas from the Grande Chartreuse
The Strayed Reveller and Other Poems
Dover Beach
Thyrsis
Scholar Gypsy
On Translating Homer
New Poems
On the Study of Celtic Literature
Essays in Criticism
Culture and Anarchy
Literature and Dogma
Mixed Essays
Friendship's Garland
God and the Bible

D.G. Rossetti (1828-1882)

The Blessed Damozel
World's Worth
Ave
The White Ship
Sister Helen
Eden Bower
The House of Life
Ballads and Sonnets

Christina Georgina Rossetti (1830-1894)

The Goblin Market
The Prince's Market
A Pageant and Other Poems

William Morris (1834-1896)

The Defence of Guenevere
The Life and Death of Jason
The Earthly Paradise
A Dream of John Bull
News from Nowhere
A Tale of the House of the Wolfings
The Roots of the Mountains
The Story of the Glittering Plain
The Sundering Flood
Hope and Fears for Art
Signs of Change

A.C. Swinburne (1837-1909)

Atalanta in Calydon
Erechtheus
Tristram of Lyonesse
Chasteland
Bathwell
Mary Stuart
William Blake : A Critique
A Study of Shakespeare
A Study of Ben Jonson
Songs Before Sunrise

Edward Fitzgerald (1809-1883)

Euphranor : A Dialogue on Youth
Translation of Rubaiat

Thomas Carlyle (1795-1881)
Sartor Resartus
The French Revolution
Heroes and Hero-Worship
Past and Present
The Letters and Speeches of Oliver Cromwell
Latter-day Pamphlets
Life of John Sterling
History of Frederick the Great
Chartism

John Ruskin (1819-1900)
The Modern Painters
Salsette and Elephanta
The Seven Lamps of Architecture
The Stones of Venice
The Two Paths
Unto This Last
Munera Pulveris
Time and Tide by Wear and Tyne
Fors Clavigera
Sesame and Lilies
The Crown of Wild Olive

T.B. Macaulay (1800-1859)
History of England from the Accession of James II
Lays of Ancient Rome

Charles Dickens (1812-1870)
Pickwick Papers
Nicholas Nickleby
Martin Chuzzlewit
Dombey and Son
David Copperfield
Bleak House
A Tale of Two Cities
Great Expectations
Our Mutual Friend
Edwin Drood
Oliver Twist
Little Dorrit
Baraby Rudge
The Uncommercial Traveller
A Christmas Carol
Hard Times
Old Curiosity Shop

William Makepeace Thackeray (1811-1863)
Vanity Fair
Barry Lyndon
Pendennis
Henry Esmond
The New Comes
The Virginians
Adventures of Philip
The Book of Snobs
The History of Pendennis
Lovel the Widower
The Round about Papers
The English Humorists of the Eighteenth Century
The Four Georges
Rebecca and Rowena
The Rose and The Ring
Ivanhoe—the Legend of the Rhine

George Meredith (1828-1909)
The Ordeal of Richard Feveral
Evan Harrington
Emilia in England
Rhoda Fleming
Vittoria
The Adventures of Harry Richmond
Diana of the Crossways
One of Our Conquerous
The Amazing Marriage
The Egoist
Beauchamp's Career
The Tragic Comedians

Charlotte Bronte (1816-1855)
Jane Eyre
Shirley
The Professor
Villette

Emily Bronte (1818-1848)
Wuthering Heights

George Eliot (1810-1880)
(Mary Ann Evans)
Adam Bede
The Mill on the Floss
Silas Marner
Scenes of Clerical Life
Life of Jesus
Romola
Fleix Holt the Radical
Daniel Deronda
Middlemarch

Benjamin Disraeli (1804-1881)
Vivian Gray
Sybil : Or the Two Nations
The Voyage of Captain Popavilla
Henrietta Temple
Coningsby : or the New Generation
Tancred : or the New Crusade
The Wondrous Tale of Alroy and the Rise of Iskander
Contarini Fleming : A Psychological Autobiography

R.L. Stevenson (1850-1894)
Travels with a Donkey in the Cevennes
An Inland Voyage
Virginibus Pueresque
New Arabian Nights
Treasure Island
The Strange Case of Dr. Jackyll and Mr. Hyde
Kidnapped
The Black Arrow
The Master of Ballantrae
Catriona
Underwords
A Child's Garden of Verses

Thomas Hardy (1840-1828)
Under the Greenwood Tree
Desperate Remedies
A Pair of Blue Eyes
Two on a Tower
Far From the Madding Crowd
The Return of the Native
The Mayor of Casterbridge
Tess of the D'Urbervilles
Jude the Obscure
The Hand of Ethelberta
The Trumpet Major
The Woodlanders
The Well-beloved
A Laodicean
A Group of Noble Dames
Life's Little Ironies
Wessex Poems
The Dynasts
A Changed Man
Winter Words
The Waiting Supper and Other Tales

MULTIPLE CHOICE QUESTIONS

1. *Confessions of an English Opium Eater* is written by:
A. De Quincey B. Coleridge
C. Byron D. Leigh Hunt

2. William Godwin was a:
A. Psychologist B. Statesman
C. Scotsman D. Philosopher

3. *Don Juan* by Byron is written in:
A. blank verse B. rhyming couplets
C. ottava rima D. quatrains

4. The educational novel written by Maria Edgeworth is:
A. *Waverly*
B. *Belinda*
C. *Ivanhoe*
D. *Northanger Abbey*

5. Coleridge's *Biographia Literaria* critically analyzes the works of:
A. Byron B. Wordsworth
C. Keats D. Shelley

6. *"Bliss was it in that dawn to be alive, But to be young was very heaven!"* These lines have been attributed to:
   A. Wordsworth B. Shelley
   C. Keats D. Byron
7. *The Essays of Elia* is written by
   A. De Quincey B. Charles Lambs
   C. Hazlitt D. Cobbett
8. The publication of Wordsworth's Lyrical Ballads coincides with the
   A. French Revolution
   B. War for American Independence
   C. Industrial Revolution
   D. Invention of the steam engine
9. The poem Coleridge wrote as a result of an opium-induced dream was:
   A. *The Solitary Reaper*
   B. *Christabel*
   C. *Rime of the Ancient Mariner*
   D. *Kubla Khan*
10. Byron's poem, *The Vision of Judgment,* is an attack on the works of:
    A. Coleridge B. Keats
    C. Shelley D. Southey
11. *The Stones of Venice* is a book about:
    A. History of Venice
    B. Landscapes
    C. Romantic Literature
    D. Gothic Art
12. Hopkins and Patmore were:
    A. religious poets B. nature poets
    C. war poets D. critics
13. Swinburne, Rossetti and Morris together were known as the:
    A. Decadent poets
    B. Pre-Raphaelite poets
    C. War poets
    D. Absurd poets
14. Christina Rossetti's work containing poems for children is:
    A. *The Earthly Paradise*
    B. *Scholar Gypsy*
    C. *Goblin Market*
    D. *The House of Life*
15. Swinburne's masterpiece known for its choral passages is:
    A. *Atalanta in Calydon*
    B. *Cain*
    C. *Sohrab and Rustam*
    D. *Queen Mab*
16. *Childe Harold* is a poem by:
    A. Coleridge C. Southey
    B. Byron D. Shelley
17. *Prometheus Unbound* is written by:
    A. Browning B. Tennyson
    C. Shelley D. Spenser
18. *Adonais* is an elegy on:
    A. Keats
    B. Arthur Hallam
    C. Byron
    D. Shakespeare
19. John Keats is famous for his:
    A. odes B. plays
    C. blank verse D. masques
20. *Tales from Shakespeare* was written by:
    A. Coleridge
    B. Lamb and his sister Mary
    C. Wordsworth
    D. Byron

ANSWERS

1	2	3	4	5	6	7	8	9	10
A	D	C	B	B	A	B	C	D	D
11	**12**	**13**	**14**	**15**	**16**	**17**	**18**	**19**	**20**
D	A	B	C	A	B	C	A	A	B

THE MODERN AGE (1880-ONWARDS)

As the 20th century dawned, new values replaced the old ones and shaped the literature of Great Britain. England fast lost its imperial image as her colonies revolted and fought for independence. Industrialization progressed by leaps and bounds and the two World Wars brought economic depression. All this affected the content of literature. Writers sought new vehicles of expression. The findings of **Sigmund Freud** in the realms of psychology took novelists to the subconscious mind. A great number of writers who became famous men of letters in English came from Ireland **(G.B. Shaw, W.B. Yeats, James Joyce and Samuel Beckett)** and from America **(T.S. Eliot and Ezra Pound)**. Socialism became a practising creed and feminism raised her head. Dogmatic Christianity was more or less ignored. Although great strides were made in scientific inventions, science could not provide suitable answers to the deep questioning of the human mind resulting in ethical philosophy. The age saw the end of feudalism. Victorian reticence and prudery gave way to decadence in literature. English writers came under the influence of the French Parnassians and Symbolists. Scandinavia and Russia represented by **Ibsen** and **Tolstoy** also influenced the British men of letters. Many a poet wished to fight free from the fixed rules of versification and wrote in free verse. Many imitated the American poet **Walt Whitman**. English literature became more expansive in its concerns. The life and culture of foreign lands were depicted. Although **Kipling** was an imperialist, his works go beyond England. Being born in India, his works give a graphic view of the country. The great Celtic Revival under Yeats brought a new strain to English literature. Finally, the theatre, lying dormant for a century, now woke up with renewed vigour.

Criticism

The Age began with scholarly works in literary history. **Leslie Stephen (1832-1904)** wrote biographical and critical essays. He produced *The English Utilitarians and the Dictionary of National Biography*. He was an agnostic and rationalist. **A.C. Bradley (1851-1935), H.J.C. Grierson (1866-1960)** and **Edward Dowden (1843-1913)** were other famous critics. Bradley is famous for his critical work on Shakespeare's tragedies.

Walter Horatio Pater (1839-1894) propounded the literary doctrine *Art for Art's Sake* which was a quest for the most refined pleasure. The exquisite in art came from a reflection of the past. He eulogized the accomplishments of the Renaissance. His prose style was rich, musical and classical. His works include *Studies in the History of the Renaissance* (1873) and *Marius the Epicurean* (1885).

John Addington Symonds (1840-1893) was another admirer of the Renaissance. **Oscar Wilde (1856-1900)**, more known as a novelist and dramatist, gave a wider dimension to the theory of Art for Art's Sake by spicing it with wit and paradox. **George Saintsbury (1845-1933)** and **Sir Walter Raleigh (1861-1922)** were other famous critics.

Poetry

Most of the poetry written in this period are the works of those more renowned as novelists: Robert Louis Stevenson, Rudyard Kipling and Thomas Hardy. William Butler Yeats, who pioneered the Celtic Revival, Thomas Steams Eliot, whose *Wasteland* is a watershed leading to modern poetry, Gerard Manley Hopkins, the Catholic poet, are the famous poets of this period.

Rudyard Kipling (1865-1936) wrote on imperialist themes in *Barrack Room Ballads* (1892), *The Seven Seas* (1896) and *Five Nations* (1903). These poems were aimed by their rugged music to rouse people to protest. He combined folk-music with music-hall chorus. It had the sound of drum beats and bugle-calls and even the refinements of chamber music. The poetry of imperialism, heroism of national policy, contained slang and even biblical allusions. In fact, his popularity was that of Walt Whitman, the national poet of America. Many of his subjects were from India, like the poem *Gunga Din*.

W.E. Henley (1849-1903) also wrote poetry which praised Britain's colonial power. *The Song of the Sword, For England's Sake* and *London Voluntaries* are some of his better-known poems.

There were also a group of poets called the Decadents. They were aesthetes and their doctrine was *'Art for Art's Sake'*. **Oscar Wilde** was the leading poet of the group. *The Ballad of Reading Gaol* (1898) is his famous work inspired by his crime and imprisonment.

A group of poets had a pessimistic view of life. **John Davidson (1857-1909), Ernest Dawson (1867-1900)** and **A.E. Housman (1859-1936)** are some of these poets. But the leading pessimist of the age was **Thomas Hardy (1840-1928)**, better known as a novelist. He published *Wessex Poems* (1898) after the novel *Jude the Obscure* failed to receive public acclaim. His poetry was musical and highly individual. He had a disillusioned view of life. From 1903 to 1908, he produced the vast poetical work *The Dynasts*, written under the background of Napoleon's struggle against Europe combining real history with symbolic flashes. His poem, *To an Unborn Pauper Child,* reveals his utter dejection with life: *'Breathe : hid heart',* it begins.

Francis Thompson (1859-1907) and **Gerard Manley Hopkins (1844-1889)** were religious poets of the beginning of the twentieth century. Thompson's poem, *The Hound of Heaven* is a masterpiece. It describes God as a Heavenly Hound chasing man to capture his soul and man fleeing Him in the pleasures of life. The Jesuit, Hopkins invented a new type of verse called *'sprung rhythm'*. It was filled with strange word coinages and is difficult for the ordinary reader to understand. His poetry reflects the conflict within him between his attraction to Roman Catholicism and his joy for the beautiful creation. He wrote a number of religious poems of which *The Wreck of the "Deutschland"* is one of the best. It describes the death of five Franciscan nuns on board the ship, *Deutschland*.

Irish, English and Continental influences met in **W.B. Yeats (1865-1939)**. He was born in Ireland but came to live in London. He was influenced by the strange mystical visions of William Blake, by pre-Raphaelite refinement and even the mysticism and occultism of the Orient, especially of India. His poetry is an attempt to revive Celtic mysticism and Irish mythology. Apparently it was Yeats who introduced Rabindra Nath Tagore to the West. He also came under the influence of Verlaine, a French symbolist poet. His best poetry is in *The Wild Swans at Coole* (1919), *The Tower* (1928) and *The Winding Stair* (1933). Some of his well-known poems are: *Easter* (1916), *The Second Coming, Byzantium, A Prayer for my Daughter, Leda and Swan, Sailing to Byzantium, Meru, Lapis Lazudili, Among School Children,* etc. His progress as a poet can be assessed by comparing the beautiful but simple *Lake Isle of Innisfree* with the beautiful and profound *Byzantium.*

The towering poet of the 20th century is **Thomas Steams Eliot (1888-1965)**. Eliot came on to the scene when the West was passing through tremendous upheavals — belief in religion, especially of the Church was fading, democracy was the new experiment in politics, and many modernist trends were noticeable in literature. Eliot proclaimed himself "a royalist in politics, an Anglo-Catholic in religion and a classicist in literature". Tradition, according to him, was not the dead past but the past living in the present. In his essay *Tradition and the Individual Talent*, he states that "the talent of an artist shows itself not where he differs from the ancients but where, in his work, they assert their immortality". Eliot's poetry shows metaphysical, symbolist and imagist strains, but his individual talent shines forth unmistakeably. An eclectic philosophy, borrowed from his own Christianity and Buddhism and the Upanishads informs his poetry. His poetry, especially *The Wasteland* (1922) is a poem that describes the zeitgeist (spirit of the times) and the *angoisse metaphysique* (metaphysical anguish) of life in post-World War Europe. It begins with the sentence *"April is a cruel month"* and this sets the strain for the whole poem. A brooding sense of futility and human inanity pervades modern life. Eliot achieves this effect by a combination of literary allusions to the past which stirs associations, and by what is called as the *objective correlative*. This last technique means that images are described which call up an emotion or a feeling. His other poems are *The Lave Song of J. Alfred Prufrock* and *Four Quartets* (1944). These lines from the *Four Quartets* may sum up the disillusionment of the times: *"Footfalls echo in the memory/Down the passage one could not take / To the door one could not open"*. Eliot was a poet of spiritual regeneration.

As the century proceeds, a host of poets make their mark **Stephen Spender (1909-1995), W.H. Auden (1907-1973), C. Day Lewis (1904-1972), Louis MacNeice (1907-1963)** — all of them wrote with a Social awareness, exposing the horror of the bourgeois culture and capitalist exploitation and the terror of totalitarianism.

We cannot end this section of the early modern twentieth century without a reference to **Rupert Brooke (1887-1915), Wilfred Owen (1893-1918)** and **Siegfried Sassoon (1886-1967)** popularly known as the "War poets". They had served the Armed Forces in the First World War, and after 1918, disillusioned by the horrors they had witnessed took their pens to write against the war. The poem *The Soldier* is one of the finest lyrics in the English language. It describes the poet's sense of impending death in battle and his love for his country: *"If I should die/Think only this of me/That there is a part of England/Buried in some foreign land"*. Another poem is Sassoon's *Everyone Sang,* which describes the exultation felt by the soldiers returning home after the General Armistice was signed. They are described as *freed birds*.

Novel

Just like poetry, the novel of this century reflects the great passions and strivings of the age. The discoveries of **Sigmund Freud (1856-1939)** revealed the relationship of man's behaviour to his subconscious mind. The subconscious contains impressions of past experiences which influence a person's attitudes and behaviour. These discoveries led not only to new methods of psychiatric treatment but also to new dramatic techniques in the art of the novel. The stream-of-consciousness method used by James Joyce and Virginia Woolf spring from these discoveries. The modern novel is more and more concerned with an analysis of human behaviour. The focus shifts from a description of the external atmosphere to the thoughts of the characters.

Thomas Hardy's works are tinged with a gloomy pessimism reminiscent of Schopenhauer, and an analogy may be found in his works to Flaubert and Zola from France. Hardy's country Dorsetshire and the surroundings become the 'Wessex' of his novels. His work is full of realistic descriptions of the countryside. The places, full of pre-historic and Roman remains, heaths, have a character, and influence the people living there. The pre-historic past presses on the life of today. He is adept at delineating rustic characters. Man is a puppet of fate and an uncontrollable destiny drives him along life. A bitter helplessness pervades his novels *Far from the Madding Crowd* (1874), *The Return of the Native* (1878), *The Mayor of Casterbridge* (1886), and *Jude the Obscure* (1895). His success reached a climax with *Tess of the d'Urbervilles* (1891). His *Tess of the D'UrberviUes* and *Jude the Obscure,* because of their frank handling of sex and religion, aroused the hostility of the reading public. These two books, however, present Hardy's most moving indictments of the human situation.

The works of George Robert Gissing (1857-1903) produce a sense of absolute dejection. He worked as an ill-paid hack in the poor districts of London and described these places vividly in his books. Although impressed by Charles Dickens, his writings show none of Dickens' humour. One bitter, wretched world, a miserable London, exists in his works. Thus *Demos, a Story of English Socialism* (1886) describes the futility of socialist agitation, *The Nether World* (1889), the wretchedness of the London slums, *New Grub Street* (1891), the hopeless lot of a penniless writer, and *The Odd Women* (1893), the plight of unmarried women. His style is as bare and unaffected as his ideas.

Robert Louis Stevenson (1850-1894) stands in contrast to Hardy and Gissing in his recreation of the life of action and adventure. Although he suffered from an incurable malady, he did not lose faith in himself. He brought out *An Inland Voyage* (1878), *Travels with a Donkey in the Cevennes* (1879), *The Silverado Squatters, Treasure Island* (1833), *Kidnapped* and *The Master of Ballantrae* (1889) among others. The last three are very popular among children the world over. He also wrote children's adventure classics like *The Treasure Island* (1883), *Dr Jekyll and Mr. Hyde* (1886) and *Kidnapped* (1886). In *Dr. Jekyll and Mr Hyde* he touches upon the dual nature of man his good and evil aspects. His style is vivid and full of interesting details.

Another great novelist was the Pole, **Joseph Conrad (1857-1924)**, who perfected his knowledge of English and wrote in a vivid style with a strong foreign accent. His experience of sailing life and work in the English merchant service gave him the ideas to write masterpieces like *The Nigger of the Narcissus* (1897), and *Lord Jim: A Tale* (1900). Like the Slavs he was preoccupied with the problem of human misery. *Lord Jim* and *The Heart of Darkness* (1902) show his anger at what the white man had done to exploit Africa and other nations. A trait of his narrative technique is the gradual picture of his character formed from fragmentary descriptions of witnesses. He has a rich, sensuous prose style full of striking imagery.

Rudyard Kipling wrote stories about Indian life: *Plain Tales from the Hills* (1888) and *Soldiers Three* (1888). *Plain Tales from the Hills* depicts an Englishman's encounter with the strange East. Kipling was born in Bombay and spent his early life in India. He knew the land and its customs, its people and languages. His best book is *Kim* (1901), the story of a half-Irish boy, who speaks the language of the rustics of India and accompanies a Buddhist Lama on his search for "Nirvana" or Salvation. Kipling is adept at describing the sights and smells of India and its colourful people with their racy dialects. He also wrote two animal epics entitled, *The Jungle Book* (1894) and a series of short stories for children like *Captains Courageous* (1897), *Just So Stories* (1902) and *Puck of Pook's Hill* (1906). Kipling was influenced by Carlyle's doctrine of energy. As a spokesman of the Imperialist theme he believed that it was ideal for a person to sacrifice himself for his tribe. He believed that especially the white man was ordained to rule and lead nations. His works praise Britain's hegemony over her colonies.

Shortly after Kipling, came H. G. Wells and John Galsworthy who were Socialists and criticized the English society. **H.G. Wells** (1866-1946) began by writing stories with a semi-scientific flavour like *The Time Machine* (1895), *The Island of Dr Moreau* (1896), *The Invisible Man* (1897) and *The War of the Worlds* (1898). The stories are ingenuously plotted and thrill and disturb the readers. Later on Wells' interest shifted to social problems. He became a member of the Fabian Society. He wrote *Mankind in the Making* (1903) describing how society would look like when reformed by socialism. He also satirized the society in *Love and Mr Lewisham* (1900), *Kipps* (1905). *Tono-Bungay* (1909) and *Marriage* (1912). He does not glorify Britain's past and he scorns the existing institutions of his country. He wrote a number of remarkable books after the outbreak of World War I in 1914. These show his restless self-examining spirit. Some of these are *Mr Britling Sees it through* (1916) and *The Undying Fire* (1919).

In the works of **John Galsworthy (1867-1933)** we find an artistic conscience. Like Wells, he also attacked the concept of property and commercialism in his novels. He too exposed and criticized national prejudices, especially those existing among his own class, the landed gentry. He was widely read in Continental Literature and was especially influenced by France and Russia. Turgenev with his noble realism was his ideal. He is a detached and impartial observer of his country's decadent values. He advocates a fearless search for truth. *In The Island Pharisees* (1904) he exposes the stagnation of thought among English privileged classes. A similar theme is touched in other novels like *The Country House* (1907), *The Patrician* (1911) and *The Dark*

Flower (1913) where country squires, aristocracy and artists are critically studied. *The Forsyte Saga* (1922) is his masterpiece. It is a natural history of the rich upper-middle class family. He describes their attitude to events like the Great War, the growth of socialism, unemployment and the coal strike.

Enoch Arnold Bennett (1867-1931) wrote a number of different types of novels presenting a detailed picture of an industrial district in the provinces. He is a realist like the French nationalists. His masterpiece is *The Old Wives' Tale* (1908).

G.K. Chesterton (1874-1936) was a champion of tradition and he refuted and opposed the attacks of his contemporaries against English society in *Orthodoxy* (1908), *The Napoleon of Notting Hill* (1904). He believed in tradition sanctified by ages of experience and even in the religious bond between men. His style is effective with the use of imagery and comparison and he spices it with plenty of humour.

James Joyce (1882-1941) pioneered a new type of novel with the *stream-of-consciousness* technique. Characters in *Ulysses* (1922) unreel themselves by a sort of interior monologue. Speech is mimicked and styles are parodied. *Ulysses* is modelled on the *Odyssey* of Homer and set in the slums of Dublin. The thousand pages of this novel cover just one day in the life of Leopold Bloom and Stephen Dedalus. Joyce coined words from several languages and was a master craftsman with wit and conceits. His other famous work is the autobiographical *A Portrait of the Artist as a Young Man* (1916) which describes his adolescence and sensuous tendencies.

Virginia Woolf (1882-1941) continued the stream-of-consciousness technique. Her works *To the Lighthouse* (1927) and *Mrs Dallaway* (1925) reveal the hidden inner life of her characters.

E.M. Forster (1879-1970) was the novelist of cultural relations. In **A Passage to India** (1924) he studies the conflict between the west and the east and takes a favourable stand for the latter. *Where Angels Fear to Tread* (1905) studies how the cultural divide between an Italian girl and her English husband leads to the ruination of their marriage and life.

D.H. Lawrence (1885-1930) was a prolific writer. His outspoken views on sexual relations raised much hue and cry. He considered sex the religion of the blood. His novels were dubbed pornographic. He believed in the free expression of human personality, in being guided by unrestrained primitive instincts. In *Sons and Lovers* (1913) he studies the relationship of son and mother and the social disparity of a father, a coalminer and a mother, a teacher. The novel is autobiographical. Other works by him are *The Rainbow* (1915), *Women in Love* (1921), and *The Plumed Serpent* (1926). *The Rainbow,* suppressed as obscene, treats the conflict between man and woman. *Lady Chatterley's Lover* (1928) was canned for being obscene.

George Orwell (1903-1950) wrote novels which were an indictment of totalitarian government: *Animal Farm* (1945) and *Nineteen Eighty-Four* (1949). **Aldous Huxley's** *Brave New World* (1932) is a prophetic book about the future of civilization in the context of scientific advancement.

Drama

After Shakespeare, **George Bernard Shaw (1856-1950)** is the great playwright whose works enlivened the British stage. Shaw, like Ibsen, believed in drama as a vehicle for ideas. He had a rich Irish sense of humour and his plays are satires on various social and philosophical themes. His general technique was to discuss the problem of his play first in its preface. Often this preface is longer than the play itself. *Widowers' Houses* (1892) was his first play. In this he discusses the problem of Housing. In *Mrs Warren's Profession* (1894) he lays bare the profession of a prostitute. In *Arms and the Man* (1894) the theme is the chocolate-cream soldier. Shaw was an iconoclast breaking well-established idols or myths. Thus this play disillusions us of the romantic image of a soldier. He is not one who is willing to die for his country, but one who loves his life. When the enemy is weak, he attacks, but withdraws and takes to his heels if the enemy is strong. George Bernard Shaw had a keen interest in the English language and formulated a standard pronunciation for it. He studies the theme of how language can influence one's rise in the social ladder. Professor Higgins succeeds in teaching a flower-girl to rid herself of a cockney accent and to speak well enough to pass for royalty! In *Man and Superman* we see Shaw as a master conversationalist. Ideas are discussed without much action taking place in the play. *The Apple Cart* (1929) shows the weaknesses of democracy. Although an Irish man, Shaw did not write on Irish themes as such.

Oscar Wilde reminds one of the Restoration playwrights Sheridan and Congreve in his comedy of manners. His style is full of paradox and verbal wit. Some of his famous plays are *Lady Windermere's Fan* (1892), *A Woman of No Importance* (1893) and *The Importance of Being Ernest* (1895).

John Galsworthy's plays *Strife* (1909), *Justice* (1910) and *Loyalties* (1922) were based on the theme of class exploitation.

W.B. Yeats contributed to the Irish drama. His Celtic theme comes through in *The Countess Cathleen* (1892) and *The Land of Heart's Desire* (1894). **Sean O'Casey** (1884-1964) and **J. M. Synge** (1871-1909) were other noted Irish playwrights. The latter's plays, *The Playboy of the Western World* (1907) and *Riders to the Sea* (1904) are famous.

T.S. Eliot's contribution to the modern theatre were religious and moral plays. He uses the Greek "chorus" style in *Murder in the Cathedral* (1935) to heighten the dramatic effect of the murder of Thomas Becket by the Archbishop of Canterbury's men. *The Family Reunion* (1939) is a play about sin and expiation. Eliot pruned verse to sound like prose. This is done dexterously in *The Cocktail Party* (1949) and *The Confidential Clerk* (1953) where characters speak verse which sounds like prose.

A group of playwrights came to be known as the "Angry Young Men". **John Osborne (1929-1994)** was the most prominent of them. His play *Look Back in Anger* (1956) catches the mood of the frustrated youth in post-War England. In his plays, he exposes the wretchedness of the working class.

Harold Pinter (1930-2008) mixes comedy and horror in his plays like *The Birthday Party* (1958).

Another group of dramatists drew their inspiration from France. *The Absurd Theatre*, as it was called, began in France with Albert Camus, Jean Genet and Ionesco as its pioneers. In England, **Samuel Beckett (1906-1989)** was the Irish dramatist of this school. His plays *Endgame* (1955), *Krapp's Last Tape* (1958) and *Waiting For Godot* (1906) show the meaninglessness of human action and the unrelieved gloom of existence.

MAJOR AUTHORS AND THEIR WORKS

George Bernard Shaw (1856-1950)

Widowers' Houses
Candida
You Never Can Tell
Man and Superman
Back to Methuselah
Saint Joan
Heartbreak House
The Philanderer
Mrs. Warren's Profession
Caesar and Cleopatra
John Bull's Other Island
Major Barbara
The Doctor's Dilemma
Getting Married
The Apple Cart
Pygmalion
The Dark Lady of the Sonnets
Plays Pleasant and Unpleasant
The Millionaire
The Intelligent Woman's Guide to Socialism
Everybody's Political What is What
Cashel Byron's Profession
Love Among the Artists
Androcles and the Lion
The Devil's Disciple
The Man of Destiny

W.B. Yeats (1865-1939)

The Land of Heart's Desire
The Countess Cathleen
The Shadowy Waters

The Hour-glass
The Resurrection
The King's Threshold
On Baile's Strand
The Cat and the Moon
Ideas of Good and Evil
Discoveries
The Wind among the Reeds
The Wanderings of Oisin
The Tower
The Winding Stair and Other Poems
Lake Isle of Innisfree
Byzantium

John Galsworthy (1867-1933)

The Silver Box
Strife
The Skin Game
The Man of Property
Justice
Loyalties
Escape
The Inn of Tranquility
The Forsyte Saga
The Country House
Fraternity
The Patrician
The Dark Flower
Saint's Progress
Maid in Waiting
Flower Wilderness

Rudyard Kipling (1865-1936)

Kim
The Jungle Book
Barrack-room Ballads
Departmental Ditties
The Seven Seas
The Five Nations
Tales from the Hills
Soldiers Three
Life's Handicap
The Phantom Rickshaw
Many Inventions
The Day's Work
Just-so Stories for Little Children
Rewards and Fairies
Debits and Credits

H.G. Wells (1866-1946)

The Time Machine
Love and Mr. Levisham
Kipps
The History of Mr. Polly
Mr. Britling Sees It Through
Christina Albertas Father
The Wonderful Visit
The Island of Dr. Moreau
The Invisible Man
The War of the Worlds
The First Men in the Moon
The Food of the Gods
Marriage
Experiment in Autobiography
The Contemporary Novel

Joseph Conrad (1857-1924)

The Nigger of the 'Narcissus'
Typhoon
Lord Jim
Victory
Almayer's Folly
An Outcast of the Islands
Youth
Heart of Darkness
The Secret Agent
The Shadow of Line
Suspense-A Napoleonic Novel

Arnold Bennett (1867-1931)

The Old Wives' Tale
Clayhanger
Riceyman Steps
Buried Alive
Hilda Lessways
These Twain
Sacred and Profane Love

The Pretty Lady
The Love Match
The Author's Craft

Walter de la Mare (1873-1956)

Peacock Pie
Memoirs of a Midget
Songs of Childhood
Bells and Grass
The Traveller
Early the Morning
Love

T.S. Eliot (1888-1965)

The Waste Land
Prufrock and Other Observations
Gerontion
The Hollow Men
Ash Wednesday
Four Quartets
Sweeney Agonistes
Murder in the Cathedral
The Rock
The Family Reunion
The Cocktail Party
The Confidential Clerk
The Sacred Wood
After Strange Gods
The Elder Statesman
The Idea of a Christian Society
What is a Classic?
For Lancelot Andrews
The Use of Poetry and the Use of Criticism
Elizabethan Essays
Points of View

Virginia Woolf (1882-1941)

The Voyage Out
Jacob's Room
Mrs. Dalloway
To The Light House
The Waves
Flush
Orlando : A Biography
The Common Reader
Roger Fry
The Death of the Moth
Mr. Bennett and Mrs. Brown
A Room of One's Own
Between the Acts (Unfinished)

E.M. Forster (1879-1970)

Abinger Harvest
Two Cheers for Democracy
A Passage to India
Howard's End
The Hill of Devi
The Celestial Omnibus
Collected Short Stories
Where Angels Fear to Tread
The Longest Journey
The Story of the Siren
A Room with a View
The Eternal Moment

James Joyce (1882-1941)

Ulysses
Portrait of the Artist as a Young Man
Finnegans Wake
Dubliners

D.H. Lawrence (1885-1930)

Sons and Lovers
Woman in Love
Lady Chatterly's Lover
The Rainbow
The White Peacock
Kangaroo
The Plumed Serpent

Aldous Huxley (1894-1963)

Point Counter Point
The Burning Wheel
Those Barren Leaves
Brave New World
After Many a Summer
Eyeless in Gaza

Antic Hay
Time Must Have a Stop
Crome Yellow
The Defeat of Youth
The Perennial Philosophy
The Devils of Loudun

George Orwell (1903-1950)

The Animal Farm
The Road to Wigan Pier
Nineteen Eighty-Four
Burmese Days
Keep the Aspidistra Flying

Oscar Wilde (1854-1900)

The Sphinx
The Ballad of Reeding Gaol
The Canterville Ghost
De Profundis
The Duchess of Padua
The Importance of Being Earnest
An Ideal Husband
Lady Windermere's Fan
Salome
The Picture of Dorian Gray
The Happy Prince and the Other Tales

Harold Pinter (1930-2008)

The Birthday Party
The Dumb Waiter
The Care Taker
A Night Out
The Home Coming
Old Times
Silence

MULTIPLE CHOICE QUESTIONS

1. The British novelist and poet who described India best was:
A. Virginia Woolf B. Graham Greene
C. Rudyard Kipling D. Aldous Huxley

2. Rupert Brooke, Wilfred Owen and Siegfried Sassoon are together known as:
A. Flower Poets B. War Poets
C. Poets of Revolt D. Patriotic Poets

3. Walt Whitman was the national poet of:
A. England B. Poland
C. America D. France

4. *The Wreck of the Deutschland* is a:
A. war poem B. historical poem
C. romantic poem D. religious poem

5. *Sprung rhythm* was invented by:
A. Gerard Manley Hopkins
B. T.S. Eliot
C. Auden
D. Yeats

6. The Celtic Revival was begun by:
A. George Bernard Shaw
B. W.B. Yeats
C. J.M. Synge
D. James Joyce

7. *The Wasteland* is written by:
A. T.S. Eliot B. John Galsworthy
C. Thomas Hardy D. Virginia Woolf

8. Hardy is famous for his poem:
A. *The Hound of Heaven*
B. *The Dynasts*
C. *Four Quartets*
D. *Wild Swans of Coole*

9. The Irish dramatist, who wrote absurd plays, was
A. W.B. Yeats B. Samuel Beckett
C. Sean O'Casey D. J.M. Synge

10. *Everyone Sang* is a poem about:
A. socialism B. music
C. war D. death

11. *The Family Reunion* — a play, is written by:
A. W.B. Yeats B. T.S. Eliot
C. Cecil Day Lewis D. Louis MacNiece

12. Gissing's *The Odd Women* is a work on:
A. plight of unmarried women
B. poverty of slum-dwellers

C. war and love
D. the life force

13. *Ulysses* is written by:
A. Virginia Woolf B. George Orwell
C. Arnold Bennett D. James Joyce

14. *The Patrician* is written by:
A. Kipling B. H.G. Wells
C. Henry James D. Galsworthy

15. *Look Back in Anger* is written by:
A. A.J. Cronin B. Aldous Huxley
C. D. H. Lawrence D. John Osborne

16. *The Old Wives'* Tale is written by:
A. Robert Gissing B. Galsworthy
C. H.G. Wells D. Arnold Bennet

17. Robert Louis Stevenson wrote stories about:
A. adventure B. human nature
C. war D. nature and man

18. *The Invisible Man* is written by:
A. D.H. Lawrence B. H.G. Wells
C. Kipling D. Dickens

19. *Nigger of the Narcissus* is written by:
A. Hardy B. Eliot
C. Lawrence D. Conrad

20. Sex was considered the religion of the blood by:
A. D.H. Lawrence B. Ibsen
C. G.B. Shaw D. Oscar Wilde

ANSWERS

1	2	3	4	5	6	7	8	9	10
C	B	C	D	A	B	A	B	B	B
11	**12**	**13**	**14**	**15**	**16**	**17**	**18**	**19**	**20**
B	A	D	D	D	D	A	B	D	A

GREAT LITERARY MARVELS

CANTERBURY TALES

by Chaucer

'Canterbury Tales' is a collection of stories in verse by Chaucer. These tales are told by twenty-nine pilgrims who are going on a visit to the shrine of St. Thomas-a-Becket at Canterbury.

Each tale is a complete unit in itself without being intended to be linked with other tales. But, in the narration which is fictional in essence, we have head-links which are actually connecting passages. The headlinks are descriptions of the pilgrims as well as the events that take place in the course of the journey besides valuable digressions.

In those days, the people were very fond of pilgrimages for the sake of religious devotion and fun and they generally travelled in groups to face the dangers of the journey. The tales are written and descriptions of pilgrims given as if Chaucer himself had met such characters and had some experiences like those given.

The pilgrims meet at the Tabard Inn in Southwark on the eve of their departure and there they plan the journey. Chaucer himself is one of the pilgrims and the host of the Inn, Harry Bailly, not only gives a hearty welcome to the pilgrims but also accompanies them to the shrine.

Since the journey is quite tedious, each pilgrim is required to tell two tales on the journey towards the shrine and two during the return journey. But, Chaucer could complete only twenty four tales during his life time and in this sense, the Canterbury Tales is only a fragment.

An important aspect of the tales which brings Chaucer near to a dramatist and a novelist is that the tales differ in character as widely as do those by whom they are told.

The Knight tells, a chivalrous tale, the Clerk a devotional tale while the Miller's and the Reeve's tales are coarse and farcical in complete harmony with their own characters.

UTOPIA

by Thomas More

The period when Renaissance was in full bloom, Utopia was written by Sir Thomas More who lived from 1478-1535. He was imbued with the spirit of humanism.

The Greek word "Utopia" means "nowhere". Hence, it is in this light that Sir More tried to present an imaginary ideal republic of his dreams, which was of course, impossible to be achieved on this earth.

Utopia was originally written in Latin and was published in 1516. Later, it was translated into Italian and French. It was much later, after death of More, that its English translation appeared.

The Important characters in the book are :

1. The writer himself.
2. Peter Giles—writers's friend
3. Raphael Hythloday—a Portuguese traveller.

The book comprises two parts. In part one the protagonist (Hythloday) describes his voyaging with the explorer, Amerigo Vespucci.

In part two Hythloday describes the country of Utopia.

COMMENTS :

Utopia Glorifies

1. A democratic society.
2. A socialistic society with public control over wealth.
3. Religious tolerance
4. Economic equality
5. Peace and prosperity (upto a limit)
6. Love of this world.
7. Love of nature and natural way of living.
8. Love of beauty.
9. Love of the common man.
10. Love of human dignity.

Utopia Condemns

1. Aristocracy
2. Elitism
3. Asceticism and stoicism
4. Other worldliness
5. Fanaticism and bigotry.
6. False Chivalry
7. A Luxurious way of life
8. Scholasticism
9. Narrow-mindedness
10. War, Jingoism and Chauvinism.

GORBODUC

by Thomas Norton & Thomas Sackville

The other name of Gorboduc is Ferrex and Porrex. It is known for being the first regular English tragedy. It was written by Thomas Norton and Thomas Sackville and was first staged in 1562, that is, two years before the birth of Shakespeare. The work became a model for the Renaissance dramatists. It is, in essence, a Senecan tragedy of revenge.

The important characters in this tragedy are :

1. Gorboduc, The king of England
2. Ferrex—Gorboduc's elder son
3. Porrex—Gorboduc's younger son
4. Videna—The Queen
5. The murderers of the king and the queen
6. The nobles
7. The common people, etc.

The story in a nutshell: After the king divides his kingdom between his two sons, the latter begin to quarrel as a result of which Porrex kills Ferrex. The latter is so much loved by the queen that she kills Porrex. The people rise in revolt and kill the king and the queen. The nobles thereafter kill the murderers of the royal couple. This leads to a bloody civil war. There is chaos and anarchy as the question of success remains unsolved.

Senecan Features

1. Division into five acts.
2. Revenge as the chief motive.
3. A chain of murders—one murder leading to the other.
4. A ghost as one of the characters.
5. Lack of humour and any comic relief.
6. All-pervading seriousness and blood and thunder.
7. Avoidance of bloodshed on the stage, as it is reported by the characters through dialogues and monologues.

8. A plethora of rhetorical speeches by the characters.
9. Appearance of the chorus at the end of each act.

The use of blank verse in a drama was for the first time made in Gorboduc.

ASTROPHEL AND STELLA

by Philip Sidney

Astrophel and Stella is a sonnet series written by Sir Philip Sidney, Sidney is known more as a critic for his 'Apologie for Poetry' than as a poet, though his poetic claim is not altogether rejectable. His chief position as a poet rests on Astrophel and Stella.

Significance

1. The work is significant in the sense that it is perhaps the first work in English literature written in the white heat of passion, arising out of a personal and intimate experience.
2. In spite of artificiality of certain sonnets and general Petrarchan extravagance in the series, the work, having arisen out of real experience and genuine feelings, does not altogether look unreal.
3. It sounds real in several respects as in the apostrophe to the moon, in minute, vivid details and descriptions, etc.
4. Though the excessive use of conceits, hyperboles and embellishments mars the series in certain respects, yet its overall significance for the English literature cannot be underestimated.
5. Sidney was, no doubt, influenced by Petrarch. Yet he tries to assert himself every now and then by following a rhyme scheme other than the Petrarchan.
6. His most frequently used rhyme scheme is abba, abba, cdcd, ee. In other words, his sonnets end with a couplet in the Shakespearean style.

DOCTOR FAUSTUS

by Christopher Marlowe

The play opens with the chorus which announces the theme of the play i.e., the story of a scholarly doctor who has his end because of excessive lust for knowledge in the fields of magic and necromancy.

At the start Faustus looks at several fields of study such as Logic, Medicine, Law, Divinity, etc. But he finally settles at Magic. Then appear the Good Angel and the Evil Angel. The former warns Faustus against studying Magic book. He asks him to study the holy books. But the latter encourages him to study the Magic book.

The End of Faustus: His end is as tragic as it can be. He has not indulged or little indulged in sensual pleasures. What makes his sin more serious in theological circles in his association with Satan and the Satanic forces-demons, ghosts, devils etc. So, he gets no forgiveness and relief of any kind despite all his wailings and is taken away to hell by the Devils.

THE WINTER'S TALE

by Robert Green

Robert Greene's prose novel 'Pandosto' or 'The Triumph of Time' was published in 1588 and reprinted in 1607. This became the source for Shakespeare's *The Winter's Tale* which seems to have been composed in 1610 or 1611.

The title signifies an old wives' tale told to the curious children before they go to bed. Hence, such a tale can contain fairy-tale, exaggerative or legendary elements which may be far from reality because of some romantic, imaginary, unreal, absurd persons, incidents and situations.

Characters

Polixenes—the King of Bohemia, Leontes—the King of Sicilia, Hermione—Leontes's wife, Mamillus—Son of Leontes, Camillo—a Gicilian Lord, Cleomenes & Dion—courtiers, Paulina—Antigonus's wife, Emilia—the queen's lady, Florizel—the son of the king of Bohemia, Florizel—known as Doricles, Paulina.

BARTHOLOMEW FAIR

by Johnson

It is one of the most famous of Jonson's comedies which pleases all but hurts none. It is an authentic picture of the London of Queen Elizabeth's times. It was first staged in 1624, in manuscript form. It was published later in 1631.

There is a broad spectrum of humanity in the work at all levels, chiefly low level. Thus we have in the play gallants, gulls, cutpurses and bawds, lovers, squires, servants and justices of peace, etc.

Important Characters

1. **Bartholomew Cokes:** He is a foolish young squire.
2. **Waspe:** He is servant to Cokes who accompanies him to the fair.
3. **Grace Wellborn:** She is the fiance of Waspe.
4. **Edgeworth:** He is a cutpurse.
5. **Nightingale:** A ballad singer and companion and accomplice of Edgeworth.
6. **Adam Overdo:** A justice of peace.
7. **Zeal-of-the Land Busy:** He is a Puritan who becomes an object of mockery.
8. **Dame Purecraft:** She is a rich widow.
9. **Winwife:** He is a London gallant who is Busy's rival in wooing Purecraft.
10. **Quarlous:** He is a gamester but he is guised as a madman. He is Busy's friend, with whom he finds himself in a quarrel. He at last wins the hand of Purecraft.

Plot: There is virtually no plot in the play but only a presentation of a plethora of incidents and episodes which are mostly left undeveloped. Jonson's chief aim is to hold a mirror to the London life of his times.

The main incidents are

1. Cokes being relieved of purse, sword, cloak and marriage licence at the hands of Edgeworth.
2. Overdo being taken for a pickpocket and put in the stocks.
3. Waspe and Busy being put in the stocks for fighting and creating nuisance.
4. Overdo's escape from the stocks.
5. Quarlous's disclosing to Overdo the real face of Edgeworth.
6. Overdo's invitation to all to dinner.
7. Quarlous's winning of the hand of Purecraft.

Thus, the play proves Jonson to be a gentle satirist who has an ocean of sympathy with his characters of all kinds.

PARADISE LOST

by John Milton

Needless to say that the said Epic is the greatest heroic poem in English literature and one of the greatest of its kind in world literature.

A true epic on classical lines though with several diversional elements, as it is, it has twelve books.

A bookwise "Argument of Paradise Lost" is given by W.J. Long, which may be summarised as under :

Book I

It contains *inter alia*,

(*i*) a statement of the subject, the Fall of Man, and

(*ii*) a noble invocation for light and divine guidance.

Thereafter, in it, we have—

(*i*) description of Satan and the rebel agents. Satan's physical size, his gigantic shield, etc. are on supernatural lines, as can be visualised for a devil of his kind, as in a true epic in particular.
Satan's great power of oratory is also there before us.

(*ii*) the ouster of the rebel angels from heaven by the Almighty.

(*iii*) the diabolical plot of the rebel angels to wreak their vengeance on God by beguiling Adam and Eve, God's children and first parents of mankind, from their state of innocence by bringing about their fall by eating the forbidden fruit in the Eden.

(*iv*) a description of the sulphurous hell-fire and the eternal agonies undergone by the damned spirits there.

(*v*) the raising of Satan's palace, Pandemonium.

Book II

It contains, *inter alia*,

(*i*) a description of the council of devils in the Pandemonium.

(*ii*) Satan's desire to take up the task of beguiling Adam and Eve upon himself.

(*iii*) his journey to the gates of hell, guarded by Sin and Death.

Book III

It contains *inter alia*—

(*i*) God's behest to Raphael to warn Adam and Eve of the imminent danger of disobedience to them.

(*ii*) Son of God's offer to take upon himself the sin of the impending disobedience of man.

(*iii*) Satan's meeting with Uriel, the Angel of the sun, for the purpose of learning the way to earth, the abode of God's new creation.

(*iv*) Satan's journey to the earth in the guise of an angel of light.

Book IV

It contains, *inter alia*—

(*i*) The scenes of Paradise and of Adam and Eve being in the state of innocence.

(*ii*) Eden being guarded by an angel.

(*iii*) The arrest of Satan when he is trying to tempt Eve in a dream.

(*iv*) the setting free of Satan in an unconvincing way.

Book V

It contains, *inter alia*—

(*i*) the description by Eve of her dream to Adam.

(*ii*) Adam and Eve's routine life.

(*iii*) Raphael's visit to Eden.

(*iv*) Raphael's description of the revolt of the fallen angels.

Book VI

It contains, *inter alia*—

a continuation of Raphael's description of the revolt of the fallen angels.

Book VII

It contains a description of the story of creation by Raphael.

Book VIII

It contains Adam's description to Raphael of himself and his meeting with Eve.

Book IX

It contains an account of Satan's temptation of Eve.

Book X

It contains, *inter alia*—

(*i*) God's judgement on Adam and Eve.

(*ii*) Sin and Death's construction of a highway through chaos to the earth.

(*iii*) Satan's return to Pandemonium.

(*iv*) Adam and Eve's repentance.

(*v*) the turning of fallen angels into serpents.

Book XI

(*i*) Acceptance of Adam's repentance by God.

(*ii*) Michael's departure to bring into effect Adam and Eve's banishment from Eden.

(*iii*) Michael's prophecy regarding the destiny of man.

Book XII

It contains *inter alia*—

(*i*) Continuation of Michael's prophecy.

(*ii*) Learning by Adam and Eve of future redemption of mankind.

(*iii*) Adam and Eve's departure out of Eden.

Given below are some extracts from Book I:

The lines given below state the theme: The Fall of Man and present an Invocation to the Muse and the Holy spirit (*i.e.* the spirit of God):

THE WAY OF THE WORLD

by Congreve

As the play opens, we find two men Mirabell and Fainall talking to each other in a Chocolate House.

We learn that Fainall is married to Lady Wishfort's daughter, Arabella who is referred to as Mrs Fainall in the play. We also learn, that Mirabell loves Lady Wishfort's niece, Millament. Lady Wishfort is not only Millament's aunt but also her guardian.

It is learnt that Mirabell often went to Wishfort's house ostensibly to court her but actually to meet Millament. This pretence of Mirabell is at last exposed by Mrs. Marwood.

An enigmatic situation is now created for Millament. Since Lady Wishfort has learnt about Mirabell's sham, she forbids any meeting between him and Millament, Further, in order to inherit the lady's wealth, she has to marry according to her wish. This means that if she marries Mirabell against her wishes, she is likely to be deprived of the fortune of the lady who is fifty-five.

Mirabell has his own plot. He arranges marriage between his servant, Waitwell and Lady Wishfort's maid servant, Foible. The purpose of this marriage is that Waitwell is presented by Mirabell as his (imaginary) uncle, named Sir Rowland.

As Foible has been taken into confidence, she would impress upon Lady Wishfort that Sir Rowland, a wealthy man, has in his heart a deep love and wants to marry her. Through this plan Mirabell wanted to cause embarrassment to Lady Wishfort by revealing the identify of Sir Rowland later and thus compelling her to allow Millament to marry him.

A hindrance is created in the execution of the plot when Mrs. Marwood, Fainall's mistress comes to know about the plan, and she makes her lover aware of it. Besides, not only Millament but also Mrs. Fainall know about this plot.

Mrs. Fainall had once been Mirabell's mistress and in her heart of hearts, she still loves him. Hence, she also does not want that Mirabell should marry Millament, as her heart is burning with the fire of jealousy.

Mr. Fainall is a mean fellow, and he finds it an easy opportunity to blackmail Lady Wishfort. For this, he threatens to divorce Mrs. Fainall. It is further another proof of his avaricious nature that in a deed which is in his possession, he has already arranged the settlement of major part of Mrs. Fainall's estate in his own favour.

It is at the most critical moment when Sir Rowland and Lady Wishfort are busy in constructive prospects and Mirabell and Millament have agreed to marry each other, that Fainall makes his appearance.

Thus Mirabell's apple-cart is disturbed. However, Foible reveals the secret of Fainall's love affair with Mrs. Marwood. However, Fainall, rising on the crest of the situation sets forth certain conditions to remain silent. The conditions concern the fortunes of Mrs. Fainall and Millament and the marriage of Lady Wishfort.

Just then Waitwell presents a deed which is executed by Mrs. Fainall before her marriage with Fainall. In it, she has conferred her then estate on Mirabell. Thus the deed with Fainall becomes infructuous.

The net result of this *deus ex machina* is that Mirabell and Millament now have no obstacle in tying the nuptial knot to each other.

SENSE AND SENSIBILITY AND PRIDE AND PREJUDICE

by Jane Austen

In essence, the novel *Sense and Sensibility* is a satire on sentimentalism. Elinor represents sense, while sensibility is represented by her sister Marianne. The story, like all stories of Jane Austen, is very simple, but interesting.

Mrs. Henry Dashwood with her three daughters Elinor, Marianne and Margaret, is left in a very straitened situation on the death of her husband. They have to retire to Devonshire where they begin to live in a very humble cottage.

Edward Ferrars is the brother of Mr. John Dashwood. John is the step son of Mr. Henry Dashwood. He had been entrusted by the latter to take care of his wife and daughter after his death. But he does not discharge his responsibilities in this respect.

Edward and Elinor fall in love with each other. Marianne falls in love with a poor, unscrupulous young man, John Willoughby.

Willoughby suddenly leaves for London. Marianne and Elinor go after him. But Willoughby says that he is going to be married to a rich heiress. Elinor also learns that even her lover, Edward, has been untrue to her, as he is already engaged to Lucy Steel who is the niece of Edward.

Edward's mother is not happy with his engagement to Lucy, and settles her property on his younger brother, Robert, who is a fool of the first water. Then Robert and Lucy are married, while Edward stands rejected. Then Edward marries Elinor. Marianna who has been wooed by Colonel Brandon, marries him.

Immature style of Jane Austen is evident in this novel, but her future greatness and maturity is also visible here in seed form. The novel was completed in 1797, though it was published in 1813.

The story of Pride and Prejudice which is regarded as her best work and was published in 1813 is well-known to all scholars and need not be given here. It is in this novel that all the plot and stylistic perfection of Jane Austen comes into play. It is here that the dialogues are most lively, characters life like and her humour at its best.

Whereas in Sense and Sensibility, her characters such as Mrs. Jennings, her stupid daughter, her uncouth son-in-law and Mr. Palmer are some of the humorous characters they are no match for Mr. Collins, Mrs. Bennet, Catherina de Borough and others of Pride and Prejudice.

DAVID COPPERFIELD (1849-50)

by Charles Dickens (1812-70)

David Copperfield is perhaps the most popular novel of Dickens. It is an autobiographical novel in which Dickens's power of characterization, depicting humorous and pathetic situations and characters is perhaps the best brought out. The novel is told in the first person.

THE MAYOR OF CASTERBRIDGE

by Thomas Hardy

It was published serially in 1886. It is the story of a man who brings doom upon himself.

THE MILL ON THE FLOSS (1860)

by George Eliot (1819-80)

The Mill on the Floss is the most popular novel of George Eliot. It is also perhaps her most autobiographical novel. The story represents the typical Victorian problem of morality and a moral order which spares nobody.

The Mill mentioned in the title of the novel is the imaginary mill 'Dorlcote Mill' owned by Mr. Tulliver. The mill is situated on the river Floss.

The two main characters in the novel are:

(*i*) Tom Tulliver, and

(*ii*) Maggie Tulliver.

THE WASTELAND

by T.S. Eliot

When the Wasteland was published in book form in 1922, it was soon realized to be the beginning of the emergence of the Modernist Poetry.

Earlier the Georgians and the Imagists had appeared and disappeared but their effect, particularly that of the latter, had been retained in the inner recesses of the minds of the writers, poets included, even though superficially the movement of Imagism had all but spent itself.

It was because Ezra Pound who had occupied a pivotal position in the movement which had such protagonists as Hilda Doolittle and Aldington, also was instrumental in giving the final shape, as were now have, to Eliot's poem.

The Wasteland depicts the collapsing civilization of Europe and, connotatively, the fall of values in the modern world. The poem is highly realistic in this sense, but it promises vaguely some possibility of redemption through some everlasting philosophies such as that of the Buddha and the Upanishadas.

It cannot be disputed that the overwhelming picture of pessimism, death and desolation in the poem is to a great extent the result of the annihilation and mayhem which was witnessed in the First World War that ended in 1917. Then there emerged a particularly distressing mood in the twenties and this mood of depression of the entire period all over the world is very deftly brought about in the poem.

The poem's merit does not lie just in depicting a particular mood, but in its employment of complex symbolism and references to mythology, history, culture, religion and literature from varied sources in modern and medieval world and even the remote ancient times.

SAINT JOAN

by G.B. Shaw

It is one of the most famous plays of G.B. Shaw. It is this play which won him the Nobel Prize. The play was first produced in 1923.

Historical Background to Saint Joan: Saint Joan is a historical play which is based on the life and career of a real character, Joan of Arc. She was a common country girl, who was born in 1412. As a girl, she heard divine voices and had divine visions. But she was sent to the stake on the charges of heresy in 1431.

Social, political and religious conditions of the period are closely related to the story of Joan of Arc.

It was in 1415 that the English forces under the leadership of their young king, Henry V defeated Charles VI, the French King at Agincourt—a decisive battle which aroused waves of nationalism in England.

As a result of this humiliating defeat, the French king had to accept certain most unpleasant terms such as :

1. He had to sign a treaty with the English King in 1420.
2. According to it, he had to :
   (*i*) disown his own son, the Dauphin, declaring him as illegitimate.
   (*ii*) marry his infant daughter to the English king.
   (*iii*) allow the English to keep with them large area of France which they had conquered.

It is to be noted that at that time, France was not one united country. It consisted of a number of estates which were under the control of different feudal lords or barons.

TO THE LIGHT HOUSE

by Virginia Woolf

Virginia Woolf's most famous novel, Mrs. Dalloway was published in 1925. Two years later, another masterpiece of hers was published in 1927.

It is the only novel of Mrs. Woolf which has a Three Part Structure :

(*i*) Part I: The Window
(*ii*) Part II: Time Passes
(*iii*) Part III: The Lighthouse.

The main characters in the novel are:

1. **Mrs. Ramsay:** She is a middle-aged charming woman, a mother of eight children. She is the central figure in the novel.
2. **Mr. Ramsay:** He a scholar and philosopher of great repute and has won several academic honours.
3. **Charles Tansley:** He is an intelligent young student of Mr. Ramsay.
4. **Minta Doyle:** He is a young man who loves Paul Rayley.
5. **Paul Rayley:** She loves Doyle.
6. **Augustus Carmichael:** He is an old man and poet.
7. **Lily Briscoe:** She is a painter.
8. **William Bankes:** He is an old friend of Mr. Ramsay's.
9. **James Ramsay:** He is six year old child of Ramsays.
10. **Cam :** Janes's sister.

The scene is laid in the island of Skye in the Hebrides.

The story is autobiographical in nature in the sense that:

(*i*) Mr. and Mrs. Ramsay resemble Mrs. Woolf's parents.
(*ii*) Lily Briscoe greatly resembles Mrs. Woolf herself.

The novel whether more artistic than Mrs. Dalloway or not, has earned as much if not more popularity than Mrs. Woolf's other masterpiece.

The novel is written on the stream-of-consciousness technique:

(*i*) In the *Window,* not only the personality of Mrs. Ramsay is revealed, but also we have the personality of Mr. Ramsay before us which is laid bare through the eyes of Lily Briscoe, Charles Tansley, William Bankes, etc.
(*ii*) In *Time Passes*, we learn more about Mrs. Ramsay and others through the memory of the Charwoman, Mrs. Mc Nab.
(*iii*) In *Lighthouse* we have another focus on Mrs. Ramsay through the memory of Lily Briscoe.

The novel is poetic, as usually all of Mrs. Woolf's novels are.

ADVENTURES OF HUCKLEBERRY FINN

by Mark Twain

The novel opens with a warning to the reader:

"Persons attempting to find a moral in it will be banished; persons attempting to find a plot in it will be shot."

Although Mark Twain wrote this novel as a companion to Tom Sawyer, yet it is much more than that. However, a link with the earlier novel is established in the first chapter.

Huck is adopted by the widow Douglas to "civilize" him. The money which is found at the end of Tom Sawyer is put by Judge Thatcher on interest and it fetches a dollar to each boy 'all the year round.'

Huck is not much interested in Douglas' prescriptions of a strict disciplined moral life. Twain attains a technical tour de force by shifting narrative to the first person. This enables Twain to establish *point of view*. Huck is the model of *radical innocence* and *instinctive knowledge*.

SONS AND LOVERS

by D. H. Lawrence

The family of Morels lived in the mining village of Betswood. Mrs. Morel who has had a puritan nourishment, still upholds the values of refinement and nobility. She gets enamoured of Morel's rich ruddy face and merry laughter as well as wavy black hair. Mr. Morel is also captivated by her. The two get married.

The two have an antithetical nature and temperament. Whereas Mrs. Morel is a puritan lady, Mr. Morel is fond of a sensuous, luxurious life. He tries to domineer over his wife. But she rebels against this and the result is that even the children dislike Mr. Morel.

The estrangement between the couple becomes intense when one day, out of jealousy, Mr. Morel clips off the curls of the young William, whom his mother loves so such.

Mrs. Morel does not give up her efforts to reform her husband. But he rather goes more and more astray in his fondness for drinking, etc.

The couple had two more children. Morel tries to entertain the children, but often, the more Mrs. Morel instigates them against him, the more he teases them.

Mrs. Morel is frightened of her estranged relationship with her husband and focuses all her attention on her sons. She wants to possess her first child William whose love affair with Lily she condemns. But the boy dies of pneumonia.

Then Paul Morel, the third child, and the hero of the novel, falls ill. He is suffering from bronchitis. She nurses him tenderly and virtually treats him as her lover. This is how the famous Oedipus complex gets manifested in the novel.

Paul has relationship with three women, that is, his mother, Miriam and Clara. Among these, Miriam is his beloved.

The relationship between Paul and Miriam develops as Paul goes to the Willey Farm with his mother. He offers to teach her French and algebra and thus a friendship develops between the two. But, as Lawrence himself points out, their friendship is "chaste" and purely spiritual.

This relationship between Paul and Miriam cannot become an everlasting one since Mrs. Morel is afraid that Miriam is going to suck Paul's soul and she herself can ill-afford to lose her son. Paul too realises that as long as his mother is alive, his relationship with any woman cannot be permanent.

Paul is interested not only in a spiritual relationship with Miriam. He wants to have with her a physical contact also, but this she denies to him.

Since Paul cannot get physical satisfaction from Miriam, he enters into physical union with a married woman, Clara, who lives separately from her husband. But, the problem is that the woman is unable to satisfy Paul spiritually. The result is that Paul is thrashed by Clara's husband to his complete discomfiture.

Since Paul feels that his failure with both the women, Miriam and Clara, has been because of his mother's possessive nature towards his soul, he begins to hate her. But, when she falls ill with cancer, he tries to arrange the best medical treatment for her.

Being no longer able to witness the agonising misery of his mother, he ends the story of her life by administering morphia to her.

Now, it was impossible for Paul to establish relationship with any woman. He had to be lonely, and there was no escape for him from this state of affairs.

HAMLET

by Shakespeare

Introduction: The king of Denmark has recently died. On his death, his son, Hamlet, the Prince of Denmark, who is a student at the University of Wittenberg, is summoned to the Danish Court.

Hamlet feels miserable that his father's throne has been seized by his uncle, Claudius and his mother has married him.

Ophelia: Another shock comes to Hamlet when his beloved, Ophelia, rejects his suit on the advice of his father, Polonius.

The Ghost: Hamlet learns from his friend, Horatio, and two officers that they have sighted his father's ghost. As Hamlet himself encounters the ghost, the latter tells him the reality that his father had been poisoned by his uncle. The ghost also burdens Hamlet with the responsibility of avenging his death.

The spies: Claudius appoints two spies, Rosencrantz and Guildenstern to keep a watch on Hamlet. The latter arranges the staging of a play "The Murder of Gonzago" to which the king is also invited. The king's abnormal behaviour while watching the play (in which the murder of a king in a manner similar to that in which Hamlet's father is killed is staged) convinces Hamlet of Claudius's guilt.

Having been convinced of Claudius's and his mother's collusion in the murder of his father, Hamlet scolds his mother in a closed room. But as he hears an echo from behind the curtain, he thrusts his rapier at the person hidden. This is how Polonius who was eavesdropping gets killed.

Cause of Hamlet's Madness: Claudius tries his best to know the real cause of Hamlet's "madness," "ecstasy" or distraction, but having failed in his effort, he decides to send him out to England.

In the Ship: In the ship with the two spies, Rosencrantz and Guildenstern, Hamlet opens the sealed letter which contains the orders for his execution on his reaching England. He cleverly replaces these orders for the execution of the spies who lose their life in the venture.

Ophelia's Madness and Death: On learning about the death of her father, Ophelia goes mad, while her brother Laertes burns with the desire for revenge which is sharpened by Claudius.

The Duel: As Ophelia's dead body is being lowered in the grave, Hamlet grapples with Laertes. The two have a bloody duel in which both of them are badly wounded.

Claudius's end: When the two fighters are dying the villainy of Claudius is divulged by Laertes and Gertrude, the Queen. Hamlet kills Claudius with his poisoned rapier and soon Fortinbras arrives to be the next ruler of Denmark.

A Dialogue between the ghost and Hamlet

There are several extremely interesting scenes in Hamlet. Hamlet's dialogue with the ghost of his father is one of them. Here are the following lines which need no explanation.

MACBETH

by Shakespeare

Macbeth was the Lord of Glamis. He was related to Duncan, the king of Scotland. As the play begins, he returns with another general, Banquo, after crushing the rebellion of the Lord of Cawdor.

The Three Witches: When the two generals were returning, they met three witches, one of whom addressed Macbeth as the Lord of Cawdor. Macbeth felt greatly excited as he heard the witches' prophecies that he would soon be king and Banquo's descendants would also be kings. Thereafter, they disappeared.

Macbeth's Promotion: Soon thereafter, Macbeth was informed by two nobles that he had been made Lord of Cawdor by the king. This further thrilled Macbeth as he realized that the prophecy of the witches had come out true. He was so curious and enthusiastic that he wanted that the second prophecy of the witches that he would become the king should also turn true as early as possible.

Duncan's visit to Macbeth's Castle: The king Duncan wanted to visit Macbeth's castle to honour him. Meanwhile, Macbeth informed his wife through a letter regarding the witches' prophecies.

Lady Macbeth's Ambition: Lady Macbeth was even more ambitious than Macbeth and wanted to see him king. As Macbeth reached home, at the earliest, she incited her husband to murder Duncan to make the prophecy come out true. Macbeth was hesitant in accepting this advice.

Duncan was warmly welcomed by the Macbeth couple. He loved the peaceful atmosphere of the castle and went to sleep peacefully and without an iota of suspicion in his mind.

Lady Macbeth continued inciting her husband and even called him a coward when he expressed hesitation and his feeling of non-propriety in killing a guest who was also one of their kins.

The couple drugged the guards and they went into a sound sleep. Then Lady Macbeth herself went to kill Duncan, but now the king's face seemed to her as that of her father. So, she could not execute her plan.

The Bloody Dagger: Thereafter, Macbeth went into the king's room, but as he saw the vision of a bloody dagger, he changed his mind. Yet again, he took courage and struck a dagger into Duncan's heart and killed him.

The Voice: As Macbeth told his wife about the deed, he heard a voice: "Macbeth shall sleep no more." As Macbeth was now terribly overtaken by fear and madness, Lady Macbeth, showing greater courage, put the blood-covered dagger by the side of the guards and stained their clothes with blood to put the blame on them.

The Porter: Soon, the gate knocked. As the porter opened the gate, two of Duncan's nobles entered and went into the king's room where they found him dead.

Duncan's sons: As the news of the king's murder was conveyed to Macbeth, he killed the two guards. Meanwhile, as the news reached Scotland, the king's sons began to run for safety. The elder one, Malcom fled to England. Macbeth was then proclaimed king of Scotland.

Banquo: Macbeth was satisfied that the witches' second prophecy had also turned out to be true, but he feared Banquo. It was because the witches had also prophesied that Banquo's descendants would be kings. Hence, to perpetuate his kingdom Macbeth made up his mind to kill not only Banquo but also his son, Fleance.

The Banquet: Macbeth hit upon a plan. He invited all the nobles to a banquet. As Banquo and his son were on their way to Macbeth's castle, two assassins hired by Macbeth waylaid Banquo and his son. In the attempt, Banquo was killed but his son escaped.

Banquo's Ghost: Macbeth saw Banquo's ghost seated in a chair at the banquet. He even heard the ghost's whispers. Those present there were surprised to note Macbeth's strange behaviour.

For a brief period, the ghost disappeared, but soon it appeared again. Macbeth began to tremble and cry wildly. His such behaviour made him a suspect in the eyes of the guests.

The Witches Again: Macbeth went to consult the witches again. As he saw them, they called three ghosts. Macbeth was told the following three prophecies in turn :

(*i*) Macbeth should beware of Macduff.

(*ii*) No man born of woman could harm Macbeth.

(*iii*) Macbeth could never be defeated until Birnam Wood came to Dunsinane hill.

Lady Macbeth's mental state: Lady Macbeth was in an extremely depressed mood. As such she committed suicide. Macduff had run away to England. It was reported to Macbeth that the Birnam wood was marching towards Dunsinane hill. Macbeth felt puzzled. Soon, it was known that the green branches of the wood were being carried by Malcom's soldiers who were marching towards Macbeth.

Macbeth and Macduff: A fight started between Macbeth and Macduff face to face besides their soldiers fighting with their opposites. As Macduff told Macbeth that he was taken from his mother's womb, Macbeth felt so much discouraged that he got killed without a fight. The witches' prophecies had come full circle on Macbeth, as all his ambition was finally dashed to the ground with true poetic justice meeting out to him, which is perhaps not present in any other of Shakespeare's plays.

Macbeth is a great poet and *inter alia,* Macbeth is a wonderful piece of lyrical and dramatic poetry.

ARMS AND THE MAN

by G. B. Shaw

The young, romantic Raina is standing in her balcony to enjoy the beauty of the night in that month of November in 1885. She has all the romantic ideas of heroism of her lover Major Sergius Saranoff who is out taking part in the war between the Bulgarians and the Serbs.

Suddenly, there comes an intruder. He is a Swiss officer, Captain Bluntschli. He threatens Raina with his pistol and orders her to keep quiet.

Soon, a Russian army officer enters Raina's room to search for the fugitive. Raina hides Bluntschli behind the curtain. She tells the officer that nobody has entered her room.

As the officer goes away, Raina offers some chocolate cream to the fugitive. He tells her that he always carries chocolates to the war in place of cartridges. Then he goes to sleep.

It is the 6th of March, 1886. As Major Petkoff, Raina's father returns from the war, he is welcomed by Raina and her mother, Catherine. Major Sergius also comes. He has resigned from the army as he has not been given promotion.

The two family servants, Nicola, the man-servant and Louka, the maid-servent are already engaged. But when Sergius and Louka are alone, Sergius embraces Louka. She tells him that Raina loves a Swiss officer and would marry him.

Bluntschli comes to return the coat lent to him by Raina and Catherine. Major Petkoff instructs Bluntschli to prepare papers for sending three regiments. The papers are then delivered to the messengers.

Raina has already learnt from Bluntschli about non-heroic part of Sergius in the army. Sergius thinks that she is no longer loyal to him.

At last Raina is married to Bluntschli to which both Petkoff and his wife agree. Louka gets married to Serguis.

In this way, the myth of both the heroism of a soldier and the romance of love is exploded by Shaw in his own inimitable, interesting and simple way.

THE PORTRAIT OF A LADY

by Henry James

It is perhaps Henry James' most important novel which was written in 1881. James believed in images rather than in a story. Yet, if the novel is to be studied as a story, it can be said to be the psychological study of Isabel Archer a young American girl who leaves America with her aunt Mrs. Touchett and goes to Europe in a sort of what may be called her spiritual odyssey.

☛ 1. While portraying Isabel, Henry James had the model of his cousin Mary Temple called "Minny" in his mind. The young girl died in 1870 when she was only 24.
2. The European tour is arranged as once dreamed by Minny, though she got no opportunity to fulfil her dream.
3. Minny had died of T.B.; here we find Ralph dying of the same disease.
4. Gardencourt is a 16th Century English mansion– the kind of architecture Henry cherished.
5. Henry was particularly fond of painting and architecture.
6. Isabel's European odyssey comprises a visit to several countries, *e.g.* England, Italy, France, Greece, Turkey and Egypt.
7. It is to be noted that Henry James had a high regard for the European culture with its vast history, but he had no fondness for his native, American culture which had no history except that worth the name.
8. Isabel is shown as having fondness for Browning and George Eliot, as Minny also had. Besides she is also interested in the German philosophy.

THE GUIDE

by R.K. Narayan

Written in 1958, The Guide which won R.K. Narayan the Sahitya Akademi Award is one of his best novels and a masterpiece giving ample proof of his *tour de force* in the matter of artistic technique.

There are two distinct aspects of the story of The Guide. One half of it is supposed to be told by Raju, the hero, to one of his followers (as he turns from a tourist guide to a saint). The entire life story of Raju is however put in a flashback and told as such by the author. This technical achievement is a rare triumph in the modern artistic style.

Again, to understand more clearly, the story of Raju as saint forms the objective aspect and that of Raju as a tourist guide the autobiographical aspect. This artistic pattern is woven in the entire novel and this is what makes it artistically unique.

Simply speaking, it is the story of Raju's life and death. Raju has to indulge in several vocations and avocations, such as:

(*i*) as a food vendor at the railway station.
(*ii*) as a tourist guide.
(*iii*) as a sentimental adulterer.
(*iv*) as a manager to a dancing girl, Rosy.
(*v*) as a prisoner.
(*vi*) as a reluctantly holy martyred saint.

The setting is, as usual with Narayan, Malgudi town. It is at the newly set up railway station that Raj becomes a vendor. As a tourist guide also, he is quite successful.

One day Rosy, the dancer, and Marco, her husband, an archaeologist, engaged Raju as their guide. There were often quarrels between the husband and the wife.

Raju fell in love with Rosy and spent most of his time with her. He wanted to make her a famous dancer. Rosy's husband at last left her and she now lived with Raju. She was his 'snake-girl'.

Raju who was too ambitious, crossed the limit of propriety. He got addicted to habits such as gambling, drinking, etc. But when he forged the signature of Rosy on an important document, he was caught by Rosy's husband. He had to spend two years in jail. Then Rosy parted ways with him.

After completing his jail term, Raju went to a village, Mangal. There the people mistook him for a saint. Raju, depending on the art of simulation and dissimulation, found it a golden opportunity to be something, and if still dilly-dallying, he willy-nilly took it upon himself to be a holy man.

It was Raju's misfortune that his test was too near and too hard and it was beyond his imagination and comprehension. As usual, the villages were a superstitious lot, and as the famine hit the village, they expected of Raju to do some miracle to appease the rain God.

Raju had no grounding in such machinations of the so-called holy men and he had to go on a fast into death to cause the rain god to show his mercy. Once started, it was now impossible to give up the fast, as the whole area had been converted into a hubbub of pilgrims, tourists, visitors and mediamen who were reporting every now and then on Raju's determination and condition.

The days passed by and yet there was no sign of a cloud. It was the twelfth day of his fast. Raju was too weak to walk or even talk. Somehow he managed to reach the bank of the river, the venue of his prayer for rain. He collapsed uttering the words, "Velan, it's raining in the hills. I can feel it coming up under my feet, up my legs."

GORA

by R.N. Tagore

Written in 1923, it is perhaps the most famous novel of Tagore. It is a patriotic novel which expresses the voice of Resurgent India which is arousing to shake up the shackles of slavery. The novel expresses true secularism and a fusion of the oriental and the occidental. Even Gourmohan, the hero, the son of an English lady is brought up in a Hindu household and stands for that universal blend of ideologies and cultures which is so characteristic of Tagore.

MULTIPLE CHOICE QUESTIONS

1. Who wrote *"The Lady's Not for Burning"*?
A. Barrie B. Christopher Fry
C. Robert Bridges D. T.S. Eliot

2. Who wrote the poem *"Brahma"*?
A. T.S Eliot B. Emerson
C. Whitman D. Frost

3. The writer of *Walden* is
A. Tennyson B. Whitman
C. Thoreau D. Frost

4. In *'Sons and Lovers'* Lawrence has depicted the life of
A. factory workers B. miners
C. farmers D. animals

5. Who wrote *Kim*?
A. Kipling B. Tagore
C. Lawrence D. Narayan

6. *'The Hairy Ape'* is a famous play by
A. Barrie B. Eugene O'Neill
C. Christopher Fry D. T.S. Eliot

7. Who is the writer of *Frankenstein*?
A. George Eliot B. Jane Austen
C. Mary Shelley D. Emile Bronte

8. Who wrote the *'Cries of Children'*?
A. Robert Browning B. Elizabeth Barrett
C. Thomas Hood D. Cowper

9. Which poet is known as poet's poet?
A. Shakespeare B. Milton
C. Spenser D. Shelley

10. Who wrote the maximum number of sonnets?
A. Shakespeare B. Milton
C. Sidney D. Wordsworth

11. The name of William Golding's first novel is
A. The Inheritors B. Lord of the Flies
C. Pincher Martin D. The Pyramid

12. The author of *Erewhon* is
A. Hardy B. Marquese
C. Samuel Butler D. Cervantes

13. Which of the following is a *Comedy of Manners*?
A. The Way of the World
B. The Duchess of Malfi
C. The Lady's Not for Burning
D. The Hairy Ape

14. Which one among the following is not a pessimist?
A. Gissing B. Browning
C. Hardy D. Thomson

15. Charles Reade's drama *"Drink"* was adapted from a work of
A. Goethe B. Zola
C. Mallarwe D. Tennyson

16. Which one among the following was not a utilitarian?
A. Rousseau B. James Mill
C. Ricardo D. Bentham

17. *'The Praise of Folly'* was written by
A. Walter Raleigh B. Thomas Moore
C. Charles Lamb D. Ruskin

18. Who wrote: *"In Praise of Idleness"*?
A. Bertrand Russell B. Thomas More
C. Charles Lamb D. Hazlitt

19. The real name of Saki is
A. H.H. Munro B. Samuel Butler
C. George Orwell D. The Duke

20. Who started: *"The Tatler"*?
A. Addison B. Swift
C. Steele D. Stevenson

21. Who is believed to be the writer of *"On the Sublime"*?
A. Aristotle B. Longinus
C. Plato D. M. Arnold

22. Name the author of *"An Essay on Dramatic Poesie"*
A. Dryden B. Sidney
C. Shelley D. Arnold

23. Who is the writer of *"Culture and Society"*?
A. Cleanth Brooks
B. Eliot
C. Bertrand Russell
D. Raymond Williams

24. The writer of the *'Mirror and the Lamp'* is
A. Hume B. Lionel Trilling
C. M.H. Abrams D. Sean Lucy

25. The writer of *"Provide Provide"* is
A. Whitman B. Frost
C. Yeats D. Auden

26. Who wrote *"Desire Under the Elms"*?
A. Arthur Miller B. Osborne
C. Eugene O'Neill D. Shaw

27. Who is the writer of *"A Severed Head"*?
A. Iris Murdoch B. Paul Scott
C. Goldwing D. Huxley

28. *'Das Kapital'* is written by
A. Engel B. Freud
C. Marx D. Lawrence

29. *"Waiting for Godot"* is written by
A. Samuel Beckett B. Ibsen
C. Brecht D. Chekhov

30. Who is the writer of *"A House for Mr. Biswas"*?
A. Salman Rushdie B. V.S. Naipaul
C. Vikram Seth D. R.K. Narayan

31. What figure of speech has been used in the following line?

"Milton! thou should'st be living with us at this hour." —***Wordsworth***

A. Hyperbole B. Simile
C. Metaphor D. Apostrophe

32. Which figure of speech has been used in the term : *"immemorial elms"*?
A. Allegory B. Rhyme
C. Alliteration D. Oxymoron

33. Which play of Shaw is also sometimes called *"The Chocolate Soldier"*?
A. Arms and the Man
B. Candida
C. Pygmalion
D. Saint Joan

34. Which one among the following cannot be deemed to be a writer of the *"Problem Play"*?
A. G.B. Shaw
B. Galsworthy
C. Harley Granville-Barker
D. Eliot

35. Who is the writer of *"Metamorphoses"*?
A. Ovid B. Dante
C. Petrarch D. Virgil

36. The book *"Euphues"* was written by
A. Greene B. Jonson
C. Dryden D. John Lyly

37. Who can be said to be the greatest writer of the *Comedy of Humours*?
A. Dryden B. Ben Jonson
C. Congreve D. Etherege

38. Which one among the following is not a play by Ben Johnson?
A. Volpone
B. Alchemist
C. Every man out of His Honour
D. The Way of the World

39. Who is the writer of the book *"Prince"*?
A. Ovid B. Boccaccio
C. Machiavelli D. Montaigne

40. Who is the writer of the essay *"Simulation and Dissimulation"*?
A. Montaigne B. Lamb
C. De Quincey D. Bacon

41. Who wrote: *"We are hollow men"*?
A. Eliot B. Yeats
C. Tagore D. Ezekiel

42. By which character is the following line in Shakespeare's Julius Caesar spoken?

"I'm well-armed in honesty"?

A. Caesar B. Cassius
C. Brutus D. Cicero

43. *'The Way of All Flesh'* was written by
A. Swift B. Congreve
C. Butler D. Addison

44. Who is the writer of *"The Good Companions"*?
A. A.G. Gardiner B. Chatterton
C. Hazlitt D. J.B. Priestley

45. Who is the writer of the poem *'Vagabond'*?
A. MacNeice B. Masefield
C. Sir Henry Newbolt D. Rupert Brooke

46. *"Gullathea"* in written by
A. Spenser B. Herbert
C. Lyly D. Shelley

47. Who wrote: *"The Harp of India"*?
A. Govind Chunder Dutt
B. Michael Madhusudan Dutt
C. Henry L.V. Derozio
D. V.K. Gokak

48. *"King Porus—A Legend of Old"* is written by
A. Henry Derozio
B. Toru Dutt
C. Sarojini Naidu
D. Michael Madhusudan

49. Who is the writer of the poem *"The Dance of the Eunuchs"*?
A. Nissim Ezekiel B. Kamala Das
C. Daruwallah D. A.K. Ramanujan

50. Which Indian poet wrote the poem *"The Trojan War"*?
A. Vikram Seth B. Keki N. Daruwalla
C. Sri Aurbindo D. Tagore

51. Which of the following works is by H.G. Wells?
A. All in a Garden Fair
B. The Invisible Man
C. A Child of the Jago
D. Point Counter Point

52. Who wrote : *"The Ideal of a Christian Church"*?
A. John Keble
B. Newman
C. Nash
D. William George Ward

53. Which of the following odes is not by Keats?
A. Ode on Intimations of Immortality
B. Ode to a Nightingale
C. Ode on a Grecian Urn
D. Ode to Autumn

54. Which of the following works is not that of David Hume?
A. Treatise of Human Nature
B. The Rise and Fall of the Roman Empire
C. Political Discourses
D. History of Great Britain

55. Who is the writer of *'The School for Scandal'*?
A. Ben Jonson B. R.B. Sheridan
C. Congreve D. Webster

56. Who is the writer of the poem *"The Canonization"*?
A. Milton B. Dryden
C. Donne D. Chaucer

57. Name the writer of the poem *"Wind Hour"*?
A. Hopkins B. Eliot
C. Dryden D. Yeats

58. Who is the writer of the poem *"Adam's Course"*?
A. Eliot B. Tagore
C. Yeats D. Shelley

59. Who wrote the poem: *"Lay Your Sleeping Head"*?
A. Auden B. Yeats
C. Stephen Spender D. Ted Hughes

60. The play *"The Birthday Party"* is written by
A. G.B. Shaw B. Galsworthy
C. Harold Pinter D. Osborne

61. The poem *'The Song of the Shirt'* was written by
A. Mrs. Browning B. Pope
C. Shelley D. Thomas Hood

62. *Sir Roger* was originally the creation of
A. Addison B. Dryden
C. Steele D. Milton

63. Who wrote: *"Areopagitica"*?
A. Charles Lamb B. Hazlitt
C. De Quincey D. Milton

64. *'The Selfish Giant'* is a story written by
A. Tagore B. Oscar Wilde
C. Maupassant D. Tolstoy

65. Who wrote : *"Four Quartets"*?
A. T.S. Eliot B. W.B. Yeats
C. W.H. Auden D. Philip Larkins

66. Who wrote : *"Look Back in Anger"*?
A. Steinbeck B. Christopher Fry
C. John Osborne D. Barrie

67. Who wrote : *"The Devils of Loundun"*?
A. Bertrand Russell B. Aldous Huxley
C. J.B. Priestley D. Hazlitt

68. Who wrote: *"Principles of Human Knowledge"*?
A. Milton B. John Bunyan
C. Nash D. George Berkeley

69. Who wrote : *"Liber Amoris"*?
A. Lamb B. Hazlitt
C. Byron D. Wordsworth

70. *"A Railway Clerk"* is a poem by
A. Keki N. Daruwallah
B. Nissim Ezekiel
C. Shiv K. Kumar
D. Jayanta Mahapatra

71. Who rendered into English the ancient Greek tragedy *"Atlanta in Calydon"*?
A. Swinburne
B. Shelley
C. Tennyson
D. Arthur Hugh Clough

72. *The Deserted Village* was written by
A. Cowper B. Goldsmith
C. Keats D. Johnson

73. *'Savitri'* is an epic written by
A. Tagore
B. Prem Chand
C. Aurobindo
D. Bankim Chandra Chatterjee

74. The anthem *"Vande Mataram"* occurs in
A. Godan B. Anand Math
C. Gora D. Train to Pakistan

75. *'All Fool's Day'* is an essay written by
A. Charles Lamb B. Hazlitt
C. A.G. Gardiner D. R.C. Stevenson

76. The drama *Tamburlaine* is written by
A. Shakespeare B. Marlowe
C. Lyly D. Green

77. The book *"Appreciations"* was written by
A. Morris B. Arnold
C. Walter Pater D. Christina Rossetti

78. *"The Admirable Crichton"* was written by
A. Steinbeck B. T.S. Eliot
C. Trollope D. James Barrie

79. *"The Death of a Salesman"* was written by
A. James Barrie B. Eugene O'Neill
C. Arthur Miller D. None of these

80. The Restoration period is said to have started from
A. 1660 B. 1676
C. 1625 D. 1645

81. Who wrote *Don Juan*?
A. Shakespeare B. Tennyson
C. Byron D. T.S. Eliot

82. Who wrote *The Life of Johnson*?
A. Boswell B. Macaulay
C. Churchill D. Sir Walter Raleigh

83. *Priest's Nun's Tale* was written by
A. Spenser B. Charles Lamb
C. Tennyson D. Chaucer

84. Who is said to have first used the term "Metaphysics"?
A. Matthew Arnold B. Sidney
C. Donne D. Dr. Johnson

85. The writer of *Volpone* is
A. Johnson B. Milton
C. Jonson D. Shelley

86. Which is the correct chronological sequence?
A. Spenser—Chaucer—Milton—Donne
B. Spenser—Wordsworth—Tennyson—T.S. Eliot
C. Milton—Shakespeare—Philip Larkin—Keats
D. Auden—Eliot—Shelley—Keats

87. *Pilgrim's Progress* was written by
A. Milton B. Shelley
C. Swinburne D. John Bunyan

88. The writer of the line : *"Stone walls do not a prison make"* is
A. Lovelace B. Milton
C. W.B. Yeats D. T.S. Eliot

89. *"Monkey's Paw"* is a
A. Poem B. Drama
C. Short story D. Novel

90. Lyrical Ballads appeared in
A. 1690 B. 1798
C. 1802 D. 1800

91. Dunciad was written by
A. Dryden B. Pope
C. Tennyson D. Shelley

92. Bernard Shaw got the Nobel Prize for
A. Pygmalion
B. Man and Superman
C. Saint Joan
D. None of these

93. The Victorian Period is marked by
A. Great political upheavals
B. Great social security
C. Great wars
D. Economic deprivation

94. Swift is known mainly as
A. an essayist B. a poet
C. a satirist D. a short story writer

95. Who is the writer of the novel *"The Village"*?
A. Khushwant Singh B. Anita Desai
C. Mulk Raj Anand D. R.K. Narayan

96. The most famous writer of the heroic couplet is
A. Dryden B. Chaucer
C. Spenser D. Pope

97. *Macflecknoe* is a poem written by
A. Dryden B. Pope
C. Tennyson D. Yeats

98. Who wrote *'Everyman in His Humour'*?
A. Shakespeare B. Jonson
C. Milton D. Keats

99. *'Indian Jugglers'* is an essay by
A. De Quincey B. Gardiner
C. Hazlitt D. Lamb

100. Who wrote *'The Gropes of Wrath'*?
A. Pearl Buck B. Hemingway
C. Virginia Woolf D. John Steinbeck

101. *Adonais* is the eulogy written on the death of
A. Coleridge B. Byron
C. Keats D. Wordsworth

102. Who wrote *Mother*?
A. Tolstoy B. Maxim Gorky
C. Chekhov D. Hardy

103. Who is associated with *Malgudi*?
A. Narayan
B. Anand
C. Manohar Malgonkar
D. Anita Desai

104. The author of *Beowulf* is
A. Bede B. Cynewulf
C. Chaucer D. Unknown

105. The Anglo-Saxon period is often said to be from 450 to ......
A. 900 B. 1000
C. 1050 D. 1100

106. *"To a Mountain Daisy"* is a poem by
A. Wordsworth B. Shelley
C. Keats D. Burns

107. Who wrote: *"The Devil's Disciple"*?
A. Galsworthy B. Barrie
C. Shaw D. Fry

108. Who wrote *"The Decline and Fall of the Roman Empire"*?
A. Walter Raleigh B. Trollope
C. Smollett D. Edward Gibbon

109. Richard Hooker was a prose writer of the
A. Victorian period B. Romantic period
C. Elizabethan period D. Chaucerian age

110. Alexander Dumas was
A. an English writer B. an American writer
C. a French writer D. a German writer

111. Name the author of *"1984"*
A. George Orwell B. Graham Greene
C. Naipaul D. James Joyce

112. Who is the creator of *Wessex*?
A. Dickens B. Smollett
C. Meredith D. Hardy

113. Whose novel *"The Foundation Pit?"* was discovered only a few years ago?
A. Andrey Platanov B. Cherneshevysky
C. Jane Austen D. George Eliot

114. The novel *"We"* was written by
A. Andrey Platanov B. Tolstoy
C. Maxim Gorky D. Zamayatin

115. Name the writer of *"What Is To Be Done"*
A. Zamayatin B. Gorky
C. Cherneshevysky D. Chekhov

116. Name the writer of the novel *"Les Miserables"*
A. Virginia Woolf B. Mrs. Radcliffe
C. Victor Hugo D. James Joyce

117. Which of the following novels is not by Salman Rushdie?
A. Midnight's Children
B. Grimus
C. The Moor's Last Sigh
D. The Lighthouse

118. A sonnet comprises
A. 16 lines B. 14 lines
C. 12 lines D. 20 lines

119. Who is renowned for his outstanding work *"Holy Sonnets"*?
A. Donne B. Herrick
C. Milton D. Pope

120. Which of the following is not written by Hugo Charteris?
A. Pictures in the Wall
B. A Piece of String
C. The Old Boys
D. The Boarding House

121. Name the figure of speech for which Lyly is chiefly remembered
A. Malapropism B. Euphuism
C. Melodramaticism D. None of these

122. *Utopia* was written by
A. Walter Raleigh B. Sir Thomas Moore
C. Daniel Defoe D. None of these

123. The other name for *Euphues* is
A. The Anatomy of Melancholy
B. The Anatomy of Joy
C. The Anatomy of Wit
D. None of these

124. *Ferrex and Porrex* is the other name for
A. The Spanish Tragedy
B. Dr. Faustus
C. Goboduc
D. None of these

125. Which one among the following belongs to the group known as University Wits?
A. Shakespeare B. Congreve
C. Dryden D. Marlowe

126. *Astrophel and Stella* is a
A. play B. novel
C. sonnet sequence D. short story

127. What is the Greek meaning of *'Utopia'*?
A. An ideal place
B. A healthy place
C. A lovely place
D. Not a place (=*ou*=not; *topos*=a place)

128. The word "Volksgeist" means
A. The spirit of the age
B. (As per) tradition, custom and consensus
C. The essence of something
D. None of these

129. Which one of the following was a contemporary of Chaucer?
A. Spenser B. Herrick
C. Robert Graves D. John Gower

130. The famous work of Boccaccio is
A. Decameron
B. Divine Comedy
C. Essays
D. A collection of sonnets

131. The writer of *"The Swan and the Eagle"* is
A. M.K. Naik B. C.D. Narasimhaiah
C. Bruce King D. V.K. Gokak

132. Who wrote the poem: *"The Lake Isle of Innisfree"*?
A. Yeats B. Eliot
C. Spender D. Auden

133. Who wrote : *"The Lives of the Poets"*?
A. Boswell B. Hazlitt
C. Macaulay D. Dr. Johnson

134. Who wrote: *"The Interpretation of Dreams"*?
A. Marx B. Jung
C. Freud D. Darwin

135. Who wrote : *"Principles of Literary Criticism"* (in 1924)?
A. T.R. Leavis B. Kenneth Brooke
C. I.A. Richards D. A.G. Gardiner

136. Whose book "Language" (1933) is considered *"The Bible of American Linguistics"*?
A. Robert A. Hall B. Bloomfield
C. Bernard Bloch D. Edward Sapir

137. Which of the following poems is not by Frost?
A. Design B. Birches
C. Reluctance D. Michael

138. The famous soliloquy *"To be or not to be"* occurs in
A. Macbeth B. King Lear
C. Hamlet D. Othello

139. Which is the *'Odd man out'* in the following?
A. Paradise Lost B. The Ramayana
C. Essay on Man D. Iliad

140. Which Italian poet is most famous for his sonnets?
A. Petrarch B. Dante
C. Ovid D. None of these

141. Which one among the following was not a contemporary or predecessor of Shakespeare?
A. Marlowe B. Kyd
C. Fry D. Greene

142. Who among the following was not a prose writer?
A. Ascham B. Coleridge
C. Hooker D. Raleigh

143. Who among the following was not a character writer?
A. Wordsworth
B. Joseph Hall
C. John Earle
D. Sir Thomas Overbury

144. Who among the following was not an essayist of the seventeenth century?
A. Halifax
B. Sir Thomas Browne
C. Hazlitt
D. Sir William Temple

145. About whom has it been said :
"He knew small Latin and less Greek"
A. Ben Jonson B. Shakespeare
C. Milton D. Aristotle

146. Who said about Shakespeare:
"He was not of age but of ages"?
A. Jonson B. Johnson
C. Dryden D. Arnold

147. Who wrote: *'Modern Painters'*?
A. Rossetti B. Reynolds
C. Hazlitt D. Ruskin

148. Which one of the following is not the work of Lamb?
A. Of Style B. All Fools' Day
C. Dream Children D. Grace Before Meat

149. Who is stated to have said :
"veni, vidi, vici"?
A. Julius Caesar B. Alexander
C. Napoleon D. Homer

150. Who wrote : *"The Advancement of Learning"*?
A. Pope B. Tennyson
C. Bacon D. Eliot

151. The writer of *'A Pair of Blue Eyes'* is
A. Thackeray B. Dickens
C. George Eliot D. Thomas Hardy

152. *Hard Times* was written by
A. Thackeray B. Dickens
C. Trollope D. Marquese

153. Which of the following poets was most impressed by the German philosophy?
A. Chaucer B. Wordsworth
C. Coleridge D. Southey

154. The two cities referred to in *"A Tale of Two Cities"* are
A. London and Paris
B. London and Rome
C. Rome and Paris
D. Moscow and Rome

155. *The Peasant's Bread* is a story by
A. Maupassant B. Tagore
C. R.K. Narayan D. Tolstoy

156. *The Financial Express* was written by
A. Raja Rao B. R.K. Narayan
C. Tagore D. Mulk Raj Anand

157. *"Negative Capability"* is a term associated with
A. Tagore B. Shelley
C. Keats D. Coleridge

158. The most impressive treatment of "imagination" has been given by
A. Coleridge B. Shelley
C. Eliot D. Yeats

159. *Lady Chatterley's Lover* was banned because it was considered
A. obscene B. revolutionary
C. obscurantist D. None of these

160. *For Whom The Bell Tolls* was written by
A. Marquese B. Hemingway
C. Hawthorne D. None of these

161. Which one was not one of the Lake poets?
A. Shelley B. Wordsworth
C. Southey D. Coleridge

162. *The Theory of Catharsis* is associated with
A. Plato B. Dryden
C. Aristotle D. Sidney

163. Who wrote *'In Defence of Poetry'*?
A. T.S. Eliot B. Yeats
C. Keats D. Shelley

164. *'The Playboy of the Western World'* is a play by
A. Barrie B. Synge
C. Fry D. Eliot

165. *'Silent Woman'* is a play by
A. Marlowe B. Shakespeare
C. Ben Jonson D. Lyly

166. The Scene of *Beowulf* is laid in
A. England B. France
C. Spain D. None of these

167. *"Kidnapped"* was written by
A. Dickens B. Thackeray
C. Hardy D. R.L. Stevenson

168. *'The Prisoner of Zenda'* was written by
A. Sterne B. Trollope
C. Anthony Hope D. George Eliot

169. What was the full name of Cervantes?
A. Jim Cervantes B. John Cervantes
C. Miguel de Cervantes
D. Sir Roger Cervantes

170. Besides being a poet, Chaucer was
A. a trader B. a manufacturer
C. a teacher D. a diplomat

171. Who won The Booker of Bookers?
A. Arundhati Roy B. Khushwant Singh
C. Mulk Raj Anand D. Salman Rushdie

172. Who wrote: *"The Battle of Books"*?
A. Bacon B. Hazlitt
C. Swift D. None of these

173. Who wrote: *"Nectar in a Sieve"*?
A. Mulk Raj Anand
B. Manohar Malgonkar
C. Kamala Markandaya
D. Pearl S. Buck

174. *'The Good Earth'* was written by
A. Raja Rao
B. R.K. Narayan
C. Pearl S. Buck
D. Kamala Markandaya

175. The writer of *'The Dove Found No Rest'* is
A. Pearl S Buck B. Hemingway
C. Raja Rao D. Dennis Stoll

176. Who wrote: *"So Many Hungers"*?
A. Bhabani Bhattacharya
B. Kamala Markandaya
C. Manohar Malgonkar
D. Chaman Nahal

177. Who is the writer of *"The Middleman and Other Stories"*?
A. Mulk Raj Anand B. Bharati Mukherjee
C. Tagore D. Prem Chand

178. Cicero was a Roman
A. philologist B. physician
C. orator D. None of these

179. Who is the writer of *"Gita Rahasya"*?
A. Tulsi Das B. Vivekananda
C. Shivananda D. B.G. Tilak

180. *'The Rubaiyat of Omar Khayyam'* was translated into English by
A. Robert Browning B. Tennyson
C. Fitz Gerald D. Hopkins

181. Name which is not the work of Marlowe
A. Richard I B. Tambarlaine
C. The Jew of Malta D. Dr. Faustus

182. Name the writer of the poem *"The Weary Blues"*
A. Longfellow B. Whitman
C. Frost D. Langston Hughes

183. Which of the following poems is not written by Robert Lowell?
A. In the Cage B. Dolphin
C. Good Morning D. The Old Flame

184. Which of the following poems is written by Wallace Stevens?
A. Red Sun Blues B. Sunday Morning
C. From Survivor D. "Going"

185. Which of the following poems is not written by Philip Larkin?
A. Art Grass B. Sad Steps
C. Traveller D. Church going

ANSWERS

1	2	3	4	5	6	7	8	9	10
B	B	C	B	A	B	C	B	C	D
11	12	13	14	15	16	17	18	19	20
B	C	A	B	B	A	B	A	A	C
21	22	23	24	25	26	27	28	29	30
B	A	D	C	B	C	A	C	A	B
31	32	33	34	35	36	37	38	39	40
D	C	A	D	A	D	B	D	C	D
41	42	43	44	45	46	47	48	49	50
A	C	C	D	B	C	C	D	B	C
51	52	53	54	55	56	57	58	59	60
B	D	A	B	B	C	A	C	A	C
61	62	63	64	65	66	67	68	69	70
D	C	D	B	A	C	B	D	B	B
71	72	73	74	75	76	77	78	79	80
A	B	C	B	A	B	C	D	C	A
81	82	83	84	85	86	87	88	89	90
C	A	D	D	C	B	D	A	C	B
91	92	93	94	95	96	97	98	99	100
B	C	A	C	C	D	A	B	C	D
101	102	103	104	105	106	107	108	109	110
C	B	A	D	C	D	D	D	C	C
111	112	113	114	115	116	117	118	119	120
A	D	A	D	C	C	D	B	A	B
121	122	123	124	125	126	127	128	129	130
B	B	C	C	D	C	D	B	D	A
131	132	133	134	135	136	137	138	139	140
B	A	D	C	C	B	D	C	C	A
141	142	143	144	145	146	147	148	149	150
C	B	A	C	B	A	D	A	A	C
151	152	153	154	155	156	157	158	159	160
D	B	C	A	D	B	C	A	A	B
161	162	163	164	165	166	167	168	169	170
A	C	D	B	C	D	D	C	C	B
171	172	173	174	175	176	177	178	179	180
D	C	C	C	D	A	B	C	D	C
181	182	183	184	185					
A	D	C	B	C					

3 Great English Authors & Their Works

WILLIAM SHAKESPEARE (1564–1616)

Life

William Shakespeare was born on 23rd April 1564 at Stratford-on-Avon. His father was a grain-dealer. His business deteriorated when William was yet a child and so William could not study more than a few years in the local grammar school and left it at the age of about 13 to help out in his family's business. He married at the age of 18 to Anne Hathaway, who was eight years his senior. They had three children, but the marriage was not happy. According to tradition, William was caught poaching deer and rabbits in Thomas Lucy's park at Charlecote. He was lynched and ran away from home, gradually reaching London. There he got a job as a holder of visitors' horses at a theatre. He later on got a job as an actor and is supposed to have done the roles of the type of Ghost in *Hamlet* and Adam in *As You Like it.* Shakespeare very soon got the hang of the theatre and began revising plays or writing plays based on English translations of Greek and Latin stories. These plays were very successful with audiences and provoked the jealousy of rivals like Greene who denounces Shakespeare in a pamphlet entitled *A Groatsworth of Wit* (1592). Greene describes him as "an upstart crow beautified with our feathers, that with his Tyger's heart wrapped in a player's hide ....".

From then on there was no stopping of Shakespeare's upward rise in career. He was attached to and wrote his plays for the Earl of Leicester's Players. In 1595, his name appears on the Payroll of the Lord Chamberlain's and finally of the King's Servants. These companies performed at The Rose, The Curtain and The Theatre. The company finally bought the Globe and Shakespeare, growing prosperous, became a partner of the Globe Theatre and later of the Blackfriars.

Shakespeare wrote and published for twenty years from 1591 to 1611. During this period he wrote 37 plays and more than 154 sonnets. The first 126 of the sonnets are addressed to a man Mr. W.H., the Earl of Southampton, who introduced him to the important courtiers, and the remainder to a "dark lady". He grew prosperous day by day, acquired estate, got his father to apply for a coat of arms and became a gentleman by inheritance. He bought New Place, the largest house at Stratford and retired there after 1611. After a drinking bout in 1616, he fell sick and died untimely.

Works

Shakespeare wrote the famous love poems, *Venus and Adonis* (1593) and *The Rape of Lucrece* (1594) dedicated to the Earl of Southampton. These poems in themselves entitle him to a place among the immortals. But he was destined to become famous and known to posterity as England's greatest dramatist. He began, as was the custom of the times, by collaborating with Marlowe and Kyd in revising and touching up old plays like *Titus Andronicus,*

Henry VI and *Richard III.* The exact sequence of dates in which his plays came out is not known, but only sixteen were published in quarto form during his life-time. There were copyright laws at the time and unscrupulous writer 'pirates' took down bits of the plays as they were enacted and published them in different editions. In 1623, seven years after his death, two of Shakespeare's friends and fellow-actors, Heminge and Condell, published all his plays as the first folio in memory of their worthy friend. This folio contains all the plays except *Pericles.* There are references to Shakespeare's plays in *Palladis Tamia, Wit's Treasury* (1593) by Francis Meres. The date of composition is guessed by topical and contemporary allusions in the plays and the tone and metre used.

In the earlier plays there is in general a youthful exuberance, a lot of verbal wit, strange conceits and light-heartedness. The blank verse used is end-stopped (the sense ends with each line) and rhyming couplets are used. As the plays grow in maturity and Shakespeare's art advances he uses run-on lines in which the sense of one line carries on to the next. This allows the verse to express a greater range of emotions. Still later on, feminine endings are used, that is, a number of unstressed syllables are added at the ends of lines. In the last plays, rhyme completely disappears.

Shakespeare's plays were written in three periods. Although their date of writing is based on conjecture, the periods give a clue to the gradual development of his art.

Early Period (1590-1596)

Henry VI (three plays), *Richard III, Richard II, Love's Labour Lost, A Midsummer Night's Dream, Romeo and Juliet.*

Middle Period (1596-1608)

Herry IV (two plays), *The Merchant of Venice, As You Like It, Julius Caesar, Hamlet, Othello, Macbeth, Twelfth Night King Lear, Antony and Cleopatra,* etc.

Late Period (1608-1613)

Cymbeline, The Tempest, Pericles, The Winter's Tale, etc.

The above are some of the 37 plays he wrote. An analysis of the plays reveals some common characteristics of the different categories like comedies and tragedies. The comedies are boisterous and farcical. They show Shakespeare's immature period. *The Merchant of Venice* (1596) is one of his most popular comedies with several episodes woven together. In those days when the Christians hated the Jews, Shakespeare's portrayal of Shylock in sympathetic tones caused a stir. *A Midsummer Night's Dream* (1595), the one play for which Shakespeare did not borrow the story, takes us to a wonderland of fairies, the impish Puck Goodfellow and Bottom whose scenes are the most hilarious in all Shakespeare. In this play, Theseus says *"The lunatic, the lover, and the poet/Are of imagination all compact."* This line refers to Shakespeare's own weird fancies as he creates them in his plays. *The Merry Wives of Windsor* (1600) was written on the behest of Queen Elizabeth. The character Falstaff is one of Shakespeare's best creations. According to the critic Hazlitt, Falstaff is all laughter and merriment, "laughing 3 inches below the skin". *Much Ado about Nothing* (1598) contains bracing wit-combats between Benedick and Beatrice. *As You Like It* (1600) provides glimpses of an emotionally rich life in the forest of Arden. *Twelfth Night* (1601) is a hilarious comedy. Through Malvolio, Shakespeare satirizes Puritanism.

Histories like *Richard III* (1593) and *Richard II* (1596) show the influence of Marlowe on Shakespeare. He wrote the three parts of *Henry VI* (1591-92) in collaboration with Marlowe. Most of these histories show the patriotic victory of kings.

The tragedies show Shakespeare's maturity in character delineation. *Titus Andronicus* (1594) is a horror play. *Romeo and Juliet* (1594) is a romantic tragedy which has become immortal. The four great tragedies of Shakespeare are psychological plays which show how a man of high rank falls from grace, becomes a plaything of destiny and ends up wretchedly all because of a "fatal flaw" in his character. In Greek tragedy, man was a complete puppet whose destiny was in the hands of the gods. Shakespeare often alludes to this: *"As flies to wanton boys are we to the gods/They kill us for their sport"*. But he gives his tragic characters "will-power". The tragic flaw in their characters, however, becomes the cause of their undoing. Thus with *Julius Caesar* (1599), it is his inordinate ambition; with *King Lear* (1605) it is dotedness and bad temper; with *Hamlet* (1601), it is over-refinement of thought leading to indecision; and with *Othello* (1604), it is simplicity causing suspicion. *Timon of Athens* (1607) is the tragedy of a misanthrope. *Coriolanus* (1606) depicts how pride leads to downfall. The last plays — *Pericles* (1608), *Cymbeline* (1609), *The Winter's Tale* (1610) and *The Tempest* (1611) have happy endings. With *The tempest* Shakespeare bid farewell to the theatre just as Prospero in the play puts away his wand and magic books.

To estimate the complete contribution of Shakespeare to English literature and the literature of the world is a difficult task. Thousands of books have been written on Shakespeare by scholars from all over the world and his plays have been translated into all the major languages. They are enacted everywhere and the Russians even claim he was a Slav! Even after 400 years his fame is on the rise. In *Julius Caesar,* Brutus says, *"How many times will this scene of ours be acted over/In states unborn and accents yet unknown"*. This indeed was a prophetic statement about his own plays.

Dryden stated that Shakespeare had 'a universal mind' and Ben Jonson said, "Shakespeare was not of an age but for all times." Indeed Shakespeare's characters — a gallery of 800 — are types of characters that have inhabited this planet throughout the human history. Shakespeare could enter into his characters and present them so vividly that they are more real than life itself. Master of the whole keyboard of emotions and expressions, the subtlest feelings are expressed in his plays. No wonder we quote him the most after the Bible.

Another aspect of his genius is that he excelled many of his contemporaries in whatever they invented. Thus he took Marlowe's 'mighty line' or the blank verse and made it a supple instrument for expressing many intense feelings. Ben Jonson described the 'humours' or human moods in his plays; Shakespeare bettered him in the description of greed, vice, folly and virtue.

Many have expressed doubt about his claim to the authorship of 37 plays in just 20 years. Yet there is no cause for doubt here. After all, he borrowed the stories from Latin and Greek translations and enlivened them with his genius. One of the sources of his Roman histories like *Julius Caesar,* for example, was Plutarch's *Lives of the Noble Romans* translated by North.

Shakespeare undoubtedly had many demerits, but these are overwhelmed and eclipsed by his outstanding gifts. Shakespeare, not being educated more than a few years in grammar school, was thrown upon his own resources. He observed Nature and human behaviour very keenly and had rare intuition and imagination. So he was trained in the school of life. His faults of grammar so prevalent in his plays are glossed off as poetic licence. In fact, he created his own grammar, using nouns as adjectives and inventing syntax. These have become expressions so apt, it is impossible to change or correct them without reducing the impact.

What was Shakespeare's philosophy? Was he a Christian? Shakespeare's ideas as expressed through his noble characters show universal virtue free from dogma and any religious denomination. They are virtues in the human spirit. He was capable of seeing good in all people.

"There is a soul of goodness
In things evil
Distil it if we may".

His advocacy of the cause of Shylock, the Jew, in the days when rank hatred existed for them among the Christians, shows the truth of the above lines. It reinforces the view that Shylock was a man *"more sinned against than sinning"*. Portia's speech on mercy and forgiveness in *The Merchant of Venice* is one of the most beautiful passages of his plays: *"The quality of mercy is not strained/It droppeth like the gentle rain from above/This mightiest in the mightiests"*.

The great range and variety of human behaviour treated by Shakespeare gives his plays an everlasting interest. We may ascribe to the Bard what he himself makes Enobarbus say of Cleopatra:

"Age cannot wither her
Nor custom state her infinite variety".

IMPORTANT POINTS

Life

1. He was born on or about 23 April, 1564 at Stratford-on-Avon, Warwickshire.
2. His father was a prosperous tradesman.
3. He was sent to a Grammar school where he learnt "small Latin and less Greek."
4. Later misfortunes overtook the family.
5. In his 19th year, he married Anne Hathaway, who was eight years his senior.
6. His marriage seems to have been an unhappy one.
7. (*i*) There are several anecdotes why he left for London, but we need not study them here.
   (*ii*) It is almost certain that he went to London in or about 1587 to seek fortunes there.
8. It was the time when drama was being popularized by the University Wits.
9. (*i*) There are again several stories how he came on the stage, but what we are concerned here is that soon he gained popularity and appeared on the stage as an actor.
   For example, he acted in Ben Jonson's "Everyman in His Humour."
   (*ii*) Soon alongwith being an actor, he became a playwright also.
10. It is certain from the deathbed words of Greene who called him an "upstart" that by 1592, Shakespeare had quite established himself as a playwright.
11. Soon he became a shareholder in prestigious theatres such as the Globe and the Blackfriars.
12. (*i*) He also purchased property in London and Stratford.
    (*ii*) It is clear that he had become sufficiently prosperous.
13. However, misfortunes were not late in visiting him :
    (*i*) His only son died in 1596.
    (*ii*) His father died in 1601.
    (*iii*) His mother died in 1608.
14. Still, financially he was sound.
15. Between 1610 and 1612 he retired to his hometown, Stratford, where he bought the largest house in the town named the New Place.
16. As his health broke down, he died on 23rd April, 1616.

Works

In all, he wrote :

(*i*) 37 plays
(*ii*) Two narrative poems:
   (*a*) Venus and Adonis
   (*b*) Lucrece
(*iii*) 154 sonnets:
   (*a*) 126 addressed to a man—a patron or friend.
   (*b*) the rest 28 addressed to a dark lady.

His dramatic work is generally divided in four periods:

1. **The First Period (1588-93) :** It was the period of apprenticeship and experiment. It included:
   (*i*) Revision of old plays such as:
      (*a*) Henry VI
      (*b*) Titus Andronicus,
   (*ii*) the first comedies such as :
      (*a*) Love's Labour's Lost
      (*b*) Two Gentlemen of Verona
      (*c*) The Comedy of Errors, and
      (*d*) A Midsummer Night's Dream, and
   (*iii*) the first attempt at writing a tragedy—Romeo and Juliet.
2. **The Second Period (1594-1600) :** It was the period of the great Comedies and Chronicle Plays, such as
   (*a*) Richard II
   (*b*) King John
   (*c*) The Merchant of Venice
   (*d*) Henry IV Part I

(*e*) Henry IV Part II
(*f*) Henry V
(*g*) The Taming of the Shrew
(*h*) The Merry Wives of Windsor
(*i*) Much Ado About Nothing
(*j*) As You Like It, and
(*k*) Twelfth Night

3. **The Third Period (1601-08):** This was the period of his great tragedies and sombre comedies, such as
(*i*) Julius Caesar
(*ii*) Hamlet
(*iii*) All's Well That Ends Well
(*iv*) Measure for Measure
(*v*) Troilus and Cressida
(*vi*) Othello
(*vii*) King Lear
(*viii*) Macbeth
(*ix*) Antony and Cleopatra
(*x*) Coriolanus
(*xi*) Timon of Athens

4. **The Fourth Period (1608-12):** This was the period of later comedies or what are known as "Dramatic Romances"—
(*a*) (*i*) Cymbeline
(*ii*) The Tempest
(*iii*) Winter's Tale
(*b*) There are two other plays of this period which are only partly written by Shakespeare
(*i*) Pericles
(*ii*) Henry VIII

☛ Henry VIII was completed by his friend, Fletcher (1579-1625) after his death.

Characteristics

1. No single writer has contributed to literature as much literary work as Shakespeare has done.
2. There is "infinite variety" in his work.
3. He was indisputably a versatile genius—a deft master both at prose and verse of all kinds:
(*i*) blank verse
(*ii*) rhyme
(*iii*) dramatic verse
(*iv*) narrative verse, etc.
4. He is the most often quoted among all the English writers.
5. He is one of the greatest poets and dramatists of the world, probably the greatest.
6. It is said that he is the only man in the history of mankind who has said all that is worth-saying.
7. He himself might not be a great thinker, but he could reproduce the borrowed matter in an original form such as none else perhaps could do.
8. No other writer, not even Dickens, has been able to produce so many living and throbbing characters as he has done.
9. It is estimated that he coined more than 15000 (some say, about 18000) words which he contributed to the English language.
10. He is the single writer who has given such a solid footing to the English language that its undying endurance over the centuries can hardly ever be doubted.
11. Needless to say his command over the language he uses is unrivalled.
12. Though a romantic writer, he is all the same the master of realism.
13. He steered the drama clear of stiff classical rules based on ancient masters, and made it a national movement.
14. With all the brutalities as shown by him like other dramatists, unlike them, he upheld the moral law such that truth triumphs in the long run, though poetic justice is not essentially done.
15. Thus his dramas are true to life and human nature.
16. There is a mixture of tragedy and comedy in his dramas as in life.
17. He is the master of true humour and has genuine sympathy with mankind.

Shakespeare's Faults

Like everyone he too is not without faults. Here are listed some of his faults:

1. The feeling of hastiness is evident at places in his works.
2. At places, he uses claptrap methods and means to cater to the 'groundlings', thus sacrificing some of the essential elements of genuine drama, consistency of character and propriety.
3. At places his psychology is hopelessly crude and unconvincing; his style vicious; his wit forced and poor; his tragic language bombastic.
4. At some places there are factual errors in his dramas such that the story, plot, scenes and characters start seeing unreal, *e.g.*
   (*i*) The modern Switzerland in 'Winter's Tale' is shown as having a sea-coast.
   (*ii*) There are trees of coconut and palm-dates side by side in 'As You Like It'.
   (*iii*) Sometimes, the "mistaken identity" scenes as in 'The Merchant of Venice' and 'Twelfth Night' seem unreal.

JOHN MILTON (1608–1674)

Life

John Milton was born on December 9, 1608 in London. His father was a lawyer-cum-banker. Although a Puritan, he loved art and literature and was known as a musician. Milton was trained in music and inherited a love for music. He was charming and aloof. After his education at St. Paul's School he joined Christs' College, Cambridge. But he was rusticated from college for protesting against the curriculum.

Even while he was at Cambridge, he wrote Latin and Italian poems. The best one was *Ode on the Morning of Christ's Nativity* written at the age of twenty-one. In this poem he celebrates the end of paganism and "the death of Pan". The style is rich with Elizabethan devices.

He refused ordination as minister or taking holy orders under the Church of England because this would have fettered his liberated conscience. He settled at Horton near London and devoted himself to writing poems. *L' Allegro* and *Il Penseroso* and two masques *Arcades* and *Comus* and the famous elegy, *Lycidas,* are the works of this period.

In 1638 he left for a tour of the Continent. He won many friends in Italy because of his interest in and mastery of Latin and Italian. But before he could go to Greece, he heard of the conflict between the King and the Parliament and hurried back to England to support the latter. He also taught for a time at a school and wrote a tract on education.

Between 1640 and 1660 he wrote prose pamphlets and some sonnets. When the Commonwealth was established, he was appointed Latin Secretary to the department of foreign affairs. He married Mary Powell in 1643. The marriage was an unhappy one. The daughter of a Cavalier Royalist, she could not tolerate Milton's puritanical ways and left him after marriage. He was much aggrieved and wrote tract pleading for a change in divorce laws. Mary returned to him after two years and he had three daughters by her.

Milton turned fully blind in 1653. Andrew Marvell and others assisted him in his work of writing. He accepted his blindness as the will of God in his beautiful sonnet *On His Blindness: "They also serve who only stand and wait"*.

He married Catherine Woodcock after his first wife died. But Catherine also expired within fifteen months. When monarchy was restored, Milton lost his post and was arrested. He was soon released. He lost some of his property. Now Milton set himself to writing the work that was to make him immortal. In 1667, he completed the *Paradise Lost.* During this period he married for the third time. He finished *Paradise Regained* and *Samson Agonistes* in 1671. He died on November 8, 1674.

Milton was a tolerant Puritan. That is why he got along well with a Royalist father-in-law and a Catholic brother. In later life he became an Arian and did not accept Christ as the divine son. He kept away from wine and women in order to concentrate on higher goals. An unshakeable idealist, he could not understand man completely. His desire to reform mankind was too ambitious and failed. His poetry is remembered today for its magnificent grandeur rather than for any message.

Works

There are four clear-cut periods in Milton's career as a poet: (1) At Cambridge till 1632, (2) At Horton from 1632 to 1638, (3) The period of journalism from 1640 to 1660, (4) The final period of his masterpieces.

The period of his youth produced the famous *Ode on the Morning of Christ's Nativity* (1629). The poem is marred by exaggeration and metaphysical conceits in describing his devotion to the infant Jesus. He also wrote a number of Latin and Italian poems which have been translated into English.

In 1632, he wrote the exquisite *"L' Allegro"* and *Il Penseroso.* The titles only are in Italian. The poems and their spirit are quite English. The first one describes the poet's thoughts in a gay mood and *Il Penseroso* describes the gloomy side of his thinking. The poems are written in octosyllabic couplets and have a haunting music. *L'Allegro* means *'the cheerful man'* and describes his revels, his delight in a castle or a theatre and *Il Penseroso,* his pensive thoughts. Dr. Johnson is said to have admired these poems very much. The poems depict not so much natural scenes as moods of the mind. Milton seeks pure pleasure. In *L'Allegro*, it is Mirth, fresh, rosy and vigorous, dancing on tiptoe. In *Il Penseroso,* divine Melancholy is presented as a pensive nun *"devout and pure .... with even step and musing gait".*

Milton's inner conflict, the moral problem before him, is the theme in the masques *Arcades* and *Comus.* Although these are Renaissance in form, the spirit is grave, austere and Miltonic. *Comus* (1634) is a paean to chastity. It is obviously didactic and lacks any dramatic power to thrill. A young, immaculate heroine is confronted by the magician, Comus, who is drunk and sensual. He tries to have her beautiful virginity, but she is successful in warding him off. The poem is full of discourses and learned reminiscences of the classics and lyrical grace. The morality is high and only the select few could appreciate it.

In *Lycidas* (1637) Milton laments the death of a friend by drowning. The elegy asks the question that if a young man full of promise is carried away in the prime of youth then what avails in this life? Pleasure, therefore, calls him to *"sport with Amaryllis in the shade, Or with the tangles of Neaera's hair".* But another voice, that of fame, calls him away to a life of virtue.

Milton wrote in prose for twenty years. He also composed some exquisite sonnets including the one *On His Blindness* where he regrets he might be incapable of performing God's wish on earth because of his impairment, but consoles himself that even through poetry he can fulfill his life:

"And that one talent which is death to hide
Lodged with me useless
But Patience to prevent that murmur soon replies
They also serve who only stand and wait".

The Restoration of 1660 deprived him of his post for sometime. Poverty, blindness and leisure brought forth his best works: *Paradise Lost* (1667), *Paradise Regained* and *Samson Agonistes* (1671). Here we read in magniloquent lines through great biblical allegories of his personal unhappiness and a nation's agony. He is Beelzebub Satan and Samson in rebellion. Thrown out of Heaven by God, Satan exhorts:

"What though the field be lost
All is not lost
The unconquerable will to survive".

He wrote in blank verse only and used choruses in *Samson Agonistes. Paradise Lost* is his magnum opus, a Puritan's meditation of the Bible or his interpretation of it. The story of Adam and Eve becomes the drama of conscience, the exposure to temptation. The Bible has the ingredients of his own life. *Paradise Regained* is a reply to *Paradise Lost.* This poem is an allegory based on the story of Christ's fast for forty days where he resists the three temptations of Satan and destroys the latter's reign on earth. Christ is seen not as divine incarnation, but as a superman. In fact, Milton himself is Christ, like in that he resists the great temptation for worldly fame by mastering Greek culture and becoming a poet. Literature, philosophy and art are all vain compared to the true wisdom of the Bible.

In *Samson Agonistes,* we again see Milton. He is Samson betrayed by Delilah. He is alone and isolated, blind and helpless, the last of the Republicans among the triumphant Royalists. He lashes out against woman, as the inferior of the human race, deceitful and untrustworthy. The poem is like a Hellenic drama, but lacks movement. There is unending dialectics and reasoning.

IMPORTANT POINTS

Life

1. Milton got a very good education and this, combined with his matchless genius, enabled him to achieve things never attempted, much less achieved, by any poet so far.
2. (*i*) His father became a puritan and Milton inherited all the qualities of virtue, purity, discipline and austerity from him.
   (*ii*) However, Milton by natural bent of mind was a great lover of art, music and literature. Hence the qualities of Hebraism and Hellenism blended in him in equal measure.
3. Thus Milton was :
   (*i*) a religious man
   (*ii*) a great scholar
   (*iii*) a lover of music, if not a musician
   (*iv*) a great epic poet
   (*v*) a politician
   (*vi*) a radical in thought
   (*vii*) a lover and crusader of liberty and freedom, particularly that of the press and the soul.
   (*viii*) a reformer
   (*ix*) a lover of beauty in man and nature
   (*x*) He had spirit of devotion and dedication to cause and duty.
4. Milton imbibed the love of religion, art, music and literature and even politics from his father and those of generosity and charity from his mother.
5. From 1632 onwards, Milton withdrew to the country home of his father in Horton where he led an almost solitary life studying deeply the classics in various languages such as :
   (*i*) Greek (*ii*) Latin
   (*iii*) Hebrew (*iv*) French
   (*v*) Italian (*vi*) Spanish
   (*vii*) English, etc.
6. Not only this, Milton also got a mastery over such disparate subjects as:
   (*i*) music (*ii*) science
   (*iii*) mathematics (*iv*) theology, etc.
7. (*i*) Thereafter, Milton went on a continental tour.
   He visited France, Switzerland and Italy.
   (*ii*) He met Grotius, the Dutch scholar in Paris, and Galileo in Florence where he was serving a jail term.
8. As Civil War broke out in England, Milton hurried back to England.
9. In His "Tenure of Kings and Magistrates," Milton asserted the divine right of the people to take the action necessary for their self-defence and protection, as against the Divine Right of the King asserted earlier by James I and now by Charles I.
10. (*i*) Milton was married in 1643 to Mary Powell.
    (*ii*) She was not a woman of high calibre and, moreover, she was fond of a luxurious life.
    (*iii*) To cap it all, she belonged to a Royalist family.
11. (*i*) Just a month after their marriage, the girl deserted Milton.
    (*ii*) It was then that Milton wrote :
    (*a*) "Doctrine and Discipline of Divorce," and
    (*b*) "Tetrachordon"

(*iii*) This he did to justify the repudiation of marriage from his side.

(*iv*) Milton's arguments were not taken with pleasant approval by the people of England.

12. (*i*) After the death of his wife he married the second time.

(*ii*) After her death he wrote his famous sonnet: "Methought I saw my late espoused saint."

(*iii*) He married the third time in 1663.

(*iv*) Now, Milton had been stone blind since 1652 and his third wife was like a nurse to him.

13. (*i*) He wrote "Defensio pro Populo Anglicano"—a controversial work but containing powerful prose.

(*ii*) However, his best prose work is "Areopagitica" in which he fights the cause of freedom of press like a true crusader.

Works

Early works : Among his early works, we have :

1. On the Morning of Christ's Nativity
2. L'Allegro
3. Il Penseroso
4. The Masque of Comus (1634)
5. Lycidas
6. Sonnets

Characteristics

1. **On the Morning of Christ's Nativity:** Long points out, "In his early work Milton appears as the inheritor of all that was best in Elizabethan literature, and his first work, the ode "On the Morning of Christ's Nativity" approaches the high-water mark of lyric poetry in England."

2. **L'Allegro and Il Penseroso:**

(*i*) These poems belong to Milton's Horton period.

(*ii*) The former is about the happy man, and the latter about the sad man.

(*iii*) Long writes on **L'Allegro:**
"The air is sweet; birds are singing; multitude of sights, sounds, fragrances, fill all the senses; and to this appeal of nature the soul of man responds by being happy, seeing in every flower and hearing in every harmony some exquisite symbol of human life."

(*iv*) **In Il Penseroso,** we have inter alia:

(*a*) a scene of twilight and the appearance of the moon.

(*b*) "a quiet thoughtfulness.... which is not sad, though like all quiet moods, it is akin to sadness, and which sounds the deeps of human emotion in the presence of nature." (Long)

3. **Comus**

(*i*) According to Long, it "is in many respects the most perfect of Milton's poems".

(*ii*) In Comus, we have inter alia:

(*a*) dance and music

(*b*) gorgeous visual scenery

(*c*) the hoary past moral purpose but so consummately delineated by Milton—
The Triumph of Virtue over vice.

4. **Lycidas**

(*i*) It is an elegy written by Milton on the death of his college friend, Edward King.

(*ii*) It is a blend of "high moral purpose with the noblest poetry." (Long)

(*iii*) There is abundance of supernatural element in the poem in the form of nymphs, fauns, satyrs, etc.

(*iv*) So, the poem is an unrivalled example of "Pagan Renaissance."

5. **Sonnets**

(*i*) Milton made use of the form which is known as Miltonic, Italian or Petrarchan in his sonnets instead of the Shakespearean form.

(*ii*) Instead of love, Milton directed his sonnets towards such subjects as:

(*a*) fulfilment of duty

(*b*) unflinching patriotism

(*c*) music and harmony

(*d*) undying love for political struggle

(*e*) undeterrable faith in God and His creation.

(f) justification of ways of God to man which he later endeavoured most vehemently, elaborately and consummately in Paradise Lost.

(iii) That is why Wordsworth says of him:

"Thy soul was like a star and dwelt apart;
Thou hadst a voice whose sound was like the sea—
Pure as the naked heavens, majestic, free."

(iv) Some of his famous sonnets are:
  (a) On Arriving at the Age of Twenty Three
  (b) On His Deceased Wife
  (c) The Massacre in Piedmont
  (d) On His Blindness

(v) Unlike Wordsworth who wrote 500 or more sonnets, Milton did not write many sonnets.

6. **Paradise Lost**

(i) Its theme is the Fall of Man.

(ii) In it Milton wanted to justify the ways of God to man.

(iii) No doubt, it is Milton's greatest and best work which has made him immortal.

(iv) According to Lamartine, it is "the dream of a Puritan fallen asleep over his Bible."

(v) It was composed by Milton when he had fully lost his eye-sight.

(vi) Paradise Lost has 12 books like any true epic.

Book I: It contains *inter alia*:

(i) A noble invocation
(ii) A description of Satan and his legions,
(iii) The description of the rebel angels' plot to wife out the state of innocence of Adam and Eve, our first parents, as created by God.

Book II: It contains *inter alia*:

(i) The great meeting of the devils
(ii) The start of Satan's journey to cause temptation of Adam and Eve.

Book III: It contains *inter alia*:

(i) God's despatch of Raphael to undertake the warning of Adam and Eve about the impending danger.
(ii) The Son of God's offer of personal sacrifice to take upon himself the punishment to man for disobedience to God.
(iii) Satan is also seen again.

Book IV: It contains *inter alia*:

(i) The scene of Paradise
(ii) Satan is caught while tempting Eve in a dream, but is not punished.

Book V, VI: It contains *inter alia*:

(i) Eve's narration of her dream to Adam.
(ii) Scenes of their daily routine
(iii) Arrival of Raphael, etc.

Book VII: It contains the story of creation as told by Raphael.

Book VIII: It contains Adam's narration of his own story, etc.

Book IX: It describes Satan's temptation of Eve, etc.

Book X: It contains *inter alia*:

(i) God's judgement upon Adam and Eve.
(ii) Their repentance
(iii) Satan and his followers' changing into hissing serpents.

Book XI: It describes :

(i) God's acceptance of Adam's repentance, but His ordering of his banishment from Eden.
(ii) Michael's departure to execute God's orders.

Book XII: It describes *inter alia* :

(i) Adam and Eve's having the assurance regarding their future redemption.
(ii) Man's first ancestors' being turned out of paradise "hand in hand."

Comments: The poem is :

(i) a triumph of Milton's most artistic blank verse.
(ii) a triumph of the Epic art.
(iii) an assertion of the Puritan view-point.
(iv) a perfect expression of Milton's own love of music, liberty, justice, etc.
(v) a triumph of sublimity and what is called "the grand style."

(*vi*) a justification of man's ways to God, instead of God's ways to man, as Milton claimed to assert.

(*vii*) the unrivalled character of Satan which resembles Milton's own in many respects.

(*viii*) a triumph of Hebraism.

(*ix*) a triumph of the subjective art.

(*x*) a triumph of the Elizabethan wonder, which earned Milton the title : "A belated Elizabethan".

7. **Paradise Regained**

(*i*) It is a bare poem as compared to Paradise Lost in the matter of style, as is shorn of ornate prosody.

(*ii*) It has wonderful lines and passages showing Milton's :

(*a*) purity and loftiness of mind

(*b*) most exquisite scenery and imagery

(*iii*) Here, Christ, who spurns the tempter, is, in fact, Milton himself as 'In Paradise Lost' Milton is often identified with Satan, who loves liberty above anything else, at least in the first two books.

(*iv*) The theme of the poem is "Christ's temptation in the wilderness."

8. **Samson Agonistes**

(*i*) Samson was an Israeli wrestler who was blind and much maligned.

(*ii*) He was a champion of liberty.

(*iii*) Milton can indisputably be identified with him.

(*iv*) The poem is "a pure tragedy, with all the passion and restraint which marked the old Greek dramas." (Long)

(*v*) The climax is reached when Samson chained with the central pillar of a dome where his tormentors are making merry, brings down the whole structure which destroys all.

WILLIAM WORDSWORTH (1770–1850)

Life

William Wordsworth was born on April 7, 1770 at Cockermouth in the cumberland highlands. His father was a lawyer and land agent. He lost both the parents by the age of fourteen. His school days at Hawkeshead was full of joy, spent in games and reading. He joined St John's College, Cambridge when he was seventeen and went on a walking tour of France during one of his vacations. Taking his degree in 1791 he went to France to stay. The cause of the French Revolution — liberty and equality — attracted him much. He spent 1797-98 mostly with Coleridge and published *Lyrical Ballads* in collaboration with him. After this he visited Germany with his sister Dorothy. Finally he returned to Grasmere in the Lake district of England. Here he published the second volume of the *Lyrical Ballads* and married his cousin Mary Hutchinson.

Wordsworth's life was spent in quiet contemplation and meditation in the beautiful Lake district. Here nature inspired him to write his poetry. He also visited Wales, Scotland and Ireland. He was left a legacy of money by a kind man and got a job as sinecure — distributor of stamps. A man of simple living and high thinking, he could lead a comfortable life and devote himself to poetry. In 1842, the Government provided him a pension of £ 300 a year.

Earlier Wordsworth's poetry received no recognition. In fact, there was adverse criticism of it. But during the last two decades of his life, recognition came to him. He received an honorary degree from the Universities of Durham and Oxford. In 1843 he was appointed poet-laureate. He died in 1850.

Wordsworth was of hardy north-country stock. In austerity he reminds us of Milton. Wordsworth's egotism came in the way of appreciation of the poetry of others.

Works

Most of Wordsworth's voluminous work is dull and prosaic. Only a few works like *The Prelude* and *The*

Excursion make him worthy of the recognition he received as poet-laureate. First and foremost, Wordsworth was the High Priest of Nature. While Cowper, Burns, Blake, Byron, Shelley and Keats all loved Nature 'it was only the external forms'. To Wordsworth Nature was where the Spirit of the Supreme Being dwelt. Nature revealed God's peace and mystery. He had a mystic understanding of Nature. Nature showed the bonds that united all forms of life together — birds, animals and humans. To love all was the message of Nature, Nature was a great teacher. In his own words:

> *"One impulse from a vernal wood*
> *May teach you more of man,*
> *Of moral evil and of good,*
> *Than all the sages can".*

To be able to learn such lessons, Wordsworth advocated a receptive heart. If one bared oneself to the influence of Nature one received wisdom, health, beauty, grace and peace of mind. In one of his *Lucy* poems he says:

> *"And beauty born of murmuring sound*
> *Shall pass into her face".*

When England went to war with France, his mind was in conflict between patriotic loyalty and his love and admiration for the Revolution. War shattered all hopes. He returned to Nature to restore his faith in divine providence and found Nature a great healer.

Nature was a teacher of morals. *"Stern Daughter of the voice of God,"* he called her. His attitude to Nature developed in stages. First, he saw the visionary gleams of childhood in the *Ode on the Intimations of Childhood.*

> *"There was a time when valley, rock and hill*
> *Seem'd apparelled in celestial light".*

Later he developed a passion for Nature which gave him *"aching joys."* Finally, Nature in all its manifestations gave him a lesson in living: *"the meanest flower that blows"* gave him *"thoughts that do often lie too deep for tears".*

Once when Wordsworth was returning home from Cambridge, he passed through a very beautiful landscape of mountains and the sea and that moment of enchantment with Nature was a flash of illumination. He realized that his mission of life was to teach mankind. He wished to bring mankind back to Nature for healing and morals. He set out to write the long poem *The Recluse,* consisting of two parts *The Prelude* (1850) and *The Excursion* (1814). He could not finish the work. Wordsworth claimed that his work as a poet was to teach and this is what he does. The poem is marred by too much moralizing.

Wordsworth felt that the real characters for his poetry must be common, noble men, not Lords and Ladies. He, therefore, wrote a number of poems like *The Idiot Boy, Harry Gill* and *Peter Bell* (1819) in which metre is ignored and common everyday speech is used. The effect is prosaic poetry — dull and ineffective. The real great poetry of Wordsworth is that which springs from his genius, not his poetic beliefs. Wordsworth's great poetry shows spiritual depths of calm reflection. As he writes in *Laodamia,* his classical poem, *"For the Gods approve / The depth and not the tumult of the soul".*

Wordsworth wrote a great variety of poems — odes, lyrics and almost 400 sonnets of which *Upon Westminster Bridge, On Milton* and *The World is too much with Us* are famous.

According to Wordsworth, poetry was "emotion recollected in transquillity". *The Solitary Reaper, To a Highland Girl, The Daffodils, Tintern Abbey* and the *Immortality Ode* were written after some time had elapsed from the event described. These events were moments of perception and when the time had passed the emotions stirred by those moments surfaced clearly. These emotions are then put into words.

IMPORTANT POINTS

Life

1. He was born at Cockermouth, Cumberland. (A poet/critic has called him "the gander of Cockermouth").
2. He got education at Hawkeshead School, Lancashire, and Cambridge.

3. He paid two visits to France :
   (*i*) The first time in 1790
   (*ii*) The second time in 1791-92.

   Long divides his life into four periods :
   (*i*) *1770-87:* It belongs to his childhood and youth-Cumberland.
   (*ii*) *1787-97:* This period covers :
      (*a*) his life at Cambridge
      (*b*) his travels abroad which enabled him to be influenced by the revolutionary ideas.

☛ We know that his revolutionary enthusiasm died soon with :
   (*i*) the excesses of the Revolution including what is called "The Reign of Terror,"
   (*ii*) the rise of tyrannical Napoleon
   (*iii*) 1797-99: This period was very significant as it enabled him to understand his own abilities and take full advantage of them.
   (*iv*) 1799-1850: It was practically a period of retirement in the lake region of his birth and childhood and to remain in direct touch with nature.

Works

1. His "Lyrical Ballads"—a book which is often considered the start of the Revival of Romanticism in England appeared in 1798.
2. His Preface to the Lyrical Ballads is considered important in the history of Criticism of English literature.
3. (*i*) He intended to write a single great poem under the caption "The Recluse."
   (*ii*) The poem was intended to give a comprehensive treatment of: (*a*) nature, (*b*) man and (c) society.
   (*iii*) His intention was that his "The Prelude"—the Growth of a Poet's Mind—should introduce the Recluse.
   (*iv*) (*a*) The first book of The Recluse "The Home at Grasmere" was published posthumously in 1888.
   (*b*) The name of the second book was 'The Excursion.'
   (*c*) The third was never completed by the poet.

His most famous poems are :

1. The Prelude
2. Tintern Abbey
3. Ode on Intimations of Immortality.
4. Ode to Duty or Education of Nature
5. The Rainbow
6. The Solitary Reaper
7. Michael
8. To a Skylark
9. Yarrow Revisited
10. Lucy Gray
11. She Dwelt Among the Untrodden Ways
12. Daffodils

He also wrote a large number of sonnets such as :

1. On Milton
2. On Westminster Bridge
3. The World is Too Much With Us, etc.

Characteristics

1. He was a great lover of nature.
2. He felt the presence of a spirit in nature, that is, the spirit of nature.
3. He believed in pantheism.
4. He believed that nature could bestow peace, sympathy, love, joy and other virtues on man.
5. He did not like to depict nature "red in tooth and claw."
6. He believed that nature gave purity to man and ennobled his heart.
7. He was a great lover of the common man and the rustic and rural life.
8. He loved the child and thought that because of its innocence, purity of thought and nearness to God, childhood was the golden period of human life.
9. He loved all creation and all kinds of creatures, including the smallest and most insignificant animals and insects.

10. He believed that "nature never did betray the heart that loved her."
11. He himself practised what he preached and spent most of his time in the company of nature.
12. His poetry is full of :
    (*i*) vivid descriptions of scenes of nature.
    (*ii*) simple human affections.
    (*iii*) fervent adulations of childhood and love of animals.
    (*iv*) depictions of country and village life.
    (*v*) sweet and haunting music.
    (*vi*) personal reminiscences and memories
    (*vii*) autobiographical tones
    (*viii*) adulation of simplicity and homeliness.
    (*ix*) tones of true theism and fervent faith in greatness, goodness and benignity of nature.
13. Although much of his later poetry is dull and interesting, yet it contains flashes of imaginative lines and good poetry.

JOHN GALSWORTHY (1867–1933)

John Galsworthy was an English novelist and playwright. His notable works include *The Forsyte Saga* (1906–1921) and its sequels, *A Modern Comedy* and *End of the Chapter*. He won the Nobel Prize in Literature in 1932.

Life

John Galsworthy was born on 14 August 1867 at Kingston Hill in Surrey, England, the son of John and Blanche Bailey (nee Bartleet) Galsworthy. His family was wealthy and well established, with a large estate in Kingston upon Thames that is now the site of three schools: Marymount International School, Rokeby Preparatory School, and Holy Cross. He attended Harrow and New College, Oxford, training as a barrister, and was called to the bar in 1890. However, he was not keen to begin practising law and instead travelled abroad to look after the family's shipping business. During these travels he met Joseph Conrad, then the first mate of a sailing-ship moored in the harbour of Adelaide, Australia, and the two future novelists became close friends. In 1895 Galsworthy began an affair with Ada Nemesis Pearson Cooper (1864–1956), the wife of his cousin Major Arthur Galsworthy. After her divorce ten years later, they married 23 September 1905 and stayed together until his death in 1933. Before their marriage, they often stayed clandestinely in a farmhouse called Wingstone in the village of Manaton on Dartmoor, Devon. From 1908 he took out a long lease on part of the building and made it their regular second home until 1923.

From the Four Winds, a collection of short stories, was Galsworthy's first published work in 1897. These and several subsequent works were published under the pen name John Sinjohn, and it would not be until *The Island Pharisees* (1904) that he would begin publishing under his own name, probably owing to the death of his father. His first full-length novel, *Jocelyn* was published in an edition of 750 under the name of *John Sinjohn* – he later refused to have it republished. His first play, *The Silver Box* (1906), – in which the theft of a prostitute's purse by a rich 'young man of good family' is placed beside the theft of a silver cigarette case from the rich man's father's house by 'a poor devil', with very different repercussions – became a success, and he followed it up with *The Man of Property* (1906), the first in the Forsyte trilogy. Although he continued writing both plays and novels, it was as a playwright that he was mainly appreciated at the time. Along with those of other writers of the time, such as George Bernard Shaw, his plays addressed the class system and social issues, two of the best known being *Strife* (1909) and *The Skin Game* (1920).

He is now far better known for his novels, particularly *The Forsyte Saga,* his trilogy about the eponymous family and connected lives. These books, as with many of his other works, deal with social class, upper-middle class lives in particular. Although sympathetic to his characters, he highlights their insular, snobbish, and acquisitive attitudes and their suffocating moral codes. He is viewed as one of the first writers of the Edwardian era who challenged some of the ideals of society depicted in the preceding literature of Victorian England. The depiction of a woman in an unhappy marriage furnishes another recurring theme in his work. The character of Irene in *The Forsyte Saga* is drawn from Ada Pearson, though her previous marriage was not as miserable as that of the character.

Through his writings he campaigned for a variety of causes, including prison reform, women's rights, animal welfare, and the opposition of censorship. During World War I he worked in a hospital in France as an orderly after being passed over for military service. He was elected as the first president of the PEN International literary club in 1921, was appointed to the Order of Merit in 1929 — after earlier turning down a knighthood — and was awarded the Nobel Prize in 1932. He was too ill to attend the Nobel awards ceremony, and died six weeks later on 31 January 1933 of a stroke at his London home.

John Galsworthy lived for the final seven years of his life at Bury in West Sussex. In accordance with his will he was cremated at Woking with his ashes then being scattered over the South Downs from an aeroplane, but there are also memorials in High gate 'New' Cemetery and in the cloisters of New College, Oxford (the latter cut and placed in the cloisters by Eric Gill). The popularity of his fiction waned quickly after his death but the hugely successful adaptation of *The Forsyte Saga* in 1967 renewed interest in his work.

A number of John Galsworthy's letters and papers are held at the University of Birmingham Special Collections.

In 2007, Kingston University, London opened a new building named in recognition of his local birth. Galsworthy Road in Kingston, location of Kingston Hospital, is also named for him.

Works

- *From the Four Winds,* 1897 (as John Sinjohn)
- *Jocelyn,* 1898 (as John Sinjohn)
- *Villa Rubein,* 1900 (as John Sinjohn)
- *A Man of Devon,* 1901 (as John Sinjohn)
- *The Island Pharisees,* 1904
- *The Silver Box,* 1906 (his first play
- *The Man of Property,* 1906 – first book of *The Forsyte Saga* (1922)
- *The Country House,* 1907
- *A Commentary,* 1908
- *Fraternity,* 1909
- *A Justification for the Censorship of Plays,* 1909
- *Strife,* 1909
- *Fraternity,* 1909
- *Joy,* 1909
- *Justice,* 1910
- *A Motley,* 1910
- *The Spirit of Punishment,* 1910
- *Horses in Mines,* 1910
- *The Patrician,* 1911
- *The Pigeon,* 1912
- *The Eidest Son,* 1912
- *Quality,* 1912
- *Moods, Songs, and Doggerels,* 1912
- *For Love of Beasts,* 1912
- *The Inn of Tranquillity,* 1912
- *The Dark Flower,* 1913
- *The Fugitive,* 1913
- *The Mob,* 1914
- *The Freelands,* 1915
- *The Little Man,* 1915
- *A Bit's Love,* 1915
- *A Sheaf,* 1916
- *The Apple Tree,* 1916
- *Beyond,* 1917
- *Five Tales,* 1918
- *Indian Summer of a Forsyte,* 1918 – first interlude of *The Forsyte Saga*
- *Saint's Progress,* 1919

- *Addresses in America,* 1912
- *The Foundations,* 1920
- *In Chancery,* 1920 – second book of *The Forsyte Saga*
- *Awakening,* 1920 – second interlude of *The Forsyte Saga*
- *Awakening,* 1920 – second interlude of *The Forsyte Saga*
- *The Skin Game,* 1920
- *To Let,* 1921 – third book of *The Forsyte Saga*
- *A Family Man,* 1922
- *The Little Man,* 1922
- *Loyalties,* 1922
- *Windows,* 1922
- *Captures,* 1923
- *Abracadabra,* 1924
- *The Forest,* 1924
- *Old English,* 1924
- *The White Monkey,* 1924 – first book of *A Modern Comedy* (1929)
- *The Show,* (1925
- *Escape,* 1926
- *The Silver Spoon,* 1926 – second book of *A Modern Comedy*
- *Verses New and Old,* 1926
- *Castles in Spain,* 1927
- *A Silent Wooing,* 1927 – first Interlude of *A Modern Comedy*
- *Passers By,* 1927 – second Interlude of *A Modern Comedy*
- *Swan Song,* 1928 – third book of *A Modern Comedy*
- *The Manaton Edition,* 1923–26 (collection, 30 vols.)
- *Exiled,* 1929
- *The Roof,* 1929
- *On Forsyte Change,* 1930
- *Two Essays on Conrad,* 1930
- *Soames and the Flag,* 1930
- *The Creation of Character in Literature,* 1931 (The Romanes Lecture for (1931).
- *Maid in Waiting,* 1931 – first book of *End of the Chapter* (1934)
- *Forty Poems,* 1932
- *Flowering Wilderness,* 1932
- *Over the River,* 1933
- *Autobiographical Letters of Galsworthy: A Corres-pondence with Frank Harris,* 1933
- *The Grove Edition,* 1927–34 (collection, 27 Vols.)
- *Collected Poems,* 1934
- *Flowering Wilderness,* 1932 – second book of *End of the Chapter*
- *One More River* (originally *Over the River*), 1933 – third book of *End of the Chapter*
- *Punch and Go,* 1935
- *The Life and Letters,* 1935
- *The Winter Garden,* 1935
- *Forsytes, Pendyces and Others,* 1935
- *Selected Short Stories,* 1935
- *Glimpses and Reflections,* 1937
- *Galsworthy's Letters to Leon Lion,* 1968
- *Letters from John Galsworthy* 1900–1932, 1970

IMPORTANT POINTS

1. Galsworthy's early works which were written over the pseudonym "John Sinjohn" were all rejected by the publishers.
2. (*i*) His first work which made him widely known was 'The Man of Property' (a novel).
   (*ii*) It deals with middle-class Victorian society.
3. In 1904 he published his play "Island Pharisees", which reappeared as "The Pigeon" in 1922.
4. The same year (1922) was published "The Forsyte Saga.
5. In all, he wrote about thirty works of fiction. According to Long, the best among them all is "Indian Summer of a Forsyte."
6. Galsworthy is better known as a play-wright than a fiction writer.
7. His plays are what now we know as "Problem Plays."

8. His most famous plays among his thirty plays are :
   (i) Strife (For this work he received the Nobel Prize for Literature)
   (ii) Justice (1910)
   (iii) Loyalties (1922)
   (iv) The Silver Box (1909)
   (v) Escape (1926)

The Skin Game was adapted and directed by Alfred Hitchocock in 1931. It starred C.V. France, Helen Haye, Jill Esmond, Edmoud Gwenn, and John Longden.

Escape was filmed in 1930 and 1948. The latter was directed by Joseph L. Mankiewicz, starring Rex Harrison, Peggy Cummins, and William Hartnell. The screenplay was by Philip Dunne.

One More River (a film version of Galsworthy's *Over the River*) was filmed by James Whale in 1934. The film starred Frank Lawton, Colin Clive (one of Whale's most frequently used actors), Diana Wynyard, and featured Mrs. Patrick Campbell in a rare sound film appearance.

The First and the Last, as short play, was adapted as *21 Days*, starring Vivien Leigh and Laurence Olivier.

Galsworthy's short story *The Apple Tree* was adapted into a radio play for Orson Welles's *Lady Esther Almanac* radio series on CBS, first broadcast on 12 January 1942; the play was again produced by Welles for CBS on *The Mercury Summer Theatre* of 6 September 1946. The 1988 film *A Summer Story* was also based on *The Apple Tree.*

The Patrician was broadcast on NBC University Theater of the Air radio show on 24 February 1950.

Characteristics

In the works of **John Galsworthy (1867-1933)** we find an artistic conscience. Like Wells, he also attacked the concept of property and commercialism in his novels. He too exposed and criticized national prejudices, especially those existing among his own class, the landed gentry. He was widely read in Continental Literature and was especially influenced by France and Russia. Turgenev with his noble realism was his ideal. He is a detached and impartial observer of his country's decadent values. He advocates a fearless search for truth. *In The Island Pharisees* (1904) he exposes the stagnation of thought among English privileged classes. A similar theme is touched in other novels like *The Country House* (1907), *The Patrician* (1911) and *The Dark Flower* (1913) where country squires, aristocracy and artists are critically studied. *The Forsyte Saga* (1922) is his masterpiece. It is a natural history of the rich upper-middle class family. He describes their attitude to events like the Great War, the growth of socialism, unemployment and the coal strike.

WALT WHITMAN (1819-1892)

Walter "Walt" Whitman (May 31, 1819 — March 26, 1892) was an American poet, essayist and journalist. A humanist, he was a part of the transition between transcendentalism and realism, incorporating both views in his works. Whitman is among the most influential poets in the American canon, often called the father of free verse. His work was very controversial in its time, particularly his poetry collection Leaves of Grass, which was described as obscene for its overt sexuality.

Born in Huntington on Long Island, Whitman worked as a journalist, a teacher, a government clerk, and—in addition to publishing his poetry—was a volunteer nurse during the American Civil War. Early in his career, he also produced a temperance novel, *Franklin Evans* (1842). Whitman's major work, *Leaves of Grass*, was first published in 1855 with his own money. The work was an attempt at reaching out to the common person with an American epic. He continued expanding and revising it until his death in 1892. After a stroke, towards the end of his life, he moved to Camden, New Jersey, where his health further declined. He died at age 72 and his funeral became a public spectacle.

Whitman's sexuality is often discussed alongside his poetry. Though biographers continue to debate his sexuality, he is usually described as either homosexual or bisexual in his feelings and attractions. However, there is disagreement among biographers as to whether Whitman had actual sexual experiences with men.

Whitman was concerned with politics throughout his life. He supported the Wilmot Proviso and opposed the extension of slavery generally. His poetry presented an egalitarian view of the races, though his attitude in life reflected many of the racial prejudices common to nineteenth-century America and his opposition to slavery was not necessarily based on belief in the equality of races per se. At one point he called for the abolition of slavery, but later he saw the abolitionist movement as a threat to democracy.

Works

Whitman's work breaks the boundaries of poetic form and is generally prose-like. He also used unusual images and symbols in his poetry, including rotting leaves, tufts of straw, and debris. He also openly wrote about death and sexuality, including prostitution. He is often labeled as the father of free verse, though he did not invent it.

Whitman wrote in the preface to the 1855 edition of Leaves of Grass, "The proof of a poet is that his country absorbs him as affectionately as he has absorbed it." He believed there was a vital, symbiotic relationship between the poet and society. This connection was emphasized especially in "Song of Myself" by using an all-powerful first-person narration. As an American epic, it deviated from the historic use of an elevated hero and instead assumed the identity of the common people. Leaves of Grass also responded to the impact that recent urbanization in the United States had on the masses.

Walt Whitman has been claimed as America's first "poet of democracy", a title meant to reflect his ability to write in a singularly American character. A British friend of Walt Whitman, Mary Smith Whitall Costelloe, wrote: "You cannot really understand America without Walt Whitman, without *Leaves of Grass*... He has expressed that civilization, 'up to date,' as he would say, and no student of the philosophy of history can do without him."

Whitman's vagabond lifestyle was adopted by the Beat movement and its leaders such as Allen Ginsberg and Jack Kerouac in the 1950s and 1960s as well as anti-war poets like Adrienne Rich and Gary Snyder. Lawrence Ferlinghetti numbered himself among Whitman's "wild children", and the title of his 1961 collection Starting from San Francisco is a deliberate reference to Whitman's *Starting from Paumanok*. Whitman also influenced Bram Stoker, author of *Dracula*, and was the model for the character of Dracula. Stoker said in his notes that Dracula represented the quintessential male which, to Stoker, was Whitman, with whom he corresponded until Whitman's death. Other admirers included the Eagle Street College, an informal group established in 1885 at the home of James William Wallace in Eagle Street, Bolton, to read and discuss the poetry of Whitman. The group subsequently became known as the Bolton Whitman Fellowship or Whitmanites. Its members held an annual 'Whitman Day' celebration around the poet's birthday.

Whitman's poetry has been set to music by a large number of composers; indeed it has been suggested his poetry has been set to music more than any other American poet except for Emily Dickinson and Henry Wadsworth Longfellow. Whitman is a 2009 inductee of the New Jersey Hall of Fame.

IMPORTANT POINTS

1. He was the first really powerful true American poet.
2. He had his first influences from his own family, *e.g.*
   (i) On the side of his father :
   He imbibed the spirit of love of freedom, and patriotism and enlightened revolutionary idealism from his father.
   (ii) On the side of his mother:
   (a) His mother was a Quaker.

(b) He learnt from her deeply mystic qualities which we find strewn all over his poetry and which make him the "poet of the soul."

3. Some of the other things which influenced or attracted him were :
   (i) Democracy
   (ii) the urban multitudes
   (iii) Journalism—The career enabled him to observe and be a genuine and keen spectator rather than a participant in life's activities.
4. This was upto 'The Leaves of Grass'
5. His real genius got exploded only in
   (i) The Leaves of Grass (1855)
   (ii) The 4th edition of the book appeared in 1866.
6. With the passage of time, his love of the universe grew continuously.
7. (i) He believed in *Unanimism,* that is ensembling, that is collectivity, wholeness amplitude or totality rather that partliness or partiality.
   (ii) Hence, his aesthetics may be called the "Aesthetics of Unanimism"
8. There is a lot of controversy regarding the unity of the Leaves of Grass, but there is a general feeling of its being, in the real sense, the epic of modern America.
9. Whitman is studied in various roles such as:
   (i) As a Poet of Democracy
   (ii) As a Mystic Poet
   (iii) As a Symbolist
   (iv) As a Cataloguing Poet
   (or Poet having a catalogue technique or style)
   (v) As a Romantic poet
   (vi) As a Modern Poet
   (vii) As a poet known for his special style.
   (viii) As a representative poet of America, etc.
10. Some of his most read poems are :
   (i) Song of My Self
   (ii) Song of the open Road
   (iii) Crossing Brooklyn Ferry
   (iv) Passage to India
   (v) What is Grass?
   (vi) I think I could Turn and Love with Animals
   (vii) A Hub for the Universe
   (viii) When Lilacs Last in the Dooryard Bloom'd
   (ix) Out of the Cradle Endlessly Rocking
   (x) O Captain! My captain!
   (xi) There was a child went forth
   (xii) I Hear America Singing
   (xiii) I saw in Louisiana a Live-Oak grossing
   (xiv) Poets to come
   (xv) One's Self I Sing
   (xvi) I Hear It was Charged Against Me
   (xvii) Scented Herbage of My Breast
   (xviii) Prayer of Columbus
   (xix) A Glimpse
   (xx) On the Beach at Night.

P.B. SHELLEY (1792-1822)

Percy Bysshe Shelley, a controversial English writer of great personal conviction and one of the epic poets of the 19th century, is best known for his classic anthology verse works such as *Ode to the West Wind* and *The Masque of Anarchy*. He is also well known for his long-form poetry, including *Queen Mab* and *Alastor*. He went on many adventures with his second wife, Mary Shelley, the author of *Frankenstein.*

Shelley was born on August 4, 1792, at Field Place, near Horsham, Sussex, England. The eldest son of Timothy and Elizabeth Shelley, with one brother and four sisters, he stood in line to inherit not only his grandfather's considerable estate but also a seat in Parliament. He attended Eton College for six years beginning in 1804, and then went on to Oxford University.

Shelly began writing poetry while at Eton, but his first publication was a Gothic novel, *Zastrozzi* (1810), in which he voiced his own heretical and atheistic opinions through the villain Zastrozzi. That same year, Shelley and another student, Thomas Jefferson Hogg, published a pamphlet of burlesque verse, "Posthumous Fragments of Margaret Nicholson," and with his sister Elizabeth, Shelley published *Original Poetry; by Victor and Cazire*. In 1811, Shelley continued this prolific outpouring with more publications, and it was one of these that got him expelled from Oxford after less than a year's enrollment: another pamphlet that he wrote and circulated with Hogg, "The Necessity of Atheism." Shelley could have been reinstated with the intervention of his father, but this would have required his disavowing the pamphlet and declaring himself Christian. Shelley refused, which led to a complete break between Shelley and his father. This left him in dire financial straits for the next two years, until he came of age.

Shelly, that same year, at age nineteen, eloped to Scotland with Harriet Westbrook, sixteen. Once married, Shelley moved to the Lake District of England to study and write. Two years later he published his first long serious work, *Queen Mab: A Philosophical Poem*. The poem emerged from Shelley's friendship with the British philosopher William Godwin, and it expressed Godwin's freethinking Socialist philosophy. Shelley also became enamored of Godwin and Mary Wollstonecraft's daughter, Mary, and in 1814 they eloped to Europe. After six weeks, out of money, they returned to England. In November 1814 Harriet Shelley bore a son, and in February 1815 Mary Godwin gave birth prematurely to a child who died two weeks later. The following January, Mary bore another son, named William after her father. In May the couple went to Lake Geneva, where Shelley spent a great deal of time with George Gordon, Lord Byron, sailing on Lake Geneva and discussing poetry and other topics, including ghosts and spirits, into the night. During one of these ghostly "seances," Byron proposed that each person present should write a ghost story. Mary's contribution to the contest became the novel *Frankenstein*. That same year, Shelley produced the verse allegory *Alastor, or The Spirit of Solitude*. In December 1816 Harriet Shelley apparently committed suicide. Three weeks after her body was recovered from a lake in a London park, Shelley and Mary Godwin officially were married. Shelley lost custody of his two children by Harriet because of his adherence to the notion of free love.

Shelley, in 1817, produced *Laon and Cythna*, a long narrative poem that, because it contained references to incest as well as attacks on religion, was withdrawn after only a few copies were published. It was later edited and reissued as *The Revolt of Islam* (1818). At this time, he also wrote revolutionary political tracts signed "The Hermit of Marlow." Then, early in 1818, he and his new wife left England for the last time. During the remaining four years of his life, Shelley produced all his major works, including *Prometheus Unbound* (1820). Traveling and living in various Italian cities, the Shelleys were friendly with the British poet Leigh Hunt and his family as well as with Byron.

On July 8, 1822, just shy of turning 30, Shelley drowned while sailing his schooner back from Livorno to Lerici, after having met with Leigh Hunt to discuss their newly printed journal, *The Liberal*. Despite conflicting evidence, most papers reported Shelley's death as an accident.

Shelley's body was cremated on the beach in Viareggio, where it had washed ashore. Shelley's ashes were interred in the Protestant Cemetery in Rome. More than a century later, he was memorialized in Poet's Corner in Westminster Abbey.

IMPORTANT POINTS

Life

1. He was born in Sussex in 1792.
2. His parents belonged to the class of nobility.
3. As a child, Shelley was highly fanciful like Blake.
4. After having got a brutal treatment in his Scotch public school, he joined Eton. But being a highly sensitive boy who held self-respect above anything else, he revolted against the tyrannical system in the new school.
5. Of course, he was ridiculed and called 'Mad Shelley' by other boys.
6. (*i*) While at Oxford, he published his pamphlet "The Necessity of Atheism."
   (*ii*) In writing this, he was influenced by the philosophy of Hume.
   (*iii*) He was expelled from the university for this.
7. (*i*) First Shelley married Harriet Westbrook, a mere school girl whose parents never agreed to this marriage.
   (*ii*) Even Shelley's own parents disinherited him for this.
8. (*i*) Later, as Shelley came under the influence of Godwin—an anarchist philosopher—he eloped with his daughter, Mary, who later wrote "Frankenstein's Monster" which is so famous for its title if not much for its contents.
   (*ii*) Sadly, this elopement, however, led to Harriet's well-known suicide.
9. Just as Byron had earlier left England in 1816, never to return, Shelley did the same in 1818, though for reasons of health mainly and partly of hostility against his ideology of revolt, anarchism or cynicism (whatever we may call it), etc.
10. His shifting to Italy proved a boon, since—
    (*i*) here he wrote his best poetry
    (*ii*) here he was able to get the friendship of such personalities as: (*a*) Byron (*b*) Leigh Hunt (*c*) Trelawney, etc.
11. Shelley met with a tragic death in 1822 while sailing in a boat off the Italian coast.

Works

1. Alastor (or the Spirit of Solitude) (1816):
   (*i*) It expresses Shelley's endless love for wandering in search of a dream girl who is the model of beauty.
   (*ii*) The poem is illusory in nature and lacks reality.
2. Prometheus Unbound (1818-20):
   (*i*) In this lyrical drama whilst Prometheus steals fire from heaven for mankind, Shelley, according to Long, "is the prophet of science and evolution."
   (*ii*) Studied in the proper prospective, the work suggests hope and promise for goodness to prevail at last.
   (*iii*) In his poem "The Cloud" Shelley takes recourse to exact geographical phenomenon. Similar is the case in 'Ode to the West Wind'. Because of his correct use of geographical and scientific facts, he is sometimes called "the scientist poet."
3. Other Revolutionary works: Besides Promentheus, Shelley's other revolutionary works are:
   (*i*) Queen Mab (1813)
   (*ii*) The Revolt of Islam (1818)
   (*iii*) The Witch of Atlas (1820)
   (*iv*) Hellas (1821)
4. "Epipsychidion" (1821) is Shelley's work of Platonic love.
5. Perhaps Shelley's only work based on reality is his drama "The Cenci". Here below is an extract:

JOHN KEATS (1795-1821)

John Keats was one of England's greatest poets. He is specially known for his love of the country and sensuous descriptions of the beauty of nature, his poetry also resonated with deep philosophic questions. Elabourate word choice and sensual imagery characterise Keats' poetry.

John Keats was born on October 13, 1795 in Moorfields, London. His father died when he was eight and his mother when he was 14; these sad circum-stances drew him particularly close to his two brothers, George and Tom, and his sister, Frances Mary.

Keats was well educated at a school in Enfield, where he began a translation of Virgil's Aeneid. Keats, who was barely five feet tall, was not known at school for his enthusiasm for books, but his fighting. "My mind has been the most discontented and restless one that ever was put into a body too small for it," he wrote.

In 1810, he was apprenticed to an apothecary-surgeon. His first attempts at writing poetry dated from about 1814, and included an 'Imitation' of the Elizabethan poet, Edmund Spenser.

In 1816, he became a Licentiate of the Society of Apothecaries and was allowed to practise surgery. Before devoting himself entirely to poetry, Keats worked as a dresser and junior house surgeon. In London, he had met Leigh Hunt, the editor of the leading liberal magazine of the day, The Examiner. He introduced Keats to other young romantics, including Shelley, and published in the magazine Keats's sonnet, O Solitude.

Keats's first book, Poems, was published in 1817. Sales were poor. It was about this time, Keats started to use his letters as the vehicle of his thoughts of poetry. They mixed the everyday events of his own life with comments with his correspondence. Among others T.S. Eliot considered the letters in The Use of Poetry and the Use of Criticism "certainly the most notable and most important ever written by any English poet," but also said about Keats's famous Hyperion: "it contains great lines, but I do not know whether it is a great poem."

His greatest works were written in the late 1810s, among them, Lamia, The Eve of St. Agnes, the great odes and two versions of Hyperion. He worked briefly as a theatrical critic for The Champion.

Keats toured the north of England and Scotland in the summer of 1818, returning home to nurse his brother, Tom, who was ill with tuberculosis. After Tom's death in December, he moved into a friend's house in Hampstead, now known as Keats House. There he met and fell deeply in love with a young neighbour, Fanny Brawne. During the following year, despite ill health and financial problems, he wrote an astonishing amount of poetry, including The Eve of St-Agnes', La Belle Dame sans Merci, Ode to a Nightingale and To Autumn.

His second volume of poems appeared in July 1820. It gained a huge critical success. However, Keats was suffering at that time from tuberculosis. Keats rallied a little at first, and was able to take gentle walks and rides, but by early December, he was confined to bed, extremely ill with a high fever. Severn nursed him devotedly throughout the next few distressing and painful weeks. Keats died peacefully, clasping his friend's hand, on February 23, 1821.

In spite of early harsh criticism, Keats's reputation grew after his death. The poet's letters were published in 1848 and 1878. His works have influenced among others The Pre-Raphaelites, Oscar Wilde and Alfred Tennyson.

IMPORTANT POINTS

Life

1. He was born in London in 1795.
2. His father was a hostler and stable keeper.
3. Both his parents died before he was fifteen.
4. It is said that his guardians cheated him and his brothers and sisters.

5. At first, he started the profession of a surgeon but later abandoned it.
6. He was greatly impressed by Spenser, particularly his Faerie Queene which he read most fervently.
7. Byron and some other critics and literary men held, the view that savage criticism of Keats' "Endymion" in the Blackwood Magazine shortened the life of this young poet, but Matthew Arnold does not subscribe to this view.
8. Since he was suffering from tuberculosis and could not tolerate the severity and coldness of the British climate, he left for Italy, where in Rome, he settled with his friend Severn, but soon he breathed his last in February, 1821.

Works

1. His first work was 'Endymion' which although immature and imperfect, has flashes of beautiful and charming lines in it.
2. Odes : Keats is most famous for his odes, some of which are named below:
   (*i*) Ode to a Nightingale
   (*ii*) Ode on a Grecian Urn
   (*iii*) Ode of Psyche
   (*iv*) Ode to Autumn
   (*v*) Ode of Indolence

   (**Note:** He is undeniably the greatest ode writer in English literature.)
3. His last volume which was composed in 1820, comprised the following poems :
   (*i*) Lamia
   (*ii*) Isabella
   (*iii*) The Eve of St. Agnes, etc.
4. (*i*) Keats left his stupendously planned work: "Hyperion" a mere fragment.
   (*ii*) The poem was to be a wonderful epic on a grand scale but were never completed.
   (*iii*) It is in this work that the following celebrated line occurs :
   "For it's the eternal law that the first in beauty shall be the first in might."

Note: (*i*) Keats is considered by many the greatest romanticist, had always been a lover of beauty. Thus, we have—

(*ii*) 'A thing of beauty is a joy for ever.'

—Endymion

(*iii*) 'Beauty is truth, truth beauty,
That is all ye know on earth
and all ye need to know."

—Ode on a Grecian Urn

(*iv*) One of his most famous poems is :
"La Belle Dame Sans Merci":
"O what can ail thee, knight -ate arms,
Alone and palely loitering?
The sedge is withered on the lake,
And no birds sing."

As a Sonneteer: Keats did not live to write many sonnets, but the few sonnets he wrote, are some of the best in English literature. Some of them are:

(*i*) When I have fears that I may cease to be
(*ii*) Human Seasons
(*iii*) On Looking Into Chapman's Homer
(*iv*) Bright Star! .....

BEN JONSON (1573-1637)

Ben Jonson was only second to Shakespeare as a playwright. He had a chequered career. He was educated at Westminster School, but did not go up to university. Both Oxford and Cambridge Universities, however, honoured him. Jonson did stints as bricklayer, soldier and then actor. Being of a hot temperament, he picked up quarrels with fellow-actors and even killed one in a brawl for which crime he was branded in the left hand. He was both an admirer and a rival of Shakespeare. He offended King James and the Scots by his comedy *Eastward Hoe!* (written with George Chapman and John Marston), was imprisoned and almost lost his ears and nose. He lived for sometime with William Drummond, the Scottish poet, at Hawthornden. Drummond has left us an account of Ben Jonson's fiery nature. Like Samuel Johnson later on, Jonson later on, Jonson behaved like a literary dictator in the last period of his life gathering fawning admirers who were called the tribe of Ben. He died a poor man. On his tomb in Westminster Abbey, it is inscribed "O rare Ben Jonson!".

Ben Jonson was a neo-classical and revived the theories of drama that existed among the classical Greeks and Romans. Thus unlike Shakespeare, he maintained the classical rules of the unities of time, place and action in his plays. In this way, he wished to reform the Elizabethan theatre. Although he worshipped Shakespeare "this side of idolatory", he derided his lack of classical taste. At the Mermaid Tavern, he had witty combats with Shakespeare. Jonson did a lot of research into historical facts and documented his famous plays *Sejanus* and *Catiline* which turned out to be dull and pedantic. He was more successful in comedies and attacked romantic conventions used by his contemporaries. The comedies are realistic portrayals of the fads and follies of contemporary London. The best of his comedies are *Everyman in His Humour* (1598), *Epicoene or The Silent Woman* (1609), *The Alchemist* (1610) and *Volpone* (1605), the story of criminals.

Ben Jonson's comedies were "comedies of humour". In medieval medical parlance, a honour was one of the four fluids — choler, bite, phlegm and blood which determined a person's disposition by its preponderance. Thus choler or rather too much of it made one bad-tempered. Ben Jonson thus used it to mean a typical trait or idiosyncracy of a person. He exaggerated this and blew it out of all proportions to create comedy. Characters are given tell-tale names like Morose in *Epicoene*. Thus his characters were personifications of various qualities and resembled moralities. This was a method Charles Dickens was to employ later on, but on a larger canvas. Morose in Ben Jonson's play is eccentric about noise. He cannot tolerate the least noise. He oils his locks and doors and lives in a narrow street where no traffic is possible. His house is carpeted to absorb sound. Servants communicate in signs and one loses the job if the boots squeak. Morose agrees to his nephew marrying if he can get a perfectly silent woman. This he finds. But after marriage the wife becomes a loud mouth. The nephew celebrates the marriage with a noisy band. Horrified, Morose looks for a divorce. Here too he meets with disaster since he accosts two lawyers wrangling noisily. The nephew agrees to get rid of his wife if Morose leaves him an inheritance. He gets Morose to make a bond for this. Then he pulls of his wife's wig to reveal a boy!

Jonson's other plays are tedious and satirical — *Everyman out of His Humour* (1599), *Cynthis's Revels* (1600) and *The Poetaster* (1601). Jonson also wrote pastoral drama. His *Eastward Hoe!* gives a realistic picture of London life that surpasses all of Shakespeare's descriptions of the city. His plays contain some very beautiful lyrics like *"Drink to me only with thine eyes"*.

Ben Jonson was original and showed great technical skill in plot construction. His language is witty and vigorous, but his characters are not immortal because satire dominated his plays. Jonson's style was coarse and he was more concerned about his own age.

JOHN DONNE (1573-1631)

John Donne led a dissipated and tempestuous life before he took religious orders and rose to become Dean of St. Paul's. He wrote both secular and religious poems depicting his great ambivalent nature — passionate eroticism and deep meditation. Donne despised convention which followed Spenser's style of ornate language and smooth lyricism. To rebel against this he adopted a crabbed style and used a deliberately colloquial language. Ben Jonson, who otherwise admired him, said that for not keeping metre properly Donne deserved hanging. Donne's subjects were not allegory, pastoral or platonic love, but as mentioned earlier, a wild and passionate love. He was given the name of metaphysical because he and his followers like Henry Vaughan, George Herbert and Crashaw affected the metaphysical philosophers. They were all learned men and exhibited their learning by subtlety of thought or philosophical rumination as expressed in their poetry. The idea of his poem *The Extasie* could be described or expressed in straight and simple language, but Donne invests it with strange arguments and it requires tortured imagination to understand his reasoning. Thoughts and feelings are blended in a strange manner. Preposterous conceits are used. Conceits are images in which two contrastive ideas are yoked together or the sense jumps abruptly from the sublime to the ridiculous. Thus his mandrake song — *"Go and catch a falling star/ Get with child a mandrake root/ Tell me where all past years are/ Or who cleft the Devil's foot"* — describes how after travelling far and wide as man reports that there is no woman existing who is fair and true. Donne was unkind to the opposite sex. In one of his poems, he describes how after his death he would visit his disdainful mistress and as a ghost watch her making love to her new lover.

In some of his divine poems like *Death, be not proud,* he displays great forcefulness of reasoning. Because of the obscurity of his thoughts, Donne lost his admirers in the 18th and 19th centuries, but T.S. Eliot and the moderns revived interest in him, by having recourse to imagery and metre like his to express a tortured conscience.

JOHN DRYDEN (1631-1700)

Dryden was the greatest man of letters in the Restoration Period. In fact, he dominated the literary scene in poetry, prose and drama and the dates of his life 1640 to 1700 are known as the *Age of Dryden* and covers the reigns of Charles II, James II and William III. After 1660, a decisive change came over English thought and style. It became practical and utilitarian and shunned the speculative and the imaginative. One reason for this was the influence of French models like Moliere in literature. English writers copied French plots. Secondly, the writers were dissatisfied with the past. The Renaissance with its emphasis on wonder and imagination had ruled long. The grandeur of Milton was too much for the common masses, Shakespeare's great works were followed by degenerate writers, and the Puritans had made literature very moralistic and morose. Now there was a general desire for change. It is in this light that Dryden's works must be considered.

Life

Dryden was born in 1631 in a respectable family and was educated at Westminster School and Trinity College. His earlier poems: *"Heroic stanzas on the Death of Oliver Cromwell"* (1659), and *Astraea Redux* (1660) were based on contemporary events, the latter on the happy Restoration of Charles II. He was married to an Earl's daughter and wrote plays for fifteen years to make a decent living. During the Great Plague he withdrew to the country where he composed the famous *Essay of Dramatick Poesie.* He became the poet laureate after Davenant. When the revolution came he was deprived of the post of poet laureate because he wrote *The Hind and the Panther* (1687) in defence of the Roman Catholic Church. He spent the remaining twelve years of his life in writing plays and translating Virgil and the *Fables.* He died in May 1700 and was buried in Westminster Abbey.

Dryden had no fixed religious or political loyalties and changed sides to suit his needs. He was patronized by the king and more than once got involved in brawls.

Works

Poetry

Some of his poems are:

1. *Heroic Stanzas on the Death of Cromwell* — written in quatrains (1659).
2. *Astraea Redux* to celebrate the return of Charles II — written in heroic couplets (1660).
3. *Annus Mirabilis* (Wonderful Year) describing the Great Fire of London and the Dutch War (1667).
4. *To the Memory of Mrs. Anne Killigrew.*

5. *Song for St. Cecilia's Day* (1687).
6. *Alexander's Feast* (1697).

The first three were based on contemporary events. The last three are known still for their lyrical beauty. *Alexander's Feast* is the best poem in which the power of music is brought out through the sound and rhythm of the words and lines.

Absalom and Achitophel (1681) is one of the best political satires in English. It was written in the background of the bogus Popish Plot. The anti-Catholics used the opportunity to stir up a hysteria against Catholics and James who was to succeed Charles to the throne. The anti-Catholics also tried to get the Exclusion Bills passed in Parliament to prevent James from succession, but the King dissolved the Parliament. The Earl of Shaftesbury tried to put the Duke of Monmouth on the throne, but was arrested. But when he was acquitted, the Whigs struck a medal to acknowledge him as a hero. Dryden based it on the story from the Bible. Charles II is portrayed as David, Duke of Monmouth is Absalom and Shaftesbury, his evil counsellor, is Achitophel. The poem derides Shaftesbury who flees to Holland and dies in exile. The satire is immortal for its wonderful pen-pictures of the Earl of Shaftesbury and the Duke of Buckingham (Zimri).

Dryden wrote other satires like *The Medal* (1682) again on Shaftesbury. Shadwell, a former friend of Dryden, wrote a counter to this entitled, *The Medal of John Bayes*. To this last Dryden replied with another, *Mac Flecknoe* (1682) — satirizing Shadwell.

In Dryden's age, politics and religion were mixed up and Dryden wrote verse arguing for or against the Church. He wrote *Religio Laice* (religion of the layman) which is a defence of the Church of England against the Roman Catholic Church. When he became a convert to the Catholic faith, he wrote *The Hind and the Panther.* The Roman Church is a milk-white Hind and the Anglican is represented as a fierce Panther. The argumentation is remarkable.

Dryden wrote free translations / paraphrases of Virgil and the *Fables* or *Tales* of Chaucer and Boccaccio.

In most of his poetry, Dryden shows his mastery of the heroic couplet often interspersed with triplets.

Drama

When Dryden began writing plays, the Restoration stage underwent significant changes. The theatre companies called the King's Players and the Duke of York's Players, got patents to stage plays, and theatre began to be patronized exclusively by the aristocracy. The Royalists used the stage to ridicule the Puritans and their excessive pre-occupation with morality. Stage machinery like scenery came to be used and actresses took parts instead of boys for female roles. Shakespeare's plays like *Romeo and Juliet* were rewritten with happy endings. Dryden joined the Restoration drama scene by vulgarizing *The Tempest* by adding coarse touches to it. French drama, especially Moliere's comedies and Corneille's tragedies, began to influence Restoration drama. Restoration tragedy was called 'heroic' since the hero and the heroine were grand and declaimed speeches in decasyllabic couplets full of rant and bombast. Love and honour were of an extravagant type and heroic feats were accomplished. Owing to his mastery of the heroic couplet, Dryden excelled others in this. His *The Conquest of Granada* (1669-1670) has a preface defending heroic drama. He defended the use of rhyme in the *Essay of Dramatick Poesie*. He also wrote blank verse tragedies like *All for Love* (1678) in the Elizabethan tradition. This play is his own version of Shakespeare's *Antony and Cleopatra* and is probably his best. Comedy is more characteristic of Restoration literature. Here too Dryden led the age. Although his first comedy *The Wild Gallant* (1663) was a failure. he, wrote the successful *Marriage a la Mode.*

Prose

Dryden was also the greatest prose writer of his age. He wrote essays, prefaces to his plays, dedications, prologues to his works of poetry, propounding his views on literature. Dryden's prose style was plain, elegant, forceful and modern. His *Preface to the Fables* written in a conversational style consists of the wonderful appreciation of Chaucer's personality and genius. *The Essay of Dramatick Poesie* (1668) is a dialogue between four friends representing and comparing the merits of classical, French, Elizabethan and the new English drama. His defence of rhyme in drama and his praise of Shakespeare stand out as excellent prose pieces. Dr. Johnson aptly called Dryden the Father of English Criticism.

DANIEL DEFOE (1659-1731)

Daniel Defoe belonged to the Age of Queen Anne which is also known as the *Age of Prose*. The political satire was the speciality of the works of fiction or novels. Journalism began with periodical essays in *The Tatler* and *The Spectator*. Prose style became simple, plain and was moulded to express clearly narration, description, exposition argument and speculation.

Daniel Defoe, who is world-renowned for his novel *Robinson Crusoe,* began his career as a journalist and went on to novels. He belonged to the Dissenting Schools where a modern and practical education was given. Having failed to start a number of trades, he took to writing pamphlets where his flair for controversy found expression. His first verse satire was *The True-Born Englishman* (1701), in which he defended King William III who was being ridiculed by his English subjects for being Dutch. In his second work *The Shortest Way with the Dissenters* (1702), he argues that the best way of tackling dissenters is to liquidate them. He was convicted of sedition and was imprisoned. In the prison he wrote *A Hymn to the Pillory*. He became a hero in the public eye and was released on the instance of Lord Oxford. He started a non-political paper *The Review* (1704) discussing current politics. A ghost story *True Relation of the Apparition of one Mrs Veal* came out in 1706 in this paper and was much acclaimed.

He joined Lord Oxford as a secret agent and negotiated the Union in Scotland. He was arrested for writing some anti-Jacobite pamphlets but then released on bail. He became a Tory journalist and spied on the Tories for the Whigs. It was late in life when he was sixty that he published *Robinson Crusoe* (1719) and other works like *Moll Flanders* (1722), *Captain Singleton* (1720), *Colonel Jack* (1722), etc. He wrote prolifically on travel, trade and other subjects. His heroes are low characters like pirates and prostitutes. *A Journal of the Plague Year* (1722) is notable for its authentic account of the plague of 1664-65. Gifted with a versatile and powerful imagination, Defoe's stories are narrated by a fictitious hero. He uses a lot of vivid details. A puritan by upbringing, he moralizes and writes for a free conscience. His *Review* trail-blazed the essays of Steele and his novels were the cue for the great works of Richardson and Fielding.

JONATHAN SWIFT (1667-1745)

Jonathan Swift was born posthumously in Ireland. His uncle brought him up sending him to Trinity College, Dublin. Being hot-tempered and vitriolic by nature, he said that his uncle had given him the education of a dog. He worked as secretary to Sir William Temple but could not tolerate subordination. He was ordained a minister in Ireland, but finding the life dull, returned to work for Temple for the rest of his life. In 1697, he defended Temple and his favour for the Ancients in *The Battle of the Books,* published in 1704.

After Temple's death he returned to find work in Ireland. From 1699 to 1710 he socialized with the Whigs like Steele, Addison and Congreve in London. He took to writing pamphlets to support the Church and the Whigs. One of these was *Argument against Abolishing Christianity.* He also contributed essays to the *Tatler* denouncing the vulgar style of the journals of the time.

When he found that his support of the Church and the Whigs did not pay him, he switched his favours to the Tories. He became the editor of the Tory paper *The Examiner.* He wrote pamphlets like *The Conduct of the Allies* (1711) to support the cause of peace with France and ending of the War of Spanish Succession. His *Journal to Stella* is a work of great merit. The Tories made him Dean of St Patrick's Cathedral, Dublin, for his services. But he was disappointed because he wanted to be a Bishop. When Queen Anne died and the Tories fell, he became entirely heart-broken and lived the last thirty years in exile in

Ireland, a country he detested. But the wretchedness of the poor moved him to write for their cause in various pamphlets like *Drapier's Letters* (1724), *A Short View of the Present State of Ireland* and the famous *A Modest Proposal. Gulliver's Travels* came out in 1726. He suffered from a disease of the brain and became insane in the end. His will, strangely, bestowed part of his income to set up a lunatic asylum.

Swift was a bundle of contradictions. Although he loved and was admired by two women, and political bigwigs sought his company, he was a great misanthrope or hater of mankind, as the mad ravings in his novels reveal. Since he suffered from congenital deformity and abnormality in the brain, his callousness and snobbery are understandable. He could snub lords and ladies in his writings.

A Tale of the Tub (1704) is an argument among the three faiths prevalent — Roman Catholicism, Anglicanism and Puritanism. Basing his satire on reason, he attacked religion, science and philosophy. *Journal to Stella* is based on his relationship with Esther Johnson whom he loved. He also loved Vanessa and the triangle of love was an interesting phenomenon of his personality. The journal consists of letters which show Swift's rarely soft, human nature and gives details of his daily life from 1710-1713.

A Modest Proposal was written to call public attention to the plight of poor children in Ireland. Swift recommended that the best solution was that the rich should devour infants and poor children upto the age of eighteen months. A rather repulsive proposal!

The most famous work of Swift which has become the children's classic is his satire *Gulliver's Travels* (1726). The hero finds himself ship-wrecked at Lilliput, a land of diminutive humans. He mocks at their wars, civil strifes and pomp. There are disputes between the high heels and the low heels and between the Big-endians and the Little-endians on the fatuous question of whether eggs should be broken on their big or their little heads! The satire was aimed at the religious and political controversies of his time. When Gulliver reaches Brobdingnag, he encounters a race of giants. To them, he represents *"a race of pernicious, odious vermin"* or humans. At Laputa, Swift aims his satire at the philosophers, historians and scientists of the time. At the Academy of Projectors, a scientist is engaged for the past eight years in extracting sunshine from cucumbers! Later on he pours vitriol on Houyhnhnms, horses who can reason and the Yahoos full of animal corruption.

Swift was gifted by a very mordant style of satire and wrote out of sheer malice and bitterness. While we admire his genius, we are repelled by his hatred of mankind.

RICHARD STEELE (1672-1729)

Richard Steele was a colourful man who had a chequered career. Born in Ireland, he was educated in the Charterhouse school at London and then went off to Oxford where Addison was a classmate. He left Oxford without a degree and joined the army. He soon became a captain for having written a poem to support the Whigs when Queen Mary died. Although partly puritanical, he was a licentious like a Restoration Cavalier and was falling into debts for his extravagance. He wrote *Christian Hero* (1701) to show the importance of religion in ennobling man. He married twice. He was gentleman waiter to Prince George of Denmark, Queen Anne's husband. He edited the *"London Gazette"* and then brought out a number of papers in succession, like *The Tatler* (1709), *The Spectator* (1711), *The Guardian* (1713), *The Englishman* (1713), etc. He was appointed member of Parliament in 1713, but when he favoured Hanoverian succession in his pamphlet *The crisis,* he was expelled. He apologized for this in another autobiographical tract. With the accession of George I, he returned to parliament and was knighted. He became the manager of Drury Fane Theatre. He kept writing essays for journals till he left London in 1724 because of financial problems. He also wrote a number of comedies whose interest today is merely historical.

JOSEPH ADDISON (1672-1719)

Joseph Addison's father was a clergyman. He went to school at Charterhouse and to college at Oxford. At both places Richard Steele was his fellow student. He became a classical scholar and a fellow of Magdalen College. He won an annual pension of 300 pounds by writing poems to flatter William III and the ministers. He could use his finances to travel across the Continent for four years during which he learnt a lot about public life. With the death of the King his pension was stopped. He then turned to the Whigs for favours and praised their policies in *The Whig Examiner*. He celebrated the British victory at Blenheim in *The Campaign* (1704) and was promoted to parliament. When the Tories came to power, he engaged in writing for the newspapers begun by Richard Steele — *The Tatler, The Spectator* and *The Guardian*. When the Whigs returned, he defended their policies again in *The Freeholder*. In 1716, he married the Countess of Warwick and towards the end of his life became a Secretary of State.

ALEXANDER POPE (1688-1744)

Alexander Pope was born in London and as a child lived at Binfield in Windsor Forest. His father was a linen-draper. As a poor Catholic he was denied a good education and was taught by a family priest and at a Catholic school. He suffered from congenital deformity and was always physically weak which is generally regarded as the reason for his peevish, spiteful and revengeful nature. His works, like Swift's, are often motivated by malice and he uses poetry to lampoon and lambaste other writers like Addison, Grub Street hacks, Theobald and Colley Cibber. When he was jilted by Lady Montagu, a bluestocking, he made her the subject of a vulgar satire. His habits showed him to be miserly. He wrote on the reverse blanks of letters and on scraps of paper. Swift called him the "paper-saving Pope". He encouraged younger writers, and the saving grace in his character was is affection for his mother whom he tended very lovingly in her old age. He already had paternal property and his translation of Homer proved a bonanza, bringing him 10,000 pounds. He bought a house at Twickenham and made a beautiful garden. There he lived a comfortable life.

Pope's first collection of poems *Pastorals* was written in 1709 when he was only sixteen. In 1711, he published *An Essay on Criticism,* which brought him into the poetic limelight. In this work, he uses a verse very near to prose in form. The work sums up the art of poetry as propounded by Horace under the influence of Boileau, the French poet-critic. We see here Pope's mastery of terse epigrammatic style that has made him the most quoted writer after Shakespeare. His style is a counterpart of the pithy maxims of Francis Bacon in prose. Pope took Dryden's heroic couplet and made it smoother but rigid. Pope subordinates the content or matter to the form. Some of his more famous lines often quoted are:

"A little learning is a dangerous thing".
"To err is human, to forgive divine".

In his satire, *The Rape of the Lock,* published in 1714, he satirizes the fashions of high society in mock-heroic style. In probable imitation of Boileau's *Lutrin,* he creates an epic where spirits like gnomes and fairies take part. The context is the trivial matter of one Lord Petre who clips off a lock of hair from Arabella Fermor's head. This leads to a quarrel between their families. Pope brings in all the paraphernalia of fashionable society — tea parties, billet-doux and lap-dogs. According to Doctor Johnson, the poem is the most ingenious of Pope's works.

Eloisa to Abelard treats of the love between a theologian teacher of Paris and Eloisa who has dedicated her life to God. Their love is carried out through the passionate lines of correspondence.

Pope translated the *Iliad* in ten years and followed it up with a translation of the *Odyssey* for which Fenton and Broome helped him. Since Pope's verse, or rather the couplets he wrote, are mechanical in structure, it is difficult to distinguish contributions made by others to the translation. Many scholars criticized the translations as unauthentic in the sense that he could not bring in the grandeur of the classics into his works. But for the general public it was a great boon. For the first time they had the classic stories in language comprehensible to them.

In 1725, Alexander Pope published an edition of Shakespeare which was berated by the Shakespeare scholar Theobald for its many factual errors. Pope wrote *The Dunciad* (the *'Iliad'* of Dunces) to avenge himself on Theobald. He also attacked hack writers of Grub Street and the mediocre actor-dramatist Colley Cibber who had been made poet laureate. The poem is a merciless attack on dullness.

It is said that Pope took Dryden as his model and the *Dunciad* was inspired by *MacFlecknoe*. But instead of imitating the gracious Dryden, Pope was bent on personal revenge and malice.

An Essay on Man (1733-34) is again verse in aphorisms. Its aim was to *"vindicate the ways of God to man"*. It elaborates the general philosophy common to most religions that man cannot understand God's inscrutable ways and therefore finds faults with the universal order. Our vision cannot 'see' the mysterious perfection of Creation. The famous lines, often quoted, are:

"All Nature is but Art, unknown to thee;
All Chance, Direction which thou canst not see:
And spite of Pride, in erring Reason's spite
One truth is clear, Whatever is, is Right".

Epistle to Dr. Arbuthnot (1735) has an autobiographical element in it. The satire is famous for the portrayal of Addison, or Atticus in the poem.

Pope's stature as a poet has undergone shifts since his times. In his own age, he was looked upon as a genius of the heroic couplet, the best wit of the times. But when Wordsworth and Coleridge published their *Lyrical Ballads* in 1798, they derided his stiff, epigrammatic style and his malicious wit. His image fell very low in the 19th century for writing poetry that was almost prose. In modern times, poetry that seeks deviated ways to express thoughts is extolled and so Pope is back in the list of the greats.

Pope himself laid down the main principle of his poetry.

"True wit is nature to advantage dressed,
What oft was thought but ne'er so well express'd".

'Nature' in Pope's times human nature and behaviour in general. Pope mechanized Dryden's couplet by sticking to the iambic beat with well-marked caesuras or pauses. He forced all his ideas into the straight-jacketted body of his verse. His poetry is full of moral principles and has given us a great number of pithy, epigrammatic statements to be quoted in our essays and speeches.

SAMUEL JOHNSON (1709-1784)

Doctor Samuel Johnson was the literary dictator of the third part of the 18th century. Although his contribution to poetry and drama is admirable, he is chiefly known for his prose works — biographies, criticism, letters, prefaces, essays and the dictionary. He has become known to the world more through the biography of him written by his devoted disciple and secretary, Boswell. Boswell's masterly protrayal of Johnson is one of the best biographies in English literature. It paints Johnson bigger than life and makes his personality overshadow his great contributions to literature. The biography, in fact, made both the master and the disciple immortal. It has given us numerous anecdotes from the life of Samuel Johnson and numerous quotations of the great man of letters.

Samuel Johnson, the son of a bookseller, was born at Lichfield. From early childhood he knew poverty and had to struggle for subsistence when he drifted to London in 1737. Johnson found London full of corruption and wretchedness of the poor. In his famous poem *London* (1738), he describes the crimes, intrigues, squalor, slums and poverty of the metropolis. He finds a vast concourse of humanity engaged in the worship of Mammon, the god of gold. He is tired of the inane human quest for glory and fame. He describes the lives of the great and famous in his poem, *The Vanity of Human Wishes* (1749).

After *The Tatler* and *The Spectator* the art of essay-writing died down. Johnson revived it and brought out *The Rambler* (1750-52) and *The Idler*. The first one was not well received since it was of a serious, moralizing type. The latter was in the lighter vein and was much acclaimed. Johnson also wrote a tragedy, the *Irene* (1749), on the neo-classic model. He wrote *Rasselas* (1759) to pay for the charges of his mother's funeral. Later on he became famous and was acknowledged as a great master of literature. The government gave him a pension of 300 pounds annually which allowed him to live comfortably for the rest of his life with a circle of admirers at the coffee-house and club. Johnson defined "Pension" in his famous dictionary as an allowance given to a person for *"treason to his country"*. This, of course, does not show his ingratitude but strange humour. Johnson first proposed his idea of composing his famous dictionary to Lord Chesterfield in a letter. The Lord did not respond and Johnson felt snubbed. Later on when after eight years of monumental hard labour, Johnson's dictionary, the first ever in the English language, came out. Chesterfield wanted to cash on it for fame by writing a preface. Johnson then wrote a famous excerpt taking Chesterfield to task. The dictionary is unique in that the definitions are often subjective and contain Johnson's personal opinions. For instance, Oats is described as a grain used to feed horses in England, but supports the people in Scotland!

A group of book-sellers deputed Johnson to write on the *Lives of the Poets*. The work was finished in 1781, and is his contribution to literary criticism. A staunch neo-classicist, he judges poets by the rules of the classics. Although he points to Shakespeare's disregard of the unities, he allows concessions in his case saying there is always an appeal from criticism to nature. Pope is Johnson's great poet for observing a strict mechanical metre. Johnson is callous to the imaginative flights of the poets. The shortcoming of the *Lives* is the selection of poets. Many minor poets are discussed and important contemporaries are left out.

Today, the image of Doctor Johnson, the eccentric, far overshadows his contributions to literature. Boswell described him as a bundle of contradictions. He could be humorous in public always, yet he suffered from melancholic depression throughout his life. He married a widow, twenty years older than himself. Johnson was always cynical of people. When Boswell first introduced himself as coming from Scotland, Johnson replied, *"That is something most of your countrymen cannot help"*.

Johnson's literary style, which was pedantic, ponderous and full of Latinisms, goes by the name of Johnsonese. Today we admire him as the greatest man of letters of his age.

THOMAS GRAY (1716-1771)

Thomas Gray has his own unique place in English literature. He is famous today and remembered chiefly for his long poem *Elegy Written in a Country Churchyard* (1751). General Wolfe is said to have commented "I would rather be remembered as the man who wrote the Elegy than the conqueror of Quebec!" Palgrave would have left it out of his Golden Treasury because of its length had Tennyson not insisted. Doctor Johnson who was usually hard on Gray, praised its universal nature — it echoed the finer sentiments of all mankind.

Gray was educated at Eton and Cambridge and because he had independent means of money, he lived a quiet scholarly life in the university. He was extremely will-read in the Greek classics and traces all poetry to its Hellenic source in his *Progress of Poesy*. He also studied European literature and produced *The Descent of Odin* from Icelandic myths. The undergraduates of his college played a practical joke on him startling him on a false fire alarm. This made him shift from Peterhouse to Pembroke. His mother lived estranged from his ill-tempered father and this might have contributed to the melancholic strain in most of his poetry. The Elegy is a meditation on the futility of all human endeavour. Notice these off-quoted lines:

Full many a gem of purest ray serene
The dark unfathom'd caves of ocean bear.
Full many a flower is born to blush unseen,
And waste its sweetness on the desert air.
The boast of heraldry, the pomp of pow'r
And all that beauty, all that wealth e'er gave,
Awaits alike th' inevitable hour.
The paths of glory lead but to the grave".

Another poem *The Bard* is one of the best Pindaric odes in the English language. It is based on the Welsh legend of King Edward's cruel conquest of Wales. It describes how Edward had all the Welsh bards killed and one bard survived and gathered with the ghosts of slain bards to curse Edward and foretell his doom in the Wars of the Roses: *"Ruin seize thee, ruthless king!"*. The Tudors would reign supreme and the great poets of the Elizabethan age would achieve eminence. The surviving bard hurls himself from a mountain into a river below.

Gray was also capable of humour as may be seen in his *Ode on the Death of a Favourite Cat*. A Lord's cat is drowned in a water jar while trying to catch goldfish in it. Gray makes the comments: "A fev'rite has no friend" and "What female heart can gold despise? What cat's averse to fish?" Gray wrote other odes like *On Spring, On a Distant Prospect of Eton College,* and *On Adversity.*

Gray has written less but whatever he has produced is sterling poetry, a mixture of classical restraint and romantic imagination and varied, regular music.

OLIVER GOLDSMITH (1728-1774)

Goldsmith is remembered today for his famous poems *The Deserted Village* (1770) and *The Traveller* (1764). Also well-known are his poems, *Elegy on the Death of a Mad Dog,* the fine lines beginning "When lovely woman stoops to folly", and *Retaliation*.

Oliver Goldsmith was the son of an Irish clergyman. After school, he attended Trinity College, Dublin. He was temporarily sent out of college for some misdemeanour, but rejoined to obtain a degree in 1749. He was rejected from the priesthood and for a time worked as a tutor to support his family. He studied medicine at Edinburgh and then at Leyden, Holland. He went on a walking-tour of some countries in Europe and wrote down his experiences in his poem *The Traveller* in which he describes the different gifts of scenery and culture bestowed by Nature on different countries. On return to England, he had stints at different jobs — chemist's assistant, proof-reader, school master and even a roving player. He worked as a hack-writer for sometime. In 1759, he published *an Enquiry into the Present State of Polite Learning in Europe.* He edited a periodical called *Bee*. He wrote prolifically for magazines like Smollett's *British Magazine*. He brought out a series of *Chinese Letters in the Public Ledger*. His works included histories, biographies and books of popular science.

An interesting event led to the publication of his novel, *The Vicar of Wakefield,* in 1766. He was pestered by his landlady for not paying his rent. She put pressure on him to accept marriage with her. Flustered, he sent a message to Doctor Johnson who arrived soon after and discovered the manuscript of *The Vicar* and sold it off for 60 pounds.

Goldsmith's enemies like Garrick and Boswell exaggerated his vices. It is true Goldsmith was unpleasant in appearance, extravagant and led a luxurious life-style and got into debt for it. Despite all this, we cannot deny his contribution to literature. The characters of his essays, poems and plays stand out unforgettably.

Goldsmith was inspired by the Restoration comedy and wrote *The Good-natured Man* (1768) and *She Stoops to Conquer* (1773) which are anti-sentimental comedies. As Goldsmith writes in the preface of the latter play, the true spirit of comedy had died since the sentimental comedy of his times had no laughter in it. It was merely a maudlin display or tear-jerker making the reader and audience indulge in sobs. To regain health it was necessary to restore gaiety and laughter. For this he pleads with Doctor Johnson to administer the cure. *The Good-natural Man* was produced at Covent Garden in 1768. Doctor Johnson recommended the play. The play portrays a character called Croaker who is Benjonsonian in his '*humour*'. It is the story of Mr Honeywood, a warm-hearted simpleton who gives money in charity without finding out the genuine neediness of the recipients. In the end his uncle opens his eyes to his folly.

She Stoops to Conquer is a much more successful play. It was produced at Covent Garden in 1773. It has numerous sub-plots but all pivot around *The mistakes of a night,* the other title of the play. The characters of the son-pampering Mrs Hardcastle, Tony Lumpkin, the mischievous scoundrel son of Mrs Hardcastle and of the ambivalent Marlow are unforgettable. Some scenes are uproariously funny — the servants being trained to entertain guests, Tony Lumpkin takes his guests round and round the house in the dark to land them in a horse-pond.

WILLIAM BLAKE (1757-1827)

William Blake was a revolutionary eighteenth century poet. He admired Milton but did not use his blank verse. In fact, he wrote his poetry in a type of rhythmical prose. He was far beyond his time. Of the Romantic vein of which he was a forerunner, he exercised his imagination to the extreme. So much so that he reaches levels of obscurity impossible to fathom.

Blake was the son of a London hosier and himself took to painting nad engraving. His earlier poetry was written as commentary to his book of paintings. Most of his earlier poetry is simple and imbued with a lyrical sweetness. They are contained in two anthologies — *Songs of Innocence* (1789) and *Songs of Experience* (1794). His latter poetry is very mystical and difficult to understand. Blake had mystic visions of God and angels in childhood and they are described in his poetry. He created a symbolism of his own. The horrors of the French Revolution shocked him and this is symbolized in his poem *The Tyger:*

"Tyger, Tyger, burning bright!
In the forests of the night.
What immortal hand or eye
Could frame thy fearful symmetry?"

Christ as Eternal goodness was symbolized by the Lamb. *The Songs of Innocence,* therefore, represent experiences under divine grace and *The Songs of Experience,* the power of evil in the world.

Blake's contemporaries thought of him as insane and one living in a strange, unreal world. But Wordsworth described Blake thus: "The madness of Blake interests us more than the sanity of others".

JANE AUSTEN (1775-1817)

Jane Austen was the daughter of a Hampshire rector. She and her sisters were educated at home. Jane's life was spent at country parishes and at the health resort at Bath. Her life was hardly disturbed by any major upheaval and was for the most part uneventful. Even the Napoleonic Wars of the time never touched her thinking. Her brothers were in the navy, and naval exercises took place in her village. Naval officers like Wickham and Wentworth appear in her novels as only eligible bachelors for the girls. Jane Austen was intensely familiar with the social life of Hampshire and she makes this the limited canvas of her novels. A country mansion drawing room and a few young girls and boys were enough stuff for her to mould her novels. Witty dialogues, understatements and humour are used to delineate characters — an art in which she had no equal in her age. Her novels are *comedies of manners* and she excels in them and is probably unique in this genre. Her characters belong to the middle class which she knew very well and portrayed in six wonderful novels. *Pride and Prejudice, Sense and Sensibility, Mansfield Park* and *Emma* were published between 1811 and 1815. *Northanger Abbey* and *Persuasion* were published posthumously in 1818. These dates do not correspond to the dates of writing. For instance *Northanger* was published last but was the first to be written, in 1797.

In the beginning, Jane Austen could not get a publisher easily, but she emerged into limelight when the novel *Emma* was praised in the *Quarterly Review* by an anonymous writer who later on turned out to be Walter Scott, the great Scottish novelist. He wrote, "That young lady has a talent for describing the involvements and feelings and characters of ordinary life which is to me the most wonderful I ever met with .... the exquisite touch which renders, ordinary commonplace things and characters interesting, from the truth of the description and the sentiment, is denied to me".

Jane Austen did not practise any new or invented art of novel writing, yet her plots are most ingeniously constructed, the sub-plots dovetailing wonderfully. She did not seek to moralize, either. All she set out to do and succeeded in, was to entertain her readers by a faithful representation of life around her. She was not romantic in view and her descriptions are most matter-of-fact. She ridiculed the Radcliffian novel of terror and mystery in *Northanger Abbey*. She ridicules Marianne's sentimental nature in *Sense and Sensibility*. Her novels are one around of domestic work, balls, gossips, teas, love-affairs, visits and money matters — the common paraphernalia of any human life. Touched by her sparkling wit, these trivial affairs burst into life.

She was adept at charting the sentiments of love in a female heart. It is not so much the hero and heroine who impart life to her novels as the secondary characters — the Collins and the Bennetts. She does not indulge in hairsplitting psychology like Henry James or Virginia Woolf. A few broad strokes are enough to assess a character. Characters have both their good and bad sides. Even villains like Wickham Willoughby, Crawfords, Frank Churchill display gaiety and charm.

Irony is a major device in character portrayal. In *Sense and Sensibility* the selfishness of John Dashwood is revealed through ironic dialogue in which John begins by intending to give 3000 pounds to his step-mother and step-sisters. He whittles this down gradually to zero and finally reasons out that they had better give him something! She is excellent in exposing hypocrisy and the foibles of society. Mrs Musgrove in *Persuasion* is ridiculed as exhibiting hysterical grief (crocodile tears) on her deceased son.

Financial wholeness is the bedrock of a happy life. A realist by nature, Austen believed that we cannot change the world, but must adjust ourselves to it. She derided people who claimed superiority on the basis of birth, but she acknowledged class distinctions as no snobbery.

ALFRED TENNYSON (1809-1892)

Lord Alfred Tennyson was the third son of a Lincolnshire clergyman and went to Louth Grammar School and Trinity College, Cambridge. His earlier poetry received scant praise from critics. They include *Poems by two Brothers* (1827), *Timbuctoo* (1829) which received the Chancellor's prize, *Poems, Chiefly Lyrical* (1830) and the Volume *Lady Shalott and Other Poems* (1833). In 1842, he published two slim anthologies, revising some older poems. These won recognition. In 1850, he was made Poet Laureate. In the same year, he published his famous elegy *In Memoriam,* on the death of a friend Arthur Hallam. He became a peer in 1884. He died at the age of 83 in 1892.

When Tennyson brought out his two volumes of poetry in 1842, people claimed him as a successor to Keats because of his romantic spirit. But he did not ignore the classical correctness of form in which there are no redundant ornaments of style. There is a great sense for pictures and sounds but this is not overdone. He shunned adherence to any strict poetic diction or too much imagination and imbued his poetry with philosophy. He also, like Wordsworth, wrote to instruct his readers. He wanted to enlighten and edify his readers. He came to be regarded a prophet who voiced the thoughts of the Victorians.

As a youth, Tennyson believed in the grandeur of his country, in the institution of Parliament and democracy. He also believed that science would help to take the world to glorious heights. But as time went on he was filled with doubts. In religion, the Darwinian theory of man's evolution from natural selection of species threatened the biblical story of Adam and Eve and weaned men away from their traditional faith. Socialism was leading to too much materialism. Tennyson warned his country-men not to take up any extreme stand. Scientific progress must not drive out religious feelings of charity and love.

The Princess (1847) deals with women's rights, the need to give them a higher education. Tennyson's thoughts on religion come through in *In Memoriam* (1850) and *The Idylls of the King* (1859, 1869, 1889). In *Maud* (1855) he exposes the folly of materialsm.

One of Tennyson's demerits was that his narration in the longer poems like *In Memoriam* is rambling and vague. *Maud* is excellent for its diverse metre but is on the whole unbalanced and melodramatic. *The Princess* is very popular with its romance, humour, pathos, songs and philosophy.

Tennyson's excellence lies mainly in his lyrical gifts especially in his shorter poems. He displays domestic pathos and rustic humour in *Enoch Arden* (1864) and a number of poems. In these he describes the life of ordinary men and women he knew in Lincolnshire and the Isle of Wight. He is quite authentic in his description of farmers, cobblers and people of the common classes.

Tennyson was aware of evil in his age. He described Earth as "teeming with liars, and madmen and knaves, and wearied of Autocrats, Anarchs and slaves". Yet he was optimistic of a bright future for humanity. He was a seer and spoke from the depths of the heart. No wonder his poems strike us and we quote so much from his poems now-a-days. Here are some of the more popular lines:

"There lives more faith in honest doubt
Believe me, than in half the creeds"
(In Memoriam)

" 'tis better to have loved and lost
Than never to have loved at all".
(In Memoriam)

"For men may come and men may go,
But I go on forever". (The Brook)

"The old order changeth, yielding place to new,
And God fulfils himself in many ways
Lest one good custom should corrupt the world".
(Morte d' Arthur)

Tennyson suited his verse to different themes, moods, feelings and atmosphere. Rhyme and blank verse were used to match form and matter. Many poems are replete with graphic descriptions of nature. For example, in *Mariana* he describes Mariana's farm-house which is decaying and desolate:

"With blackest moss the flower-pots
Were thickly crusted, one and all;
The rusted nails fell from the knots
That held the pear to the gable-wall".

There is a nostalgia and pathos in the lines of his poems *Break, Break, Break* and *Tears, idle tears*; there is a yearning *For the days that are no more.*

Tennyson was hailed as a prophet of his age.

ROBERT BROWNING (1812-1889)

Robert Browning was educated at home and in private schools. His father was a clerk in the Bank of England. His mother was of mixed stock and a dissenter. In 1846, he married the poetess Elizabeth Barret. He lived in Italy until her death in 1861. After this he returned to London. He died in 1889 and was buried in Westminster Abbey.

His major works include:

Pauline (1833) in which he shows his admiration for an anonymous poet who may be guessed to be Shelley.

Paracelsus (1835) is the story of a Swiss physician who searched for perfect knowledge and the secrets of the universe. But having no power to love, he did not achieve his goal.

Sordello (1840) is a poem based on the life of a 12th century poet. This poem is very difficult to understand.

Browning also wrote two plays, *Strafford* (1837) and *A Blot on the 'Scutcheon* (1843). Among other well-known poems are *Pippa Passes* (1841), *The Pied Piper of Hamelin, The Lost Leader, My Last Duchess* and *Andrea del Sarto. The Ring and the Book* (1868-1869) is one of the longest poems in the English language and was his masterpiece.

Robert Browning was a complete contrast to Tennyson. While Tennyson interested himself in the political affairs of the Victorian times, the glory of England and democratic traditions, the Parliament of Man, Browning's poetry shows no reference to the political or religious questions of his times. *Home Thoughts from Abroad,* however, does show some patriotic feelings. While Tennyson's mind was filled with the doubts about God and faith, Browning strongly believed in God. Browning was a philosopher and did not care much for beauty and melody like Keats and Tennyson did in their poetry. He is more like John Donne, filled with intellectual curiosity for the strange and unconventional. He did not ignore the beauties of Nature as is evident from his poems *Pippa Passes* and *Saul.*

According to Browning, God and Immortality are unquestioned truths of existence. God is evident in the love that is visible in man and Nature. He believed that as man evolved from age to age, his ideals in life became higher. Man must struggle ceaselessly to overcome his failures and imperfections: *"Ah, but a man's reach should exceed his grasp/ Or what's a Heaven for"?* Failures are stepping stones to success. His philosophy is a positive one. He was an optimist, *"God's in His heaven and all's right with the world".*

Browning's love for his wife, Elizabeth Barrett, inspired many of his love poems, like *By the fireside* and *O Lyric Love.*

Browning's poetry is famous for the technique known as the *dramatic monologue*. Characters are made to speak out their minds and unfold their hidden thoughts. This was a device to etch out characters like the Bishop Bloryam and in this he excelled.

One of the demerits of Browning's poetry is obscurity. The common reader cannot understand his poetry. He chose events and characters from the past like Fra Lippo Lippi and Andrea del Sarto. Not many were interested among them. His style is compressed leaving out pronouns and grammatical connectives which makes the meaning vague. But he is popular today for his simpler poems like *The Pied Piper* and *A Grammarian's Funeral.*

CHARLES DICKENS (1812-1870)

Life

Charles Dickens was the son of a navy office clerk, John Dickens. The young Charles moved with his father from Postmouth to Chatham and then to London. His father underwent many financial problems and had to spend time in debtor's prison in Marshalsea. Charles survived by working in a blacking factory and roaming the streets of London as a vagrant. These bitter experiences left a deep, traumatic effect on his life and were recreated in his novels in the characters of David Copperfield, Little Nell, Oliver, Paul Dombey and Pip. Charles Dickens did not get a smooth education, breaking off from schools according to whether his father could pay or not. The schools he went to were also centres of persecution. When he was only fifteen he became a lawyer's clerk and at 19, a reporter of Parliamentary speeches. At 21, he became a reporter on *The Morning Chronicle* to which he contributed various imaginary sketches of social life which were later published as *Sketches by Boz* (1836). Dickens wrote his masterpiece *Pickwick Papers* in monthly installments in 1836-37. In 1937, Queen Victoria came to the throne. The world of characters he created caught the imagination of the people like anything and he became a resounding success. He also became rich at 25.

In 1848, his wife Catherine left him since she believed he was having an affair with Ellen Ternan, an actress. The scandal sent tremor through the literary world.

Dickens visited America twice, in 1842 and 1867, and also the Continent, and read out his works in a dramatic style. At the age of 59, he died of cerebral bleeding and was buried at Westminster Abbey.

Works

The Pickwick Papers was his masterpiece. It firmly enthroned Dickens in the hearts of the readers throughout Europe, America and later in the whole English-speaking world. Almost 300 characters were created in this series. Each character is a universal type that may be found in any age and land. In this, Dickens is compared to Shakespeare. Dickens created almost 2000 character-types. His unique gift for minute description is unparalleled. Dickens' characters are household words today. We have come to describe people as Pickwickian or Dickensian when they display oddity or eccentricity. Thus the loyal Sam Weller, a servant, is a type of the witty, resourceful and loyal; Jingle as a rascal using a clipped telegraphese; the wily Uriah Heep; the incorrigible optimist Micawber and hundreds of others are types of the universal panorama of human beings.

Dickens' novels are loosely constructed. His later novels like *Bleak House* (1852), *David Copperfield* (1849), *Great Expectations* (1860) which show a maturer craftsman at work, are appealing because of their humour and pathos. Dickens used his novels to muster public opinion against many social injustices. Thus *Nicholas Nickleby* (1838) is a satire on the horrible condition of Yorkshire schools like Dotheboys Hall with its cruel schoolmaster Squares. Later on these schools were forced to close down. Dickens called his weekly *Household Words (1849), a gentle mouthpiece of reform. Most of his satire was garbed in humour, so it did not hurt.* In *Household Words* and *All the Year Round* (1859), Dickens campaigned for free trade, abolition of Corn Laws, improvement of sanitation, etc. He exposed the appalling conditions of labour in the Midlands and the North in *The Curiosity Shop* (1840) and *Hard Times* (1854). This led to reform in factory laws. Thanks to Dickens' description of debtor's imprisonment in *Little Dorrit* (1855) the laws were altered, Fleet Prison and Marshalsea (where his father was imprisoned) were demolished. Dickens ridiculed obstructive bureaucratic interference through his description of the Barnacles and the Civil Service. His suggestive name for bureaucratic red tape was the Circumlocution Office. Although Dickens had no faith in the functioning of Parliament, he was in favour of democracy if practised in spirit. Bernard Shaw remarked that *Little Dorrit* was a more revolutionary book than Marx's *Das Capital*!

Dickens came to be known as the family novelist of the Victorians. His main aim was to convey moral precepts to his countrymen through a personal relationship in his serialized publications. In *Martin Chuzzlewit* (1843), he condemns selfishness and greed; in *Dombey and Son* (1846), pride is reviled; *Our Mutual Friend* (1864) shows the corrupting influence of wealth; the most sublime is his teaching of unselfish love and generosity in *A Christmas Carol* (1843). Dickens lived in an age of sexual prudery. It was very corrupt to mention 'sex'. Marriage was the only sacred bond. He shows how Emily who is seduced by Steerforth in *David Copperfield* is disgraced by society.

Some of the demerits of Dickens' writings have been described as: (*a*) he is often verbose, using more words than necessary; (*b*) his plots are not properly constructed; (*c*) he does not describe sublime thoughts, and (*d*) his novels are too grounded in the Victorian age to have any meaning now. Many critics have refuted these charges. If there are faults of diction in Dickens it is owing to his irregular education. But, like Shakespeare, his very faults are qualities of his genius. His powerful, graphic descriptions, the dialogues he puts into his characters — all remain unsurpassed despite oddities of syntax. He was educated in the cruel school of life and he was a keen observer. His descriptions and characterization give his novels an enduring value. It is ridiculous to say that Dickens does not deal in sublime thoughts. Love and charity are the essence of Christ's doctrines and like Christ's own simple language in the gospels, Dickens uses a layman's diction to express these.

Dickens is certainly the greatest novelist of English literature.

MATTHEW ARNOLD (1822-1888)

Matthew's father was the headmaster of Rugby College and he was educated at Rugby and Balliol College, Oxford. In 1851 he was appointed Inspector of Schools and he married the daughter of a judge. He was Professor of Poetry at Oxford for ten years. His famous poems are *The Strayed Reveller and other poems* (1849), *Empedocles on Etna* (1852), *Sohrab and Rustum* (an epic based on the Shah-Nama of Persia), *Switzerland, Dover Beach* and *The Scholar Gypsy.*

Matthew Arnold was a versatile writer trying his hand in poetry and criticism. In his age he was seen as a prophet and apostle of culture. His literary criticism is contained in the preface of his *Poems* (1853 volume) and in *Essays in Criticism* (1865, 1889). He was also a prose writer of renown.

Arnold's poetry reflects most the Victorian loss of faith in the face of materialism and the progress of science. His famous poem, *Dover Beach,* best brings this out.

"The sea of Faith
Was once, too, at the full and round earth's shore
Lay like the fold of a bright girdle furl'd.
But now I only hear
Its long withdrawing melancholy, roar ......"

Arnold admired the classical rule of clarity of expression which must be subordinated to the thought. He condemned poets including Shakespeare who used ornamental patches with no solid thought content. Arnold did not use much rhyme. *Sohrab and Rustum* is in blank verse. From Wordsworth and Goethe he learnt to use poetry to convey morals. In *Resignation,* he recommends that we reflect on life calmly and impersonally.

Arnold used poetry to express experiences about "actions, human actions, possessing an inherent interest in themselves". He also used poetry to convey personal feelings of a deep nature. *The Forsaken Merman, Scholar Gypsy, Thyrsis* and even *Sohrab and Rustum* are romantic poems in which his own feelings are uppermost. Thirteen of his poems including two *Obermann* poems and *Grande Chartreuse* are elegiac and contain his philosophy.

Arnold was influenced by the Greek classical form in poetry, but lacked their joy. Peace which is the aim of life, according to him, is difficult to achieve in the sick hurry of Victorian living. There is, therefore, a nostalgic desire to live in the past like his scholar gypsy who joins a roving band. His Obermann retires to a Swiss mountain to meditate and Empedocles cannot bear society or solitude and throw himself into the Crater at Etna. For Arnold, the best path was one of quiet work and self-dependence. *Love Nature* and *Know Thyself,* he prescribes. Like Wordsworth he believed that Nature had a healing touch. Arnold defined poetry as "a criticism of life" and, though intellectual in spirit, it is not cold and unspontaneous.

GEORGE BERNARD SHAW (1856-1950)

George Bernard Shaw was an Irish protestant playwright based in the United Kingdom. He was uniquely the winner of the Nobel Prize in Literature and an Academy Award for writing adapted screenplay.

George Bernard Shaw was born on 1856 in Dublin, in a lowermiddle-class family of Scottish-Protestant ancestry. His father was a failed corn-merchant, with a drinking problem and a squint, and his mother was a professional singer, the disciple of Vandeleur Lee, a voice teacher claiming to have a unique and original approach to singing.

When Shaw was just short of his sixteenth birthday, his mother left her husband and son, and moved with Vandeleur Lee to London, where the two set up a household, along with Shaw's elder sister, Lucy. There, Shaw's mother worked as a clerk for an estate office.

In 1876, Shaw left Dublin and his father, and moved to London. He went with his mother's *menage*. There he lived with his mother and sister while pursuing a career in journalism and writing. The first medium he tried as a creative writer was prose, completing five novels before any of them were published. He read voraciously, in public libraries and in the British Museum reading room.

In 1891, at the invitation of J.T. Grein, a merchant, theatre critic, and director of a progressive private new-play society, The Independent Theatre, Shaw wrote his first play, *Widower's Houses*. For the next twelve years, he wrote close to a dozen plays, though he generally failed to persuade the managers of the London Theatres to produce them. A few were produced abroad; one (*Arms and the Man*) was produced under the auspices of an experimental management; one (*Mrs Warren's Profession*) was censored by the Lord Chamberlain's Examiner of Plays and several were presented in single performances by private societies.

In 1898, after a serious illness, Shaw resigned as theatre critic, and moved out of his mother's house where he was still living to marry Charlotte Payne-Townsend, an Irish woman of independent means. Their marriage lasted until Charlotte's death in 1943.

In 1904, Harley Granville Barker, an actor, director and playwright, twenty years younger than Shaw who had appeared in a private theatre society's production of Shaw's *Candida*, took over the management of the Court Theatre on Sloane Square in Chelsea and set it up as an experimental theatre specializing in new and progressive drama. Over the next three seasons, Barker produced ten plays by Shaw, and he began writing new plays with Barker's management specifically in mind.

Over the next ten years, all but one of Shaw's plays, (*Pygmalion* in 1914) was produced either by Barker or by Barker's friends and colleagues in the other experimental theatre managements around England. With royalties from his plays, Shaw, who had become financially independent on marrying, now became quite wealthy. Throughout the decade, he remained active in the Fabian Society, in city government , and on committees dedicated to ending dramatic censorship, and to establishing a subsidised National Theatre.

The outbreak of war in 1914 changed Shaw's life. For Shaw, the war represented the bankruptcy of the capitalist system, the last desperate gasps of the nineteenth-century empires, and a tragic waste of young lives, all under the guise of patriotism. He expressed his opinions in a series of newspaper articles under the title, *Common Sense About the War*.

After the war, Shaw found his dramatic voice again and rebuilt his reputation, first with a series of five plays about "creative evolution," *Back to Methuselah*, and then, in 1923, with *Saint Joan*. In 1925, he was awarded the Nobel Prize for Literature. He donated the cash award towards an English edition of the Swedish playwright, August Strindberg, who had never been recognised with a Nobel prize by the Swedish Academy. Shaw's plays were regularly produced and revived in London. He lived the rest of his life as an international celebrity, travelling the world, continually involved in local and international politics. And he continued to write thousands of letters and over a dozen more plays.

In 1950, Shaw fell off a ladder while trimming a tree on his property at Ayot St. Lawrence in Hertfordshire, outside London, and died a few days later of complications from the injury, at the age of 94. He had been at work on yet another play (*Why She Would Not*). In his will, he left a large part of his estate to a project to revamp the English alphabet. After that, the project failed, the estate was divided among the other beneficiaries in his will: the National Gallery of Ireland, the British Museum, and the Royal Academy of Dramatic Art.

THOMAS HARDY (1840-1928)

Thomas Hardy was born near Dorchester (the country which was to be part and parcel and permanent landscape of his novels). By profession he was an architect and his sense of symmetry and design may be responsible for the perfect organization of the plots of his novels. His first great novel *Far from the Madding Crowd* (1874) brought him fame and money and he was able to devote himself more completely to his literary pursuits. He married twice, the second time in 1914 at the age of 74. In 1910, he was awarded the Order of Merit.

Hardy wrote many novels of which five are world-famous. *Far from the Madding Crowd* is about Bathsheba Everdene, a farmer who is loved by a shepherd called Gabriel Oak who serves her for many years with devotion. But Bathsheba falls in love with a selfish sergeant Troy and she realizes the greater, more permanent love of Gabriel Oak. She marries him.

Hardy's second great novel is *The Return of the Native* (1878). His great work of tragedy is *The Mayor of Casterbridge* (1886) which contains his vision of life. Man has very little free will and the great power of the universe control him as seen in the fate of Henchard who in a drunken state sells his wife and undergoes unlimited sorrows. A blind Universal Will controls destiny. Shakespeare believed that a tragic flaw was responsible for the downfall of his great characters. Hardy went much further and truly echoes Shakespeare's words, *"As flies to wanton boys are we to the gods. They kill us for their sport"*. Hardy's other great tragic novel *Tess of the D'Urbervilles* (1891) ends with the lines *"The President of the Immortals had finished his sport with Tess"*. Hardy's novel, *Jude the Obscure* (1895) deals with the social question of marriage.

Hardy was a pressimist. He knew the rustic life of his Dorsetshire very well and used this as the landscape of his novels. In fact, landmarks like Egdon Heath assume the nature of a character in the novel. Hardy described the seasons and aspects of Nature very realistically and the past plays an important role. Historical relics like Stonehenge, Roman roads and references to Napoleonic Wars are all there.

Hardy usually wrote in plain and direct style and his portrayal of rural life is unromantic. But sometimes he clutters his language with technical words. His rustics have a sense of humour which is too sophisticated to believe. His women characters are passionate and impulsive and love is a major theme in his fiction. His plots do not seem convincing. Many events are obviously contrived and seem quite illogical. There are too many coincidences.

Hardy was also a poet. He used his poetry to express his philosophy of fatalism. In fact, he took to writing poetry because his last novel, *Jude the Obscure,* was not well received by critics and readers. His *Wessex Poems,* a volume of poems, came out in 1898. He wrote the long novel or epic *The Dynasts* (1903, 1906, 1908) with the Napoleonic Wars as the background. Other notable poems by him are: *The Darkling Thrush* and *To an Unborn Paper Child.*

Hardy is certainly one of the greatest literary figures of English literature.

ROBERT FROST (1874-1963)

IMPORTANT POINTS

1. He could not get good response from the American publishers in the beginning.
2. (*i*) His first volume of poems: "A Boy's Will" was published in 1913 by an English publisher.
   (*ii*) His second volume "North of Boston" was published by the same publisher in 1914.
   (*iii*) His first poem "The Butterfly" had already appeared in "The Independent" (New York) in 1894.
3. When he lived in Beaconsfield, England, most of his friends were Georgian poets.
4. Some of his other works which appeared later were :
   (*i*) Mountain Interval (1916)
   (*ii*) New Hampshire.... (1923)
   (*iii*) West-Running Brook (1928)
   (*iv*) A Further Range (1936)
   (*v*) A Witness Tree (1942)
   (*vi*) Steeple Bush (1947)
5. His "Complete Poems" appeared in 1949, at the end of which were placed two of his verse dramas:
   (*i*) A Masque of Rcason (1945) and
   (*ii*) A Masque of Mercy (1947)
6. In his life, Frost received four Pulitzer Prizes, Poet Laureateship of New England and several other honours.
7. Before his death, he had become a national poet.
8. In his "The Figure a Poem Makes" (1949) which is a kind of Preface to his "Collected Poems," he gave his comments on a poem :
   (*i*) "(A poem) begins in delight and ends in wisdom.... it runs a course of lucky events, and ends in a clarification of life...."
   (*ii*) "The artist.... matches a thing from some previous order in time and space into a new order."
9. Some of the more famous poems of Frost are :
   (*i*) Neither Out Far Nor in Deep
   (*ii*) Birches
   (*iii*) The Onset
   (*iv*) The Pasture
   (*v*) Provide, Provide
   (*vi*) Mending Wall
   (*vii*) The Road Not Taken
   (*viii*) After Apple-Picking
   (*ix*) Two Tramps in Mud Time
   (*x*) Stopping By Woods on a Snowy Evening
   (*xi*) Directive
   (*xii*) Meetting and Passing
   (*xiii*) The Gift Outright
   (*xiv*) A Considerable Speck
   (*xv*) The Death of a Hired Man
   (*xvi*) West, Running Brook
   (*xvii*) Home Burial
   (*xviii*) Departmental
   (*xix*) Snow
   (*xx*) The Tuft of Flowers
   (*xxi*) Mowing
   (*xxii*) Acquainted with the Night
   (*xxiii*) The Need of Being Versed in County Things
   (*xxiv*) I Will Sing You One—O
   (*xxv*) Blueberries, etc.
10. Frost is studied on several levels:
   (*i*) As an American poet
   (*ii*) As a poet of nature
   (*iii*) As a poet of New England
   (*iv*) As a Rural poet
   (*v*) As a Modern poet
   (*vi*) As a poet of Truth
   (*vii*) As a poet of known for new type or techniques, etc.
   (*viii*) As a poet of New England/of New Hampshire, in particular.

ERNEST HEMINGWAY (1899-1961)

IMPORTANT POINTS

1. His novels and stories portray the real events honestly, where toughness and courage are the rule rather than the exception and emotion of often held in abeyance—a method reminiscent of Ezra Pound by whom he was influenced immensely.
2. Some of his works are :
   (*i*) The Sun Also Rises (1926)
   (*ii*) A Farewell To Arms (1929)
   (*iii*) To Have and Have Not (1937)
   (*iv*) For Whom the Bell Tolls (1940)
   (*v*) The Old Man and The Sea (1952)
   (This novelette won him the Nobel Prize in 1954)
3. He committed suicide in 1961.
4. He wrote several other books on :
   (*i*) fiction
   (*ii*) bull fighting
   (*iii*) big game hunting in Africa, etc.
   (*iv*) stories
5. Among his works which appeared posthumously, there are a number of poems also.

NATHANIEL HAWTHORNE (1804-1864)

IMPORTANT POINTS

1. He regarded himself as a romancer rather than a novelist.
2. He chiefly employed the device of symbolism in his novels.
3. He is a great novelist and allegorist.
4. He is constantly preoccupied with the themes of sin and evil, believing pride to be the principal sin.
5. Some of his works are :
   (*i*) The Scarlet Letter (1850)
   (*ii*) The House of Seven Gables (1851)
   (*iii*) The Blithedale Romance (1852)
   (*iv*) The Marble Faun (1860)
6. (*i*) He had already produced a juvenile novel; and a few short stories which were later on published "Twice Told Tales" in 1837.
   (*ii*) Some of these stories had earlier appeared in the "The Token."
   (*iii*) Some of the popular stories were :
   (*a*) An Old Woman's Tale
   (*b*) My Kinsman, Major Molinex (1832)
   (*c*) The Gray Champion (1832)
   (*d*) Young Goodman Brown (1835)
   (*e*) Wakefield (1835), etc.
7. In 1846, his collection of 25 short stories, historical sketches and histories was published under the caption "Moses From an Old Mouse."
8. In 1884, he produced a history book for children under the caption: "Grandfather's Chair."

Characteristics

1. He is a great symbolist and allegorist.
2. He is fond of writing romances.
3. He is interested in the study of the Puritan conscience and the Calvinistic idea of the damnation of Man.
4. His chief theme is the impact of sin on the human soul.
5. He tries to introduce the supernatural element in his works, as, for instance, in The Scarlet Letter.
6. Henry James has complained of a lack of intricacy in the rendering of human reality in his novels.
7. Another complaint against him is the tightness of structure (as in the Scarlet Letter) which sometimes encroaches upon his otherwise imaginative and suggestive poetic style.

8. A deep psychoanalytic approach is writ large on almost every page of his novels.
9. The intention to destroy the human soul is something unpardonable in his view.
10. The social, economic, religious and political aspects emerge in one sweep in his novels.
11. His novels present suggestive comments on such themes as :
    (*i*) Puritanism in general.
    (*ii*) Human relations on all planes such as:
        (*a*) sexual
        (*b*) conjugal
        (*c*) filial, etc.
    (*iii*) mystery of life.
    (*iv*) Characteristics of sin.
    (*v*) value of repentance and redemption.
    (*vi*) relationship with the past.
    (*vii*) unexplored human psyche.
    (*viii*) deviation of best intentions from their path.
    (*ix*) Calvinistic Puritanism which enshrines chiefly:
        (*a*) depravity of man
        (*b*) Pre-destined nature of punishment for sinfulness.
        (*c*) Not all are saved.
        (*d*) God's grace has its own independent way of working.
        (*e*) Those saved have to surrender their will to God.
12. Nature (as in the Forest Scene in The Scarlet Letter) as the representative of the Immanent Spirit.
13. The divine spark in man himself, (as in Pearl's elfin beauty).
    Significance of intuition and imagination, as per transcendental doctrine, vis-a-vis the English eighteenth century stress correctness and refinement. (This may not be so marked in Hawthorne as in the main Transcendentalists like Emerson and Thoreau).
14. The intrinsic coherence of symbols despite their apparent incoherence, etc., etc.

EMILY DICKINSON (1830-1886)

IMPORTANT POINTS

1. She led a secluded life during the last 25 years of her life.
2. During this period, she cut herself up from all worldly contact except with some intimate friends.
3. (*i*) In her life she wrote more than one thousand lyrics, but she never cared to get them published during her lifetime.
   (*ii*) During her life, only six of her poems were published.
4. Her poems often are about :
   (*i*) life and death.
   (*ii*) the mystery of death.
   (*iii*) some mystic experiences.
   (*iv*) visions.
   (*v*) sound comments on various aspects of human life and destiny.
   (*vi*) a sympathetic attitude to pathos of life.
   (*vii*) expression of a poignant wit.
5. They contain :
   (*i*) economy of expression.
   (*ii*) novelty of expression.
   (*iii*) new experiments even in simple old metres.
   (*iv*) an aphoristic tone at places.
   (*v*) mystic obscurity or ambiguity at other places.
6. After her death, her poems were published in a number of volumes.
   Some of her well-known poems are mentioned below :
   1. Success is counted Sweetest:
      "Success is counted sweetest
      By those who ne'er succeed.
      To comprehend a nectar
      Requires sorest need."

2. This is my Letter to The World.
3. I Never Saw a Moor
4. I Had Been Hungry
5. Hope is The Thing With Feathers
6. A Bird Came Down The Walk
7. The Sky is Low, the Clouds are Mean
8. A Light Exists in Spring
9. Before I God My Eye Put Out
10. The Heart Asks Pleasure First
11. The Brain Is Wider Than the Sky
12. I Taste A Liquor Never Brewed
13. A Narrow Fellow in the Grass
14. I Heard a Buzz when I Died
15. I Years Had Been from Home
16. A Bird Came Down the Walk
17. I Felt A Funeral in My Brain
18. Safe In Their Alabaster Chambers
19. Much Madness is Divinest Sense
20. The Soul Selects Her Own Society, etc.

Here are some extracts from her works :

1. Because I could not stop for Death,
He kindly stopped for me;
The carriage held but just ourselves
And Immortality. —The Chariot
2. How dreary to be somebody!
How public, like a frog
To tell your name the livelong day
To an admiring bog! —Life
3. I never saw a moor,
I never saw the sea;
Yet know I how the heather looks,
And what a wave must be.
—Time and Eternity
4. My life closed twice before its, close;
It yet remains to see
It Immortality unveil
A third event to me. —Parting
5. How much can come
And much can go,
And yet abide the world!
—There Came a Wind
6. Parting is all we know of heaven,
And all we need of hell. —Parting

ARTHUR MILLER (1915)

IMPORTANT POINTS

1. Whereas O'Neill was the pioneer of American drama in the pre-First World War period, Miller and Tennessee Williams were the only two important American dramatists during the post war period.
2. (*i*) He got admission in the University of Michigan in 1934.
   (*ii*) There he won the first Avery Hopwood Prize for the play: "The Grass Still Grows."
3. Some of his important works are :
   (*i*) Situation Normal (1944): It is a volume of sketches pertaining to life in the army.
   (*ii*) The Man Who Had All the Luck: It is his first novelistic play.
   (*iii*) Focus (1945): It is his successful novel.
   (*iv*) All My Sons (1947): It is his first highly successful play.
   (*v*) Death of a Salesman (1949): It is generally considered his masterpiece.
   (*vi*) The Crucible (1953): This play is a kind of modern parable.
   (*vii*) (*a*) A Memory of Two Mondays (1955)
   (*b*) A View From the Bridge (1955)
   In these two plays, Miller's main focus is on the common man.
   (*viii*) Misfits: In this play, the central theme is the effect of maladjustment in a matrimonial alliance.
   (*ix*) After the Fall (1964): This emotional play is modelled on the stream of consciousness technique.
   (*x*) Incident at Vichy (1964): It is a long one-act play based on the theme of individual gilt.
   (*xi*) The Prince (1968): This play depicts a family feud between two brothers.

S.T. COLERIDGE (1772-1834)

IMPORTANT POINTS

Life

1. Coleridge was born in Devonshire in 1772.
2. His father Rev. John Coleridge was a vicar and incharge of a primary school. He was an honest, sincere, religiously minded man who left the indelible mark of his personality on his children, including S.T. Coleridge.
3. Coleridge, was a precocious child who could read at three and recite from memory a great part of the Bible and the Arabian Nights.
4. It was at the Charity School of Christ's Hospital where he was sent when he was ten and where he made friendship with Lamb.
5. As a boy, he was largely poor and neglected but he was a great dreamer.
6. In 1791, he joined Cambridge as a charity student but left in 1794 without taking a degree.
7. Now, he met the youthful Southey with whom he planned to establish Pantisocracy (an ideal society), on the banks of the Susquehanna.
8. The plan regarding Pantisocracy failed and Coleridge went to Germany to study.
9. Thereafter, he went to Rome.
10. He started a paper "The Friend" which was devoted to truth and also started lectures on poetry and fine arts; he gained a good success, but since he was not regular in his engagements, his audiences ultimately dwindled.

Early works

Among his early poems, we have:

(i) A Day Dream
(ii) The Devil's Thoughts
(iii) The Suicide's Arguments
(iv) The Wanderings of Cain.

Later works

His later works which have made him immortal are:

1. Kubla Khan

It is just a fragment. It is commonly known that he composed the poem in a dream which he remembered and started writing as he woke up but was interrupted and forgot beyond what he had written (54 lines).

2. Christabel

(i) This poem is also a fragment.
(ii) Here, the heroine, Geraldine, is a German woman who, in fact, is a pure young girl who has fallen under the spell of a sorcerer.
(iii) The poem contains:
  (a) exquisitely poetic lines.
  (b) grotesque musical tones.
  (c) element of supernaturalism.
  (d) an atmosphere of awfulness.

3. The Rime of the Ancient Mariner

(i) It is Coleridge's most famous poem and as Long points out, "one of the world's masterpieces."
(ii) It was a part of the Lyrical Ballads which appeared in 1798.
(iii) The story is too well-known to be recounted.
(iv) Some of the important elements in the poem are:
  (a) supernaturalism
  (b) wonderful narration
  (c) triumph of story-telling art
  (d) exquisite poetry
  (e) sweet, luscious music
  (f) triumph of simplicity over complexity
  (g) wonderfully smooth sailing lines
  (h) a well-knit plot and anecdotes
  (i) an element of suspense
  (j) a true vindication of the moral purpose
  (k) a queer atmosphere
  (l) exact geographical positions
  (m) gorgeous scenery, as if painted.
  (n) deep pathos
  (o) value of repentance
  (p) futility of boastful human endeavours.

(*q*) final predominance of fate and mysterious divine power ruling over mankind and all creatures.
(*r*) a true account of the life on the sea during Coleridge's days.
(*s*) freedom from obscurity of any sort despite the element of mystery and suspense.
(*t*) vindication of the "willing suspension of disbelief, etc. etc.

Coleridge's Shorter poems

Some of such poems are

1. Ode on Dejection
2. Frost at Midnight
3. Fears in Solitude
4. Love Poems
5. Hymn Before Sunrise in the Vale of Chamouni
6. Work without Hope
7. Religious Musing, etc.

Prose works

1. His most well-known prose-work is Biographia Literaria, or Sketches of My Literary Life and Opinions (1817).
2. His other prose works are :
   (*i*) Aids to Reflection (1815)
   (*ii*) Lectures on Shakespeare (1849)

As a Philosopher

As such, he was greatly influenced by the German idealistic philosophy which he introduced into England.

As a Music lover and critic

It is well-known that he loved music and was a keen, constructive critic of it.

EMINENT INDIAN WRITERS

MULKRAJ ANAND (1905-2004)

He was greatly influenced by Premchand on the one hand and Tagore on the other.

Some of his famous novels are :

1. The Village (1939)
2. Across the Black Waters (1940)
3. The Sword and the Sickle (1942)
4. Untouchable (1933) (his first novel)
5. Seven Summers (1951)
6. Private Life of an Indian Prince (1953)
7. The Big Heart (1945)
8. Coolie (1936) (It was recast in seventies)
9. Two Leaves and a Bud (1937)
10. The Old Woman and the Cow (1960)
11. The Road (1961)
12. Death of a Hero (1963)
13. Confession of a Lover (1976)
14. Morning Face (1968)

AUROBINDO GHOSE (1872-1950)

1. He was known as the "firebrand" of India.
2. He was a poet, a saint, a philosopher, statesman, yogi and a prophet.
3. He is one of the pre-Independence Titanic trio of Indian poets—Tagore, Aurobindo and Sarojini Naidu.
4. He is chiefly known for his
   (*i*) Savitri (1953) a poetic epic on a grand scale.
   (*ii*) The Life Divine (1939-40)
   (*iii*) Essays on Gita
5. He is a great exponent and proponent of ancient Indian thought.
6. According to R. K. Singh, "Aurobindo is sympathetic to the modernist trends in writing and study of poetry and, in fact, himself adopts some of the methods followed by the modern poets."
7. To quote Mr. Singh again, "In Aurobindo's literary order, poetry is a means of spiritual expression that helps to open the consciousness..."

BANKIM CHANDRA CHATTERJEE (1838-94)

1. He is generally called 'The Father of Bengali fiction.'
2. Today he is most known for his patriotic bent of mind.
3. In all he wrote 14 novels.
   (*i*) Some of them are historical.
   (*ii*) Others are social.
   (*iii*) Still others are philosophical with stress on renunciation and non-attachment.
4. Some of his novels are :
   (*i*) *The Poison Tree* (*1884*)*:* It is a story of Hindu life in Bengal of the period
   (*ii*) Kapalkundala (1885)
   (*iii*) Durgeshnandini (1890)
   (*iv*) Krishnakanta's Will (1895)
   (*v*) The Two Rings (1897)
   (*vi*) Rajmohan's Wife (1904) (published posthumously)
   (*vii*) Anand Math (1884)

NIRAD C. CHAUDHURI (1897-1999)

1. He came into limelight with the publication of his "The Autobiography of an Unknown Indian." (1951).
2. His other important works are:
   (*i*) A Passage to India (1959)
   (*ii*) Continent of Circe (1966) (He received the Duff Cooper Memorial Prize).
   (*iii*) The Intellectual in India (1967)
   (*iv*) To Live or Not to Live (1970)
3. He is known for his most correct and chaste prose for which he has earned much acclaim from the scholars and critics, including Khushwant Singh.

ANITA DESAI (Born-1937)

1. She is a renowned novelist and short story writer.
2. Some of her famous novels are :
   (*i*) Cry, the Peacock (1963)
   (*ii*) Voices in the City (1965)
   (*iii*) Bye-Bye, Blackbird (1971)
   (*iv*) Fire on the Mountain (1977)
   (*v*) Clear Light of Day (1980)
3. Her collection of short stories is captioned "Games at Twilight" (1978)

M.K. GANDHI (1869-1948)

1. His famous work in English is "My Experiments with Truth."
2. The work is an important autobiographical writing which is held in high esteem for its truthfulness, frankness, simplicity and directness of expression in non-ornamental effective English.

KAMALA MARKANDAYA (1924-2004)

1. She is one of the modern novelists and is known for her:
   (*i*) Nectar in a Sieve (her first novel) (It is a novel on miserable rural life).
   (*ii*) Some Inner Fury (1955) (It is a novel of violence and destruction)
   (*iii*) A Silence of Desire (1960) (It is a novel urging the readers to speak out frankly to unburden their hearts).
   (*iv*) Possession (1963) (The problem of possession is discussed in this novel).
   (*v*) A Handful of Rice (1966) (It depicts the life of the poor classes in Madras).
   (*vi*) The Coffer Danus (1969)
   (*vii*) The Nowhere Man (1972)
   (*viii*) Two Virgins (1973)
   (*ix*) The Golden Honeycomb (1977)
   (*x*) Pleasure City (1982).

KHUSHWANT SINGH (Born-1915)

1. He is known for his novels :
   (*i*) Train to Pakistan (his masterpiece)
   (*ii*) I Shall Not Hear the Nightingale (1959). (It describes the social life of a Sikh family during the pre-Independence period).

2. "The Mark of Vishnu" is another of his well-known works.
3. Some of his known stories
   (*a*) Karma
   (*b*) When Sikh Meets Sikh
   (*c*) The Rape, etc.
4. He is also known for his:
   (*i*) A History of the Sikhs
   (*ii*) Translation of Japji Sahib, etc.
4. His regular columns appear weekly in some dailies, *e.g.* :
   (*i*) 'With Malice Towards One And All'—The Hindustan Times.
   (*ii*) 'This Above All'—The Tribune.
5. Mulk Raj Anand is stated to have said that Khushwant Singh's "Train to Pakistan" is likely to last, while about his other creative literary work, one may have some doubts.
6. Among his latest work is "Truth, Love and Little Malice."

MAX MULLER (1823-1900)

1. He was a famous Indologist, German orientalist and linguist, who unearthed a lot of ancient Indian history and Sanskrit scriptures, the Rig Veda, in particular, of which he published six colossal volumes, for which he had got an assignment from the East India Company in 1847.
2. Actually he was a student of Sanskrit, who started comparative study of languages and "Avesta" (in 1845) which is the renowned sacred book of the Zoroastrians.
3. He gave seven lectures on Indian and ancient Indian philosophy at Cambridge University, which have now been published by Rupa & Co. under the caption: "India : What Can it Teach Us?"
4. He distnguishes the highest wisdom of Greece and India by using the terms "to know ourselves" and "to know our self", respectively.
5. Muller makes very appreciative comments on the Rig Veda and the Vedic Religion.

SAROJINI NAIDU (1879-1946)

1. She is a well-known Indian English poet who started writing poetry at a very early age and she was inspired by Edmund Gosse to choose Indian themes and scenery rather than imitating the English classics.
2. She is now known as 'The Nightingale of India.'
3. She took a keen interest in India's struggle for freedom.
4. Some of her works are :
   (*i*) The Golden Threshold (1905)
   (*ii*) The Bird of Time (1912)
   (*iii*) The Broken Wing (1917)
   (*iv*) The Sceptred Flute (1946)
   (*v*) The Feather of the Dawn (1961) (It appeared posthumously)
5. Some of her famous poems are :
   (*i*) The Queen's Rival
   (*ii*) Palanquin Bearers
   (*iii*) To My Fairy Fancies
   (*iv*) The Pardah Nashin
   (*v*) Awake
   (*vi*) Village Song
   (*vii*) The Soul's Prayer
   (*viii*) Fishermen of Coromondel
   (*ix*) It You Call Me
   (*x*) Caprice
   (*xi*) Summer Woods
   (*xii*) Songs of Radha
   (*xiii*) The Bird Sanctuary, etc.

PRITISH NANDY (Born-1947)

1. He was the editor of the 'Illustrated Weekly of India' and has now Telecast a T.V. serial over the Doordarshan: "Hungama Unlimited."
2. (*i*) He is a prolific poet, though he is still not considered one of the best.
   (*ii*) Most of his poetry has been dismissed by critics as mere experimental gimmickry. Such was Saleem Peeradina.

(*iii*) Even Nissim Ezekiel dubbed him to be a poetaster.

3. Some of his works are :
   (*i*) Gods and Olives (1967)
   (*ii*) On Either Side of Arrogance (1968)
   (*iii*) From the Outer Bank of the Brahmputra (1969)
   (*iv*) Riding the Midnight River (1975)
   (*v*) In secret Anarchy (1979), etc.
4. He has written a number of anthologies and translated a number of poets including Agyeya, Amrita Pritam, Kaifi Azmi etc.
5. He has also written some short stories and a verse play.

R.K. NARAYAN (1906-2001)

1. Of the three great novelists, Narayan, Anand and Rao, it is Narayan who has won the maximum accolade both in India and abroad.
2. One of his great achievements is his creation of the famous town of Malgudi like Hardy's Wessex.
3. Narayan is the true master of humour, irony, realism, romance and artistry.
4. Most of his novels and stories depict the life of people of South India.
5. It is sometimes held that Narayan lacks true pathos, genuine depth of feeling, realistic description of poverty and misery, the elements which go in for making a novelist a great one.
6. However, he has earned much popularity as a novelist, and within the range of his own art, he cannot be taken except with due regard and attention.
7. Some of his famous novels are :
   (*i*) Swami and Friends (1935)
   (*ii*) Bachelor of Arts
   (*iii*) The English Teacher
   (*iv*) The Financial Expert
   (*v*) Mr. Sampath (1949)
   (*vi*) The Guide (1958)
   (*vii*) The Man-eater of Malgudi
   (*viii*) The Dark Room (1939)
   (*ix*) Waiting for the Mahatma
   (*x*) The Vendor of Sweets
   (*xi*) The Painter of Signs (1976)

   (He won the Sahitya Akademi Award for 'Guide' in 1961)

R.K. Narayan as a short story writer

1. Some of his stories have appeared in the following collections:
   (*i*) Malgudi Days
   (*ii*) Dodu and Other Stories
   (*iii*) Cyclone and Other Stories
   (*iv*) Gods, Demons and Others

   Narayan has written a few hundred stories, most of them quite interesting and highly readable:
2. Some of his famous short stories are :
   (*i*) The Golden
   (*ii*) A Career
   (*iii*) The Snake Song
   (*iv*) Man Hunt
   (*v*) A Willing Slave
   (*vi*) An Astrologer's Day
   (*vii*) The Doctor's word
   (*viii*) God of Troubles, etc.

JAWAHARLAL NEHRU (1889-1964)

1. He needs no introduction as a freedom fighter, statesman and first Prime Minister of India.
2. Some of his literary works are :
   (*i*) An Autobiography (1936)
   (*ii*) Glimpses of World History (1939)
   (*iii*) Discovery of India (1946)
3. Children enjoy reading his "Letters from Father to His Daughter."
4. He is known for his simple, chaste, poetic English which is a model of natural style.

AMRITA PRITAM (1919-2005)

1. She is the most famous Punjabi Author.
2. She won the Jnanpith Award for her "Kagaj Te Kenvas" in 1981.

3. Her best known autobiographical work which appeared in the seventies is "Rasidi Ticket."
4. (*i*) Her "Shadows of words : An Autobiography" (a transcreation of the Hindi original by Jyoti Sabharwal) has been published by Macmillan in 2002.
   (*ii*) The book presents "an inner journey down the memory lane" presented by the author, who considers old age the best part of her life, like the last sips of tea, which are "usually the sweetest."

SARVAPALLI RADHAKRISHNAN (1888-1975)

1. He is known as an outstanding educationist and a philosopher who presented the Hindu/Indian viewpoint to the world.
2. His works include
   (*i*) An Idealist View of Life (Lectures)
   (*ii*) Indian Philosophy (1923, 1927)
   (*iii*) The Hindu View of Life (1932)
   (*iv*) An Idealist View of Life (1932)
   (*v*) Eastern Religious and Western Thought (1939)
3. He wrote in a very simple, intelligible prose-style.

RAJA RAO (1908-2006)

1. His famous works are:
   (*i*) The Serpent and the Rope (1960)
   (*ii*) Kanthapura (1938)
   (*iii*) The Cat and Shakespeare (1965-66)
2. (*i*) He was awarded the Sahitya Akademi Award for his 'The Serpent and the Rope' in 1964.
   (*ii*) He was also decorated with Padma Bhushan in 1969.

Raja Rao as a short story writer

1. He is also a well-known short story writer.
2. His first collection of short stories was "Jauni" which was published in France in 1930.
3. The collection: "The Cow of the Barricades" was published in 1947
4. Some of his famous short stories are :
   (*i*) Akkayya
   (*ii*) The Little Gram-shop
   (*iii*) Kanaka Pal
   (*iv*) Narsiga

ARUNDHATI ROY (Born-1961)

She made her debut with her novel: "The God of Small Things" which won her the Booker Prize in 1997, besides a handful amount running into crores as royalty for less than four hundred pages which comprise the said novel.

SHOBHA DE (Born-1948)

1. She is a renowned contemporary Indian English novelist and T.V. serial script writer.
2. Some of her novels are prescribed in universities in England and Australias.
3. Her T.V. serial "Swabhiman" which ran into numerous episodes was telecast over the Doordarshan.
4. (*i*) She has become even more popular with her serial "Kittie Party" telecast over the Zee T.V.
   (*ii*) According to the Tribune, it "is a clever insight into the mind of today's urban Indian women poised at the crossroads of modernity and tradition."

RABINDRANATH TAGORE (1861-1941)

1. Tagore was a versatile genius. He was a :
   (*i*) poet
   (*ii*) novelist
   (*iii*) short story writer
   (*iv*) dramatist
   (*v*) musician
   (*vi*) actor (in dramas)
   (*vii*) painter
   (*viii*) statesman and a host of other things.
2. Some of his famous novels are :
   (*i*) The House and the World (1919)
   (*ii*) The Wreck (1921)
   (*iii*) Gora (1923)

SWAMI VIVEKANANDA (1863-1902)

He is a well-known Indian seer, prophet, recluse preacher, lecturer and poet, who:

(i) made the ancient Indian philosophy known to the whole world at the Parliament of Religious in Chicago, USA.

(ii) Brought about a wave of resurgence among the Indian masses through his stirring spiritually inspired speeches which were also full of:

(a) patriotic fervour

(b) love for universal brotherhood.

(c) spirit of social uplight, etc.

NISSIM EZEKIEL (1924)

1. He is a famous Bombayite who has written on all aspects of the mega-city.
2. He worked as an editor of the Quest and Poetry India and later became President of PEN (India).
3. He is also a poetry and an art critic. He is, however better known as a poet.
4. Some of his works are :
   (i) A Time to Change (1952)
   (ii) Sixty Poems (1953)
   (iii) The Third (1959)
   (iv) The Unfinished Man (1960)
   (v) The Exact Name (1969)
   (vi) The Sleepwalkers (1969)
   (vii) Snakeskin and Other Poems (1974)
   (viii) Hymns in Darkness (1976)
   (ix) Latter Day Psalms (1982).
5. He won the Sahitya Akademi Award in 1983.
6. He had worked as a good samaritan collecting funds from Israel for the poor Bombay Jews children before he had to be hospitalised for Alzhmeir's Disease.

Some of his most famous poems are :

1. Night of the Scorpion.
2. Poet, Lover, Birdwatcher.

K.N. DARUWALLA (1937)

1. He wrote short stories and his critical work has also often appeared in journals, but he is known more for his poetry.
2. He is one of the judges who decide the poetic works at competitions held by the All-India (English) Poetry Society and Sahitya Akademi, New Delhi.
3. He won the Sahitya Akademi Award for Poetry in 1984.
4. In his poetry, he is virtually a social protester, but he is known for his vivid imagery and accuracy of description.
5. He is one of the most famous living Indian English poets, who says about himself, "I am not an urban writer and my poems are rooted in the rural landscape. My poetry is earthy, and I like to consciously keep it that way..."
6. He has published many collections of poems.

   Some of them are :
   (i) Under Orion (1970)
   (ii) Apparition in April (1971)
   (iii) Crossing of Rivers (1976)
   (iv) Winter Poems (1980)
   (v) The Keeper of the Dead (1982)
   (vi) Landscapes (1987)
   (vii) The Map-Maker (Pub. by Ravi Dayal) (2002)
7. His poems have appeared in :
   (i) Opinion
   (ii) Poetry Australia, Sydney
   (iii) Transatlantic Review, London
   (iv) Triquarterly—Illinois
8. Some of his well-known poems are :
   (i) The Epileptic
   (ii) The Ghaghra in Spate
   (iii) Rumination
   (iv) Death of a Bird
   (v) Fire-Hymn
   (vi) Routine

(vii) Old Sailor (The opening poem of "The Map Maker")

(viii) The Birth of Maya } included in "The Map Maker"
(ix) Draupadi

9. The famous collection of his short stories is entitled : "Sword and Abyss."
10. Some of the qualities of his poetry are :
    (i) faithful depiction of north Indian landscape.
    (ii) element of social protest.
    (iii) a bitter, satiric tone.
    (iv) concrete statuesque imagery.
    (v) complete surrender of self to the poetic art.
    (vi) crude earthiness.
    (vii) mainly a rural atmosphere.
    (viii) bringing into full poetic display of his experience in the police department :
    "A crowd senses a mishap before it sees one."

RUSKIN BOND (1934)

Ruskin Bond is known internationally as one of India's most prolific writers in English for children, young adults, and adults. He was awarded the Padma Shri in 1999 for contribution to children's literature.

Ruskin Bond was born in Kasauli, Himachal Pradesh in 1934. He grew up in Jamnagar (Gujarat), Mussoorie, Dehradun, and Shimla. When he was 10, his father passed away in 1944 during the World War II, not to the war but to the malaria, and he was raised by his mother. He has two half-brothers from his mother's remarriage after his father's death.

For a while, he attended Hampton Court School, which is still in existence on Mussoorie's Mall Road, once the town's major promenade. He completed his schooling at Bishop Cotton School in Shimla, from where he graduated in 1952. Given his childhood in various hill stations, most of his writings revolve around the foothills of the Himalayas, especially the greater Doon Valley.

As a young man, Ruskin Bond spent four years in the Channel Islands and London, having moved there with his family, as was common for many Anglo-Indian and domiciled British families to have done in the years after 1947. Bond, to the surprise of his family, returned to India alone in 1956, and since then, he has never left the country since.

He has lived in Mussoorie since 1962. A lifelong bachelor, he moved to Landour by himself, but over the decades, an extended foster family has grown around him. Among blood relatives, Bond has a sister, who lived in England but now too may have returned to India.

At the time, Ruskin Bond moved there, Mussoorie and Landour were losing population given the decline of the boarding schools of the area and the gradual departure of the once-dominant expatriate classes, primarily British and American missionaries.

Bond initially moved to Landour for the "peace and quiet". **Things** are rather different now in Mussoorie, **which** is **often** described as "Delhi's Chandni Chowk on a Hillside", though the Landour Cantonment where Bond lives is much calmer. Earlier he lived in Mussoorie proper, in Maplewood Cottage just below Wynberg-Allen School, until 1976.

Ruskin was seventeen when his first novel, *The Room on the Roof*, came out. The book won the *John Llewellyn Rhys Prize* in 1957. *Vagrants In The Valley* was also written in his teens and picked up from where *The Room On The Roof* left off.

In 1992, Ruskin Bond received the 'Sahitya Academy Award' for English writing in India for, *Our Trees Still Grow In Dehra.*

In 1994, his much acclaimed collection of his non-fiction writing; *Rain In The Mountains, Delhi Is Not Far* and *The Best Of Ruskin Bond*, were also published.

In 1997, Bond's autobiography, *Scenes from a Writer's Life*, was published. He has written over three hundred short stories, essays and novels, including *Vagrants in The Valley*, *The Blue Umbrella*, *Funny Side Up*, *A Flight of Pigeons* and more than 30 books for children. He has also published two volumes of autobiography. *Scenes from a Writer's Life* describes his formative years growing up in Anglo-India; *The Lamp is Lit* is a collection of essays and episodes from his journal.

Ruskin Bond was awarded Padma Shri in 1999. His interest in the paranormal led him to write popular titles like, *Ghost Stories from the 'Raj'*, *A Season of Ghosts*, *A Face in the dark and other hauntings.*

His novel, *The Flight of Pigeons*, has been adapted into the film *Junoon*. *The Room on the Roof* has been adapted into a BBC-produced TV series. Several stories have been incorporated in the school curriculum in India, including "The Night Train at Deoli", "Time Stops at Shamli" and *Our Trees Still Grow in Dehra*. In 2007, the Bollywood director Vishal Bhardwaj made a film based on his popular novel for children, *The Blue Umbrella*. The movie won the National Award for Best Children's film.

Ruskin Bond made his maiden foray on the big screen with a cameo in Vishal Bhardwaj's film *7 Khoon Maaf* (2010) based on short story Susanna's Seven Husbands. He was conferred with Lifetime Achievement Award by Delhi government for his contribution in Literature, especially in Child Literature.

He now lives with his adopted family in Mussoorie.

Collections

- Garland of memories
- Ghost stories from the Raj
- Funny side up
- Rain in the mountains-notes from the Himalayas
- Our trees still grow in Dehra
- Dust on the mountain
- A season of ghosts
- Tigers forever
- A town called Dehra
- An island of trees
- The night train at Deoli
- A face in the dark and other hauntings
- Potpourri
- The advantages of Rusty
- The lost Ruby
- Crazy times with Uncle Ken
- The death of trees
- Tales and legends from India
- Time stops at Shamli
- Grandpa tickles a tiger
- Four feathers
- School days
- The tiger in the Tunnel
- The parrot who wouldn't talk
- The doctor
- The hop nature boy and other poems

Novels

- The room on the roof
- Vagrants in the valley
- Scenes from a writer's life
- A flight of pigeons
- Landour days — A writer's journal
- The sensualist by Ruskin Bond
- The road to the Bazaar
- The panther's moon
- Once upon A monsoon time
- The India I love
- The Kashmiri storyteller
- The blue umbrella
- The tiger in the tunnel
- Delhi is not far
- Animal stories
- Funny side up
- Ruskin Bond's children omnibus
- Maharani (Book)
- Angry River
- Roads to Mussoorie
- All roads lead to Ganga

VIKRAM SETH (1952)

Vikram Seth was born on June 20, 1952 at Kolkata. His father, Prem, was an employee of a shoe company who migrated to post-partition India from West Punjab in Pakistan. Vikram Seth's childhood was spent in the town of Batanagar near Calcutta, Patna, and London. His mother Leila Seth was the first woman judge of the Delhi High Court as well as the first woman to become Chief Justice of a state High Court. She was the Chief Justice of Shimla High Court. Leila gave her law exams when she was pregnant with Vikram Seth's younger brother and gave birth to child just a few weeks after her exams.

Although born in India, Vikram Seth spent some of his early years in London. However, he returned to India in 1957 and completed his primary education from The Doon School in Dehradun. For his higher studies, he returned to UK and joined the

Tonbridge School. He later went to Corpus Christ College, Oxford where he studied philosophy, economics and politics. The beautiful years spent in this college not only earned him a degree, but also helped him to explore his interest in poetry and writing. From then he worked towards poetry and other forms of writing. He even enrolled for Ph.D. in Stanford University but could never complete it because of his inclination towards writing. Having lived in London for many years, he loved the people and culture of the country. That was why he bought a residence near Salisbury, UK. He took his undergraduate degree in philosophy, politics and economics from Oxford University. He was enrolled in postgraduate economics courses at Stanford University and was also attached to Nanjing University for his intended doctoral dissertation on Chinese population planning. He has travelled widely and lived in Britain, California, India and China.

Vikram Seth is well known for some of his noted works. He possesses the art of creating a living and breathing world that keeps the readers focused and engaged. He has published six books of poetry and three novels. In 1986, he wrote *The Golden Gate*, his first novel. It is a novel in verse about the lives of a number of young professionals in San Francisco. Seth had encountered Charles Johnston's 1977 translation of it in a Stanford second-hand bookstore and it changed the direction of his career, shifting his focus from academic to literary work. The likelihood of commercial success seemed highly doubtful — and the skepticism of friends as to the novel's viability is facetiously quoted within the novel; but the verse novel received wide acclaim and achieved healthy sales. After the success of *The Golden Gate*, Seth took up residence in his parents' house back in Delhi to work on his second novel, *A Suitable Boy* (1993). Though initially conceived as a short piece detailing the domestic drama of an Indian mother's search for an appropriate husband for her marriageable Indian daughter against the background of the formative years of India after independence, the novel grew and Seth was to labour over it for almost a decade. The 1474-page novel is a four-family saga set in post-independence, post-Partition India, and alternately satirically and earnestly examines issues of national politics in the period leading up to the first post-independence national election of 1952, inter-sectarian animosity, the status of lower caste people such as the jatav, land reform and the eclipse of the feudal princes and landlords, academic affairs, inter- and intra-family relations and a range of further issues of importance to the characters. The novel was, despite its formidable length, a best-seller, and propelled Seth into the public spotlight. *'A Suitable Boy'* won the W.H.Smith prize in 1993. It also won the prestigious Booker's award for 1994. Seth's third novel, *An Equal Music* (1999), set in contemporary Europe, focuses on the lives of classical musicians and their music. Some readers and critics complained that Michael, the protagonist, was simply not a likeable (or unlikeable) enough character to sustain interest throughout a substantial novel and that the focus on the music for its own sake can be trying for the uninitiated. However, Paolo Isotta, one of Italy's most significant music critics, wrote in the influential newspaper *Il Corriere della Sera* of the Italian translation that no European writer had ever shown such a knowledge of European classical music, nor had any European novel before managed to convey the psychology, the technical abilities, even the human potentialities of those who practice music for a living.

The Rivered Earth, released in late 2011, consists of four libretti taking inspiration from the Salisbury house where English poet George Herbert lived and died which also serves the illustration for the book cover. The libretti are written to accompany music by Alec Roth, and quite a few of the pieces were adjusted and rewritten to suit Roth's style. The venue for the libretti is churches, including Salisbury church. The four parts are entitled *'Songs in Time of War'*, *'Shared Ground'*, *'The Traveller'* and *'Seven Elements'*. They are inspired from Chinese and Indian poetry and even George Herbert's house which Seth later bought. Two Lives, is a non-fiction family memoir written at the suggestion of his mother, and published in October 2005. It is a memoir of the marriage of his great uncle and aunt. It focuses on the lives of his great-uncle (Shanti

Behari Seth) and German-Jewish great aunt (Henny Caro) who met in Berlin in the early 1930s while Shanti was a student there and with whom Seth stayed extensively on going to England at age 17 for school. The award of the commander of the order 3 of the British Empire was given to Seth on February 2001. Vikram Seth is also the author of a travel book, *From Heaven Lake: Travels Through Sinkiang and Tibet* (1983), an account of a journey through Tibet, China and Nepal that won the Thomas Cook Travel Book Award, and a libretto, *Arion and the Dolphin: A Libretto* (1994), which was performed at the English National Opera in June 1994, with music by Alec Roth. His poetry includes *Mappings* (1980), *The Humble Administrator's Garden* (1985), winner of the Commonwealth Poetry Prize (Asia), and *All You Who Sleep Tonight: Poems* (1990). His children's book, *Beastly Tales from Here and There* (1992), consists of ten stories about animals told in verse. Vikram Seth was also commissioned by the English National Opera to write a libretto based on the Greek legend of Arion and the Dolphin. The opera was performed for the first time in June 1994. At home in Delhi where he stays with his parents and maintains an extensive library and his vast paper work.

Vikram Seth's magnum opus fictional system, *A Suitable Boy* is set in Brahmpur, a fictionalized Northern Indian city on the banks of the Ganges River. The action takes place sometime around in 1950 to 1952, four to five years after India gained independence from Great Britain in 1947.

After winning The Connect Award in 1993 for *A Suitable Boy*, Seth came into limelight with a slew of interviews, talk shows, and book signings on his book tour etc. But many readers and critics alike were utterly disappointed and dismayed when *A Suitable Boy* was left out of the race for the Booker Prize in 1993. Seth's work was not among the six novels nominated for the prize, which was ultimately awarded to *Paddy Clarke Ha Ha Ha* on October 26, 1993. However it won the 1994 Commonwealth Writers Prize. *A Suitable Boy* is a fictional system which very realistically depicts the social and political life of post independence India. The story revolves around four families-the Kapoors, Mehras, Chatterjis and Khans.

Novels

- *The Golden Gate* (1986)
- *A Suitable Boy* (1993)
- *An Equal Music* (1999)
- *A Suitable Girl* (upcoming, 2016)

Poetry

- *Mappings* (1980)
- *The Humble Administrator's Garden* (1985)
- *All You Who Sleep Tonight* (1990)
- *Beastly Tales* (1991)
- *Three Chinese Poets* (1992)
- *The Frog and the Nightingale* (1994)

Children's Book

- *Beastly Tales* (1991)

Others

- *From Heaven Lake: Travels Through Sinkiang and Tibet* (1983)
- *Two Lives*
- *The Rivered Earth*

Awards

- 1983 – Thomas Cook Travels Book Award for *From Heaven Lake: Travels Through Sinkiang and Tibet*
- 1985 – Commonwealth Poetry Prize (Asia) for *The Humble Administrator's Garden*
- 1993 – Irish Times International Fiction Prize (shortlist) for *A Suitable Boy*
- 1994 – Commonwealth Writers Prize (Overall Winner, Best Book) for *A Suitable Boy*
- 1994 – WH Smith Literary Award for *An Equal Music*
- 1999 – Crossword Book Award for *An Equal Music*
- 2001 – EMMA (BT Ethnic and Multicultural Media Award) for Best Book/Novel for *An Equal Music*
- 2005 – Pravasi Bharatiya Samman
- 2007 – Padma Shri in Literature & Education
- 2013 – The 25 Greatest Global Living Legends in India

MULTIPLE CHOICE QUESTIONS

1. Who says that all the sweet scents of Arabia cannot remove the stench of blood and all the seven seas cannot wash off the blood of Duncan from the hands?
A. Lady Macbeth B. Malcolm
C. The Witches D. Macbeth

2. No man of woman born will be able to kill Macbeth. So the witches prophesied. But Macduff succeeds in killing him because he was born from:
A. a goddess
B. a miracle
C. a Caesarean operation
D. a test-tube

3. Lady Macbeth's sleep-walking is a result of her:
A. deep sense of guilt B. overactive brain
C. dreams D. pretence

4. Which of these plays by Shakespeare does *not* use 'cross-dressing' as a device?
A. *As You Like It*
B. *Julius Caeser*
C. *Cymbeline*
D. *Two Gentlemen of Verona*

5. The etymological meaning of the word "trope" is
A. gesture B. turning
C. mirror D. desire

6. In the late seventeenth century a "Battle of Books" erupted between which two groups?
A. Cavaliers and Roundheads
B. Abolitionists and Enthusiasts for slaves
C. Champions of Ancient and Modern Learning
D. The Welsh and the Scots

7. Shakespeare's sonnets:
A. do not carry a dedication.
B. are dedicated to James I of England.
C. are dedicated to Mary Arden.
D. are dedicated to an unknown "Mr. W.H."

8. Which of the following poems uses *terza rima*?
A. John Keats's "Ode to a Nightingale"
B. P.B. Shelley's "Ode to the West Wind"
C. William Wordsworth's "The Solitary Reaper"
D. Alfred Tennyson's "Ulysses"

9. When one says that "someone is no more" or that "someone has breathed his/ her last", the speaker is resorting to
A. euphism B. euphony
C. understatement D. euphemism

10. Which of the following are "companion poems"?
A. "Gypsy songs" and "Songs and Sonnets"
B. "L'Allegro" and "Il Penseroso"
C. "The Good Morrow" and "The Sun Rising"
D. "Full Fathom Five" and "Hark, Hark! the Lark"

11. Arrange the following in ascending order in terms of size:
1. epic 2. epigram
3. stanza 4. sonnet
A. 1 2 3 4 B. 2 1 3 4
C. 2 3 4 1 D. 1 3 4 2

12. Hyperbole is
1. an extravagant exaggeration
2. a racist slur
3. a metrical skill
4. a figure of speech
A. 1 is correct
B. 1 and 4 are correct
C. 1 and 3 are correct
D. 3 is correct

13. The poetry of Wordsworth and Coleridge was notably influenced by...
A. The Napoleonic Wars
B. The Glorious Revolution
C. The French Revolution
D. Poor Laws

14. "He's not the brightest man in the world" is an example of :
A. Chiasmus B. Hyperbole
C. Litotes D. Simile

15. *Prosody studies*:
A. Line endings
B. Meanings of words
C. Patterns of prose
D. Metrics

16. *"Formal Criticism"* relates to the structure of:
A. Literary devices B. Myths
C. Content D. Form

17. A *"Foot"* in prosody is a basic unit of :
A. rhyme
B. length
C. rhythmic measurement
D. height

18. "Iambus" is a metrical foot consisting of :
A. two syllables B. three syllables
C. four syllables D. one syllable

19. An "Idyll" is usually a poem about a :
A. picturesque city life
B. panoramic view of nature
C. picture of industrial society
D. picturesque country life

20. The rhyme scheme of the Shakespearean sonnet is :
A. abab, cdcd, efef, gg
B. abba, cddc, effe, gg
C. abab, cdcd, efef, gh
D. aabb, ccdd, eeff, gg

21. Pope's "Essay on Criticism" sums up the art of poetry as taught first by:
A. Aristotle B. Horace
C. Longinus D. Plato

22. A particle is:
A. a patchwork of words, sentences, passages
B. a satirical poem
C. a love song
D. a collection of lines from different poems

23. "Careless she is with artful Care/Affecting to seem unaffected" is an example of:
A. irony B. paradox
C. simile D. metaphor

24. A metrical foot containing a stressed, followed by an unstressed, syllable is:
A. anapaest B. iamb
C. trochee D. dactyl

25. The rhyme scheme of a Spenserian sonnet is:
A. abba, cbcb, cdcd, ee
B. abab, bccb, ccdd, ee
C. aabb, bcbc, ccdd, ee
D. abab, bcbc, cdcd, ee

26. Using the expression "Crown" for the monarchy is an example of:
A. Metonymy B. Synecdoche
C. Irony D. Metaphor

27. Dr. Johnson's *A Dictionary of the English Language* was published in:
A. 1755 B. 1756
C. 1757 D. 1758

28. A figure of speech in which two terms opposite in meaning are placed side-by-side in one phrase is known as:
A. paradox B. oxymoron
C. sarcasm D. antithesis

29. A stanza of eight iambic pentametres on the pattern of ab, ab, ab, cc is known as:
A. Rhyme royal
B. Ottava rima
C. Tennysonian stanza
D. Spenserian stanza

30. In the assertion "Four out of five people suffer from *dreaded* pyorrhoca", the writer wants to arouse the feeling of:
A. Sympathy B. Fear
C. Hatred D. Ill-will

31. Which novel earned Galsworthy the reputation of a novelist?
A. Jocelyn
B. Country Mouse
C. The Island Pharisees
D. Fraternity

32. In 1929, which honour was conferred upon Galsworthy?
A. Order of merit B. Order of demerit
C. Booker Prize D. All of the above

33. Which play of Galsworthy is a study in social pride and social convention?
A. The Mob B. The Skin Game
C. The Loyalties D. The Silver Box

34. Which play made Galsworthy famous as a dramatist?
A. Justice B. The Silver Box
C. Loyalties D. None of these

35. What is the title of Galsworthy's collection of essays?
A. The Inn of Tranquility
B. The River of Tranquility
C. The Ocean of Tranquility
D. None of the above

36. Which play of Galsworthy dramatizes strike?
A. Mob B. Justice
C. Strife D. None of these

37. What is the name of Galsworthy's first play?
A. Loyalties B. Joy
C. Justice D. Silver Box

38. The Essays and Stories—The White Monkey, The Silver Spark, Swan Song, A Slient Wooing and Passers by were collected together as
A. awakening B. a modern tragedy
C. a modern comedy D. None of these

39. In 1931, Oxford University and Princeton University conferred upon Galsworthy
A. Knighthood B. Honorary Doctorate
C. Both A and B D. None of these

40. Galsworthy is the chief exponent of
A. romantic tales B. adventures tales
C. problem plays D. None of these

41. A poem that captures the essence of a moment in a simple image is:
A. Lyric B. Ballad
C. Ode D. Haiku

42. The word 'nature' in the eighteenth century literature stands for :
A. Nature of writing B. External nature
C. Human nature D. The Universe

43. Who is given credit for first using the term "romantic"?
A. Friedrich Schlegel B. Kant
C. Coleridge D. Schiller

44. Heroic Couplet is a pair of :
A. Rhyming iambic pentameter lines
B. Unrhyming iambic pentameter lines
C. Rhyming iambic hexameter
D. Unrhyming iambic hexameter

45. Heroic quatrain is.:
A. a stanza in blank verse
B. eight line stanza in iambic hexameter
C. four line stanza in iambic pentameter
D. six line stanza in iambic pentameter

46. Victorian Age witnessed a clash between:
A. faith and reason
B. tradition and modernity
C. oriental and occidental civilization
D. romanticism and neo romanticism

47. The historical novel began in:
A. Restoration Period
B. Augustan Age
C. Victorian Period
D. Romantic Period

48. Internal rhyme is :
A. the basic rhythmic structure of a poem
B. rhyming of two words in alternative lines
C. rhyming of two or more words in the same line of poetry
D. all the lines of a poem ending with the same line pattern

49. "Fancy" deals with:
A. "Fixities and definities"
B. "Imagination and Reason"
C. "Judgement and Memory"
D. "Structure and Superstructure"

50. The early religious drama is associated with:
A. Superstitions and beliefs
B. Mysteries and histories
C. Interludes and mysteries
D. Miracles and morality

51. Shakespeare was born at:
A. London B. Stratford-on-Avon
C. Leicester D. Edinburgh

52. Shakespeare married:
A. Portia B. Imogen
C. Anne Hathaway D. Lucy

53. Shakespeare's first job in a London theatre was:
A. acting as a ghost
B. translating plays
C. to write plays
D. holding visitor's horses

54. Shakespeare first wrote his plays for:
A. Earl of Leicester's Players
B. The Globe
C. The King's Players
D. The Shakespeare Society

55. Shakespeare wrote:
A. 20 plays B. 35 plays
C. 24 plays D. 37 plays

56. His sonnets are mostly addressed to:
A. Queen Elizabeth
B. Ben Jonson
C. The Earl of Southampton
D. The Duke of Edinburgh

57. *Venus* and *Adonis* is a poem of:
A. Two Sisters B. Victory
C. Love D. Greek art

58. The play written in collaboration with Marlowe was:
A. Winter's Tale
B. Merchant of Venice
C. Titus Andronicus
D. Hamlet

59. Portia is a character in the Shakespearean play:
A. Merchant of Venice
B. Twelfth Night
C. The Tempest
D. Romeo and Juliet

60. The Shakespearean play which describes the assassination of a Roman general is:
A. Macbeth B. Julius Caesar
C. Othello D. Richard II

61. The fourth witch is the name usually given to:
A. One of Duncan's royal maids
B. An invisible spirit
C. Macduff's wife
D. Lady Macbeth

62. The witches prophesy that Macbeth cannot be killed till a forest comes moving down towards him. This forest is:
A. Dunsinane B. The Black Forest
C. Brinam Wood D. The Scottish Forest

63. Duncan wants to make which one of these his successor to the throne?
A. Malcolm, his own son
B. Macbeth
C. Banquo
D. Fleance

64. In the beginning of the play, Macbeth is shown returning from:
A. a tour B. a holiday
C. battle D. an expedition

65. Lady Macbeth is described as:
A. masculine B. frail as any woman
C. kind-hearted D. dull and powerless

66. Lady Macbeth does not wish to kill the sleeping Duncan because:
A. he resembles her father
B. it is not proper for a woman
C. her husband is the one who will succeed him
D. it is not proper to kill the enemy in sleep

67. Duncan is a guest of the Macbeths at:
A. Edinburgh Castle B. Dunsinane
C. Buckingham D. Inverness Castle

68. A speech in which an actor reveals his innermost thoughts is called a:
A. Soliloquy B. Aside
C. Chorus D. Loud thinking

69. The dagger that Macbeth sees in the air is:
A. his own dagger held by a spirit
B. a projection of his imagination signifying the murder of his conscience and peace
C. some other object resembling a dagger
D. suspended from a thread

70. Who says "I have supped too much with horrors/And know the taste of blood"?
A. Banquo B. Duncan
C. Macbeth D. Lady Macbeth

71. In tragedy, human beings are shown coming to terms with forces larger and greater than themselves. These forces are:
A. Devils B. Fate or Death
C. Circumstances D. Natural calamities

72. The cause of the downfall of a Shakespearean hero is:
A. *hubris* or pride
B. God's will
C. a bad woman
D. some wrong decision

73. The book which influenced Shakespeare the most in introducing witches in *Macbeth* was:
A. Demonology
B. Chronicles of Scotland
C. Discovery of Witchcraft
D. Written by King James I

74. Shakespeare's Macbeth is an important source of information about the history of:
A. Scotland
B. England of his own times
C. Ireland
D. The world

75. The belief in Elizabethan times that the King was God's representative or image on earth led to the theory of the:
A. Divine Right of Kings
B. Great Chain of Being
C. Natural Order
D. Witchcraft

76. According to the Elizabethans anything that went contrary to the natural order was:
A. good B. strange
C. revolutionary D. evil

77. In Tudor England, women's role in society was:
A. more important than men
B. that of a slave
C. equal to men
D. secondary to men

78. Widows could not protect their property, and if they showed bold ideas, they were accused of being:
A. thieves B. wrongful owners
C. witches D. greedy

79. In the beginning of *Macbeth*, the three witches meet:
A. in a health
B. in a ruined building
C. in a forest
D. in a barn

80. What title do the witches use to hail Macbeth?
A. General B. Victor
C. Glamis D. King

81. According to Galsworthy, which play made a great sensation, especially in Parliamentary and official circles?
A. The Mob B. Justice
C. The Skin Game D. The Eldest Son

82. John Galsworthy was awarded the Nobel Prize for literature in
A. 1942 B. 1932
C. 1922 D. 1912

83. The masterpiece of Galsworthy is
A. The Forsyte Saga B. The Freelands
C. Fraternity D. The Patrician

84. Galsworthy deals with the inadequacy of the administration of justice and the attitude of different types of people towards and escaped prisoner in the play
A. Escape B. The Show
C. Jocelyn D. None of these

85. Which universities awarded D. Litt to Galsworthy?
A. Oxford and Princeton University
B. Cambridge and Sheffiled University
C. Oxford and Cambridge
D. None of the above

86. Which novel of Galsworthy illustrates the breaking down of inhibitions and barriers as the result of war?
A. Saint's Progress B. Fraternity
C. Jocelyn D. None of these

87. What is "The White Monkey"?
A. A pet B. A book
C. A poem D. A painting

88. D. Litt was conferred upon Galsworthy in the year
A. 1929 B. 1930
C. 1940 D. None of these

89. The Forsyte Saga includes two interludes. Name the interludes.
A. Indian Autumn of Forsyte Tales and Awakening
B. Indian Winter of Forstye Tales and Awakening
C. Indian Summer of Forsyte Tales and Awakening
D. None of these

90. Galsworthy's Forsyte Saga is said to be an English parallel to
A. Milton's Paradise Lost
B. Thomas Mann's Buddenbrooks
C. Seth's A Suitable Boy
D. Shakespeare's Hamlet

91. The expression "murderous innocence" is an example of
A. Oxymoron B. Zeugma
C. Chiasmus D. Pun

92. Which of the following works of John Milton is an elegy?
A. *Lycidas* B. *L'Allegro*
C. *Camus* D. *Paradise Lost*

93. The rhyme scheme of the Spenserian sonnet is
A. abab bcbc cdcd ee
B. abab cdcd efef gg
C. abba cddc effe gg
D. abba abba cde cde

94. A monosyllabic rhyme on the final stressed syllable of two lines of verse is called
A. monorhyme B. feminine rhyme
C. masculine rhyme D. eye rhyme

95. A sequence of repeated consonantal sounds in a stretch of language is
A. alliteration B. acrostic
C. assent D. syllable

96. English Iambic Pentameter was brought to its first maturity in
A. sonnet B. dramatic verse
C. lyric D. elegy

97. The Restoration comedy has been criticized mainly for its
A. excessive wit and humour
B. bitter satire and cynicism
C. indecency and permissiveness
D. superficial reflection of society

98. Sexual possessiveness is a theme of Shakespeare's
A. *Coriolanus*
B. *Julius Caesar*
C. *Henry IV Part–I*
D. *A Midsummer Night's Dream*

99. Johnson's *Dictionary of the English Language* was published in the year
A. 1710 B. 1755
C. 1739 D. 1759

100. The first complete printed English Bible was produced by
A. William Tyndale B. William Caxton
C. Miles Coverdale D. Roger Ascham

101. *'Fluency'* in language is the same as:
A. the ability to put oneself across comfortably in speech and/or writing
B. the ability to command language rather than language commanding the user
C. glibness
D. accuracy

102. What is a mock-heroic poem? A mock-heroic poem
A. mocks at heroic pretensions in poets and critics
B. mocks heroism, an exaggerated virtue in all epics
C. uses a heroic style to deride airs and affectations
D. uses a mocking style to deride heroes and hero-worship

103. In drama, an aside is addressed
A. to an audience by an actor; the words so spoken are not meant to be heard by other actors on the stage.
B. to other actors on the stage; the words so spoken are not meant to be heard by the audience.
C. by the playwright to the audience.
D. by the protagonist to his/her antagonist

104. Which of the following is not a revenge tragedy?
A. *Hamlet*
B. *The Duchess of Malfi*
C. *Volpone*
D. *Gorboduc*

105. "The pen is mightier than the sword" is an example of
A. simile B. image
C. conceit D. metonymy

106. An epilogue is
A. prefixed to a text which it introduces.
B. suffixed to a text which it sums up or extends.
C. a piece of writing or speech that formally begins a book.
D. a piece of writing or speech that bears no relation to the text at hand.

107. Items in a published book appear in the following order:
A. Index, Copyright Page, Bibliography, Footnotes
B. Copyright Page, Bibliography, Index, Footnotes
C. Copyright Page, Footnotes, Bibliography, Index
D. Bibliography, Copyright Page, Index, Footnotes

108. Which of the following statements on The Prelude by William Wordsworth is/are not true?
1. *The Prelude* was published posthumously.
2. In this poem, Wordsworth records his development as a poet.
3. The poem runs to 14 books; at crucial stages the poet celebrates the sublime natural scenery in developing his spiritual, moral and imaginative nature.
4. Poems like "Michael", "The Old Cumberland Beggar", "She dwelt among the untrodden ways", "Nutting" etc. are the highlights of this volume.

A. 1 to 4 are true B. 1 is not true
C. 4 is not true D. Only 3 is true

109. One of the following *Canterbury Tales* is in prose, identify.
A. *The Pardoner's Tale*
B. *The Parson's Tale*
C. *The Monk's Tale*
D. *The Knight's Tale*

110. A 'curtal sonnet' consists of
A. 11 lines B. 12 lines
C. 13 lines D. 14 lines

111. The first folio of all of Shakespeare's plays were published in:
A. 1616 B. 1638
C. 1640 D. 1623

112. The only play missing from the first folio is:
A. The Winter's Tale
B. The Merry Wives of Windsor
C. Pericles
D. A Midsummer Night's Dream

113. Shakespeare wrote his plays in:
A. Rhyming couplets B. Blank verse
C. Quatrains D. Iambic metre

114. The Jew with whom Shakespeare showed sympathy in one of his plays is:
A. Morose B. Barabbas
C. Nicodemus D. Shylock

115. Puck Goodfellow in *A Midsummer Night's Dream* is a/an:
A. impish fairy B. courtier
C. moneylender D. soldier

116. The downfall of Shakespeare's tragic characters is owing to:
A. the Will of God
B. a fatal flaw in character
C. destiny
D. evil advisers

117. Shakespeare got the plot of most of his plays from:
A. Existing plays
B. Ben Jonson
C. The original classics
D. Translations of Greek, Roman and other European stories.

118. Although Macbeth is a murderer, he is still the hero because:
A. he wants to become the king
B. his life ends tragically
C. he shows uncommon intelligence and vitality
D. he refuses to surrender

119. The part of a play where all the major themes and characters are introduced is known as:
A. Revelation B. Exposition
C. Chorus D. Introduction

120. Among Shakespeare's 37 plays, *Macbeth* was .... in order of being published.
A. 28th B. 26th
C. 30th D. 35th

121. Feminine ending refers to :
A. a stressed final syllable in a line of verse
B. the ending of a poem in a stressed syllable
C. the ending of a poem in an unstressed syllable
D. an unstressed final syllable in a line of verse

122. Johnson's edition of Shakespeare appeared in:
A. 1752 B. 1765
C. 1791 D. 1760

123. After Shakespeare made his debut as a London playwright, he was described as an 'upstart crow' by :
A. Robert Greene
B. Thomas Lodge
C. Christopher Marlowe
D. John Lyly

124. The term 'metaphysical poets', was first used by:
A. Ben Jonson B. Dr. Johnson
C. Helen Gardner D. Dryden

125. Which are the figures of speech used in the following lines by Blake?
"Tyger, tyger, burning bright
In the forest of the night,
What immortal hand or eye
Could frame thy fearful symmetry?"
A. simile and personification
B. irony and synecdoche
C. apostrophe and synecdoche
D. metonymy and apostrophe

126. More's Latin Masterpiece *Utopia* was translated into English in :
A. 1551 B. 1498
C. 1516 D. 1532

127. The Gutenberg Bible was first published in:
A. 1456 B. 1516
C. 1449 D. 1498

128. Restoration Comedy marks the restoration of :
A. women's rights B. democracy
C. monarchy D. human rights

129. "Hamartia" means :
A. reversal of fortunes
B. purgation of emotions
C. depravity
D. error of judgement

130. The term "gothic", a category of fiction, also applies to:
A. architecture B. painting
C. music D. theater

131. "John is six feet tall and 240 lb" is an assertion of:
A. a fact B. a judgement
C. an opinion D. an inference

132. What is the pseudonym of John Galsworthy?
A. John Gals B. Elia
C. John Sinjohn D. Boz

133. "I wandered lonely as a cloud" makes an assertion that:
A. The poet travelled with the cloud
B. The poet moved aimlessly with the cloud
C. Both the poet and the cloud were lonely
D. The poet moved as aimlessly as the cloud

134. Which was Galsworthy's first published novel?
A. Jocelyn B. A Man of Devon
C. Villa Rubcin D. The Science

135. The First Folio of Shakespeare's plays appeared in:
A. 1664 B. 1631
C. 1623 D. 1650

136. Restoration comedy begins with:
A. Congreve B. Sheridan
C. Dryden D. Etherege

137. The soul of tragedy, according to Aristotle is:
A. Thought B. Character
C. Plot D. Spectacle

138. "United we stand, divided we fall" is an example of:
A. Antithesis B. Bathos
C. Tautology D. Litotes

139. A metre in which an unaccented syllable precedes the accented is called:
A. anapaestic B. dactylic
C. catalectic D. iambic

140. Which play analyses the impact of modern publicity on private domestic tragedy?
A. The Show B. Escape
C. Jocelyn D. None of these

141. Miracle plays are based on the lives of :

A. Knights B. Crusaders
C. Pilgrims D. Saints

142. A metrical foot consisting of an unstressed syllable followed by a stressed syllable is:

A. dactyl B. trochee
C. iamb D. anapaest

143. Using "the Bench" for the judiciary is an example of :

A. metaphor B. irony
C. synecdoche D. metonymy

144. Four feet, comprising a monosyllable, trochee, dactyl and first paeon is often called:

A. running rhythm
B. sprung rhythm
C. blank verse
D. rhymed verse

145. "Essays of Elia" are:

A. political ideology
B. economic disparity
C. literary criticism
D. personal impressions

ANSWERS

1	2	3	4	5	6	7	8	9	10
A	C	A	B	B	C	D	B	D	B
11	12	13	14	15	16	17	18	19	20
C	B	C	C	D	A	C	A	D	A
21	22	23	24	25	26	27	28	29	30
A	A	B	C	D	B	A	B	B	B
31	32	33	34	35	36	37	38	39	40
C	A	C	B	A	C	D	C	B	C
41	42	43	44	45	46	47	48	49	50
D	C	A	A	C	A	B	C	B	A
51	52	53	54	55	56	57	58	59	60
B	C	D	A	D	C	C	C	A	B
61	62	63	64	65	66	67	68	69	70
D	C	A	A	C	A	A	A	B	C
71	72	73	74	75	76	77	78	79	80
B	A	D	B	A	D	D	C	A	C
81	82	83	84	85	86	87	88	89	90
B	B	A	A	B	A	B	B	C	B
91	92	93	94	95	96	97	98	99	100
A	A	A	C	A	A	C	D	B	C
101	102	103	104	105	106	107	108	109	110
A	C	A	C	D	B	C	C	B	A
111	112	113	114	115	116	117	118	119	120
D	C	B	D	A	B	D	C	B	A
121	122	123	124	125	126	127	128	129	130
C	B	A	B	D	A	A	C	D	A
131	132	133	134	135	136	137	138	139	140
A	C	D	A	C	A	C	A	B	A
141	142	143	144	145					
D	C	C	B	D					

4 Literary General Knowledge

NOBEL PRIZE FOR LITERATURE 2000–2013

Year	Laureate	Country	Language	Genre(s)
2000	Gao Xingjian	China, France	Chinese	novel, drama, literary criticism
2001	V. S. Naipaul	United Kingdom Trinidad & Tobago	English	novel, essay
2002	Imre Kertesz	Hungary	Hungarian	novel
2003	J. M. Coetzee	South Africa	English	novel, essay, translation
2004	Elfriede Jelinek	Austria	German	novel, drama
2005	Harold Pinter	United Kingdom	English	drama
2006	Orhan Pamuk	Turkey	Turkish	novel, screenplay, essay
2007	Doris Lessing	United Kingdom	English	novel, drama, poetry, short story, memoirs
2008	J. M. G. Le Clezio	France Mauritius	French translation	novel, short story, essay
2009	Herta Muller	Germany Romania	German	novel, poetry
2010	Mario Vargas Llosa	Peru Spain	Spanish drama	novel, short story, essay
2011	Tomas Transtromer	Sweden	Swedish	poetry, translation
2012	Mo Yan	China	Chinese	novel, short story
2013	Alice Munro	Canada	English	short story

MAN BOOKER PRIZE (2000-2013)

Year	Winner	Book	Genre	Country
2000	Margaret Atwood	The Blind Assassin	Novel	Canada
2001	Peter Carey	True History of the Kelly Gang	Historical novel	Australia
2002	Yann Martel	Life of Pi	Fantasy novel	Canada
2003	DBC Pierre	Vernon God Little	Novel	Australia, Mexico
2004	Alan Hollinghurst	The Line of Beauty	Historical novel	United Kingdom

Year	Winner	Book	Genre	Country
2005	John Banville	The Sea	Novel	Ireland
2006	Kiran Desai	The Inheritance of Loss	Novel	India
2007	Anne Enright	The Gathering	Novel	Ireland
2008	Aravind Adiga	The White Tiger	Novel	India
2009	Hilary Mantel	Wolf Hall	Historical novel	United Kingdom
2010	Howard Jacobson	The Finkler Question	Novel	United Kingdom
2011	Julian Barnes	The Sense of an Ending	Novel	United Kingdom
2012	Hilary Mantel	Bring Up the Bodies	Historical novel	United Kingdom
2013	Eleanor Catton	The Luminaries	Historical novel	New Zealand

FAMOUS BOOKS AND AUTHORS

Book	Author
A Secular Agenda	Arun Shourie
A Suitable Boy	Vikram Seth
Accession of Extinction	D.R. Mankekar
Adam Beda	George Eliot
Adonis	P.B. Shelley
Adventures of Huckleberry Finn	Mark Twain
Adventures of Sherlock Holmes	Arthur Conan Doyle
Adventures of Tom Sawyer	Mark Twain
Advise and Consent	Allen Drury
Affluent Society	J.K. Galbraith
After the Dark Night	S.M. Ali
Age of Reason	Jean Paul Sartre
The Agony and the Ecstasy	Irving Stone
Airport	Arthur Hailey
Alchemist, The	Ben Jonson
Alice in Wonderland	Lewis Carroll
All is Well that Ends Well	William Shakespeare
All Quite on the Western Front	Erich Maria Remarque
All the President's Men	Carl Bernestin and Bob Woodward
All the Prime Minister's Men	Janardhan Thakur
All things Bright and Beautiful	James Herroit
Ambassador's Journal	J.K. Galbraith
Ambassador's Report	Chester Bowles
An American Tragedy	Theodore Drieser
An Autobiography	Jawaharlal Nehru
An Eye to China	David Selbourne

Book	Author
An Idealist View of Life	Dr. S. Radhakrishnan
An Unknown Indian	Nirad C. Choudhury
Anandmath	Bankim Chandra Chatterjee
Ancient Mariner	Samuel Taylor Coleridge
And Quiet Flows the Don	Mikhail Sholokhov
Androcles and the Lion	George Bernard Shaw
Animal Farm, The	George Orwell
Anna Karenina	Count Leo Tolstoy
Another Life	Derek Walcott
Answer of History	Mohammed Raza Pahlavi
Antony and Cleopatra	William Shakespeare
Ape and Essence	A. Huxley
Apple Cart	George Bernard Shaw
Arabian Nights	Sir Richard Burton
Area of Darkness	V.S. Naipaul
Arms and the Man	George Bernard Shaw
Around the World in Eighty days	Jules Verne
Arrangement, The	Elia Kazan
Arrival and Departure	Arthur Koestler
Arrowsmith	Sinclair Lewis
As You Like It	William Shakespeare
Ascent of the Everest	Sir John Hunt
Asian Drama	Gunnar Myrdal
Asia and Western Dominance	K.M. Panikkar
Atoms of Hope	Mohan Sundara Rajan
August 1914	Alexander Solzhenitsyn
August Coup, The	Mikhail S. Gorbachev
Autumn Leaves	O. Pulla Reddi
Babbit	Sinclair Lewis
Back of Methuselah	George Bernard Shaw
Backward Place, A	Ruth P. Jhabwala
Bandicoot Run	Manohar Malgonkar
Bangla Desh The Unfinished Revolution	Lawrence Liftschultz
Banyan Tree, The	Hugh Tinker
Beast and Man	Murry Midgely
Beginning of the Beginning	Acharya Rajneesh
Betrayal of Pearl Harbour	James Rusbridge and Eric Nave
Bend in the Ganges, A	Manohar Malgonkar

Book	*Author*
Ben Hur	Lewis Wallace
Bermuda Triangle	Charles Berlitz
Berry Patches	Yevgeny Yevtushenko
Best and the Brightest, The	David Halberstan
Between the Lines	Kuldip Nayar
Beyond Modernisation, Beyond Self	Sisir Kumar Ghose
Big Breach, The	Richard Tomlinson
Big Fisherman, The	Lloyd C. Douglas
Biographia Literaria	Samuel Taylor Coleridge
Birth and Death of Sun	George Gamow
Bitter Sweet	Noel Coward
Black Arrow, The	Robert Louis Stevenson
Blind Ambitions	John Dean
Blind Beauty	Boris Pasternak
Blind Men of Hindustan ! Indo-Pak Nuclear War	General K.S. Sundarji
Bliss was it in that Dawn	Minoo Masani
Bloodline	Sidney Sheldon
Blue Bird	Maurice Macterlink
Bone People, The	Kerl Hulme
Born Free	Joy Adamson
Bread, Beauty and Revolution	Khwaja Ahmed Abbas
Breakthrough	Gen. Moshe Dayan
Bride for the Sahib and other Stories, A	Khushwant Singh
Bride's Book of Beauty, The	Mulk Raj Anand
Broken Wings	Sarojini Naidu
Brothers Karamazhov	Fyodor Dostoevsky
Bubble, The	Mulk Raj Anand
Bunch of Old Letters, A	Jawaharlal Nehru
Butterfield-8	John O' Hara
By Love Possessed	James Cozzens
Caesar and Cleopatra	George Bernard Shaw
Cancer Ward	Alexander Solzhenitsyn
Candida	George Bernard Shaw
Candide	Voltaire
Canterbury Tales	Geoffery Chaucer
Cardinal, The	Henry M. Robinson
Centennial	James Michener

Book	*Author*
Cherry Orchard	Anton Chekov
Chesaplake	James A. Michener
Children of Gebelawi	Naguib Mahfouz
Childe Herolds Pilgrimage	Lord Byron
China Passage, A	J.K. Galbraith
China's Watergate	Leo Goodstadt
Chinese Betrayal	B.N. Mullick
Chronicle of a Death Foretold	Gabrel Garcia Marquez
Class, The	Eric Segal
Climate of Treason	Andrew Boyle
Comedy of Errors	William Shakespeare
Common Sense	Thomas Paine
Comus	John Milton
Communist Manifesto	Karl Marx
Confessions	J.J. Rousseau
Confessions of a Lover	Mulk Raj Anand
Confessions of an Opium Eater, The	Thomas Dequicey
Confidential Clerk	T.S. Eliot
Conquest of Self	M.K. Gandhi
Conservationist, The	Ms. Nadine Gordimer
Continent of Circle	Nirad C. Choudhury
Coolie	Mulk Raj Anand
Coup, The	John Updike
Count of Monte Cristo	Alexander Dumas
Court Dancer	Rabindra Nath Tagore
Covertly Papers	Joseph Addison
Cresent Moon	Rabindra Nath Tagore
Crescent over Kashmir	Anil Maheshwari
Crime and Punishment	Fyodor Dostoevsky
Crisis into Chaos	E.M.S. Namboodiripad
Crisis in India, The	Ronald Segal
Critique of Pure Reason, A	Immanuel Kant
Crown and the Loincloth, The	Chaman Nahal
Crown of Wild Olive, The	John Ruskin
Cry My Beloved Country	Alan Patan
Culture in the Vanity Bag	Nirad C. Choudhury
Curtain Raisers	K. Natwar Singh
Dangerous Summer, The	Ernest Hemingway

Book	*Author*
Darkness at Noon	Arthur Keostler
Dark Room, The	R.K. Narayan
Das Kapital	Karl Marx
Daughter of the East	Benazir Bhutto
David Copperfield	Charles Dickens
Day in Shadow, The	Nayantara Sehgal
Days of His Grace	Eyvind Johnson
Dean's December	Saul Below
Death of a City	Amrita Pritam
Death of a Patriot	R.E. Harrington
Death of a President	William Manchester
Death, The Supreme Friend	Kakasaheb Kalelkar
Debacle	Emile Zola
Decameron	Giovanni Boccaccio
Decline and Fall of the Roman Empire	Edward Gibbon
Decline and Fall of Indira Gandhi	D.R. Mankekar and Kamala Mankekar
Decline of the West	O Spengier
Delhi	Khushwant Singh
Democracy Means Bread and Freedom	Piloo Mody
Democracy Redeemed	V.K. Narsimhan
Descent of Man	Charles Darwin
Deserted Village	Oliver Goldsmith
Die Blendung	Elias Canetti
Dilemma of our Time	Harold Joseph Laski
Diplomacy in Peace and War	J.N. Kaul
Discovery of India	Jawaharlal Nehru
Distant Drums	Manohar Malgonkar
Distant Neighbours	Kuldip Nayar
Divine Comedy	A. Dante
Divine Life	Swami Sivananda
Doctor's Dilemma	George Bernard Shaw
Dolls's House, A	Ibsen
Don Juan	Lord Byron
Don Quixote	Saavedra Miguel de Cervantes
Double Helix, The	J.D. Watson
Dragon's Teeth	U.B. Sinclair
Dream in Hawaii, A	Bhabani Bhattacharya
Dream of Fair to Middling Women	Samuel Beckett

Book	Author
Dreams Roses and Fire	Eyvind Johnson
Dr. Jekyll and Mr. Hyde	Robert Louis Stevenson
Dynamics of Social Change	Chandra Shekhar
Earth	Emile Zola
Earth Mother, The	Pupul Jayakar
Economic Planning of India	Ashok Mehta
Economics of the Third World	S.K. Ray
Education of Public Man	Hubert Humphery
Eight Lives	Raj Mohan Gandhi
Elegy Written in a Country Church Yard	Thomas Grey
Emile	J.J. Rousseau
Emma	Jane Austen
End of Era	C.S. Pandit
Ends and Means	Aldous Huxley
Envoy to Nehru	Escott Reid
Essays for Poor to the Rich	John Kenneth Galbraith
Essays of Elia	Charles Lamb
Essays on Gita	Sri Aurobindo Ghosh
Eternal Himalayas	Major H.P.S. Ahluwalia
Eternal India	Indira Gandhi
Executioner's Song	Norman Mailer
Expanding Universe	Arthur Stanley Eddington
Eye of the Storm, The	Patric White
Face to Face	Lasse & Mrs. Lisa Berg
Faces of Everest	Maj. H.P.S. Ahluwalia
Facts are Facts	Khan Abdul Wali Khan
Fall of a Sparrow, The	Salim Ali
Family Reunion	T.S. Eliot
Far From the Madding Crowd	Thomas Hardy
Far Pavilions, The	M.M. Kaye
Faraway Music, The	Svetlana Allilueva
Farewell the Trumpets	James Morris
Farewell to Arms, A	Ernest Hemingway
Farm House	George Orwell
Father and Sons	Ivan Turgenev
Faust	J.W. Von Goethe
Fidelio	L. Beethoven
Fifth Horseman, The	Larry Collins and Dominique Lapierre

Book	*Author*
Final Days, The	Bob Woodward and Carl Bernstein
Finding a Voice-Asian Women in Britain	Amrit Wilson
Fire Next Time, The	James Balbwin
First Circle	Alexander Solzhenitsyn
Flames form the Ashes	P.D. Tandon
Flounder, The	Gunter Grass
Food Nutrition and Poverty in India	V.K.R.V. Rao
For Whom the Bell Tolls	Ernest Hemingway
Forbidden Sea, The	Tar Ali Baig
Forsyte Saga	John Galsworthy
Forty Nine Days	Amrita Pritam
Freedom At Midnight	Larry Collins and Dominique Lapierre
French Revolution	Thomas Carlyle
Friends and Foes	Sheikh Mujibur Rehman
Friends not Masters	Ayyub Khan
From Here to Eternity	James Jones
From India to America	L. S. Chandrashekhar
From Raj to Rajiv	Mark Tully & Zaheer Masani
Gandhi and Stalin	Louis Fisher
Gardener	Rabindra Nath Tagore
Gathering Storm	Winston Churchill
Glimpses of World History	Jawaharlal Nehru
Godfather, The	Mario Puzzo
God of Small Things, The	Arundhati Roy
Gold Bat, The	P.G. Wodehouse
Golden Gate	Vikram Seth
Golden Threshold, The	Sarojini Naidu
Gone with the Wind	Margaret Mitchel
Good Earth	Pearl S. Buck
Grammar of Politics	Harold Joseph Laski
Grapes of Wrath	John Steinbeck
Great Challenge, The	Louis Fishcer
Great Depression of 1990, The	Ravi Batra
Great Expectations	Charles Dickens
Great Gatsby	F. Scott Fitzgerald
Great Illusion	Norman Angel
Great Tragedy	Z.A. Bhutto
Guide, The	R.K. Narayan

Book	Author
Gulag Archipelago	Alexander Solzhenitsyn
Gulliver's Travels	Jonathan Swift
Hamlet	William Shakespeare
Handful of Dust, A	Evelyn Waugh
Harry Potter	J.K. Rowling
Heat and Dust	Ruth P. Jhabwala
Heir Apparent	Dr. Karan Singh
Henderson, the Rain King	Saul Below
Henry Esmond	William Thackeray
Hero of our Times	Richard Hough
Heroes and Hero Worship	Thomas Carlyle
Higher than Hope	Fatima Meer
Himalayan Blunder	Brigadier J.P. Dalvi
Hindu Civilization	J.M. Barrier
Hinduism	Nirad C. Choudhury
Hindu View of Life	Dr. S. Radhakrishnan
Hounds of Baskervilles, The	Arthur Conan Doyle
House Divided	Pearl S. Buck
House for Mr. Biswas, A	V.S. Naipaul
Huckleberry Finn	Mark Twain
Human Factor	Graham Greene
Humboldt's Gift, The	Saul Bellow
Humour	Ben Johnson
Hunchback of Notre Dame	Victor Hugo
Hungary Stones	Rabindra Nath Tagore
I Am Not an Island	K.A. Abbas
I Follow the Mahatma	K.M. Munshi
Idiot, The	Fyodor Dostoevsky
Idols	Sunil Gavaskar
Idylls of the King	Alfred Tennyson
If I am Assassinated	Z.A. Bhutto
Illiad	Homer
Importance of Being Earnest	Oscar Wilde
In Afghanistan's Shadow	Salig S. Harrison
In Evil Hour	Gabriel Garcia Marquez
In a Free State	V.S. Naipaul
In Memorium	Alfred Lord Tennyson
In Search of Gandhi	Richard Attenbrough

Book	Author
In Search of Identity	Anwar-al-Sadat
India A Wounded Civilization	V.S. Naipaul
India Changes	Taya Zinkin
India Discovered	John Keay
India Divided	Rajendra Prasad
India from Curzon to Nehru and After	Durga Das
India Remembered	Percival and Margaret Spear
India of Our Dreams	M.V. Kamath
India, The Critical Years	Kuldip Nayar
India Today	Rajni Palme Dutt
India We Left	Humphry Trevelyan
India Wins Freedom	Maulana Abul Kalam Azad
Indian Home Rule	M.K. Gandhi
Indian Muslims	Mohammed Mujeeb
Indian Muslims The Need For a Positive Outlook	Wahiduddin Khan
Indian Philosophy	Dr. S. Radhakrishnan
Indian War of Independence	V.D. Savarkar
India's China War	Neville Maxwell
India's Priceless Heritage	N.A. Palkhivala
India	Magasthenes
Indira's India	S. Nihal Singh
Indira Gandhi's Emergence and Style	Nayantara Sehgal
Inheritance of Loss, The	Kiran Desai
Inner Circle, The	Jonathan Frost
Inside Asia (also, Inside Europe and Inside Africa)	John Gunter
Inside Third Reich	Albert Spencer
Intimacy	Jean Paul Sartre
Invisible Man	H.G. Wells
Iron in the Soul	Jean Paul Sartre
Isabella	John Keats
Islamic Bomb	Stev Weissman and Herbert Krounsney
Island in the Steams	Ernest Hemingway
Is Paris Burning	Larry Collins and Dominique Lapierre
Ivanhoe	Sir Walter Scott
Jane Eyre	Charlotte Bronte
Jazz	Toni Morison

Book	Author
Jean Christopher	Roman Rolland
Jinnah-India-Partition Independence	Jaswant Singh
Jobs for Millions	V.V. Giri
Judgement, The	Kuldip Nayar
Judge's Miscellany, A	M. Hidayatullah
Jullius Caesar	William Shakespeare
Jungle Book	Rudyard Kipling
Justice of Peace Ke Aansu	Janardan Prasad Singh
Kashmir-Behind the Vale	M.J. Akbar
Ken Attendant Godot	Samuel Backett
Kenilworth	Sir Walter Scott
Kidnapped	Robert Louis Stevenson
Killer Angels	Michael Shaara
Kim	Rudyard Kipling
King of Dark Chamber	Rabindra Nath Tagore
King Lear	William Shakespeare
Kipps	H. G. Wells
Kissinger Years, The	T.N. Kaul
Kublai Khan	Samuel Taylor Coleridge
L'Allegro	John Milton
La Divine Comedia	A. Dante
Lady Chatterley's Lover	D.H. Lawrence
Lady of the Lake	Sir Walter Scott
Last Days of Pompeii	Edward George Lytton
Last Maharaja, The	Jean Louis Nou and Jacques Pouchepadass
Last Thing	C.P. Snow
Laws Versus Justice	V.R. Krishna Iyer
Lead Kindly Light	Vincent Shean
Le Contract Social (The Social Contract)	J.J. Rousseau
Leaders	Richard Nixon
Leaves of Grass	Walt Whiteman
Letters from the Field	Margaret Mead
Les Miserables	Victor Hugo
Leviathan	Thomas Hobbes
Life Divine	Aurbindo Ghosh
Life of Dr. Johnson	James Boswell
Light that Failed	Rudyard Kipling
Lines of Fate	Marek Kharitonov

Book	Author
Lipika	Rabindra Nath Tagore
Living Room	Graham Greene
Lolita	V. Nabokov
Long Walk to Freedom	Nelson Mandela
Look Back in Anger	John Osborne
Lord of the Files	William Golding
Lost Child	Mulk Raj Anand
Lost Honour	John Dena
Lotus Eaters	A Tennyson
Love Story	Eric Segal
Lycidas	John Milton
Macbeth	William Shakespeare
Magic Mountain	Maharishi Ved Vyas
Main Street	Sinclair Lewis
Major Barbara	George Bernard Shaw
Making of a Midsummer Night's Dream, The	David Selbourne
Malgudi Days	R.K. Narayan
Malti Madhav	Bhavabhuti
Malavikagnimitra	Kalidas
Man and Superman	George Bernard Shaw
Man Eaters of Kumaon	Jim Corbett
Man of Destiny	George Bernard Shaw
Mankind and Mother Earth	Arnold Toynbee
Man, The Unknown	Lewis Carroll
Man for All Seasons, A	Robert Bolt
Man for Moscow	G. Wynne
Many Worlds	K.P.S. Menon
Marriage and Morals	Bertrand Russel
Masters, The	C.P. Snow
Maurice	E.M. Forster
Mayor of Casterbridge	Thomas Hardy
Mein Kampf	Adolf Hitler
Memories of Hope	Charles de Gaulle
Memories of Malgudi	R.K. Narayan
Men who Kept the Secrets	Thomas Powers
Men who Killed Gandhi, The	Manohar Malgonkar
Merchant of Venice	William Shakespeare
Middle Ground, The	Margaret Drabble

Book	Author
Middle March	George Eliot
Midnight's Children	Salman Rushdie
Midsummer Night's Dream, A	William Shakespeare
Mill on the Floss	George Eliot
Miser, The	Moliere
Mistaken Identify	Nayantara Sehgal
Moby Dick	Hermann Melville
Modern Painters	John Ruskin
Moon and Six Pence	W. Somerset Maugham
Moonlight Sonata	L Beethoven
Mother	Maxim Gorky
Mother India	Katherine Mayo
Mountbatten and Independent India	Larry Collins & Dominique Lapierre
Mountbatten and The Partition of India	Larry Collins & Dominique Lapierre
Mrs. Gandhi's Second Reign	Arun Shourie
Much Ado About Nothing	William Shakespeare
Murder in the Cathedral	V.S. Eliot
Muslim Dilemma in India	M. K. A. Baig
My Days	R.K. Narayana
My Early Life	M.K. Gandhi
My Experiments with Truth	M.K. Gandhi
My India	S. Nihal Singh
My Life and Times	V.V. Giri
My Music, My Love	Ravi Shankar
My Own Boswell	M. Hidayatullah
My Presidential Years	R.Venkata Raman
My Struggles	E.K. Nayanar
My Truth	Indira Gandhi
Mysterious Universe	James Jens
Naked Came the Stranger	Penelope Ashe
Naked Face, The	Sidney Sheldon
Naked Triangle, The	Balwant Gargi
Nana	Emile Zola
Nature of Mass Poverty, The	J.K. Galbraith
Nehru Family and Sikhs	Harbans Singh
Netaji Dead or Alive	Samar Guha
New Dimensions of India's Foreign Policy	Atal Bchari Vajpayee
Nine Days' Wonder	John Mansfield

Book	*Author*
Nineteen Eighty-four	George Orwell
1999-Victory Without War	Richard Nixon
Nixon in White House	Seymour M. Hersh
Non-Violence in Peace and War	M.K. Gandhi
Nuclear India	G.G. Mirchandani and P.K.S. Namboodari
O'Jerusalem	Larry Collins and Dominique Lapierre
Occasion for Loving	Nadine Gordimer
Odyssey	Homer
Of Human Bondage	W. Somerset Maugham
Old Man and the Sea	Ernest Hemingway
Oliver Twist	Charles Dickens
Omeros	Derek Walcott
One Day on the Life of Ivan Denisovich	Alexander Solzhenitsyn
One Hundred Years of Solitude	Gabriel Marquez
One World	Wendell Wilkie
One World to Share	Sridath Ramphal
Origin of Species	Charles Darwin
Oscar and Lucinda	Peter Carey
Othello	William Shakespeare
Other Side of Midnight, The	Sidney Sheldon
Our Films, Their Films	Satyajit Ray
Paddy Clarke Ha Ha Ha	Roddy Doyle
Pakistan Papers	Mani Shankar Aiyer
Painted Veil	W. Somerset Maugham
Painter of Signs	R.K. Narayan
Pair of Blue Eyes, A	Thomas Hardy
Pakistan Crisis	David Loshak
Pakistan Cut to Size	D.R. Mankekar
Pakistan, The Gathering Storm	Benazir Bhutto
Paradise Lost	John Milton
Paradise Regained	John Milton
Passage to England, A	Nirad C. Choudhury
Passage to India, A	E.M. Forster
Past and Present	Thomas Carlyle
Patriot, The	Pearl S. Buck
Personal Adventure, A	Theodore H. White
Peter Pan	J. M. Berrie
Pickwick Papers	Charles Dickens

Book	*Author*
Pilgrim's Progress	John Bunyan
Plans for Departure	Nayantara Sehgal
Portrait of India	Ved Mehta
Post Office	Rabindra Nath Tagore
Power and Glory	Graham Greene
Power That Be	David Halberstan
Prelude	William Wordsworth
Premonitions	P.N. Haksar
Price of Power	Kissinger
Pride and Prejudice	Jane Austen
Prince	Nicolo Machiaveli
Principla	Issac Newton
Prison and Chocolate Cake	Nayantara Sehgal
Prison Diary	Jaya Prakash Narayan
Prisoner of Zenda	Anthony Hope
Prisoner's Scrapbook, A	L.K. Advani
Professor, The	Charlotte Bronte
Promises to Keep	Chester Bowels
Pygmalion	George Bernard Shaw
Pyramids of Sacrifice	Peter L. Berger
Rage of Angels	Sidney Sheldon
Ragtime	E.L. Doctorow
Rainbow, The	Pearl S. Buck
Rains Came	Louis Bromefield
Rape of Bangladesh	Anthony Mascarenhas
Rape of the Lock	Alexander Pope
Razor's Edge	W. Somerset Maugham
Rebel, The	Albert Camus
Rebirth	Leonid Brezhnev
Red and Black, The	Stendhal
Red Badge of Courage	Stephan Crane
Red Star over China	Edgar Snow
Reflections of the French Revolution	Edmund Burke
Reminiscences of the Nehru Age	M.O. Mathai
Reprieve	Jean Paul Sartre
Republic	Plato
Resurrection	Count Leo Tolstoy
Return of the Native, The	Thomas Hardy

Book	Author
Returning to the Source	Acharya Shree Rajneesh
Revenue Stamps, The	Amrita Pritam
Rich Like Us	Nayantara Sehgal
Riding the Storm	Harold MacMillan
Rights of Man	Thomas Paine
Rise and Fall of the Great Powers	Paul Kennedy
Rivals, The	R.B. Shridan
Road to Folly	Leslie Ford
Robe, The	Lloyd C. Douglas
Robinson Crusoe	Daniel Defoe
Romeo and Julliet	William Shakespeare
Samler's Planet	Saul Bellow
Sands of Time	Sidney Sheldon
Satanic Verses	Salman Rushdie
Sanctuary	William Faulkner
Scarlet Letter	Nathaniel Hawthorne
Scarlet Pimpernal	Baroness Orczy
Sceptred Flute	Sarojini Naidu
Scholar Extraordinary	Nirad C. Choudhury
School for Scandal, The	R.B. Sheridan
Scope of Happiness, The	Vijayalakshmi Pandit
Search for Home, A	Sasthi Brata
Sense and Sensibility	Jane Austen
Sense of Time, A	H.S. Vatsyayan
Sesame and Lilies	John Ruskin
Seven Lamps of Architecture	John Ruskin
Seven Summers	Mulk Raj Anand
Shadow from Ladakh	Bhabani Bhattacharya
Shalimar	Manohar Malgonkar
Shall We Tell the President	Jeffrey Archer
Shape of Things to Come	H.G Wells
Shame	Salman Rushdie
She Stoops to Conquer	Oliver Goldsmith
Ship of Fools	Katherine Anne Porter
Shivaji, The Great Patriot	Lala Lajpat Rai
Shoes of the Fisherman, The	Morris West
Silas Marner	George Eliot
Six Characters in Search of an Author	Lugi Pirandello

Book	Author
Slave, The	Issac Bashevis Singer
Small Land	Leonid Brezhnev
Sohrab and Rustam	Matthew Arnold
Song of India, The	Sarojini Naidu
Sonnets, The	William Shakespeare
Sons and Lovers	D.H. Lawrence
Sound and the Fury, The	William Faulkner
Spaniard in the Works, A	John Lennon
Spirit of the Age	William Hazlitt
Spy Catcher	Peter Wright
St. John	George Bernard Shaw
Story of My Life	Moshe Dayan
Story of Real Man	Nikolayev Polevol
Strangers and Brothers Omnibus	C.P. Snow
Sunny Days	Sunil Gavaskar
Study of History, A	Arnold Toynbee
Swami and Friends	R.K. Narayan
Sword and the Sickle	Mulk Raj Anand
Tale of a Tub, A	Jonathan Swift
Tale of Two Cities, A	Charles Dickens
Tales from Shakespeare	Charles Lamb
Talisman	Sir Walter Scott
Tarzan of the Apes	Edger Rice Burroughs
Tears of D'Urberviles	Thoms Huardy
Tempest, The	William Shakespeare
Thank You, Jeeves	P.G. Wodehouse
The Garden of Life	Naveen Patnaik
The White Tiger	Arvind Adiga
Thieves in the Night	Arthur Koestler
Thirteenth Sun	Amrita Pritam
Three Musketeers	Alexander Dumas
Thorn Birds	Colleen McCollough
Thousand Days, A	Arthur M. Shlesinger
Through the Indian Looking Glass	David Selbourne
Through the Looking Glass	Lewis Carroll
Times Machine	H.G. Wells
Time to be Happy	Nayantara Sehgal
To Live or not to Live	Nirad C. Choudhury

Book	*Author*
Tom Jones	Henry Fielding
Train to Pakistan	Khushwant Singh
Traveller, The	Olive Goldsmith
Treasure Island	Robert Louis Stevenson
Trial, The	Franz Kafka
Trinity	Leon Uris
Triumph	John Kenneth Galbraith
Tropic of Cancer	Henry Miller
Tryst with Destiny	L. S. Gopalan
Twelfth Night	William Shakespeare
Twenty Years After	Alexander Dumas
Two Leaves and a Bud	Mulk Raj Anand
Two Women	Alberto Moravia
Ulysses	James Joyce
Uncle Tom's Cabin	H.B. Stowe
Unhappy India	Lala Lajpat Rai
Universe Around Us	James Jeans
Unto this Last	John Ruskin
Untold Story	General B.M. Kaul
Upturned Soil, The	Mikhail Sholokhov
Utopia	Thomas Moore
Valley of Dolls	Jacqueline Susann
Vanity Fair	William Thackeray
Vendor of Sweets, The	R.K. Narayan
Vicar of Wakefield	Oliver Goldsmith
Victim, The	Saul Bellow
View From Delhi, A	Chester Bowles
View From the UN	U. Thant
Village by the Sea, A	Anita Desai
Village, The	Mulk Raj Anand
Virginians, The	William Thackeray
Voice of Conscience	V.V. Giri
Voice of Freedom , A	Nayantara Sehgal
Voice of the Voiceless	Ruth Harring
Waiting for Godot	Thomas Becket
Wake up India	Annie Besant
Walls of Glass, The	K.A. Abbas
War and Peace	Count Leo Tolstoy

Book	Author
War of the Worlds, The	H.G. Wells
Waste Land	T.S. Eliot
Way to all Flesh	Samuel Butler
Way of the World, The	William Congreve
Wealth of Nations	Adam Smith
Week with Gandhi, A	Louis Fisher
We Indians	Khushwant Singh
We, the People	N.A. Palkivala
Where the Grass is Greener	David M. Smith
White House Years	Henry Kissinger
Wings of Fire	A.P.J. Abdul Kalam
Willhelm Meister	J.W. Von Goethe
Without Fear or Favour	Neelam Sanjiva Reddy
Witness to an Era	Frank Moraes
Woman's Life, A	Guy de Maupassant
Wonder That Was India, The	A.L. Basham
Worthy it is	Odysseus Elytis
Wreck , The	Rabindra Nath Tagore
Wuthering Heights	Emile Bronte
Year of the Upheaval	Henry Kissinger
Year of the Vulture, The	Amita Malik
Yesterday and Today	K.P.S. Menon
Zhivago, Dr.	Boris Pasternak
Zulfi, My Friend	Piloo Mody

FAMOUS AUTHORS IN DIFFERENT LANGUAGES

English	William Shakespeare, John Milton, Chaucer, Spenser, Lord Byron, P.B. Shelley, John Keats, Francis Bacon, T.S. Eliot, Cecil Dlay Lewis, Alduous Huxley, W.B. Yeats Bunyan, Dryden, Dr. Johnson, Alexander Pope, Robert Browning, Charles Lamb, Charles Dickens, Thomas Hardy, W.M. Thackeray, George Eliot, Alfred Tennyson, Robert Bridges, George Bernard Shaw, D.H. Lawrence, Oliver Goldsmith, Sheridan, Walter Scott, William Wordsworth, S.T. Coleridge, Henry Fielding, Somerset Maugham, J.K. Rowling.
French	Imile Zola, Gustave Flaubert, Moliere, Proudhon, Jean Paul Sartre, Le Sage, Victor Hugo, Alexander Dumas, Balzac.
German	Goethe, Hoffman, Lessing, Schelling, Schaupenhuer, Heinrich Heine, Guenter Grass
Russian	Tolstoy, Mikhail Solokhov, Turgenev, Dostoevsky, Maxim Gorky, Techov, Alexander Salzhenitsyn, Boris Pasternak
Greek	Homer, Aesop, Aristophanes, Euripedes, Herodotus, Hesoid, Theocritus, Xenophon, Aeschylus, Sophocles

Latin	Dante, Boccacio, Terence, Virgil, Ovid, Horace, Seneca
Norwegian	John Bojer, Ibsen
Persian	Ghalib, Umar Khyyam, Abul Fazal, Amir Khusro, Faiz, Firdausi, Mohd. Iqbal Saddi
Spanish	Juan Valera, Lope De Vega, Cervantes

FAMOUS CHARACTERS AND THEIR CREATORS

Character	*Creator*	*Character*	*Creator*
Adam	Milton	James Bond	Ian Fleming
Alice	Lewis Carroll	Juliet	William Shakespeare
Ancient Mariner	Coleridge	Jessica	William Shakespeare
Ariel	William Shakespeare	Jean Valjin	Victor Hugo
Antonio	William Shakespeare	Jacques	William Shakespeare
Anna Karenina	Leo Tolstoy	Jeeves	P.G. Wodehouse
Bassomio	William Shakespeare	King Arthur	Tennyson
Bertie Wooster	P.G. Wodehouse	Kim	Rudyard Kipling
Brutus	William Shakespeare	Long John Silver	R.L. Stevenson
Beatrix	Thackery	Macbeth	William Shakespeare
Beatrice	William Shakespeare	Micawber	Charles Dickens
Christian	John Bunyan	Miranda	William Shakespeare
Cordelia	William Shakespeare	Mephistopheles	J.W. Von Goethe
Cleopatra	William Shakespeare	Mellors	D.H. Lawrence
Clare	Thomas Hardy	Malaprop	Sheridian
Claudius	William Shakespeare	Oliver Twist	Charles Dickens
David Copperfield	Charles Dickens	Peggotty	Charles Dickens
Dushyanta	Kalidas	Priyangbada	Kalidas
Don Quixote	Cervantes	Portia	William Shakespeare
Eliza Doolittle	George Bernard Shaw	Pip	Charles Dickens
Estella	Charles Dickens	Perry Mason	Erle Stanley Gardner
Faust	J.W. Von Goethe	Pickwick	Charles Dickens
Gora	Rabindranath Tagore	Rip Van Winkle	Washington Irving
Hamlet	William Shakespeare	Sam Weller	Charles Dickens
Harry Potter	J.K. Rowling	Surpanakha	Valmiki
Hyde	R.L. Stevenson	Shylock	William Shakespeare
Hercule Poirot	Agatha Christie	Sherlock Halmes	Arthur Conan Doyle
Hawkins	R.L. Stevenson	Shakuntala	Kalidas
Hector	Homer	Sancho Panza	Cervantes Saavedra
Ivanhoe	Sir Walter Scott	Tess	Thomas Hardy
Iago	William Shakespeare	Watson	Arthur Conan Doyle
		Zhivago	Boris Pasternak

GREAT POETS

Language	*Poet*
Hindi	Surdas, Tulsidas, Keshav
Sanskrit	Valmiki, Vedvyas, Kalidas
Bengali	Rabindra Nath Tagore
Urdu	Mirza Ghalib
Persian	Sheikh Saadi
Latin	Virgil
Greek	Homer
English	Shakespeare
German	Goethe
Italian	Dante
French	Sully Proudhone
Punjabi	Waris Shah

GREAT INDIAN AUTHORS AND POETS IN ENGLISH

Kamala Das; Manohar Malgonkar; R.K. Narayan; Raja Rao; Mulk Raj Anand; Bhabani Bhatacharya; Sasthi Brata; Arun Joshi; Chaman Nahal; K.A. Abbas; Anita Desai; R. Prawer Jhabwala; Kamla Markandaya; Khushwant Singh; Manoj Dass.

WELL KNOWN QUOTATIONS

1. What's in a name? That which we call a rose By any other name would smell as sweet
— *Shakespeare: Merchant of Venice*
2. Patriotism is the best refuge of a scoundrel
— *Samuel Johnson*
3. Reading maketh a full man; conference a ready man; and writing an exact man
— *Francis Bacon*
4. It is excellent to love a giant's strength but it is tyrannous to use it like a giant
— *Shakespeare: Measure to Measure*
5. Water, water everywhere
Not any drop to drink
— *S.T. Coleridge: The Ancient Mainer*
6. It is strange but true, for truth is always strange
— *Byron: Don Juan*
7. Virtue is its own reward
— *Cicero: De Fintibus*
8. Frailty, thy name is woman
— *Shakespeare: Hamlet*
9. We don't fear to negotiate, but we do not negotiate out of fear — *J.F. Kennedy*
10. Give us good mothers and I shall give you good nation — *Napoleon*
11. I came, I saw, I conquered — *Julius Ceaser*
12. For fools rush in where angels fear to tread
— *Pope*
13. Generations to come, it may, will scarce believe that such a one as this ever in flesh and blood walked upon this earth — *Einstein*
14. Government of the people, by the people, for the people — *Lincoln*
15. East is east and west is west and never the twain shall meet — *Kipling*
16. Swaraj is my birth right
— *Bal Gangadhar Tilak*
17. Cowards die many times before their death: The valiant never taste of death but once
— *Shakespeare: Julius Ceaser*
18. Where ignorance is bliss, It is folly to be wise
— *Grey*
19. I know nothing except the fact of my ignorancc — *Socrates*
20. We are such stuff as dreams are made of and our little life is rounded with a sleep
— *Shakespeare: The Tempest*
21. Only free men negotiate. I shall never negotiate while I am still a prisoner
— *Nelson Mandela*
22. Truth and non-violence are my God
— *Mahatma Gandhi*
23. Let a hundred flowers bloom and let a thousand schools of thought contend
— *Mao Tse-tung*
24. Jai Jawan, Jai Kisan— *Lal Bahadur Shastri*
25. Eureka! Eureka! — *Archimedes*

26. Some are born great, some achieve greatness and some have greatness thrust upon them — *Shakespeare*

27. Where wealth accumulates, men decay — *Goldsmith*

28. Power tends to corrupt and absolute power corrupts absolutely — *Lord Acton*

29. Man is by nature a political animal — *Aristotle*

30. I have nothing to offer but blood, toil, tears and sweat — *Winston Churchill*

31. The woods are lovely, dark and deep
But I have promises to keep
And miles to go before I sleep
— *Robert Frost*

32. We have made a tryst with destiny — *Pt. Nehru*

33. Eli, Eli, Lamma Sabcathani (My God, my God, why last thou forsaken me) — *Jesus Christ at the Cross*

34. If winter comes can spring be for behind — *Shelley*

35. Man does not live by bread alone — *Bible*

36. Nothing is good or bad, thinking makes it so — *Shakespeare: Hamlet*

37. Garibi hatao — *Indira Gandhi*

38. Aram haram hai — *Jawaharlal Nehru*

39. Quit India — *Mahatma Gandhi*

40. Jai Jawan, Jai Kisan, Jai Vigyan — *Atal Behari Vajpayee*

41. A thing of beauty is a joy for ever; Its loveliness increases; It will never pass into nothingness. — *Keats: Endymion*

42. A little knowledge is a dangerous thing — *Pope*

43. Beauty is truth, truth beauty that is all. Ye know on earth, all all ye need to know — *Keats: Ode on a Grecian urn*

44. All the world is a stage and all the man and women merely players — *Shakespeare: As you like it*

45. Some books are to be tested, others to be swallowed and some few to be chewed and digested — *Bacon*

46. Better to reign in hell than serve in heaven — *Milton: Paradise lost*

47. The child is father of the man — *Wordsworth: My heart leaps up*

48. A single step for man — a giant leap for mankind — *Neil Armstrong*

49. Dilli Chalo— *Netaji Subhash Chandra Bose*

50. To be or not to be — that is the question. — *Shakespeare: Hamlet*

MULTIPLE TYPE QUESTIONS

1. Which Indian diplomat and author's work is *The Flying Troika*?

2. Name the Indian author and journalist, settledin New York, who became blind at the age of 3, and is a writer for *New Yorker*.

3. Who is credited to have authored the first modern Indian novel in English, *Rajmohan's Wife*?

4. Which British Prime Minister (1951-55), won Nobel Prize for literature?

5. Name the Indian writer and social critic, whose work includes *Autobiography of an Unknown Indian*.

6. Which English satirist's work is *Gulliver's Travels?*

7. Which India-born British writer's controversial book *The Satanic Verses* made Iran's spiritual leader Ayatollah Khomeini sentence him to death?

8. Which French novelist and dramatist's works include *Jean-Christophe* (a ten-volume novel), biographies of Mahatma Gandhi and Vivekananda?

9. Which Indian president authored the *Hindu View of Life?*

10. Which Hindi writer's real name was Dhanpat Rai?

11. Name the Hungarian author of *Darkness at Noon*.

12. Name the ghost who narrates the stories to king Vikramaditya.

13. Who wrote the famous sea-story *The Cruel Sea*?

14. Which country is the setting for the famous story of *Alibaba and the Forty Thieves*?

15. Name the authors of the following books:

A. *Making Peace with Partition*

B. *The Grapes of Wrath*

16. Who wrote the book *Pather Panchali*?

17. Which staunch socialist leader of India wrote *Prison Diary*?

18. Who wrote *Small is Beautiful: A study of Economics as if people Mattered*?

19. Who is considered the Father of comedy?

20. Who wrote the book *Somnium*, regarded by some people as the first science fiction to be written?

21. Name the British historian who authored the adage "power tends to corrupt and absolute power corrupts absolutely".

22. Which Indian Sanskrit scholar and poet wrote *Kadambari* and *Harsha Charita*?

23. Which Italian author and humanist, also called the Father of the Novel, wrote *Life of Dante*?

24. Who said it— "All the world is a stage And all the man and women merely players"?

25. Name the French educationist, who as a (blind) teacher of the blind, devised the touch system of reading and writing for blind.
(**Clue:** She died in the year 2000.)

26. Name the authentic book on statecraft by Chanakya (Kautilya) (4th century B.C.).

27. Which English poet wrote *The Canterbury Tales*?

28. Who wrote the following books:

A. Secrets of the World's Inspirational Women (Westland);

B. Gandhi : A Political and Spiritual Life

C. *Brushes with History : Autobiography of Dr. K.K. Birla*

29. Which football player's autobiography, released in 2007, is titled 'Moments'?

30. Along which famous road is Rudyard Kipling's novel *Kim* set?

31. Who are the authors of following works?

A. *Hidden Love*

B. *My Book of Human Rights*

C. *Devil May Care*

D. *A Prisoner of Birth*

32. Who was the first English writer to win Nobel Prize for Literature?

33. Whose autobiography is titled *Freedom in Exile*?

34. Who wrote *The Dream of the Red Chamber*, China's greatest novel?

35. Name the author of following Books—

A. *Reconciliation, Islam, Democracy and the West;*

B. *My Country: My Life* (Autobiography);

C. *Good-bye Shahzadi: A Political Biography of Benazir Bhutto.*

36. Which Indian freedom-fighter and staunch nationalist's work is *India Wins Freedom*?

37. Who has written the Tales Of The Future?

38. Which American historian wrote the 10-volume *History of the United States*?

39. *Songs of Innocence* is the work of which English poet, philosopher and artist?

40. Who is the author of *'The Enchantress of Florence'*?

41. Which Greek Philosopher and educator's work, *Dialogues,* includes the *Republic,* the longest and one of the most celebrated works?

42. What do you call the art of compiling dictionaries?

43. What was the pseudonym of Lewis Carroll?

44. Give the title of the book Jim Corbett wrote on animals.

45. Who is called the Father of English poetry?

46. What is the term for 'the fear of books'?

47. Which former Indian Prime Minister's autobiography is titled *The Insider*?

48. What is the title of famous Musician Pt. Ravi Shankar's autobiography?

49. A. Which book is considered China's greatest novel?

B. Who wrote it?

50. A. Who wrote *Mahatma Gandhi and his Apostles*?

B. What was the title of the book on Mahatma Gandhi by Romain Rolland?

51. Who wrote the book *The Great Indian Novel*?

52. Who wrote the famous sea-story *The Rover*?

53. Dr. Samuel Johnson's biography was written by ....

54. Name the Sanskrit writer who wrote the famous *Kamasutra*.

55. Which English author is known for his works like *The Time Machine, Kipps* and *The Outline of History*?

56. Which English writer developed the stream-of-consciousness technique and is known for works like *To the Lighthouse, Mrs. Dalloway* and *Orlando*?

57. Which Indian authored *Bread, Beauty and Revolution*?

58. A business tycoon of world fame, authored *Business @ the Speed of Thought*. Name him.

59. Who wrote the following books:

A. *Conquest of Self*

B. *Devdas*

60. Give the names of the authors of following books:

A. *The Book of Negroes*

B. *The God of Small Things*

C. *Hungary Stones*

D. *The Water Babies*

61. Name the sister of forceful novelist Charlotte Bronte who wrote *Wuthering Heights*.

62. Which Libyan leader and military dictator wrote *The Green Book*?

63. Which former British Prime Minister's autobiography is titled *Full circle*?

64. Which is the longest biography in publishing history?

65. Who is the author of best sold series of Harry Potter?

66. What is the pen name of K.K. Nair, who wrote a 10 volume *History of Literature*?

67. Who is the author of '*The Kalam Effect – My Years with the President*'?

68. Which is the longest single-volume novel of the 20th century?

69. Which Pakistani Prime Minister's autobiography is titled *Daughter of the East?*

70. Name the Russian-American novelist, poet, and an authority on butterflies, whose *Lolita* is world famous.

71. Name the German poet who wrote a poem appreciating Kalidasa's *Shakuntala*.

72. Who created the character 'Tarzon'?

73. In Arthur Conan Doyle's novels, who narrates the Sherlock Holmes stories?

74. Which English novelist and playwright wrote detective thrillers including *The Four Just Men* and *The Ringer*?

75. This 19th century Irish author and dramatist authored *An Ideal Husband*. Who was he?

ANSWERS

1. Kumara Padmanabha Shivashankar Menon (1898-1982).

2. Ved Mehta (b. 1934).

3. Bankim Chandra Chattopadhyaya (1834-94). He is often called the 'Father of the Indian novel'.

4. Sir Winston Churchill (1874-1965).

5. Nirad C. Chaudhary (1897-1999).

6. Jonathan Swift (1667-1745).

7. Salman Rushdie (b. 1946).

8. Romain Rolland (1866-1944).

9. Dr. Sarvepalli Radhakrishnan (1888-1975).

10. Munshi Premchand (1880-1936).

11. Arthur Koestler (1905-83).

12. Betaal.
13. Nicholas Monsarrat.
14. Persia.
15. A. Radha Kumar.
B. John Steinbeck.
16. Bibhuti Bhushan.
17. Jayaprakash Narayan.
18. Ernst Schumacher.
19. Aristophanes.
20. Johannes Kepler.
21. John Acton (1834-1902).
22. Banabhatta (7th Century).
23. Giovanni Boccaccio.
24. Shakespeare.
25. Louis Braille (1809-52).
26. *Artha Shastra.*
27. Geoffrey Chaucer.
28. A. Zerbanoo Gifford.
B. Kathryn Tidrick.
C. Sonia Gandhi.
29. Christiano Ronaldo.
30. Grand Trunk Road.
31. A. Angshumita Deka.
B. Jaya-shree Gupta.
C. Sebastian Faulks.
D. Jeffrey Archer.
32. Rudyard Kipling, in 1907.
33. Dalai Lama.
34. Cao Chan (he wrote 80 of the 120 chapters). Following his death in 1763, Kao Eh finished it.
35. A. Mrs. Benazir Bhutto;
B. Lal Krishna Advani;
C. Shyam Bhatia.
36. Abul Kalam Azad (1888-1958).
37. Jayant Narlikar.
38. George Bancroft (1800-1891).
39. William Blake (1757-1827).
40. Salman Rushdie.
41. Plato (427-347 B.C.). He was a pupil of legendary Socrates and teacher of Aristotle.
42. Lexicography.
43. Charles Lutwidge Dodgson.
44. *Man-eaters of Kumaon.*
45. Geoffery Chaucer.
46. Bibliophobia.
47. P.V. Narasimha Rao.
48. *My Music and My Life.*
49. A. *The Dream of the Red Chamber.*
B. Cao Chan wrote 80 of the 120 chapters of the book. Following his death in 1763, Kao Eh finished it.
50. A. Ved Mehta.
B. *Mahatma Gandhi.*
51. Shashi Tharoor.
52. Joseph Conrad.
53. James Boswell.
54. Vatsyayana (5th century A.D.).
55. Herbert George Wells (1866-1946).
56. Virginia Woolf (1882-1941).
57. Khwaja Ahmad Abbas.
58. Bill Gates.
59. A. Mahatma Gandhi.
B. Sarat Chandra.
60. A. Lawrence Hill.
B. Arundhati Roy.
C. Rabindranath Tagore.
D. Charles Kingsley.
61. Emily Bronte (1818-48).
62. Col. Muammar al Gaddafi (1924-2011). (He took power in a coup in 1969 and became President in 1977).
63. Sir Anthony Eden.
64. The ongoing biography of Sir Winston Churchill, coauthored by his son Randolph and the historian Martin Gilbert (both UK).
65. J.K. Rowling.
66. Krishna Chaitanya.
67. P.M. Nair.
68. *A Suitable Boy* (p. 1349) by Vikram Seth.
69. Benazir Bhutto.
70. Vladimir Nabokov (1899-1977).
71. J.W. Von Goethe.
72. Edgar Rice Burroughs.
73. Dr. Watson.
74. Edgar Wallace (1875-1932).
75. Oscar Wilde (1854-1900).

5 Glossary of Literary Terms

ABRIDGED EDITION: Condensed or shortened version of a work.

ABSENCE: It is a modern term which is used to explain a work of art on the basis of aspects which are absent rather than those which are manifestly present in the work.

ACRONYM:

1. A word formed from the initial letters of other words, *e.g.*
   NOIDA for New Okhla Industrial Development Authority.
2. The word may be considered synonymous to 'acrostic'.

ACROSTIC: It is a form of literary exercise in which the first letters of each line in a poem form a word as we read downwards. *e.g.*

"Wait, O little child, wait!
In the wind lies thy message,
Not in the hubbub of the worldly;
Else you may repent, says the sage."
(The word formed is "WINE")

ACT: Major division in a dramatic work.

ADAGEL: Maxim or proverb.

ADDENDUM: Addition or appendix to a book.

AESTHETIC REALISM:

1. According to Hudson, "Esther Waters" by George Moore was a landmark in this movement toward aesthetic realism.
2. This movement was the vehicle of the new realists of which Moore and Gissing were representatives.
3. According to Hudson, "they mistook mere ugliness for frankness and "seeing life steadily and seeing it whole."

ALEXANDRINE:

1. It is a line of six iambic feet instead of five.
2. It is not known for certain how this line originated.
3. It appears that it was evolved by Spenser by adding the Alexandrine to the eight-line stave (a b a b b c b c) of Chaucer that he used in *the Monkeys Tale*.

ALIENATION EFFECT: It was a term devised by the famous German playwright, Bartolt Brecht, who wanted to bring home the need, for realization of a kind of 'alienation' of the audience and the actors from the stage during the performance of a play, as the play being a play and not a part of real life.

ALLEGORY: When the abstract or spiritual ideas are presented through living images, the result is the allegory.

Examples of Allegorical Works

(*i*) The Pilgrim Progress
(*ii*) The Scarlet Letter
(*iii*) The Faerie Queene
(*iv*) Morality Plays, such as "Everyman".
(*v*) Seven Deadly Sins in Dr. Faustus, etc.

ALLITERATION: It signifies the repetition of initial consonant sounds, *e.g.* The furrow followed free.

ALLUSION: Allusion is a reference to a well- known person, place, event, literary work, or work of art. Writers often make allusions to stories from the Bible, the Mahabharata, Greek or Roman mythology, plays by Shakespeare, famous quotes by historical figures such as Mahatma Gandhi, political and historical events, and to other materials with which they can expect their readers to be familiar. By using allusions, writers can bring to mind complex ideas simply and easily. Gandhi used an allusion to the writings of the Bible when he said, "An eye for an eye turns the whole world blind."

ALMANAC: Book or table comprising a calendar of days, weeks and months indicating special occasions or events.

ANAGNORISIS: It means Discovery or Reversal in a Tragedy.

ANAGRAM: Letters or word or phrase which, when re-arranged, form a new word.

ANAPAEST: It comprises two unaccented syllables followed by an accented one:
(*i*) Redeploy
(*ii*) Introduce
(*iii*) Camouflage

ANDROCENTRISM: The term implies the predominance of man in all social and intellectual activities.

ANECDOTE: Brief account or story about an individual.

ANGRY YOUNG MEN: It was a movement which came into existence in the second half of the twentieth century, mainly as a result of Osborn's play: "Look Back In Anger."

ANNOTATION: Textual comment on a book.

ANTAGONIST: Antagonist is a character or force in conflict with a main character, or protagonist. In the Harry Potter series, for example, Voldemort is the antagonist. Not all stories contain antagonists; however, in many stories the conflict between the antagonist and the protagonist is the basis for the plot.

ANTHOLOGY: Collection of poetry or prose from diverse sources.

ANTITHESIS:

1. It signifies the setting of one thing against another, often of opposite sense *e.g.*
   'A *friend never* betrays, an *enemy always* does.'
2. 'Antithesis' can be expressed in literature also by presenting two aspects (of life) side by side, *e.g.* the real and the marvellous.

APHORISM: Short statement of a truth or dogma couched in memorable terms.

APHORISTIC ESSAY: Aphoristic Essays are impersonal essays. They are pithy and short essays packful of the author's knowledge, wisdom and philosophy of life. They are rugged and abrupt and difficult to understand on account of their depth of thought.

APOSTROPHE: It implies an exclamatory address to a person. (usually a dead one), some inanimate object or an abstract idea, *e.g.*
"Milton! thou should'st be living with us at this hour..."

ARCHAISM: It is a word or phrase which is no longer in use, *e.g.* loon, quoth, yclept, eftsoon(s), etc.

ARCHETYPAL APPROACH TO CRITICISM:

1. This Approach is also called Mythological, Ritualistic or Totemic Approach.
2. It endeavours to study literature on the basis of myth.

AREOPAGITICA: This is the name of Milton's famous prose pamphlet, pleading for freedom, freedom of the press, in particular.

ARGOT: Slang or coarse vernacular language.

ASIDE:

1. It is a kind of device similar to "soliloquy" (being probably comparatively brief) when a character speaks to himself.
2. The best example of an "aside" may be Shylock's words : "How like a fawning publican he looks" in Act, I sc. 3 of The Merchant of Venice.

ASSONANCE: Unlike the alliteration (which signifies the repetition of consonant sounds), it signifies the repetition of vowel sounds, *e.g.*
I *hear* him *bear* the mark of a *seer* on his head.

AUTOBIOGRAPHY: A form of nonfiction in which a person tells his or her own life story. Notable examples of autobiographies include Gandhi's My Experiments with Truthand Nehru's Towards Freedom. A memoir is a first-person account of personally or historically significant events in which the writer was a participant or an eyewitness and is a particular kind of autobiography.

AUTO SUGGESTIVE TEXT: The texts of certain very ancient books are not found in their authentic forms. Different editors or publishers modify them in their own way. Efforts should be made to discover their real or authentic form.

AVANT-GARDE: Without going into historical aspects of the word, one can say that it implies those (persons) who support or create the newest ideas, fashions (generally literary or artistic), techniques, styles, etc. in an art, piece of literature, etc.

BALLAD: The word 'Ballad' literally means 'a dance-song'. They generally sang of the brave deeds and heroic exploits of historical or legendary heroes and knights.

BATHOS:

1. It is a term to denote anticlimax.
2. It is generally used when there is sudden descent or fall from the sublime to the trite or ridiculous, *e.g.*
   Delay not thine departure hence,
   For thou mightst have a hot pudding, Awaiting thee.

BELLES LETTERS: Essays on literary studies and the aesthetics of literature.

BIBLIOGRAPHY: List of works on a particular subject or author.

BIOGRAPHY: An account of a person's life.

BLANK VERSE: Poetry with unrhymed line endings (usually written in iambic pentameters).

BLURB: These are the words of praise or description of a book in a nutshell, inserted usually by the publisher on the cover page or jacket of the book, to attract the reader's eye.

BOUND VERSE: Verse based on metrical pattern.

BURLESQUE: Burlesque is defined as 'an incongruous imitation'. It imitates the matter or manner of a serious literary work, or literary genre, but makes the imitations funny and amusing by a ridiculous disparity.

BOWDLERIZE: To 'cleanse' a work by omitting or cutting out indecent passages, phrases or words.

CACOPHONY: When the excessive use of high sounding words is made such that the meaning is lost or diminished in value in the sound, the result is cacophony instead of euphony.

CADENCE: Rhythm and phrasing of language.

CAESURA:

1. In classical prosody, 'Caesura' means "break between words within a metrical foot." (Concise Oxford).
2. In English prosody, it means "pause about middle of line." (ibid.).
3. A Caesura "which does not immediately follow the ictus" is known as 'Feminine Caesura' (Chambers 20th century).

☛ In modern connotation, Caesura implies natural pause in a line of verse and not an unnatural or forced one.

CAMPUS NOVEL: The Campus Novels deal with the life and problems of students in colleges and universities. They highlight the problems of education and careers of students during this formative period.

CANON: Collection of works established as genuine.

CANTO: Division of an epic or narrative poem.

CAPTION: Short description accompanying an illustration.

CARICATURE: The chief characteristics of characters are sometimes so exaggerated by the author that the characters look like some humorous or even funny creatures. The result is the creation of caricatures. This is what Dickens (more than any other author) has done.

CATASTROPHE: The final end of the tragedy is called catastrophe. At this point the hero or the heroine or both meet their tragic death. The tragic end comes through Hamartia and Perpheteia. It signifies the complete (often sudden) devastation of the fortunes of a character (often the hero and/or the heroine) in a play or piece of fiction.

CATALOGUE: List of books or works.

CATHARSIS: This is the term used for the ousting of the emotions of pity and fear in the tragedy.

CAVALIER POETS: The Cavalier Poets were associated with the Court of Charles I. They wrote witty and polished lyrics of live and gallantry. The group included Richard Lovelace, John Suckling, Thomas Carew and Robert Herrick.

CHARACTER: Character is a person or an animal that takes part in the action of a literary work. The following are some terms used to describe various types of characters:

- main character is the one on whom the work focuses
- major characters include the main character and any other characters who play significant roles
- minor character is one who does not play a significant role
- round character is one who is complex and multifaceted, like a real person
- flat character is one who is one-dimensional
- dynamic character is one who changes in the course of a work
- static character is one who does not change in the course of a work

- protagonist is the leading character or main character in a drama, movie, novel or other fictional work
- antagonist is a character or a force which actively opposes or is hostile to the main character or protagonist

CHARACTERIZATION: Characterization the act of creating and developing a character. There are two primary methods of characterization: direct and indirect. In direct characterization, a writer simply states a character's traits, as when F. Scott Fitzgerald writes in his story "Winter Dreams," "He wanted not association with glittering things and glittering people—he wanted the glittering things themselves." In indirect characterization, character is revealed by one of the following means:

1. the words, thoughts or actions of the character
2. descriptions of the character's appearance or background
3. what other characters say about the character
4. the ways in which other characters react to the character

CHORUS: The term Chorus is taken from Greek drama. In English drama it is applied to a character who speaks the Prologue and Epilogue and also communicates to the audience the exposition, setting and offstage events in the play.

CHRONICLE OR HISTORICAL PLAY: A Chronicle or Historical play deals with the life of a king or with some important historical event. However, the dramatist weaves an imaginative or highly emotional garb around it to make it appealing to the spectators sitting in the theatre.

CIPHER: Writing that employs substitution or transposition of letters.

CLASSIC:

1. A classic (in reality, any book) is "the expression of man" as an individual.
2. It is also the expression of his mindset and the stance taken by him.

CLICHE: Any word, phrase or expression that has lost its real effect for having been too frequently used by authors or laymen is called a cliche which may otherwise be quite lovable, *e.g.*

(*i*) The news is too good to be true.
(*ii*) The sorrow was too deep for tears.
(*iii*) Thanking you in anticipation, etc.

CLIMAX:

1. It is the main point of interest in a play or novel which is reached usually in the third act (or sometimes 4th or a 5th act of a play) or towards the end.
2. The resolution often takes place after the Climax or the forces for it start working or increase their intensity after it.

COLLOQUIAL:

1. In speech, the use of certain words and phrases which are not acceptable in standard speech.
2. Such colloquial expressions should be avoided in all formal speech or writing.

COLONIALISM: The term differs from 'colonization' as the term may imply political or economic control of policies in a political unit without real annexation of land.

COLONISATION: Literarily, the most significant modernist theories in the matter of

(*i*) colonisation
(*ii*) post-colonisation
(*iii*) decolonisation, and
(*iv*) neo-colonisation have been provided and practised by—

(*a*) Ngugiwa Thiong'o
(*b*) Soyinka
(*c*) Achebe Chinua, etc.

COMEDY: Comedy, in general, is a play of love, romance and marriage, joy and delight, wit and humour, light satire and irony exposing the follies and foibles of man good-humouredly. It deals with the light and trivial occurrences of life which are treated in such a manner that the ludicrous and comic element predominates.

COMEDY OF HUMOURS: Ben Jonson was the principal exponent of the Comedy of Humours. The Comedy of Humours was actually satirical comedy based on the classical concept of humours.

COMEDY OF MANNERS: The Comedy of Manners exhibited the artificial manners and low moral values of the high class society of the Restoration Age. They largely displayed the intrigues, witty remarks, sparkling dialogues and verbal fencings between gentleman and sophisticated ladies.

COMIC RELIEF: It is the name given to the brief light or comic dramatic action within the performance of a regular serious play to bring about a relief to the spectators to regain their real selves, for a short while to relax their strained nerves and prepare for further action, often more serious and culminating into breath-taking, gasping climax before denouement.

CONCEIT:

1. A conceit is a far-fetched or highly complex and even obscure or unintelligible comparison between two, often dissimilar, persons or objects.
2. It was commonly used by the Elizabethans particularly the Metaphysical poets, especially Donne.

CONCORDANCE: Alphabetical index of words in a work, or works by a single author.

CONFIDANT/CONFIDANTE:

1. In a play when a character takes upon himself/herself the task of some secret or information characteristic about a character to another, the character indulging in such an activity is known as a "confidant" (mas.) or "confidante" (fem.)
2. Such information or secret is generally in the matter of love.
3. A good example of a 'confidante' is Nerissa in the Merchant of Venice.

CONFLICT: Conflict a struggle between opposing forces. Sometimes this struggle is internal, or within a character; at other times this struggle is external, or between a character and an outside force. Conflict is one of the primary elements of narrative literature because most plots develop from conflicts

CONNOTATION:

1. It signifies the suggested or implied meaning of word as against the transparent or literary meaning.
2. Connotative devices are brought into play by the artists, poets in particular to enhance pleasure and acceptability conveyed by words and other expressions.
3. Poets like Keats and T.S. Eliot frequently resort to the device of suggestiveness which is akin to connotation.

CONSONANCE: Consonance the repetition of similar final consonant sounds at the ends of words or accented syllables. Emily Dickinson uses consonance in the following lines:

But if he ask where you are hid
Until tomorrow–happy letter!
Gesture, coquette, and shake your head!

CONSUMMATION:

1. When a work achieves complete satisfaction on all counts—literary as well as artistic, it is consummation that results.
2. An artist who has the knack, calibre or skill to make this achievement, is a consummate artist.

COPYRIGHT: Protective law to prevent pirating or plagiarism of an author's work.

COUPLET: Two successive rhyming lines in poetry.

COURT COMEDY: It is opposed to the Domestic Comedy in the sense that instead of domestic scenes it contains other elements which attract a different kind of audience, *e.g.*

(*i*) endless play of words
(*ii*) elaborate dialogues
(*iii*) repartees, jests, retorts, etc.

CYCLE: Group of works united by an overall theme.

DACTYL: Dactyl means one accented syllable followed by two unaccented ones, *e.g.*

(*i*) Lazily
(*ii*) Separate
(*iii*) Unspoken.

DEISM: A "deist" is a theist who believes in the existence of God but rejects the idea of a revealed religion.

DENOTATION: Denotation the objective meaning of a word, independent of other associations that the word brings to mind.

DENOUEMENT: The conclusion of a comedy is called denouement. Here all the obstacles and tangles that came in the path of true love are resolved and the lovers get happily married.

DESCRIPTION: Description a portrayal, in words, of something that can be perceived by the senses. Writers create descriptions by using images.

Description is one of the major forms of discourse and appears quite often in literary works of all genres.

DESCRIPTIVE CRITICISM OR PRACTICAL CRITICISM: Descriptive Criticism is a study or evaluation of individual works or authors. The critic evaluates their aims, methods and effects, and brings out their aesthetic beauty, emotional effect and literary significance by whatever criteria he deems fit.

DETONATION: When a word refers to its literal meaning independent of the meaning which the author may intend to convey, it is the device of "Detonation" which is at play.

DIABOLUS EX MACHINA:

1. The term literally means "devil out of the machine".
2. When all of a sudden a person or an event spoils the whole good game, causing unmitigated misery, it is the work of "Diabolus Ex Machina".
3. Thus, the term signifies sudden, unexpected turn of events for a plightful situation.

DIALECT: Manner of speaking pertaining to a particular class or geographical region.

DIALECTIC:

1. It was used originally to refer to the nature of a logical argument.
2. Later, it began to be linked to Kant, Hegel and Marx in varying forms.
3. The three generally accepted aspects of 'dialectic' are:
   (i) *Thesis:* It is akin to the (original) idea.
   (ii) *Antithesis:* It implies the inherent opposition in the thesis, which may operate after some time.
   (iii) *Synthesis:* It implies the resolution of the conflict to evolve a higher (or final) truth.

DIALOGUE:

1. Dialogue is something very important in any poetic or prose play or a piece of prose fictions.
2. (i) The nature of the dialogue, including its language depends upon the kind of the play—a tragedy, comedy, romance, etc. or the kind of the scene prevailing there at the time and place of the dialogue.
   (ii) Much also depends upon the taste of the spectators or audience which again is related to the spirit of the age.

A DIALOGICAL NOVEL: It is a kind of novel in which a number of voices, interactive in the scheme, operate in work, resulting in a kind of dialogue (or series of dialogues) as against the Monologic Presentation.

DIARY: Sequential private record of personal and other events kept by an individual.

DICTION:

1. It refers to the selection, arrangement and order of words.
2. The term which has become more popular in literary world is "Poetic Diction" to which a lot of space has been devoted by Wordsworth in his "Preface to Lyrical Ballads."

DICTIONARY: Book containing the words of a language, and their definitions, alphabetically; two-language dictionaries contain the corresponding words of both languages and their meanings, also alphabetically; any book that gives words and phrases about a particular subject, arranged alphabetically.

DIDACTIC: A work is didactic in nature when it undertakes to teach a moral, *e.g.* much of Wordsworth's poetry.

DIDACTIC LITERATURE: Didactic Literature is that form of literature that directly seeks to teach some moral or religious lesson. Allegorical works like Spenser's *Faerie Queene* or Bunyan's *Pilgrim's Progress* are didactic literature. Most of the eighteenth-century literature is didactic.

DIGEST: Publication where works are abridged.

DIGRESSION:

1. When a writer, instead of carrying on the main plot or incident, starts indulging in a side story, dialogue or descriptive narration, it is digression that results.
2. Digression gives extraneous pleasure which is not inherent in or indispensable to the main story.
3. Digression can sometimes enhance the value of a work but more often it mars its spirit.

DOCUMENTARY: Form of fiction or drama based on documentary evidence provided by newspapers, recent historical reports or other contemporary or recent factual evidence.

DOGGEREL: Rough, ill-constructed verse.

DOMESTIC COMEDY:

1. One of the earliest examples of the Domestic Comedies is "Gammer Gurton's Needle" (Cir. 1562)
2. It presents realistic life of the peasant class of its times.
3. It is full of fun and coarse humour.

DOUBLE ENTENDRE: Ambiguity in a word or expression, one of whose meanings is usually bawdy or frivolous.

DOMESTIC NOVEL: The domestic novels present the day-to-day domestic life of the middle-class families and their friends and relations. The festivals and festivities, functions and celebrations, birthdays and marriage are graphically described in them.

DRAMA: Drama is a long literary composition in prose or verse, developed through dialogues and action to be presented on the stage. While every other form of literature is complete in itself; drama remains incomplete without a stage.

DRAMATIC IRONY: It is a device occurring in a drama when a character on the stage is unaware of a fact which the audience know and understand.

DRAMATIC MONOLOGUE: 'Monologue' literally means 'Dialogue with the self'. In the Dramatic Monologue there is only one character who expresses out his own innermost feelings and thoughts through a long poetic speech. It offers a psychological analysis of the solo-speaker.

DRAMATIS PERSONAE: Characters in a play.

DUOLOGUE: Conversation between two characters in a play, story or poem.

EDITION: Total number of copies of a book printed from unchanged set of type.

ELECTICISM: The term implies the gleaning of facts or ideas from different sources instead of depending on just one source (or a few sources).

ELEGY: Serious meditative poem; often lamenting death.

EMPATHY: In a play or novel, when the reader or spectator begins to feel like the hero/heroine or some particular character as if he/she were that character, it is "empathy" which is at play.

EMPIRICISM: Empiricism implies the importance of experiment and experience in the matter of gaining knowledge.

ENCYCLOPAEDIA: Comprehensive work encompassing and describing many aspects of knowledge; specialist work covering compreh-ensively a subject or discipline.

EPIC: The Epic is the greatest and most sublime form of poetry. The Epic is a long poem, divided into several books, celebrating the life, heroic deeds and achievements of a national hero, whether historical or legendary.

EPIC STYLE:

1. It is a style which is dignified and exalted (as grand style is), as:
   (*i*) *Paradise Lost* by Milton
   (*ii*) *Aeneid* by Virgil
   (*iii*) *Iliad* by Homer
   (*iv*) *Hyperion* by Keats, etc.
2. Sometimes, it is, also referred to as 'heroic' style.'

EPIGRAM: A brief, pointed statement, in prose or in verse, often characterized by use of some rhetorical device or figure of speech.

EPILOGUE: It is the last item in a work of art (as in a drama) which often declares or comments upon the conclusion of the work.

EPIPHANY: Epiphany a sudden revelation or flash of insight.

EPISTLE: Direct address to another person, a 'letter' in the form of verse.

EPISTOLARY NOVEL: The Epistolary Novel is a novel of which the plot develops through the medium of letters. The characters exchange their thoughts and views through letters. There is very little dialogue face to face.

EPITAPH: Valediction to dead person or persons; inscription on a tomb or grave.

EPITHET: It comprises a word or group of words to describe the chief characteristics of a person, *e.g.*
   (*i*) Alexander the Great
   (*ii*) The Holy Bible.

EPONYMOUS: Person whose name becomes the title of the work.

ERASTIANISM:

1. It implies the doctrine that the state should have supremacy over the church in ecclesiastical matters.
2. Erastianism was one of the doctrines which was vehemently opposed by the followers of the Oxford Movement
3. The doctrine is probably wrongly ascribed to Erastus.

ESSAY: Short composition, usually in prose, discussing a topic or variety of topics.

EUPHEMISM: When an unpleasant expression has to be made in a comparatively pleasant or less harsh way, the mellowed or toned down words which are used express euphemism, *e.g.*
   (*i*) Instead of saying about a person "He acted foolishly, we can say, "He should have acted more wisely."

(*ii*) Instead of saying about a person that he has died, we sometimes say, "God Almighty has called him" or "He has left for his heavenly abode."

EUPHONY:

1. It signifies the pleasant combination of words which create desirable rhythms and tonal effects without interfering with the intended meaning.
2. An excessive use of such devices can lead to tautology or bombasticism and sound superficial or facile.
3. The generally accepted antonym of euphony is "Cacophony".

EUPHUISM: An ornate, floral style of writing popularized by Lyly.

EXPOSITION: It signifies a way of writing where explanations are not withheld or suppressed but manifestly made clear to the reader for immediate response based on clarity.

FABLE: A short narrative in prose or verse, often with animals, that points a moral.

FICTION: General term for an imaginative work, usually in prose.

FIGURATIVE LANGUAGE: writing or speech not meant to be taken literally. Writers use figurative language to explain ideas in vivid and imaginative ways.

For example, Emily Dickinson begins one poem with this description:

It sifts from leaden sieves,
It powders all the wood.

By describing the snow as if it were flour, Dickinson renders a precise and compelling picture of it.

FIGURE OF SPEECH (OR OF RHETORIC): It signifies the unusual use of words to heighten their effect.

FIRST PERSON: Style of novel, etc., in which narrator is a character.

FLASHBACK:

1. When a writer while presenting a situation suddenly refers to a past situation or event, it is the device of "flashback" that he exploits.
2. Browning, T.S, Eliot and Stream of consciousness novelists, in particular, take advantage of this device.

FOIL: Foil is a character who provides a contrast to another character. In the Arthur Conan Doyle detective stories, Dr. Watson provides a foil to Sherlock Holmes.

FOLK TALE: Story handed down by word of mouth from generation to generation.

FOOT: In poetry, rhythmic unit of two or three syllables.

FORESHADOWING:

1. It is a device in which the author himself prepares the spectators (or readers) for the catastrophe or some important event which may be on the cards.
2. Such a device checks the readers, etc. from suffering from the malady of disbelief.
3. Shakespeare is probably one of the greatest masters of this device, and it is sometimes believed that one of the main reasons of Shakespeare's grand success was his convincing mastery over the technique of foreshadowing.

FOREWORD: Short introduction to a work.

FREE VERSE (VERS LIBRE): Poetry free from mechanical restrictions such as metre and rhyme, cadenced according to meaningful stress.

FUSTIAN: It means the use of pompous, ornate, Euphuist or bombastic language.

GAZETTEER: Geographical dictionary or index.

GENRE: Genre a division or type, of literature. Literature is commonly divided into three major genres: poetry, prose and drama. Each major genre can in turn be divided into smaller genres. Poetry can be divided into lyric, concrete, dramatic, narrative, and epic poetry. Prose can be divided into fiction (novels and short stories) and nonfiction (biography, autobiography, letters, essays, and reports.) Drama can be divided into serious drama, tragedy, comic drama, melodrama, and farce.

GHOST WRITER: Person who undertakes literary work for another who takes the credit.

GLOSSARY: Alphabetical list of unfamiliar or uncommon words, usually appended to work in which they appear.

GOTHIC: Gothic the use of primitive, medieval, wild, or mysterious elements in literature. Gothic novels feature places like mysterious and gloomy castles, where horrifying, supernatural events take place.

GROTESQUE: Grotesque the use of bizarre, absurd, or fantastic elements in literature. The grotesque is generally characterized by distortions or striking incongruities.

HAIKU: A Haiku is a Japanese poem of seventeen syllables, in three lines of five, seven and five traditionally evoking images of the natural world.

HAMARTIA: Hamartia is the 'tragic flaw' in the character of the tragic hero who is basically a good and great man. This 'tragic flaw' becomes the cause of his fall, doom and death.

HAPLOLOGY: Omission in utterance of a sound resembling neighbouring sounds.

HAPLOGRAPHY: The inadvertent writing once of what should have been written twice.

HEROIC COUPLET: A couplet written in iambic pentametre is known as a 'heroic couplet'.

HEROIC DRAMA: Heroic drama was mainly written in the Restoration Age principally by Dryden. It tried to emulate the dimensions of Epic or Heroic poetry. Its hero was a great warrior whose fate affected the fate of an empire, such as Dryden's *All For Love*.

HEROIC VERSE: A poem written in heroic couplets is known as 'heroic verse,' *e.g.* Pope's poems such as:

(*i*) Essay Man
(*ii*) Essay in Criticism
(*iii*) The Rape of the Lock, etc.

HISTORICAL NOVEL: The Historical Novel draws its theme from some important historical event. But around this historical event the novelist weaves some imaginative and artistic environment to make it an interesting and arresting theme for a novel.

HOMILY:

1. It is a term pertaining to a work which instead of laying stress on artistic or aesthetic standards, undertakes to urge the readers on to a high moral life.
2. It is just like a sermon in a church.
3. Such are the most of the poems of Longfellow.

HOMOGRAPH: It implies a word which has the same spelling and pronunciation as another, but is different in meaning and origin from the other, *e.g.* :

(*i*) bear (*n*) an animal
(*ii*) bear (*v*) (to) tolerate
(*iii*) bear (*v*) (to) carry

HOMONYM:

1. It is "a word having the same sound and perhaps the same spelling as another, but a different meaning and origin"
2. Hence, *Homonymous* means: " having the same name : having different *significations* and origin but the same sound." (ibid.)

HYPERBOLE: It is a figure of speech which expresses an exaggerated statement to heighten the effect of a rhetorical statement, *e.g.*

(*i*) O child, may you never die!
(*ii*) Child is Father of the Man

IAMBIC PENTAMETER: Iambic Pentameter a line of poetry with five iambic feet, each containing one unstressed syllable followed by one stressed syllable. Iambic pentameter may be rhymed or unrhymed. Unrhymed iambic pentameter is called blank verse, which Shakespeare often used in his plays.

IDIOM: Form of expression of phrase peculiar to its language and possessing a meaning other than its literal one.

IDOLATRY: It means the worship of an image which is believed to be the abode of a superhuman being.

IDYLL: The origin of Idyll may be traced back to the Greek poet Theocritus, Idylls are small lyrical poems generally describing the scenes and pleasures of rural countryside. They depict country life as realistically and pictorically as possible.

IMAGE: Image is a word or phrase that appeals to one or more of the five senses—sight, hearing, touch, taste, smell.

IMAGERY: Imagery is the descriptive or figurative language used in literature to create word pictures for the reader. These pictures or images are created by details of sight, sound, taste, touch, smell, or movement. The following stanza, from Kuangchi C. Chang's "Garden of My Childhood," shows how a poet can use imagery to appeal to several sense:

I ran past the old maple by the terraced hall
And the singing crickets under the latticed wall.
And I kept on running down the walk
Paved with pebbles of memory big and small
Without turning to look until I as out of the gate
Through which there be no return at all.

IMAGISM: School of poetry (early 1900s) concerned with precise language, direct treatment, and freedom of form.

IMPERIALISM: It means the state policy for a country (as of England and certain other European countries, in particular during certain periods of history) to expand its area by annexing foreign lands and subduing the natives.

IMPERSONALITY: It means that the author himself should not be palpably visible in a piece of literature, in other words, the work should be done on highly objective lines.

IMPRESSIONISTIC CRITICISM: Impressionistic Criticism is that branch of criticism in which the critic evaluates a work by the impressions it makes upon his own mind. He expresses the attitudes and feelingful responses the work evokes in him as an individual.

INDIANISM: When an expression is commonly used in India but is not used by the English, it is called an "Indianism," *e.g.*

(*i*) 'demise' instead of 'death'

(*ii*) 'bearer' instead of 'waiter'

(*iii*) 'left for his heavenly abode' instead of 'died,' etc.

INTERIOR MONOLOGUE:

1. It is a device, as used by James Joyce in *Ulysses*, to express the thoughts, feelings and emotions of a character on usually more than one levels of consciousness.
2. It is a sort of inner debate which may or may not be conflict in essence.

INTERLUDES: The interludes were generally short entertainments inserted within a longer play or amidst some other festivities or festivals. Their primary function was to entertain the audience by humour or even by farce.

INTRODUCTION: Essay stating author's intention to reader.

INVERSION: It is the figure of speech (much used by Milton but ridiculed by many modern critics) in which words are presented in their unnatural order, *e.g.*

O God's glory I sing,

And to His Mercy I pray.

IRONY: It is a device used to convey a meaning which is the opposite of the apparent meaning, *e.g.* What a brave son of India Jai Chand was!

JINGLE: Verse or verses with strong rhyme and rhythm.

JOURNAL: Paper, periodical or magazine.

JUDICIAL CRITICISM:

1. It is the kind of criticism which is a sort of judgement on a writer or his work of art.
2. Such kind of best example is Pope's *"Essay on Criticism"*.

LEGEND: Story about a particular person containing myth and historical fact; explanation of symbols on a map or chart.

LETTER: Letter is a written message or communication addressed to a reader or readers and generally sent by mail. Letters may be private or public, depending on their intended audience. Letters to the editor are a common form of public letter.

LEXICON: Dictionary, especially for Classical and Middle Eastern languages.

LIMERICK:

1. It is a kind of humorous verse written in five jingling lines.
2. The form seems to have derived "from a refrain formerly used, referring to 'Limerick' in Ireland."

LINGUISTICS: The scientific study of language.

LITOTES:

1. It is akin to "understatement" which is sometimes used by writers to emphasise the desired meaning, *e.g.* India is not lagging in Information Technology.
2. However, more often it is an "understatement used ironically, especially using a negative to express the category as :

   'I shan't be sorry when it's over' meaning 'I shall be very glad', or 'It was no easy matter' for 'It was very difficult.'

LOCAL COLOR: Local Color a literary work of characters and details unique to a particular geographic area. Local color can be created by the use of dialect and by descriptions of customs, clothing, manners, attitudes, scenery, and landscape.

LYRIC: A Lyric is a short musical composition meant to be sung to the accompaniment of a lyre by a single singer. Now the term is used for any short non-narrative poem expressing a single thought or feeling of the poet.

LYRIC POEM: Lyric Poem a melodic poem that expresses the observations and feelings of a single speaker. Unlike a narrative poem, a lyric poem focus on producing a single, unified effect. Types of lyric poems include the elegy, the ode, and the sonnet.

MANUSCRIPT: Book or work written by hand.

MAXIM: Short statement or even sentence containing a general truth about human conduct and human nature.

MELODRAMA:

1. It was a crude form of drama which appealed to the groundings who were not much interested in the artistic minuteness such as the plot, characterization, etc.
2. They wanted only entertainment through striking scenes and absorbing movement of incidents and situations.

METAPHOR: A figure of speech in which one thing is spoken of as though it were something else. The identification suggests a comparison between the two things that are identified as in "death as a long sleep" or "the sleeping dead." A mixed metaphor occurs when two metaphors are jumbled together. For example, thorns and rain are illogically mixed in "the thorns of life rained down on him." A dead metaphor is one that has been overused and has become a common expression, such as "the arm of the chair" or "nightfall." Metaphors are used to make writing more vivid and meaningful.

METAPHYSICAL: The term 'metaphysical' was first used by Dryden in his assessment of the poetry of John Donne. The metaphysical poets were men of learning, and to show their learning was their whole endeavour.

METAPHYSICAL SCHOOL OF POETRY: The term 'Metaphysical' was first used by Dryden and further extended by Dr Johnson. It refers to a group of seventeenth-century poets who employed far-fetched imagery, abstruse arguments, scholastic philosophical terms, and subtle logic.

METRE: The rhythmical pattern if a poem. The pattern is determined by the number and types of stresses or beats in each line. To describe the meter of a poem, scan the lines. Scanning involves marking the stressed and unstressed syllables as follows, with the stressed syllables in bold and the unstressed syllables in italics:

"*Me* **thinks** *the* **la***dy* **doth** *pro***test** *too* **much**"
(Shakespeare's *Macbeth*)

The weak and strong stresses are then divided by vertical lines (/) into groups called feet. The following types of feet are common in poetry written in English:

1. Iamb: a foot with one unstressed syllable followed by one stressed syllable, as in the word: a**round**.
2. Troche: a foot with one stressed syllable followed by one unstressed syllable, as in the word: **bro**ken
3. Anapest: a foot with two unstressed syllables followed by one stressed syllable, as in the phrase: in a**flash**
4. Dactyl: a foot with one stressed syllable followed by two unstressed syllables, as in the word: **ar**gument

Lines of poetry are often described as iambic, trochaic, anapestic or dactylic. Lines are also described in terms of the number of feet that occur in them, as follows:

1. *Monometre :* It means a line (or verse) with a single iamb (foot)
2. *Dimetre:* It means a line with two iambs.
3. *Trimetre:* It means a line with three iambs.
4. *Tetrametre:* It means a line with four iambs.
5. *Penta metre:* It means a line with five iambs.
6. *Hexta metre:* It means a line with six iambs.
7. *Hepta metre:* It means a line with seven iambs.

METONYMY:

1. It implies the use of the name of some person or thing for another person or thing, *e.g.*
   (*i*) Have you studied 'Milton'? (Milton here means Milton's works).
   (*ii*) In the 'light' of these remarks: ('light' here means in view of....)
   (*iii*) Sceptre and Crown (i.e. monarchy) Must tumble down.

MIRACLE PLAY: A Miracle play is basically a religious play. They deal with the lives of saints and the miracles performed by them. The life and martyrdom of a saint formed the central theme of a Miracle play.

MOCK HEROIC: When an apparent epic is presented in a light vein, it is known as a "mock heroic" poem piece of fiction, etc., *e.g. The Rape of the Lock.*

MODERNISM: Towards the close of the 20th century, a movement against such modes as realism and naturalism started in all forms of literature and art such as poetry, drama, novel, music, painting, architecture, sculpture, etc. which continued unabated during the first world war period and partly upto the middle of the century.

MODULATION:

1. Of necessity, poetry is musical.
2. As in music, to avoid poetry from falling into "monotony," there is the system of "modulation" which here means, changing the key or tone, to introduce the element of variety to give or enhance pleasure.

MONOLOGUE: Single person addressing an audience alone, in drama, verse or prose. *Interior monologue*: unspoken but thought speech in verse or prose.

MOOD: Mood is the feeling created in the reader by a literary work or passage. Elements that can influence the mood of a work include its settling, tone, and events.

MORALITY PLAY: Morality Plays are allegorical plays. They present on the stage, personified Virtues and Vices. Everyman is presented as the Hero. Satan personified as Vice, God or Christ as Virtue, and Death as the Reward of Sin.

MOTIVATION: Motivation is a reason that explains a character's thoughts, feelings, actions, or speech. Characters are motivated by their values and by their wants, desires, dreams, wishes, and needs. Sometimes the reasons for a character's actions are stated directly, but other times the motives are implied or stated indirectly.

MYSTERY PLAY: The Mystery Plays basically deal with the themes taken from the Bible. They present in chronological order major events from the creation and fall of man through Nativity, Crucifixion, Resurrection of Christ to The Last Judgement.

MYTH: A fictional tale that explains the actions of gods or heroes or the causes of natural phenomena. Myths that explain the origins of earthly life, as does the Book of Genesis in the Bible and the Rig Veda, are known as origin myths. Other myths express the central values of the people who created them.

NARRATIVE: A story told in fiction, nonfiction, poetry or drama. Narratives are often classified by their content or purpose. An exploration narrative is a firsthand account of an explorer's travels in a new land. A historical narrative is a narrative account of significant historical events. Narrative poems also tell a story in verse form. Three traditional types of narrative verse are ballads, songlike poems that tell stories; epics, long poems about the deeds of gods or heroes, and metrical romances, poems that tell tales of love and chivalry.

NATURALISM: Naturalism was a literary movement among novelists at the end of the nineteenth century and during the early decades of the twentieth century. The Naturalists tended to view people as hapless victims of immutable natural laws. Authors include Jack London and Stephen Crane. Naturalism is a form of realism.

NARRATOLOGY: It means the study of different forms and structures of a narrative work in the matter of its various syntactical, literary and grammatical frameworks.

NEOCLASSICISM: Movement of late 17th and 18th century reviving classical values in English literature, emphasizing discipline, reason and clarity.

NEOLOGISM: Newly-coined word.

NEW WAVE (LA NOUVELLE VAGUE): Movement in literature and cinema originating in France in late 1950s that attempted to eschew fixed values, revealing a character by the way he experienced objects and events, which were often meticulously described.

NOM DE PLUME: Term used to indicate a fictitious name used by a writer to represent his work.

NON-FICTION: Nonfiction prose writing that presents and explains ideas or that tells about real people, places, objects or events. Essays, biographies, autobiographies, journals, and reports are all examples of non-fiction.

NOVEL: A long work of fiction. A novel often has a complicated plot, many major and minor characters, significant theme, and several varied settings. Novels can be classified in many ways, based on the historical periods in which they are written, on the subjects and themes that they treat, on the techniques that are used in them, and on the literary movements that inspired them.

NOVELETTE: Long short-story of some 15,000 words.

NOVELLA: Prose fiction longer than a short story, shorter than a novel (about 30,000 words), concentrating upon a single event. A novella is not as long as a novel but is longer than a short story. Ernest Hemingway's *The Old Man and the Sea* is a novella.

OBSCURITY: When a writer's language is not (or not easily) intelligible to the reader, the work concerned is termed as obscure.

ODE: An Ode is a long lyrical poem, serious in subject, elevated in style and elaborate in its stanzaic structure. It is in the form of an address to the object or the person about whom it is written.

OMNISCIENT AUTHOR: It is a device used by some outstanding modern novelists to move freely from the objective narrative to the internal or subjective psyche of a character or characters and then comment freely and apparently unattached on the significance, possibility or outcome of any or some events.

ONOMATOPOEIA: The use of words that imitate sounds. Examples of such words are buzz, hiss, murmur, and rustle. Isabella Gardner uses onomatopoeia in "Summer Remembered":

Sounds sum and summon the remembering of summers
The humming of the sun
The mumbling in the honey-suckle vine
The whirring in the clovered grass
The pizzicato plinkle of ice in an auburn uncle's amber glass

ORAL TRADITION: the passing of songs, stories and poems from generation to generation by word of mouth.

ORATORY: public speaking that is formal, persuasive, and emotionally appealing.

OXYMORON: It is a figure of speech in which two apparently contradictory words or terms are used to convey, a paradoxical sense, e.g.

(*i*) 'busy-idle days' (Lamb in *Dream children*)
(*ii*) Life in Death (Coleridge in *'Rime.....'*).

PANTOMIME:

1. A Pantomime is a dramatic representation pertaining to some myth, legend or traditional tale (or it may have some fairy element in it).
2. Pantomimes became popular in England particularly in the first quarter of the 18th century.

PARABLE: A story which conveys a moral lesson is known as a parable, as for instance, the biblical parables.

PARADOX: It is a figure of speech in which a truth is brought home through the use of self-contradictory statement, *e.g.*

(*i*) Cowards die many a time before their death.
(*ii*) Discretion is the better part of valour.
(*iii*) After death, we awake into an eternal life.

PARALLELISM:

1. It is a rhetorical device where balancing sentences, phrases or words are used to enhance effect, e.g. What is important is not what you say, but what is important is what you mean.
2. Excessive use of this device leads to monotony and superficiality.

PARODY: Comic imitation of serious words, style, sense, subject of a writer to make them appear ridiculous.

PASTORAL: Literature depicting idealized rural life.

PASTORAL ELEGY: It is an elegy cast into the conventional pastoral form. It is presumed that the poet is a shepherd mourning the death of a fellow shepherd. The whole image of goats, sheep, pastures and pastoral gods and goddesses is drawn into it.

PATHETIC FALLACY: When nature is shown as sympathising with human lot, the device used is called "pathetic fallacy," *e.g.*

(*i*) Byron's description of the battle of Waterloo in Childe Harold's Pilgrimage.
(*ii*) The behaviour of slow-moving nature in Tennyson's "Lotos-eaters".

PEDANTRY: The term refers to the excessive display of knowledge such as:

(*i*) Foreign words and phrases
(*ii*) Allusions
(*iii*) Archaic words
(*iv*) High sounding and sesquipedalian words
(*v*) Cataloguing, etc.

when these are not strictly needed within the context of the work.

PERIODIC SENTENCE: A sentence in which the Principal clause occurs at the end when it is preceded by one or more subordinate clauses, such that the sense is clear only when the whole sentence is read, is known as a 'periodic sentence'.

PERIODICAL: Magazine or journal published regularly.

PERIPETEIA: Peripeteia means sudden change in the fortune or position of the hero from good to bad, or high to low. This reversal of fortue happens due to Hamartia in the character of the hero.

PERIPHRASIS:

1. It means a round about way of saying a thing, *e.g.* An idle singer of an empty day, etc.
2. The term is close to circumlocution and euphemism in sense and effect.

PERSONAL ESSAY: According to Hudson, true essay is essentially personal. Montaigne says, "I am myself the subject of my book". In the Personal essay the author gives his own experiences, impressions of reactions about the subjects taken up for writing his essays.

PERSONIFICATION: A figure of speech in which a non-human subject is given human characteristics. In "April Rain Song," Langston Hughes personifies the rain:

Let the rain kiss you
Let the rain sing you a lullaby.

Effective personification of things or ideas makes them seem vital and alive, as if they were human.

PERSUASION: Writing or speech that attempts to convince a reader to think or act in a particular way. Persuasion is used in political arguments as well as in advertising, editorials and sermons.

PESSIMISTS: Although in English literature, we have a number of pessimist poets or a good number of poets expressing at times pessimistic ideas or writing sometimes in a pessimistic mood, yet two of the poets are known in particular, as "Pessimists." They are:

(*i*) Thomas Hardy
(*ii*) A.E. Housman

PHILOLOGY: Study of literature, language and linguistics.

PICARESQUE: Chronicle of adventures of a rogue; originated in 16-century Spain.

PINDARIC ODE: The Pindaric Odes are written on the model of the odes written by Pindar, the great Greak poet. They are choric in character and designed to be sung by a troupe of dancers in churches or public halls.

PLAGIARISM: Wrongful appropriation and publication of another's work as one's own.

PLATITUDE: It means a truth or generalization which is too well-known mainly because of its overuse, *e.g.*

Truth is evergreen.

PLEONASM:

1. It means the use of words more than those which are absolutely necessary, *e.g.*
   (*i*) He sat *down* on the ground.
   (*ii*) He looked up *high* towards the sky.
   (*iii*) He has got *sole* monopoly over such kind of business.
2. In essence, it is akin to Tautology or circum-locution.

PLOT: The plan or sequence of events in a literary work. In most novels, dramas, short stories, and narrative poems, the plot involves both characters and a central conflict. The plot usually begins with an exposition that introduces the setting, the characters, and the basic situation. This is followed by the inciting incident, which introduces the central conflict. The conflict then increases during the development until it reaches a high point of interest or suspense, the climax. The climax is followed by the end, or resolution, of the central conflict. Any events that occur after the resolution make up the denouement. The events that lead up to the climax comprise the rising action. The events that follow the climax comprise the falling action.

POEM: Literary work which may be in rhyme, blank verse or a combination of the two.

POETIC DICTION:

1. Diction stands chiefly for choice of words.
2. In poetry, poetic diction is unavoidable as mere metre is not enough to make a poem a literary piece of work.
3. In other words, mere versification or combination of words in rhyme or any other verse form does not make poetry.
4. The poets resort to several devices in this regard, some of which are :

(i) Use of similes, metaphors, symbols, inversions, and other figures of speech as such as hyperbole, irony, antithesis, personification, etc.
(ii) Omission of some parts of speech or grammatical rules.
(iii) Use of archaic or uncommon words,
(iv) Change in order of words, etc.
(v) Use of picturesque phrases and expressions
(vi) Use of other ornamental devices such as epithets
(vii) Use of highly musical lies, fanciful flights etc.

POETIC JUSTICE: The term 'Poetic Justice' was coined by Thomas Rhymer. It means exact reward or punishment given to a character according to his good or bad deeds. This exactness of justice is possible only in the world of poetry.

POETIC LICENCE: By 'Poetic Licence' it is meant a certain amount of liberty enjoyed by the poets in the use of grammar, word-order or coinage of words in order to produce greater poetic effects.

POETRY: One of the three major types of literature, in which form and content are closely connected, like the two faces of a single coin. Poems are often divided into lines and stanzas and often employ regular rhythmical patterns, or meters. Most poems make use of highly concise, musical, and emotionally charged language. Many also make use of imagery, figurative language, and special devices such as rhyme.

POINT OF VIEW: The perspective or vantage point from which a story is told. Three commonly used points of view are first person, omniscient third person, and limited third person.

In *first person point of view*, the narrator is a character in the story and refers to himself or herself with the first-person pronoun "I."

The two kinds of *third-person point of view, limited* and *omniscient*, are called "third person" because the narrator uses third-person pronouns such as "he" and "she" to refer to the characters. There is no "I" telling the story.

In stories told from the *omniscient third person point of view*, the narrator knows and tells about what each character feels and thinks.

In stories told from the *limited third-person point of view*, the narrator relates the inner thoughts and feelings of only one character; and everything is viewed from this character's perspective. The *Harry Potter* series by J.K. Rowlings is told from the limited third-person point of view.

PORNOGRAPHY: Work in which there is a deliberate emphasis on the sexual behaviour of characters, in order to arouse sexual excitement.

POTBOILER: Work written essentially to gain the author a livelihood.

PRECIS: Concise statement; short summary of a work.

PREFACE: Introduction to a work.

PRE-RAPHAELITE SCHOOL OF POETS: A group of painter-poets led by D.G. Rossetti founded the Pre-Raphaelite School of poetry. Other poets of this school were Christina Rosetti, Swinburne, and William Morris. They wrote highly sensuous, pictorial and symbolical poems which could be painted with equal effect.

PROLOGUE: It is often the original statement by the writer (as in a drama) which highlights the chief aim of the work which is going to be unfolded or staged.

PROPAGANDA: Work devoted to the dissemination of an idea or belief, usually biased.

PROPHETIC NOVEL: The Prophetic Novels try to forecast what the future would be like. They do not claim to be absolutely correct. They only give a tentative picture of the future on the basis of the tendencies prevailing in the present.

PROSE: The ordinary form of written language. Most writing that is not poetry, drama or song is considered prose. It occurs in fiction and nonfiction.

(MODERN) PROSE STYLE:

1. The English prose style started by Bacon, flourished in the hands of Addison and Steele and numerous essayists and prose stylists that followed.
2. As a fine example of the latest modern prose style, Naipaul who won the Nobel Prize for Literature in 2001 deserves to be mentioned.

PROSODY: Study of the handling of language in poetry.

PROSOPOPAEIA: This figure of speech is used when:

(i) The past (called the Historic Present) is written in the present tense:

Sohrab and Rustam clash with their full might.

(ii) The (anticipated) future is written in the present tense:

Here, we go to our new house tomorrow with all our belongings carried in a lorry and then tucked in elegant mahogany almirahs.

PSEUDONYM: Name other than the true one used by an author to represent his work.

PSYCHOLOGICAL NOVEL: The Psychological Novels are also known as the "Stream of Consciousness Novels'. These novels probe into the working of human psychology at the conscious, subconscious and unconscious levels.

PSYCHOLOGICAL PROCESS: It is the process applied to the study of a piece of literature to penetrate another's mind and to study the activities, utterances, etc. of various characters, as, for instance, to arrive at the exact nature of Hamlet's madness whether there was "method" in it or not.

PUN:

1. When a word gives several meanings (often for fun) as in a play, it is the "pun" that is used.
2. Shakespeare is a great master of this device.
3. **Example :**
   (*i*) This is the *book.*
   (*ii*) It means
      (*a*) any book
      (*b*) a holy book, often the Bible.

REALISM: Literature that attempts to depict life objectively and faithfully.

REFORMATION: Reformation was a religious Movement led by Martin Luther in the fifteenth century. It protested against the practices of the Roman Catholic Church. It advocated complete faith in the Bible and in one's own soul for salvation.

REFRAIN: Phrase, line or lines repeated at intervals or at the end of a stanza in poetry.

REGIONAL NOVEL: The Regional Novel is a novel which describes the social and family life, customs and manners, language and dress, occupations and professions of the people of a particular region. The entire novel is woven around these factors of the region.

RENAISSANCE: The term Renaissance literally means re-birth on revival. In Art and Literature it meant the rebirth or revival of Greek art, literature, culture and pattern of life which had been partly or largely destroyed by the repeated invasions of the Turks.

REVIEW: Notice or critical article on musical, artistic or literary work.

REVUE: Theatrical entertainment made up of sketches, dances, songs, recitals and improvised pieces, usually humorous, satirical or topical.

RHETORIC: Art of using language, in speaking or writing, to persuade. The persuasive style (rather than the content) of a work.

RHYTHM:

1. It signifies the measured regular beat or movement of sounded words in language.
2. Rhythm is a must in poetry as well as prose, as it introduces or enhances the element of pleasure, interest and curiosity.

RHYME: Echoing sound or audible similarity in two or more words, especially at endings. Device used to construct much poetry.

RIDDLE: Puzzle, question or enigma; conundrum.

ROMAN A CLEF: Novel based upon actual people under disguised names.

ROMANCE: Tale of chivalry, originally written in verse (Medieval times); term applied now to any wonderful or mysterious tale far removed from reality.

ROMANCE LANGUAGES: Languages which have emerged straightaway from Latin and/or Greek, are called Romance Languages.

ROMANTICISM: Romanticism has been variously defined by various critics and scholars. According to Walter Peter, "Romanticism is the addition of curiosity to the desire of beauty.

ROMANTIC COMEDY: The Romantic Comedy is basically a love comedy. There is usually a story of triangular love with two heroes and one heroine, or two heroines and one hero, but finally the play ends in happy marriage.

SAGA: Lengthy prose work, sometimes in several parts, describing the history and events surrounding medieval kings, warrriors and, recently, fictitious families.

SATIRE: Dryden defines the Satire as "a literary composition whose principal aim is to ridicule folly or vice. The true end of Satire is the amendment of vices by correction." A healthy satire good-humouredly exposes one's folly or vice.

SCIENCE FICTION: Literature based on scientific fact or fantasy, on earth or on other worlds in space, often set in periods in the distant future.

SEMANTICS: Branch of linguistics dealing with meaning, and the change of meaning, in words.

SEMIOLOGY: General study or science of signs with which humans communicate with each other (including words and their use in every context).

SERMON: Verbal instruction of some length, usually religious.

SHORT STORY: Work of fiction usually revolving around single event.

SIC: Included in brackets after a printed word or quoted passage to indicate that it is quoted accurately, however actually incorrect.

SIMILE:

1. When we draw comparison between two persons by using (usually 'like', as-so or as) it is the 'simile' that we make use of, *e.g.*
   (*i*) As red as a rose
   (*ii*) As happy as a lark
   (*iii*) She looked like a violet, half-hidden behind the rock.
2. *An Exaggerated Simile:* It is a simile in which the sense is clearly exaggerated, *e.g.*
   (*i*) He ran as fast as lightning
   (*ii*) He has in himself the force as much as there is in ten horses.

SLANG: Colourful and vernacular language of the street, marketplace, barrackroom, workplace, sportsplace and playground.

SOLILOQUY: Kind of monologue in which a stage character expresses his thoughts and feelings.

SONG: Poem or verse set to music.

SONNET: 14-line poem of set rhyme-scheme; Elizabethan (Shakespearean) *ababcdcdefefgg*, Italian *abbaabba cdcdcd* (or *cdecde*).

STANZA: A group of lines in a poem that are considered to be a unit. Many poems are divided into stanzas that are separated by spaces. Stanzas often function just like paragraphs in prose. Each stanza states and develops a single main idea.

STREAM OF CONSCIOUSNESS: A narrative technique that presents thoughts as if they were coming directly from a character's mind. Instead of being arranged in chronological order, the events of the story are presented from the character's point of view, mixed in with the character's feelings and memories just as they might spontaneously occur in the mind of a real person. Stream-of-consciousness writing reveals a character's complex psychology and presents it in realistic detail.

STROPHE AND ANTI STROPHE:

1. Strophe is "the song sung by the chorus (in a Greek play) as it moved towards one side, answered by an exact counterpart."
2. Anti-Strophe is the term for the Strophe, "as it returned : part of any ode thus answered..."

STYLE: A writer's typical way of writing. Style includes word choice, tone, degree of formality, figurative language, rhythm, grammatical structure, sentence length, organization-in short, every feature of a writer's use of language. Ernest Hemingway in The Old Man and the Sea and Aravind Ardiga in The White Tiger, for example, use a simple or informal prose style that contrasts with V. S. Naipaul's more formal style of writing.

STOCK MATERIAL: Material necessary for a writer to write.

STOCK CHARACTERS: Characters that are commonly found in most of pieces of dramas or fiction.

STOCK SITUATIONS: Situations which are frequently presented by authors in their works.

SUSPENSE: A feeling of growing uncertainty about the outcome of events in a literary work. Writers create suspense by raising questions in the minds of the readers. Suspense builds until the climax of the plot, at which point the suspense reaches its peak.

SYMBOL: Anything that stands for or represents something else. A conventional symbol is one that is widely known and accepted, such as a voyage symbolizing life or a skull symbolizing death. A personal symbol is one developed for a particular work by a particular author. Examples include Melville's white whale in *Moby Dick.*

SYNTHESIS, POETRY OF: The term "Poetry of Synthesis" is referred to by I.A. Richards, and it has been thus explained by Cleanth Brooks—

"... a poetry which does not leave out what is apparently hostile to its dominant tone, and which, because it is able to fuse the irrelevant and disordant, has come to terms with itself and invulnerable to irony."

STRUCTURE: The structure meant is a structure of meaning, evaluations and interpretations; and the principle of unity which informs it seems to one of balancing and harmonizing connotations, attitudes and meanings.

SUBLIMITY: It is a term which is used to describe inexplicable beauty which is beyond any rules to describe or measure.

SYMBOLISM: French poetic movement of late 19th century that developed as revolt against realism, concentrating on evoking emotions by use of indirect suggestion (symbol and metaphor); flourished in Russia at turn of century as literary movement, and later in British novel.

SYNECDOCHE:

1. This figure of speech is used when the understanding of one thing by means of another is employed.
2. This can be done in several ways, some of which are mentioned below :
   (*i*) When a part stands for a whole or genus, e.g. We have fifty *hands* in our factory.
   (hands = workers)
   (*ii*) When a whole or genus stands for a part, e.g. He belongs to a different *world* from yors (world = category, social set-up, economic status, etc.)
   (*iii*) When an individual represents a class, *e.g.* He is the *Nestor* of our village.
   (Nestor = the oldest man)

SYNTAX: It means:

(*i*) The way a sentence is constructed
(*ii*) Arrangement of words in writing (or in speech) according to the rules of grammar
(*iii*) Rules pertaining to this system or arrangement.

SYNONYM: A word similar in meaning to another.

SYNOPSIS: Outline of the main points of a work; a summary.

TALE: Spoken or written narrative.

TAUTOLOGY: Overuse of synonyms or repetition of ideas in sentence.

THEME: A central message or insight into life revealed by a literary work. An essay's theme is often directly stated in its thesis statement. In most works of fiction, the theme is only indirectly stated: a story, poem, or play most often has an implied theme. In some forms of didactic literature, which is intended to be morally instructive, such as a fable or a parable, the theme can be stated outright at the end as the "moral of the story." In some modern literature, the theme can be very subtle and abstract.

THESIS: Long essay or treatise on a subject, usually expository; work presented to examiners for academic qualification.

THIRD PERSON: Style of novel, etc., in which narrator is outside action.

TONE: The writer's attitude towards his or her subject, characters, or audience. A writer's tone may be formal or informal, friendly or distant, personal or pompous.

TRACT: Short printed treatise on religious or political subject.

TRAGEDY: The Tragedy is the tragic story of a good and great man who, on account of a slight flaw in his character, passes through a harrowing emotional and spiritual crisis, and finally meets his doom and death.

TRAGEDY OF BLOOD (AND THUNDER):

1. It was basically a melodramatic presentation of horrible, gory scenes.
2. The first famous tragedy of this kind is Kyd's "Spanish Tragedy".

TRAGIC-COMEDY: A Tragic-Comedy is an artistic combination of both tragedy and comedy. It develops as a tragedy to the point of climax, and then takes a happy turn and finally ends into a happy denouement.

TRAGIC FLAW: In Shakespeare's tragedies, in particular, we often find a particular flaw in the character of the hero which ultimately leads to the fall of his destiny, along with the fall of his state or estate.

TRANSFERRED EPITHET: When an epithet is transferred from a person to a thing, it is known as a 'transferred epithet', *e.g.*

(*i*) It is a *foolish* idea
(*ii*) Let *happy* days come.

TRANSLATION: Rendering of a work into another language.

TREATISE: Formal work examining a subject and the principles underlying it.

TROCHAIC LINE METRE:

1. A line in verse is known as a *"trochaic" line* when the first, third and other odd syllables in it are accented (as in the 'Iambic metre') irrespective of the length of the line.
2. A poem comprising such lines is known as having been written in the "Trochaic" metre.

UNDERSTATEMENT: It is practically the opposite of hyperbole and is sometimes used by the writers to emphasise indirectly the desired meaning.

VADE MECUM: Manual or handbook carried for frequent reference.

VERISIMILITUDE: It is the likeness of truth presented in a work of art that makes it similar to the characteristics or situation in real life and that enables the readers to accept it ungrudgingly as truth (and may be, sometimes, more than real happening in life).

VERNACULAR: Domestic or native language.

VERSIFICATION: Study of how traditional verse is constructed.

WIT: Dryden defines (in "Annus Mirabilis") wit as "delightful imagining of persons, actions, passions or things."

YARN: Story or tale, sometimes improbable and far-fetched.